The
System
of
Industrial
Relations
in
Canada

Second Edition

Alton W. J. Craig

Faculty of Administration
University of Ottawa

Prentice-Hall Canada Inc., Scarborough, Ontario

To Dorothy

Canadian Cataloguing in Publication Data

Craig, Alton W. J. (Alton Westwood Joseph), 1931-
  The system of industrial relations in Canada

Includes index,
Bibliography: p.
ISBN 0-13-881194-6.

1. Industrial relations - Canada. I. Title.

HD8106.5.C63 1985   331'.0971   C85-099504-3

©1986 by Prentice-Hall Canada Inc.
Scarborough, Ontario

Prentice-Hall, Inc., Englewood Cliffs, New Jersey
Prentice-Hall International, Inc., London
Prentice-Hall of Australia, Pty., Ltd., Sydney
Prentice-Hall of India Pvt., Ltd., New Delhi
Prentice-Hall of Japan, Inc., Tokyo
Prentice-Hall of Southeast Asia (Pte.) Ltd., Singapore
Editora Prentice-Hall do Brasil Ltda., Rio de Janeiro
Prentice-Hall Hispanoamericana, S.A., Mexico

ISBN 0-13-881194-6

Production editors: Mary Land, Maureen Chill
Designer: Steven Boyle
Manufacturing buyer: Sheldon Fischer
Typesetter: Cundari Group Ltd.
Printed and bound in Canada by John Deyell Company

3 4 5 JD 90 89 88

Contents

3 Theories of the Labour Movement 46

4 The History and Philosophy of the Canadian Labour Movement 64

8 Forms of Third-Party Assistance in the Negotiation Process 199

9 Administration of the Collective Agreement 232

10 Collective Bargaining in the Public and Parapublic Sectors 253

11 The Outputs of the Canadian Industrial Relations System 284

Preface

Organized into an open-systems framework, the discussions presented in this edition fulfil the need of introductory undergraduate and graduate courses for a detailed, integrated analysis of the industrial relations system in Canada. Cases on certification, contract negotiation, unfair labour practice, fair representation, and arbitration supplement the major issues brought to light within the text. The short cases have been chosen for their suitability to first-level study, the long cases for their suitability to advanced study.

A particularly useful approach to understanding the multidisciplinary nature of industrial relations, open-systems theory concerns itself with the actors in an industrial relations system and with the translation by these actors of both the constraints imposed by the environment and the goals, values and power of the actors into system outputs. The three actors in an industrial relations system — unions, management, and third parties — affect and are affected in turn by the other actors and by the environment. I have conceptualized these interrelationships in the form of a feedback loop.

There are critics of open-systems theory. These writers attribute to the theory an inappropriate emphasis on stability, harmony, and the collective regulation of industrial relations behaviour.[1] The truth is that open-systems theory presupposes neither cooperation nor conflict to be the essential determinant of the union-management relationship. Indeed this theory avoids generalizations about the attitudes and behaviour of unions and management altogether, leaving these topics wholly problematic.

Action theory, on the other hand, makes the collective regulation of industrial relations its central focus. Problems common to workers and management, according to action theory, may inspire varying solutions which may be agreed upon through collective bargaining. Action theory addresses not industrial relations, therefore, but negotiation—one part only of industrial relations—and fails entirely "to acknowledge that which takes place beyond the bargaining table."[2]

Marxism, another analytical approach to the study of industrial relations, views industrial relations as an arena of conflict between societal classes, more specifically between capital and labour.[3] According to the Marxist, the capitalist seeks to buy labour at the lowest possible price and then to combine it with other factors of production to produce the highest possible profit. The worker, on the other hand, seeks to sell labour at the highest possible price—at least an amount which the worker considers commensurate with the value to production of that particular labour. The union functions to pool power in favour of the worker.

Karl Marx, however, failed to predict the tremendous effect of state power over conditions in the workplace. Since the time of Marx, governments in the industrialized world have legislated hours of work, minimum wages, health and safety, and human rights protection. This state intervention has eradicated the extremes of exploitation which Marx believed would spark the overthrow of the capitalist society and usher in the era of a classless society.

To my mind, familiarity with the psychology and objectives of North American workers and unions diminishes the appeal of Marxist theory to industrial relations analysis in this country. To begin with, the notion and practice of the mixed economy—the combination of private and public enterprise—is strongly entrenched here. Canadian workers and unions, moreover, appear neither to be particularly class conscious nor amenable to revolutionary doctrine. In fact, our unions have proven to be among our most conservative institutions.

Given the limitations of Marxism, action theory, and other partially developed alternatives too numerous to discuss here, I believe open-systems theory to be the most suitable framework available. In response to some of its critics, however, I have modified the open-systems framework somewhat. In Chapter One, I define my version of the open-systems industrial relations framework, describing the complex interrelationships between the industrial relations system and environmental subsystems. In Chapter Two, I discuss the characteristics and effects of the environment (the economic, ecological, political, legal, and social subsystems) on the actors, inputs, and outputs of the industrial relations system.

In the next three chapters, I deal with the labour movement. Chapter Three sets out major labour theories in the context of four questions central to the labour movement: (1) How do we explain the origin or emergence of labour organizations? (2) How do we explain the pattern of growth and development of labour organizations? (3) What are the ultimate goals of the labour movement? and (4) Why do workers join labour organizations? Chapter Four discusses the history and philosophy of the Canadian labour movement, emphasizes central labour organizations in Canada, and shows how American events have influenced them. Chapter Five analyzes the general structure and statistical parameters of the labour movement, discusses the Canadian Labour Congress and its components, and proceeds to a freshly expanded treatment of union governance, including union conventions, democracy, officers and their tenure, leadership, and the growing importance of women to all these areas. The chapter closes by examining some of the relationships between American unions and their Canadian branches, particularly as manifested in the establishment of a Canadian Auto Workers Union.

Chapter Six compares private-sector labour legislation among jurisdictions from one end of the country to the other. After presenting a historical overview of the legislation, the chapter proceeds to show how different jurisdictions deal with recognition disputes, mandatory third-party assistance in interest and rights disputes, jurisdictional disputes between unions, and public policy questions, drawing attention to philosophical issues where pertinent.

Chapter Seven discusses the negotiation process—the mechanism for converting inputs into outputs—and includes such topics as the structure of negotiating units, the preparation of demands and counter-demands, and the strategy and tactics used by the parties at different stages of bargaining. The chapter also points out the importance of bargaining power in determining specific outcomes of negotiations and examines the factors contributing to bargaining power. Discussions of good-faith bargaining and concession bargaining are new with this edition.

Chapter Eight considers the forms of third-party assistance provided by government agencies or private individuals in the event that the parties fail to settle through bilateral negotiations. Using the latest research findings, forms of third-party assistance—both voluntary and mandatory—are compared among eleven jurisdictions. Once a collective agreement is entered into, the problem arises of living with it for its duration: that is, of making it work for the union, management, and workers. Chapter Nine examines grievance procedures and the arbitration of contract interpretation disputes, drawing heavily on the jurisprudence which has been accumulating rapidly from recent arbitration and court decisions.

Chapter Ten sets out problems peculiar to labour relations in the public and parapublic sectors. To this edition, I have added discussions on the history and structure of public-sector unions, the controversy surrounding comparisons of wages between public and private sectors, and workstoppages. A comprehensive diagrammatic comparison of legislative provisions among the jurisdictions supplements this part of the book.

Chapter Eleven describes three outputs of the Canadian industrial relations system: (1) organizational outputs, (2) worker outputs, and (3) industrial conflict. Representative collective agreement clauses are clearly set out and their effects on both the industrial relations system and the environmental subsystems discussed. The postscript, new to this edition, closes the book by raising crucial questions about the future roles and interrelationships of unions, management, and government. Legal decisions arising from cases under the Charter of Rights and Freedoms, many of which will likely alter greatly the nature of Canadian industrial relations, are also brought to the reader's attention. Finally, in response to Shirley Carr's 1986 ascendancy to CLC leadership, I point out the expanding future for women in the Canadian labour movement.

---

notes

1 For one of the more recent critiques of theory in industrial relations, see G. Shienstock, "Towards a Theory of Industrial Relations," Vol. XIX, No. 2, *British Journal of Industrial Relations* (July 1981), pp. 170-89 and particularly pp. 171-73 for a critique of "the systems model."
2 *Ibid.*, p. 180.
3 For a good summary of the Marxist approach, see Schienstock's article, pp. 180-84.

Acknowledgements

The Humanities and Social Science Research Council (formerly the Canada Council) provided much appreciated financial assistance in the preparation of Chapters Six and Ten which deal with legislation in the private sector and the public and parapublic sectors respectively. Special thanks are also extended to Warren Stroud, Phillip Brazeau, and Dick Van Wyck—former students in the Faculty of Law of the University of Ottawa—for their assistance on these two chapters. Industrial relations practitioners interviewed from Vancouver to St. John's provided many insights which helped in the preparation of these two chapters.

Former colleagues and more recently acquired ones in Labour Canada were extremely helpful and readily provided assistance when it was needed. Gratitude is due to Dr. Garfield Clack, Barry Maloney, Ken Ross, Michael Legault, Lucy Nobert, Fred West, Michel Gauvin, Robert Dupuis, J. C. Roy, and Nicole Marchand for providing very useful information and helpful suggestions. Very special thanks are due to Fred Longley of the Labour Canada Library for his extensive and generous assistance.

Miss Mary Kehoe, M.A., Assistant Editor, Public Relations Department of the Canadian Labour Congress, provided very constructive comments on drafts of the three chapters on the labour movement for the first edition. Professor Bryan Downie of Queen's University provided very helpful advice on Chapters Six and Eight of the first edition. I am particularly grateful to Professor Joseph B. Rose of McMaster University who provided extensive comments on all chapters of the first edition of the book and to Professor Roy J. Adams of McMaster University who made me more aware than I had been of the role of the Canadian trade union movement in politics, particularly during its early years. My gratitude is also extended to Professor S. Muthuchidambaram of the University of Regina for helpful suggestions on a number of chapters and to Professor Allan Patterson of the University of Manitoba for keeping me abreast of legislative changes which took place in that province.

The reviewers selected by Prentice-Hall Canada for both editions of the book provided constructive and useful suggestions on the entire manuscripts.

I am grateful to my associates at the Faculty of Administration, University Of Ottawa, especially Professor A. V. Subbarao. In addition, the M.B.A. students during the Fall of 1981 and the third-year students during the Spring of 1982 who used bound copies of the original manuscript provided much useful feedback. I am more than grateful to the late Frank Hintenberger, Associate Editor of Prentice-Hall Canada who persuaded me about ten years ago to begin the writing of this book—a dream that I had harboured ever since graduating from Cornell University in 1964. His replacement, Executive Editor Cliff Newman, and Special Projects Editor Marta Tomins were extremely helpful in finalizing the manuscript for the first edition, and Charles Macli did an excellent job of editing it. I have been greatly assisted by Elynor Kagan in finalizing the second edition, and Maureen Chill did an excellent job of editing it.

The typing and retyping of most chapters of the first edition of this book were very capably done by Mrs. Donna Curtis. Donna's dedication to this project and her penchant for excellence were very much appreciated. Thanks are also extended to Mrs. Louise Moreau and the secretarial staff of the Faculty of Administration, University of Ottawa, for their generous assistance. I would like to make a special dedication of Chapter Six to the memory of Jerry Friedman, an M.B.A. student at the University of Ottawa who assisted me with that chapter. Finally, my sincere thanks are extended to a friend and very wise counsellor, Dr. A. G. Catterson, for helping me over the many frustrating hurdles that usually accompany the writing of a textbook.

This book serves in part as a tribute to my mother and my late father whose generosity and moral support I will always appreciate. Very special thanks go to my wife, Dorothy, for all the encouragement and support she has given me over the years and for the help that she has given me in the preparation of this second edition. I dedicate this book to her as an expression of my sincere and continuing gratitude. My thanks are also extended to our three children—Michael, Ann Marie, and Robert—for their encouragement and support. I am particularly indebted to Robert for showing me how to use my word processor, and for getting me out of trouble many times in the preparation of this edition.

Tables

James C. Fish, *The Financial Post*

1

A Framework for the Analysis of Industrial Relations Systems

Introduction

This chapter[1] presents a systems framework for the study of industrial relations. An analysis of industrial relations systems should not only seek to explain the many events which occur at the workplace, but should also be comprehensive enough to show how these events influence and are influenced by the society at large. In the past, research in this area has lacked methodological strength and as a result has been characterized by conceptual vagueness and a seeming inability to relate findings to any broad and coherent system of knowledge.

If the study of industrial relations is to develop into a respected and intellectually challenging discipline, more serious attempts must be made to specify, precisely define its essential factors, and show how these fit into a broader system of interdependent variables and propositions. J. T. Dunlop made a significant contribution in this regard with his book, *Industrial Relations Systems*.[2] Since then, there have been scattered attempts to develop more systematic approaches. While the present chapter is set forth as an analytical tool for the purpose of this book, it by no means constitutes a theory of industrial relations.[3] It is hoped, however, that it may someday serve as the basis for attempts to develop such a theory.

One of the major factors creating difficulties in the area of industrial relations is that researchers have neither precisely defined their fundamental concerns nor specified the analytical apparatus which would assist them in considering pertinent data.[4] In this connection, a promising approach is that of open-systems theory in which the subject matter consists of a set of interrelated factors operating in a larger environment. This approach implies that the system under study receives, in addition to its own internal inputs, external inputs from its environment. It then transforms these inputs into outputs which flow into pertinent environmental subsystems — legal, political, economic, etc.

Using this simplified explanation of open systems theory, it is possible to define industrial relations as comprising *a complex of private and public activities operating in a specified environment and concerned with the allocation of rewards to workers for their services and with the conditions under which these services are rendered.* The *complex of private and public activities* includes all structural arrangements and processes related to the field of study. *Operating in a specified environment* implies that an industrial relations system functions dynamically in relation to the environmental subsystems of a given society. *Rewards to workers for their services* are the material, social, and psychological rewards that workers receive for the performance of their work. Some of these rewards, such as the monetary ones, may become costs to the employer or to the economy, depending on whether a firm is analyzed as a micro unit or the economy is analyzed as a macro unit. The *conditions under which services are rendered* are the physical and other circumstances under which work is performed.

The Main Components of the Framework

As noted above, the main concerns of any industrial relations system are the allocation of rewards to workers and the physical and other conditions under which work is performed. These concerns form the foundation for the framework outlined in Figure 1.1. Subsequent chapters will prepare the ground for a more detailed discussion of outputs in Chapter 11.

The framework developed here and diagrammed in Figure 1.1 relies on David Easton's input-output model for its analysis of political life.[5] As with any such device, this one abstracts from empirical phenomena and summarizes the basic categories of variables required for an analysis of industrial relations systems.

The analytical system presented here consists of four basic components: (1) internal inputs expressed as the goals, values, and power of the participants (actors) in the system, which are conditioned by the flow of effects from environmental subsystems (external inputs); (2) the complex of private and public processes for converting the inputs into outputs; (3) the outputs, comprising the material, social and psychological rewards workers receive in exchange for services; and (4) a feedback loop through which the outputs flow not only directly into the industrial relations system itself but also into the environmental subsystems. Through the feedback loop, outputs can shape the subsequent goals, values, and power of the actors in the industrial relations system as well as influence the actors in other environmental subsystems.

The Inputs of an Industrial Relations System

As stated above, the inputs of an industrial relations system are of two types: internal inputs (goals, values, and power of the actors in the system) and external inputs (the flow from environmental subsystems of effects which modify the goals, values, and power of these actors).

Inputs from Within the System

In order to discuss internal inputs, one must first look at goals, values, and power in relation to each of the actors in the industrial relations

Figure 1.1

A Framework for Analyzing Industrial Relations Systems
(A Structural-Functional Approach)

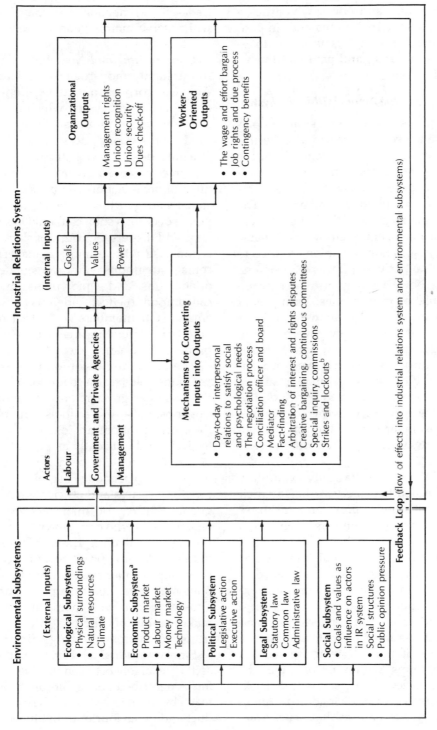

Industrial Relations System

Actors — **(Internal Inputs)**

Labour

Government and Private Agencies

Management

Goals

Values

Power

Organizational Outputs
- Management rights
- Union recognition
- Union security
- Dues check-off

Worker-Oriented Outputs
- The wage and effort bargain
- Job rights and due process
- Contingency benefits

Mechanisms for Converting Inputs into Outputs
- Day-to-day interpersonal relations to satisfy social and psychological needs
- The negotiation process
- Conciliation officer and board
- Mediator
- Fact-finding
- Arbitration of interest and rights disputes
- Creative bargaining, continuous committees
- Special inquiry commissions
- Strikes and lockouts[b]

Environmental Subsystems

(External Inputs)

Ecological Subsystem
- Physical surroundings
- Natural resources
- Climate

Economic Subsystem[a]
- Product market
- Labour market
- Money market
- Technology

Political Subsystem
- Legislative action
- Executive action

Legal Subsystem
- Statutory law
- Common law
- Administrative law

Social Subsystem
- Goals and values as influence on actors in IR system
- Social structures
- Public opinion pressure

Feedback Loop (flow of effects into industrial relations system and environmental subsystems)

[a]This model presupposes but does not explicitly show the interrelationship between the various societal subsystems.

[b]A work stoppage may also be considered an outcome or output of the industrial relations system.

system, since it is the interrelationships of the actors' goals, values, and power which determine the system's internal inputs and, in part, its outputs. First, however, it is necessary to examine in detail the roles and nature of the actors within the system.

Roles and Nature of the Actors Within the System

In exploring industrial relations systems, particularly those aspects referred to as collective bargaining, we are engaged essentially in the study of unions and corporations, their organizational relationships and behaviour. The term *actor* designates both individuals and groups. The principal actors in an industrial relations system are individual managers, management teams, workers, and associations or unions formed to represent the collective concerns of workers. Third parties, however, may also become involved in public or private roles. Examples of public actors are labour relations boards or similar agencies established by government to designate bargaining agents for specified groups of workers and to resolve any union-management difficulties which may arise as a result. Examples of private actors include law firms, consulting agencies, or private individuals who often assist management and unions, separately or jointly, to resolve their differences.

Unions Unions are basically voluntary associations formed to protect workers in their relationships with their employers and to express the concerns of members who might otherwise be powerless when confronting a large corporation or government bureaucracy. Although unions, like other organizations, seem to have a life of their own, they are far from monolithic institutions, and in fact contain a variety of subgroups whose needs vary and whose expectations must be met, at least to a minimal degree, if unions are to be seen as credible. Subgroups within unions may be classified by skill level, age, sex, ethnic background, and degree of participation in union activities. Union leaders are, or should be, aware

of the demands of competing subgroups so that trade-offs in negotiations may be fashioned which serve members adequately.

Corporations and Non-Profit Organizations In the highly industrialized societies of North America, corporations as legal entities are by and large the means by which labour, capital, and other factor-inputs are brought together to produce the goods and services society wants. To a great degree, ownership of capital and other resources has been divorced from the management of organizations. Thus, a corps of professional managers has evolved to make major corporate decisions subject to only loose control by large and dispersed groups of shareholders. As is the case with unions, management cadres contain subgroups with divergent demands and orientations, and senior management may be called upon to effect trade-offs between, for example, staff members (industrial relations experts) and operating managers (in marketing, production, finance, etc.).

The above discussion on profit-seeking corporations holds true also for non-profit organizations such as governments, government agencies, hospitals, and schools. The objectives of these organizations are to deliver services as effectively and efficiently as possible, whether it be pension benefits by a government department, mail by Canada Post, high quality health care, or effective and efficient educational programs. Cadres of managers exist in these organizations who do not own the means of producing or delivering the services to the community. As in profit-seeking corporations, subgroups of managers within these organizations may have their own particular objectives. Those managers with competing objectives must make trade-offs before they meet union negotiators across the bargaining table.

Similarly, industrial relations in the unionized sector are largely between the two organizational forms described above, although the decisions made by them have a direct bearing on the conduct and behaviour of individuals in the workplace. Organizations, however, do not interact *per se*. It is individuals at various levels whose interactions constitute the relationships between formal organizations. As we shall see later, collective agreements contain provisions concerning these organizational relationships.

Goals, Values, and Power of the Actors

Goals Goals are the objectives or needs which an individual or group seeks to achieve. The goals of a formal or informal group are normally defined through agreement. However, specific individuals within groups may dissent from group goals and analysis of industrial relations systems, therefore, must be sensitive to the goals of these individuals.

As Maslow has indicated, there is a hierarchy of basic needs which motivates individual behaviour. These range from physiological (life-sustaining) needs to safety, love (social acceptance), esteem (recognition), and finally self-actualization.[6] According to Maslow, these needs are listed in order of basic relative strength. It should be noted that when one need is satisfied it no longer serves as a motivator and is supplanted by the next higher one. Most of the literature in the field of organizational behaviour seems to suggest that, in North America today, physiological needs and the need for safety are satisfied for the greater part of the population and that now high-level needs (social acceptance, esteem, self-actualization) motivate individuals. Although other writers have classified individual needs in slightly different ways, they all stress the importance of organizational climate and quality of work in promoting or thwarting the satisfaction of high-level needs. For this reason, psychological and social rewards are now taking on a new significance in the workplace, particularly among young members of the labour force, whether managers or workers.

Values Values are the norms or standards which an actor observes in establishing the relative importance of objectives and the means of attaining them. Faced with a variety of solutions to any given problem, an actor will choose the one which promises the greatest satisfaction, providing it is consistent with the actor's established values.

Power Power is the ability of an actor to achieve goals despite the resistance of others, and is made up of at least two elements: (1) a strong attachment to a desired object or to one already possessed but threatened; and (2) an ability to impose sanctions. Power thus initially lies in a commitment to an issue or series of issues. Where there is no commitment, there is no inducement to impose sanctions irrespective of the ability to do so. Sanctions may be of three types: (1) moral, such as the use of public opinion; (2) economic, such as strikes, work-to-rule and lockouts; and (3) physical, such as intimidation or physical violence.[7]

Each actor, at any time, possesses specific goals, values and power. In the study of industrial relations, it is easy to obtain some measure of the goals of the parties, but difficult to evaluate their values and power. Over time, however, certain qualititative assessments are possible; for example, fluctuations in the importance of some goals and in an actor's commitment to them or fluctuations in the factors which influence the power of a given party. These qualitative judgements nonetheless identify only whether or not a specific input has increased or decreased in strength or importance, and do not constitute precise quantitative evaluations of goals, values, and power.

Generally, organized labour in North America has the very pragmatic objective of obtaining "more, more and more now," as stated by Samuel Gompers, first President of the American Federation of Labour (AFL). However, this is not to suggest that labour is concerned only with its own needs. To varying degrees, unions embrace an egalitarian norm which manifests itself as a concern for the welfare of all workers. This has been demonstrated by union support for various social initiatives, such as support for higher minimum wages to improve the lot of non-union workers in small establishments. R. B. Freeman and J. L. Medoff, two Harvard economists, have recently analyzed a large computerized data base and concluded that unionism raises productivity in the United States. While reducing wage inequities, however, unionism also reduces profits. More success has been experienced with union initiatives directed toward legislation of broad social importance than with those demonstrating special interests.[8]

Even when unions seem guided by Gomper's formula, they recognize that certain goals take precedence over the desire for increased wages and benefits. An example of this type of priority-setting can be found in those cases where unions have agreed to lower wage demands in order to keep companies operating and so avoid unemployment among their membership. For example, in 1984 Alberta's electricians agreed to a wage and benefit freeze in favour of greater job security. The agreement contained a novel clause whereby the union and contractors could agree to cut the basic hourly wage before bidding on a job in order to compete with cheaper, non-unionized contractors.[9] Unionized employers have been having difficulty in competing for jobs in the construction industry for a number of years because non-unionized wages have been lower than those in the unionized sector of the industry.

The objective of obtaining more — more profits, a greater share of the market, increased growth and greater control over the workplace — is attributed also to management in the private sector which has traditionally been guided by the competitive norm, although oligopolistic and monopolistic industries exert a fair amount of control over the North American market. In the public sector, bureaucratic management attempts to provide reliable services for the lowest possible cost: the Federal Government refers to reliable service as *effectiveness* and low costs as *efficiency*. Both private

industry and government, however, recognize the desirability of reconciling personal and organizational objectives. For this reason, writers in the fields of personnel and organizational behaviour stress the mutual benefits of increased productivity, decreased absenteeism, lower worker turnover and improved morale.

In North America, government and private agencies, acting as third parties in the collective bargaining process and guided by the goal of maintaining industrial peace between labour and management, have assisted them in resolving disputes without work stoppages or in ending work stoppages once they have begun. Governments for their part have been involved for some time in labour standards legislation covering employment issues such as minimum wage and hours of work. In recent years, some government-sponsored agencies have also attempted to regulate bargaining outcomes by using wage-and-price controls such as those which existed in the United States from 1971 to 1973 and in Canada under the Anti-Inflation Program of 1975 to 1978, by imposing restraint programs of 6% and 5% in 1983 and 1984 respectively in the federal public sector, and by implementing similar restraint programs in certain provincial public sectors. In addition, government interest in health and safety, equal pay for work of equal value, and the quality of worklife is increasing.

While all three actors in the system have distinct goals and values, general agreement does exist; this consensus keeps the system functioning. Because some actors represent different subgroups in our society, however, distinct goals and values are maintained. And where these different goals and values clash, so do the actors.

Our analytical scheme presupposes neither conflict nor harmony as those of some others do; for example, the schemes of Marx (conflict) and of Dunlop (harmony). Our framework enables both analyst and practitioner to observe given situations and determine for themselves whether these situations are characterized by conflict or harmony, stability or instability. Jack

Barbash, writing on collective bargaining in the United States, observes that,

> [it] is...a *co-operative* form of conflict in which the parties — or for that matter the *partners* — seek to exchange what they want from each other. Unlike *competitors* who seek to oust one another, bargainers seek a mutually agreeable exchange.[10]

He also contends that collective bargaining is perceived by the actors as an adversary game, the outcome of which determines the way available funds are distributed between wages and profits. He asserts further that "conflict, latent or manifest, is the essence of industrial relations, but it is almost invariably followed by the *resolution* of conflict."[11]

In accepting in principle Barbash's formulation of the essence of contract negotiations, one should always keep in mind that conflict does not always express itself overtly. In many cases conflicting parties adopt an accommodative approach to negotiations whereby both sides gain. For example, negotiations completed by the Letter Carriers' Union and Canada Post in early 1982 resulted in a sharing of productivity gains so as to create a situation in which "we all win."[12]

The power of any one actor, as stated above, lies in the ability of that actor to attain objectives despite the resistance of others. The power of any one actor also varies according to conditions in the environment and industrial relations system. For example, a very buoyant economy increases labour's power, wheras a slack economy increases management's power. The recent recession has proven this. A very militant union membership, moreover, will support a labour leader at the bargaining table more than an apathetic union membership will. Likewise a government may or may not exercise some degree of power, depending on how much economic, political, or social clout it perceives itself to have. For example, the United States government exerted considerable power over both labour and management in a number of industries in 1966 by releasing stockpiles of basic materials and thus maintaining or lowering prices for these commodities.

How important then is power in contract negotiations? A recent book by two American authors goes so far as to assume that "bargaining power is the pivotal construct for a general theory of bargaining."[13] Bacharach and Lawler further content that power "pervades all aspects of bargaining and is the key to an integrative analysis of context, process, and outcome."[14] This formulation accords notably with the ideas presented in this book and, furthermore, is consistent with the idea of a contract zone — that area in which the positions of the two principal actors overlap and in which bargaining power helps to define a specific point of settlement. As a general rule, both unions and management prefer to reach a settlement within this zone, rather than initiate a work stoppage. The contract zone will be discussed in greater detail in the chapter "The Negotiating Process."

The preceding discussion has illustrated how the goals, values and power of the actors in the industrial relations system create its internal input variables. The following section will examine external conditioning inputs from environmental subsystems into the industrial relations system.

External Conditioning Inputs into the Industrial Relations System

Environmental inputs act as external conditioning inputs and impose a range within which internal inputs and outputs fall. Within this range, however, outputs are determined by the goals, values and, in particular, the power of the actors in the system. This suggests that the outputs are not deterministic in the Marxist sense but that the actors have some degree of control over both inputs and outputs. The following environmental subsystems have significant conditioning effects on the industrial relations system: (1) the ecological subsystem, (2) the economic subsystem, (3) the political subsystem, (4) the legal subsystem, and (5) the social or cultural subsystem. Each of these will be discussed briefly.

Ecological Subsystem The ecological subsystem is a society's physical surroundings and the way it adjusts to them. For example, the climate in Canada has an influence on several industries: it closes many of our inland ports for a good part of the year and slows down construction activities. Consequently, the seasonal nature of these and other industries will have a bearing on the timing of negotiations and the level of rewards granted or obtained for workers. Furthermore, the availability of key resources to a region has serious consequences for the inputs and outputs of its industrial relations system. The energy crisis has shown how the concentration of important energy resources in particular areas of the world has had an impact on the economies and industrial relations systems of dependent countries. During the Winter of 1973, for example, many industries in the United Kingdom operated only three or four days a week in order to conserve energy during this period of shortage.

Although an ecological subsystem influences an industrial relations system, it is of course unable to respond to the outputs from that system. In this, an ecological subsystem differs from other societal subsystems in which conscious decision-making mechanisms exist to analyze industrial relations outputs and to modify subsequent system inputs.

Economic Subsystem The economic subsystem, comprising the product, labour, and money markets as well as the level of technological progress also conditions the inputs and outputs of the industrial relations system. As stated previously, a period of high economic activity promotes high rates of inputs and outputs, whereas a period of slow economic activity produces the opposite effect. Other macroeconomic conditions, such as inflation, unemployment, and interest rates, also exert a substantial influence on industrial relations.

The product market acts to establish a ceiling on outputs, since consumer demand for a given product influences the producer's (manage-

ment's) willingness and ability to provide increased wages and benefits. The labour market, by contrast, acts to establish the minimum inputs and outputs needed to attract sufficient numbers of workers into the labour force of a specific firm. The money market is affected by monetary and fiscal policies, as well as the interest-rate structure. These in turn operate to accelerate or decelerate economic activity and thus act indirectly as conditioning factors.

Double-digit inflation on a world-wide scale during the late 1970's and early 1980's demonstrated how difficult it is for countries to manage monetary and fiscal policies to keep prices and wages from rising too rapidly. This realization has given rise to various forms of governmental and other institutional structures to cope with rising wage demands as workers have attempted, through the industrial relations system, to maintain or increase their real wages. Wage and price controls — and the increasing incidence of escalator or cost-of-living clauses in North American collective agreements — are evidence of the many ways in which governments and unions try to cope with inflation.

Technological change, by affecting the capital-labour ratio, job structure, requisite skills, and productivity, has wide-spread impact on the inputs and outputs of the industrial relations system. The Canadian federal government and a number of provincial governments have gone so far as to pass legislation that will help protect workers from the adverse consequences, in human terms, of technological change. Other countries have tried to cope with the same type of problem by using a variety of so-called redundancy schemes, whereby all employers contribute to a fund from which workers who are made redundant by technological changes receive benefits such as lump sum payments, subsidized retraining, and relocation grants to assist them to move to areas where there is a demand for labour.

Political Subsystem The political subsystem influences the industrial relations system in many ways, only a few of which will be noted here. One major determinant of such influence is the political structure itself. The formation of centralized systems of collective bargaining is easier in unitary states than it is in decentralized states. Such is the case in a number of European countries, where highly-structured systems allow private parties to view the outputs of their industrial relations systems in relation to the economy of the country as a whole. Canada, with its highly decentralized federal system of government, has one of the world's most decentralized industrial relations systems. Such a system leaves members of small negotiating units with the feeling that their outputs have little effect on the total national scene.

For this reason, the executive branch of the political subsystem may intervene to play a direct role in protecting what it perceives to be the public interest. Such intervention has been used frequently in both Canada and the United States in an attempt to achieve settlements between unions and management without work stoppages. In addition, the political subsystem often operates through its legislative branch by enacting or modifying labour relations legislation to establish general "rules of the game" or *ad hoc* measures to cope with particular disputes. On several occasions, the Canadian Parliament has used *ad hoc* measures in the form of Acts of Parliament ordering railway, postal, and other workers back to work with minimum settlements though these have sometimes been subject to change by further negotiation or arbitration or both.

Legal Subsystem The legal subsystem, comprising statutory, common, and administrative law, also affects the industrial relations system. First, this subsystem legislates procedural rules determining how unions and management are to conduct themselves in both everyday activities and in negotiations. Second, this subsystem legislates labour standards such as minimum wages, maximum hours, health and safety standards, and equal pay for work of equal value and

thus conditions external inputs by describing a society's idea of acceptable working conditions. Third, common law, both that which predates statutory law and that which flows from the legal interpretation of statutory law, has a significant bearing on what the actors in the system may or may not do. Fourth, perhaps in a more direct way, administrative law issuing from bodies such as labour relations boards established by labour relations statutes plays a very decisive role in the industrial relations system. The various administrative tribunals in their interpretation and implementation roles help to fill gaps in the general provisions of statute law. Much more will be said about this topic in the chapter "Legislation Governing Collective Bargaining in the Private Sector."

Social or Cultural Subsystem The social or cultural subsystem acts as a comprehensive conditioning input. Since all the actors in the industrial relations system are part of society, they share at least some goals and values. This minimal consensus on goals and values keeps the industrial relations system functioning at both the micro and macro levels. Consensus, however, may be jeopardized to the extent that the goals and values of subgroups differ. If consensus breaks down, the public may pressure social, political, or economic leaders to intervene in a dispute if the dispute appears to be disruptive to either an important part or the whole of society. The political system may then take action to resolve the dispute by legislating or otherwise imposing guidelines.

At times the involvement of the political subsystem may be extensive enough to transform a bipartite system into a tripartite one in which government wields heavy influence on labour and management. For example, when the unions bargaining in the public sector of Quebec in 1972 and 1982 formed a common front and engaged in strikes disrupting essential services such as schools and hospitals, the Government of Quebec legislated the workers back to work. Some labour leaders, moreover, were imprisoned for encouraging workers to violate back-to-work injunctions. Similar action has been taken by some of the other provinces to order striking teachers and other essential workers back to work.

While the subsystems described above condition the inputs of the industrial relations system, they do not operate in a vacuum. There is, as the preceding section has pointed out, an articulation between the social or cultural subsystem and the political sybsystem. Likewise, articulations among the various other subsystems may develop, depending upon the problem to be resolved. In Table 1.1, the arrows among the subsystems depict some of these interrelationships.

One of the major tasks to be accomplished in the study of industrial relations is to define precisely the inputs from within the system (internal inputs) and the role of environmental subsystems as they condition these inputs. To develop quantitative measures of each variable to assess their individual impact or to combine these measures into some kind of composite index would be ideal. This is a difficult task, but interesting approaches have been suggested by Syed M. A. Hameed in an article which appeared in the July 1967 issue of the *British Journal of Industrial Relations* and by John Anderson in *Industrial Relations*.[15]

Procedures for Converting Inputs into Outputs

Unilateral Decisions Procedures for converting inputs into outputs take various forms. Sometimes outputs may be determined by one party alone, be it employer or state. In the non-unionized sectors of North America, it is the employer (whether in the private or public sector) who establishes the levels of rewards offered to workers and who regulates the conditions under which they work. In making these determinations and in attempting to recruit and retain labour of a calibre suitable to the employer, the employer is guided by general societal conditions.

Bipartite Negotiations Alternatively, inputs may be converted into outputs through bipartite negotiations between labour unions (or worker associations) and management. In the United States and Canada, this method predominates among organized sectors of the economy where most agreements are reached by the two private parties themselves.

Within the bipartite system, three sets of negotiations are possible. First, competing groups within a union may debate and agree upon goals. Second, a similar process may take place within management: for example, a sales manager may be most concerned with the delivery dates of products or services, whereas a production manager may be chiefly interested in keeping costs down. Some compromises may have to be made. Third, following these two sets of intraorganizational negotiations, bilateral negotiations take place in an attempt to reach a settlement.[16]

Third-Party Assistance If the two parties fail to reach a settlement, third-party assistance may be necessary. In Canada, we have a compulsory, two-stage conciliation process (to be explained fully later) in most of our political jurisdictions, to which both unions and management must submit before a strike or lockout is deemed legal. In the United States, parties wishing to renew a collective agreement must, under federal law, notify the Federal Mediation and Conciliation Service in advance of the expiration of an existing agreement. While mediation is often used in the United States, it is not compulsory except under the eighty-day injunction issued when the President declares a dispute to involve national health and safety. Interestingly enough, in most political jurisdictions in Canada the two-stage compulsory conciliation process is giving way to a one-stage process in which the emphasis is placed on mediation.

Compulsory arbitration exists for some essential sectors of the economy, where there are negotiations but no strike or lockout options. As the means for resolving disputes in some public and parapublic sectors in various Canadian provinces, arbitration is mandatory. Voluntary arbitration is an optional route, however, for dispute settlement among workers covered by the *Public Service Staff Relations Act*.

If these or other forms of third-party assistance fail to produce a settlement (i.e., convert inputs into outputs), then a settlement is usually determined by a trial of strength. This may take the form of a strike by workers or a lockout by management. Eventually, however, one or more forms of third-party assistance must be used in order to produce an agreement satisfactory to both sides. It is important to recognize that, when a strike or lockout occurs, this is an output of the industrial relations system and may have serious consequences for both environmental subsystems and actors in the industrial relations system itself.

It should be pointed out that industrial relations consist not only of periodic negotiations but also of day-to-day relationships among individuals in the workplace. Collective agreements cannot contain provisions that anticipate every action taken by management or unions on a daily basis. Hence all political jurisdictions in Canada require that collective agreements provide for the ongoing resolution of conflicts over the interpretation or application of clauses in current collective agreements. Such provision takes the form of a grievance procedure, the final stage of which usually results in binding third-party arbitration. While not required under United States law, some 90% or more of collective agreements in that country do contain such clauses. The grievance procedure and its resulting decisions work to evolve an elaborate jurisprudence or an industrial constitution which helps to regulate daily behaviour in the workplace.

Nonunionized Sector

So far we have been discussing the processes used in the unionized sector of the economy where the collective bargaining model prevails. Since only 40% to 50%[17] of the Canadian labour force participates in collective bargaining, we should now give some attention to the systems which apply to the nonunionized sector. An American scholar has recently identified three major worker relations systems within the nonunionized sector of the American economy, in addition to the collective bargaining model. He has named these the administrative model, the civil service model, and the legal model.[18] These models are pure types, but there may be articulations among them: for example, the collective bargaining model is supported by the legal model.

Administrative Model The administrative model, unilaterally established by the employer, is implemented throughout the hierarchy of an organization. Many of the rules and procedures take written form such as personnel policies and handbooks, while others take the form of custom. This subsystem is characterized by an implicit contract expressing a whole set of expectations which management and workers have regarding wages and working conditions; in times of financial hardship, it is understood that the employer has the unilateral right to change whatever he deems necessary to change. The items included under this model bear a striking resemblance to those in the collective bargaining model, primarily because employers have usurped the methods of the unionized sector, often in the hope of keeping their organizations union-free.

Civil Service Model The civil service model combines collective bargaining with the administrative model: administration is by a government agency acting under special law, procedures for grievances comprise a many-tiered hierarchy, final review is by a public service commission, and representation may be chosen from among external experts including worker associations. There are explicit, detailed, and legally binding procedures for discipline, reduction in force, and other personnel functions. Most of the regulations are internally generated, setting them apart from those of the collective bargaining model. Since workers at all levels of government in Canada are unionized and act in many ways like their counterparts in the collective bargaining model of the private sector, the civil service model does not apply as well to the Canadian public sector as it does to the American public sector.

Legal Model The legal model is concerned with both process and substantive outcome, but emphasizes employment relations law which comprises a body of regulations concerning compensation and working conditions. A Canadian writer[19] has recently written about laws governing the unorganized in Canada, some of which are similar to those in the American model. In Canada, laws exist which govern unemployment insurance, minimum wages, maximum hours, paid holidays, paid vacations, and occupational health and safety. Workers in some Canadian jurisdictions may refuse to perform duties which they consider hazardous. Laws also exist in Canada which prohibit discrimination on the basis of race, creed, colour, sex, and national ancestry, among other things. In some jurisdictions, laws prohibit discrimination on the basis of age and require equal pay for work of equal value while, in practically all jurisdictions, there is provision for maternity leave. In three jurisdictions (the federal, Quebec, and Nova Scotia) laws permit nonunionized workers to appeal dismissals which they feel have not been for just cause. Their cases may go all the way to impartial third-party arbitration. Human rights legislation in a number of jurisdictions prohibits sexual harrassment. In 1984 the Federal Government enacted legislation to require employers in industries under federal jurisdiction to develop policies on sexual harrassment and to publicize these policies within their organizations.

At common law, workers had few rights attached to their jobs. Employment could be terminated provided the employer gave reasonable notice, and many conditions of employment had

no legal support. This situation caused much controversy. In response, a growing body of labour standards legislation (including most of the items discussed above) can now be brought to bear to form minimum or maximum conditions, depending on those being regulated. These standards, however, usually lag behind practices developed in the unionized sector.

While protection for individuals has been growing, so too has support for group action, particularly in the area of health and safety. Through joint union–management and worker–management committees, Saskatchewan workers and management accomplished much in the field of health and safety during the 1970's, resolving issues quite successfully on their own. One of the major reasons for their success was the assurance felt by both workers and management that government was committed to making them the prime agents for ensuring compliance.[20] The *Ontario Occupational Health and Safety Act* requires the establishment of similar committees consisting of at least two people. Worker members are selected by workers where no union exists, and by union members where unions do exist.

The idea of universal committees in nonunionized as well as unionized sectors was introduced under the *Federal Labour Adjustment Benefits Act* of 1982 which deals with redundancies. When an employer plans to terminate the employment of fifty or more workers within a four-week period, a joint planning committee of not less than four members must be established. In nonunionized sectors, workers are entitled to select the members of such a committee, just as union members are in the unionized sector. These joint committees are charged with developing adjustment programs to eliminate the necessity for terminating employment, or to minimize the impact of termination on redundant workers and help them find other employment. In attempting to reach its objectives, a joint planning committee may choose to deal with matters normally pertaining to collective agreements. The mandate of these committees

— that "the members shall cooperate and make every reasonable effort to develop an adjustment program as expeditiously as possible"[21] — reflects the obligation of parties in the unionized sector to bargain in good faith.

As workers involved in labour–adjustment–benefits committees learn what it is like to deal with employers on a united rather than individual basis, the likelihood of their forming unions may increase. At the same time, the scope of these committees, according to one observer, may grow to include not only redundancy but technological change, health and safety, training, and possibly the joint management of pension plans. Furthermore, the idea of dividing responsibility for these matters among separate committees will be superseded, he predicts, by the idea of a general-purpose committee responsible for co-ordinating all these different matters, the boundaries of which to a large extent overlap. The term *unorganized*, he adds, may become archaic. "Should collective employment decision making become as widespread as the current trend suggests it might, the term will cease to have any real meaning. Everyone will be organized."[22] Another writer, however, sees these initiatives as obstacles to the formation of unions since, he argues, governments may appear to be doing so much that little will remain for unions to do.[23]

Hence nonunion workers are now protected by a large number of laws and regulations, many of which are based on benefits obtained through the collective bargaining process. New measures deal with just cause for dismissal in nonunionized firms in three jurisdictions. In addition, the idea of joint committees in nonunionized organizations gives workers a chance to have an input into policies affecting them.

We need hardly take sides with one or the other of these views. It is useful to note, however, that nonunionized workers in some jurisdictions already have some say about how their rewards and the conditions under which they work are determined. Whether these workers remain satisfied with what they have or whether they opt for the advantages (and disadvantages) of collective bargaining in a bid to improve their lot is a crucial question.

Informal Relationships In the preceding section, we have been discussing the formalized procedures for converting inputs into outputs. Equally important, however, are the host of informal relationships between managers, workers and managers, workers themselves, and workers and their union leaders. To a large extent, the participants satisfy their social and psychological needs at this level. The literature of industrial psychology and organizational behaviour recognizes the existence of informal relationships among the actors and, in order to thoroughly understand industrial relations systems, these relationships must undergo a close and rigorous examination.

We know that many individual and group needs are satisfied through informal relationships more than through formal organizational structures and activities, but organizational needs, too, are often best met informally, as numerous studies have shown. Issues such as boredom on the assembly line or with routine jobs, absenteeism, turnover, and quality of worklife are receiving increasing attention. Research is now being conducted on the quality of worklife and experimentation is being undertaken to overcome some of the malaise that plagues many organizations. Some studies deal with patterns of interpersonal relations, while others examine the nature of work itself.

The Outputs of an Industrial Relations System

The main function of an industrial relations system is the allocation of rewards to workers for their services and the determination of the conditions under which they are to work. Since collective bargaining first began in North America, collective agreements, which cover most material outputs, have grown from small documents into fairly large ones. This increase in size reflects the number of items that have been added through negotiations over the years and the refinements and elaborations of what were once simple provisions.

The outputs of industrial relations systems can be subdivided into two major types: those oriented toward organizations and those oriented toward workers. (The former would not exist in non-unionized organizations.)

Clauses oriented toward organizations are concerned with (1) management rights, (2) union recognition, (3) union security, and (4) dues check-off. These clauses represent both the relationships between organizational entities and the relationships between these entities and their members.

Clauses oriented toward workers are concerned with (1) the wage and effort bargain, (2) job rights and due process, and (3) contingency benefits. The wage and effort bargain is concerned with reconciling the services workers provide for an organization with returns in the form of wages, cost-of-living (COLA) clauses, hours of work, etc. Job rights and due process involve such things as the role of seniority in promotions, layoff, recall, and various aspects of the grievance procedure. Contingency benefits include such things as supplementary unemployment benefits (SUB), pension plans, hospital and medical plans, etc., some of which will be covered in Chapter 11.

In addition to outputs oriented toward organizations and outputs oriented toward workers, there is a third kind of output: conversion mechanisms. Conversion mechanisms — particularly strikes and lockouts — can have an impact not only on the organization and workers, but also on the public which is not a direct participant in the industrial relations system.

Industrial relations concerns itself with changes in outputs, as well as with their relative levels between occupations and industries. Good comparative studies should examine industrial, national, and international trends. One must, moreover, be concerned not only with the rate of change in any one output, but with the emphasis placed on different types of output under different circumstances. For example, it is generally assumed that during periods of high unemployment or rapid technological change, emphasis is placed on various job and income security provisions; whereas during periods of high employment, emphasis is placed on wages and other direct forms of benefits.

From these observations a number of questions arise. To what extent do variations in wages for the same types of jobs (wage differentials) act as an allocative mechanism in the labour market? How does one account for variations in wages among industries and the stability of inter-industry wage differentials over substantial periods of time? To what extent do fringe benefits, which in North America are largely tied to the firm, impede labour mobility? How can workers be trained for the new jobs arising from technological change? What keeps some workers in low-income areas despite the visible material advantages of moving to higher-income areas? A fair amount has been written on these topics by labour economists and should be incorporated into the study of industrial relations.

Because industrial relations is concerned not only with substantive or material rewards for employment, but also with types of social and psychological rewards (often as critical as material rewards in determining the satisfaction or dissatisfaction of workers), several questions arise: In what ways may informal relationships enhance the needs of the individual and at the same time meet the needs of the organization? What types of communication channels most satisfy the individual and at the same time most serve the organization? What types of processes best lend themselves to individual or group decision-making? Under what circumstances may the individual and the organization gain more from participatory than directive management? What conditions allow the individual to achieve his or her potential and at the same time meet the needs of the organization? What types of organizational structures best respond to the needs of both the organization and the individual? What kind of job redesign — horizontal or vertical — motivates workers to produce more and better products and services for the organization and and its clients? (Horizontal job redesign adds a greater variety of duties at the same level of difficulty. Vertical job redesign adds more challenging duties and opportunities for decision-making.) Does satisfaction lead to higher productivity, as we once thought, or does higher productivity lead to greater satisfaction? These are but a few of the many social and psychological questions for which some answers are beginning to appear, yet the glut of books and articles on organizational behaviour in recent years has not resulted in a systematic inventory of findings in these critical areas.

The Feedback Loop

So far, we have been discussing the outputs of an industrial relations system in terms of rewards to workers for their services and the conditions under which they work. However, one should not only consider the outputs of the system solely in these terms, but look also at the effects of outputs on the economic or service unit under study (be it a plant, hospital, company, industry or country) and on the other subsystems of a society. The relationship of the industrial relations system to various environmental subsystems constitutes a feedback loop.

Conceptually, the outputs of the industrial relations system can be viewed as inputs into environmental subsystems: the industrial relations system conditions environmental subsystems. Conversely, the environmental subsystems condition the industrial relations system. This mutual conditioning occurs not only between the industrial relations system and environmental subsystems, but between the outputs of the industrial relations system and its actors, and is a direct interaction, free of intermediate forces. A good example of this direct, internal conditioning is the beneficial effect on the morale and productivity of workers of satisfactory wages, fringe benefits, and working conditions.

There are a number of reasons why the feedback loop is part of the present framework. From a scientific point of view, observing how the outputs of the industrial relations system return to it in the form of external conditioning inputs to sustain or transform the system itself incorporates a dynamic dimension into the framework. From the point of view of public or private policy, it is essential to investigate the consequences of the outputs of the industrial relations system for societal subsystems. For example, what is the impact of strikes on the economic, legal, political and social subsystems? How do wages and other outputs affect costs, prices, and employment at both the organizational and societal level? How do the outputs of the industrial relations system influence community attitudes towards labour and management, and what part do these attitudes play in shaping public policy in areas such as incomes policies, the right to strike, and other questions which affect the outputs of the industrial relations system? How do these outputs affect a country's ability to compete with other countries? It may be difficult to establish objective measures with which to assess these effects; nevertheless, attempts should be made to develop means of analyzing and predicting the behaviour of unions and management and of assessing the effects of industrial relations systems (its outputs) on society as a whole.

The Analytical, Explanatory, and Predictive Power of the Framework

This part of the chapter will illustrate at micro and macro levels the problems of analysis, explanation, and prediction. At the micro level, the closer the goals, values, and power of the actors in the industrial relations system, the less likelihood there is of any major internal conflict unless one of the actors (e.g., the union) demands concessions the other (e.g., the employer) is not prepared to make. Under the Canadian system, where conciliation or mediation is compulsory in all jurisdictions before a work stoppage may be deemed legal, a government agency charged with conciliation or mediation is likely to become involved as a third party to resolve such disputes. Thus, in Canada a bipartite system can be transformed into a tripartite one.

At the macro level, if the political authorities perceive the outputs of the industrial relations system as important factors in such problems as excess inflation, balance of payments deficits, etc., they are likely to take substantive steps such as imposing wage and price guidelines or controls. Such action is based on the assumption that the collective bargaining process enables unions to push wages and prices higher than

they would be under free competition in labour and product markets. In transforming a bipartite system into a tripartite system, the imposition of wage and price guidelines by government resembles arbitration by government agencies, at least for as long as the government controls are in force.

Another example of the transformation of a bipartite system into a tripartite one may occur during a major strike in an essential industry or service. As mentioned above, Parliament has on several occasions passed special *ad hoc* legislation ordering striking railway, postal and other workers back to work. Similar legislation has also been used by provincial authorities to end strikes. Whether this is the best way to handle these kinds of disputes is the subject of much debate.[24] Undoubtedly, such measures are taken only when political authorities feel that they have strong public support and when it

---

Figure 1.2		**Dunlop's Framework in Diagram Form**

Actors
Labour
Management
Specialized government and
private agencies

Ideology
A set of ideas and beliefs held by
the actors that legitimizes the
role of each and that serves to
bind the system together.

Contexts
1 Technological Characteristics
— Skill levels
— Variable or fixed workplace
— Size of work group
— Job content
— Relation of workplace to
residence
— Stable or variable workplace
— Etc.

2 Market
— Labour and product
— Competitive to monopolistic
— Local to international
— Size of enterprise
— Scope of market
— Secular expansion or
contraction
— Ratio of labor costs to total
costs
— Labour market stringency
— Etc.

3 Budgetary
— Funds available (very important
for public sector)

4 Distribution of power in the larger
society
— which of the actors has more
access to the sources of power?

Rules
1 Procedures for determining
substantive rules (such as
negotiations)

2 Substantive rules (such as
wages, hours, fringe benefits)

3 Procedures for applying
substantive rules to specific
situations (such as grievances)

appears that the *ad hoc* legislation will be adhered to by the actors in the system. Not only is the feedback loop a useful tool for explaining and predicting the behaviour of actors in the industrial relations system but, by applying it to the analysis of the consequences of a strike and the degree to which the public supports the strike, it enables political authorities to legitimize their intervention in disputes.

Application of the Framework to the Three Kinds of Industrial Relations Systems Coexisting in North America

From what has been stated above, it is relatively easy to show how the framework may be applied to the three types of industrial relations systems found in North America. In the bipartite system where collective bargaining takes place between employers and unions without a third party, internal inputs and environmental constraints (external inputs) impinge on the actors as they formulate their demands and negotiate collective agreements without the use of outside assistance. This occurs in a very large percentage of the cases in North America. In formulating their demands, the actors are influenced by environmental constraints. The outputs of the actors in turn feed back directly into the industrial relations system and also into the environmental subsystems, sometimes modifying these environmental subsystems to the extent that they in turn will condition the goals, values, and power of the actors in the next round of negotiations.

The only difference between the bipartite and tripartite systems is that in the latter case some outside agency (in the form of government, private, or some other mediator) may be used to help the parties resolve their differences. In most cases, the role of the third party is to assist the parties to reach agreements, sometimes within the confines of formal or informal wage guidelines.

Where no union exists, the employer determines the outputs of the industrial relations system. He is normally guided by conditions in the surrounding labour market area and by the kinds of settlements that are being negotiated in bipartite or tripartite systems. An example of this kind of employer is the Dominion Foundry and Steel Company (Dofasco) in Hamilton, Ontario. The workers there are not unionized but enjoy the benefits of a profit-sharing programme. Officials at Dofasco keep a close eye on what happens in the highly unionized Stelco plant nearby. The outputs of the bipartite system at Stelco greatly influence the outputs of Dofasco since the two companies operate in the same areas of the labour market and use similar kinds of technology.

Conclusion

This chapter has proposed a framework for the analysis of industrial relations systems and shown how this framework can be used as an explanatory or predictive instrument as well as how it might be applied to the analysis of the bipartite, tripartite, and non-organized systems that coexist in North America. With further elaboration, this framework may serve as a foundation for developing a theory of industrial relations systems in which a series of propositions will be postulated to explain the relationships among the variables. However, that kind of elaboration is the subject of another book — a more generic book than this one. The intent of this chapter has been to lay down the rudiments of the framework and of the analyses and explanations of phenomena described in the following chapters, to anticipate the sequence of these chapters, and to make some predictions where these seem appropriate.

For those wishing to use another framework — as an alternative to the one presented here or for comparative purposes — there is Dunlop's work[25] which in large measure inspired me to write this chapter. A schematic presentation of Dunlop's framework appears on the opposite page.

questions

1 Discuss and explain in detail the main components of the systems approach presented in this chapter.

2 Discuss the major similarities and differences between Dunlop's framework and the one presented in this chapter.

3 What impact, if any, might a major wage increase have on the price of a firm's products or services? What other factors would you include in discussing the impact of a wage increase?

4 In what ways, if any, does the provincial deficit and budgeted expenditures affect labour-management relations in the public sector?

5 Does the systems framework presented in this chapter give you any idea of what you will be studying in this course? Be specific about your expectations and use examples where possible.

6 Do you think that the systems framework

presented in this chapter takes into account all of the factors present in any industrial relations system, particularly that of your province? Elaborate and give examples.

7 Take a firm or industry with which you are familiar and analyze its industrial relations system in terms of the framework presented in this chapter. What problems, if any, are inherent in your analysis?

8 What modifications do you think are necessary to the present framework to render it more useful in analyzing industrial relations problems?

9 Do you consider this systems framework applicable equally at the firm, industry and national levels?

10 Does the systems framework apply equally well to both unionized and nonunionized sectors of the economy? Elaborate.

notes

1 The present chapter represents a refinement of two previous articles by the author: Alton W. J. Craig, "A Model for the Analysis of Industrial Relations Systems," a paper first presented at the 1967 meeting of the Canadian Political Science Association and published in *Canadian Labour and Industrial Relations: Private and Public Sectors,* ed. H. C. Jain (Toronto: McGraw-Hill Ryerson Limited, 1975), pp. 2-12; and, "A Framework for the Analysis of Industrial Relations Systems," a paper given to the Third World Congress of the International Industrial Relations Association in London, England, in September 1973 and published in *Industrial Relations and the Wider Society: Aspects of Interaction,* eds. B. Barrett, E. Rhodes, and J. Beishon (London: Collier Macmillan, 1975), pp. 8-20.

The diagram shown at the beginning of this chapter, which summarizes my concept of the industrial relations system, is not comparable to the one contained in *Canadian Industrial Relations: The Report of the Task Force on Labour Relations,* Privy Council Office (Ottawa: December 1968), p. 10. The latter has been erroneously attributed to me, but is not appropriate to my analysis of industrial relations. A similar misattribution, incidentally, is made in *Union-Management Relations in Canada,*

eds. John Anderson and Morley Gunderson (Don Mills: Addison-Wesley, 1982), p. 7.

2 J. T. Dunlop, *Industrial Relations Systems* (New York: Henry Holt and Co., Inc., 1958).

3 For those interested in attempts to develop industrial relations theory, see *ibid;* and C. Kerr, J. T. Dunlop, F. H. Harbison, and C. A. Myers, *Industrialism and Industrial Man* (Cambridge: Harvard University Press, 1966). For some more recent attempts, see the following: R. J. Adams, "Competing Paradigms in Industrial Relations," Vol. 38, No. 3, *Relations Industrielles/Relations* (1983), pp. 508-31; S. M. A. Hameed, "A Critique of Industrial Relations Theory," Vol. 37, No. 1, *Relations Industrielles/Relations* (1982), pp. 15-31; V. Larouche et E. Deom, "L'approche systématique en relations industrielles," Vol. 39, No. 1, *Relations Industrielles/Relations* (1984), pp. 114-43; G. Schienstock, "Towards a Theory of Industrial Relations," Vol. XIX, No. 2, *British Journal of Industrial Relations* (July 1981), pp. 170-89; and K. F. Walker, "Towards Useful Theorizing about Industrial Relations," Vol. XV, No. 3, *British Journal of Industrial Relations* (November 1977), pp. 307-16.

4 For a good critique of the current status of industrial relations research, see G. Strauss and P. Feuille, "Industrial Relations Research: A

Critical Analysis," Vol. 17, No. 3, *Industrial Relations* (October 1978), pp. 259-77; and Schienstock, "Towards a Theory of Industrial Relations."

5 David Easton, Pt. 1, *Systems Analysis of Political Life* (New York: John Wiley and Sons, Inc., 1955).

6 Abraham H. Maslow, Ch. 4, *Motivation and Personality*, 2nd ed. (New York: Harper and Row, 1970).

7 J. R. Commons, *The Economics of Collective Action* (New York: Macmillan Co., 1950), pp. 76-77.

8 R. B. Freeman and J. L. Medoff, *What Do Unions Do?* (New York: Basic Books, Inc., Publishers, 1984), p. 247.

9 "Alberta's Electricians Accept Three-year Freeze on Wages," *Globe and Mail* (September 28, 1984), p. 4.

10 Jack Barbash, "Collective Bargaining and the Theory of Conflict," Vol. XVIII, No. 1, *British Journal of Industrial Relations* (March 1980), p. 87.

11 *Ibid.*, p. 86.

12 Wilfred List, "Productivity Deal Puts Letter-Carrier Raise in Line, Warren Says," *Globe and Mail* (January 15, 1982), p. 5.

13 Samuel Bacharach and Edward J. Lawler, *Bargaining: Power, Tactics and Outcomes* (San Francisco: Jossey-Bass Publishers, 1981), p. 43.

14 *Ibid.*

15 Syeed M. A. Hameed, "Theory and Research in the Field of Industrial Relations," *British Journal of Industrial Relations* (July, 1967); John C. Anderson, "Bargaining Outcomes: An IR Systems Approach," Vol. 19, No.2, *Industrial Relations* (California) (1979), pp. 126-43.

16 R. E. Walton and R. B. McKersie, *A Behavioral Theory of Labor Negotiations* (New York: McGraw-Hill, 1965) for a good analysis of what they consider to be the four subprocesses of contract negotiations. This significant book received a great deal of attention shortly after its publication, but there has been little follow-up work along the same lines.

17 R. J. Adams, "Estimating the Extent of Collective Bargaining in Canada," No. 223, Faculty of Business, McMaster University, Research and Working Paper Series (Hamilton: April 1984), p. 16.

18 J. W. Garbarino, "Unions Without Unions: The New Industrial Relations," Vol. 23, No. 1, *Industrial Relations* (Winter 1984), pp. 40-51.

19 R. J. Adams, "The Unorganized: A Rising Force?" No. 201, Faculty of Business, McMaster University, Research and Working Paper Series (Hamilton: April 1983).

20 *Ibid.*, pp. 10-11.

21 *The Labour Adjustment Benefits Act* (Bill C-78, 1982), s. 60.13(3).

22 R. J. Adams, "The Unorganized: A Rising Force?" p. 19.

23 C. R. Brookbank, "The Adversary System in Canadian Industrial Relations: Blight or Blessing?" Vol. 35, No. 1, *Relations Industrielles/Industrial Relations* (1980), p. 34.

24 For a good discussion of political involvement in essential services, see *Collective Bargaining in the Essential and Public Service Sectors*, ed. Morley Gunderson (Toronto: University of Toronto Press, 1975). This book resulted from a conference in which a small group of academics and practitioners discussed various ways of dealing with disputes in the essential and public service sectors.

25 For the major components of Dunlop's framework, see J. T. Dunlop, Chs. 1-4, *Industrial Relations System* (New York: Henry Holt and Co., 1958). For an abbreviated form of Dunlop's framework, see E. W. Bakke, C. Kerr, and C. W. Anrod, *Unions, Management and the Public*, 3rd ed. (New York: Harcourt, Brace and World, Inc., 1967), pp. 3-9.

2

The Environment of the Canadian Industrial Relations System

Peter Redman, *The Financial Post*

Introduction

As indicated in the preceding chapter, industrial relations do not operate in a vacuum but rather within the larger environment of society. Furthermore, other societal subsystems act as external conditioning inputs into the industrial relations system. Included among these are: (1) the ecological subsystem, (2) the economic subsystem with its various components, (3) the political subsystem, (4) the legal subsystem, and (5) the social subsystem. Not only do these subsystems condition the inputs and outputs of the industrial relations system, but the outputs of the industrial relations system in turn feed back into the environmental subsystems and quite frequently give cause for action in one or more of them.

To deal with the various components of the environmental subsystems in detail would be an enormous undertaking. There have been entire books written on individual environmental subsystems and a complete analysis of them simply cannot be given here. Rather, this chapter will attempt a brief outline of the major components of each subsystem. Also where possible, this chapter will attempt to include some historical data and their implications for the evolution of a system of industrial relations in Canada.

The Ecological Subsystem

The ecological subsystem is one of the external inputs but, as indicated in Chapter 1, it differs from the other subsystems in that it has no decision-making mechanism to respond to the outputs of the industrial relations system.

Canada is the world's second largest country (next to the Soviet Union) with a total land and fresh water area of almost ten million square kilometres. Over 55% of the land area, however, is not suitable for producing forest or vegetable products. In addition, about 97% of the Canadian population lives within 24% of Canada's total land area.[1] The vast majority of people lives along its southern perimeter and, quite often, there is a greater degree of interaction between Canadians and Americans in the border states than among people in different regions in Canada. The proximity of Canadians and Americans makes for a good deal of cultural commonality and in many cases for close north–south ties in the North American labour movement. These close labour links between the two countries are extremely important since many Canadian union leaders take their cue from what is happening in the American industrial relations system. Some writers refer to this as the demonstration effect.

The severe weather patterns in Canada also have a substantial influence on industrial relations in those industries that are particularly sensitive to climatic variations. Construction and shipping are two industries which are seriously affected by climate. In the construction industry, workers attempt to negotiate generous wage increases so that their incomes during the peak employment season can tide them over the cold winter months when there is little construction activity. The same is true of workers who operate ships on the Great Lakes and the St. Lawrence River since these waterways are usually frozen over during the winter.

Seasonal variations influence not only the level of outputs or benefits, but may also have a significant impact on the timing of negotiations. From a union's point of view, its bargaining power is highest at the beginning of the active season, whereas the employer's bargaining power is greatest during the closed season. Unions on the St. Lawrence Seaway try to bring their negotiations to a head either in the early part of the shipping season or before the end of the shipping season when attempts escalate on the part of shipping companies to complete their shipments before the Great Lakes and St. Lawrence River freeze over. Hence, seasonal variations may have an impact not only on the substantive outputs of an industrial relations system in seasonal industries but also on the timing of periodic negotiations.

The Economic Subsystem

In our discussion of the economic subsystem, I will indicate first the trends in inflation and incomes policies. This will be followed by a discussion of the product market, the labour market, the capital and technology market, and the money market. Capital is linked with technology because capital (money) really does not mean anything until it is translated into some form of technology which is capable of turning out a saleable product or service. A brief description of each of these markets will outline their significance for the evolution and operation of the Canadian industrial relations system.

Inflation

Inflation erodes real income and therefore has a significant impact on the industrial relations system of a country. In times of inflation, both unionized and non-unionized workers will normally seek to restore their real wages.

| Table 2.1 | | | Consumer Price Indexes: Standard Classifications | | | | 1961-1984 (1981=100) | |

Year	All Items	Food	Housing	Clothing	Trans-portation	Health and Personal care	Recreation and reading	Tobacco and alcohol
D	130000	130001	130131	130222	130316	130344	130375	130417
1961	31.6	26.2	32.3	40.6	32.4	31.8	38.6	37.2
1962	32.0	26.7	32.7	41.0	32.4	32.4	38.9	37.7
1963	32.6	27.5	33.1	42.0	32.4	33.2	39.5	37.7
1964	33.2	28.0	33.6	43.0	32.7	34.3	40.1	38.4
1965	34.0	28.7	34.2	43.8	34.0	35.9	40.7	39.1
1966	35.2	30.6	35.1	45.5	34.7	37.0	42.0	40.0
1967	36.5	31.0	36.6	47.7	36.2	38.9	44.1	41.0
1968	38.0	32.0	38.3	49.2	37.2	40.5	46.2	44.8
1969	39.7	33.3	40.3	50.5	38.9	42.4	49.0	46.5
1970	41.0	34.1	42.3	51.5	40.4	44.3	50.7	47.0
1971	42.2	34.4	44.2	52.2	42.1	45.2	52.3	47.8
1972	44.2	37.0	46.2	53.6	43.2	47.4	53.8	49.1
1973	47.6	42.4	49.2	56.3	44.3	49.7	56.1	50.6
1974	52.8	49.4	53.5	61.7	48.7	54.0	61.0	53.4
1975	58.5	55.7	58.9	65.4	54.4	60.2	67.3	59.9
1976	62.9	57.3	65.4	69.0	60.3	65.3	71.3	64.1
1977	67.9	62.0	71.5	73.7	64.5	70.2	74.7	68.7
1978	73.9	71.6	76.9	76.5	68.3	75.2	77.6	74.3
1979	80.7	81.0	82.3	83.6	74.9	82.0	82.9	79.6
1980	88.9	89.8	89.0	93.4	84.5	90.2	90.8	88.6
1981	100.0	100.0	100.0	100.0	100.0	100.0	100.0	100.0
1982	110.8	107.2	112.5	105.6	114.1	110.6	108.7	115.5
1983	117.2	111.2	120.2	109.8	119.8	118.2	115.8	130.0
1984	122.3	117.4	124.7	112.5	124.8	122.9	119.7	140.6
				([%] change)				
1961	1.0	1.5	0.4	1.4	0.2	0.6	1.1	0.5
1962	1.2	1.9	1.2	0.9	−0.1	2.0	1.0	1.3
1963	1.7	3.2	1.1	2.5	0.0	2.5	1.3	0.2
1964	1.8	1.6	1.5	2.5	1.1	3.3	1.7	1.8
1965	2.5	2.6	1.8	1.8	3.8	4.7	1.5	1.7
1966	3.7	6.4	2.8	3.8	2.3	3.0	2.9	2.3
1967	3.6	1.3	4.3	5.0	4.3	5.2	5.0	2.6
1968	4.0	3.3	4.6	3.0	2.7	4.1	4.9	9.1
1969	4.5	4.3	5.2	2.8	4.5	4.8	5.9	3.8
1970	3.4	2.3	4.9	1.9	4.0	4.5	3.5	1.2
1971	2.8	1.1	4.6	1.5	4.1	2.0	3.3	1.7
1972	4.8	7.6	4.6	2.6	2.6	4.8	2.8	2.7
1973	7.6	14.6	6.5	4.9	2.7	4.9	4.2	3.1
1974	10.9	16.3	8.7	9.6	9.9	8.6	8.8	5.5
1975	10.8	12.9	10.0	6.0	11.7	11.4	10.4	12.0
1976	7.5	2.7	11.1	5.6	10.8	8.5	6.0	7.1
1977	8.0	8.3	9.4	6.8	7.0	7.4	4.7	7.1
1978	8.9	15.5	7.5	3.9	5.8	7.2	3.9	8.1
1979	9.2	13.2	7.0	9.2	9.7	9.1	6.9	7.2
1980	10.2	10.7	8.1	11.7	12.8	9.9	9.5	11.2
1981	12.5	11.4	12.4	7.1	18.4	10.9	10.1	12.9
1982	10.8	7.2	12.5	5.6	14.1	10.6	8.7	15.5
1983	5.8	3.7	6.8	4.0	5.0	7.0	6.5	12.6
1984	4.3	5.5	3.8	2.4	4.2	3.9	3.4	8.2

Source: Canada Department of Finance, *Economic Review: April 1985* (Ottawa: Supply and Services Canada, 1985), Reference Table 43, p. 119. Reproduced by permission of the Minister of Supply and Services Canada.

Table 2.2

Indexes of Real Income 1947-1984

Year	Real net national income			Real personal income			Real personal disposable income			Real wages and salaries and supplementary income and military pay		Real average weekly wages and salaries [1]
	Per capita	Per house-hold	Per em-ployee	Per capita	Per house-hold	Per em-ployee	Per capita	Per house-hold	Per em-ployee	Per paid em-ployee	Per em-ployee [1]	
						([%] change)						
1948	0.5	−3.6	1.8	−0.6	−4.7	0.6	0.0	−4.0	1.3	−0.5	−	−
1949	−0.6	−0.7	3.4	−2.1	−2.2	1.9	−1.4	−1.5	2.6	2.0	−	−
1950	3.9	11.1	4.6	1.3	8.3	2.0	2.1	9.1	2.8	2.3	−	−
1951	4.9	3.6	4.6	4.5	3.2	4.2	3.1	1.8	2.9	1.0	−	−
1952	7.3	9.4	9.2	4.9	7.0	6.8	3.9	6.0	5.8	5.6	−	−
1953	0.9	−0.4	2.3	2.6	1.3	4.0	2.2	0.9	3.6	6.0	−	−
1954	−4.4	−4.0	−1.7	−3.0	−2.6	−0.3	−3.0	−2.6	−0.3	1.8	−	−
1955	6.6	5.6	7.0	5.0	4.0	5.4	5.3	4.3	5.7	2.3	−	−
1956	6.9	6.7	5.1	6.3	6.1	4.5	5.8	5.6	4.1	4.3	−	−
1957	−2.3	−1.0	−1.7	0.5	1.8	1.2	0.2	1.4	0.8	1.6	−	−
1958	−1.3	−1.4	2.0	0.3	0.2	3.6	1.4	1.2	4.7	−0.5	−	−
1959	1.4	0.6	0.9	1.8	1.1	1.3	1.0	0.3	0.5	1.4	−	−
1960	0.7	0.6	1.3	2.1	2.0	2.7	1.3	1.1	1.8	1.9	−	−
1961	0.5	0.2	1.1	−1.0	−1.3	−0.5	−1.4	−1.7	−0.9	2.2	−	−
1962	5.3	4.6	4.3	5.5	4.8	4.5	5.6	4.9	4.7	1.9	1.1	1.6
1963	3.7	3.0	3.1	2.8	2.1	2.2	2.8	2.1	2.2	1.9	1.4	1.9
1964	5.2	4.3	3.4	3.7	2.9	1.9	2.7	1.9	0.9	2.9	2.4	2.5
1965	5.4	4.6	3.3	6.1	5.3	4.1	5.7	4.9	3.7	3.3	3.4	3.2
1966	6.7	6.0	4.3	6.6	6.0	4.2	4.5	3.9	2.2	3.3	3.9	2.4
1967	2.0	0.6	1.0	4.2	2.7	3.1	2.6	1.2	1.6	3.6	4.0	3.2
1968	3.8	2.2	3.4	4.0	2.5	3.7	2.6	1.1	2.3	1.4	2.1	2.7
1969	5.1	3.7	3.4	5.3	3.8	3.6	3.2	1.7	1.5	3.9	3.4	3.2
1970	1.1	−0.4	1.4	2.7	1.1	3.0	1.0	−0.5	1.3	2.8	3.0	3.9
1971	6.3	4.9	5.2	7.2	5.9	6.1	7.0	5.7	5.9	4.9	5.0	6.0
1972	7.2	5.2	5.2	7.6	5.6	5.6	8.1	6.1	6.1	3.5	3.7	4.3
1973	9.4	7.3	5.4	7.6	5.5	3.6	7.9	5.8	3.9	2.0	2.4	0.2
1974	6.5	4.5	3.7	5.8	3.8	3.0	5.0	3.1	2.3	3.3	3.2	−0.3
1975	1.6	−0.0	1.4	3.9	2.2	3.7	4.7	2.9	4.4	3.4	3.5	3.3
1976	4.3	2.2	3.5	3.9	1.8	3.1	3.0	0.9	2.2	5.8	5.5	3.6
1977	−0.8	−2.5	−1.4	1.1	−0.7	0.5	0.9	−0.8	0.3	0.6	0.2	1.4
1978	2.7	0.9	0.3	2.6	0.9	0.2	3.7	2.0	1.3	−1.6	−2.1	−1.4
1979	3.9	2.0	0.8	1.9	0.0	−1.1	2.2	0.3	−0.9	−1.2	1.2	−0.6
1980	1.3	−0.2	−0.4	1.4	−0.2	−0.4	1.3	−0.3	−0.5	−1.2	−0.9	−0.6
1981	−1.2	−2.9	−2.6	4.2	2.4	2.7	3.3	1.4	1.7	0.5	0.5	0.2
1982	−7.3	−8.8	−3.0	−1.9	−3.5	2.6	−2.2	−3.8	2.3	0.2	−0.2	−0.8
1983	3.4	1.9	3.6	−0.7	−2.1	−0.5	−1.3	−2.7	−1.1	−0.8	−1.0	1.4
1984	2.7	−0.9	1.2	1.8	−1.8	0.3	1.6	−2.0	0.1	−0.4	−0.6	1.1

[1] For 1983 and 1984, this series is based on special synthetic estimates released by Statistics Canada following changes to its Survey of Employment, Payroll and Manhours. These synthetic estimates will terminate in 1985.

Source: Canada Department of Finance, *Economic Review: April 1985* (Ottawa: Supply and Services Canada, 1985), Reference Table 13, p. 83. Reproduced by permission of the Minister of Supply and Services Canada.

As veteran reporter Wilfred List stated in 1981,

> workers today are readily receptive to the argument that they should not only be able to make up for losses to inflation in the previous contract and cushion themselves against future inflation, but should also be able to improve their real income.[2]

The government's inability to control inflation and its defense of high interest rates were increasing inflationary expectations, according to List, and raising union goals at the bargaining table. He went on to say that

> This could lead to a new wage-and-price spiral as intense as the one that led to controls in 1975. In the end, it could produce irresistible pressures for renewed controls even though the controls had no lasting benefits and soured industrial relations.[3]

Tables 2.1 and 2.2 indicate that the Canadian economy has in fact undergone two recent periods of rapid inflation. The first one occurred from 1972 to 1974 when inflation, as measured by changes in the consumer price index (CPI), went from 2.8% in 1971 to close to 11% in 1974 and 1975. Real income, however, increased by 4.3% in 1972 and dropped to -0.3% in 1974. Subsequently, real income increased from 1975 to 1978, with 1976 registering the highest gain of 3.6% — these were the years that wage and price controls were in effect. The second recent period of inflation started in 1977 with an 8% increase in the CPI and culminated in 1981 with a 12.5% increase in the CPI. Real income, as measured by changes in real average weekly wages and salaries, decreased every year except one from 1978 (-1.4%) to 1982 (-0.8%). These reductions in real income resulted, at least in part, from the recession. Inflation moderated greatly during 1983 and 1984, however, when the CPI increased by only 5.8% and 4.3% respectively. These reductions in the rates of inflation resulted in reductions in annual average changes in major collective agreements — changes which went from 13.1% in 1981 to only 5.6% and 3.9% in 1983 and 1984 respectively in the noncommercial sector.[4] Hence, the hypothesized positive relationship between inflation and wage changes has held true for most of the period since 1972.

To summarize the above discussion we need simply to remark that both negotiated wage settlements and wages and salaries in general are very sensitive to changes in the rate of inflation. During inflationary periods, cost-of-living allowances (COLA) clauses tied to changes in the CPI become popular means of maintaining real incomes for union members. (See the section in Chapter 11 which deals with COLA clauses.)

Incomes Policies and Their Impact The Federal Government's policy of dealing with inflation has been concentrated on monetary and fiscal policies. However, even with record high interest rates and other measures taken by the government, inflation continued to increase until 1983 and 1984. In light of this failure, there has been discussion in some quarters of an incomes policy which might take the form of wage and price guidelines or wage and price controls. Canada has had experience in the recent past with both of these.

During 1969 and 1970, Canada had a Prices and Income Commission whose mandate was

> to inquire into and report upon the causes, processes and consequences of inflation and to inform those making current policy and income decisions, the general public and the Government on how price stability may best be achieved.[5]

Although it had no specific mandate to propose a voluntary wage guideline, the Commission unilaterally announced in June 1970 an upper limit of 6% for annual wage and salary adjustments with provision for exceptions. In fact, increases averaging from 8% to 9% were negotiated by unions and management during the time this voluntary program was in effect. According to the Commission's final report, the guideline was strongly opposed by worker groups and did not gain the necessary support of the general public and government. When the informal restraint program was terminated at the end of 1970, the common view was that although the 6% upper limit may have had a positive influence in reducing wage and salary increases, any such effect had been quite small.[6]

Prior to the June budget of 1975, the Minister

of Finance tried unsuccessfully to develop a voluntary wage and price control program in consultation with labour, management, and the provincial governments. On October 14, 1975 after having failed to achieve a consensus on a voluntary plan, the government announced the immediate implementation of measures to provide for "the restraint of profit margins, prices, dividends, and compensation in Canada." The *Anti-Inflation Act*, as it was termed, was passed by the Commons on December 3, 1975, and lasted for three years. Mandatory wage and price guidelines were given effect on October 14, 1975 and further detailed guidelines, as established by the Anti-Inflation Board, were subsequently issued. Analysis of wage settlements shows that actual settlements were about 4.5% lower than predicted; factors other than the controls program, however, may have been partially responsible for these results.[7]

During the Winter and Spring of 1982, Prime Minister Trudeau tried several times to get the provinces to agree to some form of voluntary restraint program. He also met with high-ranking individuals from the business community and, during the summer, held several meetings with representatives from the labour movement. Labour support, however, was not forthcoming.

In his Budget speech of June 28, 1982, the Minister of Finance put forward the idea of an incomes restraint program of 6% in the first year and 5% in the second year of a two-year program. While appealing to all Canadians to lower their income demands to 6% then 5%, he indicated that the Federal Government would be applying the 6 and 5 program to Ministers of the Crown, Members of the Senate and House of Commons, and federal public servants. It was his wish that the action taken by the Federal Government would serve as an example for other governments and groups to follow.

Following the Budget, the Government introduced Bill C-124 which became the *Public Sector Compensation Restraint Act* of August 1982. This act subjected federal workers to the 6 and 5 wage guidelines for the next two years, during which time existing agreements with public service unions were automatically extended.

While unions, and particularly public-sector unions, were very hostile to the program, they did not cause major disruptions to services. Although many unions in the private sector were not only hit hard by lay-offs but had to deal with companies in financial difficulties, these unions did not engage in illegal actions on behalf of public-sector unions.

Employer reaction generally favoured the Federal Government's move to restrain wages in the federal public sector and while many business leaders doubted the effectiveness of the 6 and 5 program, they too supported the restraint on wages.

Provincial responses to the 6 and 5 program were initially negative. However, it was not too long before most of the provinces initiated programs of their own. The British Columbia restraint program was probably the most controversial of them all, since many social services were substantially reduced. Many union rallies were organized to protest cutbacks in government expenditures.

Thus far we have been discussing some of the recent macroeconomic factors in the Canadian economy. We shall now turn our attention to more specific aspects of the Canadian economic system, starting with the product market.

The Product Market

Some goods produced in Canada are intended for both domestic and export markets whereas others are intended for the domestic market only. We shall deal first with Canada's exports. About 25% of the total production of goods and services in Canada is destined for export markets. In 1974, about two-thirds of Canada's exports were sent to the United States and over two-thirds of our imports were received from that country.[8] Canada's major commodities exports and imports for 1984 are shown in Table 2.3. In 1984 motor vehicles and parts and other fabricated materials constituted the two most important categories of exports. However, over 30% of exports consisted primarily of unfinished goods such as crude petroleum and natural gas, ores and concentrates, wheat, wood pulp, lumber, and other crude materials.

As indicated in Table 2.3, most of the merchandise imported into Canada in 1984 consisted of finished goods. Crude petroleum and other raw materials accounted for only about 15% of imports. This stands in sharp contrast to the 30% of unfinished goods which were exported.

Because the development of a manufacturing base represents the best prospects for long-term economic stability, it is important for Canadian industry to expand both domestic and foreign markets for its finished goods. To accomplish this, it must maintain high levels of productivity and low labour costs per unit of output relative to other trading partners — especially the United States. For this reason it is in the interests of both employers and unions to assess the possible effects of wage increases on the competitive position of a given industry or firm.

An example of what can happen when our costs get out of line with those in the United States occurred in the period from 1974 to 1975. At that time, not only did the average hourly wage rate in Canada surpass the American figure, but the unit labour costs also increased at a higher rate. As the chief economist for the Canadian Manufacturers Association noted, the result was that (with wage settlements going as high as 15% to 20%) "manufacturing fell apart, imports flooded in and exports fell off."[9] One might also add that wage and price controls were imposed in October 1975.

The last column of Table 2.4 shows, "Labour Compensation Per Unit of Output" for the Canadian economy. Note that the increases in compensation for 1974 and 1975 were 13.3% and 17.2% respectively in the manufacturing sector; the data for 1981 (13.7%) and 1982 (13.5%) indicate another potential problem for the Canadian economy. The year 1984 showed a marked difference from previous years: labour compensation per unit of output increased by only 0.5% and output per person hour increased by 6.4%.

Table 2.3	Merchandise Trade Detail: Exports and Imports 1984	
	Exports (%)	Imports (%)
Wheat	4.1	
Animals and other edible products	5.6	6.2
Ores and concentrates	3.3	
Crude petroleum and natural gas	7.6	3.6
Other crude materials	4.9	4.9
Lumber	3.9	
Woodpulp	3.5	
Newsprint	4.3	
Fabricated metals	7.2	
Other fabricated materials	13.2	17.6
Motor vehicles and parts	26.5	27.3
Other machinery and equipment	12.5	28.8
Consumer goods and Miscellaneous	3.0	9.9
Special transactions trade	–	1.6
Totals	99.6	99.9

Source: Department of Finance, *Economic Review, April 1985* (Ottawa: Supply and Services Canada, 1985), Reference Tables 67 and 68, pp. 147-48.

Declining productivity is of great concern to both employers and unions, for it may put employers at a competitive disadvantage in international markets and thus cause layoffs. In fact, the recent recession saw the introduction of what is termed "concession bargaining" in which unions gave up some of the benefits which they had earlier won. Concession bargaining was more prevalent in the United States than in Canada and reflected a greater concern with job security than it did with real income gains.

In 1982, for example, American auto workers gave up eight paid holidays, other benifits, and reportedly conceded $3.5 million in wages and benefits.[10] In 1984, negotiations in the U.S. auto industry emphasized job security. After record profits in 1983 and 1984, negotiations saw two American auto companies agree to establish "job banks" to maintain income and provide retraining for workers who might lose their jobs due

Table 2.4   Index of Productivity and Costs: Manufacturing Industries 1961-1983 (1971 = 100)

Year	Output	Persons employed	Total person-hours	Labour compensation	Output per person employed	Output per person-hour	Labour compensation per person employed	Labour compensation per unit of output
D	143083	240186	240246	240546	240306	240336	240576	240636
1961	54.4	83.6	84.4	46.9	65.1	64.4	56.1	86.1
1962	59.4	85.8	87.6	50.1	69.2	67.8	58.3	84.3
1963	63.4	88.0	90.1	53.3	72.1	70.4	60.6	84.1
1964	69.5	92.0	94.6	58.1	75.6	73.5	63.2	83.6
1965	75.8	96.7	99.4	64.1	78.4	76.2	66.3	84.6
1966	81.5	101.3	103.4	71.9	80.5	78.9	71.0	88.2
1967	83.9	101.7	103.1	77.2	82.5	81.4	75.9	92.0
1968	89.1	101.0	102.5	82.4	88.3	86.9	81.6	92.4
1969	95.8	102.9	104.1	89.9	93.1	92.0	87.3	93.8
1970	94.5	100.6	101.2	94.0	94.0	93.4	93.5	99.5
1971	100.0	100.0	100.0	100.0	100.0	100.0	100.0	100.0
1972	107.7	103.1	103.2	110.6	104.5	104.4	107.2	102.6
1973	119.9	107.8	107.2	126.7	110.4	111.0	117.5	106.4
1974	123.4	110.0	108.7	148.7	112.2	113.5	135.2	120.5
1975	116.2	107.5	105.1	164.0	108.0	110.6	152.6	141.2
1976	123.5	108.0	105.6	189.7	114.4	116.9	175.7	153.5
1977	125.9	105.8	103.6	206.8	118.9	121.6	195.4	164.3
1978	132.0	109.2	107.1	228.2	120.9	123.3	209.0	172.9
1979	139.6	113.2	110.2	260.3	123.4	126.7	230.0	186.4
1980	135.5	112.8	109.4	285.3	120.1	123.9	252.8	210.5
1981	137.0	113.0	108.4	327.8	121.2	126.4	290.0	239.3
1982	121.3	104.2	98.7	329.6	116.5	122.9	316.4	271.6
1983	128.6	102.7	98.3	350.5	125.2	130.8	341.3	272.6
([%] change)								
1962	9.2	2.6	3.8	6.8	6.3	5.3	3.9	−2.1
1963	6.7	2.6	2.9	6.4	4.2	3.8	3.9	−0.2
1964	9.6	4.5	5.0	9.0	4.9	4.4	4.3	−0.6
1965	9.1	5.1	5.1	10.3	3.7	3.7	4.9	1.2
1966	7.5	4.8	4.0	12.2	2.7	3.5	7.1	4.3
1967	2.9	0.4	−0.3	7.4	2.5	3.2	6.9	4.3
1968	6.2	−0.7	−0.6	6.7	7.0	6.8	7.5	0.4
1969	7.5	1.9	1.6	9.1	5.4	5.9	7.0	1.5
1970	1.4	−2.2	−2.8	4.6	1.0	1.5	7.1	6.1
1971	5.8	−0.6	−1.2	6.4	6.4	7.1	7.0	0.5
1972	7.7	3.1	3.2	10.6	4.5	4.4	7.2	2.6
1973	10.6	4.6	3.9	14.6	5.6	6.3	9.6	3.7
1974	3.6	2.0	1.4	17.4	1.6	2.3	15.1	13.3
1975	−5.8	−2.3	−3.3	10.3	−3.7	−2.6	12.9	17.2
1976	6.3	0.5	0.5	15.7	5.9	5.7	15.1	8.7
1977	1.9	−2.0	−1.9	9.0	4.0	4.0	11.2	7.0
1978	4.8	3.2	3.4	10.3	1.7	1.4	7.0	5.2
1979	5.8	3.7	2.9	14.1	2.1	2.8	10.0	7.8
1980	−2.9	−0.4	−0.7	9.6	−2.7	−2.2	9.9	12.9
1981	1.1	0.2	−0.9	14.9	1.0	2.0	14.7	13.7
1982	−11.5	−7.8	−8.9	0.5	−3.9	−2.8	9.0	13.5
1983	6.0	−1.4	−0.4	6.3	7.5	6.4	7.9	0.4

Source: Canada Department of Finance, *Economic Review: April 1985* (Ottawa: Supply and Services Canada, 1985), Reference Table 40, p. 115. Reproduced by permission of the Minister of Supply and Services Canada.

to subcontracting, automation, or productivity gains. The Ford agreement included a four-year ban on closing any of its seventeen assembly plants or forty-eight parts factories.[11]

Both collective agreements provided for a wage increase of 15¢ per hour in the first year of the three-year agreements. But it was estimated that this raise, plus lump-sum payments, profit-sharing and cost-of-living adjustments would provide GM workers with about $12,000 over the three years.[12] Despite the 1984 prosperity, officials of both companies expressed concern over high labour rates, and problems in competing with the Japanese auto industry. Nevertheless, their settlements may have influenced other negotiations in which concessions were granted in the depth of the recession.

The present depreciation of the Canadian dollar relative to the American dollar may help offset some of these figures in the short run; but, should the Canadian dollar return to near par with the American dollar, it will be extremely important for the participants in the industrial relations system in many industries in Canada to keep a close watch on the costs of imports and exports. As mentioned previously, labour is one factor — and a serious one — but productivity is equally if not more important in these complex relationships.

We indicated earlier that some industries in Canada are primarily domestically oriented and include various types of construction and a number of goods-producing industries, all of which are protected by high tariff walls. While Canada is a party to the General Agreement on Tariffs and Trade (GATT), it has agreements nevertheless with some member countries of GATT to continue its tariffs in a number of industries. However, in recent rounds of GATT negotiations there have been attempts to get Canada to lower its tariffs on many products. While tariff rates have decreased by 14% between 1947 and 1980, they will decrease by an average rate of about 9% between 1980 and 1988.[13]

One industry highly protected by tariffs is the clothing industry, particularly manufacturers of knitted garments, knitted fabrics, and knitted goods. The tariff on this Canadian industry is 20% in relation to the British preferential tariff, 27.5% in relation to the most-favoured nation tariff, and 55% in relation to the general tariff.[14] Should the tariffs on these protected products be lowered, employers and workers in the industries involved would be seriously affected. Workers and management would have to negotiate means to lower costs (including labour costs) and increase productivity. As well, some plants would undoubtedly close with unfortunate consequences for all concerned.

The brief discussion above should be sufficient to indicate the importance of the product market to the industrial relations system. It is important for both management and unions to cooperate when competing in international markets. In domestic markets too, where the demand for goods or services is elastic, prices and wages should not be pushed up so high as to reduce sales and hence employment in these sectors.

The Labour Market

Ostry and Zaidi define

> the supply of labour at any given time [as] a *schedule* or *function* relating the quantity of man-hours (of standard efficiency) offered in response to varying levels of wage-rates per hour.[15]

While this definition refers to person hours of standard efficiency, the fact is that labour is not homogeneous. Workers are endowed with various degrees of ability, education, and training which to some extent determine the various forms of labour known as occupations. These range from the most highly skilled and trained types of occupational categories to the lowest, commonly called the unskilled level. Fortunately, there are many functions to be performed in industry and commerce which require the full

Table 2.5 Labour Force by Major Industry Group 1911-1983[a]

	1911		1931		1941		1951		1961		1971		1983	
	Number (1000s)	[%]	Number (1000s)	[%]	Number (1000s)	[%]	Number (1000s)	[%]	Number (1000s)	[%]	Number (1000s)	[%]	Number (1000s)	[%]
Total Civilian Labour Force	2,725.2	100.0	3,917.6	100.0	4,196.0	100.0	5,214.9	100.0	6,342.3	100.0	8,626.9	100.0	12,183	100.0
Primary	1,067.6	39.2	1,293.3	33.0	1,320.6	31.5	1,111.7	21.3	903.3	14.2	720.1	8.4	853	7.0
Agriculture	931.6	34.2	1,124.0	28.7	1,082.3	25.8	827.2	15.9	640.4	10.1	481.2	5.6	513	4.2
Forestry and Fishing	77.8	2.9	97.5	2.5	145.0	3.5	180.6	3.5	143.6	2.3	99.9	1.2	340	2.8
Mining	58.2	2.1	71.8	1.8	93.3	2.2	103.9	2.0	119.3	1.9	139.0	1.6		
Secondary	672.9	24.7	1,093.5	27.9	1,209.9	28.8	1,717.1	32.9	1,963.1	31.0	2,245.5	26.0	2,911	23.9
Manufacturing	473.7	17.4	800.0	20.4	983.9	23.4	1,364.7	26.2	1,494.7	23.6	1,707.3	19.8	2,167	17.8
Construction	199.2	7.3	293.5	7.5	226.0	5.4	352.4	6.7	468.4	7.4	538.2	6.2	744	6.1
Tertiary	896.9	32.9	1,530.4	39.1	1,657.4	39.5	2,328.8	44.7	3,344.1	52.7	4,979.4	57.8	8,419	69.1
Electricity, Gas and Water	10.6	0.4	28.1	0.7	25.9	0.6	62.0	1.2	70.5	1.1				
Transportation and Communication	181.3	5.7	317.0	8.1	292.3	7.0	433.5	8.3	500.2	7.9	678.9	7.9	948	7.8
Trade	259.9	9.5	395.6	10.1	468.4	11.2	711.3	13.6	931.8	14.7	1,269.3	14.7	2,067	17.0
Finance	36.9	1.4	93.1	2.4	90.4	2.2	144.2	2.8	229.7	3.6	358.1	4.2	641	5.3
Community and Business Service	191.7	7.0	251.4	6.4	277.7	6.5	431.2	8.3	764.4	12.1	2,041.4	23.7	3,811	31.3
Recreation Service	9.1	0.3	18.8	0.5	17.7	0.4	28.7	0.6	39.8	0.6				
Personal Service	129.2	4.7	325.6	8.3	367.9	8.3	314.4	6.0	444.4	7.0				
Government Service	78.2	2.9	100.8	2.6	117.2	2.3	203.5	3.9	363.3	5.7	631.7	7.3	848	7.0
Industry not Stated	87.8	3.2	0.5	0.0	8.0	0.2	57.2	1.1	132.0	2.1	681.9	7.9	104	0.9

[a]No estimates are available for 1921.

Source: For the years 1911 to 1971, Sylvia Ostry and Mahmood A. Zaidi, *Labour Economics in Canada*, 3rd ed. (Toronto: Macmillan of Canada, 1979), p. 109. Copyright © Sylvia Ostry and Mahmood A. Zaidi, 1979. Reprinted by permission of Macmillan of Canada, a division of Gage Publishing Ltd. For the year 1983, Statistics Canada, *Labour Force Annual Average, 1975-1983*, Catalogue No. 71-525 (Ottawa: Supply and Services Canada, 1984), p. 179.

range of skills workers bring to the labour market.

As indicated in Table 2.5, the total labour force may be broken down into three major industry groups. These are primary industries such as agriculture, forestry, fishing, and mining; secondary industries such as manufacturing and construction; and tertiary industries such as transportation and communication, trade, finance, and a variety of community and personal services. One of the more dramatic changes indicated in Table 2.5 is the pronounced reduction in agriculture from 34.2% of the labour force in 1911 to 4.2% in 1983. (This figure by itself implies that there has been a significant movement from rural areas into urban centres.) The secondary sector increased from 24.7% in 1911 to 32.9% in 1951 and decreased to 23.9% in 1983. The most pronounced change has been in tertiary industries where employment rose in personal service sectors (excluding government) from 12.0% in 1911 to 23.7% in 1971. An additional significant increase has been that from 9.5% in 1911 to 17% in 1983 for wholesale and retail trade.

Table 2.6 represents workers organized by industry for the year 1982. As can be seen from this table, public administration, construction, transportation, communications, and other utilities are the most highly unionized. Fishing, trapping, and manufacturing are around 44% and the forestry sector about 39% unionized. The service sector, however, is only about 26% unionized, and trade a mere 9%. Thus, from the union point of view, there is much potential for organization, particularly in service industries and trade.

Participation and Unemployment Rates by Sex and Age Groups from 1966 to 1984 Table 2.7 gives the participation and unemployment rates by sex and age groups for the period 1966 to 1984. The participation rate for males between fifteen and twenty-four years of age increased from 64.1% in 1966 to 69.9% in 1984. The female participation rate for the same age group in-

Table 2.6   Workers Organized by Industry 1982

Industry group	[%] workers unionized
Public administration	68.7
Construction	61.8
Transportation, communications, and other utilities	54.0
Fishing and trapping	45.4
Manufacturing	44.3
Forestry	39.3
Mines, quarries, and oil wells	32.9
Service industries	26.3
Trade	9.0
Finance	3.0
Agriculture	0.2

Source: Statistics Canada, *Annual Report of the Minister of Supply and Services Canada under the Corporations Labour and Unions Returns Act, Part 11-Labour Unions 1982,* Catalogue No. 71-202 (Ottawa: Supply and Services Canada, August 1984), p. 60. Reproduced by permission of the Minister of Supply and Services Canada.

creased from 48.4% to 63.6%. What these figures mean is that more young people of both sexes are entering the labour force. These increases have potentially serious consequences for the industrial relations system. For example, persons in the fifteen- to twenty-four year old age group have not gone through the hard times associated with a depression, nor have they suffered the severe discipline that the Second World War imposed on both civilian and military personnel. In addition, this group brings new expectations to the workplace since its level of education is higher than that of previous groups and its expectations are conditioned by having grown up in an era of great affluence. In addition, people of this age are not as predisposed as older people to accept the discipline which is characteristic of many types of employment.

A study of Canadian work values conducted from 1973 to 1974 by the Department of Manpower and Immigration attempted to define the work ethic and to find out how satisfied people

Table 2.7 — Participation and Unemployment Rates by Sex and Age Groups 1966-1984

	Participation rates						
	Male			Female			
Year	Total	15-24	25+	Total	15-24	25+	Total
D	767420	767430	767389	767552	767562	767521	767288
	767685	767697	767656	767752	767763	767730	767610
	767985	768143	767129	768005	768171	767165	767860
				[%]			
1966	79.8	64.1	84.9	35.4	48.4	31.2	57.3
1967	79.3	64.1	84.5	36.5	49.1	32.3	57.6
1968	78.6	63.3	84.0	37.1	49.8	32.8	57.6
1969	78.3	62.7	83.8	38.0	50.2	33.8	57.9
1970	77.8	62.5	83.3	38.3	49.5	34.5	57.8
1971	77.3	62.7	82.7	39.4	50.8	35.4	58.1
1972	77.5	64.4	82.3	40.2	51.2	36.2	58.6
1973	78.2	66.8	82.3	41.9	54.2	37.6	59.7
1974	78.7	68.9	82.2	43.0	56.0	38.5	60.5
1975	78.4	68.8	81.9	44.4	56.8	40.0	61.1
1976	77.6	67.9	81.1	45.2	56.8	41.1	61.1
1977	77.7	68.9	80.9	46.0	57.5	42.1	61.6
1978	78.1	69.7	81.1	47.9	59.0	44.1	62.7
1979	78.5	71.3	81.0	49.0	61.0	45.0	63.4
1980	78.4	71.0	80.7	50.4	62.6	46.4	64.1
1981	78.4	72.3	80.5	51.7	63.2	48.1	64.8
1982	77.0	69.3	79.5	51.7	62.3	48.5	64.1
1983	76.7	69.2	79.1	52.6	62.8	49.6	64.4
1984	76.6	69.9	78.6	53.5	63.6	50.6	64.8

	Unemployment rates						
	Male			Female			
	Total	15-24	25+	Total	15-24	25+	Total
	767421	767431	767390	767553	767563	767522	767289
	767686	767698	767657	767753	767764	767731	767611
	767898	768146	767130	768008	768174	767166	767863
				[%]			
1966	3.3	6.3	2.6	3.4	4.8	2.7	3.4
1967	3.9	7.2	3.0	3.7	5.5	2.8	3.8
1968	4.6	8.7	3.5	4.4	6.5	3.3	4.5
1969	4.3	8.3	3.2	4.7	6.5	3.7	4.4
1970	5.6	11.2	4.1	5.8	8.6	4.4	5.7
1971	6.0	12.0	4.3	6.6	9.8	5.0	6.2
1972	5.8	11.9	4.1	7.0	9.6	5.7	6.2
1973	4.9	10.0	3.4	6.7	9.2	5.4	5.5
1974	4.8	9.6	3.3	6.4	8.9	5.1	5.3
1975	6.2	12.5	4.3	8.1	11.4	6.5	6.9
1976	6.3	13.2	4.2	8.4	12.1	6.6	7.1
1977	7.3	14.9	4.9	9.4	13.8	7.4	8.1
1978	7.5	15.0	5.2	9.6	13.8	7.7	8.3
1979	6.6	13.2	4.5	8.8	12.7	7.0	7.4
1980	6.9	13.7	4.8	8.4	12.6	6.5	7.5
1981	7.0	14.1	4.8	8.3	12.3	6.7	7.5
1982	11.1	21.1	8.2	10.9	16.1	8.8	11.0
1983	12.1	22.4	9.2	11.6	17.0	9.6	11.9
1984	11.2	19.4	8.9	11.4	16.2	9.7	11.3

Source: Canada Department of Finance, *Economic Review: April 1985* (Ottawa: Supply and Services Canada, 1985), Reference Table 28. p. 103. Reproduced by permission of the Minister of Supply and Services Canada.

were with their jobs. Young people placed greater emphasis on their peer group for self-fulfillment than did any other group. As the Report indicates,

> Twenty per cent of those under 24 years, as compared with approximately 10 per cent of older Canadians, indicated that friends were the key to self-fulfillment. These young people relied equally on work and less on the family than did other age groups.[16]

In addition, the survey found that young people were slightly more likely than older people to disagree with the statements "I want a boss who is strict," and "I like a job where I'm carefully supervised all the time."[17] A very important finding was that the sixteen- to nineteen-year olds, when asked what single factor would be most important in inducing them to change jobs, placed as much stress on interesting work and the opportunity to use their talents as on salary or advancement.[18]

Because it appears that young workers will be looking for pleasant jobs with relatively good pay, a high degree of challenge, and not too much supervision, employers and unions may soon have to experiment with quality-of-life projects and job enrichment in order to build more satisfaction into the jobs of the future. Some of the more senior management and union representatives may also have a difficult time adjusting to the attitudes of young, highly educated workers. However, if these representatives do not respond in a positive way, young workers may attempt to gain greater control within unions and management and try themselves to exercise more influence on the structure of jobs.

As Table 2.7 indicates, the participation rate of male workers twenty-five years and older decreased from 84.9% in 1966 to 78.6% in 1984 whereas the participation rate for female workers in the same age group increased from 31.2% to 50.6%. The significant increase in the participation rate of women in the labour force has a number of implications for trade unions

and industrial relations. On the trade union side, if organized labour wants to expand into some areas of employment it will have to exert greater effort to organize women in the labour force.

From an industrial relations point of view, having a fairly high proportion of women in an organized workplace will probably increase the number of demands made. This became very evident during the 1981 postal strike in Canada when the Canadian Union of Postal Workers (whose membership is about 40% women) struck for a substantial time in order to acquire paid maternity leave. Not only will unions have to respond to the needs of women, but women may also seek to play a much more effective and continuing role in the operations of trade unions. This will be a relatively new phenomenon for both the managers of organizations and trade union leaders. Already, there are a number of high profile women in some of the larger unions in Canada — their number is likely to increase in the near future.

Turning now to the unemployment rates, Table 2.7 indicates that the unemployment rate for males between the age of fifteen and twenty-four years increased from 6.3% in 1966 to 19.4% in 1984 whereas for females within the same age category the unemployment rate increased from 4.8% to 16.2%. This reflects a softening in the market for goods and consequently for labour, and usually the first to be laid off are the younger, less experienced workers. The unemployment rate for males twenty-five years and older increased from 2.6% in 1966 to 8.9% in 1984 and for females of the same age group from 2.7% to 9.7%. The recent recession had its most devastating effects on the young.

The significance of the above statistics relates particularly to the fifteen- to twenty-four year old age group. Since the unemployment rates in this group are higher during times of recession than in times of prosperity, now would perhaps be an opportune time to provide these young workers with training programs in occupations where vacancies do or will exist. One recommendation has been to conduct an advertising campaign to attract the nineteen- to twenty-four-year-olds into apprenticeship programs for occupations where there are existing or projected labour shortages. It is a waste of resources to have substantial numbers of these people unemployed and it would represent a real investment in human capital if these people could be attracted into apprenticeship programs whether financed jointly by management and unions or by government, management, and unions. Such apprenticeship or other types of training programs would doubtless alleviate the financial burden on the unemployment insurance and welfare programs.

One can argue, however, that industry, along with other groups, has a social responsibility to help people in this age group grow into productive members of society.[19] In the past, government and the private sectors have not embraced this strategy. As a result, representatives of provincial governments and private employers have been obliged to go to Europe to recruit the kind of skilled tradesmen that a comprehensive, indigenous apprenticeship could otherwise have provided.

In September 1978, however, the Federal Government inaugurated the Critical Trades Skill Training Program to which substantially increased federal funds were allocated to assist the private sector in training workers or prospective workers for certain high-skilled trades. This scheme represented an excellent opportunity for unions and management to cooperate in increasing the supply of skilled labour and tackling the often intractable problem of unemployment among youth. While this program was phased out during the Summer of 1985, the Conservative government announced six new programs under the title of "Canadian Jobs Strategy." These programs are designed (1) to help workers whose jobs are threatened due to changing technology and economic conditions, (2) to assist young people and women facing difficulties

entering the labour market by providing them with a combination of training and work experience, (3) to provide meaningful assistance for the long-term unemployed, (4) to ensure that critical-skill shortages are alleviated, (5) to offer help to workers in communities facing chronic high unemployment, plant closures, mass lay-offs, or severe economic decline, and (6) to stimulate the search for innovative solutions to labour market problems. Some of these objectives are new; others combine existing programs while giving them new directions.[20]

Unemployment for Canada and by Region from 1966 to 1985 As Table 2.8 indicates, Canada's unemployment rate remained fairly stable (around 7% to 8%) from 1975 to 1981, but rose dramatically to 11.0% in 1982 and to 11.9% in 1983. However, it dropped to 11.3% in 1984 and to an estimated 10.5% in June 1985. These intolerable rates of unemployment have policy makers and other concerned groups very worried. The Canadian Mental Health Association contended in 1984 that "Canadians must sacrifice [a] part of their jobs and income to the unemployed to avert social disaster."[21] The Conference Board of Canada, a non-partisan economic forecasting organization, launched "an $800,000 study on the controversial issue of job-sharing and national income supplements."[22]

While the national unemployment rate is very high, there is substantial variation between regions. On the whole, the Prairie region suffered the least unemployment from 1966 to 1984, followed by Ontario. However, the Atlantic region, which usually suffers high unemployment rates, has had problems in this regard from 1975 to 1984 and Quebec has not fared much better during the same period. British Columbia, on the other hand, has had an unemployment rate slightly above the national average for some years and slightly below it for other years. While Quebec's pattern may be at least partly attributed to substantial unemployment in the

Eastern Townships, it is difficult to explain the persistently high unemployment in the province of British Columbia in recent years.

If the classical and neo-classical economic theories held true, we would not have major variations in unemployment rates or in wage rates in different regions. According to neo-classical theory, labour in regions with a high unemployment rate would migrate to those parts of the country where the unemployment rate is low and where wages are higher. If the theory actually worked in practice, what would happen is that people from the Atlantic region, for example, would move to Ontario or the Prairie Region and by creating a greater supply of labour would reduce wage rates in areas of low unemployment. This would presumably in-

crease overall employment, while reducing the unemployment rate in regions which now have high unemployment.

However, it is well known that the labour market does not operate the way that neo-classical economics suggest it should. Specifically, social and psychological ties often outweigh material advantage. For this reason, unions and management along with government should normally attempt to attract industry to areas of high unemployment in order to stimulate employment in these areas. Unfortunately, in times of extreme economic dislocation, such a solution is not always feasible.

Unemployment and Recession   Given the current downturn in the Canadian economy, it

Table 2.8
Unemployment, Canada and by Region 1966-1984

Year	Unemployed						Unemployment rate					
	Canada	Atlantic region	Quebec	Ontario	Prairie region	British Columbia	Canada	Atlantic region	Quebec	Ontario	Prairie region	British Columbia
D	767891		769840	769903		769921	767863		769842	769905		769923
	(Thousands of persons)						[%]					
1966	251	32	86	72	29	33	3.4	5.2	4.1	2.6	2.3	4.6
1967	296	33	100	92	33	39	3.8	5.3	4.6	3.2	2.6	5.1
1968	358	37	124	107	43	47	4.5	5.8	5.6	3.6	3.2	5.9
1969	362	40	137	99	45	42	4.4	6.2	6.1	3.2	3.3	5.0
1970	476	39	160	139	70	67	5.7	6.0	7.0	4.4	5.0	7.7
1971	535	47	171	178	74	65	6.2	7.0	7.3	5.4	5.2	7.2
1972	553	53	178	171	78	73	6.2	7.6	7.5	5.0	5.3	7.8
1973	515	57	169	152	70	66	5.5	7.7	6.8	4.3	4.6	6.7
1974	514	64	169	164	53	64	5.3	8.3	6.6	4.4	3.4	6.2
1975	690	77	214	242	65	92	6.9	9.8	8.1	6.3	4.0	8.5
1976	726	87	233	239	71	96	7.1	10.8	8.7	6.2	4.1	8.6
1977	849	103	284	278	86	98	8.1	12.5	10.3	7.0	4.8	8.5
1978	908	106	308	298	97	99	8.3	12.5	10.9	7.2	5.2	8.3
1979	836	101	278	278	84	95	7.4	11.6	9.6	6.5	4.3	7.6
1980	865	99	294	297	88	88	7.5	11.1	9.8	6.8	4.3	6.8
1981	898	104	314	293	96	91	7.5	11.5	10.3	6.6	4.5	6.7
1982	1,314	129	413	440	165	166	11.0	14.3	13.8	9.8	7.6	12.1
1983	1,448	139	427	474	217	192	11.9	15.0	13.9	10.4	9.7	13.8
1984	1,399	147	400	423	221	208	11.3	15.4	12.8	9.1	9.8	14.7

Source: Canada Department of Finance, *Economic Review: April 1985* (Ottawa: Supply and Services Canada, 1985), Reference Table 33, p. 108. Reproduced by permission of the Minister of Supply and Services Canada.

would seem appropriate to discuss the impact of exceptionally high unemployment rates on this country's industrial relations system. In June 1984, Canada reached its highest unemployment rate since the Depression. The estimated unemployment rate for the country as a whole decreased to 10.5% in June 1985. On the same date, estimated unemployment rates for the provinces were as follows: 23.3% in Newfoundland, 11.5% in Prince Edward Island, 14.1% in Nova Scotia, 15.3% in New Brunswick, 11.8% in Quebec, 7.7% in Ontario, 8.7% in Manitoba, 7.9% in Saskatchewan, 9.8% in Alberta, and 14.8% in British Columbia.[23]

With both high unemployment and inflation rates, most countries in the Western world are unable to find economic policies to reduce simultaneously the high inflation and unemployment rates. Canada's emphasis on reducing inflation may cause high unemployment rates for some time unless government priorities and policies change. The present high level of unemployment is hitting not only blue-collar workers but also white-collar occupations not usually thought to be subject to high levels of unemployment. For example, the unemployment rate for clerical workers increased from 6.6% in December 1981 to 8.3% in March, 1982.[24] In 1985, however, interest rates dropped dramatically. Low finance charges on cars made 1985 the most successful year in a long time for a number of automobile companies, particularly GM and Ford.

With inadequate theories to explain the twin problems of high inflation and high unemployment, governments are left with piecemeal approaches. Simple theories of inflation such as "demand-pull" or "cost-push" are inadequate to explain this situation. Economists and other theorists are thus of little help to government and business during the present economic crisis. Some companies are cutting back on office staff and reducing salary levels for their office workers, and many American companies and unions are negotiating wage freezes and reduced

benefits (such as paid holidays) for workers.

At the time of writing this chapter, Canadian unions and the President of the Canadian Labour Congress were arguing against some of the American initiatives. The 1984-85 negotiations in the auto industry in Canada saw the Canadian section split from the United Automobile Workers Union to form a separate Canadian union. The director of the Canadian UAW contended that the international UAW had interfered unduly in the 1984 Canadian negotiations. This subject will be discussed in more detail in Chapter 5.

Personal Income Per Capita at Federal and Provincial Levels from 1951 to 1984 Table 2.9 showing personal income per capita by province as a percentage of personal income per capita for the nation as a whole provides the basis for a number of interesting comparisons. Throughout most of the period from 1955 to 1983, Ontario has led all of the other provinces in terms of per capita income. Overall, it has been closely followed by British Columbia which, in some years, actually exceeded the Ontario per capita income. Alberta follows British Columbia, although in recent years it has been increasing more rapidly than that of any of the other provinces. Manitoba and Saskatchewan have roughly the same income per capita although there are some variations from year to year. Quebec, for a number of years somewhat lower in income per capita than Manitoba and Saskatchewan, has more recently slightly surpassed the per capita income of these two provinces, except for Saskatchewan from 1977 to 1980. The four Atlantic provinces are by far the lowest in terms of per capita income with Newfoundland being the lowest of the four.

Hence, what we have in Canada is a number of "rich" provinces and a number of "poor" provinces as measured in terms of personal income per capita. The low levels in the Atlantic provinces provide one of the major reasons for the transfer of payments from the Federal Government's general tax revenues to the provinces with the lowest per capita incomes.

From an industrial relations point of view, these provincial differentials may have serious ramifications with respect to negotiating collective agreements. In some industries which bargain on a multi-provincial basis there is the question of whether or not there should be wage differentials to take into account local labour market conditions. A motion at the 1982 convention of the Public Service Alliance of Canada to provide for regional variations for federal workers came close to being accepted by the delegates.

Table 2.9											Personal Income Per Capita, Canada and by Province 1955-1983	
Year	Nfld.	P.E.I.	N.S.	N.B.	Que.	Ont.	Man.	Sask.	Alta.	B.C.	Y.T.& N.W.T.	Canada
(Personal income per capita, by province, as a [%] of personal income per capita at the national level)												
1955	53.1	49.4	73.8	66.0	86.5	119.5	94.4	8.9	99.8	123.3	109.4	100.0
1956	53.5	58.7	72.0	65.8	86.3	117.8	97.0	93.5	104.6	121.3	130.1	100.0
1957	54.5	51.4	73.9	65.3	88.1	119.6	93.7	77.8	99.2	121.5	125.6	100.0
1958	53.6	53.2	74.2	65.7	87.0	119.0	99.0	83.1	104.1	116.1	114.6	100.0
1959	54.0	59.1	75.6	66.9	86.7	118.8	99.1	82.3	101.6	117.0	111.6	100.0
1960	55.6	56.9	76.4	68.1	87.1	117.8	99.5	89.3	99.8	115.3	105.7	100.0
1961	58.2	58.8	77.8	68.0	90.1	118.4	94.3	71.0	100.0	114.9	96.6	100.0
1962	56.0	60.4	75.6	66.3	89.2	116.9	97.6	93.2	99.8	112.0	87.9	100.0
1963	56.3	58.4	75.5	67.0	88.6	117.2	94.3	98.2	98.2	112.2	88.8	100.0
1964	56.9	60.7	75.9	68.5	90.3	117.3	95.8	84.5	96.0	113.3	86.2	100.0
1965	59.2	60.1	74.7	68.4	89.9	116.5	93.8	90.1	97.0	113.7	80.5	100.0
1966	59.9	60.1	74.8	68.9	89.2	116.4	91.9	93.1	100.0	111.6	80.8	100.0
1967	61.0	62.1	76.7	69.3	90.5	116.2	95.4	81.3	99.1	110.8	82.4	100.0
1968	61.5	63.9	76.6	70.4	89.0	117.0	96.6	84.7	100.3	108.3	85.9	100.0
1969	61.0	62.8	77.4	70.1	88.4	117.9	93.8	80.5	100.0	109.6	88.2	100.0
1970	63.4	66.5	77.4	72.0	88.7	118.4	92.9	72.5	99.2	108.8	94.6	100.0
1971	63.6	63.7	77.5	72.3	88.7	117.0	94.1	80.3	99.0	109.0	86.8	100.0
1972	63.9	66.1	79.8	73.6	89.5	116.1	93.6	78.8	98.4	109.4	88.1	100.0
1973	64.0	70.2	79.9	73.3	89.2	113.6	96.0	91.5	99.6	110.9	88.3	100.0
1974	67.3	66.6	79.5	74.3	90.6	111.8	94.7	96.1	100.2	110.2	93.4	100.0
1975	68.6	70.2	79.1	77.2	91.2	109.9	96.4	104.0	103.0	108.1	91.5	100.0
1976	68.3	67.8	78.4	75.3	93.5	109.5	93.0	98.7	101.8	108.7	93.3	100.0
1977	68.7	67.5	79.6	74.8	93.7	109.5	92.5	91.6	102.3	110.1	96.9	100.0
1978	66.9	71.0	80.6	74.9	93.9	108.9	92.3	92.0	103.5	110.2	96.8	100.0
1979	66.9	69.1	80.3	75.1	93.5	108.3	90.6	92.0	107.5	110.6	98.6	100.0
1980	65.3	70.6	78.9	72.9	94.2	107.6	88.8	91.9	109.1	111.5	101.5	100.0
1981	65.5	66.9	77.1	70.8	93.5	107.3	92.6	98.9	110.9	109.0	104.4	100.0
1982	66.9	69.4	78.8	72.0	93.1	107.8	93.8	96.8	110.4	107.3	102.2	100.0
1983	67.8	74.3	80.4	74.1	92.5	109.2	93.1	93.7	108.2	105.9	105.5	100.0

Source: Canada Department of Finance, *Economic Review: April 1985* (Ottawa: Supply and Services Canada, 1985), Reference Table 17, p. 90. Reproduced by permission of the Minister of Supply and Services Canada.

In some cases, collective agreements do make differentials, and the Irving Pulp and Paper Company is a good example of a company which insists on keeping its rates in line with local levels of income. On the other hand, large pulp and paper companies, such as International Paper and Abitibi which bargain on a multi-provincial basis, have collective agreements which contain the same pay rates for their plants in Ontario, Quebec, and the Atlantic provinces. The higher rates paid by large companies may make it hard for companies based in low income areas to attract a sufficient quantity and quality of labour. Consequently, differences in provincial per capita income, apart from generating transfer payments, also prove to be quite significant with respect to negotiations which cross the boundaries of some provinces.

Capital and Technology

Capital and technology will be discussed together since capital does not mean very much until it is converted into the technological structures needed to produce goods and services. Canadian industry, until recently, has generally not been as capital intensive as industry in the United States. Since Canada operates behind high tariff walls in some industries, there is little incentive for employers in some industries to become more highly capital intensive. One has merely to walk through a number of Canadian and American automobile parts producers to notice the differences in the technology in the two countries. In addition, relatively high tariff walls do not push Canadian companies to try to achieve economies of scale, and hence make more effective use of their technological resources and produce goods at lower costs.

A 1978 Royal Commission had the following to say about Canadian industry:

> That Canadian firms are scale-inefficient has become a cliché both in the literature of industrial organizations in Canada and among businessmen. Until 1975 relatively lower wages in Canada as

compared with the United States partially masked the effect of low productivity in Canada. When the wage relationship reversed in 1975, the future of the manufacturing sector in Canada looked bleak indeed: low productivity, compounded by high costs of both labour and capital, was rapidly making large segments of Canadian industry uncompetitive internationally. One proposed solution to this predicament was the Economic Council of Canada's recommendation, in its study *Looking Outward*, that Canada move towards multilateral free trade since then all firms would be open to international competition and would have free access to world markets. They would then be forced to move towards their most efficient scale of operation at product, plant and firm levels.[25]

A Canadian authority on productivity has recently claimed that Canada is now more capital intensive than the United States "which makes Canada the most capital intensive country in the world."[26] Yet for some years now, there have been substantial numbers of Canadians who have argued that Canada relies too heavily on foreign investment and that it should somehow acquire more control over its own investment and its own affairs. The Canadian economy is often called a "branch-plant economy." The Royal Commission whose *Report* we quoted above has the following to say about foreign ownership in Canada:

> Canadian industry features a higher proportion of foreign ownership than does any other developed country, and the presence of foreign ownership and foreign subsidiaries in Canada contributes to Canada's dependence on capital and technology from abroad. Repatriation of dividends and interest charges at the rate of $2.5 billion per year reduces the growth of domestic pools of capital. Because of their backing by their parent firms, multinational subsidiaries are often able to obtain capital in Canada on more favourable terms than domestic companies of the same size. Technology is often imported rather than developed in Canada because it is cheaper and less risky to buy or license from foreign firms than to maintain indigenous research and development.[27]

The estimated book value of capital employed in non-financial industries in 1954 was 28.2

billion dollars but it had increased to 129.7 billion dollars in 1974. Canadian ownership of capital employed and controlled in Canada was 64% in the years 1969, 1970, and 1971 — down from a high of 72% in 1954. The percentage of Canadian controlled capital in 1974 was 67%. The United States accounted for a vast majority of the percentage of capital employed and controlled in Canada between 1954 and 1972. It varied from 24% in 1954 to 28% in 1967-1970 and in 1974 it was 25%. The percentage of capital employed and controlled by other foreign countries varied from 4% in 1954, to 7% for a good part of the 1960's to 9% in 1971 and 1972 and 8% in 1973 and 1974.[28]

When one looks at the assets of foreign controlled corporations as a percentage of industry assets one discovers startling contrasts. Using this criterion in 1974, one finds heavy foreign involvement in tobacco products (99.8%), mineral fuels (74%), textile mills (60%), machinery (67.6%), transportation equipment (79.6%), and petroleum and coal products (94.4%). These examples contrast with lows of 11.5% in printing, publishing and allied industries, 15.5% in clothing, and 21.9% in beverages.[29]

From these figures one can see the very high degree of foreign ownership and control of industry in Canada both generally and in specific industries. This factor was the major reason the Trudeau government set up the Foreign Investment Review Agency to exercise some restraint on the rate of foreign investment and acquisitions in Canada. The Mulroney government has renamed the agency Investment Canada and has adopted a more permissive stance toward foreign investment.

This high degree of foreign control in Canadian industry may have serious implications for industrial relations policies and practices. In some cases, companies may try to import their industrial relations practices from the country of ownership into Canada. If the two cultures are somewhat compatible, the problems may not be too great. A more serious feature of the high degree of foreign ownership is that, should Canadian subsidiaries become unprofitable,

they may very well be closed down and their assets removed to other countries. This happened to an Oshawa plant in the Summer of 1980 — many workers with years of seniority lost benefits they otherwise would have been entitled to.

Plant closures became such a serious problem in Ontario that the provincial government set guidelines on plant closure. For example, Part XII, section 40(2) of the Ontario *Employment Standards Act* requires an employer to give specified notice of layoff ranging from eight to sixteen weeks depending on the numbers of workers to be laid off.[30] In addition, section 40(a) provides that where the employment of fifty or more workers is to be terminated, severance pay shall be given to each worker who has been employed for five or more years at the rate of his or her regular pay per week multiplied by the number of years that the worker has been with the firm, up to a maximum of twenty-six years. Heavy fines have been given to employers who have failed to comply with these provisions.

As a concluding comment on this section, we should add that Canadian industry probably would not be as highly developed as it is today if it had not been for foreign investment. However, this development does not preclude a certain vigilance concerning the effects of foreign-controlled organizations on industrial relations and workers in this country.

The Money Market

The diagram which sets out the environmental constraints operating on industrial relations systems includes the money market as an important aspect of the economic system that may have an impact upon industrial relations in Canada. This market may be defined as capital available for investments of different types and interest rates payable on bank loans or long-term securities. While it is unnecessary to elaborate greatly on cash flows, note that the high interest rates of recent years (if they are any predictor of what is to happen in the future) must cause us concern with respect to the cost of borrowing money. High interest rates seriously curtail purchases of houses, cars, and other durable goods and, as a consequence, affect employment and capital investment in these industries. Unionized workers in a number of industries in the United States (e.g., airlines, trucking, meat packing, rubber and steel) have negotiated wage cuts, wage freezes or improved productivity arrangements to help protect their jobs and income. These were negotiated in addition to the Ford and GM agreements.[31]

So far there have been few recorded cases of Canadian union members taking wage cuts. However, many unions that did make wage concessions during the worst years of the recession are beginning to recover lost ground. Also the devalued Canadian dollar has had serious implications both for our exports (which should have been aided by the devalued dollar) and for imports (which will cost more because of the devalued Canadian dollar). Thus, we have imported some of our inflation in recent years because of the high prices that must be paid in Canadian dollars to buy finished products or other goods on international markets.

What the present monetary system may do with respect to the long-term development of Canadian industry is very difficult to predict, but should the Canadian dollar soon approach par with the American dollar, many companies will be in difficulty, especially if they wish to operate in international markets. Here again, the money market would be of concern to those involved in Canada's industrial relations system in industries which rely fairly heavily on export markets, and in particular on the exportation of manufactured products.

Some Concluding Comments on the Economic Subsystem

What we have tried to do in this section on the Canadian economic system is to discuss in some detail the implications of various aspects of the Canadian economic system for industrial relations policy and practice. We first commented on the roles that projected inflation and real income losses are likely to have on our industrial relations system. We also discussed briefly the

impact of previous incomes policies. We have commented on the Canadian import and export situation and the extent to which we rely on both imports and exports to keep our economic system running. We have also commented briefly on the degree of foreign ownership of Canadian assets and some of its potential implications for Canada's economic development and for industrial relations practices in particular. Finally, we have commented on the money market and how shifts here may have serious implications not only for domestic developments in Canada but also on the country's foreign trade. All of these factors act as important conditioning inputs and outputs of the industrial relations system.

The Political Subsystem

Canada is a federation in which certain powers are granted to the Federal Government and other powers are granted to the provincial legislatures. Section 91 of *The Constitution Act, 1867* spells out the powers of the Federal Government and Section 92 spells out the powers of the provincial legislatures. The most important provisions relating to federal power regarding industrial relations include the preamble of Section 91 which gives the Federal Government the right to make laws for the "Peace, Order and Good Government of Canada." There are thirty-one enumerated items in Section 91, of which the following may be considered pertinent to the constitutionality of labour relations:

> The Regulation of Trade and Commerce (2); Unemployment Insurance (2A); Postal Service (5); Navigation and Shipping (10); Sea Coast and Inland Fisheries (12); Ferries between a Province and any British or Foreign Country or between two Provinces (13); Banking, Incorporation of Banks and the Issue of Paper Money (15); Savings Banks (16); The Criminal Law, except the Constitution of Courts of Criminal Jurisdiction, but including the Procedure in Criminal Matters (27); and Such Classes of Subjects by this Act assigned exclusively to the Legislatures of the Provinces (29).[32]

Section 92 lists those areas which are within the exclusive domain of the provincial legislatures. There are sixteen headings altogether, the most important of these with respect to the constitutionality of labour legislation being:

> Municipal Institutions in the Province (8); Property and Civil Rights in the Province (13); Generally all Matters of a merely local or private Nature in the Province (16); and Local Works and Undertakings other than such as are of the following Classes: (a) Lines of Steam or other Ships, Railways, Canals, Telegraphs, and other Works and Undertakings connecting the Province with any other or others of the Provinces, or extending beyond the Limits of the Province; (b) Lines of Steam Ships between the Province and any British or Foreign Country; (c) Such Works as, although wholly situate within the Province, are before or after their Execution declared by the Parliament of Canada to be for the general Advantage of Canada or for the Advantage of Two or more of the Provinces (10).[33]

Note that most of the industries or services over which the Federal Government now claims jurisdiction as far as labour relations are concerned are the exceptions to the provincial ones listed under Section 92(10) (a) and (b). This is a very unusual way (through the back door) for a federal government to gain jurisdiction over labour relations in a number of industries. Banking, moreover, has recently been included under Part V of the *Canada Labour Code* and the only apparent justification for including it under federal jurisdiction is under heading 15 or 16 of Section 91 of *The Constitution Act, 1867.*[34]

The early decisions on the Canadian Constitution were largely in favour of extensive federal jurisdiction. However, the Judicial Committee of the British Privy Council (the court of last resort until 1949 when it was replaced by the Supreme Court of Canada) soon began to make decisions which favoured increased provincial jurisdiction. The most celebrated instance in the industrial relations field is the *Snider* case in which a federal statute was overturned, the Judicial Committee deciding that it was beyond the powers of the Federal Government. John Porter, in his classic book, *The Vertical Mosaic*, has the

following to say about the Judicial Committee:

> gradually through the decisions of judges in the United Kingdom, whose knowledge of Canada could at the most be slight, the relative weight of responsibility went to the provinces and away from the central government. The federalism which resulted from the decisions of the Judicial Committee of the Privy Council left Canada after the 1930's politically and socially incapacitated.[35]

The Constitution Act, 1867 (formerly the *BNA Act*) and its interpretation by judicial authorities has had a significant impact upon the Canadian industrial relations system. This will be spelled out in detail in the chapter "Legislation Governing Collective Bargaining in the Private Sector." The Federal Government may, in the future, find means to assume more responsibility in the industrial relations field. Much will depend upon what amendments, if any, are made to the recently repatriated Canadian Constitution, especially any new division of powers between the federal and provincial governments. For this reason, any person active in the industrial relations field cannot help but be critically concerned with the future interpretations of the new Canadian Constitution.

As Canadians are well aware, they live in a federal state with a central government and ten provincial governments, along with two territories. The powers of the two levels of government vary, the Federal Government having more control during wartime periods and the provincial governments generally having more control during times of peace and prosperity. The Federal Government is bicameral, with an elected House of Commons and a Senate to which members are appointed. At the provincial level, there is only one level of the legislature which is usually referred to as the Legislative Assembly. Ours is a parliamentary system, with members of the governing party voting along party lines rather than as individuals. The same voting pattern is also true of the opposition parties. Our Prime Minister is the leader of the party which has enough seats to form the government.

Standing in contrast to the Canadian system are the presidential forms of government, such as that of the United States. In that country, the populace at large votes for the President, Vice-President and Members of the Senate and House of Representatives. Canada now has three major political parties at the federal level — the Liberal, Conservative, and New Democratic parties. At the provincial level there are usually two parties (in some cases three) which generally correspond to the parties at the federal level. The parties in British Columbia and Quebec, however, do not correspond to federal parties.

The significance of Canada's political system is that the Federal Government has jurisdiction over only about 10% of the labour force while the provinces have jurisdiction over the remaining 90%. There is, therefore, the potential for divergences of policies between the two levels of government, and an even greater potential for such divergences among the provinces. This makes it difficult for employers and unions operating across provincial boundaries to achieve consistency of policy and programs among their various branches across the country.

The partisan nature of the Canadian political system makes it difficult to determine how individual members of the parties feel about labour relations and labour policies. Internal differences among members are usually ironed out in caucuses where members vote along party lines. This is different from the American system in which each senator or member of Congress votes as an individual and it is possible to see how a party vote is divided on labour issues. In fact, the American Federation of Labour–Congress for Industrial Organization (AFL–CIO) keeps a running record of how each senator and member of Congress votes on issues of importance to the labour movement. Also, the American labour movement is able to "reward its friends and punish its enemies," an ability that first AFL President Samuel Gompers recommended be used by labour in politics. Under the Canadian system, labour has no such power.

While lobbying by politicians takes place on both sides of the border, it is much more common in the United States since individual senators and members of Congress play a more important role in shaping government policy in that country. Although party bosses play an important role in American politics, they do not have the control over government policy that party leaders have in Canada, particularly the leader of the party which forms the government of the day. This is important for Canadian unions and employers to realize, especially while commenting on white papers or presenting their cases before parliamentary committees studying labour issues. The same is true at the provincial level. This is one reason why we have provincial federations of labour in Canada, as well as provincial arms of the Chamber of Commerce and the Canadian Manufacturers Association. Hence, both trade unions and employers must understand the political system if they hope to play a role in the formulation of government policies, either by supporting political parties or by spending money lobbying at the senior levels of government.

The Legal Subsystem

Canada's legal system consists not only of the Constitution, but also of the statutory law passed by the Federal Government and the provincial legislatures as well as court interpretation of such law. In addition, much common or case law has been built up over the years out of which general legal principles have emerged.

As far as the labour movement and collective bargaining are concerned, it is noteworthy that trade unions were illegal under the *Combines Act* until 1872. A trade union represented up to that time, in effect, a combination that presumably acted against the common good. This supposition, known in the United States as the "criminal conspiracy doctrine," also had a lengthy period of existence in that country. Following the Toronto's printers' strike in 1871, criminal law was amended and a *Trade Unions Act* was passed.

Following the *Snider* case of 1925 (a case in which federal authority was challenged) federal jurisdiction was trimmed to only about 10% of the labour force with the ten provinces claiming jurisdiction over the remaining 90%. As a consequence, legal developments vary from one jurisdiction to another, making it very difficult to keep up with the many amendments that are taking place across Canada in the industrial relations field — yet union and management must keep abreast of and adhere to these changes in regulation. In recent years, moreover, various jurisdictions have been passing increasingly more substantive legislation concerning compulsory dues check-off and advance notice of technological changes. The role of the legal system will be spelled out in greater detail in the chapters "Legislation Governing Collective Bargaining in the Private Sector" and "Collective Bargaining in the Public and Parapublic Sectors."

As well as laws relating to industrial relations *per se*, there is labour standards legislation in all jurisdictions in Canada. This legislation covers, for example, hours of work per day and per week, overtime pay beyond normal hours, and minimum wages for adults and young people. Any industrial relations practitioner or student must be aware of these labour standards because they set limits (maximums or minimums) on the outputs of collective bargaining.

A number of jurisdictions in recent years have also passed human rights acts or their equivalent which forbid discrimination in employment on the basis of race, colour, religion, age, and sex among other factors. In a couple of cases, workers who were retired at a so-called compulsory retirement age applied to their respective provincial human rights commissions which ruled that such retirements contravene human rights legislation. This is just one example of the important interface developing between industrial relations and human rights legislation. Some jurisdictions have also passed legislation relating to health and safety in the workplace. The appointment of joint committees on safety and the use of improved work methods to avoid accidents are two outcomes of such legislation which affect the industrial relations system. Legislation on sexual harrassment, moreover, is now enabling persons subjected to unwanted sexual innuendos, threats, and actions to be heard before independent tribunals.

Legislation without implementation would not be worth the paper on which it is written. As a consequence, we have tribunals and agencies which administer the legal provisions in industrial relations and related fields. For example, labour relations boards are charged with applying statute law to a specific set of facts and develop in this process important jurisprudence referred to as administrative law. In addition, the executive branch of government acts to resolve disputes when the regular administrative machinery appears incapable of doing so in specific cases.

As we shall see in the chapter "The Administration of the Collective Agreement," arbitration boards are now handing down very important decisions, and a substantial body of arbitrable jurisprudence is building up. Again, people involved in industrial relations should be aware of the general principles which are emerging from arbitration decisions and analyze these principles to ensure that they do not violate the principles inherent in the provisions of their collective agreemtns. If any of these administrative tribunals exceed their jurisdiction or act against generally accepted legal principles, the courts often intervene at the request of either unions or management and may make rulings which override the tribunals' decisions.

The Social Subsystem

The social system of any country consists of a set of values and beliefs which serve to guide interaction between individuals and groups and to provide norms for individual and group behaviour. These values and beliefs provide cohesion and unity within a country but there may be secondary systems of value and belief which differentiate people within that country. For example, managers may have a different set of beliefs and values from those who work under them, particularly workers at the lower level of the occupational hierarchy. To the extent that there are *differences* among the people at the top and bottom of organizations, there is likely to be a certain amount of *conflict* inherent in that organizational setting.

A person born into a specific society normally acquires in the course of growing up the values and beliefs of that society. This is what sociologists call "the socialization process." However, younger generations may adopt value systems which differ from those of their parents or grandparents and, in the course of a society's development, they may change the basic value and belief systems of their society. For example, the men and women in Canada and other countries who went through the Great Depression and World War II may find their values and beliefs at odds with those of the generation born in the 1950's and 1960's who have grown up in a permissive and affluent society. Any observer of behaviour at the workplace or of an industrial relations system will know that there is a significant difference in thinking between those under thirty and those over thirty years of age.

The important role that values play in every society is succinctly stated by John Porter:

> Besides providing cohesion and unity, value systems give a sense of rightness to the social order and legitimacy for particular practices and usages, including class and power structures, within a given society. For individuals, the value system with which they have been indoctrinated provides

a view of the world and an explanation of life in society.[36]

He goes on to state that certain social mechanisms are necessary for restating and generalizing values so that they do not become so vague as to cease to perform the function of social cohesion. In particular, he places great emphasis on mass media for translating particular value systems into a meaningful and coherent whole which serves to guide behaviour.[37]

Every society has certain power groups who give direction to that society, usually through the political system in which elected representatives formulate national policy. Corporations and trade unions are two power blocs which may try to influence the political process. In some European countries, for example, the labour parties which form the government have a close tie-in with the labour movement. But, as John Porter points out, "In Canada there has been throughout the present century a close coalition between political leadership, the mass media, and the corporate world."[38] He goes on to point out that the power of labour leaders does not extend beyond their institutional roles inasmuch as labour leaders rarely share in the informal aspects of the confraternity of power. Hence, in terms of Porter's analysis of Canadian society, people involved in industrial relations should be aware that the political system is influenced to a large degree by large corporations (including the corporate mass media) and that the labour movement, while having some influence on public policy and direction, is not nearly so powerful in influencing the Canadian political system.

Another interesting and potentially increasing source of power in Canada is that of various interest or pressure groups. Among such groups we can include those of the women's movement, native peoples, and consumers. These interest groups are beginning to make their power strongly felt in political decision-making. Labour is one such pressure group, although because of its long history, it may play a more important role than many of these newer groups.

During the 1970's in Canada there was some debate on the extent to which Canadians still embraced the work ethic. The previously mentioned Department of Manpower and Immigration Work Ethic Survey and Job Satisfaction Survey confirmed that Canadians are indeed strongly committed to work. The resulting report had the following to say:

> Work was named by more respondents to the Work Ethic Survey than any other option, including family and friends, as a way [of] achieving one's goals. Canadians see themselves as industrious people to whom work contributes a feeling of success and, for a large proportion, of personal fulfillment. It is not surprising, therefore, that the vast majority of respondents... expected to get satisfaction from their work, and satisfaction, or more precisely the behaviour that it engenders, has social consequences.[39]

With respect to job satisfaction, the characteristics stressed by workers were that work should be interesting, that there should be enough information and authority to do the job, and that there should be the opportunity to develop special abilities. Things that were considered to be less important included job security, promotional considerations, pay, hours of work, and

fringe benefits.[40] What this study indicates is that not only are people in Canada strongly committed to work, but they look for jobs which offer challenge and opportunities to help develop policies — to affect the decision-making process. This is important to both business (if it wants to increase productivity and reduce absenteeism and staff turnover) and labour (if it wants to increase participation in trade-union activity, particularly at the local level). One thing that managers and union leaders should monitor is the extent to which the findings in the above surveys remain constant or change in the coming years.

Conclusion

This chapter has attempted to develop more fully the nature and role of conditioning (external) inputs for the industrial relations system. In the following chapters, other topics (e.g. contract negotiations) will be viewed in terms of the broader societal framework discussed here; and, in some cases, it will be useful to analyze the way in which societal constraints shape the various aspects of the industrial relations system.

questions

1 What are the advantages of viewing the industrial relations system within a broader environmental context? Elaborate.
2 How do the various environmental subsystems have impact on the inputs and outputs of the industrial relations system?
3 Given the specific environmental constraints operating on an organization and the goals, values and power of the actors in that organization, is it possible to predict the specific outputs of contract negotiations for the workers and employers of a particular organization? Choose an organization and explain.
4 Do you think the present constitutional division of powers between the federal and provin-

cial governments in Canada contributes to or detracts from collective bargaining in Canada? Elaborate.
5 Do environmental constraints operate on government, private industry, and parapublic institutions in Canada?
6 Do you think that it is possible to combine environmental influences into some quantitative form in order to make the outputs of an industrial relations system fairly predictable? Elaborate.
7 In your province, do the private and public sectors impose different kinds of restraints for collective bargaining? Be specific and include examples in your reply.
8 Does public opinion play a very important role

in labour–management relations in your province? Elaborate.

9 What are some of the more important constraints under which private employers operate in your province? Do they vary by industry? Be specific in your reply.

10 Do economic conditions in the United States affect the industrial relations climate in your province? Elaborate.

notes

1 *Perspectives Canada III*, Supply and Services Canada (Ottawa: 1980), p. 243.
2 Wilfred List, "Talk About Controls Spurs Union Demands," *Globe and Mail* (August 3, 1981), p. B7.
3 *Ibid*.
4 *Economic Review*, Department of Finance (Ottawa: Supply and Services Canada, 1985), Reference Table 41, p. 116.
5 Quoted in *Inflation, Unemployment and Incomes Policy — Summary Report*, Prices and Incomes Commission (Ottawa: Information Canada, 1972), Preface.
6 *Ibid.*, p. 51.
7 Frank Reid, "Wage-and-Price Controls in Canada," *Union-Management Relations in Canada*, eds. J. Anderson and M. Gunderson (Don Mills: Addison-Wesley Publishers, 1982), pp. 493-95.
8 David Stager, *Economic Analysis and Canadian Policy*, 2nd ed., (Toronto: Butterworth & Company (Canada) Limited, 1976), pp. 199-200.
9 Virginia Galt, "Labour Turmoil Worsens as Leaders Dig In," *Globe and Mail* (July 20, 1982), p. 1.
10 "Auto Pacts Aid Laid-Off Workers," *Globe and Mail* (October 16, 1984), p. B4.
11 *Ibid*.
12 *Ibid*.
13 *Labour Market Developments in the 1980s*, Employment and Immigration Canada (Ottawa: Supply and Services Canada, 1981), p. 113.
14 The Hon. Jean Chrétien, Minister of Finance, *The Budget* (April 10, 1978), p. 40.
15 Sylvia Ostry and Mahmood A. Zaidi, *Labour Economics in Canada*, 3rd ed., (Toronto: Macmillan of Canada, 1979), p. 1.
16 *Canadian Work Values*, Department of Manpower and Immigration Canada (Ottawa: Information Canada, 1975), p. 37.
17 *Ibid.*, p. 46.
18 *Ibid.*, p. 49.
19 Alton Craig, "Report on Manpower Development and Planning — Mechanical Contracting Industry," *Manpower Needs in the Mechanical Construction Industry: 1975-1980*, joint study of the Department of Manpower and Immigration, the United Association of the Plumbing and Pipefitting Industry of the USA and Canada, and the Mechanical Contractors Association of Canada, (Spring 1975), p. 25.
20 *Canadian Job Strategies*, Employment and Immigration Canada (Ottawa: June 1985).
21 "Job-sharing Proposed to Avert 'Social Disaster,'" *Ottawa Citizen* (September 24, 1984), p. A4.
22 *Ibid*.
23 Statistics Canada, *Labour Force Information for the Week Ended June 15, 1985*, Catalogue No. 71-001P.
24 Robert Stephens, "White-Collar Workers Feel The Pinch of Layoffs," *Globe and Mail* (May 1, 1982), p. 11.
25 *Report of the Royal Commission on Corporate Concentration* (Ottawa: Supply and Services Canada, March 1978), pp. 45-46.
26 D. J. Daly, "Remedies for Increasing Productivity Levels in Canada," ch. 7, *Lagging Productivity Growth, Causes and Remedies*, eds. S. Maital and N. M. Meltz (Cambridge: Ballinges Publishing Co., 1985), p. 226.
27 *Report of the Royal Commission on Corporate Concentration*, p. 4.
28 *Ibid.*, Table 8.2, p. 189.
29 *Ibid.*, p. 191.
30 *Employment Standards Act*, R.S.O. (1980), s. 40; Regulation 286, s. 4, R.R.O. (1980).
31 Wilfred List, "Canadian Unions' Hard Line Product of Complex Factors," *Globe and Mail* (March 1, 1982), p. B14.
32 Vol. 1, *Decisions of the Judicial Committee of the Privy Council Relating to the British North America Act 1867 and the Canadian Constitution 1867-1954*, (Ottawa: Queen's Printer, 1954), pp. xxxvi-xxxviii; and the 1940 and 1949 amendments thereto.
33 *Ibid*.
34 *Ibid*.
35 John Porter, *The Vertical Mosaic* (Toronto: University of Toronto Press, 1965), p. 380.
36 *Ibid.*, p. 459.
37 *Ibid*.
38 *Ibid.*, p. 539.
39 *Canadian Work Values*, p. 60.
40 *Ibid*.

3

Theories of the Labour Movement

With Godsell, *The Financial Post*

Introduction

As I pointed out in the preface, three chapters of this book are devoted to the labour movement. This chapter summarizes the major factors accounting for the emergence and development of labour movements, Chapter 4 discusses the history and philosophy of the Canadian labour movement, and Chapter 5 discusses its structure.

In speaking of trade unions today, we seem to take for granted that they have always existed, and do not consider the factors which gave rise to labour organizations or which explain their continued growth. A number of early and well respected scholars in the field of industrial relations put forth various theories that attempted to explain the emergence of trade unions, their patterns of growth, and their structure. However, in recent years, there has been little serious inquiry into trade union theory. One exception has been a study by Kerr, Harbison, Dunlop, and Myers, entitled *Industrialism and Industrial Man*.[1]

Dunlop, in an article on the development of trade unions published some years ago, suggested that theorists of the labour movement have posed at least four important questions:

1 How do we explain the origin or emergence of labour organizations?
2 How do we explain the pattern of growth and development of labour organizations?
3 What are the ultimate goals of the labour movement?
4 Why do workers join labour organizations?[2]

The writers whose works Dunlop examined were concerned solely with unionism among blue-collar workers, since white-collar unions did not then exist. Among the early commentators whom Dunlop discussed were Fabian socialist writers Sidney and Beatrice Webb.

The Webbs[3]

The Webbs defined a trade union as "a continuous association of wage-earners for the purpose of maintaining or improving the conditions of their working lives."[4] The meticulous and detailed research of the Webbs led them to conclude that, in all cases in which trade unions arose, wage-earners (currently referred to as workers) had ceased to be independent producers who owned both the means of production and the goods they created.[5]

The Webbs attributed the development of trade unionism largely to the divorce of capital from labour — a development outlined in the following terms:

> It has, indeed, become a commonplace of modern Trade Unionism that only in those industries in which the worker has ceased to be concerned in the profits of buying and selling — that inseparable characteristic of the ownership and management of the means of production — can effective and stable trade organizations be established.[6]

In effect, stable trade unions came into being, according to the Webbs, only when workers lost control of the ownership and management of the means of production — a situation characteristic of capitalism. Capitalism brought with it not only competition in the product market but also in the labour market. Hence, it is not surprising that the Webbs should have considered the fundamental objective of trade unionism to be "the deliberate regulation of the conditions of employment in such a way as to ward off from the manual-working producers the evil effects of industrial competition."[7] As long as the law protected workers from the evil effects of competition there was little need for unionism. However, the introduction by government of a policy removing such protection provided strong incentive for workers to form unions to protect their interests. The Webbs attributed the formation of British unions to three factors: (1) the divorce of labour from capital, (2) the need to regulate competition, and (3) the lack of government protection.

The Webbs were also interested in union structure and how it evolved. Leaders of early unions had to combat a trend towards what the Webbs referred to as "local monopoly," the tendency of workers to look out for themselves or their fellows in the local community rather than their trade or their fellows in the larger community of that trade.

> The natural selfishness of the local branches is accordingly always being combated by the central executives and national delegate meetings, in the wider interests of the whole body of the members wherever they may be working.[8]

Nonetheless, there seemed to be optimism about the movement from local to national unionism:

> the Trade Union world has, throughout its whole history, manifested an overpowering impulse to the amalgamation of local trade clubs into national unions, with centralised funds and centralised administration.[9]

The process of amalgamation described by the Webbs applies equally well to the modern trade-union movement.

Trade Union Methods

Unions enforced their regulations, according to the Webbs, by means of three distinct instruments: "the Method of Mutual Insurance, the Method of Collective Bargaining, and the Method of Legal Enactment."[10]

Method of Mutual Insurance The method of mutual insurance was used by unions to accumulate funds out of which benefits were paid to workers deprived of their livelihood by causes over which they had no control. These benefits were divided into two categories: "benevolent or friendly" on the one hand and "out-of-work" on the other. The benevolent fund provided sick pay, accident benefits, superannuation allowances, and burial money. The out-of-work pay or trade fund provided money to replace tools lost by theft or fire, or to compensate for unemployment caused by temporary breakdowns of machinery, employer bankruptcy, or depression in a trade.[11] As far as the Webbs were concerned, the out-of-work benefits were the important part of mutual insurance.

Mutual insurance was practised largely during the first quarter of the twentieth century when combination laws in Britain prevented the legal formation of workers into trade unions. Similar provisions in Canada's Criminal Code inhibited union activity in this country. It was only when the combination laws were amended in 1871 that British unions were able to begin to engage actively in the method of collective bargaining. Similar legislative action followed in Canada one year later.

Method of Collective Bargaining The method of collective bargaining, as discussed by the Webbs, corresponds roughly to the type of collective bargaining that is currently practised in North America and most other industrially advanced countries. "The most obvious form of permanent machinery for Collective Bargaining," the Webbs claimed, "is a joint committee, consisting of equal numbers of representatives of the employers and workmen respectively."[12]

Method of Legal Enactment The method of legal enactment referred basically to attempts by trade-union leaders and other prominent

thinkers of the time to petition Parliament to enact guarantees of at least basic minimum conditions of employment. The Webbs saw a doctrine of a national minimum emerging which encompassed such items as terms of apprenticeship, sanitation, job safety, working hours, and minimum wages for all grades of labour. This national minimum would be enforced through an elaborate labour code. In their view, trade-union officials could have a substantial input in helping government to develop the national minimum. In addition, they saw the possibility of certain unions negotiating for more than the national minimum, where these unions represented groups of workers possessing specialized skills.

The Webbs argued that trade-union regulations could be reduced to two economic devices: "the Device of the Common Rule" and "the Device of Restriction of Numbers." They found the device of the common rule to be a universal feature of trade unionism since its aim was to continuously upgrade the minimum conditions of employment applicable to all types of workers, and strongly recommended that trade-union leaders use this device.[13] By contrast, the device of the restriction of numbers (usually enforced by limiting admission to a trade through apprenticeship regulations) was seriously questioned by the Webbs, particularly if it caused injustices in the selection of apprentices by preventing many young, underprivileged boys from gaining access to apprenticeship, or by limiting the employer's freedom of choice in hiring, or both.[14]

The Webbs predicted the popularity of the method of legal enactment over mutual insurance or collective bargaining in this statement:

> Whether for good or for evil, it appears inevitable that the growing participation of the wage-earners in political life, and the rising influence of their organisations, must necessarily bring about an increasing use of the Method of Legal Enactment.[15]

Legal enactment, the Webbs noted, appeared to be characterized by peaceful conditions in industry and by an absence of friction between unions and management. Moreover, since it also set minimum standards, it approached universal coverage more closely than mutual insurance or collective bargaining did. The Webbs acknowledged, however, that the regulations established under the legal enactment method were slow to adapt to changing circumstances.[16] Like many other observers, they came to view legal enactment not as a tool for progressive reform but as a rote determined by prevailing custom.

For altering regulations and attaining objectives quickly, the Webbs admitted that the method of collective bargaining was more effective than the other two methods, and also permitted the most powerful groups to obtain benefits beyond those provided by legislation. Despite these perceived advantages, the Webbs expressed a preference for the method of legal enactment particularly if all regulations were based on the doctrine of a living wage. For them, it was a question of the labour movement's place in society and its role in working toward social justice: "Trade Unionism is not merely an incident of the present phase of capitalistic industry, but has a permanent function to fulfill in the democratic state."[17]

Although the Webbs did not develop a complete theory of the labour movement, they have developed one of the most comprehensive treatises of the labour movement. Probably more than any other writers, they have answered the four questions posed by Dunlop: (1) How do we explain the origin or emergence of labour organizations? Unions emerged as a result of the divorce of labour from capital and were intended to protect workers from the evils of competition while guaranteeing certain levels of wages and benefits. (2) How do we explain the pattern of growth and development of labour organizations? Unions grew from closely knit community trade organizations, overcoming an initial tendency toward local monopolies, to emerge as national unions. (3) What are the ultimate goals of the labour movement? Unions seek not only to obtain for their members benefits equal to

those enjoyed by workers performing equivalent duties, but to establish a national minimum for all workers. (4) Why do workers join labour organizations? Workers join unions to improve or protect their wages and working conditions.

Commons[18]

Although John R. Commons did not consider himself a theorist of the labour movement, there are in a number of his writings ideas which help to explain the formation and development of trade unions. Commons, who confined his analysis to the United States, claimed that trade unions could only be explained by recognizing "the interaction of economic, industrial, and political conditions, with many varieties of individualistic, socialistic, and protectionistic philosophies."[19] He also treated labour history in the United States as part of its industrial and political history. Commons saw two conditions in America which made trade-union development in that country different from the development of unions in other countries: the wide expanse of free land in the United States and the early granting of universal suffrage.[20]

The main explanation offered by Commons for the emergence of the American labour movement was the expansion of competitive markets. He set out his explanation, after exhaustive study, in an article entitled "American Shoemakers, 1648-1895."[21] In this article, Commons described not only the divorce of craftspeople from ownership and from the sale of their products but also the growth of many intermediary market links between the retailer and the original production unit. In order to protect themselves in this specialized distribution system among local markets, workers would unionize to ensure that competition would be based on product quality and not on the difference in wages between unionized and nonunionized labour.

Commons went on to explain that those workers who were organized into unions to great advantage in one community should help to organize unions in other communities where people worked under non-union conditions. He saw both the desirability and the possibility of workers organizing local unions in nearly all communities where workers in the same trade produced the same kind of goods. This city-by-city type of organizing explains, in large part, the rise of national unions. Hence, for Commons, the broadening of markets was the basic concept underlying the emergence and growth of the trade union movement in the United States. While he recognized the importance of changes in the methods of production, Commons gave primary emphasis to the expansion of markets:

> The vast area of the United States, coupled with free trade within that area and a spreading network of transportation, has developed an unparalleled extension of the competitive area of markets, and thereby has strikingly distinguished American [labour] movements from those of other countries.[22]

He recognized clear patterns of development in trade unionism by differentiating several periods of trade-union growth and decline and the factors which were instrumental in these changes. To summarize, Commons explained the emergence and development of the American labour movement by formulating the idea of an extension of competitive markets. It was left to one of his students, Selig Perlman, to develop a theory of the trade union movement in the United States.

Perlman[23]

In the preface to his classic study, *A Theory of the Labor Movement*, Selig Perlman indicates that he was born in Russia and first embraced the theory of the labour movement in Marxist readings. He later immigrated to North America and joined the research staff of John R. Commons at the University of Wisconsin. As a result of his studies in America, Perlman radically revised his Marxist outlook. In defining his new theory, he noted that three factors appeared to be basic to any modern labour situation:

> first, the resistance power of capitalism, determined by its own historical development; second, the degree of dominance over the labor movements by the intellectual's 'mentality,' which regularly underestimates capitalism's resistance power and overestimates labor's will to radical change; and third, the degree of maturity of a trade union 'mentality'.[24]

With respect to capitalism and its resistance power, Perlman insisted that for labour unions to develop and exist in the United States, they would need the support of the middle class. Moreover, they would have to respect the institution of private property upon which capitalism is based since, as Perlman points out, "any suspicion that labor might harbor a design to do away altogether with private property, instead of merely regulating its use, immediately throws the public into an alliance with the anti-union employers."[25]

Furthermore, the dominance of the intellectual mentality, Perlman contended, was not appropriate to the labour movement because socialist or idealist intellectualism detracted from the manualist mentality which produces and sustains a genuine trade-union movement. The manualist mentality in Perlman's theory is characterized by the workers' consciousness of the scarcity of job opportunities:

> manual groups...have had their economic attitudes basically determined by a consciousness of scarcity of opportunity, which is characteristic of these groups, and stands out in contrast with the business men's 'abundance consciousness,' or consciousness of unlimited opportunity.[26]

Perlman proposed, therefore, that a theory of the labour movement should include a theory of the psychology of the labouring man.[27]

Like Commons, Perlman pointed out that the United States with its vast regions of uninhabited land created in the mind of the worker an abundance of opportunity. Hence, unionism could take hold in the United States only when the abundance consciousness of the worker had been replaced by the consciousness of job scarcity.[28]

Although Perlman discussed some of the American unions leaning toward socialism, he indicated that trade unionism of the American Federation of Labor type (craft unionism) was a necessary counterbalance to the inevitability of big business. In Perlman's words,

> The province of the union is, therefore, to assert labor's collective mastery over job opportunities and employment bargains, leaving the ownership of the business to the employer, and creating for its members an ever-increasing sphere of economic security and opportunity.[29]

Perlman's theory, then (like that of the Webbs), seems to answer all of the questions posed by Dunlop: (1) How do we explain the origin or emergence of labour organizations? In the United States, only when the consciousness of abundance was replaced by the consciousness of job scarcity did workers adopt the idea of trade unionism. (2) How do we explain the pattern of growth and development of labour organizations? Labour organizations grew out of the resistance power of capitalism and the dominance of the manualist mentality. (3) What are the ultimate goals of the labour movement? To ensure worker control of job opportunities within the confines of the capitalist system is the ultimate goal of the labour movement. (4) Why do workers join labour organizations? Workers join unions because they see them as controlling access to scarce jobs and as providing a degree of job security. Perlman's development of the idea of a manualist mentality, his pragmatism and realistic appraisal of how American labour might survive within a capitalist system marks him as one of the most important early labour writers.

Hoxie[30]

Robert F. Hoxie's interpretation of the trade-union movement in the United States is com-

plex. He discussed not only the different structural types but, more importantly, a number of functional types of unions. Hoxie saw unions emerging as a result of social or group consciousness which is marked by a fairly unified and well-developed viewpoint and which is translated into group action. However, his group consciousness is not of the job-scarcity type characteristic of Perlman's theory, but much broader in scope. Unionism, according to Hoxie,

> appears primarily as a group interpretation of the social situation in which the workers find themselves, and a remedial program in the form of aims, policies, and methods; the organization and the specific form or structure which it takes are merely the instruments which the group adopts for propagating its viewpoint and putting its program into effect.[31]

Functional Unionism

Hoxie claimed that the essential character of unionism is functional, and went on to develop a typology of unions. Each functional type is determined through an interpretation of the group situation by the group itself and contains a remedial action program developed by this same group. To Hoxie, the functional types may be very narrow or very broad in their orientations:

> The only essential point is that the viewpoint and program, whatever their scope and character, shall command the adherence of the membership of the group so as to constitute an effective motive and guide to group action. If this condition is met the type exists.[32]

In leading up to his general characterization of types, Hoxie states that the master key to the real character of unionism is to be found in the existence of distinct sorts of unions. He feels that unionism is so pragmatic—so much a response to particular situations—that it is impossible to characterize and judge it as a whole. However, he perceives it to have developed along lines distinct enough to allow one to generalize about the different types.[33]

Hoxie's four functional types are as follows: business unionism, friendly or uplift unionism, revolutionary unionism, and predatory unionism, the two varieties of which are hold-up unionism and guerilla unionism.[34]

Business Unionism Business unionism is essentially trade-conscious rather than class-conscious. It is more concerned with the working conditions in a craft or industry than with the working class as a whole. Conservative in its orientation, it is conceived of as a negotiating institution which seeks its ends primarily through the process of collective bargaining.

Friendly or Uplift Unionism Friendly or uplift unionism is idealistic, trade- or class-conscious and sometimes inspires workers to act in the interests of society as a whole. It aspires to elevate the moral, intellectual, and social life of the worker, as well as the worker's standard of living. The major method of friendly or uplift unionism is collective bargaining but it also uses the method of mutual insurance and, on occasion, political action and cooperative enterprise. The labour organization most demonstrating the principles of uplift unionism, according to Hoxie, was the Knights of Labour.[35]

Revolutionary Unionism Revolutionary unionism is extremely radical, both in its viewpoints and actions. Unlike the two previous trade-conscious types, it is clearly class-conscious in nature. There are two variants of the revolutionary unionism type. The first one is socialist and seeks its ultimate ends by invoking class political action. "In short, it looks upon unionism and socialism as the two wings of the working class movement."[36] The second variant of revolutionary unionism stays away from socialism and collective bargaining, and focusses its energies on direct action, sabotage, and violence. Hoxie calls these two variants socialistic unionism and quasi-anarchistic unionism respectively.

Predatory Unionism Predatory unionism may be conservative or radical, trade-conscious or class-conscious, but it appears to concern itself solely with immediate ends and is conceived of as ruthless, holding little regard for ethical or legal codes of conduct. There are two variants of this particular type, the first of which is hold-up unionism. While hold-up unionism appears similar to business unionism, it is in essence primarily exclusive and monopolistic, according to Hoxie. Generally boss-ridden and corrupt, hold-up unionism may engage in "sweetheart" collective agreements in which negotiators accept bribes in exchange for agreeing to settlements which serve employers well and workers badly. Guerilla unionism is similar to hold-up unionism inasmuch as it avoids or lacks principle and uses violent methods. It operates, however, directly against employers rather than in combination with them and, unlike hold-up unionism, cannot be bought off by sweetheart agreements.

Group Consciousness

According to Hoxie, all four of the above are ideal types and no one union may be characterized strictly in terms of any one of these types. He goes on to contend that the membership of any union may include representatives of all types of unionism. Hoxie's business unionism, however, is what is often called today "bread and butter" unionism in which members merely pay dues and receive whatever benefits the union may obtain for them. Business unionism is by far the most prevalent type in North American society.

Like Perlman, Hoxie saw unions emerging to a large extent as a result of a unified group consciousness which developed within a particular environmental setting; Perlman's group consciousness was universal only insofar as it concerned itself with scarcity of job opportunities. Hoxie went further and indicated that unionism is not something which is found only among wage-earners, but that, "[i]t may exist wherever in society there is a group of men with consciousness of common needs and interests apart from the rest of society."[37]

Implicit in this quotation is the idea that trade unionism could spread to any group of individuals within society who are in close proximity and thus may develop a sense of "groupness." Hence, Hoxie's analysis applies to unions of professional, technical, and clerical workers equally well as to blue-collar workers.

Although Hoxie did an excellent job of developing a typology of unionism, he did not construct a full-blown theory of the labour movement and answered only three of Dunlop's questions: (1) How do we explain the origin or emergence of labour organizations? The origins of trade unions were explained by the emergence of a group psychology, the scope of which was much broader than that of Perlman. Furthermore, the organization of any group had within it the potential for explaining the emergence and increasing unionization of both blue-collar and white-collar workers. Large numbers of these latter workers are now being organized in Canada and other industrialized nations. (2) How do we explain the pattern of growth and development of labour organizations? Since Hoxie concentrated primarily on functional types, he did not really give an explanation for the growth of the trade union movement. (3) What are the ultimate goals of the labour movement? Hoxie's functional types differ in their objectives and methods, but do point to a relationship between unionism and capitalism. (4) Why do workers join labour organizations? The involvement of individuals in a group consciousness explains in part why workers join unions.

Tannenbaum[38]

To Frank Tannenbaum, the insecurity of the industrial worker was the critical variable in the explanation of the origin of trade unionism, and the main reason for this insecurity was the machine: "The labor movement is the result, and the machine is the major cause."[39] When Tannenbaum was writing his first book in 1921, the machine seemed to be the centre of gravity in the industrial community. Machines led to increasing urbanization, reduced the skills of workers and their income, made their jobs less secure, and determined the nature of the activities, contact, outlook, and way of life for all those people who were gathered around a machine in the conduct of their daily work. The labour movement had become, therefore, the primary instrument of self-defence for the worker, and it was the hope for greater security that drove the average worker into labour organizations.[40]

Workers joined trade unions in order to improve their bargaining power as they attempted to gain some control over the application of the machine. Also, many unions provided unemployment insurance for workers, sick benefits, disability benefits, and in many cases, death provisions for families.[41] To Tannenbaum, the labour union was the means of holding onto a fleeting and changing world:

> The labor movement serves as a means of stabilizing a dynamic world. To state it in other words, the labor movement serves to make possible the continuance of the dynamic character of our industrial organization within a social organization secure for the individual.[42]

In his second book, *Philosophy of Labor*, Tannenbaum discussed the various ways in which industry can be run, including the method used in various socialist countries, a notable example of which was the Soviet Union. He concluded that government ownership is not appropriate or effective and that

> the corporation and the union will ultimately merge in common ownership and cease to be a house divided. It is only thus that a common identity may once again come to rule the lives of men and endow each one with rights and duties recognized by all.[43]

Tannenbaum provided at least partial answers to three of Dunlop's questions: (1) How do we explain the origin or emergence of labour organizations? The quest for security could be seen not only as an explanation for the individual joining trade unions, but also as the basis for the formation of the trade union movement itself. (2) How do we explain the pattern of growth and development of labour organizations? Tannenbaum observed to some extent and predicted the increasing unionization of professional and white-collar workers. While noting that the labour movement showed no sign of abatement, Tannenbaum indicated that it "tends to include more and more the professional and the civil-service people of the community, each of whom is interested in stability and security, each of whom operates in terms of service rather than of profit."[44] To some extent, then, there is in his writing a rudimentary explanation of the growth and development of unionization among professional, technical, and clerical workers. Nowhere in his works, however, does he trace out the historical development of the trade union movement, nor does he predict the historical evolution of the future development of trade unions. (3) What are the ultimate goals of the labour movement? A new type of society was perceived to be emerging in which labour and management would play a much more cooperative role; This growing cooperation reflected labour's ultimate objective of achieving stability and security in the workplace. (4) Why do workers join labour organizations? Individual workers joined trade unions to protect themselves from the insecurity caused by the increasing use of machines in the workplace.

Marx[45]

No discussion of unions and the reasons workers join them would be complete without some comment on the contribution of Karl Marx. Marx did much of his writing in England where he deplored the poverty, poor working condi-

tions, and child labour which characterized European industrial society at that time.

In keeping with his philosophy of the overthrow of the capitalistic system and the establishment of a communist system, Marx regarded unions as one of the more important weapons in waging the class struggle. They were conceived of as class-conscious organizations which came into existence mainly to protect the worker against exploitation by the employer. They were a response to workers' needs to protect their day-to-day interests and, as Taft points out, they could only deal with short-term, day-to-day problems.[46] According to Lozovsky,

> the trade union developed originally out of the spontaneous attempts of the workers to do away with...competition, or at least to restrict it for the purpose of obtaining at least such contractual conditions as would raise them above the status of bare slaves.[47]

Labour organizations were viewed as an attempt to support revolts made inevitable by capitalist exploitation, but while labour might have been able to gain temporary concessions, it could not gain permanent relief through trade union action alone. Hence, the isolated revolts that did occur had to build continually until they culminated in a "living embodiment of the struggle between classes."[48]

In the Marxist view, if trade unions were to obtain a high degree of control over conditions in the workplace, and if they were able to satisfy the needs of workers to a high degree, then they would lose their *raison d'être*. Hence, as far as Marx and later Engels were concerned, trade unions engaged in trade-union activity *per se* were phenomena of a temporary nature intended primarily to be a political vehicle in a revolution which would overturn the ruling capitalist class and establish a classless society.

The influence of the Communist Party on Canadian society and on the Canadian labour movement is described by Norman Penner:

> The greatest impact of the Communist Party on Canadian society was during the thirties when no

other organized force was prepared to give expression to the discontent of the Depression and to initiate imaginative, militant, and effective extra-parliamentary activity on the whole host of domestic and foreign policy questions... Its members took an active and leading part in building the trade-union movement and were partly responsible for making this period the most momentous in Canadian labor history.[49]

A reading of Penner's chapter "The Communist Party, the Trade Unions, and CCF" leaves one with the impression that this claim overstates the relation between the Communist Party and trade unionism in Canada.

With respect to the four questions that Dunlop posed, Marx provided at least partial answers to three of them: (1) How do we explain the origin or emergence of labour organizations? The search for short-term gains and protection from competition provided a partial answer for the rise of trade unions. (2) With respect to the patterns of growth of trade unions, Marx had nothing to say. (3) What are the ultimate goals of unions? They were seen as being in the forefront in the overthrow of the capitalist class and in the formation of a classless society. (4) Why do workers join labour organizations? Workers joined trade unions to seek relief from the evil effects of capitalism and to maintain a level of subsistance above that of slaves.

Bakke[50]

In a classic article written in 1945 and fostered by the Division of Labour Studies at the Yale Institute of Human Relations, E. Wight Bakke tried to discover why people join or do not join unions. By interviewing a cross-section of workers, he isolated the fact that people were more willing to become union members if they thought such action would enhance opportunities for successful living:

> The worker reacts favourably to union membership in proportion to the strength of his belief that this step will reduce his frustrations and anxieties

and will further his opportunities relevant to the achievement of his standards of successful living.[51]

A worker, therefore, would react unfavourably if he felt that joining a union would have the opposite effect.

Bakke and his associates involved in this study found that a worker believed himself to be living successfully if he was making progress towards the experience and assurance of:

1 The respect of society and respect of other people;
2 The degree of creature comforts and economic security possessed by the most favored of his customary associates;
3 Independence in and control over his own affairs;
4 Understanding of the forces and factors at work in his world; and
5 Integrity.[52]

Bakke refers to these as the workers' goals and then examines the effect that union membership may have on the desire of workers to achieve these goals.

Social Status Unions elevate the social status of some workers by providing them with opportunities to gain union office and thereby to earn the respect of their fellow workers. One example of this would be the ability of a shop steward, union official, or member of a grievance committee to talk with management about workers' problems. Holders of union office also often become members of associations involved in community projects. Furthermore, a worker who starts off as a shop steward may end up being the president of a national union. The presidents of the Canadian Labour Congress, for example, all started fairly low in the union hierarchy and were able to rise progressively to national status. Although all workers cannot achieve this kind of status, some people at least who belong to a union can advance to elected or appointed office, and in this manner acquire the respect of others.

Creature Comforts Concern over the degree of creature comforts and economic security possessed by the most favoured of one's customary associates relates to the type of "bread and butter" unionism referred to earlier. Bakke and his associates found that when workers looked at creature comforts, they did not compare themselves with the rich or most wealthy people, but rather with people in similar states of life. Hence, if unions could enable workers to enjoy creature comforts comparable to those of their usual associates, then workers would be more likely to join unions. The converse would hold if the union were seen as a hindrance to the attainment of such creature comforts.

Control Another important factor in the minds of workers is that of independence in and, specifically, control over their own affairs. Prior to the advent of unions, workers had very little bargaining power before employers: if workers approached employers with demands for more money or better working conditions, employers could very well dismiss them without any recourse to grievance procedures. Hence, unions helped to provide workers with some degree of control over the conditions of their employment, and also, through the collective bargaining process, gave them some influence within their society. In some cases, however, workers may choose to substitute union control for management control, particularly in unions which are autocratically run. Thus, merely joining a union does not automatically ensure workers control, for control as union members involves participation in union decisions and responsiveness on the part of union officers.

Information To some extent, unions are able to help workers understand the forces at work in their world through their various educational programs and publications. Most unions of any size publish a monthly newspaper in which they explain in clear, direct language developments in their industry and in the economy generally. Workers who read their union's newspaper are thus kept generally well informed of what the union is doing to improve the lot of workers in their industry and elsewhere. In addition, a number of unions conduct educational programs for workers to help them understand the nature and administration of the collective agreements affecting them.

Integrity Bakke uses the word integrity to describe a sense of wholeness, self-respect, justice, and fairness. When workers think about whether or not they should join a union, they probably ask themselves whether or not joining a union will help promote their sense of integrity. If the answer is yes, then they are likely to join, but if the answer is no, then they are likely not to join unless compelled by a union-shop security clause to do so.

Bakke concludes his article, in part, with the following statement:

> The contribution of unionism at its best is its provision of a pattern of life which offers chances of successful adjustment and goal realization, not for the few who get out of the working class but for the great majority who must stay there.[53]

The Growth of Unionism

Most of the authors whose writings we have discussed have dealt primarily with the unionization of industrial workers. As I pointed out on a number of occasions, several of the earlier writers touch upon unionization among the various categories of white-collar workers only incidentally. In recent years, however, there has been a growing amount of research into the reasons that various groups of white-collar workers are turning to unions. Many of the reasons that apply to white-collar workers apply equally well to blue-collar workers. The factors that apply to both blue- and white-collar workers will be looked at first, and those that apply to white-collar workers only will be looked at in the last part of this chapter. Our discussion of these factors will refer to the theories discussed earlier in this chapter.

Major Factors Which Determine the Growth of Unionism Among White-Collar and Blue-Collar Workers

Concentration in Large Groups The extent to which workers are concentrated in large groups determines, in great measure the degree to which they are unionized. In general, the more highly concentrated workers are in large organizations, the more likely they are to turn to unionization.[54] (Bureaucratization is the administrative answer to the problem of governing large numbers of workers.) When workers are highly concentrated, they realize that they are no longer able to strike their own bargains with their employers and thus conclude that the most effective way to improve their employment conditions under these circumstances is by forming unions and dealing collectively with the employers. The Webbs deal with this factor in their reference to the separation between labour and capital and Hoxie deals with it in terms of group consciousness.

Concern with Job Security Workers are concerned with job security which may be threatened by the introduction of new technology or by a lessening in demand for the services of certain groups, both of which have occurred among blue-collar and white-collar workers alike. The difference between these two groups of workers is that for many years blue-collar workers have been negotiating clauses in collective agreements which provide for notice of lay-off, severance pay, continuation of company-paid health and life-insurance plans, company assistance in locating new employment, and other provisions which attempt to cushion the impact of technology. Granted, unions are unable to guarantee employment to any group, but they are at least able to negotiate provisions in collective agreements which make the problem of redundancy or job insecurity less frightening to the worker.

A cursory examination of many collective agreements between school boards and teacher groups in Ontario shows clearly that teachers have in many cases negotiated clauses in their collective agreements which attempt to maintain to some degree their job security in light of the declining enrollment of students in elementary and secondary schools. University professors have clauses in many of their collective agreements which provide for recycling in cases where the demand for certain university programs has declined substantially. Recycling provisions enable professors to undergo retraining in programs where the demand is stable or increasing.

Perlman's preoccupation with the control of scarce jobs, the Webbs' concern with the separation of the worker from the means of production, and Tannenbaum's emphasis on the machine as the centre of gravity of a worker's life all concern themselves with job security in the context of technological growth.

Legislative Policy The legislative policy of governments may, to some extent, either help or hinder unionization among both blue-collar and white-collar groups. Favourable public policy is of crucial importance for the development of unionism and collective bargaining. This is particularly true of the development of unionism in the United States and Canada. Following the passage of the *Wagner Act* of 1935 in the United States — an act which encouraged unionization and collective bargaining — there was a tremendous growth of unions and collectives particularly among blue-collar workers in mass-production industries. A similar degree of growth took place in Canada following the issuance of *Order-in-Council PC 1003* in 1944, an order which was modeled largely on the principles of the *Wagner Act*.

Since 1967, there has been a phenomenal expansion of unionization among white-collar and other workers in government services, both at the federal and provincial levels. This expansion has been due in large measure to the fact that both the Federal Government and all the provincial governments have now given collective bargaining rights to their workers. In addition, all provinces have accorded collective bargaining rights to professional and white-collar workers in hospitals and in the educational sector. This protective legislation has fostered increasing unionization among various groups within these sectors. These sectors, called parapublic groups, will be dealt with in the chapter "Collective Bargaining in the Public and Parapublic Sectors."[55]

Neither Perlman nor Tannenbaum recognized the importance of favourable public policy; the Webbs, however, did draw attention to employment standards legislation, as it is called today.

Growth of the Service Sector An economic shift has occurred from primary and manufacturing industries to the service or tertiary industries. This shift has influenced the development of unionism among both blue- and white-collar workers in several ways. First, the development of the primary and secondary sectors of the economy, especially manufacturing, meant that there was a rapid rise in the proportion of the labour force which was unionized. Recently, however, employment in secondary industries has been declining and, consequently, the number of workers (primarily blue-collar workers) unionized in these industries has been declining. In Canada, the decline in the number of unionized blue-collar workers has been offset by an increase in the number of unionized white-collar workers. In the United States, however, the decline in the number of unionized blue-collar workers has been dramatic.

The substantial increase of the labour force in the service sector (which employs large numbers of white-collar workers) has not been a complete blessing for unionization because this increase has to some extent inhibited the unionization of white-collar and professional workers. Of particular significance is the fact that an increasing proportion of service-sector workers are employed in small establishments.

Small establishments are the most difficult to unionize — one reason why the degree of unionization in the service sector is not as high as it probably would be if its establishments were larger. Because women are more apt than men to be employed in small service establishments, they appear to be less susceptible to unionization even though both women and men have remarkably similar attitudes towards unions.[56]

In the retail sector a potentially significant development in unionization occurred in May 1985 when the T. Eaton Company and the Retail, Wholesale and Department Store Union concluded an agreement covering about 1,000 workers in six Southern Ontario stores in Toronto, Bramalea, St. Catharines, and a small warehouse in London, Ontario. The workers were certified in fourteen separate bargaining units, including separate units for full- and part-time workers and for office workers. A strike against the company began on November 30, 1984 and a country-wide campaign to boycott Eaton's stores was organized by the Canadian Labour Congress. Since a large number of the strikers were women, women's groups also organized boycotts against the company. About a week to ten days before the settlement, the Social Affairs Commission of the Canadian Conference of Catholic Bishops and high-ranking authorities of the United Church urged the T. Eaton Company to conclude agreements with its striking workers.

The major issues disputed were wages and pensions. The union also wanted a master agreement covering the fourteen bargaining units. However, since in Ontario workers lose their employment status after being on strike for six months, there was an incentive for the union to lower its sights on an agreement which was only slightly better than the one it rejected in January 1985. The signing of this agreement was seen by the labour movement both as a major achievement in its own right and as a major breakthrough in the retail sector.[57]

Among the theorists discussed above, only Hoxie makes reference to unionization among both white- and blue-collar workers.

Inadequate Grievance Procedures White-collar groups often have no recourse to an adequate grievance procedure. In the absence of unions, workers may be required to work overtime with neither monetary compensation nor time off, and may have no means of airing their grievance over this and other objectionable practices. From an early stage in union-management relations, collective agreements have guaranteed blue-collar workers recourse to grievance procedures. If agreement cannot be reached between various levels in the union-management hierarchy over controversial issues in the collective agreement, workers may have their grievances heard by impartial third parties whose decisions are binding.

> [T]he complaint may be very serious to the individual involved...[b]ut, whatever the nature of the specific dispute, a modern organization is not set up to deal directly with individuals. Authority for settling disputes is usually much higher up in the hierarchy than the immediate supervisor or personnel person with whom the complainant tries to bargain.[58]

White-collar workers often regard unions as instruments to resolve their grievances without fear of reprisal from bosses. Bakke is the only theorist to have referred to the grievance procedure. He did so because he recognized that this procedure allows individual workers to retain their self-respect.

Concern with Policy-Making All workers like to have an input into the formulation of policies, especially those policies which may affect their daily worklife. Blue-collar workers, for example, like to have a say in the way overtime work is allocated, and usually their collective agreements will reflect this concern. Also, they may be concerned that layoffs and recall be subject to systematic procedures rather than to the whims of superiors. For this reason collective agreements contain provisions that require supervisors to consider both a worker's seniority and ability when making decisions about layoffs and recalls.

Among white-collar workers, teachers are very concerned about class size, and nurses are concerned about the type of care patients receive. Engineers and other professional groups have similar concerns about the nature of the work they do and the control they have over the formulation of policy. Commenting on the American situation, Dennis Chamot points out that,

> Discussion with representatives of several unions that are active in organizing professionals confirms that dissatisfaction with policies relating to authority and decision-making is a major issue. For example, at most campuses where faculties have unionized in recent years, the primary concerns were job security and the somewhat related but much broader subject of university governance.[59]

One of the major ways in which professional groups and quasi-professional groups may obtain control over the formulation of policy is through collective bargaining. Individually, professionals have very little impact on the formulation of policy but collectively, through their unions or associations, they may be able to bargain with their employers over policy issues relating to authority and decision-making.

Perlman's thesis that workers want to control scarce jobs, Tannenbaum's idea that workers want something to hold onto in a changing world, and Bakke's idea that workers want some control over their affairs reflect the importance of *control* to all workers.

Poor Personnel Policies The relatively poor personnel policies practised by many managers in organizations where workers are highly concentrated is contributing to unionism. Poor personnel policies lead to dissatisfaction among workers who may turn to unions as a means of forcing managers to develop better policies. Banking, until relatively recently, has been well known as an industry with relatively poor personnel policies and practices. Although some banks have maintained poor personnel policies despite attempts by their workers to unionize (see the decisions of the Canada Labour Relations Board in some of the bank cases), most banks seem to be improving their personnel policies in an attempt to stay union-free.

In the depths of the recession in the early 1980's, some retail stores fired long-service workers who considered their income and benefits adequate. Subsequent to the firing, these same long-service workers were rehired as part-time workers with greatly reduced wages and very few benefits. This abuse of economic power facilitated the unionization of these workers and, in general, is such a short-sighted practice that no theorist need comment on it. Practically all the theories discussed here, however, would predict the same outcome: the introduction of a union.

Changes in Family Structure The emergence of the single-parent family is making unionization an economic necessity for many workers. Secondary wage-earners have now become primary wage-earners in many households, partly because of the increasing divorce rates in recent years. In the nursing profession, for example, many nurses are the sole wage-earners for their families and for them the economic benefits of employment are very significant. Nurses agonized over whether or not they should unionize, for many nurses have traditionally seen themselves as highly dedicated, devoted more to service than to income. However, after years of soul-searching, a vast majority of nurses has turned to unions in the hope of improving both their workload and their financial and job security.

Primary wage-earners are found not only among the ranks of professionals such as nurses, but are unskilled aids in hospitals, secretaries in offices, clerks in governmental agencies,

among other kinds of workers. None of the theorists discussed above mentioned single-parent families, however, because the divorce rates in their times were not nearly as high as they are today.

Factors Unique to the Development of White-Collar Unionism

A number of factors are unique to the development of unionism among white-collar workers.

Changes in Skill Levels Changes in skill levels may lead to unionism. George W. Adams points out that the bureaucratization of intellectual work and the explosion of knowledge in both new and existing fields has led to the specialization of intellectual work into minute parts. As this happens, skills are inevitably broken down and routinized to the point where professionals may be unable to practise the skills for which they were trained. Given these conditions, Adams claims that professionals may turn to collective bargaining, and implicitly to unionism, as a method of preserving or recovering what they believe to be an exclusive work jurisdiction.[60] This kind of thing is also happening among other white-collar groups.

Inadequate Legislation Canadian labour-standards legislation does not apply to professionals. These workers may be required to work very long hours, but are not protected by laws which give other workers time-and-a-half for working over eight hours a day or over forty hours a week. This is one reason resident doctors completing their internship in hospitals have frequently gone on strike in recent years. Economists, statisticians, and sociologists employed in the Federal Public Service, however, successfully negotiated a time-and-a-half agreement and thus avoided a strike. If these people had not belonged to a union or an association with collective bargaining rights, they probably would not have obtained the overtime benefits. As it stands, this particular group has set an example for those groups not protected by labour standards legislation to form unions and catch up with organized labour.

Changes in Union Image   The changing image of unions makes the idea of unionization more acceptable to professionals. No longer are unions considered radical oranizations out to destroy the basic fibre of our social and economic systems. In part, this change in image has come about as a result of more people belonging to unions and the families of unionized workers becoming more aware of what unions and collective bargaining are all about.

To counteract the growing appeal of unionism, a number of groups now provide training programs for managers on how to keep their organizations union-free. Membership lists of a number of professional associations are often used by these groups as a means of advertising their programs. These groups sponsor courses which are attended by managers in a number of important sectors of the economy. In the early 1970's when the CLC launched a major campaign to organize office workers in the financial institutions in Toronto, a program was being sponsored for employers in the same sector on how to keep their companies free of unionization.

Conclusion

This chapter has described different viewpoints on why workers join unions. In some cases the discussion has included the ultimate objective of unions and their emergence and development. We began with the Webbs who viewed unions arising largely because workers wanted to protect themselves as members of a wage-earning class who had lost control of the means of production and distribution of goods. We also discussed the work of John R. Commons who viewed the extension of competitive markets as the major factor in the formation of unions. Then we looked at the ideas of Selig Perlman, one of Commons' former students and colleagues; he saw unions emerging primarily from a consciousness of job-scarcity. Robert Hoxie thought that unions emerged as a result of a group's interpretation of the social situations in which it found itself. Robert Tannenbaum saw the labour movement springing from the rise of machines which threatened job security and other conditions of employment.

Among the more modern writers, we discussed the work of Bakke who, along with his associates, conducted a large number of interviews with workers and attempted to make some sense out of their reasons for joining unions. Bakke indicated that workers would be apt to join unions if they saw unionism as a means of reducing their frustrations and helping them enrich their lives. The final part of this chapter has described the growth of unionization among white-collar workers in professional, quasi-professional, technical, and clerical groups. Apart from the works of a few British writers (the most notable of whom is George Bain, a Canadian teaching and conducting research in the United Kingdom) there are very few prominent writers who are trying to articulate any kind of theory which would explain the emergence of unionism among white-collar groups. We did see, however, that many of the factors which explain the rise of unionism among blue-collar workers also explain the rise of unionism among white-collar workers.

questions

1 In what ways does an examination of historical theories of the labour movement help you to understand how unions operate today?

2 Give a summary of the major ideas of each of the theorists discussed in this chapter. How well do they answer the questions posed by Dunlop?

3 Does John R. Commons's idea of the expansion of markets help to explain the operation of American-based unions in Canada? Elaborate.

4 Provide Canadian examples of the four major types of unions that Hoxie developed. Explain how each union falls into one of the four major categories.

5 Using a graph with Dunlop's four questions on one axis and the name of each theorist on the other axis, develop a detailed analysis of the similarities and differences of the major theorists discussed in this chapter.

6 Is a theory of the labour movement which would apply to both blue-collar and white-collar workers possible? Why or why not?

7 What is the level of unionization in your province? How do the theories discussed in this chapter help you to answer this question?

8 How do you account for the fact that British Columbia is the most highly unionized province in Canada? What are the major factors at work in that province that are not as prevalent in the other provinces?

9 Why was it predictable that the first union to apply to represent workers in Canadian banks was a B.C. union? Why was it predictable that this union was led by women?

10 Is a theory which would explain equally well the functioning of blue-collar and white-collar unions in your province possible? Elaborate.

notes

1 C. Kerr, F. H. Harbison, J. T. Dunlop and C. A. Myers, *Industrializm and Industrial Man* (Cambridge: Harvard University Press, 1960). For an attempt to convene the writings of many American trade union theorists, see Mark Perlman, *Labour Union Theories in America* (Evanston: Row, Peterson and Company, 1958).

2 J. T. Dunlop, "The Development of Labor Organizations: A Theoretical Framework," *Insights into Labour Issues*, eds. R. A. Lester and J. Shister (New York: The MacMillan Company, 1948). This article has been reprinted in *Readings in Labor Economics and Labor Relations*, 3rd. ed., ed. Richard L. Rowan (Homewood: Richard D. Irwin, 1976), pp. 63-76.

3 Sidney and Beatrice Webb produced two classic books towards the end of the 19th century: *The History of Trade Unionism* (New York: Longmans, Green and Co., 1894) and *Industrial Democracy* (New York: Longmans, Green and Co., 1897). The revised 1920 editions of both books were used as the source reference for this chapter.

4 Webb, *History of Trade Unionism*, p. 1.

5 *Ibid.*, pp. 25-26.

6 *Ibid.*, p. 41.

7 Webb, *Industrial Democracy*, p. 807.

8 *Ibid.*, p. 79.

9 *Ibid.*, p. 833.

10 *Ibid.*, p. 150.

11 *Ibid.*, p. 152 ff.

12 *Ibid.*, p. 185.

13 *Ibid.*, pp. 791-92.

14 *Ibid.*, pp. 704-15.

15 *Ibid.*, p. 253.

16 *Ibid.*, p. 803.

17 *Ibid.*, p. 823.

18 John R. Commons et al., *History of Labour in the United States,* 2 vols. (New York: The Macmillan Company, 1918). See in particular Vol. 1 and the section by John R. Commons entitled "American Labor History — Introduction," pp. 3-21. See also, Lafayette G. Harter, Jr., *John R. Commons: His Assault on Laissez-faire* (Corvallis, Oregon: Oregon State University Press, 1962), in particular ch. 7 "John R. Commons, Student of the Labor Movement," pp. 163-204.

19 Commons, Vol. 1, *History of Labor*, p. 3.

20 *Ibid.*, pp. 4-5.

21 John R. Commons, "American Shoemakers, 1648-1895," Vol. XXIV, *The Quarterly Journal of Economics* (November, 1909). This article has been reproduced in *Readings in Labor Economics and Labor Relations*, rev. ed., ed. Richard L. Rowan (Homewood: Richard D. Irwin, 1972), pp. 93-108.

22 Commons, *History of Labor*, pp. 5-6.

23 Selig Perlman, *A Theory of the Labor Movement* (New York: Augustus M. Kelly, 1949). (The book was first published and copyrighted in Perlman's name in 1928. The book was reprinted and published in 1949 by Augustus M. Kelley of New York. It is the 1949 edition to which reference will be made in this chapter.)

24 *Ibid.*, p. x.

25 *Ibid.*, p. 161.

26 *Ibid.*, p. 6.

27 *Ibid.*, p. 237.

28 *Ibid.*, p. 8.

29 *Ibid.*, p. 253.

30 Robert F. Hoxie, *Trade Unionism in the United States* (New York: D. Appleton and Co., 1919 or 1921). The version used here is entitled Robert F. Hoxie, *Trade Unionism in the United States*, reproduced from the second revised edition of 1923, and reissued in 1966 by Russell and Russell, a division of Atheneum House Inc. The reader is advised to read the excellent introduction by E. H. Downey.

31 *Ibid.*, p. 60.

32 *Ibid.*, p. 69.

33 *Ibid.*, pp. 37-38.

34 *Ibid.*, pp. 45-52.

35 *Ibid.*, p. 47.

36 *Ibid.*, p. 48.

37 *Ibid.*, p. 59, n. 3.

38 Tannenbaum's contribution to an analysis of the labour movement is included in two of his books. They are *The Labor Movement: Its Conservative Functions and Social Consequences* (New York: G. P. Putnam's Sons, 1921) and *A Philosophy of Labor* (New York: Alfred A. Knopf, 1951).

39 Tannenbaum, *Labor Movement*, p. 29.

40 *Ibid.*, pp. 25-31.

41 *Ibid.*, p. 34.

42 *Ibid.*, pp. 35-36.

43 Tannenbaum, *Philosophy of Labor*, p. 199.

44 Tannenbaum, *Labor Movement*, p. 40.

45 The Marxist analysis of unions comes primarily from Philip Taft, "Theories of the Labor Movement," *Readings in Labor Economics and Labor Relations*, 2nd ed., eds. Lloyd G. Reynolds, S. H. Masters, and C. H. Moser (Englewood Cliffs: Prentice-Hall, 1978), pp. 246-55; and Dunlop, "Development of Labor Organizations," pp. 67-68.

46 Taft, "Theories of the Labor Movement," p. 248.

47 A. Lozovsky, *Marx and the Trade Unions*, (New York: International Publishing Company, 1935), p. 15; and quoted in Dunlop, "Development of Labor Organizations," p. 67.

48 Taft, "Theories of the Labor Movement," p. 249.

49 Norman Penner, *The Canadian Left: A Critical Analysis* and particularly Ch. 5, "The Communist Party, the Trade Unions, and CCF" (Scarborough: Prentice-Hall Canada Inc., 1977), p. 170.

50 The material for this section is taken from E. Wight Bakke, "Why Workers Join Unions," Vol. 22, No. 1, *Personnel* (July 1945), pp. 2-11; and reprinted in E. W. Bakke, Clark Kerr, and C. W. Anrod, *Unions, Management and the Public*, 3rd ed. (New York: Harcourt, Brace and World Incorporated, 1967), pp. 85-92.

51 E. Wight Bakke, "To Join or Not to Join," *Unions, Management and the Public*, p. 85.

52 *Ibid.*, p. 86.

53 *Ibid.*, p. 92.

54 George Sayers Bain, "The Growth of White-Collar Unionism and Public Policy in Canada," Vol. 24, No. 2, *Industrial Relations/Relations Industrielles*, No. 2 (1969), p. 247.

55 For an interesting discussion of the increase in unionization among government workers, see Roy Brookbank, "The Adversary System in Canadian Industrial Relations: Blight or Blessing?" Vol. 35, No. 1, *Industrial Relations/Relations Industrielles*, (1980), pp. 20-40.

56 George Bain, *Union Growth and Public Policy in Canada* (Ottawa: Labour Canada, October 1978), p. 19.

57 Lorne Slotnick, "Symbol of First Eaton's Pact Outweighs Contents for Union," and "Landmark Agreement Awaits Ratification," *Globe and Mail* (May 9, 1985). For statements on church support for Eaton's workers see Lorne Slotnick, "United Church Backs Striking Eaton's Clerks," *Globe and Mail* (May 2, 1985); and "Bishops Supporting Workers in Canadian Retail Industry," The Catholic Register (May 11, 1985), p. 8.

58 Dennis Chamot, "Professional Employees Turn to Unions," *Harvard Business Review* (May June 1976), p. 124.

59 *Ibid.*, p. 122.

60 George W. Adams, "Collective Bargaining by Salaried Professionals," Vol. 32, No. 2, *Industrial Relations/Relations Industrielles* (1977), p. 189.

4

The History and Philosophy of the Canadian Labour Movement

R. Norman Matheny, *The Financial Post*

Introduction

Before reading this chapter, it would be useful to come to some understanding of its central term: *labour movement. Labour movement* refers only to the unionized segment of the Canadian labour force; those workers and union leaders who have made a conscious decision to join trade unions and to foster their formation and development. The fact that we have a complex trade union structure in Canada does not invalidate this definition but merely makes an

analysis of the movement more difficult than it might otherwise be.

A. E. Kovacs defines the labour movement in the following terms:

> a dynamic organizational instrument created by workers and emerging as an institutional force independent of the state and the employers... Since the movement is an evolutionary force, its philosophy is also subject to alteration with the times.[1]

It might appear from the above that the Canadian labour movement comprises only one organization. However, as will be shown throughout this chapter, the Canadian labour movement has historically been characterized by more than one central labour federation.*

Within the Canadian labour movement, the primary building block is the local union at the plant or establishment level. Workers elect their own officers for and pay dues directly to the local. At a higher level, a local union may be part of a national union which organizes workers in a particular industry or occupation for all, or part, of the country. An example is the Canadian Union of Public Employees (CUPE) which in 1985 had 1,864 local unions across Canada representing some 295,961 members, mostly at the municipal level.[2] CUPE is part of the Canadian Labour Congress which is a federation of national and Canadian branches of international unions. (International unions have their headquarters in the United States; a branch, district, or lodge in Canada; and organize workers in both countries.)

Unions may also be differentiated in terms of the nature of their membership. Craft (or horizontal) unions organize strictly on the basis of a specific craft or skill. An example would be the United Brotherhood of Carpenters and Joiners of America which organizes carpenters only. An industrial union, on the other hand, organizes on a vertical basis and includes everyone in an enterprise, unskilled and skilled workers alike. The United Steelworkers Union is an example of this type of union.

While some reference will be made to the development of local unions in Canada, the ma-jor focus of this chapter will be on the development of central labour federations. Some of these federations have endured; others, though short-lived, still deserve our attention. Since international unions have played an important role in the evolution of the Canadian labour movement, parallels will be drawn between the Canadian and American federations where appropriate.

Origins

A distinguished Canadian author, Eugene Forsey, recently wrote that we usually think of trade unions as part of an advanced industrial society, and that we are often shocked to realize that unions existed in Canada as early as the War of 1812. Forsey suggests that we not be so surprised since at that time

> There were towns and cities. They had to have construction workers. They had to have tools, and stoves, therefore foundries and foundry workers. They had to have boots and shoes and clothes, therefore tailors and shoemakers. They had to have printers. And even in that simple society there were employers and employed, and their interests were not identical. The employed soon found that out, by experience; found out also the employer's strength and their own weakness in individual bargaining on terms and conditions of employment, and so started organizing to prevent their employers from taking advantage of them.[3]

Unions began in Canada between 1812 and 1859 taking the form of local unions. These local unions probably first emerged in New Brunswick and Nova Scotia. Saint John, with as many as fourteen unions in the late 1850's, was the chief centre of union activity between the late 1830's and the late 1850's. Quite surprisingly, "in the 1850's, [Saint] John (with the adjacent town of Portland) was bigger than Toronto, twice the size of Hamilton, and more than half as big as Montreal. It was the centre of flourishing shipping, shipbuilding, and lumber industries."[4] In Quebec City, too, there was a printers union in

---

*A central labour federation is an organization whose affiliates include various national unions or Canadian branches of international unions or both, directly-chartered locals, provincial and territorial federations of labour, and local labour councils. Its general purpose is to represent workers who belong to these bodies at the national level. The national unions and Canadian branches of international unions, provincial and territorial federations and local labour councils will be dealt with in more detail in the chapter, "The Structure of the Canadian Labour Movement."

1827 and, although this particular union did not last long, there were several reorganizations of it that culminated in 1872 in the formation of locals 159 and 160 of the International Typographical Union.[5] Unions of printers, shoemakers, and tailors, among others, sprang up in Montreal, Toronto, and Hamilton.

Despite its early activity, the labour movement in Canada developed relatively slowly until the 1900's. Specialization in agriculture and primary industries, the dominance of domestic production in many industries, the lack of industrial development, the small and scattered population, and inadequate transportation and communication facilities all account for this slow growth.[6]

Forsey draws some conclusions about early unions and the young Canadian labour movement in the following statement:

> From this sketchy and scattered information, several things seem clear. First, by 1859, there must have been at least 30 to 36 unions, in almost every settled part of the country. Second, except for the...ASE [Amalgamated Society of Engineers, a British-based union] branches, all seem to have been purely local, and very few seem to have had any relations with other unions. Third, there seems to have been a fairly high mortality. Fourth, certain crafts predominated, notably printers, engineers, waterfront workers, a few construction trades, moulders and foundrymen, shoemakers, and tailors. Fifth, the only organizations of the unskilled were...two longshoremen's unions.[7]

Forsey's statement characterizes the early local unions and indicates why there would be no history of central labour federations without them.

International unionism made its appearance in Canada in the 1850's. The first internationals were British organizations, of which the most important were the Amalgamated Society of Carpenters and Joiners and the Amalgamated Society of Engineers.[8] These two organizations, the only ones which operated in Canada, had Canadian members as late as the 1920's. American international unions began to appear in Canada during the early 1860's and were soon

to become the dominant force on the Canadian trade-union scene.[9] The Journeymen Shoemakers was the first American international union to enter Canada. Its first locals were in Hamilton and Toronto. The Second American international union to enter Canada was the National Union of Iron Moulders with locals in Montreal, Hamilton, Toronto, and Brantford. Canadian locals played an important role in helping the American union become incorporated by the American Congress. Both the Shoemakers and Iron Moulders conducted a number of strikes in their early years.[10]

In subsequent decades, a large number of American international unions were to have a significant impact on the development of Canadian unionism. International unions supplanted local, regional, and national unions "because of the mobility of labour across the border...and because the international unions had more money, more experience, more organizers, and more skilled negotiators and so could do a more effective job of representing the workers concerned."[11]

Prior to the formation of central federations in Canada, a number of attempts were made to combine the various unions at the local level to further their common objectives. Probably the most significant of these was the formation of the Toronto Trades Assembly in 1871 which comprised fifteen local unions. This organization played an important role in leading the movement for a nine-hour work day. It is also credited with contributing to the establishment of the *Trade Unions Act* and the *Criminal Law Amendment Act* of 1872 which freed unions from charges of criminal conspiracy; i.e., the accusation that unions worked against the interest of the state. These enactments were considered fundamental to the continued existence and formation of trade unions.

The Toronto Trades Assembly undertook to form a central federation of all labour organizations in Canada during the 1870's and led the call for a general convention which was held in Toronto on September 23, 1873. The forty delegates who attended this meeting, all of whom were from Ontario, decided to form a permanent national organization to be known as the Canadian Labour Union (CLU). Although its organizers had hoped to form a national body, the CLU never did expand to include workers outside of Ontario, and succumbed in the late 1870's to the effects of economic depression.[12]

The Emergence and Development of Central Labour Federations

Knights of Labour 1869-1910

The Knights of Labour, founded in Philadelphia in 1869, was the first major trade-union federation in the United States. This body welcomed members from all walks of life: blue-collar workers, white-collar office workers, salesmen, and others. The Knights were organized in craft or mixed locals, which combined to form district assemblies of craft or mixed memberships. For example, in some cases a local might be composed of carpenters only, whereas in others there might be a mixed local composed of carpenters, printers, and other groups. Not long after their formation in the United States, the Knights of Labour came into Canada. The first Canadian local assembly of the Knights was established in Hamilton in 1875 and by the end of the 1880's it had some 250 local assemblies organized into seven district assemblies.[13] The federation made particularly rapid progress in the Province of Quebec, partly because its structure suited the then rural society of Quebec and partly because the organization had agreed to forego one of its rituals which required the taking of a secret oath, a practice outlawed by the Catholic Church.

The federation in the United States, as in Canada, has sometimes been likened to a train station, inasmuch as people were coming in and leaving so rapidly that it was very difficult to get a true idea of its membership. However, for a while the Knights of Labour played a dominant role in the Canadian labour scene, and continued to be active in Canada even after the demise of the federation in the United States. Its success in Canada is attributable, at least in part, to its idealism and open organizational structure which, it is claimed, were well-suited to the Canadian environment.[14]

Trades and Labour Congress of Canada 1886-1956

Following the failure of the Canadian Labour Union in the 1870's, a number of attempts were made to establish a central labour federation in Canada. One of the first attempts was undertaken by the Toronto Trades and Labour Council (formerly the Toronto Trades Assembly) which, together with the Knights of Labour, held a convention in Toronto in 1883. Although that attempt was not completely successful, a new federation, the Trades and Labour Congress of Canada (TLC), was established on a permanent basis at a second convention in 1886. This body included both traditional trade unions and assemblies of the Knights of Labour, and remained in existence until the Canadian Labour Congress was formed in 1956. Although it suffered losses in membership during certain periods, it maintained some continuity in organization and policy throughout its history.

Since the Trades and Labour Congress (TLC) was in large measure influenced by and similar to the American Federation of Labour (AFL) which was formed in the United States during the same year, it might be useful to discuss the development of the AFL briefly. The AFL was a loosely knit federation of autonomous national and international trade unions representing cigarmakers, carpenters, and other crafts workers. Each union chartered by the AFL was to have exclusive jurisdiction over its trade, and no other union was to organize workers within that trade. This proscription on dual unionism made it impossible for the American Knights of Labour to belong to the AFL.

Each trade union within the AFL was an autonomous organization in the sense that it had control over most of its own activities. The AFL was primarily a clearing house that disseminated information to its members, helped coordinate their activities, and acted to resolve problems of overlapping jurisdictions among its affiliated unions.

The AFL was a pragmatic federation which reflected the philosophy of its first president, Samuel Gompers, who led the organization from 1886 to 1924 with the exception of one three-year term. Although Gompers had been a socialist while he worked in the east end of London, he concluded soon after his arrival in the United States that socialism would not take root in American soil and that a practical approach unfettered by ideology represented labour's best strategy.

A close link developed between the AFL and the TLC. Many of the international unions that became members of the AFL also had Canadian districts which helped form the TLC. The TLC, moreover, included not only Canadian branches of international unions associated with the AFL but also district councils or assemblies of the Knights of Labour, as well as strictly Canadian unions. However, the leadership of the TLC soon came to be dominated by the Canadian directors of international unions. Thus, the AFL indirectly exercised a fair degree of control over the TLC, and was sometimes a source of conflict within that body.

One conflict centred around the TLC's acceptance of the Knights of Labour. The Knights of Labour could not belong to the AFL in the United States. The AFL, moreover, frowned on the toleration of the TLC toward the practice of dual unionism among its membership, and tried to have the TLC expel the Knights of Labour. Finally in 1902, the TLC acceded to the wishes of the AFL, changed its constitution to bar dual unionism, and expelled the Knights and other national Canadian unions whose jurisdictions conflicted with those of TLC affiliates. Hence, the AFL exerted a significant impact on the TLC by effectively determining its membership through Canadian AFL branch officers.

The Canadian labour movement grew rapidly from 1902 to 1920, and particularly from 1913 onward. In 1919 union membership was over 378,000, a figure that was not exceeded until 1937. Unions affiliated with the TLC accounted for the greatest proportion of membership and, during this period, the TLC was the central labour federation in Canada.[15]

According to S. Jamieson, an industrial relations writer in Canada, the following factors were mainly responsible for trade union growth from 1902 to 1920: a favourable economic climate, support in the form of funds and personnel from the headquarters of international unions, unprecedented population growth and economic expansion, settlement of the Prairie provinces, and large-scale railway construction. In addition, labour shortages, inflation, and serious wage-price lags during and immediately after World War I created conditions favourable to organized labour.[16]

The 1920's, by contrast, were a period of slow growth for unions in both Canada and the United States. The craft nature of the TLC neither suited the mass production industries that had begun to emerge in Canada, nor was it adaptable to western Canadian economy which was characterized largely by primary industries such as mining, forestry, and logging. In the United States, employers during the 1920's launched what was known as the American plan. This plan emphasized the primacy of individualism and discouraged collectivism. The philosophy of individualism during the 1920's impeded the growth of unionism in the United States, and undoubtedly had a similar influence within branches of American firms. These factors counteracted the effects of the decade's prosperity, which normally would have encouraged union growth. In this respect, the nature of unionism during the 1920's was quite unique.

The TLC experienced an uneven pattern of growth during the 1930's and 1940's. In the early 1930's the Depression caused a decline in membership. However, from about 1935 to 1945, membership increased significantly. We noted in the previous chapter that favourable legislation is crucial in promoting unions and collective bargaining. Favourable legislation was first enacted in the United States with the *Wagner Act* of 1935. This act gave unions the right to organize and required employers to bargain in good faith. These guarantees helped the unions that belonged to the newly-formed Congress of Industrial Organization (CIO) and led to increasing demands among Canadian trade unionists for similar legislation. In Canada, unionization in the mass production industries had led to substantial increases in TLC numbers, so that by 1938 its membership was close to the previous high of 1920-21.[17] When the AFL expelled the CIO unions in 1938, the TLC followed suit the next year, which resulted in a substantial decrease in its membership. Not before well into World War II did the TLC regain its 1938 peak membership.

While the TLC professed in principle to be an autonomous labour body having no direct connection with the AFL, it soon became apparent that the TLC had become firmly committed to the policy of working in close conjunction with the AFL. Purely Canadian national or local organizations formed part of the TLC only when their jurisdictions did not conflict with those of the international unions affiliated with the AFL in the United States. Given this connection between the AFL and the TLC,

> [i]t is hardly surprising that Gompers, in November 1902, asserted that relations between the AFL and the [TLC] were now substantially the same as between the AFL and its state federations. There were in fact important differences, notably the congress's power to charter trades and labour councils...which it continued to exercise, though within limitations subsequently worked out with the AFL executive council.[18]

The TLC played a significant role in the development of organized labour in Canada. Part of its strength derived from its affiliation with the American Federation of Labour, although this association may be judged by some to have been a mixed blessing. There were, however, other strictly Canadian federations, established after 1886, which operated along nationalistic lines and in opposition to the TLC. In the following sections, some of these major indigenous or national organizations will be discussed.

Canadian Federation of Labour 1908-1927

The first of these indigenous federations was the National Trades and Labour Congress which existed under that title from 1902 until 1908 when it changed its name to the Canadian Federation of Labour (CFL). Its membership comprised mainly the Knights of Labour which had been expelled from the TLC in 1902, the Provincial Workmen's Association of Nova Scotia[19] which affiliated with the CFL in 1910, and a number of other strictly Canadian unions. Its areas of major strength were Quebec and Nova Scotia. Like some of its purely Canadian successors, the CFL was preoccupied with a predominantly nationalistic outlook and was opposed to what it considered the rigid and AFL-influenced policies of the TLC.

That the CFL failed is in part attributable to the fact that it lacked funds to compete with the organizational abilities of the international unions. The CFL also lost support among unions in Quebec, many of which chose to become part of that province's Catholic trade-union movement. In addition, the alliance between workers in Quebec and Nova Scotia was never more than a tenuous one, with the Nova Scotia section (PWA) seeking the sort of industrial strength against employers which the Quebec section, rural and locally based, could not provide.

Thus, although it continued to linger on for some time, the CFL never became a major force in Canadian labour. However, its formation and existence reflected a nationalistic preoccupation that was to characterize the Canadian union movement up to the formation of the Canadian Labour Congress in 1956. Nationalism continues to dominate the thinking of many Canadian trade-unionists.

One Big Union 1919-1956

In the early 1900's western Canada and the western part of the United States were influenced by a number of socialist labour organizations such as the American Labour Union, the American Federation of Miners and, a little later, by the Industrial Workers of the World (IWW or Wobblies). These organizations won many adherents particularly in British Columbia and Alberta, in part because there was a feeling among important union leaders in the West that the TLC was controlled primarily by people in eastern Canada. This combination of factors, among others, led to the formation of the One Big Union which "sprang suddenly into prominence during the Spring and Summer of 1919."[20] The OBU proclaimed a doctrine of revolutionary unionism and was avowedly a class-conscious movement. It sought to organize on an industrial rather than a craft basis, thus appealing to the tastes of western workers, and was composed mainly of western labour unions. Many of these western labour unions were locals of international unions. Western labour councils, including the important Vancouver Trades and Labour Council, also were part of the OBU. At the end of 1919, the OBU had a membership of over 40,000 members, representing 101 local unions with eight central labour councils and two district boards.[21] Its radicalism, however, aroused the opposition of both federal and provincial authorities and this, combined with internal dissension, led to a rapid decline in the OBU's fortunes. The OBU is not known for any contribution to the Canadian labour movement, and what remained of it became part of the Canadian Labour Congress when that body was formed in 1956.

All-Canadian Congress of Labour 1927-1940

During the early 1920's there was an attempt to revive the Canadian Federation of Labour (CFL) as a national movement, but the organization lacked leadership, an attractive philosophy and a creative purpose. Earlier, the Federation had been a protest movement against the international unions with substantial backing in Nova Scotia and Quebec, but when the Catholic unions began to take root in Quebec, the CFL lost a good deal of its support. Dissatisfaction continued, however, with the conservatism of the international craft unions. The militancy of the OBU was scarcely more attractive, and real incentive existed to form an indigenous Canadian federation, in this case the All-Canadian Congress of Labour (ACCL).

The initiative for the formation of the ACCL came from the Canadian Brotherhood of Railway Employees (CBRE), founded as a national union in 1908 and affiliated with the TLC between 1917 and 1921. (The CBRE was expelled from the TLC in 1921 because its jurisdiction conflicted with that of an international union.) The ACCL was also composed of recruits from the CFL and the OBU of 1919, and a few unaffiliated organizations.

The main objective of the All-Canadian Congress of Labour was to organize workers on an industrial rather than a craft basis, the latter being characteristic of the TLC. A critic of the TLC's conservative philosophy, the ACCL sought to free the Canadian labour movement from any form of American control. The ACCL, however, did not survive the Depression of the 1930's, although its members eventually helped form another major federation in 1940, the Canadian Congress of Labour.

Canadian Congress of Labour 1940-1956

As is often the case with events in Canadian labour history, the founding of the Canadian Congress of Labour was, in large measure, the result of actions in the American arena. In 1935, a split developed within the American Federation of Labour between the craft-oriented leadership and a group led by United Mine Workers president John L. Lewis, which favoured the establishment of industry-oriented unions. The latter group formed the Committee for Industrial Organization (CIO) within the AFL and fought for the industrial approach, and a greater political emphasis until the Federation's leadership expelled the CIO group in 1938.[22] (Thereafter, the initials CIO were to stand for a separate labour federation, the Congress of Industrial Organization.)

Following the expulsion of the CIO in the United States, the AFL pressured the TLC to follow suit with CIO-affiliates in Canada. This the TLC reluctantly did in 1939. These CIO-affiliates and the remnants of the All-Canadian Congress of Labour combined to form the Canadian Congress of Labour (CCL) in 1940.[23]

The CCL was founded on the same principle as the CIO; i.e., to organize workers on an industrial rather than a craft basis and to concentrate its efforts primarily on mass production industries. The philosophy of the CCL was political action. The CCL, for example, endorsed as the political arm of labour in Canada the Co-operative Commonwealth Federation (CCF), a socialist party and a forerunner of the New Democratic Party. Inasmuch as it was committed to an interventionist philosophy toward the role of government in union-management relations, the CCL differed from the TLC.

An early problem to be overcome by the CCL was the opposition of some former ACCL members to a merger of the CCL with the Canadian branches of international unions represented by the CIO. This difficulty was resolved when the CIO agreed that both the Canadian sections of international unions and the CCL should be completely autonomous. Nonetheless, as time went on and the number of Canadian branches of international unions in the CCL grew larger, conflicts arose as to who would control the CCL — the Canadian nationalists, the Canadian directors of international unions, or the CIO itself.

According to Canadian labour analyst Irving Abella, the period from 1940 to 1950 was marked by almost constant inner turmoil over who would control the CCL. The organization also had to contend with the spread of Communism within its ranks. With the expulsion of three major left-wing unions, however, and the diminution of Communism in another, Communism soon disappeared as a major concern for the CCL.[24] Other internal difficulties survived. One such difficulty concerned the payment of dues by international unions directly to the CCL. Another involved the question as to whether or not the CCL was empowered to settle jurisdictional disputes involving all its affiliates, including the Canadian branches of international unions. A third major dilemma was whether or not the CCL leadership could be compelled to accept into membership all CIO unions operating in Canada. In spite of the failure of the CIO to force the CCL to accept a CIO union as an affiliate,[25] the status of CIO unions with respect to CCL membership remained a contentious issue.

In 1952, these problems came to a head at the CCL convention and resulted in a clear defeat for the CCL nationalist wing. As a result, "the international unions were now clearly in control."[26] Policies of the CCL would henceforth be in line with those agreed to by these international unions. However, while the CCL was controlled by Canadian branches of international unions affiliated with the CIO, all decisions made by the CCL were binding on those affiliates in Canada. In this way the CCL maintained its autonomy from the American organization.

Despite its stormy history, the CCL demonstrated that, even with the presence of international unions in Canada, a Canadian trade-union federation which is both independent from and the beneficiary of American resources, is possible. Moreover, taking industrial unionism as a basis for organizing, the CCL was able to attract many workers to unions which had been previously neglected by the TLC in Canada. Relations between the CCL and TLC will be examined in the following section.

TLC and CCL Coexistence 1940-1956

With the formation of the CCL in 1940, there were two competing peak or national labour federations in Canada, the Canadian Trades and Labour Congress (TLC) and the Canadian Congress of Labour (CCL). On a number of occasions, the unions affiliated with these two federations competed with one another to organize the same groups of workers. Undoubtedly much money was wasted on inter-union rivalries. Sometimes, however, common interests gave rise to common action. When, for example, Prince Edward Island passed legislation in 1949 that barred international unions from operating in that province, both federations petitioned the Federal Government to disallow the provincial legislation. The initiative persuaded the Prince Edward Island government to repeal its sanctions against the activities of international unions within its jurisdiction.

The affiliates of the two federations gained greatly in membership during the 1940's, particularly during World War II when the Federal Government passed orders-in-council which encouraged the formation of trade unions and collective bargaining. *Order-in-Council P.C. 1003* of 1944 was particularly significant in terms of promoting the growth of both federations.

P.C. 1003 of February 1944 — the Wartime labour relations regulations — gave workers across Canada the right to choose a union as their bargaining agent, made provision for certification of a bargaining agent (union) by the Canada Wartime Labour Relations Board (CWLR), required employers to bargain in good faith, prohibited unfair labour practices by unions and employers, and provided for conciliation of contract negotiation disputes. The Order further specified that collective agreements were to contain no-strike and no-lockout clauses and that agreements were to make provision for handling grievances, the final step of which was binding arbitration. Thus, unions no longer had to strike to acquire bargaining rights but could apply to the CWLR Board for certification and, once certified, could force employers to negotiate with them.

Although both the CCL and TLC grew considerably during the war, the TLC continued to have the edge in numbers. By 1956 when the federations merged to form the Canadian Labour Congress, the TLC was almost twice as large as the CCL, having 47.4% of Canadian union members as compared to 28.0% for the CCL.[27]

As indicated in Table 4.1 on page 83, trade-union membership failed to grow significantly during the early 1950's. There were significant changes occurring in the economy. Of particular note was the growth of the service sector where unions were unsuccessful in organizing. Despite the merger of the CLC and TLC, membership continued to decline from 1955 to 1965 when public servants were given the right to unionize.

Mergers of the Central Labour Federations in Canada and the United States

As we emphasized earlier, the history of the formation and development of central labour federations in Canada has been very much influenced by the history and development of similar federations in the United States, as have mergers.

The merger in the United States between the AFL and the CIO took place in 1955. A number of factors accounted for this merger. First, the passage of the *Taft-Hartley Act* in 1947, which significantly amended the *Wagner Act* of 1935, was seen by both central federations as increasing management's power at the expense of labour's power. For a number of years both federations cooperated in trying to get the American Congress to amend the *Taft-Hartley Act*, but to no avail. Second, the AFL had always dealt severely with Communists and, although the CIO had accepted Communists as members of its executive bodies until 1949, the CIO amended its constitution in that year to eliminate all Communist leadership within its ranks. Third, both federations engaged in political activities that supported the Democratic Party and improvements in minimum wages and social security. Similar political philosophies drew the AFL and the CIO together.

But there were also conflicts between and within the two federations that required practical, conciliatory resolutions. Specifically, a great deal of money was being wasted by both groups as affiliates of the two federations fought to organize the same workers. More important than this competition were the deaths of the presidents of both the AFL and the CIO in November 1953 which meant that neither federation had a chief executive officer. George Meany, then Secretary-Treasurer of the AFL, was easily elected its president. A bitter battle for the leadership took place within the CIO, however; a battle narrowly won by the brilliant Walter Reuther, then President of the UAW. Reuther's control over the CIO was much weaker than Meany's control over the AFL. A merger of the CIO and AFL, therefore, was facilitated by the lack of rivalry for leadership of the merged body.[28]

Before the merger, a two-year no-raiding agreement had been signed between the affiliates of the two organizations, and a unity committee of the AFL and CIO was formed, with the president of each federation playing key roles. The merged federation — American Federation of Labour–Congress of Industrial Organization (AFL–CIO) — named George Meany as its first president. One of the major reasons for hyphenating the names of the two previous national federations was to maintain the identity of the CIO so as to permit it to control a large sum of money which had been gathered from its affiliates since 1938. This money was largely to organize non-unionized workers. A second and unofficial reason for the hybrid name lay in the feeling of CIO leaders that, if the marriage of the two federations did not work, the CIO could withdraw with its identity intact and with the money that it controlled through its Industrial Union Department. Later, however, affiliates of the former AFL began contributing to the fund.

This abbreviated account of the merger between the AFL and CIO is intended to show once again the significance of American developments upon the Canadian labour movement. When the merger took place in the United States, it was expected that the affiliates of the two organizations with branches in Canada would also try to work out a merger between the two competing federations in Canada. Although there had been previous attempts to unite the

two bodies in Canada, it is undoubtedly true that such an event would not have taken place in Canada (at least not as early as 1956) if the AFL-CIO merger had not taken place in the United States.

In Canada, both the TLC and CCL appointed committees in December 1953 to study the possibility of merger. These committees united to form a Unity Committee, which ultimately brought about the merger of the two federations. In February, 1954, a no-raiding agreement was reached by the Unity Committee, and its provisions were subsequently approved by the conventions of the two federations that same year. The no-raiding pact not only forbade raiding but, more importantly, set up mechanisms for dealing with alleged violations. Initially, the no-raiding agreement was binding only on the directly chartered locals of each federation, but affiliated national and Canadian branches of international unions were also encouraged to become parties to the accord.

On March 9, 1955, the Unity Committee reached agreement on a statement of principles which was to govern the merger of the two federations. Two months later, a complete merger agreement was announced. This agreement was unanimously approved on June 1 by the TLC and on October 12 by the CCL. A joint TLC-CCL convention, which became the founding convention of the new Canadian Labour Congress (CLC), met in Toronto on April 23, 1956. There, the constitution drafted by the Unity Committee was ratified with some minor variations and the new Congress was formally launched.[29]

The founding convention of the CLC made it clear that the CLC was to be independent of the AFL-CIO. In fact, the CLC has since that convention often taken positions in international matters diametrically opposed to those of the American federation.

In discussing the differences between the mergers in the United States and Canada, Eugene Forsey indicated his belief that ours more closely approached the perfect union than did that of the United States. He attributed this quality largely to the fact that the CCL was closer to equality with the TLC in power than was the CIO with the AFL. At the time of the merger in the United States, the AFL had 9.5 million members and the CIO had about 6 million, out of a total union membership of some 18 million — a huge discrepancy compared with the distribution of Canadian membership![30] The two Canadian organizations, Forsey added, merged more quickly at the provincial and local levels than did the American organizations at the state and local levels.[31] In contrast to the AFL-CIO, then, there was no indication that either of the Canadian organizations was contemplating pulling out of the agreement if the marriage between the two did not work. This confidence was reflected in the decision not to adopt a hyphenated name for the merged body. Furthermore, because the TLC and CCL both contained craft and industrial unions, the traditional dichotomy between these orientations did not pose a problem at the time of merger.

Canadian Labour and Politics

The TLC played an active part in politics from its beginning, an attribute that distinguished it from the AFL. Many of the early union members in Canada were of British stock and they brought the traditions of the British working class with them. When the British Labour Party came into being in 1906, the TLC gave its support to provincial labour parties in Canada. Although these provincial parties were unsuccessful, the TLC also gave its support to the development of a national labour party in 1918. Such a party was formed, but it was taken over by the Communists in 1923 at which time union support was withdrawn.[32] Forsey has suggested that as early as 1900 there were signs that the Liberal Party wanted to capture the TLC.[33] In fact, many of the progressive policies of the Liberal Party over the years have come largely from the labour movement, both before and after the for-

mation in Regina of the socialist Co-operative Commonwealth Federation (CCF) in 1933. The CCL endorsed the CCF. At its 1943 convention, the CCL confronted the issue of political affiliation squarely and resolved that, since the CCF adequately expressed the views of the CCL, the CCL would support the party and encouraged its affiliates to lend it their support also. From 1943 onward, the CCL continued to endorse the CCF although there was opposition from some of its affiliated unions.[34]

When the Canadian Labour Congress was formed in 1956 it did not immediately support a political party. However, members of the labour movement were active in the development of the New Democratic Party which was founded in 1961 to replace the old CCF. The CLC did not ally itself directly with the NDP but many of its affiliated unions did and the CLC usually played at least a nominal role in federal elections. It was only during the election campaign of 1979 that the CLC came out dramatically in support of the NDP. Previously it had provided workers for getting the labour vote out and encouraging volunteers to work for the New Democratic Party. But in the 1979 election, the CLC lent not only its workers but its financial aid in support of the party. It is difficult to tell what impact the CLC's participation had on the results of the 1979 election, although its president claims a great deal of credit for the support gained in British Columbia and in one of the Atlantic provinces. The reason for the NDP's loss in major metropolitan Ontario cities where members of the CLC and its affiliated unions were active in politics is not clear. The result brings to mind Eugene Forsey's prediction, at the 1958 Canadian Political Science Association Meeting, of the potential role of the CLC in politics:

> [E]ven if the Congress does ultimately decide on a definite line of political action...and even if all, or most, of the unions follow that line (which experience suggests they will not), it does not follow that the union *members* will pay any attention whatever.[35]

He suggested instead that individuals might cast their ballots as Maritimers, French- or English-Canadians, etc., rather than as union members.

An American example would tend to confirm this conjecture. In the 1944 election, John L. Lewis, who was then probably the most powerful union figure in the United States, withdrew his support from President Roosevelt and recommended that trade union members vote for the Republican candidate. Subsequent analysis showed that even voters in Lewis's own constituency continued to vote Democratic rather than Republican! This would seem to confirm that trade unions by themselves in North America do not have a great deal of influence on how their members vote during elections.

The American labour movement continues to support the Democratic Party since the policies of that party are much more in line with the objectives of the labour movement. In fact, in the 1984 presidential elections, the AFL-CIO endorsed the candidacy of Walter Mondale before Mondale declared his intentions to run for the Presidency![36] Similarly, the CLC, as we have noted, has been lending its support to the NDP and it will probably continue to do so as long as the NDP's policies remain in line with those of the CLC.

The Philosophy of the Canadian Labour Movement

The philosophy of the Canadian labour movement has been a fairly pragmatic one, particularly within the craft-oriented unions. This approach is derived from the pragmatic philosophy of the AFL, particularly from the methods of Samuel Gompers (its President from 1886 to 1924). When asked what labour's objective was, he said it was to obtain "more, more and more now." This American practicality is balanced by another influence in the Canadian labour movement — the experience of the unionists who came from the United Kingdom and brought with them the ideas of a working-class movement. R. J. Adams, a Canadian writer, has commented that

> Since its emergence, the [Canadian] labour movement has been pulled between the moderate, democratic socialism of Great Britain and the nonpolitical approach of U.S. labour. Perhaps because of the British link, moderate socialism is more acceptable in Canada than in the U.S. Nevertheless, many Canadian unionists subscribe fully to the U.S. approach.[37]

Canadian writer C. B. Williams hypothesizes that the present structure and philosophy of our trade-union movement is "obsolete and it is unlikely that a recasting of its structure and philosophy will be forthcoming."[38] Williams contends that the philosophy of the Canadian labour movement reflects two primary schools of thought; namely, class collaboration and class consciousness.[39] The philosophy of class collaboration characteristic of international unions accepts the existing order and government that goes along with it, and views the role of the trade-union movement as one which gains improvements in wages, hours, and working conditions from reluctant employers. The major methods of class collaboration include collective bargaining and work stoppage. The structure of class collaboration maximizes the effectiveness of collective bargaining and reflects the exclusive jurisdiction of the craft unions, the surrender of local autonomy to the central body of the craft — namely, either the international or national union. Furthermore, the cornerstone of this class-collaboration philosophy is one of self-centered self-help. Most of the activity in this type of trade-union structure and philosophy takes place at the local level rather than at the broader societal level.

The philosophy of class-conscious trade unionism, which is diametrically opposed to that of class collaboration, rejects the existing economic and political order along with its form of government.

> As replacements, it advocate[s] various degrees of reform, ranging from direct worker control of the

means of production to direct worker representation in the existing economic and political system... It de-emphasize[s] collective bargaining and the strike as the method of protest against an employer, in favour of political action and the demonstration of labour solidarity through the general or industrial strike.[40]

Williams believes that if national and international unions are to succeed in contemporary Canadian society, they must redefine their role of "self-centered self-help" and become more socially aware. National and international unions, according to Williams, must become involved in issues that have so far remained the exclusive domain of the Canadian Labour Congress. Williams concludes by stating that "Unless the Canadian trade union movement is prepared to reshape its structure and philosophy drastically, it will continue to have great difficulty in carving for itself an accommodative role in Canadian economic and social affairs."[41]

At its eleventh constitutional convention held in Quebec City in May 1976, the CLC came out with what is called *Labour's Manifesto for Canada*.[42] The *Manifesto* attacked the wage and price controls program then in place, expressed concern at the way in which decontrol mechanisms might be instituted, and reflected the CLC's hope that the decontrol program would result in a more equitable and planned society.[43] After discussing economic problems in Canada, tripartitism and national planning, and the centralization of government, the CLC's *Manifesto* went on to suggest that changes were required in the way important economic and social decisions are made. Specifically, it demanded that business and government share their power with labour. The *Manifesto* also declared:

> The 10 point programme of the Canadian Labour Congress (which had been put forward in 1975) has been put forward as an alternative to the government's anti-inflation programme. It is a social as well as an economic programme which would establish basic standards of income and housing for all Canadians — which would create

jobs and protect those who suffer most from inflation. It is a programme which has been adopted by all the affiliates of this Congress and which has been promoted and accepted the length and breadth of the labour movement.[44]

The *Manifesto* recognized that if labour is to play an effective role in shaping the country's economic and social policies it must do so from a position of strength. The strength of labour, however, according to the *Manifesto*, is fragmented among its affiliates and exists mainly at the plant level. The *Manifesto* went on to state:

> In the future the CLC must have the power which can only come from the collective strength of its affiliates. There must be agreement between all the affiliates that a full cooperative and coordinated effort will be forthcoming to guarantee that the CLC is operating from a position of strength to protect the rights, freedoms and legitimate interests of all workers. The Executive Council as a responsible decision-making body between Conventions must be assured that the policies and decisions it makes will be followed closely by all affiliates.[45]

The *Manifesto* recognized, as have many observers, that the CLC has very little power. Power in Canada's decentralized collective bargaining system resides largely with national unions and Canadian branches of international unions, particularly with the locals of these unions. Although most unions at the 1976 CLC Convention endorsed the augmentation of CLC power, generally no transfer of power from the affiliated national and international unions to the CLC was anticipated. Hence, even if the CLC were to adopt a more socially conscious and a more dynamic economic program, it is unlikely that the CLC Executive would gain the power necessary to influence the development and implementation of such a program.

Although the CLC *Manifesto* called for a form of tripartitism to oversee the development of sound economic and social programs, this objective was never reached. In 1976, the CLC withdrew from a number of government agencies, including the Economic Council of Canada, in protest against the imposition of wage and price controls in 1976. To date, it has not yet rejoined any of these agencies.

The philosophy of the Canadian Labour Congress will likely remain much the same in the forseeable future. The CLC will continue to express the labour point of view on economic and social policies. The impact of this representation, however, will probably be minimal. The CLC's major concern almost certainly will remain with bread and butter issues at the local level.

Nationalism and Multinationalism

Within the ranks of Canadian labour, there are those who argue for a stronger, more independent, nationalistic type of trade-union movement in Canada in which Canadian workers and union leaders would exercise greater control. Of great concern is the growth of multinational conglomerates. Some labour leaders, however, have been ignoring this growth, ignoring the effects that multinational conglomerates, with their shifting means of production, could have on Canada's labour-management relationships or on its labour movement. A large body of literature now exists which indicates that, unless trade unions in a number of countries take concerted action to deal with multinational conglomerates, these conglomerates may play one country off against another in their battles with trade unions. For example, if a union goes on strike against a multinational corporation in one country, that corporation may easily counteract the strike by shipping material from another country in which it operates and where workers are not on strike.

Part of the trade-union response to this kind of action is to form secretariats along broad industrial lines with headquarters in Brussels and Geneva. These secretariats put pressure on certain parts of multinational corporations if other parts are in difficulty. So far, however, Canadian unionists have not been in the forefront of the trade-union response to the multinational corporation. It remains to be seen whether an explicit concern with the national character of our labour movement can be allied to an appreciation for the need to cooperate internationally against the threat of multinationals.

One potential inhibition to international cooperation is posed by the conflicts which occur between international unions in Canada and national federations. In the following section, we shall deal with one such conflict, in this case one which arose between the CLC and the AFL-CIO.

Construction Unions Suspended from CLC in 1981

The Canadian labour movement, and more specifically the Canadian Labour Congress, has not created as many intermediary links in its organizational structure as has the AFL-CIO. The Canadian structure is a potential problem; indeed conflict has erupted between the CLC and the building trades unions, owing, in part, to the fact that the AFL-CIO has building trades councils at the provincial and local levels in Canada whereas the CLC does not.

In March 1981, the Executive Council of the CLC suspended fourteen international building trades unions with over 229,700 members for non-payment of affiliation fees effective April 30, 1981.[46] The battle between the building trade unions and the CLC officials has been going on for some time. Several other differences have been smoothed over but the fundamental conflict has never been resolved. The building trade union leaders had withheld their dues once before, nine years earlier, in an attempt to get a block voting system at CLC conventions. CLC leaders regard this system as essential to gaining a greater voice in CLC convention policies.[47] Under the existing arrangements, each local union is entitled to send to the biennial CLC conventions one delegate for each block of members numbering up to and including 1,000, and one additional delegate for each additional block of members numbering up to and including 1,000. Each delegate has one vote. The construction unions claimed that this system gave public-sector unions with a large number of small locals undue influence at the CLC conventions. According to a knowledgeable source,

> There is statistical evidence to support this argument. The Canadian Union of Public Employees... [had] 267,000 members and 1,629 locals [in 1981]. The building trade unions, with a combined membership of approximately 355,000, [had] chartered 689 locals [in 1981]... [Thus,] CUPE had almost twice as many delegates at the 1978 CLC convention as the building trades.[48]

When the CLC suspended the building trades unions from membership, it announced that a CLC Building Trades Department would be set up jointly with the provincial and territorial federations and that building trades unions would be able to join these federations. Before the rift with the building trades unions, the CLC did not represent these building trades departments. In fact, the CLC only made this change in policy immediately following the suspension of the building trades unions from membership. It should be noted that the way in which the CLC suspended the international unions allows locals of the international construction unions to join the newly formed Trades Councils and at the same time to retain their membership in international unions. To date, the CLC Building Trade Councils have been unsuccessful in attracting members and remain a "dead letter."

In addition to their dissatisfaction with the CLC voting system, the construction unions were very angry that the CLC had not intervened in the move by the Quebec Federation of Labour to create its own umbrella body for construction workers in the Province of Quebec. The QFL is a rival to the Quebec Provincial Building Trades Council, a body chartered by the AFL-CIO Building Trades Department in the United States. Only the QFL up to this point has chartered such a provincial council.

According to the President of the CLC, the demands of the building trades unions were that (1) they wanted to have the authority to appoint delegates to CLC conventions which would

mean bypassing the local union structure and denying the locals the right to elect their own delegates and run their own affairs; (2) resolutions to CLC conventions were to be the sole purview of a union's national or international headquarters rather than of its local headquarters; and (3) the CLC was to intervene and dismantle a union structure in Quebec in which the construction workers had voted to participate and which the Quebec government recognized by legislation.[49]

Related to these disputes is the difference between the political orientation of the CLC executive and the building trades union executive. Leaders of the building trades unions have a much more conservative outlook than leaders of the industrial unions. They have been less than enthusiastic about the CLC's political involvement with the New Democratic Party, an involvement which had been strengthened under President McDermott's leadership.

A New Canadian Federation of Labour 1982-

Sensing that the rift between the CLC and the international building trade unions could not be resolved, a number of Canadian directors of these unions issued a call for a new central federation. The founding convention of the Canadian Federation of Labour (CFL) was held in Ottawa on March 31 and April 1, 1982. Delegates representing about 200,000 workers and ten of the thirteen international building trade unions participated in the establishment of the new federation. Two of the larger building trades unions, the United Brotherhood of Carpenters and Joiners (92,000 members) and the Labourers International Union (52,000 members), plus the smaller 15,000 member International Association of Ironworkers did not join the new federation. All three unions are still affiliated with the CLC.

The Convention elected James McCambly, Executive Secretary of the Canadian Executive Board of the AFL-CIO Building Trades Department, as its president. Ken Rose, the Conference Chairman and an International Vice-President of the International Brotherhood of Electrical Workers (IBEW), criticized the political affiliation of the CLC with the NDP and also the confrontational tactics of former CLC President Dennis McDermott in dealing with the Federal Government. He vowed that the CFL would seek to meet with the government regarding policies of importance to workers everywhere.

The convention adopted a resolution that the CFL would not affiliate with a political party, but that it would support any party to the extent that it espoused policies consistent with those of the CFL. This position is similar to the philosophy adopted by Samuel Gompers, the long-time President of the AFL, whose slogan was to "reward our friends, and punish our enemies." Although a few delegates argued the merits of political affiliation, the resolution was enthusiastically endorsed.

Senator Edward Lawson, Canadian head of the Teamsters' Union, addressed the convention, and among other things, stated that unions must be prepared to make sacrifices to protect their members' jobs where employers are in financial trouble. This position contrasted sharply with that of Mr. McDermott who stated that workers should not accept wage freezes or wage cuts. Prime Minister Trudeau also spoke to the convention, thus marking the first time in twenty years that a Canadian Prime Minister had addressed such a labour gathering. In his speech, Trudeau invited the consultation between the Federal Government and the CFL which is currently taking place.

The Canadian Labour Congress held its conventions in May of 1982 and 1984. It did not, however, expel the unions that formed the CFL. It will be interesting to observe, over the next few years, the extent to which interunion raiding may take place as a result of the existence of two national central federations.

Thus far, we have talked mainly about the national and international unions in English-speaking Canada and have only touched on Quebec. That province, however, has a unique history of trade-union development. It is to the Quebec situation that we now turn our attention.

The Labour Movement in Quebec

In any history of the trade union movement in Canada the Confédération des Travailleurs Catholiques du Canada (CTCC) merits special consideration. The English equivalent of the French title is the Confederation of Catholic Workers of Canada. After 1929, it was identified in English as the Canadian and Catholic Confederation of Labour (CCCL). We shall use the initials CCCL, except where CTCC appears in a quotation.

As S. Jamieson states:

> The CTCC began as a movement consciously organized and controlled by Roman Catholic clergy in Quebec for the express purpose of keeping French-Canadian workers French in language and Catholic in religion in order to prevent them from becoming absorbed into 'alien' and 'secular' trade unions controlled by English-speaking Canadian or American elements."[50]

The movement had its origins in a lockout in the boot and shoe industry in Quebec City in 1900 over the questions of union recognition by employers and wage increases. The dispute was arbitrated by the Archbishop of Quebec whose recommendations were accepted. In his recommendations he called upon the unions in Quebec to change their constitutions and rules in order to bring them into line with Roman Catholic principles as laid down in Pope Leo XIII's Encyclical *Rerum Novarum* of 1891. This Encyclical emphasized the right of workers to organize into trade unions, called for collective bargaining between unions and employers and encouraged every means of settlement without a strike if at all possible.

The movement towards federation of the various local Catholic unions began in 1918 with the formation of central councils in major districts in Quebec. The CCCL was established as a permanent organization at its founding convention in Hull, Quebec in 1921. As Fraser Isbester pointed out, "Like its affiliated unions, the Confederation was church dominated [sic] and remained so until 1946."[51] At that time, the CCCL represented one-third of the organized workers in Quebec.

During and after World War II, the Catholic unions in Quebec changed quite dramatically in their orientation and behaviour. As Jamieson points out, large numbers of French Canadians were drawn into industries and trades in major urban centres where they came into contact with other unionized workers. Also, the substantial wage increases won by unionized workers outside Quebec forced the CCCL to become militant.[52] With both the TLC and the CCL attempting to organize workers in Quebec, the CCCL had to assume an aggressive role in order to organize Catholic and non-Catholic workers. Accordingly, a new, combative breed of leaders (among them a group of graduates from Laval University) was elected to fill the top executive positions in the Confederation. The outlook and behaviour of these leaders paralleled those of the leaders of rival unions.

This change in leadership was accompanied by a number of unusual and significant strikes, the most important of which was the asbestos strike of 1949. Some people have termed it the turning point in the social history of Quebec.[53] Prior to 1949, there had been a close relationship between the Church and the Duplessis government, with the Church using its influence in the Catholic trade-union movement to prevent overt labour conflicts. The asbestos strike exploded the Church-Duplessis coalition. During the seven-month strike, the Church openly supported the strikers against a large American subsidiary. This support often took the form of special funds collected from congregations after Mass. The provincial government, however, declared the strike illegal, decertified the union, as it had done in the meat-packing strike of 1947, and sent several hundred heavily-armed provincial police to the scene of the conflict.

The CCCL gained wide moral support from prominent liberal and intellectual leaders in

Quebec, as well as from affiliates of the TLC and the CCL. While the striking workers won very little monetarily, they won a great deal psychologically, for the strike lent a new sense of credibility and militancy to the CCCL.

The asbestos strike and several other strikes were important in developing close links between the CCCL, the Quebec affiliates of the CCL, and the TLC. Both the CCL and the TLC supported the CCCL in a number of other important strikes following the asbestos strike of 1949. However, the Quebec affiliates of the TLC later broke ranks and supported the Duplessis Government, leaving the CCCL and the CCL alone to protect what they considered to be the repressive nature of new labour legislation.[54]

When the CCL and the TLC formed the Canadian Labour Congress (CLC) in 1956, their provincial counterparts in Quebec merged to become the Quebec Federation of Labour (QFL). From the time of the merger onward, the QFL and the CCCL cooperated when it was to their mutual advantage to do so. Conflicts remained, however.

At the founding convention of the Canadian Labour Congress, a number of proposals were approved which sought the affiliation of the CCCL. In turn, the CCCL convention in September 1956 passed resolutions in favour of affiliation with the CLC. Joint committees of the CCCL and the CLC were set up and a number of meetings took place over the years with a view to reaching a merger agreement. These merger talks failed to make any significant progress, but by 1959, many observers still expected the merger to come about. As Isbester says,

> The 1959 convention was widely expected to be the 'unity convention.' Such was not the case. 'The fact is,' Jean Marchand said, 'that back in 1955 the principle of affiliation was adopted by the CCCL convention provided that the CCCL could keep its 'integrity' and its freedom to expand.'[55]

In retrospect, it was this unwillingness to accommodate the CCCL as a separate entity within the framework of the CLC that foiled any attempt to merge the national central federation and the central federation in Quebec.

At its 1960 convention, the CCCL changed its name to the Confédération des Syndicats Nationaux (CSN) — or, in English, the Confederation of National Trade Unions (CNTU). In addition, it streamlined and centralized its structure in order to establish a strong, independent body, capable of competing with the QFL.

The CNTU grew rapidly during the 1960's, particularly with the passage of liberal legislation in Quebec which gave collective bargaining rights to public servants, many of whom are organized by the CNTU. In addition, the CNTU became much more radical during the 1960's and 1970's than had been the case before. In early 1971, the Confederal Bureau of the CNTU published a manifesto entitled *Il n'y a plus d'avenir pour le Québec dans le système économique actuel (There Is No Longer a Future for Quebec in the Present Economic System)*. Another document was published a few months later entitled *Ne comptons que sur nos propres moyens (Let Us Rely Only on Our Own Means)*. According to Quebec author Jean Boivin, *Ne comptons* was a quasi-Marxist interpretation of the capitalist system in Quebec. Although it was not discussed at the 1972 CNTU convention owing to a perceived lack of support, *Ne comptons* received wide circulation.[56]

In 1972, the Common Front was formed from the QFL, the CNTU, and the Quebec Teachers' Corporation to bargain jointly with the provincial government on behalf of teachers and public servants. The three major groups used a "common-table" approach in order to negotiate provisions which were shared by government, school, and hospital workers. In addition, sector tables existed at which provisions particular to each sector were bargained for. When the parties failed to reach an agreement with the government, strikes were called. Spontaneous work stoppages also occurred. In the beginning, public opinion favoured the workers but as time went on it swung toward the government. At that point, the government obtained an injunction which either prohibited workers from going on strike or ordered them back to work. During the Common-Front strikes, many workers, encouraged by their leaders, disobeyed these injunctions. As a result, both the workers and the leaders of the QFL, the CNTU, and the Quebec Teachers' Corporation were jailed. In order to achieve a settlement, the leaders were released temporarily so that they could join negotiators at the bargaining table. The Common-Front strikes were the most massive strikes ever experienced in the history of the Canadian labour movement.

One important development of the Common Front was that three members of the Executive Committee left the CNTU and called meetings of dissident union leaders who strongly disagreed with the leftist ideology of the CNTU. A majority of the dissident leaders, claiming to represent more than 75,000 of the 235,000 CNTU members, voted to secede from the CNTU and form a separate federation, the Centrale des syndicats démocratiques; in English, the Centre for Democratic Unions (CDU).[57] Not too much has been heard, however, of this new federation, partly because it now has a membership of 40,000.

Although the CNTU is sometimes perceived to be the largest federation in Quebec, its membership is not nearly as large as that of the QFL. The reason for this illusion lies in the fact that more than half the membership of the CNTU comes from the public sector, and the workers in this sector have received a great deal of media attention in recent years. In 1984, the CNTU had about 211,000 members while the QFL had over 320,000 members.[58] Media exposure for the QFL may soon more accurately reflect the relative size of the QFL, since the QFL has become more radical in recent years. In the 1970's, for example, the QFL turned away from the NDP party in Quebec and announced its support for the Parti Québécois. The radicalism which the CNTU and the QFL hold in common has reduced the conflict between the two central federations and has made for a greater degree of mutual cooperation between them, particularly in the public and parapublic sectors.

A great deal of conflict remains, however, in the construction industry where the activities of several unions create a complex situation. At present the CNTU, QFL, CDU, and another union are competing for union membership in the construction industry. The employers in the construction industry negotiate through one employer association and the union with majority support must, by law, act as the main bargaining agent. Since the QFL has generally received majority support, it has become the negotiator for unionized construction workers.

Having to compete with a number of central federations in Quebec, the QFL has insisted that it is unlike other provincial federations of labour and, therefore, needs greater autonomy from the CLC to serve its members well. At the 1974 convention of the CLC held in Vancouver, the QFL sought and obtained three major concessions:

1 that it have full control over labour education in Quebec, something that other provincial federations do not have;
2 that the QFL be able to bargain with the CLC for funds which the Quebec members pay but for which they receive little benefits because of linguistic, cultural or political differences (e.g., unilingual newspapers); and
3 that the CLC give the QFL jurisdiction over local labour councils, with the right to appoint staff workers and the money to pay them.[59]

No other provincial federations enjoy these rights: they give a special status to the QFL.

Like other federations before them, the CLC (as represented by the QFL) and the CNTU may either cooperate or enter into conflict, depending upon what seems most advantageous at the time. For example, in the construction industry there have been spectacular conflicts between the CNTU and the unions affiliated with the QFL over which unions should represent workers in that industry. Although discussions have occurred over the possibility of the Quebec Teachers' Corporation joining with the CNTU, no degree of assurance has come about as yet as to whether such a merger might materialize.

In summary, the Quebec labour scene is more complex than the labour scene in any other province in Canada. The QFL, by far the largest central body, has become radical over the years and

has a special status in comparison to other provincial federations. The CNTU, more radical than the QFL, has lost membership as a result of the formation of the Center for Democratic Unionism (CDU) as well as the breakaway of about 30,000 civil servants and 5,000 aluminum workers, both of whom have remained independent.[60] The Quebec Teachers' Corporation professes an ideology somewhat similar to that of the CNTU. While QTC membership was at one time confined to primary and secondary school teachers, its charter was changed in the early 1970's to permit it to organize all categories of workers in the field of education. Now, the QTC competes for members in that field with the CNTU, CDU, and affiliates of the QFL. There have been sporadic discussions regarding the possibility of mergers between some of the competing federations, but given the volatile situation in Quebec it would be unwise to speculate on what might happen in the province in the future.

Growth of the Canadian Labour Movement

There were no reliable data on union membership until the Labour Department started collecting statistics around 1920. It has done so consecutively every year since then, with the exception of 1979. As Table 4.1 indicates, trade-union membership as a percentage of non-agricultural paid workers did not reach the 20% mark until around 1942. The major reason for the substantial growth during the 1940's was that Canadian workers were encouraged to organize by the American *Wagner Act* of 1935 which gave workers the right to form unions. Also, the Canadian Orders-in-Council during wartime encouraged unionization and collective bargaining. The return to peacetime conditions in 1947 along with favourable legislation and a high level of economic growth encouraged the growth of trade unions during the 1950's, with union membership as a percentage of the non-agricultural paid

Table 4.1				Statistics on Union Membership 1985

Year	Union membership (Thousands)	Total non-agricultural paid workers(d) (Thousands)	Union membership as % of civilian labour force	Union membership as % of non-agricultural paid workers
1911	133	—	—	—
1912	160	—	—	—
1913	176	—	—	—
1914	166	—	—	—
1915	143	—	—	—
1916	160	—	—	—
1917	205	—	—	—
1918	249	—	—	—
1919	378	—	—	—
1920	374	—	—	—
1921	313	1,956	9.4	16.0
1922	277	2,038	8.2	13.6
1923	278	2,110	8.1	13.2
1924	261	2,138	7.5	12.2
1925	271	2,203	7.6	12.3
1926	275	2,299	7.5	12.0
1927	290	2,406	7.7	12.1
1928	301	2,491	7.8	12.1
1929	319	2,541	8.0	12.6
1930	322	2,451	7.9	13.1
1931	311	2,028	7.5	15.3
1932	283	1,848	6.7	15.3
1933	286	1,717	6.7	16.7
1934	281	1,931	6.5	14.6
1935	281	1,941	6.4	14.5
1936	323	1,994	7.2	16.2
1937	383	2,108	8.5	18.2
1938	382	2,075	8.3	18.4
1939	359	2,079	7.7	17.3
1940	362	2,197	7.9	16.3
1941	462	2,566	10.3	18.0
1942	578	2,801	12.7	20.6
1943	665	2,934	14.6	22.7
1944	724	2,976	15.9	24.3
1945	711	2,937	15.7	24.2
1946	832	2,986	17.1	27.9
1947	912	3,139	18.4	29.1
1948	978	3,225	19.4	30.3
1949	1,006(a)	3,326	19.3	29.5
1950	— (b)	—	—	—
1951	1,029	3,625(a)	19.7	28.4
1952	1,146	3,795(c)	21.4	30.2
1953	1,220	3,694	23.4	33.0
1954	1,268	3,754	24.2	33.8

(continued)

			Union	Union
		Total non-	membership	membership
	Union	agricultural	as % of	as % of non-
	membership	paid workers(d)	civilian	agricultural
Year	(Thousands)	(Thousands)	labour force	paid workers
1955	1,268	3,767	23.6	33.7
1956	1,352	4,058	24.5	33.3
1957	1,386	4,282	24.3	32.4
1958	1,454	4,250	24.7	34.2
1959	1,459	4,375	24.0	33.3
1960	1,459	4,522	23.5	32.3
1961	1,447	4,578	22.6	31.6
1962	1,423	4,705	22.2	30.2
1963	1,449	4,867	22.3	29.8
1964	1,493	5,074	22.3	29.4
1965	1,589	5,343	23.2	29.7
1966	1,736	5,658	24.5	30.7
1967	1,921	5,953	26.1	32.3
1968	2,010	6,068	26.6	33.1
1969	2,075	6,380	26.3	32.5
1970	2,173	6,465	27.2	33.6
1971	2,211	6,637	26.5	33.3
1972	2,371	6,893	27.6	34.1
1973	2,591	7,181	29.2	36.1
1974	2,732	7,637	29.4	35.8
1975	2,884	7,817	29.8	36.9
1976	3,042	8,158	30.6	37.3
1977	3,149	8,243	31.0	38.2
1978	3,278	8,413	31.3	39.0
1980	3,397	9,027	30.5	37.6
1981	3,487	9,330	30.6	37.4
1982	3,617	9,264	31.4	39.0
1983	3,563	9,901	30.6	40.0
1984	3,651	9,220	30.6	39.6
1985	3,666	9,404	30.2	39.0

Table 4.1 (*continued*)   **Statistics on Union Membership 1985**

(a) Includes Newfoundland for the first time.
(b) Data on union membership for all years up to and including 1949 are as of December 31. In 1950 the reference date was moved ahead by one day to January 1, 1951. Thus, while no figure is shown for 1950, the annual series is, in effect, continued without interruption. The data on union membership for all subsequent years are also as of January.
(c) Figures for all years up to and including 1952 are as of the first week in June. Data for subsequent years are as of January.
(d) The figures shown in this column from 1921 to 1930 inclusively represent Total Non-Agricultural Workers.

Source: The figures for 1921 to 1972 are taken from Economics and Research Branch, Canada Department of Labour, *Labour Organizations in Canada* (Ottawa: Queen's Printer, 1972), pp. xxii, xxiii. The footnotes are also from this publication. The figures for 1973 to 1985 are taken from Labour Data Branch, Labour Canada, *Directory of Labour Organizations in Canada 1985* (Ottawa: Supply and Services Canada, 1985), Table 1. Reproduced by permission of the Minister of Supply and Services Canada.

Table 4.2   **The History of the Canadian Labour Movement**

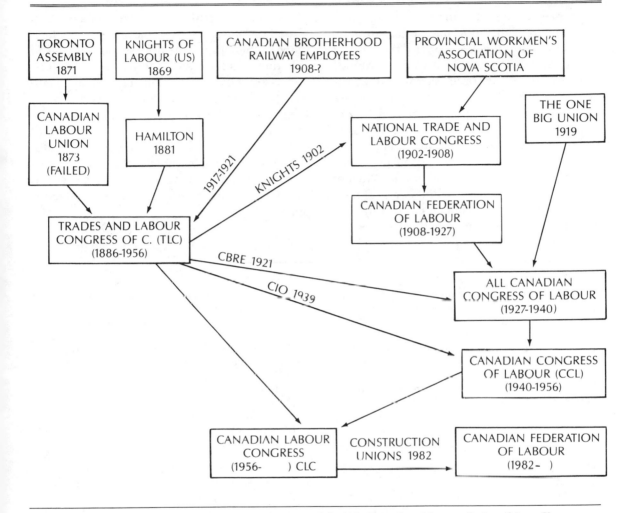

Source: Lyse Charron, MBA student, University of Ottawa (Fall 1983). Reproduced by permission of Lyse Charron.

workers stabilizing around 33%. In the early 1960's, though, the figure hovered below 30% and it was only in 1966 and 1967 that the figure again exceeded 30%. Since then it has continued to increase and now stands around 40% of non-agricultural paid workers.

The major reason for the growth since the mid-1960's is that both the federal and provincial governments have given their workers the right to bargain collectively and, in some cases, the right to strike. Many of the unions represent-

ing workers at the federal and provincial levels have joined the mainstream of the Canadian labour movement by affiliation with the Canadian Labour Congress through an umbrella association entitled the National Union of Provincial Government Employees (NUPGE). The Public Service Alliance of Canada, which represents federal public servants, is also directly affiliated with the CLC. Most provincial federations which represent civil servants have become part of NUPGE and it is now one of the largest components within the Canadian Labour Congress.

Although the majority of public-service unions have chosen to join the mainstream of the Canadian labour movement either through association with the CLC or, in the case of Quebec, the CNTU, uncertainty still surrounds the many unions of professional and white-collar workers most of which are set up on a provincial basis and have no national federation. The provincial associations of nurses, however, have joined together in a national union, but it is too early to predict whether all provincial associations will join a national union. Whether these new groups will form federations of their own, or whether they will join the CLC (or the CNTU in Quebec) is a question that remains unanswered at this time. Some of these groups, particularly teachers, have had provincial organizations for many years. No impetus seems present on their part to become part of a national Canadian labour union movement. In fact, many of them prefer the title *association* to *union*. Whether this false dichotomy between unions and associations will remain or gradually disappear is subject to speculation. Also worthy of interest are certain isolated groups of engineers that have bargaining rights with a number of companies but that belong to no overall organization. Engineers, along with the other professionals mentioned above, deserve to be watched carefully in the future by Canadian labour analysts.

---

questions

1 Discuss the criminal conspiracy doctrine that hampered union development in Canada prior to 1872. How did the legal enactments of 1872 affect unions?

2 Discuss the major central labour organizations that have existed in Canada up to the present time.

3 Why has there been such a close relationship between developments in the Canadian and American trade-union movements? Do you think that this is desirable or undesirable for Canadian workers, employers, and the country as a whole? Justify your response.

4. How do you account for the demise of indigenous Canadian federations such as the Canadian Federation of Labour (1908), the One Big Union (1919), and the All-Canadian Congress of Labour (ACCL) (1927)?

5 For what reasons have labour developments in Quebec differed from developments in the rest of Canada? What do you predict for the future of the labour movement in Quebec? Make whatever assumptions you feel are needed.

6 Why has the growth pattern of the Canadian labour movement been uneven?

7 To what extent do the theories discussed in Chapter 3 explain the emergence and growth of white-collar unionism in Canada since the mid-1960's?

8 Do you consider the unions in your province to be active enough in the political arena? Elaborate by indicating those activities in which they are or should be involved.

9 Do you think that unions in your province are influenced more by what happens in the United States than in the rest of Canada? Elaborate and give some examples.

10 Do you see any major differences between the philosophy of unions in the public and private sectors? Elaborate and give examples to support your contention.

---

notes

1 A. E. Kovacs, "The Philosophy of the Canadian Labour Movement," *Canadian Labour in Transition*, eds. Richard U. Miller and Fraser Isbester (Scarborough: Prentice-Hall Canada Inc., 1971), p. 120.

2 Labour Canada, *Directory of Labour Organizations in Canada 1985* (Ottawa: Supplies and Services Canada, 1985), p. 55.

3 Eugene Forsey, *Trade Unions in Canada: 1812-1902* (Toronto: University of Toronto Press, 1982), pp. X, 1. This book is a narration — analysis is left to the author's "youngers and betters." Nevertheless, Forsey is to be commended for providing us with a rich account of the development of our early unions. He constructs a picture that is partly at odds with

conventional wisdom. Important dates which have been erroneously used in the past are corrected by Forsey.

4 *Ibid.*, pp. 12-13.

5 *Ibid.*, pp. 14-15.

6 S. Jamieson, *Industrial Relations in Canada*, 2nd ed. (Toronto: Macmillan of Canada, 1973), p. 12.

7 Forsey, *Trade Unions in Canada*, p. 31.

8 John Crispo, *International Unionism: A Study in Canadian-American Relations* (Toronto: McGraw-Hill Company of Canada Ltd., 1967), p. 2.

9 Jamieson, *Industrial Relations in Canada*, p. 13.

10 Forsey, *Trade Unions in Canada*, pp. 32, 37.

11 *Ibid.*, p. 5.

12 H. A. Logan, *Trade Unions in Canada* (Toronto: Macmillan Company of Canada Limited, 1948), pp. 43-45.

13 *Ibid.*, p. 50; Forsey, *Trade Unions in Canada*, p. 138.

14 Jamieson, *Industrial Relations in Canada*, pp. 14-15.

15 Logan, *Trade Unions in Canada*, Table IV, p. 78.

16 Jamieson, *Industrial Relations in Canada*, p. 18.

17 *Ibid.*, p. 23.

18 Forsey, *Trade Unions in Canada*, pp. 501-02.

19 Jamieson, *Industrial Relations in Canada*, p. 17.

20 Logan, *Trade Unions in Canada*, p. 301.

21 *Ibid.*, p. 324.

22 For a brief account of the rise of the CIO, see Foster Rhea Dulles, Ch. XVI, *Labor in America*, 2nd rev. ed. (New York: Thomas Y. Crowell Co., 1960). For a more detailed account, see Walter Galenson, *The CIO Challenge to the AFL: A History of the American Labor Movement, 1935-1941* (Cambridge: Harvard University Press, 1960).

23 Eugene Forsey, "The Movement Towards Labour Unity in Canada: History and Implication," *Readings in Canadian Labour Economics*, ed. A. E. Kovacs (Toronto: McGraw-Hill Company of Canada Limited, 1961), pp. 75-76.

24 Irving Martin Abella, *Nationalism, Communism and Canadian Labour* (Toronto: University of Toronto Press, 1973), p. 167.

25 For an interesting account of the developments within the CCL and those between the CIO and CCL, see Ch. 9, Abella, "The CIO versus the CCL 1940-50."

26 *Ibid.*, p. 213.

27 Economics and Research Branch, Canada Department of Labour, *Union Growth in Canada, 1921-1967* (Ottawa: Information Canada, 1970), p. 39.

28 Dulles, Ch. XX, "The A.F. of L.-C.I.O. Merger," *Labor in America*, pp. 377-93.

29 Forsey, "Labour Unity in Canada," p. 81.

30 Dulles, *Labor in America*, p. 389.

31 Forsey, "Labour Unity in Canada," p. 86.

32 Roy J. Adams, "Industrial Relations in Europe and North America," *Union-Management Relations in Canada*, eds. J. Anderson and M. Gunderson (Don Mills: Addison-Wesley Publishers, 1982), p. 460.

33 Forsey, *Trade Unions in Canada*, pp. 496-97.

34 Richard Miller, "Organized Labour and Politics in Canada," *Canadian Labour in Transition* eds. Miller and Isbester, p. 209.

35 Forsey, "Labour Unity in Canada," p. 89.

36 A. H. Raskin, "A Fundamental Shift for Labor," Vol. XXII, No. 1, *ILR Report*, ed. M. T. Cullen (Ithaca: School of Industrial and Labour Relations, Fall 1984), pp. 15-20. This entire issue of the *Report* is devoted to the role of the American labour movement in politics.

37 Adams, "Industrial Relations in Europe and North America," p. 461.

38 C. B. Williams, "Trade Union Structure and Philosophy: Need for a Reappraisal," *Canadian Labour in Transition*, eds. Miller and Isbester, p. 145.

39 *Ibid.*, p. 162.

40 *Ibid.*, p. 163.

41 *Ibid.*, pp. 171-72.

42 *Labour's Manifesto for Canada*, approved by the CLC Convention (Quebec City: May 17-21, 1976).

43 *Ibid.*, p. 6.

44 *Ibid.*, p. 13.

45 *Ibid.*, p. 11.

46 CLC Press Release (March 11, 1981).

47 Wilfred List, "Labour Schism Looms as CLC Council Meets," *Globe and Mail* (March 9, 1981).

48 Joseph B. Rose, "Some Notes on the Building Trades–Canadian Labour Congress Dispute," Vol. 22, No. 1, *Industrial Relations* (Winter 1983), pp. 89-90.

49 CLC Press Release (March 11, 1981).

50 Jamieson, *Industrial Relations in Canada*, p. 35.

51 Isbester, "Quebec Labour in Perspective, 1949-1969," Miller and Isbester, p. 242.

52 Jamieson, *Industrial Relations in Canada*, p. 37.

53 Isbester, "Quebec Labour in Perspective," p. 242.

54 *Ibid.*, p. 246.

55 *Ibid.*, pp. 250-51.

56 Jean Boivin, "Labour Relations in Quebec," *Union-Management Relations in Canada*, eds. Anderson and Gunderson, p. 430.

57 Jamieson, *Industrial Relations in Canada*, p. 43.

58 Labour Canada, *Directory of Labour Organizations in Canada 1984*, pp. xxvi, 233.

59 Boivin, "Labour Relations in Quebec," p. 433.

60 *Ibid.*, p. 431.

5

The Structure and Functions of the Canadian Labour Movement

The Financial Post

Introduction

Central labour federations, individually and as a group, perform a number of functions for their member unions and for their workers. The union structure coordinates and directs a variety of activities at different organizational levels. Central federations such as the Canadian Labour Congress exist in every country in which trade unions are found. In a number of countries, such as Sweden and Australia, there are at least two central federations, one representing blue-collar workers and one or more representing white-collar workers. In other European countries, such as France and Italy, there are a number of central federations which are organized along religious and political lines.

In a world of big government and big business, organized labour needs a strong, unified organization to be heard. Without federations at the national level, organized labour would have no input into national public policy decisions. In Canada, labour relations policy falls primarily under the jurisdiction of the provinces, since 90% of workers fall under provincial jurisdiction. National federations, therefore, have organized at provincial levels in order to affect the formulation of provincial policies. Similarly, local labour councils exist to affect the policies of local governments.

Central labour organizations play at least two major roles: one is the political role referred to above; the other is a quasi-judicial role in the sense that central federations attempt to resolve conflicts among their constituents and to ensure that constituents follow the policies adopted at national conventions. Sub-bodies meet between conventions to assess the extent to which policies are followed, and to guide senior executive officers in the direction of federation affairs.

Before continuing with this discussion of the structure and functions of the Canadian labour movement, it will be useful to study Tables 5.1 to 5.6.

Some Statistics on the Canadian Labour Movement

Table 5.1 shows membership in those unions affiliated with and those unaffiliated with congresses. In 1985, 57.8%, less than two-thirds, of Canadian union members belonged to unions affiliated with the CLC. The CNTU, the second largest federation, had only 5.8% of all the trade-union members in Canada. A startling figure in Table 5.1 is the number of workers represented by unaffiliated national unions — it is close to 20% of union membership! In 1985, two of the larger unaffiliated national unions were the Canadian Telephone Employees' Association with 19,115 members, and the Federation of Women Teachers' Associations of Ontario with 31,400 members. Also significant is the number (2.8%) of Canadian workers represented by Canadian branches of unaffiliated international unions. Included in this group is the Teamsters Union with a Canadian membership of 91,500 workers in 1985.

Some of these unaffiliated national and international unions are strictly Canadian in origin and have remained Canadian-based. Others have at some time belonged to the CLC, but for various reasons have either withdrawn or been expelled from that body. The Teamsters, for example, were expelled from the CLC for raiding other unions.

Another way of looking at the membership of the Canadian trade union movement is to compare the proportion of workers who belong to Canadian branches of international unions to the proportion who belong to strictly Canadian unions. As indicated in Table 5.2, membership in strictly Canadian unions (including national unions, directly-chartered locals and independent local organizations) is 61.4% whereas membership in Canadian branches of international unions is now only 39.4%. These figures stand in sharp contrast to those of earlier years when about 70% of workers belonged to Canadian branches of international unions and only 30% belonged to strictly Canadian unions.[1]

The advent of unionism in the public and parapublic sectors has greatly contributed to this turnaround. The increase of Canadian membership in national unions is significant for the

Table 5.1	Union Membership by Congress Affiliation 1985	
Congress Affiliation	Membership	%
CLC	2,119,724	57.8
AFL-CIO/CLC	841,067	22.9
CLC only	1,278,657	34.9
CNTU	211,017	5.8
AFL-CIO/CFL	209,881	5.7
CSD	39,885	1.1
CCU	37,155	1.0
AFL-CIO only	144,626	4.0
Unaffiliated International Unions	104,067	2.8
Unaffiliated National Unions	703,889	19.2
Independent Local Organizations	95,444	2.6
TOTAL	3,665,688	100.0

Source: Labour Data Branch, Labour Canada, *Directory of Labour Organizations in Canada 1985* (Ottawa: Supply and Services Canada, 1985), Table 2, p. xxvi. Reproduced by permission of the Minister of Supply and Services Canada.

Canadian labour movement as a whole and especially for the CLC. Table 5.3 shows that 1985 national union membership in the CLC constituted 53.5% of total CLC membership. The increased participation of Canadian unions is bound to strengthen the nationalistic sentiment of the CLC and the Canadian policies emanating from it. In addition, many of these new national unions are more militant in their bargaining stances than many international unions.

Table 5.4 lists the seventeen largest unions in Canada with a membership of 50,000 or more. Although the United Steelworkers of America occupied first place for many years, the Cana-

dian Union of Public Employees (CUPE) is now the largest union in Canada. After this, comes the National Union of Provincial Government Employees, an umbrella association for the various unions of provincial government workers. The Public Service Alliance of Canada is the third-largest union in the country. In fact, six of the twelve largest unions in 1985 are strictly Canadian.

Table 5.5 shows a breakdown of the national and international unions by size. In 1985, forty-four unions had memberships of less than 500; five of these had less than 100 members. By contrast, eighteen unions had memberships of

Table 5.2			Union Membership by Type of Union and Affiliation 1985	
Type and Affiliation	Unions	Locals	Membership	%
International Unions	68	3,677	1,444,833	39.4
AFL-CIO/CLC	43	2,762	841,067	22.9
AFL-CIO/CFL	10	443	209,881	5.7
CLC only	3	135	145,192	4.0
AFL-CIO only	6	227	144,626	4.0
Unaffiliated Unions	6	164	104,067	2.8
National Unions	190	12,337	2,095,465	57.2
CLC	50	6,188	1,125,265	30.7
CNTU	9	1,660	210,505	5.8
CSD	3	156	18,651	0.5
CCU	20	130	37,155	1.0
Unaffiliated Unions	108	4,203	703,889	19.2
SUB-TOTAL	258	16,068	3,540,298	96.6
Directly Chartered Unions	295		29,946	0.8
CLC	63		8,200	0.2
CNTU	5		512	
CSD	227		21,234	0.6
Independent Local Organizations	209		95,444	2.6
TOTAL	762		3,665,688	100.0

Source: Labour Data Branch, Labour Canada, *Directory of Labour Organizations in Canada 1985* (Ottawa: Supply and Services Canada 1985), Table 3, p. xxvii. Reproduced by permission of the Minister of Supply and Services Canada.

Table 5.3   CLC Membership by Affiliation 1985

Type and Affiliation	Membership	%
International Unions		
AFL-CIO/CLC	841,067	39.7
CLC only	145,192	6.8
TOTAL	986,259	46.5
National Unions		
CLC only	1,125,265	53.1
Directly Chartered Local Unions	8,200	0.4
TOTAL	1,133,465	53.5
Total Membership of International and National Unions (CLC)	2,119,724	100.0

Source: Labour Data Branch, Labour Canada, *Directory of Labour Organizations in Canada 1985* (Ottawa: Supply and Services Canada, 1985), Table 4, p. xxviii. Reproduced by permission of the Minister of Supply and Services Canada.

40,000 or more; but these represented over 1,957,950 workers or more than 55% of all Canadian union members.

Union Consolidation

On the basis of these and similar figures, many commentators of the late 1950's and early 1960's have suggested that efforts be made to consolidate unions. John Crispo has made a case for consolidation on two grounds: (1) because union fragmentation is reducing the effectiveness of collective bargaining and (2) because a better structure would be needed in the event that government begins to consider seriously organized labour's advocacy of national planning.[2] Another reason to reduce the number of unions in Canada has been that small unions have neither the finances nor the personnel to serve their local unions adequately in contract negotiations, grievance handling, research, and education.

A recent study by G. N. Chaison shows an overall increase of thirty-eight unions between 1956 and 1977. Despite mergers, the number of national unions increased, Chaison claims, while the number of international unions decreased substantially.[3] Many of the new unions had existed previously, particularly public-sector unions. Since public-sector unions were merely consultative bodies, however, union statistics did not include them. Now, with the introduction of collective bargaining to the federal and provincial sectors, the presence of these unions is reflected in the statistics.

Two examples of public and parapublic-sector unions are the Ontario Public Service Employees Union (OPSEU) — formerly the Civil Service Association of Ontario (CSAO) — and the Ontario Nurses Association (ONA) respectively. These and many similar unions in the public and para-public sectors have bargained quite successfully on their own and have served their members well. In another study, however, Chaison points out that "fewer and larger unions could still provide some advantages, notably 'enhanced lobbying activity on the national level, increased organizing and strike funds, and the ability to maintain large, full-time professional staffs for research, bargaining and organizing.'"[4]

Women in Unions

Of increasing importance in recent years is the growing proportion of women in the unionized work force. As Table 5.6 on page 94 indicates, women comprised 32.3% of all union members in Canada in 1985 as compared with 17% in 1966 and 16.4% in 1962. Unionization in the public and parapublic sectors accounts for the substantial increase of unionization among women workers. Unions must now redefine some of their policies and programs to accommodate the needs of working women.

For example, more and more women are becoming aware of the appropriateness of the four-day work week to their lifestyles. Forty hours spread over four days, instead of the traditional five, allows women who have become

Table 5.4 — Unions with Largest Memberships 1984 and 1985

		Membership 1985	Membership 1984
1	Canadian Union of Public Employees (CLC)	296,000	293,700
2	National Union of Provincial Government Employees (CLC)	245,000	242,300
3	Public Service Alliance of Canada (CLC)	181,500	181,200
4	United Steelworkers of America (AFL-CIO/CLC)	148,000	148,000
5	United Food and Commercial Workers International Union (AFL-CIO/CLC)	146,000	140,000
6	International Union, United Automobile, Aerospace and Agricultural Implement Workers of America (CLC)*	135,800	110,000
7	Social Affairs Federation Inc. (CNTU)	93,000	93,000
8	International Brotherhood of Teamsters, Chauffeurs, Warehousemen and Helpers of America (Ind.)	91,500	91,500
9	Quebec Teaching Congress (Inc.)	90,000	86,200
10	United Brotherhood of Carpenters and Joiners of America (AFL-CIO)	73,000	78,000
11	Service Employees International Union (AFL-CIO/CLC)	70,000	65,000
12	International Brotherhood of Electrical Workers (AFL-CIO/CFL)	68,600	72,900
13	Canadian Paperworkers Union (CLC)	63,000	63,200
14	International Association of Machinists and Aerospace Workers (AFL-CIO/CLC)	58,600	66,600
15	Quebec Government Employees Union Inc. (Ind.)	55,200	55,200
16	Labourers' International Union of North America (AFL-CIO)	51,400	59,300
17	International Woodworkers of America (AFL-CIO/CLC)	51,200	55,800

*This became the Canadian Auto Workers Union in September 1985.

Source: Labour Data Branch, Labour Canada, *Directory of Labour Organizations in Canada 1985* (Ottawa: Supply and Services Canada, 1985), pp. xxii-xxiii. Reproduced by permission of the Minister of Supply and Services Canada.

primary wage-earners for their families three uninterrupted days per week to manage households, relationships with their children, and the stress of conducting two careers — one inside and one outside the home. Since 42% of the labour force in Canada are women, these considerations have gained considerable weight. Nurses in certain hospitals, for example, are already on four-day work schedules. Paid maternity benefits have also become a major collective bargaining issue since the 1981 agreement between the Federal Government and the Canadian Union of Postal Workers. This agreement provides for seventeen weeks of paid maternity leave.

The need for increasing numbers of women to participate in the leadership of the Canadian union movement will become more and more apparent in the years ahead. Research projects have already been undertaken which are attempting to show how the participation of women in unions affects union policies and programs.

The Structure and Functions of the CLC

Composition of the CLC

Since the Canadian Labour Congress is by far the largest federation on the Canadian scene, only *its* structure and functions will be discussed in this chapter. The previous chapter indicated that the CLC was created by the merger in 1956 of the (then) Trades and Labour Congress of Canada (TLC) and the Canadian Congress of Labour (CCL). The CLC is something like a "union of unions" since it brings together a number of national unions, Canadian branches of international unions and directly chartered locals. Table 5.7 presents the structure of the CLC

Table 5.5					International and National Unions by Size 1985	
	International Unions		National Unions		Total	
Membership Range	Unions	Membership	Unions	Membership	Unions	Membership
Under 100	3	197	2	138	5	335
100 – 199	6	790	9	1,398	15	2,188
200 – 499	0	0	24	8,271	24	8,271
500 – 999	4	3,023	16	11,313	20	14,336
1,000 – 2,499	7	12,575	43	68,541	50	81,116
2,500 – 4,999	9	28,589	31	113,747	40	142,336
5,000 – 9,999	6	42,719	25	173,343	31	216,062
10,000 – 14,999	8	97,533	13	155,611	21	253,144
15,000 – 19,999	6	104,954	6	111,002	12	215,956
20,000 – 29,999	4	90,710	6	142,754	10	233,464
30,000 – 39,999	4	129,400	8	285,740	12	415,140
40,000 – 49,999	1	40,251	0	0	1	40,251
50,000 – 99,999	7	464,286	4	301,194	11	765,480
100,000 and over	3	429,806	3	722,413	6	1,152,219
TOTAL	68	1,444,833	190	2,095,465	258	3,540,298

Source: Labour Data Branch, Labour Canada, *Directory of Labour Organizations in Canada 1985* (Ottawa: Supply and Services Canada 1985), Table 5, p. xxix. Reproduced by permission of the Minister of Supply and Services Canada.

Table 5.6 **Women Union Members as a Percentage of Total Union Membership 1962-1982**

	Number of women members	% of all members
1962	248,884	16.4
1963	260,567	16.6
1964	276,246	16.7
1965	292,056	16.6
1966	322,980	17.0
1967	407,181	19.8
1968	438,543	20.4
1969	469,235	21.2
1970	513,203	22.6
1971	558,138	23.5
1972	575,584	24.2
1973	635,861	24.6
1974	676,939	25.2
1975	711,102	26.0
1976	750,637	27.0
1977	782,282	27.7
1978	835,263	28.7
1979	890,365	29.3
1980	932,883	30.2
1981	979,862	31.0
1982	985,376	32.3

Source: Statistics Canada, *Annual Report of the Minister of Supply and Services Canada under the Corporations and Labour Unions Returns Act, Part 11 – Labour Unions 1982,* Catalogue No. 71-202 (Ottawa: Supply and Services Canada, August 1984), p. 41. Reproduced by permission of the Minister of Supply and Services Canada.

and the relationship of some of its components to the AFL-CIO in the United States. Table 5.3 shows that .4% of the membership of the CLC consists of directly chartered local unions; that is, local unions which receive their charters directly from the CLC, rather than from one of its affiliated national or international unions.

Table 5.2 shows that, in 1985, the CLC included forty-three Canadian branches of international unions which belonged to both the AFL-CIO and the CLC, and three Canadian branches of international unions which belonged only to the CLC. These forty-six Canadian

branches of international unions, appearing on the left-hand side of Figure 5.7, accounted for 26.9% of trade-union membership in Canada. Table 5.3 shows that membership in Canadian branches accounted for 46.5% of CLC membership. The suspension of the international building trade unions and the subsequent formation of the new Canadian Federation of Labour has substantially altered these figures from those of previous years.

The CLC also included fifty national unions (appearing in the right-hand box of Table 5.2) which comprised over 30.7% of all trade-union members in Canada and about 53.5% of CLC membership. (Overall in Canada, there are twelve provincial and territorial federations, over 100 local and district labour councils and more than 13,000 local unions, not including independent locals.)

Definitions of CLC components and an analysis of their functions follow. These definitions are taken from a work entitled *The Directory of Labour Organizations in Canada* (formerly *Labour Organizations in Canada*) published by Labour Canada.[5]

A Central Labour Congress

Labour Canada defines a central labour congress as:

> An organization having in affiliation various unions, directly chartered locals, provincial federations of labour, and local labour councils, for the purpose of broadly co-ordinating their activities at the national level including the relations between unions and governments and establishing relations with organized workers internationally. Congresses hold annual or biennial conventions attended by delegates from affiliated organizations at which policies are established and officers elected. The congress also organizes local unions known as directly chartered locals. Funds are obtained through a per capita tax on all affiliates.[6]

Functions of the CLC

The supreme governing body of the CLC is the biennial convention which establishes the policies which the CLC shall pursue. The con-

Table 5.7	**The Structure of the CLC-Affiliated Segment of the Canadian Labour Movement**

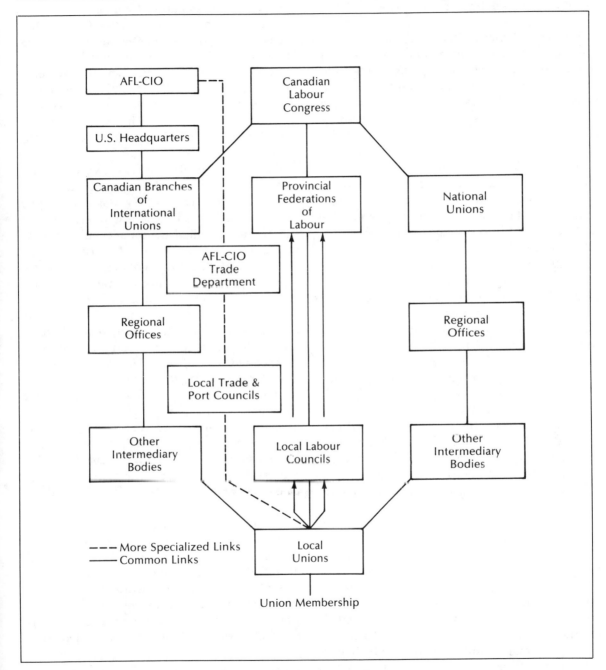

Source: John Crispo, *International Unionism* (Toronto: McGraw-Hill, 1967), p. 167.

stitution of the CLC under the article entitled "Purposes" contains thirteen sections: these elaborate upon the objectives given in the Labour Canada definition cited above.

National Policies The CLC attempts to achieve its objectives at the national level in a number of ways. Each winter it has traditionally presented its annual memorandum to the Government of Canada. Before CLC members convened from across the country, the President of the CLC outlines to the Prime Minister and his cabinet members the objectives which he thinks the Government should pursue. The memorandum, often very critical of government foreign and domestic policy, attempts to persuade Cabinet to enact measures to promote the welfare of organized labour and of the community at large.

In 1976, the CLC protested wage and price controls by discontinuing its annual presentation of an all-inclusive memorandum to Cabinet. Less formal arrangements are, however, still in place. There are, for example, meetings between the chief officers of the CLC and important government officials (including cabinet members) during which the CLC attempts to influence the formulation of government policy. In addition, when Statistics Canada releases its monthly figures on the cost of living and unemployment rate, the CLC frequently prepares press releases setting out those policies it thinks the Government should pursue in light of changes in prices, the rate of unemployment, and other economic indicators. These data are also analyzed and published in *Canadian Labour,* the CLC magazine.

On occasion, the CLC makes its positions known when the Government prepares important legislation or appoints commissions to enquire into critical social and economic issues. In February 1981, for example, the CLC presented a brief to the Parliamentary Task Force on Employment Opportunities in the 1980's. In this brief, the CLC expressed its concern with the present serious unemployment situation and proposed remedies. With the International Typographical Union, the CLC also co-authored a submission to the Kent Commission, a commission which studied the concentration of newspaper ownership in Canada.

On occasion, when Statistics Canada has released its unemployment figures, the CLC has been very quick to suggest remedies to the Government. Of course, the Government generally pays little attention to CLC recommendations. Sometimes, however, policies have been implemented very much in line with those suggested by the CLC, albeit quite a few months after the fact.

Generally, the relationship between the CLC and the Government during the McDermott/Trudeau period (1978 to 1984) was not a happy one. Announcing his proposal for establishing the CLC as "an allied and parallel political force to the federal New Democrat Party," Mr. McDermott said, "we could go on for the next 150 years switching from the Liberals to Conservatives and back and just get more of the same."[7] In response to the Federal Labour Minister's invitation to return to the Canada Labour Relations Council and the Economic Council of Canada,* the CLC President replied that "labour advice to the federal government always falls on deaf ears." The President of the Canadian Union of Public Employees at that time appeared to second Mr. McDermott's comments by observing that "in the main, Canada's unions are excluded from the decision-making process."[8] Despite these bleak appraisals, it appears that relations between the CLC and the Government will eventually return to the pattern that has existed in pre-recession years.

Another important function of the CLC is to define the organizational jurisdiction of its affiliates. When the merger of the TLC and CCL took place in 1956, the constitution of the CLC stated that the jurisdictions of affiliated unions would be as they were on the founding day of the CLC (May 1, 1956), or as subsequently

---

*In 1976, the CLC withdrew from both the Economic Council of Canada and the Canada Labour Relations Council.

granted or amended by authority of the Executive Council and the Constitution (see CLC Constitution: Article II, Section 8, page 7).

The CLC also has a mandate to promote the organization of workers in sectors that are not yet unionized, including the banking industry. In 1977, the Canada Labour Relations Board determined that a bank branch constitutes an appropriate bargaining unit. After this important decision, the CLC set up in cooperation with several other unions a committee to organize bank workers. Generally, progress has been slow. During the Summer and Fall of 1985, however, members of the fledgling Union of Bank Employees employed at the Toronto Canadian Imperial Bank of Commerce Visa Centre undertook a protracted strike. A consumer boycott, similar to that used against Eatons in 1984, was considered but not pursued because the striking workers felt such action would be ineffective in the banking industry.[9]

Jurisdictional Conflicts   Another function of the CLC is to iron out problems of conflicting jurisdictions among its affiliated members. The attempts of Automobile Workers Union and Machinists Union members to organize aerospace workers in the same plants is an example of such jurisdictional conflict. These disputes do not always lend themselves to easy resolution, since each competing union has a vested interest in maintaining its own status, position and growth. Often, the CLC finds it very difficult to accommodate competing unions. Third-party assistance, either in the form of mediation or binding arbitration may be necessary in such cases. However, if the disputing parties refuse to agree with a mediator, then the Executive Committee of the CLC will attempt to resolve the jurisdictional dispute itself.

Code of Ethics   The CLC is also responsible for enforcing its code of ethical practices set out in its Constitution. This code prescribes certain kinds of behaviour: affiliated organizations must adhere to the CLC code in order to maintain their membership in the CLC. When a union

violates any part of the code, it is the duty of the CLC executive or its elected officers to try to persuade the affiliated organization to correct its behaviour. If such an attempt fails, the same officials have the power to suspend any organization which continues to breach these standards. If the threat of dismissal or suspension is not enough to bring the offending union into line, the matter may be brought before a regular CLC convention, at which time a vote may be taken as to whether or not to expel the malefactor, be it a national union or a Canadian branch of an international union.

International Relations   The CLC is also active in international labour affairs, particularly in the International Confederation of Free Trade Unions (ICFTU). A former CLC President, Mr. Donald MacDonald, was President of the ICFTU from 1972 to 1975. Another former president, Mr. Joe Morris, was Chairman of the prestigious Governing Body of the International Labour Organization for one year in 1977.

Four functions constitute the major responsibilities of the CLC. These functions are (1) to influence the formulation and administration of public policy at the national level, (2) to keep peace within the Congress by resolving jurisdictional issues, (3) to police its ethical practices code, and (4) to represent Canadian labour on the international trade-union scene.

Provincial and Territorial Federations of Labour

Currently there are ten provincial and two territorial federations within the CLC, the territorial federations having been created in 1980. A provincial or territorial federation is defined as

> An organization formed by a labour congress at the provincial [or territorial] level which consists of the congress affiliate [sic] in the province [or territory]. It functions similarly to the congress in the appropriate provincial [or territorial] area except that it does not charter local unions. Funds are obtained through a per capita tax on all affiliates.[10]

According to Article XV, Section 2 of the CLC Constitution, all national and international unions and regional and provincial organizations affiliated with the CLC shall require their local unions, branches, or lodges to join chartered federations. Also, all local unions chartered directly by the CLC and all local labour councils shall affiliate with the provincial and territorial federations of labour.

Ontario Federation of Labour The role played by the Ontario Federation of Labour (OFL) from 1958 to 1959 is a good example of what a provincial federation may attempt to do. At that time, the Provincial Government was considering amending its labour relations legislation. The OFL presented a lengthy brief to the Ontario Government with suggestions for the enactment of measures to improve the industrial relations system in Ontario. During the Winter of 1981, another more current issue came to the fore in Ontario: the OFL outlined to the Premier of Ontario the features it desired in any legislation dealing with plant closures. As far as the OFL was concerned, what had been announced up to that point was clearly inadequate — more protection was necessary for workers who had lost their jobs.

Nova Scotia Federation of Labour The efforts of the Nova Scotia Federation of Labour (NSFL) in December 1979 to block the passage of the clearly anti-labour Michelin Bill in Nova Scotia is another example of what a provincial federation may do. This legislation prohibits the Nova Scotia Labour Relations Board from certifying workers in one plant of a manufacturing company if the operation of that plant is integrated with the operation of another plant. The bill was enacted in response to an alleged threat by Michelin Tire not to expand its operation in Nova Scotia if any of its existing plants were forced to accept unionization. Because the NSFL did not succeed in blocking the passage of this bill, the relationship between the Nova Scotia Government and the NSFL remains strained.[11]

British Columbia Federation of Labour A recent situation in which a provincial federation of labour played a very important role occurred in British Columbia in the Fall of 1983. At that time, the B.C. Government, as part of its public-sector restraint program, threatened to fire 1,600 workers. The B.C. Federation of Labour (BCFL) insisted that the government back down and agree to hire and fire workers on a strict seniority basis.[12] Following a great deal of bitterness and name-calling by both the Government and the unions, the "province signed a lucrative new contract with its employees that prevented the arbitrary dismissals that had angered unionists."[13] The President of the BCFL was also a co-leader of the Solidarity Coalition. The Coalition, composed of labour and community groups, had demonstrated massively against the government's restraint program.[14]

Thus, it may be seen that provincial federations react whenever provincial governments issue policy statements which effect the labour movement. Quite often, the executives of the provincial federations will take sharp issue with provincial initiatives, and suggest policy alternatives.

Local Labour Councils

The CLC also has what are called local labour councils, which operate at the local level in similar fashion to the CLC and the provincial federations. A local labour council is defined as:

> An organization formed by a labour congress at the city level. It is organized and functions in the same manner as a provincial federation, but within the scope of a city. Funds are obtained through a per capita tax on affiliates.[15]

The activities of the Ottawa and District Labour Council (ODLC) during the CLC's 1976 protest against wage and price controls is a good example of what a local labour council may do. The ODLC issued a very strong press release, distributed pamphlets, and used the media to urge the Government to abolish its wage and price controls program. There are also some occasions when labour organizations may have to come together to support an attack on any one of them at the local level. This type of action is usually coordinated and directed by the local labour council.

Research carried out by the Labour Council of Metropolitan Toronto in 1974 on the effects of the long delay in arbitration cases is another example of what a local labour council may do. The study contributed to Ontario's new form of expedited arbitration.[16] We will discuss expedited arbitration in the chapter "Administration of the Collective Agreement."

National Unions and Canadian Branches of International Unions

Labour Canada defines a national or international union as follows:

> The unit of labour organization that organizes and charters locals in the industries or trades as defined in its constitution, sets general policy for its locals, assists them in the conduct of their affairs, and is the medium for co-ordinating their activities. Funds are obtained from the locals through per capita dues. Unions usually hold regular conventions of delegates from the locals at which general policy is set and at which officers are elected.[17]

An international union charters locals in both Canada and the United States, while a national union restricts its activities to Canada.

As indicated earlier, the CLC consists of close to fifty Canadian branches of international unions and close to thirty national unions. Each national union usually has a mandate to organize within a particular jurisdiction (i.e., a trade or industry) which is normally spelled out in its constitution. The national union or Canadian branch of an international union serves the existing local unions within it, and organizes non-unionized workers within its particular jurisdiction.

In the early days of union development, it was easy for national unions or Canadian branches of international unions to organize in industries where large plants existed with many

workers. This was particularly true in the primary, manufacturing, and transportation and communication industries. Today, however, organization is more difficult — most of the unorganized plants are small or are located in isolated areas. This situation is perceived by many as a major challenge for existing unions.

Usually a union will have its own elected executive, appointed staff, and field officers — known as national or international representatives — who are assigned particular geographic areas. In craft unions, particularly in the construction industry, field officers who organize workers and help locals are called business agents.

Role of National or Canadian Branches of International Unions

The national union or Canadian branch of an international union* may help a local in a variety of ways. First, it may catalyze the organization of a group of workers, or it may be asked by those same workers to represent them as their collective bargaining agent. Second, during contract negotiations, the representative of the national union may assist the local negotiating committee in formulating demands and in negotiating. Third, these representatives often assist locals in handling grievances particularly when they are taken to arbitration. This assistance can be of tremendous help to local officials, who may have little experience in negotiating or in presenting grievance cases before experienced arbitrators. Although they may not publically admit as much, many employers prefer to deal with experienced national representatives rather than inexperienced local officials.

The constitutions of most national and international unions give them the power of veto over certain matters that are carried on at the local level, including the authorization of strikes and sometimes the approval of the terms of a collective agreement. For most unions the power to approve terms is largely a formality. There are

---

*Whatever applies to a national union applies also to Canadian branches of international unions.

only a very few cases on record where a national or international union has refused to accept an agreement worked out between union and management representatives at the local level, or to accept the strike decision of the majority of local union members.

One such case did occur, however, in the mid-1960's: the International Typographical Union (ITU) refused to ratify a collective agreement negotiated by the three major newspapers in Toronto and the locals of the ITU. The rationale of the ITU executive was that the accord contained objectionable provisions concerning the ways in which newspapers could introduce new technology. The ITU executive felt that these provisions might establish a dangerous precedent for negotiations elsewhere in North America. Since the workers' pension plans were administered by the union, rather than by a union-management committee, the international executive had a great deal of leverage with the local unions, which ultimately withdrew their acceptance of the agreement.

National unions assist their local unions, particularly if the latter negotiate separately, by building up reserve funds which are disbursed as benefits to striking workers should work stoppages occur. It is also not at all uncommon for one union to give donations to the striking members of another union.

The Local Union

For the ordinary worker, the most important unit within the framework of a labour movement is the local union; that is,

> The basic unit of labour organization formed in a particular plant or locality. The members participate directly in the affairs of their local including the election of officers, financial and other business matters, relations between their organization and employers, and they pay dues to the local. There are locals of international, national or regional unions, locals directly chartered by a central congress, and independent local organizations. Sometimes unions have units, similar to locals, such as lodges, branches or divisions.[18]

A worker's first contact with unionism is usually with a local. Whatever occurs during that initial contact may colour the individual's whole attitude towards unions.

Each local has its own elected officers, some of whom may contribute their time freely, others of whom may be paid on a full-time or part-time basis, depending on the size of the union. Every member has a right to take part in local meetings, to have input into the formulation of contract demands, and to vote on the ratification of contract proposals for the bargaining unit to which he or she belongs.

When union representatives organize a new plant or other establishment, they first assemble a core of union members. These union members sign union cards and then try to convince other workers to join the union. It is usually this nucleus of active members which shapes the policy and direction of the local union.

It has been estimated that only between 5% and 10% of the local members show up for regular union meetings. While this is often condemned by writers on the topic, it should be pointed out that meetings of voluntary associations normally have small turnouts. In this sense, local unions are no exception to the general rule. Only when matters arise of real importance to members (for example, the ratification of the terms of a collective agreement) will large turnouts occur at union meetings.

Within a local union, which may organize the workers of one company only or a number of small companies, members are normally elected to serve as shop stewards. Their function is to discuss grievances with workers and to represent workers in the grievance process, usually at the first level between foreman and individual. Each department or area may have one or more shop stewards. In addition, there is usually what is called a shop stewards' committee with an individual chosen from the committee as the general shop steward. The general shop steward coordinates the efforts of all committee members.

Most union constitutions provide for initiation fees. In some unions, initiation fees may be quite high. Monthly dues are normally required of members and are deducted directly from members' pay where a dues check-off clause exists in a contract. The local union in turn distributes this money according to the constitution of the national union and the by-laws of the local. Local unions are financed entirely from the dues of union members. In the case of costly strikes, however, the general strike fund of the national or international union may supplement local union funds.

As Bakke has pointed out, belonging to a local union gives the worker a chance to assume responsibility for his work environment and to feel important in relation to his fellow workers. Election to an official post within the local union brings with it a certain prestige. In like manner, election as a shop steward often provides an active trade-union member with a strong sense of purpose. In addition, union officials and shop stewards often get time off to attend national or international conventions, and to participate at important regional or local policy committee meetings at which decisions are taken on items relating to future rounds of collective bargaining, or to the organization of the union itself.[19]

Other Components of the CLC

Table 5.7 indicates that national unions and Canadian branches of international unions have regional offices which are located in various cities and large communities across the country. The *Directory of Labour Organizations in Canada* gives an indication of how many such regional offices are currently in operation.

Table 5.7 also contains a section called "Local Trades and Ports Councils." These bodies are set up to handle problems among unions or among unions and employers at the local level. A good example is the Vancouver Port's Council, a CLC affiliate which consists of the locals of the major unions representing workers engaged in the transportation of goods by ship. Most cities also have councils consisting of construction industry unions. An example of such a council is the Ottawa-Hull Building and Construction Trades Council, an AFL-CIO affiliate.

On the right-hand side of Table 5.7 is a box entitled "Other Intermediary Bodies." An example of an intermediary body is the Canadian Railway Labour Association (CRLA), a voluntary organization of eleven unions which represent a large number of Canadian railway workers. The CRLA seeks to initiate and maintain co-operative action and to coordinate policy on all matters of interest and importance to its membership. Thus, although many of the individual unions involved in the CRLA bargain with more than just the railways, the Railway Association provides them with a specific context wherein they might influence government policy in the workers' favour.

So far we have discussed the major components of the CLC, the functions of the CLC at the national level, and the role played by provincial and territorial federations and local labour councils. We have also examined the nature of national unions and the Canadian branches of international unions, and the role of local unions, local trades and ports councils, and other intermediary bodies.

The preceding chapter concerned itself with the debate in the 1930's and 1940's about the role and function of international unions in the Canadian trade-union movement. This is by no means a dead issue. At present, there is very serious controversy within the Canadian trade-union movement, especially within the CLC, over the need for Canadianization of international unions.

Concern over the Canadianization of International Unions

The question of Canadianization of international unions has been the subject of much soul-searching on the part of the Canadian Labour Congress. Dennis McDermott, former President of the CLC, considers fully independent Canadian unions to be inevitable and a product of our times. He believes the autonomy of Canadian unions is "right and proper."[20]

Foreign Control   The argument for Canadianization rests on a number of grounds. First, nationalistic perceptions portray as inordinate the degree to which the United States controls investment in Canada and influences the Canadian labour movement. Adherents to this viewpoint argue vociferously for more Canadian control over foreign investment and unions in Canada. Second, many people, both inside and outside the labour movement, feel that there are too many international unions in Canada. These people argue that, by reducing the number of unions through merger or through the development of strictly national bodies, the labour movement could serve its members more effectively than is currently possible. To some extent, many of these people see policies developed by international unions as being concerned with problems more peculiar to the United States than to Canada.

Since its election in 1984, the Conservative Federal Government has implemented a more open policy toward foreign investment than the previous Liberal Federal Government had. The crown-owned DeHavilland Aircraft of Canada Ltd., for instance, was sold by the Conservatives to the American-based Boeing Commercial Aircraft Co., one of the world's largest aerospace manufacturers. According to David Stewart-Patterson, "Opposition Members of Parliament quickly jumped on the deal, accusing the Government of selling out a vital industry to foreign interests at fire sale prices."[21] The intent of the Conservatives, apparently, was to demonstrate to the world that Canada is again ready "for business as usual."

Dues Drain   Third, some writers believe that Canadian members of international unions pay more into international trade union funds than they receive in benefits. There are also those who contend that, by being part of a continental trade-union movement, Canadian workers benefit greatly by the combined financial contributions of workers in both countries. To date, analysis of this question has been insufficient. It is still unclear whether or not Canadian workers pay more money into international unions than they receive in benefits. Certainly more research needs to be done to supplement data contained in the annual reports of the *Corporations and Labour Unions Returns Act (CALURA)*, since *CALURA* reports do not take into account many of the indirect costs assumed by international unions in serving the needs of Canadian memberships — costs such as those incurred by research activities, the production and distribution of newspapers and circulars, the payment of salaries to union officers, etc.[22]

Responses of International Unions to Canadian Concerns

To meet some of these criticisms, a number of international unions have established separate Canadian identities which take more fully into account the economic, social, and political realities of Canadian life. Large unions representing steelworkers and, until recently, the autoworkers have long had branches in this country and possess the staff necessary to provide research and policy orientations which answer to the needs of Canadian members.

Other international unions have recently shown greater sensitivity to the Canadian situation, but in varying ways. As a result, a number of important developments in the international segment of the Canadian labour movement have occurred, particularly since 1968.[23] In that year, the United Packinghouse, Food, and Allied Workers merged with the Amalgamated Meat Cutters and Butcher Workmen of North America. This merger recognized the Canadian fact by providing the Canadian section with a Canadian name: the Canadian Food and Allied Workers Union (District Council 15). Recently, this union merged in both Canada and the United States with the Retail Clerks' International Union to become in Canada Region 18 (Ontario and Western Canada) and 19 (Quebec and Eastern Canada) of the United Food and Commercial Workers International Union. This merger resulted in a Canadian membership of 140,000 in 1985.[24]

Secession from International Unions

Despite increased sensitivity by international unions to Canadian concerns, a number of Canadian sections of international unions broke away from their international counterparts during the 1970's and formed strictly Canadian unions. The first major break occurred in 1971. The Canadian section of the Communication Workers of America detached itself from the international union and established the Communications Workers of Canada (CWC) — now called Communication, Electronic, Electrical, Technical and Salaried Workers of Canada. A CLC affiliate, the CWC had 35,000 members in 1985.[25]

In 1974, the National Association of Broadcast Employees and Technicians (NABET) and the United Paperworkers International Union both split into autonomous Canadian and American organizations. NABET decided to maintain a loose multinational structure, but the Paperworkers divided into two entirely independent union organizations.[26] The Canadian section of the United Paperworkers International Union was probably the more interesting of these two new unions. The Canadian Paperworkers had about 50,000 members and was a large branch among the international unions in Canada. Prior to the establishment of an independent Canadian union, a nationwide referendum took place in which an overwhelming majority of the Canadian members voted to establish a strictly Canadian union. In some circles, it has been suggested that there were difficulties in working out the financial arrangements when the split took place within this union. The President of the international union, however, attended the founding convention of the new Canadian union and pledged to maintain harmonious relationships between the Canadian body and its American counterpart.

In 1975, special arrangements took place within the Teamsters Union. The Teamsters Union was restructured somewhat and now a new Canadian Conference exists, headed by an international vice-president who is elected by delegates from both countries at the international convention. Also, the Canadian director is now assisted by a policy committee elected by Canadians only.[27]

An interesting development occurred in 1976 within the Brotherhood of Railway, Airline, and Steamship Clerks (BRAC). In Canada, BRAC now has a separate Canadian constitution. Quadrennial conventions (the union's highest authority in Canada) set dues, hear disciplinary appeals, elect officers, and perform research and legislative functions. The three highest officers in Canada are now automatically officers of the international union.[28]

United Automobile Workers The most recent and most dramatic break between a Canadian section of an international union and its American parent was that of the Canadian section of the United Automobile Workers (UAW) in late 1984 and in September 1985 when the Canadian Auto Workers Union held its founding convention. This break was significant because of previous good relations between the Canadian section and the parent union, and also because the Canadian section had enjoyed a substantial amount of autonomy over a long period of time. The late Walter Reuther, a dynamic president of the UAW for many years, seldom interfered in the affairs of the Canadian section. However, he did so on one occasion in the 1950's at the request of the Canadian director who was having difficulties in steering the Oshawa and St. Catharines locals towards renegotiating an agreement with General Motors. Reuther settled this dispute by virtue of his excellent leadership skills.

The UAW break is all the more significant because of the 1965 automotive agreement between the American and Canadian Governments. This agreement rationalized the North American market and the facilities for manufacturing cars in both countries. Some Canadian facilities, for example, make particular models for the entire North American market. An interesting question which this break poses concerns the future investment patterns of the American headquarters of the Big Three American companies: Will the American companies continue to produce cars in Canada? There is concern that American investment in Canadian operations will, in fact, decline. List has suggested that the 1984 nine-day strike against General Motors in Canada has given rise to such thinking.[29]

The Canadian director of the UAW is assisted in his task by a Canadian Council composed of some 300 delegates from local unions across the country. The major issue leading up to the split was the alleged interference of the international union in Canadian contract negotiations in Canada. In 1984, the international office tried to influence the Canadian section of the union to agree to a contract which was practically a carbon copy of the agreement reached between the parent union in the United States and General Motors. Apparently, the current president of the international union threatened to cut off benefits for Canadian workers if they pursued goals which were at variance with the agreement negotiated in the United States.[30] However, the Canadian section had its own bargaining agenda. It refused to bow to pressures from the international office, and reached a settlement which differed from the American pattern in important ways.

The seeds of the 1984 disagreement had been sown several years earlier when the Canadian district differed from its parent union in refusing to give up concessions won years ago. The Canadian section had been arguing for some years for parity with its American counterparts.

In fact, there was a common agreement between the union and Chrysler for many years which covered plants on both sides of the border. During one bargaining year, the American consumer price index was almost incorporated into the common agreement. Because the American workers had benefitted from cost-of-living allowances based on the American consumer price index (which is calculated somewhat differently from the Canadian consumer price index), greater and more frequent wage increases were won by the American workers than those won by the Canadian workers. To rectify this disparity, the Canadian workers were given lump-sum payments in ensuing negotiations.

Apart from the demand of the Canadian section that the international union not interfere in Canadian contract negotiations, the only other issue between the two bodies was that all union staff in Canada be responsible solely to the Canadian director.[31] When the twenty-five member executive board of the international union met to discuss the demands of the Canadian section, only the Canadian director voted pro-Canadian. The executive board of the International Union is reported to have said that compliance with the demands would destroy the union. It stated that, by "definition, in an international union, the international president's involvement in any set of negotiations cannot be construed as 'interference.'"[32]

Since the board could not resolve the issues, a committee was set up to facilitate the orderly and cordial separation of the Canadian section from the international union. There was speculation that there might be difficulty in working out a financial arrangement between the Canadian section and the American headquarters. However, an amicable settlement was reached whereby the Canadian section would obtain $36 million of the $600 million American strike fund. This figure represented about 5% of the strike fund. The 125,000 Canadian membership, however, was about 10% of total union membership. It was felt that the Canadian and American unions should maintain good relations with one another since there will likely be some informal arrangement between them in future negotiations, and Canadian settlements will likely still be governed to a large extent by what happens across the border.

In September 1985, the founding convention of the new Canadian union took place in Toronto. Bob White was elected union leader and the name National Union, United Automobile, Aerospace and Agricultural Implement Workers (UAW) was selected for the union. Mr. Owen Bieber, President of the International Union, was invited to attend the founding convention but was unable to comply. His telegrammed response was that "Although we disagree with your decision to separate, we, of course, respect it. As with workers everywhere, the international union will remain a firm friend and ally of Canadian workers."[33] Thirty-six million dollars was transferred to the Canadian UAW in May 1986. The general consensus is that this sum will provide an adequate financial base for bargaining.[34]

A settlement was negotiated by White with the Chrysler Corporation of Canada during the Fall of 1985. This settlement set a pattern for the international union which achieved its own settlement shortly after the Canadian negotiations.[35] Since the relationship between the American and Canadian sections of the UAW was considered, before the split, to be among the better American-Canadian trade union relationships, it will be interesting to see if Canadian branches of other international unions will imitate the action of the Canadian UAW.

Although it is difficult to identify specific unions which are likely to form separate Canadian autonomous units in the coming years, it is inevitable that there will be a number of mergers in Canada and the United States. This will lead to the rise of more independent unions in Canada with varying degrees of affiliation to the original parent bodies. It is also possible to envisage complete breakaways. In the meantime,

national federations such as the CLC will attempt to ensure that international unions with affiliates in this country provide their Canadian components with an adequate degree of autonomy.

CLC Standards of Self-Government

The whole question of the relationship of Canadian branches of international unions to the Canadian Labour Congress has been the subject of much debate and discussion at various conventions of the CLC. The May 1970 convention of the CLC passed a resolution establishing Canadian standards of self-government for affiliated Canadian divisions of international unions. These standards were reaffirmed and expanded at the 1974 convention and now include the following five requirements:

1 Election of Canadian officers by Canadians.
2 Policies to deal with national affairs to be determined by the elected Canadian officers and/or members.
3 Canadian elected representatives to have authority to speak for the union in Canada.
4 That where an international union is affiliated to an international trade secretariat, the Canadian section of that union should be affiliated separately to ensure a Canadian presence and voice at the international industry level.
5 That international unions take whatever action is necessary to ensure that the Canadian membership will not be prevented by constitutional requirements or policy decisions from participating in the social, cultural, economic and political life of the Canadian community.[36]

Many nationalists within the CLC object to the moderation of these standards of self-government and would like to see stronger controls placed over the Canadian divisions of international unions. Hence, it is likely that there will be further developments in the Canadianization of international unions in the future.

Only a few international unions have granted self-government to their Canadian affiliates. Nevertheless, the number of self-governing unions has increased. Some unions have enjoyed self-government for some years. Since 1957, for example, authority in the International

Woodworkers has been concentrated at the regional level. "Regional directors are elected, hire staff, and administer a regional constitution. Each region has a strike fund, levies its own dues, and coordinates bargaining."[37] NABET and the Energy and Chemical Workers Union (ECWU) each have their own Canadian organizations and constitutions, and elect their own officers who may charter locals and levy dues. Interestingly enough, the executive boards in NABET for both Canada and the United States meet jointly each year, and hold their conventions at the same locations. Both organizations are of equal rank, and each pays its own expenses.[38]

There are disadvantages and advantages to increasing autonomy. One of the major limitations is cost. The 18,000-member Canadian division of BRAC levied a monthly fee of 50¢ per member to pay for a Canadian convention. The Teamsters' International office contributes 20¢ per Canadian member to support their Canadian Conference. Some unions, particularly craft unions, may see no benefits from greater autonomy. Such unions operate mainly in local labour markets and negotiate their agreements at that level. Thus, international officers play an insignificant role in these negotiations. Also, the traditions of craft unions, as we pointed out in the previous chapter, tend to be much more conservative than those of industrial unions.

Results of the Canadianization of International Unions

A recent study of a sample of twenty-nine international unions by two international scholars reveals some interesting results. For analytical purposes, the authors developed four methods: the assimilationist model, the special-status model, the self-governing model, and the sovereignty-association model. Under the assimilationist model there are few provisions for specifically Canadian issues. The Canadian divisions are treated almost exactly the same way that American divisions are treated. In the special-status model, Canada is designated as a special region, with rights and functions not

found in American regions. For example, a vice-president can be elected by Canadians, a Canadian office can be operated by Canadians, policy conferences can be organized in this country by Canadians, and union dues can be controlled and collected by Canadians. The self-governing model has the same features as the special-status model, but also provides for a separate Canadian constitution and Canadian control over strike funds.[39]

> In the sovereignty-association model, formal international ties are maintained but the U.S. headquarters exercises no authority over the Canadian section. Canadians do not pay international dues, but may contribute to an international strike fund, contract for research and other services, and coordinate bargaining strategy with Americans.[40]

Among the reasons for changing the structural links of Canadian branches of international unions, the most common one was to conform to guidelines established by the CLC conventions of 1970 and 1974. Although most craft unions made some changes, they generally resisted complying fully with the guidelines. However, the Carpenter's Union, a craft union, now has a Canadian organizer and a research officer.

What have been the results of greater Canadianization of Canadian sections of international unions?

> Overall, the evidence points to positive results from the shift to special or self-government… U.S. interviewees…noted that their unions have grown rapidly since the change, negotiate good collective agreements, require less assistance from headquarters, but still participate actively in affairs of the international… Canadian officials were also pleased with their new roles.[41]

Constitutional changes are also often accompanied by an increase in resources for Canadian operations. In addition, Canadian autonomy gives the more politically oriented Canadian unions the opportunity to debate social issues such as health insurance plans, topics which most international unions in the United States do not discuss. However, greater Canadian autonomy may lessen the ability of Canadians to influence union policies in the United States. This is a particular disadvantage in matters such as restriction of trade. Hence, greater Canadian autonomy is a mixed blessing to Canadian workers. Full and informed debate should take place before Canadian branches of international unions rush into greater autonomy for the workers they represent.

The CLC and Its Relationship to National and Canadian Branches of International Unions

Since the election of Dennis McDermott as President of the CLC, there has been at least one serious incident, apart from the building trades dispute discussed in the previous chapter, involving the relationship between the CLC and an affiliated union. This took place during the Fall of 1978, when the Canadian Union of Postal Workers (CUPW) defied special legislation to prevent a strike by inside postal workers. Although the CLC played a very low-key role in the whole affair, it came under some fairly strong criticism for allegedly not lending greater help to the members of CUPW. Mr. McDermott and the members of the CLC's Executive Committee and Executive Council had discussed very thoroughly with the leadership of CUPW the role that the CLC might be able to play in helping resolve the dispute between that union and the Post Office. However, at the request of CUPW leaders, the CLC did not publicize what it was doing.

When the CLC was criticized for its apparent failure to support CUPW, the President sent a letter to the ranking officers of all affiliated organizations, federations and labour councils indicating where the CLC, as a national federation, stood with respect to the action of any one of its affiliates. A part of that correspondence is quoted below:

> It would be foolhardy to grant to any affiliate a license to co-opt the entire labour movement in support of collective bargaining endeavours which are the private domain of the affiliate concerned,

and then have the entire labour movement march down the road to possible self-destruction. There is no question in our minds that had we embarked on the course of action that CUPW were requesting...nothing short of a general strike would have sufficed.

Apart from all of the emotion and rhetoric which results from a situation such as the post office confrontation, there is a clear-cut responsibility on the leadership of the movement to make decisions which take into consideration the welfare of all affiliates and not just the one that happens to be currently in conflict with an employer. If we permit this kind of precedent to prevail, then we could face the spectre of total anarchy; a demand from any one given affiliate to join with them in a general strike in support of their demands could result in all of us being on strike for most of the 365 days of the year. Obviously, this would become a preposterous situation.

The Canadian Labour Congress and its top leadership did not make the decision lightly. As devoted trade unionists, they were naturally reluctant to withhold support from an affiliate, but an affiliate embarking on this kind of venture has a clear-cut obligation to consult with the CLC and obtain agreement from the affiliates before expecting total unreserved support.

CUPW, in fact, made its own unilateral decision without benefit of consultation with the Canadian Labour Congress, and without prior commitment of support from the rest of organized labour. Yet they were expecting blanket endorsation for whatever course of action and related variety of activities they themselves would decide upon, up to and including the prospect of a general strike. In short, they would 'call the tune', [and] the rest of us would simply be required to 'pay the piper'. Obviously this was unacceptable, and I submit to you that anyone acquiescing to such a proposition would be guilty of abdication of leadership.[42]

When Mr. McDermott made this frank statement about the Canadian Union of Postal Workers, he was likely also delivering a message to all other national unions and Canadian branches of international unions affiliated with the CLC. In effect, he was informing them that if any union were to take drastic action without prior consultation with the CLC, it could not expect full CLC backing or support. It is interesting to note also that at the Ontario Federation of Labour Convention in the Fall of 1978, Mr.

McDermott received full support for the position that had been taken by the various authoritative bodies of the CLC. Prior to the 1980 convention, he and the President of CUPW were once more on good terms and Mr. McDermott was able to play an important role in the peaceful settlement between the Treasury Board and CUPW in the 1980 postal negotiations.[43]

Another factor which the CLC may consider when one of its member unions goes on strike is the extent to which the CLC should support the striking workers. The following section deals with this question in the context of a discussion of the merits of establishing a national CLC strike fund.

A Proposed National CLC Strike Fund

Historically, national and international unions have each developed their own strike funds. However, during the Fall and Winter of 1978 and 1979, Local 6500 of the United Steelworkers of America conducted a very lengthy strike against the International Nickel Co. (Inco) in Sudbury, Ontario. While a few other unions contributed financial aid to help the workers on strike at Inco, there was not enough money to help workers suffering from serious financial difficulties.

A former legislative director of The Canadian Brotherhood of Railway, Transport and General Workers Unions, made a proposal that serious consideration be given to setting up a centralized strike fund within the CLC. Possibly all unions in the country, or even a majority of them, might think about pooling their strike money and creating one large strike fund from which each could draw.

Administered, perhaps, by the Canadian Labour Congress, such a giant fund could serve to redress the present imbalance of power between individual unions and the multinationals [multinational corporations]. It would have to be closely regulated, of course, to ensure

strikes weren't called frivolously, or without exhausting every effort to get a peaceful settlement. Union locals would have to surrender some of their bargaining autonomy in order to justify tapping the central fund.

In practice, such a reservoir would serve more to deter than to facilitate strikes. On the union side, it would induce local unionists to consult with their top officers on contract demands and strategy, in order to qualify for strike pay. On the company side, it would discourage the precipitation of strikes designed to starve the workers into submission. The lesson of the Sudbury strike, surely, is that no one union, no matter how big or well-heeled, can single-handedly finance a lengthy strike against a much larger and wealthier corporation.

By extending the insurance principle on which any group protective plan operates — i.e., by pooling all unions' strike funds — the Canadian labour movement would be forging that bigger and better bargaining lever it so desperately needs.[44]

While this idea is certainly very interesting, particularly from a trade-union point of view, nothing has come of it yet. An important question is whether there is sufficient solidarity among the unions within the CLC to bring about the setting up of such a joint strike pool. During the fall of 1980, when members of the Communication Workers of Canada were on strike against Bell Canada, Mr. McDermott obtained over $1,000,000 from various unions within the CLC to help the striking workers.[45] It is nevertheless difficult to estimate the extent to which such efforts may be undertaken in the future.

The Governance of Unions

The question of the internal governing of trade unions is a complex one, and the most that we can do here is to give a very brief discussion of the subject. The topics which will be discussed below are (1) the union convention, (2) the union constitution and the day-to-day running of a union, (3) the tenure and turnover of union officers, (4) democracy in unions, (5) membership control within unions, and (6) due process and remedial procedures. The latter two, as well as some of the others, are related to the whole issue of democracy in unions.

Union Conventions

The union convention, which is usually held at regular intervals ranging from one to five years, is the supreme governing body of a union. Its major functions include the election of union officials and the determination of policies which will be followed by the union. Officers are usually elected by majority vote at conventions although some unions elect officers by a referendum vote. However, policies which are adopted at one convention many be modified at subsequent conventions, and new policies added. Hence, policy formulation and changes are dynamic features of union conventions.

Conventions are attended by the senior officers of the union, delegates from intermediate bodies and representatives of local unions. However, the senior officers have a great deal of control over the convention by virtue of their control over most matters which come before the convention. So, too, do senior officers control the appointment of members to the various committees which deal with these matters. One study conducted in the United States found that "in 60 of the 70 unions surveyed the major committees at conventions [were] dominated by the union's officialdom. They [were] selected by the president in 49 unions, by the executive board in 11 other unions."[46]

Most union conventions are characterized by voting on resolutions, which may come from local unions or union executives prior to the convention. Delegates from local unions may receive instructions from members on how they should vote or they may go to the conventions with no such mandate. In the latter case, the delegates may be subject to a great deal of pressure from national officers on how to vote during the convention itself. It has been ob-

served that "delegates from large locals [are] likely to submit resolutions; have delegates in attendance; and view the convention as important in the determination of policy."[47]

A study of the convention of one large Canadian union concluded that little debate occurred over resolutions presented to the delegates. This was due partly to events which occurred before the convention and partly to those which occurred during the convention itself. Pre-convention factors which limit the vitality of conventions include not knowing the location to which resolutions should be sent, the role of the union executive in screening and compiling the resolutions, and the composition of convention committees. Things which were found to hamper debate within the convention itself included lack of information on resolutions, receiving prior instructions or pressure on how to vote, and feelings of not being a free agent. These were all seen as impediments to democratic decision making.[48] On the basis of this analysis, it appears that unions should make a greater effort to ensure that delegates to conventions are able to play a more meaningful role in them.

Constitutions and Day-to-Day Running of Unions

Usually, national or international union constitutions make provisions for the election of a president, one or more vice-presidents, and a secretary-treasurer. These officials form the union executive which is responsible for looking after the day-to-day running of the union. There may also be provision for the election of vice-presidents to intermediate bodies, such as the various districts of international unions, including Canadian districts.

In addition to the officers who look after the day-to-day running of a union, there is usually a board. This board is elected at the convention to advise the executive officers on policy matters between conventions. Meetings of these bodies are held three or four times a year. Boards usually have the constitutional authority to place under trusteeship local unions whose management is suspect. This means that local democracy is at least temporarily halted until an investigation clears matters up. A trustee is appointed by the national office, and may include someone from that office or a local person who the administration deems trustworthy. The constitutions of some international and national unions may include suggestions for local union constitutions and by-laws.[49]

The elected officials of national and international unions have the authority to hire a staff of professionals which deals with matters such as research, education, legislation, and publicity. These appointed staff members may assist not only the officers at the national level, but regional representatives and local unions. National and international unions have full-time elected officers and full-time staff members. These staff members owe their appointments to their national or international presidents and, therefore, frequently become part of the political machinery of these elected officials.

Local unions also have constitutions and by-laws which guide local officers in their day-to-day activities. Some local unions have a few full-time officers while others have part-time officers, depending on the size of the local's membership. Officers are elected by the local membership. Dues are collected at the local level, and per capita contributions are made to the headquarters of the national or international union and to other bodies with which the local may be affiliated, such as provincial federations of labour and local labour councils. The most important qualification for election to the leadership of a national or international union is having worked one's way up through the ranks. Having worked on the shop-floor level and having had the experience of being a shop steward are good credentials with which to enter the running for union leadership.

Union Leaders

The managers of unions are unlike the managers of businesses. Business managers may move across companies and industries, whereas union managers normally do not. In addition, little training is available to union leaders. The Labour College of Canada is one of the few sources of union management training. Each summer, a number of union members are selected by local unions to attend the Labour College. Some unions, moreover, have in-house training programs for their members. These, however, do not involve training in management techniques.

A good deal of a union leaders' time is spent "putting out brush fires." According to D. C. Bok and J. T. Dunlop, "the key problem in union government is how to encourage innovation, a longer view of the union's role and interests, and greater effectiveness in carrying out the policies and programs of the organization."[50] However, union leaders spend a good deal of their time resolving disputes and trying to maintain cohesion among different factions within their unions, possibly assisting with the negotiation of collective agreements, handling grievances, and taking part in arbitration proceedings. Union leaders may also be active in community affairs and in community agencies.

Election and Tenure of Union Officers

Election of union officers takes place much more frequently at the local level than at the national or international levels. There is much more interaction among members at the local level, and if an incumbent official is perceived to be doing a poor job, it is easy for an ambitious individual to run against such an official in local elections. Often, however, challengers make extravagant promises and cannot deliver them — sometimes a disadvantage to such individuals when they seek higher union office.

Much of the literature on union elections at the national or international levels has noted a tendency for union leaders to perpetuate their stay in office. This is possible because of their ability to control the channels of communications. Thus, union leaders can develop and maintain prestigious national images which give them advantages over opponents. "Perhaps more important, the leader can maintain a monopoly over the political skills within the organization and is thus able to build an effective political machine. This combination of power, prestige, and skill is said to enable the union president to perpetuate his term of office."[51]

There have been several empirical studies of the turnover among presidents of strictly Canadian unions. On the basis of a study by G. N. Chaison and J. B. Rose which covered the period from 1945 to 1972, it was concluded that, in only 14.1% of the cases, turnover was attributable to union politics. The greatest proportion of these turnovers were attributed to the failure of governing bodies to nominate the incumbent for further office. Slightly over 30% of the turnovers were not political in nature. They included age, health, the onerous nature of the position, death in office, and union bars agains successive years in office. A serious limitation of this study was that, in over 50% of the cases, the reasons for retiring were uncertain. Close to 33% of the incumbents either retired or refused to run for office without giving reasons. About 20% changed jobs.[52]

Another study by Chaison and Rose indicated that union growth increased the likelihood of presidents remaining in office, presumably because of increased status, compensation, and opportunities to sharpen political skills. Also, presidents of older and larger unions tended to stay in office longer than presidents of younger and smaller unions. These findings led the authors to suggest

> that there may be a relationship between presidential turnover and stages of union growth. The early formative years for unions would be marked by relatively unstable leadership, but as unions mature...there is a more centralized organizational structure and reduced membership control of the governing process. Turnover rates decline, and there is an increase in the tenure of presidents.[53]

In general, union leadership changes frequently. This is particularly true for national unions. During the period from 1963 to 1972, nearly 80% of Canadian national unions experienced at least one presidential change. Similarly, high turnover rates were found for international unions which have their headquarters in the United States. In both countries, reasons for leaving office rarely included election defeat.[54]

Democracy in Unions

S. Muthuchidambaram claims that so much has been written on the concept of union democracy, that it "is fair to say that anybody writing on 'Union Democracy' may have almost nothing 'original' to contribute."[55] Our objective in this section is not to develop something original, but rather to summarize briefly some of the major aspects of democracy or its opposite, according to Will Herberg — bureaucracy. As Herberg has stated in a classic piece of institutional analysis, trade unions in the United States (and probably also in Canada) constitute a paradox inasmuch as they have dual natures:

> A modern labour union is, at one and the same time: (1) a businesslike service organization, operating a variety of agencies under a complicated system of industrial relations; (2) an expression and vehicle of the historical movement of the submerged laboring masses for social recognition and democratic self-expression.[56]

According to Herberg's analysis, in order to fulfull their business and service functions, unions require efficient, bureaucratic administrations, very much like those of banks or insurance companies. But unions also embody a crusading spirit of reform of which the democratic self-expression of their members is the very essence. Unions, thus, are inherently in conflict with themselves. Herberg, however, provides no instrument by which this conflict may be reconciled.

Analysts and some practitioners have been grappling with the whole problem of effective unionism for purposes of collective bargaining while trying, at the same time, to maximize the control of members over the organizations which the members themselves create. The CLC and the AFL-CIO both have codes which set out a whole array of ethical practices aimed at optimizing the control workers have over their organizations. These codes also ensure that the organizations are run honestly and democratically, and that union leaders remain responsible to rank-and-file members.

Membership Control

It has been noted by many observers that the attendance at union meetings generally runs between 10% and 15%. Even such critical issues as contract ratification and voting for union officers may bring out only a bare majority.[57] If unions leaders are adept enough to get elected as union officers, they are probably adept enough, at least most of the time, to know whether a proposed settlement can be sold to the membership. (More will be said about this matter in the chapter "The Negotiation Process.") If we compare the behaviour of workers as union members and as citizens, we may find that there are few differences as far as active involvement in governmental processes is concerned. In the 1964 American presidential campaign, for example, only 62% of the eligible voters actually voted. This is roughly the same proportion as that which voted in the 1965 Steelworkers election.[58] Hence, fairly low levels of participation, as measured by voting, are typical of the individual both as a union member and as a citizen.

When the rights of union members are perceived to be seriously jeopardized, however, all-out member participation may be expected. Those who remember the upheaval in Quebec during the Winter of 1982, when the provincial government rolled back the wages of workers in the public and parapublic sectors, realize that when workers' rights are threatened by external forces, workers will vote with their feet on the picket line. The Solidarity Coalition in British Columbia during the Summer of 1983, for instance, saw provincial restraints bring the province close to the brink of a general strike.

In summary, it seems that as long as things are going well, union members are content to delegate decision-making to the active unionists. However, if serious and contentious matters are perceived to arise internally, rank-and-file members will probably take appropriate action to protect their interests. At Inco, after having

struck for six months over the Fall of 1978 and the Winter of 1979, union members refused to be lured back to work by an offer which they perceived to be inadequate, despite the fact that this offer was recommended by their local president. Only after intensive negotiations between the union and management along with a shrewd mediator from the Ontario Ministry of Labour did the union members ratify a much improved offer. With respect to the participation of members in the affairs of their union, perhaps the issue may be stated in the form of the following hypothesis: *the more a union member perceives his or her interests to be affected by the action of a union leader, the more that union member will participate in union business.* The converse is true also.

Due Process and Remedies

Most unions have disciplinary clauses in their constitutions. Penalties include cancellation of union membership and, depending on the type of union security clause, loss of employment. Some clauses are very specific. Some are very vague and lend themselves to various interpretations. For example, clauses such as "Engaging in any activity or course of conduct contrary or detrimental to the welfare or best interests of the Association" and "Wilfully circulating false or defamatory statements or reports concerning members of the Association" are the vague types of clauses on which disciplinary action is often taken. Although there is great variation in the ways in which such behaviour is tried, often initial action is taken at the local level in which the committee investigating the case becomes both judge and jury. A person found guilty of an offence at the local level may appeal the case to the executive board of the union. If satisfaction is not obtained at that level, the case may go before a convention. At least two facts bring into question the effectiveness of this procedure. First, because of its size and number of activities, a convention is hardly an appropriate forum in which to have judgements made on such an important issue. Second, a convention may be several years down the road — this is a long time to wait for a hearing. Even worse, the courts usually will not hear such cases until internal union processes have been exhausted.

In order to hasten the appeals procedures and to provide for a fair hearing, the United Automobile Workers Union set up at its 1957 convention a Public Review Board composed entirely of independent outside persons. Under this scheme, a member who has been disciplined by a trial committee of his own local may appeal to the local union. If still dissatisfied, the member may then appeal to the international executive board, but such an appeal must be made within thirty days. If still dissatisfied, the member may appeal the case either to the convention or to the Public Review Board. Only cases involving the processing of grievances may, under some circumstances, come before both bodies. To ensure promptness, appeals must be filed within thirty days. All parties have the right to counsel, and the Board must make a public report every year.[59]

When the UAW created the Public Review Board, it was assumed that many other unions would follow suit. However, the Upholsterers Union is the only other union with an independent review board.[60] One reason other unions have not followed suit flows from the enactment in 1959 of the *Landrum-Griffin Act* which imposes very substantial controls on the internal operations of American unions. The *Landrum-Griffin Act* imposes a fiduciary responsibility on persons handling union funds, sets conditions for establishing and maintaining trusteeships over local unions, gives members a greater degree of control over their own activities, and allows candidates seeking to replace incumbent officials greater publicity in union newspapers and an appeal to the Secretary of Labour for a judicial recount if there is suspicion that union elections have been rigged. A number of recounts have occurred in fact: encumbents first declared winners have, after recounts, finished as losers. This occurred once in the Steelworkers Union and once in one of the unions which organizes electrical workers.

A recent assessment by an American writer of the effects of the *Landrum-Griffin Act* on internal union affairs concludes that

> By and large, the provisions of the Landrum-Griffin Act respecting internal union affairs have significantly advanced the cause of union democracy while doing little, if any, damage to the structure of organized labour.[61]

No comprehensive charter of rights exists for Canadian union members.

Women in Union Leadership

We noted earlier in this chapter the growing proportion of women in unions. A study done for the Canadian Advisory Council on the Status of Women concluded that in 1976, 42.6% of women trade unionists were in unions where women constituted over half the total membership in contrast to 32% in 1962. Between 1970 and 1975, women represented less than 10% of people serving on trade-union executive boards. By 1977, women constituted 28.6% of union membership and accounted for 16.7% of union executives.[62] By 1979, women accounted for 29.3% of total trade union membership.

Recently, many sectors of the Canadian trade union movement have actively encouraged women to take part in executive positions. The Ontario Federation of Labour, at its annual convention in 1983, took a significant step in creating five posts for women as vice-presidents of the 800,000-member federation. As a result, the number of vice-presidents increased from sixteen to twenty-one. Prior to this increase, there was only one woman among the sixteen vice-presidents.[63] At its 15th constitutional convention in Montreal in the Spring of 1984, the Canadian Labour Congress extended the number of vice-presidents at large from ten to fourteen, six of whom must be women.[64] Prior to the convention, a study of this subject had been done with the understanding that action would be taken at the 1986 convention.

In 1984, however, it was felt that enough studies had been done and that an affirmative action program was necessary. In his address to the convention, former CLC President Dennis McDermott acknowledged that there was no neat, orderly way in which to initiate affirmative action, but stated his position in the following terms: "We have to set an example by practicing what we preach. We can no longer tolerate our making sanctimonious lectures to employers and to governments while at the same time ignoring our own obligations."[65]

In May 1986, former CLC Secretary-Treasurer Shirley Carr replaced Dennis McDermott as President of the CLC, thus becoming the first woman to occupy that position.[66] Carr has had a long career in unions. She started in the public sector as a member of CUPE and was active in a tripartite committee of government, management, and union officials to establish the Labour Market and Productivity Centre in 1983. Generally considered more congenial than McDermott, Carr is expected to improve relations between the CLC and the Federal Government.

A women's bureau exists now in the CLC, as well as a special publishing apparatus to encourage women to participate in the decision-making process. The question of women in unions will certainly dominate much of the thinking in all ranks of the Canadian labour movement in the immediate future.

Conclusion

Given the fluid state of the Canadian labour movement at the present time, any attempts to predict what will happen in the future may have little value. Certain issues, however, such as the decline of our economy and the nationalistic orientations of certain Canadian unions, will doubtless have a profound effect on the labour movement. In particular, these may create demands on the CLC to interface effectively with government, especially at the federal level, in order to respond to the anxieties and aspirations of Canadian labour. How strong these demands will be and how effectively the CLC will respond to them is a subject for speculation.

Certainly the pressure is on the Canadian Labour Congress. The formation of the Canadian Federation of Labour in the Spring of 1982 may result in interunion raiding. It will be interesting to observe which of these two central federations will have the greater and more enduring influence in helping to shape policy at the national level. The more conservative philosophy and less provocative approach of the CFL may gain for it a more sympathetic ear among politicians in Ottawa, despite its much smaller size in comparison with the CLC.

questions

1 Discuss in detail the composition of the Canadian labour movement in the early 1980's.
2 Discuss the structure and function of the various components of the CLC.
3 Do you think that unions among professionals such as teachers, nurses, and engineers, will join the mainstream of the Canadian labour movement? Elaborate.
4 A union may be defined either as a voluntary association created by workers to improve their working conditions or as a power-accumulating and power-using entity concerned mainly with ensuring its own continued institutional existence. Do you see any major contradictions between these two definitions?
5 How do you assess the alignment of the CLC with the New Democratic Party? Has the NDP

done better in federal elections since it has received the full backing of the CLC? What conclusions can be drawn regarding the voting pattern of trade-unionists?
6 If you were an advisor to the President of the CLC, what strategy would you advise her to use in dealing with the Federal Government?
7 What is your prediction regarding future relations between the CLC and the Federal Government? Elaborate.
8 From a philosophical point of view, are there any differences in the unions operating in the public sector and those operating in the private sector? How do you explain the differences, if they exist?
9 Are union coalitions effective in your province when compared to the power of big business and big government? Elaborate.

10 Do you expect to see women occupying greater numbers of high-profile positions in Canadian trade unions in the near future? Elaborate. Do you think the election of Shirley Carr to CLC presidency will encourage women to seek leadership roles?

notes

1 Economics and Research Branch, Canada Department of Labour, *International Unions and the Canadian Trade Union Movement* (Ottawa: March 1956).

2 John Crispo, *International Unionism* (Toronto: McGraw-Hill, 1967), p. 171.

3 G. N. Chaison, "Union Mergers and International Unions in Canada," Vol. 34, No. 4, *Relations Industrielles* (1979), p. 773.

4 G. N. Chaison, "Unions: Growth, Structure, and Internal Dynamics," *Union-Management Relations in Canada*, eds. J. Anderson and M. Gunderson (Don Mills: Addison-Wesley, 1982), p. 162.

5 Labour Data Branch, Labour Canada, *Directory of Labour Organizations in Canada 1985* (Ottawa: Supply and Services Canada, 1985), pp. 287-88.

6 *Ibid.*, p. 287.

7 Wilfred List, "Working with Liberals Called Futile, So McDermott To Step Up Attacks," *Globe and Mail* (January 19, 1982), p. 1.

8 Virginia Galt, "Unions Cool to Caccia's Request for Input in Planning by Labour," *Globe and Mail* (January 9, 1982), p. B3.

9 Lorne Slotnick, "Visa Strikers Banking on Future," *Globe and Mail* (October 3, 1985), p. A23.

10 Labour Canada, *Directory of Labour Organizations 1985*, p. 288.

11 "That's Not Democracy, Mr. Buchanan," *Canadian Labour* (January 18, 1980), p. 11.

12 Jane O'Hara, "British Columbia on the Edge," *Macleans* (November 7, 1983), p. 22.

13 Ian Mulgrew, "Bennett Rules: Labour Licks Wounds," *Globe and Mail* (November 1, 1984).

14 *Ibid.*

15 Labour Canada, *Directory of Labour Organizations, 1985*, p. 288.

16 Goldblatt, *Justice Delayed* (Toronto: Labour Council of Metropolitan Toronto, 1974).

17 Labour Canada, *Directory of Labour Organizations, 1985*, p. 287.

18 *Ibid.*

19 Canadian Labour Congress, "How Unions Work," No. 2, *Notes on Unions* (Ottawa: n.d.). The Canadian Labour Congress has published a series of *Notes on Unions*. No. 2 of the series,

"How Unions Work," gives a very good description of how a union organizes, acquires its bargaining rights, and petitions the employer to negotiate with it. This article also includes a brief description of the negotiation process and the role that third parties may play in helping the two sides reach a collective agreement. A free copy of the *Notes* is available from the CLC, 2841 Riverside Drive, Ottawa K1V 8X7.

20 List, "Working with Liberals."

21 David Stewart-Patterson, "De Havilland Deal Angers MPs," *Globe and Mail* (December 3, 1985), pp. A1-A2.

22 Statistics Canada, *Annual Report of the Minister of Supply and Services Canada Under the Corporations and Labour Unions Returns Act* (Ottawa: Supply and Services Canada, July 1980), pp. 16, 69; "CALURA, Inaccurate, Incomplete, Imprecise," *Canadian Labour* (November/December, 1972), pp. 6-9.

23 Roy J. Adams, "Canada-U.S. Labor Link Under Stress," Vol. 15, No. 3, *Industrial Relations* (California: October 1976), pp. 295-312; and Crispo, *International Unionism*, p. 327.

24 Labour Canada, *Directory of Labour Organizations 1985*, pp. 146-47.

25 *Ibid.*, p. 64.

26 Adams, "Canada-U.S. Labor Link," p. 305.

27 *Ibid.*, p. 306.

28 M. Thompson and A. A. Blum, "International Unionism in Canada: The Move to Local Control," Vol. 22, No. 1, *Industrial Relations* (Winter 1983), pp. 76-77.

29 Wilfred List, "Showdown in UAW Could Lead to Historic Split," *Globe and Mail* (December 3, 1984), p. B13.

30 Lorne Slotnick, "Canadian UAW Splits from Parent Union," *Globe and Mail* (December 11, 1984), p. 2.

31 *Ibid.*, p. 1.

32 *Ibid.*

33 Lorne Slotnick, "All-Canadian UAW Opens New Chapter in History of Labour," *Globe and Mail* (September 5, 1985), p. 18.

34 Lorne Slotnick, "White Prefers UAW Deal to Long Fight," *Globe and Mail* (April 3, 1985), p. 8; and Wilfred List, "Little Change in Store

for Independent Canadian UAW," *Globe and Mail* (April 15, 1985), p. B5.

35 Wilfred List, "UAW-Canada, Chrysler Pact Shows Canadians Can Cut It," *Globe and Mail* (October 28, 1985), p. B4.

36 Canadian Labour Congress, "Canadian Standards of Self-Government," Addendum, *CLC Constitution*, pp. 48-49.

37 Thompson and Blum, "International Unionism in Canada," pp. 73-74.

38 *Ibid.*, p. 77.

39 *Ibid.*, pp. 73-74.

40 *Ibid.*, p. 74.

41 *Ibid.*, p. 83.

42 Dennis McDermott, "Ranking Officers of Affiliated Organizations, Federations of Labour and Labour Councils, Members of Executive Council," letter (November 3, 1978), p. 3. Reproduced by permission of Mr. McDermott.

43 "Strong CUPW Vote for Best Contract," *Canadian Labour* (June 20, 1981), p. 3.

44 Ed Finn, "Multi-Union Strike Fund Needed to Match Multinationals' Power," *Canadian Transport* (May 1979), p. 15.

45 Dennis McDermott, "The President's Address," Thirteenth Constitutional Convention of the CLC, *Proceedings* (Winnipeg May 5-9, 1980), p. 5.

46 W. L. Ginsburg, "Review of Literature on Union Growth, Government and Structure — 1955-1969," Vol. 1, Industrial Relations Research Association Series, *A Review of Industrial Relations Research*, eds. W. L. Ginsberg *et al.* (Madison: 1970), p. 241.

47 J. C. Anderson, "The Union Convention: An Examination of Limitations on Democratic Decision Making," Vol. 32, No. 3, *Relations Industrielles/Relations* (1977), p. 382.

48 *Ibid.*, pp. 395-96.

49 American Federation of Labour-Congress of Industrial Organization, *International Constitution of the United Packinghouse, Food and Allied Workers* (May 1962).

50 D. C. Bok and J. T. Dunlop, *Labor and the American Community* (New York: Simon and Schuster, 1970), p. 90.

51 G. N. Chaison and J. B. Rose, "Turnover Among Presidents of Canadian National Unions," Vol. 16, No. 2, *Industrial Relations* (May 1977), pp. 199-200.

52 *Ibid.*, p. 202.

53 Quoted in Chaison, "Unions: Growth," p. 165.

54 *Ibid.*

55 S. Muthuchidambaram, "Democracy as a Goal of Union Organization: An Interpretation of the United States Experience," Vol. 24, No. 3, *Relations Industrielles/Industrial Relations* (1969), p. 579.

56 W. Herberg, "Bureaucracy and Democracy in Labor Unions," *Readings in Labor Economics and Labor Relations*, Rev. ed., ed. R. L. Rowan (Homewood: Richard D. Irwin, 1972), p. 233.

57 M. Estey, *The Unions: Structure, Development and Management* (New York: Harcourt, Brace & World, 1967), p. 49.

58 *Ibid.*, p. 51.

59 United Auto Workers, *A More Perfect Union: The UAW Public Review Board* (Detroit: Solidarity House, UAW Publications, n.d.). This booklet includes the AFL-CIO Code of Ethical Practices as well as the UAW's resolution on ethical practices adopted by the 16th Constitutional Convention on April 8, 1957.

60 Ginsburg, "Review of Literature on Union Growth," p. 239.

61 T. J. St. Antoine, "The Role of Law," *U.S. Industrial Relations 1950-1980: A Critical Assessment*, eds. J. Stieber, R. B. McKersie, and D. Q. Mills (Madison: Industrial Relations Research Association Series, 1981), p. 191.

62 Julie White, *Women and Unions* (Ottawa: Supply and Services Canada, April 1980), pp. 22-23.

63 Wildred List, "Fight for Women's Equality Gains Momentum in Unions," *Globe and Mail* (December 5, 1983), p. B4.

64 *Ibid.*

65 Dennis McDermott, "The President's Address," Fifteenth Constitutional Convention of the CLC, *Proceedings* (Ottawa: May-June 1984), p. 10.

66 Lorne Slotnick, "Carr Picked for Top Job on CLC Executive Slate," *Globe and Mail* (December 12, 1985), p. A24.

Peter Redman, *The Financial Post*

6

Legislation Governing Industrial Relations in the Private Sector

Introduction

Canada is a federal state with the central government exercising jurisdiction over only about 10% of the labour force and the ten provinces claiming the remaining 90%. From a legal perspective, this makes the industrial relations system of Canada the most decentralized of any country in the world. As will be demonstrated later in this chapter, parties in the Canadian system, and especially those in the private sector who operate in more than one province, find themselves confronted with a maze of legislative provisions and with administrative machinery which may vary greatly from one jurisdiction to another. The powers of the federal and provincial governments are presented below in order to provide a context for the evolution of government policy as it applies to industrial relations.

The Division of Powers Between the Federal and Provincial Governments

When the Fathers of Confederation developed the *British North America Act* (now the *Constitution Act, 1867*)[1] they thought they had framed a constitution which had given residual powers to the Federal Government. As Dawson has pointed out, "The provinces were to be inferior bodies possessing little more prestige and authority than inflated municipalities."[2] The *Constitution Act* sets forth the powers of the federal and provincial governments in Sections 91 and 92 respectively. Section 91 contains a general grant of legislative power to make laws for the peace, order and good government of Canada. The section goes on to stipulate twenty-nine specific classes of subjects falling within the exclusive jurisdiction of the Federal Government. Section 92 sets forth the powers of the provinces and contains 16 classes of subjects.

While neither Section 91 nor Section 92 refers specifically to labour-management relations, the following provisions of Section 91 do relate either directly or indirectly to this subject: (2) The regulation of trade and commerce; (10) Navigation and shipping; (13) Ferries between a province and any British or foreign country or between two provinces; (16) Savings banks; (27) The criminal law; and (29) "[S]uch Classes of Subjects as are expressly excepted in the Enumeration of the Classes of Subjects by this Act assigned exclusively to the Legislatures of the Provinces." Among the 16 classes of subjects under Section 92 which have become relevant to industrial relations are those relating to: (8) Municipal institutions in the province; (10) Local works and undertakings; and (13) Property and civil rights in the provinces. As we shall see later, the enumerated classes of subjects in Section 92, by legal interpretation, were to have a very significant impact on the legislative structure governing policy in the field of industrial relations in Canada. It was through legal interpretation that the Federal Government found itself with jurisdiction over only about 10% of the labour force.

Public Policy Issues in Industrial Relations

Legislative policy regulating industrial relations has historically been directed to four or five major issues in Canada. These include: (1) the legal right of workers to organize into legal entities called unions or associations, a subject that was discussed in Chapter 2; (2) the process by which unions gain recognition as bargaining agents for groups of workers; (3) the duty to bargain in good faith as it applies to employers and unions in contract negotiations and the various forms of third-party assistance required or provided; (4) the application of the clauses contained in collective agreements to specific and concrete work situations; and (5) the handling of jurisdictional disputes between or among unions as to which union has the right to represent workers doing a particular type of work, especially in the construction industry. Items (2) to (5) listed above are the classical issues with which labour relations legislation and the machinery established under it have been concerned. In recent years, other policy issues have been added to the traditional list, namely: (1) the duty of fair representation of members by unions; (2) compulsory dues check-offs; (3) the imposition of first collective agreements; (4) exemption from payment of union dues for religious reasons; (5) provisions dealing with the impact of technological change on workers.

The Development of Private-Sector Legislation

Early Legislation

Before getting into a detailed analysis of the current provisions governing labour-management relations, it is necessary to examine briefly some of the more important statutes which have had a significant impact on trade unions and labour-management relations generally. This section will deal only with the federal jurisdiction. Readers may refer to other sources for information on developments in the provinces.[3]

The first major Canadian statutes were the *Trade Unions Act* and the *Criminal Law Amendment Act*, both of which were passed by Parliament in 1872 following a strike of printers in Toronto. These laws were modelled after similar legislation which had been passed in Great Britain a year earlier. Their main thrust was to free trade unions from charges of criminal conspiracy, which was considered a crime against the state, and which made the formation of unions an act punishable by fines or imprisonment or both. Although these early statutes permitted workers to unionize, employers were not required by law to recognize unions as the exclusive bargaining agents for groups of workers and were legally free to punish workers for belonging to a trade union. According to H. D. Woods, it took a 1939 amendment to the Criminal Code to prohibit the latter kind of behaviour, and, in so doing, to establish the principle that employers should not be permitted to take away the workers' right to unionize.[4]

Another important development was the *Conciliation Act* of 1900 which authorized the Minister of Labour to appoint conciliation boards to aid in the settlement of disputes when requested to do so by employers or unions or both. The *Act* was voluntary in nature so that if the unions or employers involved refused to appear before the conciliation board, they were not required to do so. The first element of compulsion came in the form of the *Railway Labour Disputes Act* of 1903, which was passed by the Federal Government after a strike on the Canadian Pacific Railway. The *Act*, as its title suggests, only covered railway transportation. It provided for a three-person board of conciliation, and was constituted in the now familiar Canadian pattern whereby the employer appoints one nominee, the union a second, and the two nominees jointly elect a third person as chairman. This law was used very infrequently and, in 1906, the *Conciliation Act* of 1900 and the *Railway Labour Disputes Act* of 1903 were combined to form the *Conciliation and Labour Act*. While this law still remains on the books, it has not been used to any great extent.*

* When the Labour Department was asked to present a brief before the Senate Committee on Science Policy, it was only under the terms of the *Conciliation Act* of 1900 and the *Conciliation and Labour Act* of 1906 that researchers could find any statutory basis for the Labour Department engaging in statistical and other research studies.

The first significant federal statute was the *Industrial Disputes Investigation (IDI) Act of 1907.*[5] The long title reads as follows: "An Act to Aid in the Prevention and Settlement of Strikes and Lockouts in Mines and Industries Connected with Public Utilities." While the term *public utility* was not explained in the statute, the term *employer* was defined in Section 2(c) as:

> Any person, company or corporation employing ten or more persons and owning or operating any mining property, agency of transportation or communication, or public service utility, including... railways, whether operated by steam, electricity or other motive power, steamships, telegraph and telephone lines, gas, electric light, water and power works.

By a 1920 amendment, the following was added to Section 2(c):

> Or any number of such persons, companies or corporations acting together, or who in the opinion of the Minister have interests in common.

The *IDI Act* was passed following a major coal strike in Lethbridge, Alberta in 1906. Its main point was that parties subject to its provisions had to submit outstanding disputes to a tripartite conciliation board for investigation and recommendations before a strike or lockout could become legal. This requirement extended the compulsory element in labour-management relations in Canada. This *Act* was also important in that it gave the Federal Government broad jurisdiction over labour relations in mining and public utilities, whether national or local. It was equally significant that the 1920 amendment should have extended application of the *Act* to multi-employer bargaining, either on a provincial or national basis. If the *Act* had not been challenged and overturned by judicial decision, this provision, along with others making the *Act* available to any trade or industry by joint agreement of both sides, would have enabled the parties involved in any national set of negotiations to establish one board to deal with their disputes.

Following the outbreak of World War I, the Parliament of Canada was called into a special session. One of the resulting laws was the *War Measures Act* of 1914 which authorized the Federal Government to take whatever steps were necessary for the security, defence, peace, order, and welfare of Canada. Under the authority of this law, the *IDI Act* was amended in 1918 to bring "industries essential to the war effort" under its provisions. A large number of Orders-in-Council were also enacted under the authority of the *War Measures Act* during World War II. These Orders-in-Council broadened the jurisdiction of the Federal Government.

In the 1920's, two cases arose which challenged the constitutionality of the *IDI Act;* both involved the application of the *Act* to local public utilities.[6] The first case, initiated by the Montreal Street Railway Company, challenged the *Act* on constitutional grounds. The statute was upheld, however, by the Supreme Court of Quebec and, upon appeal, by the Court of Review of the Montreal district which held that it was both constitutional and *intra vires* (within the power) of the Federal Parliament.[7]

The second case, and the one that ultimately led the to the *Act* being declared unconstitutional, was the now famous *Toronto Electric Power Commissioners v. Snider et al.* (hereafter referred to as the *Snider* case). The *Snider* case arose out of the refusal of the Toronto Electric Power Commission to recognize the authority of a board of conciliation and investigation appointed to deal with a dispute between the Commission and its workers. The commissioners made application to the Supreme Court of Ontario for an interim injunction to restrain the board from proceeding. The ground used in the application was that

---

Table 6.1   A Chronology of Important Statutes

1872	The *Trade Unions Act* and the *Criminal Law Amendment Act* freed unions from charges of criminal conspiracy.
1900	The *Conciliation Act* did not require the parties to appear before a conciliation board.
1903	The *Railway Labour Disputes Act* applied only to railways.
1907	The *Industrial Disputes Investigation Act (IDI Act)* required parties to appear before a conciliation board, and prohibited strike or lockout action until the board's report was handed down.
1925	The *Snider* case limited the jurisdiction of the Federal Government to a few national industries and services.
1944	P.C. 1003—The Wartime Labour Relations Regulations— contained many features of the American *Wagner Act* and the compulsory conciliation features of the *IDI Act.*
1948	The *Industrial Relations and Disputes Investigation (IRDI Act),* a federal Act, applied to only 10% of the labour force. Its provisions were like those of the Wartime Labour Relations Regulations. The ten provinces acquired jurisdiction over the remaining 90% of the labour force.
1972	Part V of the Canada Labour Code (on federal industrial relations) replaced the *IRDI Act* at the federal level. Also, legislation at the provincial level covers about 90% of the labour force. A comparison of the provisions of the eleven statutes (one federal and ten provincial) forms the subject matter of most of the remainder of this chapter.

the Federal Government did not have jurisdiction to apply the *Act* to municipal employers or to enact laws affecting civil rights. The judgement of the Appellate Division of the Supreme Court of Ontario was rendered on April 22, 1924 by Mr. Justice Ferguson. Three other justices concurred with Ferguson's decision; one dissented.

In upholding the constitutionality of the *IDI Act* falling within the competence of the Federal Government, Mr. Justice Ferguson reasoned that

> Industrial disputes are not now regarded as matters concerning only a disputing employer and his employees. It is common knowledge that such disputes are matters of public interest and concern, and frequently of national and international importance. This is so, not because the disputes may result in many plants being shut down...but because experience has taught that such disputes not infrequently develop into quarrels wherein or by reason whereof public wrongs are done and crimes are committed, and the safety of the public and the public peace are endangered and broken, and the national trade and commerce is disturbed and hindered by strikes and lockouts extending, not only throughout the Dominion, but frequently to the United States, where most of our trade unions have their headquarters. Being of opinion that the Act is not one to control or regulate contractual or civil rights, but one to authorize an inquiry into conditions or disputes and that the prevention of crimes, the protection of public safety, peace and order and the protection of trade and commerce are of the 'pith and substance and paramount purposes' of the Industrial Disputes Investigation Act and of the enquiry authorized and directed thereby, I think the legislation may and should be supported on the powers conferred upon the Dominion Parliament by Section 91, British North America Act, to make laws 'in relation to' 'the regulation of trade and commerce,' and to make laws 'in relation to' 'the criminal law' in its widest sense.[8]

Of the twelve Canadian judges who reviewed the *IDI Act*, ten upheld its constitutionality on the ground that labour disputes were of sufficient importance to the national life of Canada as to require their regulation by the Federal Government. When the *Snider* case came before the Judicial Committee of the British Privy Council, the court of last resort at the time in Canadian constitutional cases and a body far removed from the social and economic realities of Canadian life, a view was taken which differed greatly from that of the Canadian judges. The judgement was written by Justice Viscount Haldane and was handed down on January 20, 1925. The Judicial Committee held that the *Act* was unconstitutional since it interfered with property, civil rights, and municipal institutions:

> It is clear that this enactment was one which was competent to the Legislature of a Province under s. 92. In the present case the substance of it was possibly competent, not merely under the head of property and civil rights in the Province, but also under that of municipal institutions in the Province.[9]

Although many of the early decisions of the Judicial Committee gave a fairly broad construction to the federal powers, there was a marked trend in favour of provincial autonomy from 1912 to 1932, a period designated by F. P. Varcoe as the Provincial Period. As Varcoe observed, "Viscount Haldane wrote the reasons for judgement in twenty-five cases during this period, and an examination of these judgements discloses a clear purpose to protect the autonomy of the provinces."[10]

A number of leading Canadian authorities deplore the decision taken by the Judicial Committee.[11] Problems caused by provincial jurisdiction in the meat-packing industry—where negotiations have taken place on a national basis until recently—support the contention that the Committee made a mistake in the *Snider* decision. As late as 1968, four distinguished Canadian academics, declared in the *Task Force Report on Labour Relations*:

> One of our major recommendations is that there be a relaxation in the present practice of finality in determining bargaining units in order that the structure of collective bargaininug may have a better chance of finding its own level. Another set of significant recommendations bears upon conciliation and other methods of dispute settlement, especially in potential emergency disputes. Federal

policy in these areas can be applicable only to industries within its jurisdiction. In industries such as meat packing, which has proved to have many national characteristics while remaining within provincial jurisdiction, a continuing scheme of coordination will be required in order to maintain a *de facto* national bargaining unit.[12]

What the members of the Task Force had in mind is that union and management in any industry should be able to form large bargaining units without constitutional or legislative encumbrances.

Following the *Snider* case, the Federal Government passed a bill in June 1925 which attempted to salvage at least part of the *IDI Act of 1907*. The *Act*, as amended, applied to all works or undertakings which were within the legislative competence of the Federal Government, including navigation and shipping, lines of steam or other ships, railways, canals, telephones, and other works connecting one province with another. It also contained a clause enabling the Governor-in-Council to apply its provisions to any dispute considered to be of a real or anticipated national emergency. More importantly, the *Act* could be applied to any dispute which was within the legislative competence of the provinces, but which was made subject by provincial enactment to the amended federal statute. In this way, the Federal Government invited the provinces to negate the effect of the *Snider* case.

By June, 1926, five provinces — British Columbia, Saskatchewan, Manitoba, New Brunswick, and Nova Scotia — had passed enabling legislation which made the federal law applicable to provincial disputes of the nature contemplated in the original federal statute. The British Columbia legislation, which was typical of the laws enacted, stated:

> The provisions of the 'Industrial Disputes Investigation Act,' chapter 20 of the Acts of the Parliament of Canada, 1907, and amendments thereto, shall apply to every industrial dispute of the nature therein defined which is within or subject to the exclusive legislative jurisdiction of the province.[13]

By 1932, all the provinces except Prince Edward Island had taken similar legislative action. This situation remained basically unchanged until 1937 when the provinces began to pass more elaborate labour legislation of their own. This movement on the part of the provinces would undoubtedly have continued if World War II had not temporarily transferred jurisdiction over labour relations to the Federal Government. Although most of the provinces did enact legislation during World War II, the Federal Government used its authority under the *War Measures Act* of 1914 to play a dominant role in the field of labour-management relations.

Wartime Legislation Prior to P.C. 1003

Shortly after the outbreak of World War II, the Federal Government issued Order-in-Council P.C. 3495 which extended the provisions of the federal *IDI Act* to disputes between employers and workers engaged in defence projects and in industries producing munitions and war supplies. The extensive definitions of defence projects and war supplies included many kinds of materials and equipment: it has been estimated that P.C. 3495 raised the coverage of the *IDI Act* from 15% to 85% of the non-agricultural industries.[14] The Order also gave the Minister of Labour considerable discretion in determining which specific industries to bring under the jurisdiction of the Federal Government, a power which he employed extensively during the early years of World War II.

On June 19, 1940, the Federal Government issued a Declaration of Principles (Order-in-Council P.C. 2685) in an attempt to avoid wartime labour unrest. These principles were based largely on those of American labour legislation, specifically, the *Wagner Act* of 1935. The *Wagner Act* provided for the formation of unions by workers, required employers to bargain in good faith with duly certified unions, outlawed unfair labour practices by employers and workers, and, most importantly, established the National

Labour Relations Board (NLRB) to administer the *Act*.

P.C. 2685 advocated, among other things, the recognition of fair and reasonable standards of wages and working conditions; safeguards and regulations to protect the health and safety of workers; no interruption in industrial operations by strikes or lockouts; freedom of workers to organize into trade unions without interference from employers; and freedom of workers through their representatives to negotiate with employers or employers' associations concerning wages, hours, and other working conditions.[15] The Order, however, differed from the *Wagner Act* inasmuch as it provided for no administrative machinery, such as the NLRB. Nevertheless, it did set the general legislative pattern later contained in Order-in-Council P.C. 1003 of 1944. Professor Logan suggests that labour dissatisfaction with the 1940 Declaration of Principles, as expressed in suggestions put forward by the Canadian Congress of Labour, was largely responsible for the compulsory legislation that later came into being.[16]

Orders-in-Council P.C. 4020 and P.C. 4844 (June-July, 1941) established an Industrial Disputes Inquiry Commission to assist in settling disputes falling under the purview of the *IDI Act* and to investigate charges of discrimination or intimidation by employers. The Commission, composed of one or more members, could act more promptly than conciliation boards in settling disputes. In effect, the Commission also established what would become the conciliation officer role.

The right to strike in Canadian war industries was restricted by Order-in-Council P.C. 7303 of September 1941.[17] This Order made any strike in a war industry illegal until: (1) the findings of a board of conciliation had been delivered to the parties; (2) the workers had notified the federal Minister of Labour that they were contemplating a strike; (3) a vote of the workers had been taken under the supervision of the Depart-

ment of Labour, subject to whatever provisions and restrictions the Minister of Labour might impose; and (4) a majority of the workers involved voted in favour of a strike. This action was taken by the Government to prevent strikes and, thus, to ensure minimum interference with war production.[18]

Order-in-Council P.C. 1003

By far the most important piece of federal labour relations legislation in Canada during World War II was Order-in-Council P.C. 1003 of February 17, 1944, better known as the Wartime Labour Relations Regulations.[19] The Regulations combined principles taken from the *Wagner Act* with compulsory two-stage conciliation procedures for the settlement of contract negotiation disputes. They defined the rights of workers to organize into trade unions, made provision for the certification of bargaining agents (a process whereby unions acquire the right to negotiate with employers), required employers and unions to bargain in good faith for the purpose of obtaining a collective agreement, provided for a two-stage compulsory conciliation process to aid the parties in contract negotiations, required that collective agreements contain a procedure for settling disputes without stoppage of work during the term of a collective agreement, defined the unfair labour practices of employers and workers, and prohibited strikes or lockouts during contract negotiations until fourteen days after a conciliation board had handed down its report.

Sections 23 to 28 of the Order provided for the administration of the Regulations by the Wartime Labour Relations Board (WLRB) consisting of a chairman, vice-chairman, and not more than eight other members. Section 36(2) empowered the federal Minister of Labour to enter into an agreement with the government of any province to provide for the administration of the Regulations within that province. Section 39(1) gave the Minister the authority to appoint administrative officers or agencies in any province and to delegate to them powers necessary to the proper administration of the Regulations. Such agreements were intended to permit appeals from the provincial agency to the WLRB as well as to provide for reimbursement of expenses to the provinces.

As the above discussion indicates, Order-in-Council P.C. 1003 established for all intents and purposes a national labour policy from 1944 until the end of World War II. It not only gave workers the right to join unions for the purpose of collective bargaining but also to set up administrative machinery whereby they could demonstrate whether or not unions had sufficient support to be certified as bargaining agents on behalf of groups of workers. This was an important provision of the Regulations since, before that time, many strikes were conducted over the problem of union recognition. Like the NLRB in the United States, the WLRB in Canada could, upon application by a trade union, define a bargaining unit and conduct a vote, if necessary, to see if a majority of the workers in the bargaining unit supported the union named in the application as their bargaining agent. The Regulations also made it illegal for unions to strike over the issue of recognition. As well, they provided for a two-stage conciliation procedure which was to be used if the parties failed to agree through negotiations of their own. Assistance could be provided first by a single conciliation officer and then, if the impasse continued, by a conciliation board. Contract negotiation disputes, however, had not yet been taken out of the strike area. If no agreement was reached either through negotiations or with the help of third parties, unions were still free to strike and employers free to lockout. These provisions remain in operation to this day.

Another major principle contained in the Regulations was that no strike or lockout was to occur during the life of a collective agreement. As a quid pro quo for this provision, however, every collective agreement was assumed to contain a clause whereby any conflict over the interpretation or application of a provision of a collective agreement would be handled through a grievance procedure, the last step of which included binding arbitration before a tripartite board.

In preparing for the return to peacetime control over labour relations, a Dominion-Provincial Conference of Labour Ministers was held in Ottawa from October 15 to 17, 1946.[20] During this meeting, the Federal Minister made a good case for a national labour code. He indicated that since collective bargaining had been changing rapidly without regard to provincial boundaries or jurisdictions, it seemed advisable, in the interests of labour, management, and the nation as a whole, to establish laws and to set a standard pattern of administration in order to deal effectively with difficulties which might arise in labour-management relations. Most of the provinces, however, were unwilling to concede to the Federal Government the broad jurisdiction which it sought. The Federal Government concentrated, therefore, on updating legislation pertaining to workers subject to federal labour legislation.

After hearing many briefs, the Federal Government passed Bill 195 during the 1947-48 session of Parliament to become effective on September 1, 1948.[21] The new law, entitled *The Industrial Relations and Disputes Investigation Act (IRDI)*, applied to only the 10% of the Canadian labour force under federal jurisdiction. Works or undertakings covered by the *Act* included navigation and shipping, railways, canals and telegraphs, lines of steam or other ships, interprovincial ferries, aerodromes, aircraft, and lines of transport and radio broadcasting.

The *IRDI Act* was much the same as the Wartime Labour Relations Regulations: it made provision for voluntary recognition of unions by employers, certification by the Canada Labour Relations Board (CLRB) in industries within its jurisdiction, the duty to bargain in good faith, unfair labour practices by unions and employers, third-party assistance in the form of a two-stage compulsory conciliation process (officer to be followed by a board), no-strike and no-lockout restrictions, and compulsory arbitration of contract interpretation disputes.

Post-War Responses Among the Provinces

When jurisdiction over labour relations returned to the provinces in the early part of 1948, the Federal Wartime Regulations served as a general model for most of the provinces. Ontario adopted the federal legislation almost in its entirety. In 1950, however, Ontario enacted a statute which followed the federal model, but also more accurately reflected the province's industrial structure. Legislation in Nova Scotia and Manitoba was substantially the same as the federal legislation. Alberta and British Columbia consolidated previous legislation in 1947 and included some provisions from P.C. 1003. Quebec and Saskatchewan continued their legislation which differed somewhat from that of the other provinces: Saskatchewan, for example, did not until recently require labour and management to use compulsory conciliation if negotiations between the two parties fail to bring about an agreement. It should also be noted that the Saskatchewan *Trade Union Act* covers workers in both the private and public sectors. Prince Edward Island enacted its *Trade Union Act* in 1945 which required collective bargaining, but which provided machinery neither for determining questions of representation nor for settling disputes.

During the 1950's there was a general model for labour relations legislation. This model applied across the country although there were some minor variations from one jurisdiction to another. From the 1960's on, however, there have been various deviations from the standard model. It is impossible in the short space allocated for this chapter to treat the various developments for all eleven jurisdictions in Canada from the 1960's to the early 1980's. What follows is a comparison of many current provisions in labour relations legislation, dealing mainly with the traditional or classical types of disputes such as those involving union recogni-tion, contract negotiations (interest disputes), contract interpretation (rights disputes) and questions of jurisdiction. In addition, a number of recent policy initiatives are dealt with briefly.

Positive Perspectives on Unions and Collective Bargaining

In the period immediately following World War II, most of the statutes in Canada did not contain an explicitly stated positive commitment for the promotion of unionization and collective bargaining. Instead, these statutes confined themselves to definitions of major terms. Over the course of years, however, four jurisdictions — the federal, British Columbia, Manitoba and Ontario — have amended their legislation to express this commitment. The positive tone is in keeping with the following recommendation regarding federal legislation made by the Prime Minister's Task Force on Labour Relations in 1968:

> In order to encourage and ensure recognition of the social purpose of collective bargaining legislation as an instrument for the advancement of fundamental freedoms in our industrial society, we recommend that the legislation contain a preamble that would replace the neutral tone of the present statute with a positive commitment to the collective bargaining system.[22]

While the Manitoba and Ontario statutes contain only very short clauses, Part V of the Canada Labour Code commences with a full page of preambles indicating the commitment of the Federal Government to unionism, free collective bargaining and the constructive settlement of industrial disputes. A similar affirmation in the British Columbia Labour Code is contained in Section 27 which deals with the purposes and objectives of the British Columbia Labour Relations Board (BCLRB). Under Section 27, the BCLRB is charged with securing and maintaining industrial peace, and with furthering harmonious relations between employers and workers by (1) improving the practices and procedures of collective bargaining between employers and trade unions, and (2) promoting conditions favourable to the orderly and constructive settlements of disputes between employers and workers or their freely-chosen trade unions.[23]

George Bain thought it desirable that other jurisdictions include a statement of a positive commitment in their respective statutes.[24] It is almost impossible, however, to estimate what effect, if any, these affirmations have on the degree of unionization and the process of collective bargaining.

Coverage of the Statutes

The statutes of most jurisdictions in Canada governing the private sector give a broad interpretation to the range of workers covered under them. Some jurisdictions, however, do not. Alberta, Nova Scotia, and Prince Edward Island, for example, exclude from their coverage members of the medical, dental, legal, architectural, and engineering professions. Ontario excludes the same professions, except engineers, and adds to that list land surveyors and people employed in agriculture, hunting, trapping, horticulture, and domestic care.[25] Prince Edward Island, New Brunswick, and Nova Scotia statutes, however, cover police officers and accord them the right to strike.

All labour relations jurisdictions in Canada exclude workers acting in a confidential capacity in matters relating to industrial relations or who exercise managerial functions. A new provision in the Manitoba statute and a fairly recent amendment to Part V of the Canada Labour Code gives supervisors the right to collective bargaining. The latter statute is a new phenomenon in the private sector, and responds in part to recent legislation governing public and parapublic workers. In addition, following the publication of the *Report of the Task Force on Labour Relations,* a number of jurisdictions now grant collective bargaining rights to independent contractors such as taxi drivers and delivery workers for milk companies and retail stores, and others. It may reasonably be expected that in the not too distant future supervisory workers and independent contractors may be covered by the statutes of all private-sector legislation in Canada.

It is difficult to understand why some jurisdictions exclude certain categories of workers while others include these same categories. There seems to be no logical reason why *all* workers should not have the *right* to unionize and engage in collective bargaining.

Recognition Disputes

Prior to P.C. 1003 of 1944, the only ways unions could become bargaining agents for a group of workers were through voluntary recognition by employers or the use of strike action to force such recognition. P.C. 1003 changed all of this by prohibiting strikes for recognition and by establishing the Wartime Labour Relations Board through which unions could seek certification if they obtained the required level of worker support. Certain concepts are notable in the recognition dispute. The definition of the term *appropriate bargaining unit* and of the manner in which a union may gain recognition as the sole bargaining agent for a group of workers are two such notable concepts discussed in detail below.

Bargaining Units

A bargaining unit is normally a unit of workers considered to be appropriate for collective bargaining. Usually, statutes set out broad terms of reference in this regard. Labour relations boards make the fine distinctions about who should and who should not be included in units proposed by bargaining agents (unions). A typically broad definition is contained in the Ontario statute. This statute states that a bargaining unit may be a plant unit, or a sub-division thereof. The unit may consist exclusively of specialized craft or technical workers or workers

Table 6.2

The Four Classical Types of Labour Relations Disputes

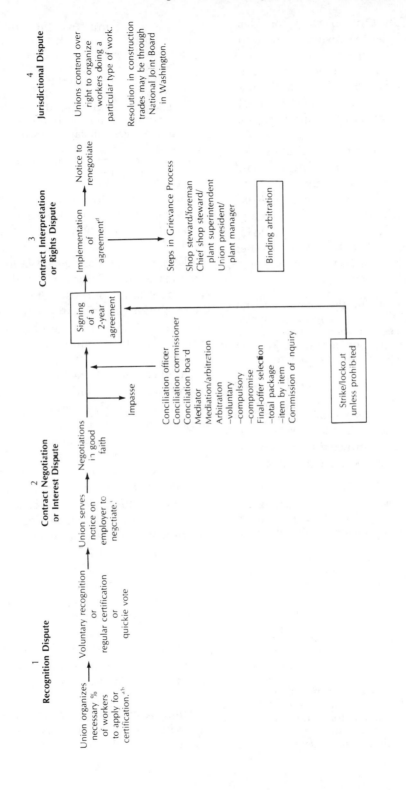

**1
Recognition Dispute**

Union organizes necessary % of workers to apply for certification.[a,b] → Voluntary recognition or regular certification or quickie vote →

**2
Contract Negotiation or Interest Dispute**

Union serves notice on employer to negotiate.[c] → Negotiations in good faith →

Impasse

Conciliation officer
Conciliation commissioner
Conciliation board
Mediator
Mediation/arbitration
Arbitration
 –voluntary
 –compulsory
 –compromise
Final-offer selection
 –total package
 –item by item
Commission of inquiry

Signing of a 2-year agreement

Strike/lockout unless prohibited

**3
Contract Interpretation or Rights Dispute**

Implementation of agreement[d] → Notice to renegotiate

Steps in Grievance Process

Shop steward/foreman
Chief shop steward/
plant superintendent
Union president/
plant manager

Binding arbitration

**4
Jurisdictional Dispute**

Unions contend over right to organize workers doing a particular type of work.

Resolution in construction trades may be through National Joint Board in Washington.

Unfair Labour Practices

a Employer fires workers for trying to unionize.
b Union uses coercive tactics in trying to organize employees.
c One or both parties fail to negotiate in good faith.
d Union fails to provide fair representation.

with diverse skills. The Ontario statute considers engineers, for example, to constitute a unit appropriate for collective bargaining, but the Board may include professional engineers in a unit with other workers if it is satisfied that the majority of the engineers agree to this.[26] Generally, at least two workers are necessary to form a bargaining unit.

A bargaining agent is a union. Unions seek to represent workers in a bargaining unit and propose the form that the bargaining unit should take. It is up to the board in each jurisdiction to determine whether or not the bargaining units proposed by unions are appropriate for collective bargaining. Unlike the statutes of other provinces, the *Nova Scotia Trade Union Act* gives a specific mandate in certification cases:

> The Board in determining the appropriate unit shall have regard to the community of interest among the employees in the proposed unit in such matters as work location, hours of work, working conditions and methods of remuneration.[27]

Labour relations boards in Canada have a long history of fleshing out the skeleton provisions contained in most provincial statutes. This detailing has occurred on a case-by-case basis. According to a study conducted by Edward E. Herman, ten criteria are used in defining appropriate bargaining units:

1 the purposes, intent, and provisions of the legislation governing the certification and determination of appropriateness of bargaining units within the particular jurisdiction;

2 the community or mutuality of interest with respect to wages, hours, and working conditions among the workers concerned;

3 the prior history and pattern of collective bargaining of the bargaining unit in question;

4 the history and nature of the proposed bargaining agent (union) and any dealings it has had with other workers of the same employer or with other employers in the same industry or area;

5 the desires of the workers concerning which bargaining agent they wish to belong to;

6 the eligibility of workers for membership in a particular labour organization;

7 the employer's administrative set-up and the way the unit fits into the company's organization;

8 the collective bargaining record of an existing bargaining agent with regard to the workers in a unit previously certified as appropriate;

9 prior decisions from which policy principles emerged concerning the establishment, or other establishments of the same employer or of identical, similar, or analogous industries; and

10 the agreement of the parties on a proposed bargaining unit.[28]

All ten criteria are not used each time a board considers a certification case. For example, a 1977 Canada Labour Relations Board certification case used only three: the community of interests of workers, the intent of the legislation under Part V of the Canada Labour Code, and the practicality of the unit for purposes of organization.[29] In the resolution of certification cases, according to Herman, boards most frequently use the criterion of the community of interests of workers.

Other considerations in defining appropriate bargaining units include the status of seasonal and part-time workers, and the choice between single-plant, multi-plant, single-employer, or multi-employer bargaining units. Those interested in pursuing the subject of appropriate bargaining units should read Herman's work *Determination of the Appropriate Bargaining Unit by Labour Relations Boards in Canada*.[30]

Political considerations may also influence the determination of bargaining units. One notable example is the Michelin Bill passed in Nova Scotia in December, 1979. Under this legislation, unions in manufacturing sectors where work is organized on an interdependent basis between plants may only be certified on a multi-plant basis—that is, *all* plants belonging to each company in question must be certified.[31] Unionization of multi-plant companies in manufacturing industries is thus very difficult.

Board Determination of Appropriate Bargaining Units Once a union has made an application to become the bargaining agent for a pro-

Table 6.3 — **A Comparison of Provisions Dealing with Certification**

Jurisdiction	% support needed to apply for certification	% support where boards are mandated to certify without a vote	% support needed to apply for a prehearing vote[ab]	% support necessary to certify a union when a vote is taken	
				50% of those in the bargaining unit	50% of those voting
Federal	35	50 or more	35		X
Newfoundland[c]	50		40	X	
Prince Edward Island	50		not specified		X
Nova Scotia	40	50 or more	N/R		X
New Brunswick	40-60	60 or more	40	X	
Quebec	35	50 or more	35	X	
Ontario	45-55	55 or more	35		X
Manitoba	45-55	55 or more	45		X
Saskatchewan	25		N/R		X
Alberta	50	50 or more	N/R		X
British Columbia[d]	45	must conduct a vote	45		X

[a]In most jurisdictions, the boards usually have the power to certify the union or bargaining agent without a vote if there is concrete evidence that over 50% of the members want the union.

[b]Includes those statutes that make specific reference to a prehearing vote.

[c]In Newfoundland, the Board may direct its chief executive officer to conduct an investigation where an application has been made and if not less than 40% and not more than 50% of members are in good standing in the union, the chief executive officer shall cause a representation vote to be taken.

[d]In British Columbia, a 1984 amendment to its Labour Code requires that a certification vote be held in every case, no matter what support the union can demonstrate that it has.

posed bargaining unit, the labour relations board must define whether or not the proposed bargaining unit is *appropriate*. Once the union has made its application, the board sends a copy of the application to the employer in question. The employer must then post the application in a place conspicuous enough to be seen by all workers concerned. Should the employer or members of the proposed bargaining unit wish to take exception to the make-up of the unit suggested by the union, they may ask the labour relations board to include or delete certain categories of workers. The board may then send a field officer to the employer's premises to investigate the request, or hold a hearing at which all parties may make their representations and petitions, or both. The board must then decide which categories of workers form a bargaining unit appropriate for collective bargaining purposes in that particular situation. This determination of what constitutes the appropriate bargaining unit in each case is noted in the certificate approving the union as the bargaining agent.

Certification of Bargaining Agents

There are three basic ways in which a bargaining agent or union may obtain recognition to represent a group of workers. These are (1) voluntary recognition, (2) the regular certification process, and (3) the prehearing vote.

Voluntary Recognition A union may organize a majority of the workers in a bargaining unit that it proposes, and then approach the employer to obtain approval as the bargaining agent for that unit. Usually, the union will either list the types of occupational categories to be included or make a general statement to the effect that the bargaining unit shall, for example, comprise "all production and maintenance workers with the exception of…." Excluded may be personnel such as the plant superintendent, supervisor, and assistant supervisor. An employer who is satisfied that the union obtained a majority of the members of the bargaining unit without the exercise of undue pressure, and who considers the bargaining unit appropriate may, according to most statutes, voluntarily accept the proposed bargaining unit and the union's right to act as the bargaining agent. This is voluntary recognition. If the employer accepts the unit and bargaining agent voluntarily, and commences negotiations with the intent of achieving a collective agreement, he becomes subject to the provisions of the statutes which allow for voluntary recognition and which specify forms of third-party assistance in the case of contract disputes.

Regular Certification A second method of union recognition is the regular certification process. This section explains the steps involved in that process, and compares the details of applying for and obtaining certification in different jurisdictions.

The certification process is initiated when a union feels that it has signed up enough workers to ensure that it has a majority of members in the bargaining unit. The union then applies to the appropriate labour relations board to become the bargaining agent for the unit. The board then determines whether or not the unit as constituted is appropriate. If the board finds the unit to be appropriate and is satisfied that the union has support from a majority of the workers, the unit may be certified without a vote. If the board is not certain that the union is supported by the

Table 6.4	Regular Certification

Union organizes required percentage of workers in proposed bargaining unit.

↓

Union makes application to board.

↓

Board defines appropriate bargaining unit.

↓

Secret vote is conducted by board.

↓

Union is certified or not, depending on support received.

workers, a secret ballot may be ordered. In 1984, British Columbia amended its Labour Code (s. 43) to require a secret ballot in every certification if the union has the required 45% support to make an application. British Columbia is now the only province in Canada where a secret ballot must be conducted in every certification case, irrespective of the support a union may have by way of signed cards. Table 6.4 outlines the certification process. However, because eleven jurisdictions exist with varying requirements for certification, the regular certification process is more complex than Table 6.4 suggests.

A former Chairman of the B.C. Labour Relations Board points out that there are two schools of thought which underly the route by which a union may acquire recognition under the regular certification process. One school of thought requires that a vote be taken in every case, drawing a parallel between secret balloting in elections for political office and secret balloting in elections for union office. According to this thinking, the secret ballot in certification cases allows the person who has signed a union card and paid the union an initial fee a chance to change his or her mind. The assumption is that the union member may have been pressured into signing a membership card and paying initial union fees. This model is followed by the National Labor Relations Board in the United States since certification on the basis of membership cards is not permitted under American law.

The other school of thought is that it should be possible—even desirable—to certify a union on the basis of majority support demonstrated by a count of membership cards. This argument rests on several grounds. First, if a union is certified on the basis of membership cards immediately, the employer has no opportunity to dissuade his workers from joining the union. Second, joining a union is only the first of a number of tests which a union member must undertake. A particularly difficult test is in negotiating a collective agreement which spells out many of the terms and conditions of employment. Frequently, strike action is necessary. At this point, genuine membership support is important for, without it, a strike cannot be called and, without a strike or a strike threat, the employer feels little compunction to settle.

The former Chairman of the B.C. Labour Relations Board underlined the circumstances surrounding certification by membership cards in this statement:

I make no secret of my preference. Trade unions should be granted certification — that legal license to bargain — on the basis of signed membership cards. The real test of whether employee support will remain steadfast will come when the trade union looks for a mandate to support its efforts at the bargaining table.[32]

In fact, he continued in the *1974 Annual Report,*

Upon receipt of the application [for certification], the Board immediately investigates the proportion of union membership among the employees. In the vast majority of cases, this investigation discloses that the union has more than a majority of the employees as members and the Board grants certification...on that basis.[33]

Figures in that report show that only about 5% of regular certification cases result in secret votes. It is ironic that the board that he chaired for five years now requires a vote by secret ballot in every certification case. Recent data from the Canada Labour Relations Board show that about 80% of certification cases are disposed of without a vote. In addition, figures from the Ontario Board indicate that votes were conducted in about 54% of the cases from 1982 to 1983 and in about 30% of the cases from 1983 to 1984.[34] It appears, then, that a vast majority of certification cases are processed without secret votes.

Prehearing Votes The third way by which a union may seek to represent workers is through a prehearing vote. This procedure is relatively new in Canadian labour legislation and is intended to be used in what one board chairman has described as messy situations. For example, if there is some indication that the employer is committing unfair labour practices, a "quickie" or prehearing vote may be ordered to measure support before management has an opportunity to infringe upon the rights of the workers.

The membership support claimed by a union in order to get a prehearing vote varies among the jurisdictions in Canada. The Ontario,

Table 6.5	Prehearing Vote

Union organizes required percentage of workers in proposed bargaining unit.

↓

Union applies for quickie vote.

↓

Board conducts vote and seals ballots.

↓

Board hears evidence and defines bargaining unit.

↓

Vote is counted.

↓

Union is certified if it has won sufficient support.

Quebec, and federal statutes allow a union to make an application for a prehearing vote on the basis of 35% support of the membership in the proposed bargaining unit.[35] The statutes of Alberta, Saskatchewan, and Newfoundland do not refer specifically to a prehearing vote. However, the boards in these provinces may arrange for such a vote.

Nova Scotia subjects every application to a quickie vote. The relevant section of the Nova Scotia statute states that "Normally the Board shall conduct the vote...no more than five working days after receipt by the Board of the application and three working days after the Board's notices are received by the employer.[36] The same provision permits the board to hold a pre-vote hearing, at which time interested parties may present evidence. This short period of five days might be appropriate for a small province like Nova Scotia where a notice may be delivered anywhere in the province in a day, but hardly for large provinces such as Ontario, Quebec, and British Columbia. The B.C. Labour Code, under section 35, enables the B.C. Labour Relations Board to take a representation vote before or after a hearing takes place. The ballots may be sealed and counted only after the parties have been given an opportunity to appear before the Board.[37] The New Brunswick statute provides that a union may request a prehearing vote where it has 40% support from members of the bargaining unit.[38] Section 13(1) of the *Prince Edward Island Labour Act* permits the Board to take a prehearing vote; presumably, the union needs the same 50% support required for a regular certification vote.[39] The recently revised Manitoba statute provides for a prehearing vote where the union has 45% membership support.[40]

Where a prehearing vote is provided for, the usual procedure is for the board to conduct it. The voters frequently include workers whose eligibility for inclusion in the proposed bargaining unit is challenged by one or another of the parties. In such cases, the board will usually place each contested ballot in an individually sealed envelope with the worker's name indicated on it. If the board decides that some of the workers in question do not form part of the bargaining unit, then the ballots of those workers are destroyed. However, should the board find in favour of these workers, their ballots are combined and counted with the rest.

After the board takes the vote, the ballot box is sealed. The ballots are not counted until the board has had a chance to hear evidence and rule on who should be included in or excluded from the bargaining unit. Only after the board has defined the appropriate bargaining unit are the ballots counted. The percentage support needed for a union to win a prehearing vote is the same as that required in the case of a regular certification vote. Figure 6.5 illustrates the sequence of events in a prehearing vote.

Post-War Certification Requirements In the period immediately after World War II, it was fairly easy to specify the conditions under which a union could be certified as a bargaining agent. Basically, support from 50% of the members in a bargaining unit was required to apply for certification. Once the board had determined whether or not the bargaining unit was appropriate and the majority of members in the bargaining unit supported the union, it would certify the bargaining agent. The onus was on the union to solicit membership support for its applications, since people who did not vote were considered not to be in favour of the union.

This practice was unfair to unions. If this rule were to hold in our political system, very few members could be elected to our parliaments. In elections for school boards, where overall support for one candidate is often as low as 15% or 20% in many municipalities, it would be impossible to elect a full complement of school trustees!

Although some jurisdictions require 50% support for the bargaining agents in a certification election, recent practice has been to accept the support of 50% of those actually voting. In jurisdictions where this norm prevails, workers who do not wish to have the union certified must get out and vote against it, since their absence no longer counts against the union. This seems to be a fair way of determining support for certification.

Support Necessary to Apply for Certification
The percentage support now required for an application for certification varies substantially among the various jurisdictions. The statutes in the provinces of Newfoundland, Prince Edward Island, and Alberta require that the union have signed up 50% of the workers in the bargaining unit in order to apply to the boards for certification. The Ontario and Manitoba statutes specify that unions may apply to the boards of these provinces if they have between 45% and 55% support. In these cases, it is mandatory for the boards to conduct a certification vote. If, however, the union has over 55% support in these two provinces, the boards must then certify the bargaining agents without a vote unless they suspect coercion.

Since the 1983 edition of this book, British Columbia and Manitoba have reversed the provisions of their statutes. Changes have also occurred to Saskatchewan's statute. In 1984, the B.C. Government went the route of requiring secret votes in all certification cases. The provision for automatic certification where a union claimed more than 55% support originated in Ontario, but was developed in British Columbia during the 1970's by the NDP. The former chairman of the B.C. Labour Relations Board reported repeated calls from employers for secret ballot votes in certification cases following the election of the Social Credit Government in the Fall of 1975. On a number of occasions, he continued, he had "to defend the existing arrangements to the Social Credit Minister of Labour, whose caucus was quite unsympathetic to the virtues of trade union representation."[41] In a white paper, the NDP Government of Manitoba

also allowed automatic certification with more than 55% support. This white paper, now legislated,[42] was harshly criticized during the Summer of 1984 by a number of employer groups through a full-page newspaper advertisement set in bold, black letters with the caption "The Dark Cloud over Manitoba."[43]

A great deal of controversy surrounded amendments to the Saskatchewan *Trade Union Act* in 1983. These amendments gave broad powers to the Board to deal with unfair labour practices and implicitly required arbitration of contract interpretation disputes. The Conservative Government argued that the amendments were necessary to industrial peace and investment capital. The official opposition, NDP, and trade unions condemned the amendments, claiming that they reflected the wishes of employers and took away worker rights which had existed since the 1940's. The amendments allow the Saskatchewan Labour Relations Board much discretion in implementing vague or ambiguous, but important, policy changes. A comparison of the provisions of the *Act* before and after the changes is beyond the scope of this chapter. Those interested in a comparison, however, should read Muthuchidambaram's work, *Legislative Background to and an Examination of the Saskatchewan Trade Union Amendment Act: Bill 40*.[44] Muthuchidambaram analyzes the amendments to the Saskatchewan *Trade Union Act* well.

In the statutes of New Brunswick and Nova Scotia, trade unions must have between 40% and 60% support of the members in the proposed bargaining unit in order to apply for certification. Under the provisions contained in Part V of the Canada Labour Code and those in the Quebec Labour Code, a union needs 35% support of the members of the proposed bargaining unit in order to make an application for certification. In the case of Part V of the Canada Labour Code, application is made to the Canada Labour Relations Board. In the case of Quebec, application is made to the Certification Commissioner General since there is no labour relations board in that province. Prior to the 1983 amendment, the Saskatchewan Board was required to conduct a secret vote when the union gained 25% support.[45] This is still true.

A listing of the requirements among jurisdictions in Canada shows the complexity of Canadian industrial relations and raises a question concerning the desirability of establishing a standard percentage of membership support necessary for certification.

A company operating under any one provincial jurisdiction will find it difficult enough to keep up to date with changing requirements. However, a company which operates under more than one provincial jurisdiction, but does not fall under the federal statute, has an extremely difficult task. This is so particularly with meat-packing companies, such as Canada Packers and Swift and Company, and pulp and paper, steel, and retail-food companies, since all negotiate on a multi-provincial basis. As we shall see later, varying requirements for conciliation make negotiations even more complex for these companies.

Support Necessary for Certification When a Vote Is Conducted Only three provinces — Newfoundland, New Brunswick, and Quebec — require as grounds for certification that a majority of those in a bargaining unit actually vote for the bargaining agent. The New Brunswick statute requires as grounds for certification that 50% of the workers in the bargaining unit actually vote for the union, unless the board is able to determine without a vote that more than 60% of the workers in the bargaining unit are members in good standing of the union.

All other jurisdictions, including the federal one, require 50% of *those voting*. The Saskatchewan statute specifies that a majority of those eligible to vote shall constitute a quorum. If quorum is attained and a majority vote in support of the bargaining agent, then that bargaining agent must be certified for that bargaining unit. In a number of jurisdictions, including the federal jurisdiction, if the board is satisfied that

a majority of the workers in a bargaining unit wish the union to represent them as bargaining agent, the board may certify that union without requiring a vote.

At the time of recognition, a trade union is certified for a certain number of occupational groups which exist at the time the application for certification is made. As new occupational categories come into existence, however, the trade union may negotiate on behalf of the workers in these new groups without applying to the respective boards for modifications to their certificate. Of the eleven statutes which deal with industrial relations in the private sector, only the Nova Scotia *Trade Union Act* refers explicitly to this particular problem. Section 26(1) of the Nova Scotia *Trade Union Act* specifies that where a trade union is certified under the *Act*, an application may be made to the Nova Scotia Labour Relations Board to amend the certificate: (1) to change the name of the union or employer, (2) to include specific additional classifications of workers in the unit, (3) to exclude specific classifications of workers from the unit, or (4) to combine previous certification orders into one order.[46] In a few other jurisdictions, these dynamic changes are dealt with by board regulations.

Decertification of Bargaining Agents

Although workers may choose a particular trade union as their bargaining agent, this does not mean that they cannot later change their minds. All statutes provide for both decertification and certification. If a certified bargaining agent is not performing well in the eyes of members of the bargaining unit, the members may, if they have majority support, apply to the appropriate labour relations board to have their union decertified. As with certification, the boards must first determine the bargaining unit. A vote is usually held: if a majority of the workers in the bargaining unit vote against the union, the union is decertified. In many cases, workers will have already chosen what they perceive to be a better union to represent them. Although no statistics are available on this particular question, it appears that where one union is decertified, another is usually certified.

Decertification provisions in the statutes are an important element of public policy. These provisions permit workers to dissociate themselves from weak, ineffective, or indifferent bargaining agents. This is as it should be, for trade unions have a moral and legal duty to represent fairly the workers for whom they are bargaining agents. If trade unions fail in this respect, workers ought to be able to seek the services of other unions.

The preceding discussion indicates that recognition disputes are no longer a cause of strikes. Three methods — voluntary recognition, regular certification, and the prehearing or quickie vote — exist whereby unions may be recognized by the employer. In addition, decertification is available to members of a bargaining unit in cases where a union is judged to be ineffectual.

As a concluding note on the certification process, it should be pointed out that an increasing number of jurisdictions are including in their statutes provisions which prevent union constitutions from barring a particular group of workers. These provisions have resulted in part from a number of court cases in which restrictive membership clauses became an issue. Section 127(3) of Part V of the Canada Labour Code is typical of these provisions:

> Where the Board is satisfied that a trade union has an established practice of admitting persons to membership without regard to the eligibility requirements of its charter, constitution or by-laws, the Board may disregard such requirements in determining whether a person is a member of a trade union.[47]

Interest Disputes

Notice of Intent to Negotiate

Once a bargaining agent becomes certified for a group of workers in a bargaining unit, both the employer and the union are obliged to bargain in good faith over the terms and conditions of a collective agreement. The first agreement may last for one, two, or three years. Before the expiration of that agreement, either party may serve notice on the other of its intent to bargain for a revised collective agreement. A conflict which develops during contract negotiations is referred to as an *interest* dispute, so as to differentiate it from a contract interpretation or *rights* dispute. In a rights dispute, the arbitrator appointed under the terms of a collective agreement is guided in his or her decision by the clauses contained in the collective agreement. In an interest dispute, there are no agreed criteria to which a third party may refer.

Once a trade union is certified and in a position to require an employer to engage in collective bargaining, it has in all jurisdictions in Canada a prescribed period of time within which it may or must give notice of intent to negotiate for a first agreement. Similarly, before an existing collective agreement expires, the statutes prescribe a certain period of time within which the bargaining agent or the employer may or must serve notice on the other of an intent to negotiate a new or revised agreement. Generally the period of time allowed runs anywhere from thirty to ninety days. A trend seems to exist, however, for a ninety-day notice period when a bargaining agent wishes to engage in collective bargaining for the revision of an existing agreement.

Provisions for Third-Party Assistance

As pointed out earlier, the *IDI Act* of 1907 provided for compulsory conciliation in contract negotiation disputes where the parties failed to reach agreement on their own. Later, P.C. 1003 of 1944 added principles from the *Wagner Act* in the United States to the compulsory conciliation procedure set out in the original *IDI Act*. While third-party assistance is not compulsory in the United States, all jurisdictions in Canada, except Saskatchewan, have continued to require third-party assistance before a legal strike or lockout may take place.

The original rationale for the use of conciliation boards assumed that publishing the recommendations of a tripartite conciliation board would bring public pressure to bear on the parties to reach a settlement. In retrospect, this assumption does not appear to have been valid, since the public is rarely aware that recommendations have been published. The major function of conciliation board reports thus serves as a useful basis for further negotiations between the parties either prior to or following a strike or lockout. The specificity of these recommendations may either help or hinder any subsequent mediators.

Until the late 1950's, most jurisdictions automatically appointed a conciliation board where a conciliation officer failed to obtain an agreement. This was done almost without regard to the nature of the dispute and irrespective of whether or not a serious public interest component existed. This automatic sequencing was often seen by the trade-union movement as a major obstacle to serious negotiations, since a legal strike or lockout could not occur until a certain period of time had elapsed after a conciliation board had handed down its report. While the use of this two-step compulsory conciliation process was intended to provide a cooling-off period, it more often served to heat things up. Since the 1950's, however, most jurisdictions have been making far less use of conciliation boards and are exercising a great deal more discretion respecting their use.

In recent years, the use of mediation as a form of third-party assistance has increased. Mediation was first tried in Ontario during the 1960's. Since that time, many other jurisdictions have adopted this approach, using the mediator to replace either the conciliation officer or the conciliation board. (In the latter case, the mediator generally submits a report with recommendations.) The following section compares the conciliation and mediation approaches currently in use in Canada.

Provisions for Initial Types of Third-Party Assistance

In most jurisdictions, the initial third party appointed is referred to as a conciliation officer. The Alberta statute, however, refers to a conciliation commissioner, and the B.C. Labour Code mentions a mediation officer. Whatever the terminology, the function of the first appointed individual is to confer with the parties to help bring about an agreement between them. Most jurisdictions specify a period of time within which a conciliation officer or similar agent must report his or her findings to the Minister. This time period may be extended by the consent of the parties or at the discretion of the Minister. If unable to reach an agreement, usually a conciliation officer will report to the Minister those items which have been agreed upon and those which are still outstanding. In most jurisdictions, the conciliation officer must advise on whether or not to appoint a conciliation board.

Some jurisdictions provide for the appointment of a mediation officer should the efforts of a conciliation officer not be successful in obtaining a collective agreement. The Ontario statute says that, where the Minister is required or authorized to appoint a conciliation officer, he may, upon written request of the parties, appoint a mediator selected by the two of them before appointing a conciliation board. The appointment of a mediator terminates any prior appointment of a conciliation officer.[48] Under the Ontario statute, the report of a mediator has the same effect and powers as the report of a conciliation board.[49]

The Manitoba *Labour Relations Act* provides, where collective bargaining has commenced, that either party may request the appointment of a conciliation officer. The Manitoba legislation also provides for the appointment of a mediator at the joint request of the two parties or on the initiative of the Minister.[50] The neighbouring province of Saskatchewan does not require conciliation. The Minister of Labour, however, has the statutory authority to establish a conciliation board.

The Quebec statute requires the Minister of Labour and Manpower to appoint a conciliation officer at the request of either party; he may, however, appoint one on his own initiative. The Quebec statute makes no reference to a concilia-

Table 6.6					Types of Initial Third-Party Assistance
Jurisdiction	Conciliation officer or similar officer	Mediator after appointment of conciliation officer	Report of mediator replaces that of conciliation officer	Report of mediator or similar officer replaces report of conciliation board	No. of days after first stage if no board is appointed before strike or lockout is permitted
Federal	X	X		X[a]	7
British Columbia[b]	Mediator				
Alberta	Mediator				6
Saskatchewan					when contract expires
Manitoba	X				
Ontario	X	X		X	14
Quebec	X				no board provided for in legislation
New Brunswick[c]	X	X	X		7
Nova Scotia	X	X		X	14
Prince Edward Island	X				21
Newfoundland[c]	X	X		X	15

[a]Under the federal statute, the report of a conciliation commissioner replaces that of a conciliation board. Also, under the statute, the Minister may appoint a mediator.
[b]The British Columbia Labour Code provides only for mediation and a strike may take place only within the three month period after its authorization by a membership vote.
[c]Provides for the appointment of one or more conciliation officers.

tion board. The New Brunswick and Newfoundland statutes provide that, at the request of either party, the Minister may appoint one or more conciliation officers to confer with the parties engaged in collective bargaining. Presumably, the appointment of more than one conciliation officer is intended to maximize the effectiveness of assistance at this stage. Although the statutes of both of these provinces make provision for the appointment of a mediator, the New Brunswick statute states that the mediator's report shall have the same effect as that of a conciliation officer and the Newfoundland statute appears to equate the appointment of a mediator with that of a conciliation board. The P.E.I. *Labour Act* authorizes the Minister to appoint a mediator instead of a conciliation board; the mediator is to have all the powers of a conciliation board. The federal statute permits the Minister of Labour to appoint a conciliation commissioner in place of a conciliation board; the report of the commissioner is to have the same effect as that of a conciliation board. In addition, Section 195 of Part V of the Canada Labour Code permits the Minister to appoint a mediator on his own initiative or upon request. (Table 6.6 compares the above provisions.)

As indicated earlier, the statutory provisions now allow for the appointment of mediators or other individuals. These provisions are a relatively recent development in the area of interest disputes. A careful assessment of the provisions among the jurisdictions confirms that the administrators of the legislation have much more flexibility now than before in using mediators rather than conciliation officers prior to the appointment of conciliation boards. This may account in part for the decline in the appointment of conciliation boards in recent years.

There has been a certain amount of criticism

of the use of conciliation boards. One of their virtues, however, is that the two nominees appointed by management and union are normally well-informed about a given industry and are therefore of great assistance to the chairman of conciliation boards in furnishing detailed knowledge about that industry. If mediators are to be effective, they should have similar expertise. Moreover, it would seem desirable to use teams of mediators or conciliation officers in attempting to improve relations in those industries which have long histories of poor labour-management relations. Ontario has developed within the Ministry of Labour a service which provides mediation teams to help repair tattered relations between unions and management.[51]

Composition and Function of Conciliation Boards

Practically all Canadian jurisdictions, with the exception of British Columbia, Quebec, and Alberta, provide for the appointment of a conciliation board should the efforts of a conciliator or mediator fail. Table 6.7 summarizes the statutory provisions. While the Saskatchewan statute does not require the appointment of conciliation boards, it does provide for the establishment of such boards on the initiative of the Minister of Labour. The fact that a jurisdiction provides for this type of third-party assistance does not necessarily mean that boards are appointed in all cases. As previously mentioned, administrators now exercise a great deal of discretion concerning the use of tripartite conciliation boards.

Where a statute provides for the appointment of conciliation boards, it will usually contain a provision which states that, within a prescribed period after the report of a conciliation officer, the Minister shall either appoint a conciliation board or notify the parties that a conciliation board will not be appointed. (The decision not to appoint a board leaves the parties free to exercise the strike or lockout option.) Conciliation boards are appointed according to a standard procedure: management and union are given a

certain period of time within which to name their nominees to the board and the two nominees agree upon a third person to act as chairman. In cases where the two nominees are unable to agree, the Minister of Labour must appoint a third person to serve as a neutral party on the conciliation board.

Conciliation boards are required to mediate a settlement between the parties. If a board cannot effect an agreement between the parties, it must recommend ways in which the outstanding issues may be reconciled. Again, most statutes require that such recommendations be submitted within prescribed time periods which may be extended either by consent of the parties or at the discretion of the Minister. Evidence suggests that, in practically all cases, boards far exceed the specified time period.

At one time, the report of a conciliation board was supposed to represent the views of the majority of its members. This often put the chairman of a board in a position of having to write recommendations agreeable to either the union or management nominee. Legislation in some jurisdictions now permits, in the absence of a majority report, that the chairman's report be taken as that of the conciliation board. This seems to be a welcome innovation, since the chairman can now take advantage of input from both sides and make recommendations acceptable to both sides or which serve as a useful basis for further negotiation.

Only when disputes have an important public interest component will jurisdictions appoint conciliation boards. This reluctance may be due in part to the criticism directed against the use of such boards, particularly against the long periods between their appointments and their reports. The Task Force appointed by Prime Minister Pearson to look into the state of industrial relations in Canada, particularly in those industries under federal jurisdiction, recommended that conciliation boards be retained but that they be appointed only at the request of both interest parties.[52] The Task Force further recommended that the conciliation boards

Table 6.7			Provisions Regarding Conciliation Boards, Compulsory Votes, etc.	
Jurisdiction	Provision made for the appointment of conciliation board or equivalent	No. of days after report before strike or lockout is legal	Supervised strike vote	Prescribed period of notice before strike or lockout may take place
Federal	X	7		
Newfoundland	X	7		
Prince Edward Island	X	7		
Nova Scotia	X	7		
New Brunswick	X	7		2 days
Quebec[a]				within 2 days
Ontario	X	7		
Manitoba	X	not specified in statute		
Saskatchewan	X			
Alberta	X[b]	14	X[b]	72 hours
British Columbia			X[c]	72 hours

[a]In Quebec, the right to strike or lockout is acquired 90 days after receipt by the minister of a request for the appointment of a conciliation officer.

[b]The Alberta *Labour Relations Act* provides for the appointment of a Disputes Inquiry Board on the initiative of the Minister of Labour. In addition, the parties may request the Minister to appoint a Voluntary Collective Bargaining Arbitration Board, the recommendations of which are binding on the parties.

[c]In British Columbia, a vote is conducted according to regulations developed by the B.C. Board.

decide whether or not they should advise on substantive issues in dispute. One of the reasons why the Task Force recommended cutting back on the availability of conciliation boards was to strengthen the role of the conciliation officer.[53]

It is also interesting to note that, when the Federal Government revised the old *Industrial Relations and Disputes Investigation Act* of 1948 and made it Part V of the Canada Labour Code in 1972-73, provision was made for the appointment of a conciliation commissioner who would have a mandate similar to that of a conciliation board, including the power to issue a report. Similarly, the emergence of the regular use of mediation in some provinces indicates clearly that governments are relying less on conciliation boards than on conciliation officers and mediators.

All statutes requiring conciliation or mediation, also stipulate that no strike or lockout may occur until after a certain period of time (usual-ly seven days) has elapsed. Under Part V of the Canada Labour Code, a strike or lockout may begin seven days after the Minister has notified the parties that he will not appoint a conciliation officer, commissioner, or board.[54]

Alberta has done away with a compulsory conciliation board and, in its place, has provided that, before or after a strike or lockout may take place, the Minister of Labour may establish a disputes inquiry board of one or more persons. Where such a board is appointed, its recommendations are given to the parties and also published in any form which the Minister thinks fit. If neither party notifies the Minister of its acceptance of the board's recommendations, the Labour Relations Board shall conduct a vote. If both parties accept the recommendations, then the recommendations are included in the terms of a collective agreement.[55]

A strike or lockout can commence in Alberta ten days after the parties have received the recommendations of a disputes inquiry board, if one is appointed, or seventy-two hours after notice has been served that a majority of the workers have voted for a strike or a majority of employer representatives have voted for a lockout. The vote may be supervised by the Board or by the parties themselves.[56] Section 115(1) of the Alberta *Act* also provides for the appointment of a voluntary collective bargaining arbitration board in the event that the parties request such a board from the Minister of Labour.

Due Process for Strikes and Lockouts

The B.C. Labour Code specifies that a strike may not take place until secret ballots show that a majority of those workers voting favour a strike. A similar provision applies to a lockout by an employers' association. Also, no strike or lockout may take place until a notice of seventy-two hours has been given.

In the cases cited above where a strike vote is required, a majority of *those voting* decides whether or not a strike will be called. The statutes of Nova Scotia and Prince Edward Island[57] specify that, where a secret vote is to be taken, the majority of those *in the bargaining unit* must approve strike action for the strike to be legal. The relevant provision of the Nova Scotia *Trade Union Act* reads as follows:

> no person shall declare or authorize a strike and no employee shall strike until after a secret vote by ballot of employees in the unit affected as to whether to strike or not to strike has been taken and the majority of such employees have voted in favour of a strike.[58]

The subtle distinction in the provisions in these particular statutes is important in light of a ruling in Saskatchewan in December 1979: the Saskatchewan Government Employees Association voted to go on strike, but less than a majority of those eligible to vote actually opted for strike action. The judge who made the ruling stated that Section 11(2)(d) of the Saskatchewan *Trade Union Act* (in effect at that time) was worded in such a way that a strike vote could be valid only

if more than 50% of the *total membership* of the union voted to strike.[59] Apparently previous strike votes were presumed to be valid if more than 50% of union members voting favoured a strike. Section 6(2)(d) of the Saskatchewan *Trade Union Act* as amended requires a secret vote, and a majority of *those voting* must vote in favour of a strike for the strike to be legal.

The requirements of other jurisdictions concerning due process for strikes and lockouts are not precisely defined. It is likely that, in many cases, a simple voting majority would suffice. Ideally, all jurisdictions should consider a strike legal as long as the strike has the support of 50% of *those voting*. Most jurisdictions now allow a majority of those voting in a secret ballot to determine whether or not a union is certified. The same logic seems desirable in determining whether or not a strike is legal. Under these rules, those wishing to vote for or against a collective agreement or strike would be obliged to get out and cast their ballots.

A new section of the Saskatchewan *Trade Union Act* (Section 45(1)) provides that, where a strike has continued for thirty days, the employer, the trade union, *or 25% of the workers in the bargaining unit, or 100 workers (whichever is less),* may ask the board to conduct a vote on the employer's last offer with a view to returning to work. If a majority of those voting accept the employer's last offer, then the strike is over and the workers must return to work. Section 45(3) makes it clear that only workers who are involved in the strike and who have not secured permanent employment elsewhere are entitled to vote. The danger of this means of ending a strike is that if 1,000 workers are on strike, 100 of them request a vote on whether or not to accept the employer's last offer, and 51 vote to accept the employer's last offer, then the strike is legally ended and all 1,000 workers must return to work.

Section 45(1) allows the employer to deal directly with the workers. In other jurisdictions, the union is involved in or itself conducts the vote. Apart from section 45(1) and the Ontario legislation, no jurisdiction specifically or expressly permits employers to communicate with workers with respect to strikes: only employers in Ontario and Saskatchewan may go over the heads of union leaders. Section 45(1) is the only legislation in Canada which gives workers the right to such a direct say in whether or not to continue a strike. The next closest thing to the provision in the Saskatchewan legislation is section 40 of the Ontario *Labour Relations Act* which permits an employer, before or after the commencement of a strike, to apply to the Minister of Labour for a vote on the employer's last offer. However, the Ontario provision does not give a similar right to workers. Ontario and Saskatchewan are the only provinces in Canada with such provisions in their legislation. In addition, Section 11(1)(a) of the Saskatchewan *Trade Union Act* expressly permits an employer to communicate with his workers.

The above discussion has concerned the policy instruments designed to resolve contract negotiation or interest disputes, the second of the four classical types referred to earlier in this chapter. If these instruments do not enable the parties to resolve their differences, then strikes and lockouts may legally take place. An exception is found in negotiations in the public and parapublic sectors where strikes are forbidden and compulsory arbitration is used in some jurisdictions. Compulsory arbitration will be detailed in Chapter 10.

Rights Disputes

As noted earlier in this chapter, one of the major policy issues dealt with by legislation is that of contract interpretation or rights disputes, the third of the classical types of disputes. Every collective agreement forbids strikes or lockouts in rights cases, but specifies procedures for their resolution. While Saskatchewan did not require arbitration of rights disputes for many years, sec-

tion 44 of the recently revised Saskatchewan *Trade Union Act* expressly prohibits strike and lock-out action during the life of a collective agreement. While there is no express provision in the new statute which requires the use of arbitration in such disputes, it is presumed to exist as the usual quid pro quo for the right to strike or lockout. In addition, sections 24, 25 and 26 imply the existence of such a provision.

A common difficulty is that contract language is general and may relate poorly to specific situations. Some provisions of collective agreements are often ambiguous or self-contradictory. Sometimes, ambiguity is deliberately incorporated because the parties at the time of negotiations have compromised on a loosely worded provision in order to expedite a settlement and avoid a strike or lockout. The parties have assumed that the wording might be referred to a third party should the need for interpretation arise at a later date.

The following provision contained in Part V of the Canada Labour Code is fairly typical of provisions requiring that rights disputes be settled by means of the grievance process, with arbitration as the final step:

> Every collective agreement shall contain a provision for final settlement without stoppage of work, by arbitration or otherwise, of all differences between the parties to or employees bound by the collective agreement, concerning its interpretation, application, administration or alleged violation.[60]

Note that, even if the collective agreement does not contain an arbitration clause, some statutes will assume it to be present. In Ontario and a number of other jurisdictions, the clause prescribed by the statute gives an arbitrator the authority to decide whether an issue is arbitrable or not. This clause anticipates objections by either party that the arbitrator lacks jurisdiction to hear the case.

In order to cope with rights disputes, most contracts specify a grievance procedure geared to the size of the company. In small companies, the procedure may contain one to three steps, with arbitration as the final step. Larger organizations may require more steps before arbitration.

Some collective agreements provide for tripartite boards of arbitration, whereas others specify a sole arbitrator. In all cases, however, arbitration is binding upon both parties. With tripartite boards of arbitration there is usually a time period within which management and union must nominate their representatives. These two nominees must then select a chairman mutually acceptable to both nominees. If either party fails to nominate a representative, or if the two nominees fail to agree upon a chairman, most statutes in Canada contain a provision whereby the Minister of Labour or chairman of the labour relations board makes the appointments.

Certain statutes also contain detailed provisions regarding the arbitration process itself, including the presentation of evidence, the calling and cross-examination of witnesses, the granting of permission to arbitrators to enter premises where infractions of collective agreements are alleged to have taken place, and so on. All jurisdictions now provide that where there is no majority decision of an arbitration board, the decision of the chairman of the board shall prevail. This provision is a welcome development, for an arbitrator can now be as objective as possible in judging a case: the acceptance of his award no longer relies upon the support of either nominee.

A recent development in practically all statutes relates to cases dealing with discharge and discipline. Until recently, if a worker was suspended or discharged for just cause, the arbitrator had no legal mandate to change the decision of management even though the penalty would appear rather drastic in some cases. Now, however, most statutes permit the arbitrator to substitute his or her judgment for that of management in such a case, unless the collective agreement prescribes a specific penalty for the infraction. More will be said about this sub-

ject in the chapter "Administration of the Collective Agreement."

Another recent development is the enforceability of awards. In most jurisdictions, the statutes provide that if an arbitration decision is not complied with within a specified period of time, it may be filed with a court and then becomes enforceable as a court order. Failure to implement an arbitration award so filed becomes a failure to comply with a court decision, with all the penalties implied therein.

There has been a great deal of criticism of the arbitration process, both in terms of the lengthy delays it involves and the costs it occasions. A similar situation exists in the United States where a few well-known arbitrators handle the vast majority of cases. In response, there has emerged the new phenomenon of expedited arbitration. Expedited arbitration was first used by the United Steelworkers Union and the ten major steel companies in the United States in 1971.[61] Its basic purposes are to reduce costs, shorten the time period from the filing of a grievance to the rendering of an arbitration award, and involve more arbitrators in the process, particularly individuals in the localities in which the disputes first arise. Parties who have used expedited arbitration find that it works well for the handling of routine grievances. The process must, nonetheless, be tailor-made to each union-management relationship.

Although expedited arbitration is beginning to find its way into a number of industries and companies, there is no wide-scale legislation dealing with it thus far. Individual jurisdictions, however, have made some effort to promote its use. During the Summer of 1979, for example, Ontario passed Bill 25 which allows either labour or management to request the Minister of Labour to refer to a single arbitrator appointed by the Minister any dispute arising from the interpretation, application, administration, or alleged violation of a collective agreement. More will be said about expedited arbitration in the chapter "Administration of the Collective Agreement."

Jurisdictional Disputes

As indicated at the beginning of this chapter, jurisdictional disputes are disagreements beween unions over the right to represent workers *by virtue of the work to be performed.* Such disputes have traditionally been found mainly in the construction industry. A good example is a situation where bathrooms are being installed in newly constructed homes. The work involves the duties both of a carpenter and a plumber/pipefitter who connects the hot- and cold-water pipes. Both the carpenters and the plumbers unions may claim to have the right to organize workers performing such work.

Although the legislative provisions dealing with certification are often able to handle the situation, in many cases the unions continue to compete with one another and the disputes are only settled by strike action. In some jurisdictions in Canada, construction industry panels of labour relations boards are effective in resolving the matter. Should these panels be unsuccessful, however, and the unions involved continue to compete, the court of last resort is the National Joint Board (NJB) in Washington, D.C. The NJB comprises an impartial chairman, four representatives of the Building and Construction Trades Department of the AFL-CIO, and four contractors' associations. There is an understanding among the international construction trade unions involved that they will be bound by whatever decision the NJB issues. A case may be brought before the NJB either by the employer or by the president of the international union involved. There have been a number of cases in Toronto and other areas of the country where a dispute was settled at this stage.

In a 1967 study, Abbé Gérard Dion of Laval University suggested that provincial entities along the lines of the National Joint Board in Washington be established in Canada, and that there be a national board to undertake a permanent liaison to ensure consistency of decisions at the provincial level.[62] To date, however, no such provincial boards have been set up and there are still a few Canadian cases which end up in Washington for final disposition.

The above section completes the discussion of the four classical disputes—recognition, contract negotiation (interest), contract interpretation (rights), and jurisdiction—and the related federal and provincial labour legislation.

Other Policy Issues

In recent years, a number of new policy issues have emerged which warrant attention. Most of these issues have started in one of the eleven jurisdictions and then spread to other jurisdictions. Some of the more important of these new policy issues include the following: (1) the replacement of workers during a legal strike, (2) the imposition of a council of trade unions, (3) the handling of emergency disputes, (4) the imposition of first agreements, (5) the arbitration of unjust dismissal cases where no collective agreement exists, (6) the accreditation of employers' associations, (7) compulsory dues check-offs, (8) the duty of fair representation, (9) religious grounds for exemption from joining or financing a union, and (10) protection from the adverse effects of technological change.

Replacement of Workers During a Legal Strike

In all jurisdictions in Canada, with the exception of Quebec, employers are permitted to replace striking workers, although such workers may regain their status as workers but not their previous jobs after the strike has ended. For a large employer with a very diversified labour force, it is practically impossible to find skilled replacements in sufficient numbers to continue operations. For example, a company such as Stelco in Hamilton would find it extremely difficult to hire replacements in many steelworking occupations. A small employer, however, may be able to hire sufficient replacements to continue normal operations during a strike.

What happens to these replacements and strikers when the strike is over? According to Paul Weiler, North American law "guarantees the striker his employee status, although not necessarily his job."[63] Workers have the right to organize, bargain through their unions for collective agreements and, except in some parts of the public sector, exercise the right to strike in order to pressure their employers to reach agreement. Workers also have some rights to job security, pension plans, etc. which cannot be transferred to other employers.

It seems reasonable to assume that striking workers should be entitled to return to their jobs after their strikes are over. But it has also been suggested that replacements hired during strikes are entitled to some form of job security. The rights of strikers and replacements is a particularly difficult public policy issue, and some exceptions have been taken to the position that the striking worker has a right only to employee status and not to his or her job.

The Ontario government has responded to this issue by including the following provision in its *Labour Relations Act:*

> Where an employee engaging in a lawful strike makes an unconditional application in writing to his employer within six months from the commencement of the lawful strike to return to work, the employer shall…reinstate the employee in his former employment, on such terms as the employer and employee may agree upon, and the employer in offering terms of employment shall not discriminate against the employee by reason of his exercising or having exercised any rights under this Act.[64]

It seems clear from this provision that in order for a worker to regain his or her previous job,

he or she may have to seek it while a strike is still on. If this interpretation is correct, this provision might place a worker under a great deal of pressure from fellow strikers.

Manitoba has a provision whereby workers may be recalled to their previous jobs according to their seniority and as such work becomes available.[65] In 1984, Manitoba amended section 10.1 to prohibit employers from hiring permanent workers during a strike.

Quebec alone extends a no-replacement right to workers. In Bill 45 of 1977, the Quebec Government included a section which has come to be known as the anti-scab provision. Under this provision, every employer is prohibited from resorting to four objectionable or unfair practices: (1) the direct replacement of workers legally on strike; (2) the hiring of additional workers prior to the commencement of a strike or lockout on the understanding that they will work during the strike or lockout period; (3) the use of workers who are in the bargaining unit on strike but who are prepared to work in another of the employer's establishments; and (4) the importation of workers from other establishments operated by the employer for the purposes of keeping a strike-bound establishment functioning. The anti-scab provision of 1977 has since been extended to include subcontractors and supervisory personnel. However, should any strike or lockout be judged to affect the health or safety of the province, the government may obtain a court order (or injunction) ordering that essential services be provided.[66]

The use of professional strikebreakers has been a controversial issue in Canada for some years. Three jurisdictions—British Columbia, Manitoba and Ontario—now consider it an unfair labour practice for employers to employ professional strikebreakers during a strike. Manitoba and Ontario also consider it an unfair labour practice for individuals to act in such a capacity. The inclusion of these provisions in the Ontario legislation in 1983 followed an incident in which a picketer was killed by a truck while walking a picket line. It would not be surprising if more jurisdictions were to add provisions to their statutes in the near future concerning professional strikebreakers.

Imposition of a Council of Trade Unions

The Labour Code of British Columbia contains a unique provision. The Minister of Labour may, according to this provision, direct the B.C. Labour Relations Board to consider whether or not a council of trade unions would be an appropriate bargaining agent for a unit of workers. Where the Board considers such a council appropriate, the Board may certify the council as the bargaining agent.[67]

Under this provision, the B.C. Board imposed a council of trade unions on the B.C. Railway in 1976. The Railway had been plagued with labour problems for years. The seven or eight unions involved negotiated separately: this resulted in a situation in which unions based new demands on settlements reached by other unions, a practice called leap-frogging. Leap-frogging escalated the number of strikes in the Railway so much that, over a five-year period, labour unrest in the Railway cost the provincial economy more than $100,000,000.[68] With the idea of bringing stability to this troubled situation, the B.C. Board took action after very careful study and did not step in until all other methods had failed, including the use of high-level neutrals. The Board concluded that the situation could not be permitted to continue. The only solution to leap-frogging, the Board claimed, was to enlarge the effective bargaining structure.

B.C. unions had tried unsuccessfully to form a voluntary council of unions, but could neither bind new unions nor stop the fair amount of union raiding going on. However, the attempt to form a council indicated a desire to rectify a bad situation. In an attempt to bring peace to this chaotic situation, the Board forced the unions to form a council and to develop a constitution which would govern the operations of the council. Under this new system, Railway unions must face a periodic set of negotiations in which all the unions participate. In addition,

before any strike action may take place, a secret strike vote must be conducted in which *all workers* take part. Each union retains its identity, however; during the life of the agreement, each one processes the grievances of its members. If any one of the unions were to feel, for example, that its wage structure differed in important respects from those of other Railway unions, the other unions would have to be persuaded of the merits of the case before it could be considered during contract negotiations.

The first two sets of negotiations resulted in peaceful settlements, but the third round of negotiations resulted in a six-week strike from December, 1979 to January, 1980. There were over 100 issues involved in the strike. However, the strike resulted in a compromise settlement which was ratified by a majority of the workers.[69]

The B.C. Board formed councils of unions in other situations including the B.C. Shipyards where about twelve unions held separate certificates and negotiated their own agreements. This situation, like that of the B.C. Railway case, was characterized by leapfrogging. In this case, however, some of the unions, including the electricians and plumbers, did not want a council since they felt that their higher wage differentials might be lost through bargaining within a council framework. The Board forced a council on the unions, however, and over the years the unions have adjusted to the council idea.

The construction unions in B.C. also bargain on a province-wide basis through a council of unions with the major building contractors who are represented by the Construction Labour Relations Association (CLRA). Many types of construction exist, however, for which negotiations do not take place through a council on a province-wide basis.

How does one assess the advantages and disadvantages of bargaining through a highly centralized structure? As the former chairman of the B.C. Board has stated, "The most obvious flaw in the growth of large bargaining units is the reduction of the capacity for self-determination by individuals or small groups within that structure."[70] In drawing on the experience of the B.C. Railway case, he implies that each union leader should cast one vote on the executive board of the council, regardless of the size of the union. Also, he indicates that key membership decisions such as contract ratification and strike votes should take place on a one-person, one-vote basis. He concludes by saying that "in developing councils of trade unions, we have proceeded on the principle of the double majority, to ensure that there will be a decent concern over the long haul for the interests of each constituency within this council framework."[71]

On March 9, 1978, the federal Minister of Labour appointed an Industrial Inquiry Commission with a mandate to look into the advantages and disadvantages of broader-based bargaining units in federal industries, particularly in the transportation, grain-handling and communication sectors. Given the limited time that the Commission had to deliver its report, it was decided to restrict the inquiry to aviation, airport services, and grain-handling. After considering the problems inherent in the lack of coordinated bargaining in these industries, and after listening to the parties of interest, the Commission expressed its preference for broader-based bargaining units in these industries, but recommended that these units be established on a voluntary basis. The Commission noted that, if voluntary efforts were not successful, the government might have recourse to legislation to effect the same end. The latter course seems more likely, since the statements made by labour and management in these sectors suggest that too many vested interests exist for parties to adopt voluntarily broader-based bargaining units.[72] The Commission might have been more effective if it had recommended a provision comparable to that contained in the Labour Code of British Columbia. The mere enactment of a clause providing for the future imposition of a council of trade unions might have been sufficient to encourage voluntary creation of the broader-based bargaining units desired by the Commission.

Handling Emergency Disputes

British Columbia and Alberta are the only jurisdictions that have provisions for handling emergency disputes in industries in the private sector. The Alberta *Labour Act* provides that, where an emergency is judged to exist or may occur that poses a threat to health or property, or where unreasonable hardship is being caused or is likely to be caused to persons who are not parties to an industrial dispute, the government may declare that all further action and procedures in the dispute be governed by the emergency provisions in the statute. The *Act* applies specifically to workers in community services such as water, heat, sewage disposal, and electrical and gas utilities. Health care workers are also included.

Following the invoking of emergency powers, the minister responsible may appoint one or more persons or create a Public Emergency Tribunal to mediate the dispute. The Tribunal has the power to make an award which will be binding on the employer, the bargaining agent, and every worker affected.[73] If an award of a Public Emergency Tribunal is not complied with, the Minister may file a copy with the court which may enforce the award as a judgment or order of the court.

Although this provision in the Alberta statute places a great deal of power in the Cabinet, the caution exercised by government officials and by the judiciary indicates that it will likely be used in a responsible manner. During the Spring of 1980, for example, when more than 6,000 Alberta nurses went on strike in defiance of a government back-to-work order, the government sought an interim court injunction to enforce the original order. The justice who heard the application for an injunction postponed his ruling on the government's request and a two-year settlement was reached before any further judicial action was required. This provision no longer applies to most nurses in the province, since section 117 of the Alberta *Labour Relations Act* requires compulsory arbitration of interest disputes for employers who operate approved hospitals as defined in the *Hospitals Act*, and all the workers of those employers. In British Columbia, under the *Essential Services Disputes Act* of 1977, the government may preempt a union's strike or employer's lockout option and substitute a strategy which includes fact-finding, mediation, and designation.

Designation means that an administrative body (such as a labour relations board) declares that a specified number of persons who would normally have the right to strike are required for the continued operation of an essential industry or service and must continue to report for duty during a work stoppage. The *Act* also specifies that, where a dispute between the parties is not resolved and where the Lieutenant-Governor in Council is of the opinion that as a consequence, (1) an immediate and serious danger to life, health or safety exists or is likely to exist, or (2) an immediate and substantial threat to the economy and welfare of the province and its citizens exists or is likely to exist, and (3) a substantial disruption in the delivery of educational services exists or is likely to exist, he may direct the Labour Relations Board to designate those facilities, productions and services which it considers necessary or essential. The *Act* further stipulates that the Board shall order the employer and trade union to continue to supply or maintain in full measure any facilities, productions and services so designated.

The provisions of the *Act* originally applied to a number of corporations including the B.C. Hydro and Power Authority, as well as to workers in health-care facilities, police officers, and firefighters, and was amended in 1978 to encompass any substantial disruption in the delivery of educational services. The B.C. statute is even broader in scope than that of Alberta. The B.C. statute also applies to those industries in the private sector, in which work stoppages may be perceived to cause a serious threat to the economy and welfare of the province.[74] (Similar legislation in Quebec will be discussed in Chapter 10.)

In all other jurisdictions, with the exception of statutes covering essential services in the public and parapublic sectors, special *ad hoc* legislation is normally used to deal with so-called emergency disputes. Given the various conditions under which such disputes may arise, the strategy of *ad hoc* legislation may be the most appropriate one. The legislation is debated in the responsible legislative assembly, where the merits and timing of the government's proposal is subject to public scrutiny. Such is not the case when special authority is vested in one or more individuals to initiate emergency procedures.

Imposition of First Agreements

If the parties to a first agreement fail to reach a settlement in negotiations, some jurisdictions provide for its imposition by an external agency. Part V of the Canada Labour Code, the Labour Code of British Columbia, The Manitoba *Labour Relations Act*, and the Quebec Labour Code all have such provisions. Labour relations boards in the first three jurisdictions, and a council of arbitration in Quebec impose first agreements on the parties concerned.

The first jurisdiction to initiate this policy was British Columbia. The policy was introduced to establish a workable union-management relationship in cases where a newly certified union made unrealistic demands which small employers could not afford or, more likely, where an employer strongly opposed to unionism stalled negotiations so long that workers would tire of the idea of unionizing. Agreements were imposed only as a last resort, after all other attempts at settlement had failed. The agreements were intended as a "trial marriage, one which could allow the parties to get used to each other and lay the foundations for a more mature and enduring relationship."[75] Decertification followed almost every case in which a first contract was imposed. This result suggests that many employers opposed to unionism succeeded in turning their workers against unions.

The relevant provision of the Labour Code of British Columbia states that, where a trade union, certified as a bargaining agent, and an employer have been engaged in collective bargaining with a view to concluding their first agreement and have failed to do so, the Ministry of Labour may, at the request of either party and after such investigation as he deems necessary and advisable, direct the B.C. Board to inquire into the dispute and settle the terms and conditions for the first collective agreement. These terms shall be binding on both sides, except to the extent that they agree in writing to any revision. The Board is, however, required to give the parties an opportunity to present evidence and to make representations. It must also take into account: (1) the extent to which the parties have, or have not, bargained in good faith in an effort to conclude a collective agreement; and (2) the terms and conditions of employment for workers covered under other agreements who perform similar functions in the same or related circumstances.[76] The provisions of Part V of the Canada Labour Code, enacted in 1977-78, are very much the same as those in the B.C. Labour Code, except that, under the federal legislation, the Board must determine the extent to which the parties have, or have not, bargained in good faith. Under both statutes, the Boards may impose an agreement for one year only.

The provisions of the Quebec Labour Code, originally enacted in 1977, allow either party to ask the Minister to submit the dispute to a council of arbitration, which may consist of a single arbitrator (Quebec no longer has a Labour Relations Board), to determine the contents of a first collective agreement in the event that the parties will likely not be able to reach agreement within a reasonable time. If the council so decides, it shall inform the parties and the Minister of its decision, and any strike or lockout in progress at that time must end. The council of arbitration, in framing a first agreement, must take into account the conditions of employment in similar undertakings or under similar circumstances. Unlike the B.C. and federal Labour Relations Boards, the council of arbitration in Quebec binds the parties to this agreement for a period of *not less than one year, nor more than two years.* As in the two other jurisdictions, the parties may agree to amend the contents of the award, in whole or in part.[77] The original pro-

Table 6.8	Jurisdictions Which Make Provision for Settlement of a First Collective Agreement	
Jurisdiction	Yes	No
Federal	X	
Newfoundland		X
Prince Edward Island		X
Nova Scotia		X
New Brunswick		X
Quebec	X	
Ontario		X
Manitoba	X	
Saskatchewan		X
Alberta		X
British Columbia	X	

vision in the Quebec Labour Code required the arbitrator to determine if the parties had been bargaining in good faith. Arbitrators, however, do not usually determine matters of good faith. Hence, the Quebec Labour Code was amended by deleting that provision.

The provision in the Manitoba *Labour Relations Act* differs from those in the jurisdictions discussed above. Either party may apply to the Labour Relations Board ninety days after certification of the union. The Board shall then notify the other party of the application, inquire into the negotiations between the parties, and proceed to settle the provisions of a first agreement. However, if the parties do not reach agreement within sixty days of the application, the Board must, within a further three days, (1) settle the provisions of the agreement, or (2) notify the parties in writing of its opinion as to whether the parties might conclude a collective agreement through their own efforts or with the assistance of a conciliation officer. If the Board decides on the second route and if the parties have not concluded an agreement within another thirty days, then the Board must determine the terms of an agreement. The Board may impose an agreement for a period of only one year.[78]

A recent study dealing with statutory provisions in different jurisdictions concludes that the mechanism for imposing a collective agreement seems to be working fairly well. It goes on to suggest, however, that policy-makers should consider other measures as well.[79] One such measure is a clause enabling small unions to combine together in the certification process to withstand stone-walling by employers who seek to destroy newly certified unions by refusing to negotiate with them.

The British Columbia experience raises some doubts about the utility of imposing first agreements. As we stated earlier, the units on which the B.C. Board imposed first agreements were subsequently decertified. The "bargaining units were small, employee turnover was high, the union was not able to retain or to rebuild its

support, and the employer remained hostile throughout the entire experience."[80] On the basis of this experience, it is suggested that the unit be quite sizeable, that the union keep an active core of supporters who are able to act effectively, and that there

> be a two-year agreement in which to engage in visible administration of the contract (that is grieving discharges, seniority cases, and the like) in order to demonstrate the value of collective bargaining in action. Only in this way will the union have the footing it needs...when it must negotiate a renewal on its own.[81]

Arbitration of Unjust Dismissal Cases Where No Collective Agreement Exists

An important policy initiative was taken by the Federal Government in its 1977-78 amendment of the Canada Labour Code. Part III of the Code was amended to include a provision dealing with the arbitration or adjudication of unjust dismissal cases for workers not covered by collective agreements. According to Section 61.5, Subsection (1) of the consolidated version of Part III of the Canada Labour Code,

> Any person (a) who has completed twelve consecutive months of continuous employment by an employer, and (b) who is not a member of a group of employees subject to a collective agreement may make a complaint in writing to an inspector if he has been dismissed and if he considers his dismissal to be unjust.[82]

A person wishing to act under this provision must first file a complaint with an inspector of Labour Canada who then endeavours to assist the parties in resolving the dispute. Where an employer dismisses a person as described in subsection (1), either the person who was dismissed or the inspector may ask the employer for a written statement giving the reasons for dismissal. The employer is legally obliged to comply within fifteen days after the request is made. If the inspector is unable to obtain a settlement, the complainant may request that the case be referred to an adjudicator. In such an event, the inspector shall report to the Minister of Labour, who may then appoint a suitable person to adjudicate the complaint.

The adjudicator must consider whether or not the dismissal of the complainant was unjust, render a decision thereon, and send a copy of the decision with reasons to each party and to the Minister. Where an adjudicator decides that a person has been unjustly dismissed, he or she may require the employer to:

1 Pay the person compensation not exceeding the amount of money that is equivalent to the remuneration that would, but for the dismissal, have been paid by the employer to the person;
2 Reinstate the person in his employ; and
3 Do any other thing...to remedy or counteract any consequence of the dismissal.[83]

Compensation is usually required to be paid for the entire period in which the wrongfully dismissed worker is out of work. If a worker has worked for another employer subsequent to wrongful dismissal and prior to reinstatement, the compensation is usually reduced by the amount of wages earned in interim employment. Sometimes, an adjudicator may order that a reprimand be removed from a worker's file in order to mitigate the consequences of wrongful dismissal.

This federal policy initiative was indeed an important one. Workers not covered by collective agreements need this provision to protect them from being dismissed at the whims of their employers. Since the Federal Government passed this legislation, the governments of Quebec and Nova Scotia have introduced similar statutes with minor variations. No doubt, other provinces will also consider implementing similar legislation in the future to protect non-unionized workers from unjust dismissal.

Accreditation of Employers' Associations

Most jurisdictions in Canada have extensive provisions for the construction industry. One recent, innovative provision has been the accreditation of employers' associations. Depending on

the jurisdiction, accreditation may cover a large or a limited geographic area. Alternatively, special provision may be made for specific sectors of the construction industry.

Prior to the accreditation of employers' associations, a union or group of unions would often strike against only one company so as to obtain a good agreement and then use that settlement as a benchmark when dealing with other employers in the industry. This tactic is known as whipsawing. The idea behind employers' associations was to create a better balance of power between labour and management and prevent any one company from signing its own agreement with the unions. Instead, the association negotiates on behalf of all member employers. Whipsawing, as a result, has been greatly reduced in the construction industry.[84]

Compulsory Dues Check-offs

Before beginning a comparison of the dues check-off provisions in Canadian legislation, it would be useful to indicate their significance to unions. In the early days of unionism in North America, dues check-off clauses did not exist. Under those circumstances, local union leaders spent a great deal of time canvassing their members for payment of union dues. Dues check-off clauses relieve the union of this duty by requiring the employer to deduct union dues from the workers' wages and forward this money to the union. Deducting dues on behalf of the union and deducting income tax on behalf of the Department of National Revenue represent the same type of bookkeeping procedure. Many employers, however, see a significant philosophical difference between these two kinds of deductions. This philosophical difference will be discussed at the end of this section.

There are several different types of dues check-off clauses. The strongest is the compulsory check-off clause under which the employer must deduct union dues from every member of the bargaining unit, and the worker

Table 6.9	Provisions Regarding Dues Check-Offs	
Jurisdiction	Compulsory dues check-off	Negotiable dues check-off
Federal	X	
Newfoundland		X
Prince Edward Island		X
Nova Scotia		X
New Brunswick		X
Quebec	X	
Ontario	X	
Manitoba	X	
Saskatchewan	X	
Alberta		X
British Columbia		X

cannot prevent the employer from doing so. A second type is the irrevocable dues check-off clause under which the worker may authorize the employer to deduct regular union dues but cannot rescind this authorization. A third provision is the revocable dues check-off clause under which the worker authorizes the employer to deduct regular union dues, but may rescind this authorization in writing. All three forms of dues check-off provisions are found in collective agreements in Canada and some provisions are required by law. It is to a comparison of these legislative provisions that we now direct our attention.

The five jurisdictions of Quebec, Ontario, Manitoba, Saskatchewan, and the Federal Government contain statutory provisions which require that collective agreements contain compulsory check-off clauses. Under the Quebec Labour Code, an employer must withhold from the salary of every worker, whether he is a member of the certified association or not, the amount stated as an assessment by such an association. The Quebec Code also requires the employer to remit assessments monthly with the names of the workers from whose wages the assessments have been deducted.[85] The provision in the Manitoba *Labour Relations Act* is similar to that of the Quebec Labour Code. Where the worker is not a member of the union,

however, the amount deducted shall not include any portion of the dues which is payable in respect of pension, superannuation, sickness, insurance, or other benefits provided by the unions.[86]

Following a series of strikes over the issue of compulsory check-off clauses in the late 1970's, the Ontario Government passed Bill 89 in 1980. Bill 89 provides that, where a union so requests,[87] a collective agreement must include a provision requiring the employer to deduct from all members of the bargaining unit, whether they are union members or not, regular union dues which shall then be submitted immediately to the union. Bill 89 was passed following the decision of the OLRB in the *Radio Shack* case requiring the employer to include a dues check-off clause in its collective agreement with the United Steelworkers Union.

The Saskatchewan *Trade Union Act* requires upon the request of a trade union representing a majority of workers in any appropriate bargaining unit that the collective agreement contain a clause making the periodic payment of union dues a condition of employment, whether the worker be a trade-union member or not.[88]

In 1984, the Federal Government amended Part V of the Canada Labour Code to require an employer to deduct union dues where the union so requested, and to forward them immediately to the union. The federal clause is similar to the Manitoba clause because it does not require workers to pay full dues to a union which provides benefits such as pensions, superannuation and sickness insurance to members of the union only.[89] Benefits for union members only are peculiar to craft unions.

All other statutes in Canada contain a provision requiring an employer to honour a written request by a worker for the deduction of union dues from his wages (revocable dues check-off). In some jurisdictions, the worker, having authorized the deduction of union dues, must allow three months to pass before revoking that authorization. Most statutes in Canada require that dues be forwarded to the union at least once a month, accompanied by a statement containing the names of all workers in the bargaining unit.

Duty of Fair Representation

A somewhat troublesome problem of great concern to the courts, and more recently to legislators, is that of reconciling the rights of an individual as a willing participant in the collective-bargaining relationship with the rights of the union as an effective collective-bargaining agent. Sometimes, collective agreements suit one group to the detriment of another. A good example of this imbalance is the gaining of benefits for full-time workers through the ero-

sion of rights for part-time workers. Most of the concern, however, has been with the administration of collective agreements. This subject will be dealt with first, but some attention will be given later to fair representation in the negotiation of collective agreements.

The Task Force on Labour Relations addressed the issue of administering collective agreements in the following terms:

> [A] troublesome issue concerns the relative rights of the collectivity and of individuals in the negotiation and administration of a collective agreement. The problem can best be illustrated in relation to the individual member's right of access to the grievance procedure and to arbitration. Normally such access is controlled by the union, and this is as it must be if collective bargaining is not to be undermined. Yet the union should be expected to exercise this discretionary power in a fair and impartial manner if it is not to have arbitrary control over its members. This suggests that a union should be able to show that it acts in good faith whenever it chooses not to pursue a member's grievance or to pursue another one contrary to his interests. This must be the limit to any concept of fair representation if responsible collective decision making within and between union and management is not to be jeopardized.[90]

Special Provisions Since the publication of the *Report of the Task Force on Labour Relations* in 1968, six jurisdictions—the federal, Ontario, British Columbia, Manitoba, Saskatchewan and Quebec—have enacted special provisions on the

Table 6.10	Jurisdictions Which Contain a Duty of Fair Representation by Unions	
Jurisdiction	Yes	No
Federal	X	
Newfoundland	X	
Prince Edward Island		X
Nova Scotia		X
New Brunswick		X
Quebec	X	
Ontario	X	
Manitoba	X	
Saskatchewan	X	
Alberta	X	
British Columbia	X	

duty of fair representation. Two jurisdictions—Newfoundland and Alberta—deal with this issue under prohibited or unfair labour practices.[91] The wording in some of the statutes makes it clear that the provisions apply to the administration of the collective agreement only. A 1983 revision of the Saskatchewan *Trade Union Act* is very specific in this respect, as is indicated in section 25.1:

> Every employee has the right to be fairly represented in grievance or rights arbitration proceedings under a collective bargaining agreement by the trade union certified to represent his bargaining unit in a manner that is not arbitrary, discriminatory, or in bad faith.

The Newfoundland provision clearly refers to grievances, but those in the Manitoba and federal acts refer to the rights of workers under a collective agreement and, presumably, to the administration of a collective agreement.

Other jurisdictions seem to impose a duty of fair representation which includes both the administration and the negotiation of the terms of collective agreements. Section 7.1 of the B.C. Labour Code, for example, contains the following provision:

> A trade union or council of trade unions shall not act in a manner that is arbitrary, discriminatory or in bad faith in representing any of the employees in an appropriate bargaining unit, whether or not they are members of the trade union or of a constituent union of the council.

This provision, part of the Labour Code enacted in 1973, applies to both contract administration and contract negotiation. The former chairman of the B.C. Board discusses a number of such cases which came before the Board, and indicates the difficult choices the Board had to make.[92] However, when the Board was called upon to impose first contracts, it usually made compensation packages generous in order to dissuade anti-union employers from engaging in further anti-union activities.

Far from being a monolithic organization, a union consists of a number of sub-groups which may be looked at in a variety of ways, such as the old versus the young, the full-time versus the part-time, male versus female, etc. Of particular importance are older workers who, over a period of years, have accumulated a number of benefits such as the right to promotions, recall from layoff, (both based in part on seniority), medical plans, and pensions. Should a collective agreement negotiated and ratified by majority vote be allowed to infringe on the rights of older workers who may find it difficult to find employment elsewhere due to their age? Surely older workers need some protection which the majority of workers in the bargaining unit may not be willing to give them.

The policy of fair representation should include both the negotiation and the administration of collective agreements. The administrative tribunals which hear these cases should examine them very thoroughly to appreciate fully the dynamics which permeate the negotiation and administration of collective agreements and the internal trade-offs which unions must make in order to be effective bargaining agents. Granted, this scrutiny puts union leaders in a very delicate position, for there is often a very fine line as to what does and what does not fall within the ambit of fair representation. While union leaders must be given some discretion, they must exercise it with caution: if they err, they should err on the side of aggrieved workers.

Joseph Rose, a long-time observer and writer on construction labour relations in Canada, has suggested that there be a duty of fair representation on the part of employers' associations with respect to their employers.[93] This suggestion is particularly relevant since all provinces except Manitoba have passed legislation enabling multi-employer associations to acquire through the process of accreditation exclusive bargaining rights for all employers they represent.

> In many respects, the accreditation process is similar to trade union certification. The acquisition of exclusive bargaining rights is normally based on majority support, the appropriateness of the bargaining unit and the employers' association being a properly constituted organization.[94]

Accreditation applies to all industries in British Columbia, but only to the construction industry in other provinces. While all employers in the construction industry in Quebec are required by law to bargain through one provincial employers' association, other models exist in the other provinces. Rose's study examined a number of aspects of accreditation, one of which was the duty of fair representation for members of employers' associations in the provinces of British Columbia and Ontario. Section 7.2 of the B.C. Labour Code states that "An employers' organization shall not act in a manner that is arbitrary, discriminatory or in bad faith in representing any of the employers in the group appropriate for collective bargaining."[95] This provision gives the B.C. Board the authority to examine the duty of fair representation by employers' associations. Section 132 of the Ontario *Labour Relations Act* also contains a duty of fair representation on the part of accredited employers' associations:

> An accredited employers' organization, so long as it continues to be entitled to represent employers in a unit of employers, shall not act in a manner that is arbitrary, discriminatory or in bad faith in the representation of any of the employers in the unit, whether members of the accredited employers' organization or not.

It would be highly desirable if all statutes which permit the formation of employers' associations also were to include a duty of fair representation. In the absence of any statute explicitly requiring fair representation, courts in Canada have generally used the common law concept of natural justice to resolve unfair representation complaints. The two major principles of natural justice are the rule against bias, and the right to a fair hearing.

The Ontario Labour Relations Board has adopted a number of standards to be applied in determining the merits of a claim. One such standard is the immediate and long-term impact of a grievance decision on the whole bargaining unit when the union declines to take such a decision to arbitration. In general, the Ontario Board has accepted the principle that the individual worker does not have an absolute right to have his claim arbitrated. Furthermore, the Ontario Board places the burden of proof on the complainant in cases involving the duty of fair representation. The complainant is further expected to exhaust all other available internal remedies within the union before initiating action before the Ontario Board. In a recent study, David McPhillips suggests that labour relations boards are uncomfortable in the role of watchdogs over unions, and recommends that governments appoint ombudsmen under their labour relations acts.[96]

Religious Grounds for Exemption from Joining or Financing a Trade Union

In five jurisdictions — the federal, British Columbia, Manitoba, Saskatchewan and Ontario — workers who have religious objections to joining or financially supporting a trade union or both may apply to the appropriate labour relations boards for exemption. The federal, Ontario, Manitoba, and Saskatchewan statutes refer to religious objections to joining trade unions and paying union dues; the B.C. statute refers only to religious objections to joining trade unions. In the Saskatchewan, Ontario and federal jurisdictions, the respective boards may not exclude such a worker from an appropriate bargaining unit as long as the worker pays an amount equivalent to union dues to a specified charity as determined jointly by the worker and the trade union or, in cases where they cannot agree, by the respective boards.

The B.C. statute, on the other hand, requires, where union membership is compulsory, that the worker make a periodic written assignment of wages to the trade union in an amount equivalent to the regular union dues and that such an assignment not be revoked without the consent of the Board. The B.C. legislation thus consciously allows for exemption from belonging to a trade union, while ensuring that a worker so exempted makes his or her regular contribution to the trade union. Under the pro-

Table 6.11   Jurisdictions Which Exempt Union Members from Payment of Union Dues for Religious Reasons

Jurisdiction	Yes	No
Federal	X	
Newfoundland		X
Prince Edward Island		X
Nova Scotia		X
New Brunswick		X
Quebec		X
Ontario	X	
Manitoba	X	
Saskatchewan	X	
Alberta		X
British Columbia	X[a]	

[a]B.C. exempts workers from union membership, but not from payment of union dues.

visions of the Manitoba *Labour Relations Act*, where a worker is relieved from an obligation to join a trade union or to make a financial contribution in terms of union dues, the bargaining agent ceases to be obliged in any way to represent or act on his or her behalf.[97]

The first edition of this book pointed out that, although only four provinces then permitted exemptions on religious grounds, it was quite possible that other jurisdictions might soon include similar provisions in their statutes. For example, Part V of the Canada Labour Code used not to provide for exemption from belonging to a trade union or paying union dues on the basis of religious belief. In 1984, however, the Federal Government enacted legislation which exempts workers from paying dues to a union for religious reasons, but requires that the equivalent of union dues be paid to charitable organizations.

In discussing exemptions and dues check-off clauses, it is appropriate to point out that much debate still exists regarding the pros and cons of compulsory unionism and compulsory payment of union dues. One school of thought contends that individuals should have the right to decide whether or not they will (1) join a trade union and (2) make payments to the union if they do not join. Other experts contend that, since all workers in the bargaining unit benefit from any provisions that the union negotiates on their behalf, all workers should belong to the union or at least make financial contributions equal to those of union members.

This debate is not a new one. As early as 1946, a six-month strike occurred in the Ford Motor Company of Canada over the issue of union security. The UAW demanded that the collective agreement between the parties contain a clause requiring all workers to become union members, whereas the company took the position that it did not wish to compel workers to belong to the union. The strike ended only when the parties agreed to submit the issue to binding arbitration. The arbitrator, Justice Ivan C. Rand, concluded that since all workers benefit from the provisions of a collective agreement, it was incumbent upon them all to support financially the trade union which had won those benefits for them. Justice Rand deplored what he called "the free-loaders,"

that is, people who receive the benefits negotiated on their behalf but who refuse to pay
union dues.[98]

Protection from the Adverse Effects of Technological Change

The problem of technological change and its impact on workers has been a major policy issue
for legislators for a number of years now. Part
V of the Canada Labour Code and the statutes
of British Columbia, Manitoba and Saskatchewan
currently provide for the reopening of negotiations when a significant or major technological
change takes place.

Part V of the Canada Labour Code defines
technological change as

> the introduction by an employer into his work,
> undertaking or business of equipment or material
> of a different nature or kind than that previously
> utilized by him in the operation of the work,
> undertaking or business; and a change in the man-
> ner in which the employer carries on the work,
> undertaking or business that is directly related to
> the introduction of that equipment or material.[99]

Other statutes define technological change in
much the same way. For example, Saskatchewan
includes in its definition of technological change:
"the removal by an employer of any part of his
work, undertaking or business."[100]

Provisions for the settlement of disputes arising out of the introduction of technological
change by the employer may be negotiated and
included in a collective agreement between the
parties. British Columbia requires a mandatory
clause in every collective agreement to cover
disputes arising from such issues as an
employer's intention to introduce technological
change, opportunities for retraining or transfer
or workers, and severance wages for workers
displaced by reason of technological change.[101]

All statutes referred to above specify that a
significant number of workers must be affected
in order for their provisions to apply. Under the
Manitoba and B.C. statutes, the question of what
constitutes a significant number of workers is
determined by an arbitration board; in Saskat-

chewan, this decision is made by the Minister.
Under Part V of the Canada Labour Code, the
Governor-in-Council may specify, on the recom-
mendation of the Canada Labour Relations
Board, either the number of workers affected or
the method for making this determination.

Under Manitoba and Saskatchewan legislation, the employer must notify the bargaining
agent at least ninety days prior to the date on
which a change is to take effect. The federal act
was amended in 1984 to require a notice of 120
days. In the Saskatchewan legislation and in a
1984 amendment to Part V of the Canada Labour
Code, notice must include information as to the
nature of the technological change and the date
upon which it is to take effect, the number and
type of workers affected, and the likely effect of
the changes on the conditions of employment.

Upon receiving notice of technological
change, a bargaining agent may serve notice
upon the employer that the union wishes to
commence negotiations with a view to revising
the terms of the collective agreement. Once the
employer has received a notice to commence collective bargaining, Part V of the Canada Labour
Code prohibits him from making the technological change until an agreement is reached with
the union, or until a legal strike or lockout takes
place.

Under the provisions of the Saskatchewan
statute and Part V of the Canada Labour Code,
if an employer fails to notify the bargaining agent
of an intended technological change, the latter
may, within thirty days, refer the matter to the
labour relations boards for determination. In
deciding the matter, the boards may order the
employer not to proceed with the technological
change for a maximum period of ninety days
and may also instruct the employer to reinstate
any staff displaced as a result of the change and
reimburse such staff for any loss of pay suffered
because of their displacement. Such an order by
a board is deemed to be a notice of technological
change.

Under the provisions of the Manitoba statute,
if the employer fails to notify the union of a pro-

posed technological change, the bargaining agent may submit to arbitration the question of whether or not the employer has instituted a technological change that affects or will likely affect the terms and conditions of employment. Where the board finds that a technological change has been made, or will be made within ninety days from submission of the matter to arbitration, the arbitration award is to be considered as a notice of technological change. A 1983 amendment to the Manitoba *Labour Relations Act* provides that, where a collective agreement does not contain provisions for adjusting to technological change, the Minister may provide for such adjustment after considering the report of a person appointed by him to look into the matter. This provision is not found in any of the other statutes in Canada.

Under the provisions of the Labour Code of British Columbia, when an employer introduces, or intends to introduce, a technological change that affects the conditions of employment of a significant number of workers, and alters significantly the basis upon which the collective agreement was negotiated, either party may refer the matter to an arbitration board under the collective agreement or pursuant to the provisions of the Code. If the arbitration board finds that a change has been or will likely be made, the board may order the employer not to proceed with the change for a maximum period of ninety days. The board may also require the employer to reinstate any worker displaced by reason of the technological change, and to pay to the worker such compensation as the board considers reasonable. Furthermore, the arbitration board may recommend that the Minister appoint a special officer to resolve the matter, or that the parties commence collective bargaining on a specified date for the purpose of revising the provisions of the collective agreement.[102] In such an event, the prohibition against strikes and lockouts during the life of a collective agreement is suspended.

When policy-makers introduced these provisions in the statutes, the intent in some jurisdictions was to encourage the parties to include voluntarily provisions in their collective agreements to cushion the impact of the effects of technological change on workers. As was noted above, the B.C. Labour Code requires that such clauses be included in every collective agreement. Whether other jurisdictions will see this problem as sufficiently serious to require amendments to their labour relations statutes remains to be seen. Given the accelerated rate of change in technology in many industries in Canada, policy-makers may find it increasingly important to include these provisions in their statutes.

Unfair Labour Practices and the Roles of Labour Relations Boards

In addition to their responsibilities in the certification process (which was discussed extensively in previous sections) and the duty to bargain in good faith, labour relations boards in Canada are charged with the responsibility of handling many other subjects in the labour relations field. One important subject is unfair labour practices.

All statutes contain provisions which prohibit employers from interfering with the workers' rights to unionize and to avail themselves of the benefits of collective bargaining. According to the deputy ministers, chairmen of labour relations boards, and senior union and management officials interviewed in the conduct of this study, the most common form of unfair labour practice is the dismissal by employers of workers for exercising the rights granted to them under the statutes. A perusal of the annual reports of a number of labour departments supports this assertion.

Unions are also prohibited from using coercion in trying to influence prospective members. Like employers, unions are required to bargain in good faith in attempting to reach or revise a collective agreement, and must meet certain conditions before they may legally strike. In some

Figure 6.12	The Radio Shack Notice

NOTICE TO EMPLOYEES

Posted by Order of the Ontario Labour Relations Board

We have issued this notice in compliance with an Order of the Ontario Labour Relations Board issued after a hearing in which both the Company and the Union had the opportunity to present evidence. The Ontario Labour Relations Board found that we violated the Ontario Labour Relations Act and has ordered us to inform our employees of their rights.

The Act gives all employees these rights:

To organize themselves;

To form, join or help unions to bargain as a group, through a representative of their own choosing;

To act together for collective bargaining;

To refuse to do any and all of these things.

We assure all of our employees that:

WE WILL NOT do anything that interferes with these rights.

WE WILL NOT threaten our employees with plant closure or discharge or with any other type of reprisals because they have selected the United Steel Workers of America as their exclusive bargaining representative.

WE WILL NOT attempt to get employees to inform on union activities and the desires of their fellow employees.

WE WILL NOT engage in surveillance of employee activities with respect to union organization.

WE WILL NOT intimidate or coerce employees in any way into withdrawing from the United Steel Workers of America or from supporting the United Steel Workers of America.

WE WILL NOT refuse to bargain collectively with the United Steel Workers of America as the certified bargaining agent representative of all employees as directed by the Board in the following units:

(1) All employees of the respondent in Barrie save and except foremen and persons above the rank of foreman, office and sales staff, persons regularly employed for not more than 24 hours per week and students employed during the school vacation period.

(2) All employees of the respondent who are regularly employed for not more than 24 hours per week and students employed during the school vacation period, save and except foremen, and persons above the rank of foreman, office and sales staff.

WE WILL NOT in any other manner interfere with or restrain or coerce our employees in the exercise of their rights under the Act.

WE WILL make whole the United Steel Workers of America for all losses suffered by reason of our refusal to bargain in good faith as directed by the Board.

WE WILL make whole all bargaining unit employees who suffered losses by reason of our failure to bargain in good faith as directed by the Board.

WE WILL comply with all other directions of the Ontario Labour Relations Board including:

(1) Providing the United Steel Workers of America with reasonable access to employee notice boards in our warehouse facility for a period of one year;

(2) providing the United Steel Workers of America with a list of names and addresses of all bargaining unit employees and to keep this list up to date for a period of one year;

(3) providing the United Steel Workers of America with a reasonable opportunity to be present and to reply to any speech made by management representatives to assembled employees;

(4) providing the United Steel Workers of America with an opportunity to address bargaining unit employees on company time and company premises for a period of time not exceeding thirty minutes following the reading of this notice.

WE WILL bargain collectively with the United Steel Workers of America as the duly certified collective bargaining representative of our employees in the above units as directed by the Board and if an understanding is reached, we will sign a contract with the Union.

RADIO SHACK

Per: (Authorized Representative)

This is an official notice of the Board and must not be removed or defaced

This notice must remain posted for 60 consecutive working days

jurisdictions, unions are also charged with the duty of fair representation on behalf of their members. Charges of lack of fair representation are handled by labour relations boards.

In all jurisdictions in Canada except Quebec, labour relations boards investigate allegations of many unfair labour practices. Hence, the boards play a fundamental and constructive role in the Canadian industrial relations system. In some jurisdictions, labour relations boards are quite large: they include a chairman, associate or vice-chairmen, and a number of union and employer representatives. Many boards with very heavy caseloads prefer to sit in panels consisting of a chairman or vice-chairman, one union representative, and one management representative. In the smaller provinces, the chairmen of labour relations boards are usually appointed on a part-time basis since the case-load is not large enough to justify a full-time appointment.

The powers of Canadian labour relations boards differ from one jurisdiction to another. The boards derive their powers from the provisions of the labour relations acts under which they were created. Where an employer has wrongly dismissed a worker for union activities, most boards have the power to reinstate the worker with compensation to cover the loss of wages. Recently, the Ontario Labour Relations Board has ordered transgressing employers to compensate workers and, in some cases, has also required them to pay interest on any monetary loss a worker may have suffered, such as lost wages, damages, and legal expenses. The extensive remedial powers of some boards are spelled out in the statutes, usually pursuant to precedents set by other boards.

The Ontario Board and most others may also certify a trade union without a vote in those situations where it appears that the wishes of the workers would not be served if a vote were ordered. It was under this authority that the Ontario Labour Relations Board certified the United Steelworkers Union at the Radio Shack operation in Barrie, Ontario, on November 24, 1978. The broad range of powers possessed by labour relations boards in Canada was demonstrated through a notice which the Ontario Labour Relations Board, in December, 1979, required Radio Shack to post on its bulletin boards for a period of sixty consecutive working days. It also required the company to send copies of the notice to the homes of workers in the bargaining units involved.[103]

This case represents one of the more blatant violations of the law by employers in recent memory. Among other things, Radio Shack threatened its workers with plant closures, undertook surveillance of staff for union activities, used other forms of intimidation and threats, and refused to bargain in good faith. This is reminiscent of similar actions taken by some employers during the 1930's, and does not depict the normal employer reaction to unionization. Rather, it is included here as an illustration of the extremes that labour relations boards must be prepared to handle. It also illustrates some of the remedies that boards must fashion for the circumstances of difficult cases.

As indicated above, some boards in Canada may also have to impose first collective agreements on employers, deal with worker complaints against their bargaining agents, and fashion remedies appropriate to the unfair practices of the unions in question. In most jurisdictions, if one party wishes to prosecute the other party in court, permission must first be granted from the appropriate labour relations board. The boards, in determining whether there are grounds for prosecution, must investigate to some extent the merits of the case before consenting to prosecute.

Conclusion

In this chapter, we have discussed major policy issues in Canadian industrial relations and have also attempted to describe the administrative machinery established by the various jurisdictions to accomplish the policy objectives set out in their statutes. Policy issues have included: the rights of workers and employers under the statutes, the certification process, the various types of third-party assistance available in the negotiation of a collective agreement where the parties fail to achieve an agreement between themselves (interest disputes), the machinery specified in the legislation for handling contract interpretation disputes during the life of the collective agreement (rights disputes), and the jurisdictional disputes between unions in the construction industry.

In addition, we have dealt with the ability of some labour relations boards to impose a first collective agreement and, to some extent, with the whole problem of unfair labour practices and the powers that boards have in rectifying these. Other policy questions discussed were the fair representation of members by unions, compulsory dues check-off, exemption from union membership on religious grounds, the special powers given boards in emergency disputes in some jurisdictions, and the establishment of employers' associations in the construction industry.

In addition to drawing comparisons among various jurisdictions, some basic philosophical questions have been raised regarding differences among jurisdictions in handling the same or similar problems: Should the certification of a bargaining agent be determined by 50% of those voting or by 50% of the membership? Why does British Columbia now require a vote in every certification case? Should the payment of union dues be compulsory? It is hoped that both students of labour relations and practitioners will give some thought to these and other questions raised in this chapter.

questions

1 Trace the evolution of labour relations legislation in Canada.
2 Do you think Canadian governments have legislated excessively in the collective bargaining field? Elaborate.
3 Identify and discuss the four classical types of labour-management disputes. Indicate how the legislation and the machinery established by it have dealt with each of these kinds of disputes.
4 Do you consider recent initiatives to have favoured unionization and collective bargaining? Elaborate.
5 The Landrum-Griffin Bill, passed in the United States in 1959, concerns itself with the internal affairs of unions with a view to ensuring the democratic elections of union officers and the financial accountability of unions. The Bill also gives the Secretary of Labour the power to conduct inquiries in cases of suspected wrongdoing. Do you see the need for similar legislation in Canada? Elaborate and give some details to support your position.
6 Using the *Radio Shack* notice, discuss some of the unfair labour practices committed by the company. What do you think of the OLRB's decision?
7 Identify and assess each of the new policy initiatives.
8 Does labour legislation in your province favour unions or management? Why?
9 Why does B.C. labour legislation require religious objectors to pay regular union dues to the union rather than to a charitable organization? Demonstrate your understanding of this legislation by identifying the philosophical questions inherent in the B.C. requirement.
10 If you were the Minister of Labour in your province, what major changes, if any, would you make in the present legislation? Elaborate.
11 Discuss the effects of legislating labour relations provisions (such as those concerning wrongful dismissal) for non-unionized workers. Compare and contrast the advantages and disadvantages of such legislative protection with those of union protection. Do you think all jurisdictions in Canada should legislate protection for non-unionized workers? If so, what parameters do you think should exist for such legislation?

notes

1 Footnote 45 gives the titles of the Acts governing industrial relations at the federal and provincial levels. However, rather than repeating the titles of the statutes, a shorter footnote form is used. For example, rather than making repeated references in our end notes to the Ontario Labour Relations Act, we refer to the R.S.O., c. 232, s. 16. This shorter form means the Revised Statutes of Ontario, Chapter 232, Section 16. In some cases the R. does not appear, as is the case of Alberta and a number of provinces. Hence, S.A. refers to the Statutes of Alberta.

2 R. M. Dawson, *The Government of Canada*, 3rd. rev. ed. (Toronto: University of Toronto Press, 1957), p. 35.

3 D. H. Woods, *Labour Policy in Canada*, 2nd. ed. (Toronto: Macmillan, 1973); Stuart Jamieson, *Industrial Relations in Canada*, 2nd ed. (Toronto: Macmillan, 1973). Jamieson's book, particularly Ch. 5, discusses in abbreviated form the material set out in Woods's book.

4 Woods, *Labour Policy in Canada*, 2nd. ed., pp. 41-42.

5 Alton Westwood Craig, *The Consequences of Provincial Jurisdiction for the Process of Company-Wide Collective Bargaining in Canada: A Study of the Packinghouse Industry* (unpublished Ph.D. Dissertation, Cornell University, 1964). Much of the material regarding the *IDI Act* and legislation up to the early 1950's is taken from the author's doctoral dissertation which is copyrighted in the author's name. A copy may be found in the Labour Canada library.

6 Canada Department of Labour, *Judicial Proceedings Respecting Constitutional Validity of the Industrial Disputes Investigation Act, 1907 and Amendments of 1910, 1918, and 1920* (Ottawa: Queen's Printer, 1925).

7 *Ibid.*, pp. 256-57.

8 *Ibid.*, pp. 21-22.

9 1925 A.C., pp. 404-05.

10 F. P. Varcoe, *The Distribution of Legislative Power in Canada* (Toronto: Carswell Company, 1954), pp. 10-11.

11 Dawson, *The Government of Canada*, and particularly the chapters dealing with the powers of the federal and provincial governments; F. R. Scott, "Federal Jurisdiction over Labour Relations — A New Look," *Proceedings, 11th Annual Conference* (Montreal: McGill University, Industrial Relations Centre, 1959), pp. 35-51.

12 *Canadian Labour Relations: Report of the Task Force on Labour Relations* (Ottawa: Privy Council Office, December, 1968), pp. 210-11. The four members who formed the Task Force on Industrial Relations were: Professor H. D. Woods, then of McGill University; Abbé Gérard Dion, of Laval University; John H. G. Crispo, of the University of Toronto; F. W. R. Carrothers, then President of the University of Calgary.

13 Quoted in B. M. Selekman, *Postponing Strikes: A Study of the Industrial Disputes Investigation Act of Canada* (New York: Russell Sage Foundation, 1927), p. 287.

14 H. D. Woods and Sylvia Ostry, *Labour Policy and Labour Economics in Canada* (Toronto: Macmillan of Canada, 1962), p. 24, footnote 21.

15 Vol. XL, No. 7, *Labour Gazette* (July 1940), pp. 678-79.

16 H. A. Logan, *State Intervention and Assistance in Collective Bargaining: The Canadian Experience, 1943-1954* (Toronto: University of Toronto Press, 1956), p. 11.

17 Vol. XLI, No. 10, *Labour Gazette* (October 1941), p. 1209.

18 *Ibid.*, p. 1209.

19 Logan, *State Intervention*; Vol. XLIV, No. 2, *Labour Gazette* (February 1944), pp. 135-43.

20 Vol. XLIV, No. 11, *Labour Gazette* (November 1946), pp. 1523-25.

21 *Industrial Relations and Disputes Investigation Act* (1948), c. 54.

22 *Report of the Task Force on Labour Relations*, p. 138.

23 Labour Code of British Columbia, s. 27.

24 George Sayers Bain, *Union Growth and Public Policy in Canada* (Ottawa: Labour Canada, October 1978), p. 29.

25 Alberta *Labour Relations Act*, R.S.A. (1980), c. L-1.1 as amended by Alberta *Labour Relations Amendment Act* (1983), c. 82, s 1(1)(k); Ontario *Labour Relations Act*, R.S.O. (1980), c. 228 as amended by 1983, c. 42, s. 3(a); The Nova Scotia *Trade Union Act*, S.N.S. 1972, c. 19 as amended and revised to June 11, 1984, s. 1(2)(b); Prince Edward Island *Labour Act*, R.S.P.E.I. (1974), Cap. L-1 with amendments to 1983, s. 7(2)(a).

26 Ontario *Labour Relations Act*, R.S.O. (1980), c. 228, s. 6(4).

27 Nova Scotia *Trade Union Act*, S.N.S. 1972, c. 19 as revised and amended to June 11, 1984, s. 24(14).

28 Edward E. Herman, *Determination of the Appropriate Bargaining Unit by Labour Relations Boards in Canada* (Ottawa: Canada Department of Labour, November 1966), pp. 12-13.

29 Canada Labour Relations Board, "Service, Office and Retail Workers of Canada, *applicant* and Canadian Imperial Bank of Commerce, *employer,* Various Branches in British Columbia" *Part I* (June 10, 1977), and *Part II,* (September, 1977).

30 Herman, *Determination of the Appropriate Bargaining Unit by Labour Relations Boards in Canada.*

31 Nova Scotia *Trade Union Act,* S.N.S. (1972), C. 19 as amended by 1978-79, c. 78, s. 1.

32 Paul Weiler, *Reconcilable Differences* (Toronto: Carswell Company, 1980), pp. 15-49, 48-49.

33 B.C. Labour Relations Board, *Annual Report* (1974), pp. 12-13.

34 Data for the Canada Labour Relations Board were received from the Research Branch of the Board. Data for Ontario were taken from the Ontario Ministry of Labour, *Annual Report* (1982-83), pp. 86-87; and Ontario Ministry of Labour, *Annual Report* (1983-84), pp. 81-82.

35 R.S.O., s. 9; R.S.Q., ss. 28, 32, 37; and R.S., s. 127.(1).

36 S.N.S., 1977, c. 70, s. 1.

37 S.B.C., 1979, c. 212, s. 35.(h).

38 S.N.B., 1971, c. I-4, s. 15(3).

39 R.S.P.E.I., 1974, Cap. L-1, s. 13.(1).

40 S.M., 1984, c. 21, s. 39(3).

41 Weiler, *Reconcilable Differences,* pp. 38-39; Caskey, "Further Attacks on Labour in British Columbia," Vol. 31, No. 7, *CAUT Bulletin* (October 1984), pp. 4, 21.

42 Honourable Mary Beth Dolin, "Information Concerning Proposed Changes in Manitoba's Legislation," (Winnipeg: Manitoba Ministry of Labour, April 1984), p. 5.

43 "The Dark Cloud Over Manitoba," *Winnipeg Free Press* (June 26, 1984), p. 19. This advertisement was sponsored by the Manitoba and Winnipeg Chambers of Commerce, the Manitoba Mining Association, and other employer organizations.

44 S. Muthuchidambaram, *Legislative Background to and an Examination of the Saskatchewan Trade Union Amendment Act: Bill 40* (Regina: Faculty of Administration, University of Regina, April 1984).

45 Part V of the Canada Labour Code, R.S., c. L-1 with amendments to October 1984, s. 127(2); Newfoundland *Labour Relations Act,* S.N. 1977, c. 64 with amendments up to 1983, s. 36.(1); Prince Edward Island *Labour Act,* R.S.P.E.I., 1974, Cap. L-1 with amendments to 1983, s. 11(1); Nova Scotia *Trade Union Act,* S.N.S. 1972, c. 19 with amendments to June 1984, ss. 23-24; New Brunswick *Industrial Relations Act,* S.N.B., 1971, c. 1-4 with amendments to 1982, s. 14; Quebec Labour Code, R.S.Q., 1983, c. C-27, with amendments to November 1983, s. 28; Ontario *Labour Relations Act,* R.S.O. 1980, c. 228 as amended by 1983, c. 42, ss. 7, 9; Manitoba *Labour Relations Act,* S.M. 1972 c. 75-Cap. L10 with amendments to August 1984, s. 31(1); Saskatchewan *Trade Union Act,* 1972, c. 137 with amendments to October 1983, ss. 6-8; Alberta *Labour Relations Act,* R.S.A. 1980, c. L-1.1 with amendments to November 30, 1983, s. 34(1); British Columbia *Labour Code,* S.B.C. 1979, c. 212 with amendments including 1984, s. 39. Under Section 28 of the Quebec Labour Code, a certification commissioner, if convinced that an association meets the requirements for certification as a bargaining agent, must certify that association in writing.

46 S.N.S., s. 26.

47 R.S., c. L-1 with amendments to October 1984, s. 127(3).

48 R.S.O. 1980, c. 228, s 17.(1).

49 *Ibid.,* s. 33.(4).

50 S.M. 1984, c. 21, ss. 83(1)(2).

51 Wilfred List, "Mediators Heal TTC's Old Wounds," *Globe and Mail* (July 3, 1979), p. 4.

52 *Canadian Industrial Relations: The Report of the Task Force on Labour Relations,* p. 169.

53 *Ibid.,* p. 168.

54 R.S., c. L-1 s. 180.(1)(d).

55 R.S.A., 1980, c. L-1.1, ss. 93-94.

56 *Ibid.,* ss. 87-90.

57 S.N.S., 1972, c. 19, s. 45(3)(a); R.S.P.E.I., 1974, c. L-1, s. 40(4).

58 *Ibid.*

59 "Union to Appeal Strike Ruling," *Globe and Mail* (December 19, 1979), p. 8.

60 R.S., c. L-1, s. 155.(1).

61 "Expedited Arbitration Breaks Grievance Logjam," *Steel Labour* (April 1973); and Ben Fischer, "The Steel Industry's Expedited Arbitration: A Judgement after Two Years," *Arbitration Journal* (September 1973), pp. 185-90.

62 Gérard Dion, "Jurisdictional Disputes," Ch. 8, *Construction Labour Relations,* eds. H. C.

Goldenburg and John H. G. Crispo (Ottawa: The Canadian Construction Association, 1968), pp. 333-75.

63 Weiler, *Reconcilable Differences,* p. 75.

64 R.S.O., 1980, c. 228, s. 73.(1).

65 S.M., 1972, c. 75-Cap. L-10, s. 11(1).

66 R.S.Q., 1983, c. C-27, ss. 109.1-2.

67 S.B.C., 1979, c. 212, s. 57.

68 Weiler, *Reconcilable Differences,* p. 168.

69 *Ibid.,* p. 170.

70 *Ibid.,* p. 173.

71 *Ibid.,* p. 177.

72 Labour Canada, *Report of the Inquiry Commission on Wider-Based Collective Bargaining,* (Ottawa: December, 1978).

73 R.S.A., 1980, c. L-1.1, ss. 148-150.

74 The British Columbia *Essential Services Disputes Act,* S.B.C., c. 113, ss. 5-8, 12; s. 18.

75 Weiler, *Reconcilable Differences,* p. 53. For a more detailed discussion of this issue, see pp. 49-55.

76 S.B.C., 1979, c. 212, s. 70.

77 R.S.Q., 1983, c. C-27, ss. 93.1-9.

78 S.M., 1984, c. 21, ss. 75.1(1)-(8).

79 S. Muthuchidambaram, "Settlement of First Collective Agreements: An Examination of the Canada Labour Code Amendment," Vol. 35, No. 3, *Industrial Relations/Relations Industrielles* (1980), pp. 387-409.

80 Weiler, *Reconcilable Differences,* p. 54.

81 *Ibid.*

82 Part 111, Canada Labour Code, R.S., c. L-1, with amendments to July, 1982, s. 61.5.

83 *Ibid.,* s. 61(9).

84 Joseph B. Rose, *Public Policy, Bargaining Structure and the Construction Industry* (Toronto: Butterworths, 1980).

85 R.S.Q., 1983, c. C-27, s. 47.

86 S.M., 1976, c. 45, s. 21.

87 R.S.O., 1980, c. 228, s. 43.

88 S.S., 1972, c. 137, s. 32.

89 R.S., c. L-1, s. 162.1.

90 *Canadian Industrial Relations: Report of the Task Force on Labour Relations,* p. 104.

91 R.S., c. L-1, s. 136.1; S.B.C., 1979, c. 212, s. 7.(1); R.S.A., 1980, c. L-1.1, s. 138(i); S.M., 1984, c. 21, s. 16; S.S., 1983, c. 81, s. 8; R.S.O., 1980, c. 228, s. 68; R.S.Q., 1983, c. C-27, ss. 47.2-.3; S.N., 1983, c. 60, s. 14.

92 Weiler, *Reconcilable Differences,* pp. 128-39.

93 Joseph B. Rose, *Employer Accreditation: a Retrospective,* Research and Working Paper Series No. 206 (Hamilton: School of Business, McMaster University, June, 1983). See in particular the section on the duty of fair representation, pp. 13-17.

94 *Ibid.,* p. 2.

95 S.B.C., 1979, c. 212, s. 7.(2).

96 David C. McPhillips, "Duty of Fair Representation: Recent Attitudes in British Columbia and Ontario," Vol. 36, No. 4, *Industrial Relations/Relations Industrielles* (1981), pp. 808-27.

97 R.S., c. L-1, s. 162.(2)-.(4) or 1984, c. 39, s. 31; S.B.C., 1979, c. 212, s. 11; S.S. 1983, c. 81, s. 5(1); S.M. 1984, c. 21, s. 33; R.S.O. 1980, c. 228, s. 47.

98 Justice Ivan C. Rand's decision in *Labour Gazette* (1946).

99 R.S., c. L-1, , s. 149.

100 S.S. 1983, c. 81, s. 43.(1)(c).

101 S.B.C., 1979, c. 212, ss. 71-78.

102 *Ibid.*

103 Ontario Labour Relations Board, "United Steelworkers of America, complainant and Radio Shack, *respondent,*" decision (December 5, 1979), para. 125, pp. 71-75.

7
The Negotiation Process

Peter Redman, *The Financial Post*

Introduction

In order to avoid any confusion about the objective of this chapter, the terms *the collective bargaining process* and *the negotiating process* need to be clarified.[1] *The collective bargaining process* constitutes a complex of activities and relationships occurring daily or continuously in the workplace, concerning both the rewards workers receive for their services and the conditions under which these services are rendered. *The negotiating process*, by contrast, occurs periodically and seeks to define the rewards and conditions of employment. Chapter 1 treats the

negotiating process as the means by which inputs (in this case, the demands of two actors, labour and management) are converted into outputs, be they working conditions or rewards to workers for services performed.

Hence, the collective bargaining process, as it is viewed here, consists of numerous subsets of activities, including negotiation and implementation of the terms of a collective agreement. The rewards for, or guides to, daily activities in the workplace are important to both workers and employers. If the terms of the collective agreement meet the needs and expectations of the workers, are spelled out clearly, and the parties share a common understanding of them, then these terms may be implemented with few difficulties. If differences do occur, however, over the meaning or application of the various clauses in the collective agreement, provisions exist for reviewing such alleged breaches. These differences are often discussed on the spot by the supervisor and worker with or without the aid of a shop steward. If such discussion does not succeed in resolving the differences, then the parties may use the grievance process, a process discussed in Chapter 9. This chapter, however, concentrates solely on the periodic negotiations which define the major terms and conditions under which workers provide their services.

The Negotiation Process

Within the organized segments of the private, public, and parapublic sectors, the negotiation process is the main instrument for converting inputs (demands) into worker-oriented and organization-oriented outputs. Should the parties fail to reach agreement through their periodic negotiations, a variety of supplementary procedures exist to help break the impasse. The use of these procedures may be prescribed by legislation or agreed upon between the parties, and occurs in both private and public sectors. The forms and functions of these supplementary procedures comprise the subject matter of the following chapter.

Among the many topics included under the rubric of industrial relations, probably none is more difficult to analyze than the negotiating process — despite the growing body of literature that has been written on the subject.[2] Rather than summarizing the several formal approaches, this chapter will explain how the negotiating process works, using the following categories: (1) negotiating units, (2) the preparation of demands, (3) the composition of negotiating committees, (4) negotiation strategy, (5) multidimensional demands, (6) bargaining power, (7) a non-deterministic approach, (8) ratification of new agreement clauses, (9) compulsory provisions, (10) the duty to bargain in good faith, and (11) concession bargaining.

Negotiating Units

The broad concept of bargaining structure and particularly the concept of the negotiating unit are complex and critical to our discussion of the negotiation process. It is crucial to understand the term *the negotiating unit* precisely in order to avoid the confusion often caused by the numerous meanings inherent in the term *bargaining structure*. Hence, we shall begin this chapter by discussing the concept of the negotiation unit, its components and determinants, and its importance for the parties involved in negotiations.

Certified Bargaining Unit   Several years ago, an excellent article pointed out the difficulty of defining the term *bargaining structure*: a number of components in the bargaining structure are not always differentiated clearly.[3] However, since we have detailed one aspect of the bargaining structure in the preceeding chapter, let us begin this discussion by defining the bargaining structure from a legislative point of view first. The discussion of the regular certification process and the quickie vote in the previous chapter pointed out that labour relations boards first determine whether or not a unit proposed by a bargaining agent is an appropriate bargaining unit, except in cases of voluntary recognition. Once this determination is made, we have what some writers call the election district[4] or, what we prefer, the certified bargaining unit. This unit may be the negotiating unit which the parties use for negotiating a collective agreement, a situation which occurs in a company consisting of one establishment only. On the other hand, a certified bargaining unit may be one of a number of building blocks in a negotiation unit which may eventually emerge by mutual agreement of the parties — a situation which typically occurs in a company consisting of more than one establishment.

Decision-Making Unit a second component, and for our purposes the most important, is a kind of negotiating unit defined as the decision-making unit through which the parties engage in formal discussions leading to a settlement of the outstanding issues. This final settlement may take the form of a first collective agreement or a renewal of the existing collective agreement. Note that both the singular and plural forms for the term *collective agreement* are used above since the settlement reached between the parties may result in one collective agreement covering all the workers in all the certified units, or it may result in as many separate collective agreements as there are certified units. Hence, the number of negotiation units may be fewer than the number of certified bargaining units. The number of certified bargaining units, however, will never be greater than the number of negotiating units.

The people in the negotiating unit may include members from some or all of the separately certified bargaining units. For example, all of the packinghouse plants of Canada Packers across the country hold separate certificates issued by the appropriate provincial labour relations boards. The parties have formed a national negotiating unit, however, which brings together not only senior representatives from the head office of the company and the union, but also company and union representatives from plants all across the country. All these people represent one large negotiating unit. The collective agreement reached by this particular unit covers over 5,000 production workers in Prince Edward Island, Quebec, Ontario, Manitoba, Saskatchewan and Alberta,[5] although some of the terms of the agreement may vary from one province to another. In Ontario, the statutory civic

holiday falls on the first Monday of August, but on other days in other provinces. Hence, single collective agreements may contain global provisions with applications which vary from plant to plant. The most common way such provisions are embodied is through master agreements with supplementary local agreements.

Unit of Direct Impact A third component of the bargaining structure is the unit of direct impact[6] — that negotiating unit which affects directly the agreements of other units. When a settlement is reached between Canada Packers and the union representing its workers, for example, the terms of that settlement are incorporated directly into the existing collective agreement between the union and Swifts. This pattern began during World War II and has contained to the present time.

Appropriate Bargaining Unit With respect to the concept of appropriate bargaining unit referred to in previous sections, one board chairman has pointed out that labour relations boards are confronted with two competing concepts when they are called upon to define such a unit. The boards may look to the appropriate bargaining unit first as the one through which the union has sufficient worker support to give it the greatest chance of acquiring bargaining rights with the employer. This was a major consideration of the Canada Labour Relations Board in a 1977 decision[7] when it found a branch of a bank to be the appropriate unit, rather than all of the workers of a trans-Canada bank, as the employer wanted. In looking down the road a few years into the future, the boards may realize that the unit most appropriate for certification purposes may not be the most appropriate for negotiation purposes later on. This conflict has been pointed out by Paul Weiler:

[It] is a common experience of labour boards to find that these two uses of the 'unit' point in opposite directions when the board must decide on the precise boundaries of an appropriate unit. What looks like an optimal structure for long-range negotiations may also be worlds removed from any grouping of employees within which the trade union could hope to obtain majority support in the short run.[8]

The appropriate bargaining unit, the negotiating unit, and the unit of direct impact represent three overviews of the concept of bargaining structure. For the purpose of this chapter, we will be concerned mainly with the negotiating unit as our unit of analysis. There will be some discussion, however, of the unit of direct impact as it relates to pattern bargaining.

Determinants of Negotiating Units

Legislative Framework One of the major determinants of the negotiating unit is the legislative framework. This framework serves as the foundation on which the union-management relationship is built. In Canada, there are two aspects to the legislative foundation. First, Canada is a highly decentralized state in which 90% of workers fall under provincial jurisdiction and only 10% fall under federal jurisdiction which includes only a few industries such as transportation and communications. Hence, most of our certified bargaining units are confined to the provincial level. However, there is nothing preventing the parties from informally or extra-legally forming multi-provincial negotiating units which include a number of separately certified bargaining units. These broader types of negotiating units are found in industries such as meat-packing, automobile and steel manufacturing, canning, and pulp and paper production.

Decentralization Second, most labour relations boards in Canada usually define the appropriate bargaining unit as including both production and craft workers at the establishment level. Some even include professional engineers if the majority of these workers wish

to be included in such a unit. The major exception to this means of definition occurs in British Columbia where unions are often certified as bargaining agents for all the establishments of a company, and where councils of trade unions may be certified as bargaining agents for all of the workers affected directly by employers' associations in any industry. Weiler has stated that "British Columbia has the only open-ended accreditation provision in Canadian labour law, one which is available to employer associations in any industry whatsoever (rather than simply in the construction industry, as in most other Canadian jurisdictions)."[9] The major point to keep in mind here is the strong emphasis placed on single-establishment certification by most provincial labour relations boards. This emphasis contributes greatly to Canada's decentralized negotiation structure.

Some governments play a centralizing role in the public sector where, as in British Columbia and Ontario, the negotiating units are two-tier: one for working conditions only and others for wages only. As we shall indicate in Chapter 10, bargaining agents for public-sector workers are named by some provincial statutes.

Market Forces Another major determinant of negotiation structure is the role played by market forces. As A. R. Weber has pointed out, unions have generally sought negotiating units which are "coextensive with the specific market(s) encompassed by their jurisdictions."[10] As a general rule, industrial unions press for negotiating units which are as broad as the scope of the product market, while craft unions are more concerned with conditions in local labour markets. A good example of an industrial union is the United Auto Workers. Until recently, the UAW tried to reach similar agreements with the Big Three for workers in both Canada and the United States. A good example of a craft union is one which operates in the construction industry. In both situations, unions are trying to take labour out of competition in order to require companies to compete on a basis other than wages.

Centralization The employer's operations may have a significant effect on the nature of the negotiating unit. Unions will attempt to obtain company-wide negotiations, for example, when the employer operates autonomous establishments. This is particularly true in industries such as meat-packing where each plant of a company operates as an autonomous unit. If one plant is struck, the company can usually supply that market from another plant which is located nearby. It was for this reason that the United Packinghouse Workers Union (now the United Food and Commercial Workers International Union) won the right to national negotiations with the Big Three meatpacking companies during World War II — a right which this union and its successors have, until recently, clung to despite the fact that the companies operate under provincial jurisdiction.

The United Steelworkers Union has also carried on joint negotiations with the Southern Ontario and Quebec plants of the Steel Company of Canada despite the fact that this industry also operates under provincial jurisdiction. No agreement is acceptable to the union unless it meets the minimal demands of the big local union at both Stelco in Hamilton and Notre Dame in Montreal. Hence, some unions are strong enough to obtain and maintain multi-provincial negotiating units despite the fact that the employers with whom they deal fall under provincial jurisdiction.

In some cases, however, it is employers who initiate more centralized forms of negotiation in order to increase their bargaining power with one or more large unions. This practice occurs in much of the clothing and printing industries in Ontario and Quebec as well as the trucking industry in a number of provinces where negotiations take place through multi-employer bargaining councils. By joining together and forming a consolidated structure these small companies minimize the economic harm which might be inflicted on them by large unions. For example, the Council of Printing Industries of Canada, which includes various locations in Ontario and Quebec, negotiates with the Graphic Arts International Union on behalf of fifty-five companies.[11] Most of these small companies would not be able to withstand a lengthy strike by this major union.

In some cases, both unions and employers prefer larger negotiating units in order to obtain uniformity of fringe benefits[12] and to facilitate administration. From the workers' point of view, however, centralized bargaining may not seem desirable, since workers may have little input into the negotiation process.[13] In addition, internal trade-offs between union and management may be much more difficult in such large structures. Managers at the local level may also object to highly-centralized negotiation structures, especially if these structures erode the decision-making powers which managers presume to be part of their own function. Administrators in hospitals and schools in the Province of Quebec are isolated from the negotiation process because of the very highly-centralized negotiations which take place in the parapublic sectors in that province. Chapter 10 will deal in detail with the legislative structure of negotiations in Quebec.

An enormous diversity of negotiation structures exists in Canada. Negotiations and collective agreements take place almost every day. There is no such thing in Canada as a major national case around which all others revolve, as in the Australian metal industries case. Some calendar years, however, see much more activity than others, particularly when many of the groups in the federal and provincial public sectors come up for negotiations during the same year.

It should also be mentioned that the highly unionized public sectors in Canada at the federal, provincial and municipal levels have made for somewhat more centralized negotiation structures than would otherwise exist. The increased incidence of unionization in these sectors since 1964 has seen a pronounced shift in the direction of multi-establishment negotiating units. In the federal and provincial sectors, negotiations for each major group of workers takes place for all workers in the group no matter how scattered the workers may be across the country or province.

Pattern Bargaining What the system of negotiations in Canada lacks in centralized negotiation structure may be made up for in part through the adoption of pattern bargaining. As indicated earlier, the outcome of a particular set of negotiations may have a significant impact on other negotiations. The phenomenon of pattern bargaining revolves around the notion of the unit of direct impact. Pattern bargaining tends to occur where negotiations in one industry or locality serve as a fulcrum for negotiations in other industries or localities. One major study concluded that "wage spillovers can only be found for bargaining units in similar industries within a region."[14] Some examples of pattern bargaining will be given here as examples of the extent to which they do operate by industry and area.

The auto industry has traditionally been characterized by informal pattern bargaining between the UAW and one of the Big Three companies. In these negotiations, the UAW focuses its efforts on one company while dragging on negotiations with the other two companies. Once the target settlement is reached, the UAW then uses it as a standard with which to negotiate with the other two large companies. A similar situation exists in the steel industry where the United Steelworkers Union will use either Stelco in Hamilton or Algoma Steel as a target, and then use the settlement reached with the target as a standard with which to conclude an agreement with the other company.

J. C. Anderson gives an example of a formal, intercity pattern-bargaining situation which is unique: In British Columbia where fire fighters' negotiations in that province are dominated by the outcome of collective bargaining in Vancouver,

> Over 80 percent of the municipalities in the province with collective agreements have included a provision agreeing to either settle for the same salary as the Vancouver fire fighters or to give some fixed proportion (for example, 90 percent) of the base Vancouver salary to their fire fighters."[15]

As we stated above, this kind of iron-clad pattern bargaining is unusual, but it demonstrates how pattern bargaining may actually act as an almost perfect substitute for a broader negotiating unit.

Since we have discussed the negotiating unit, its components and determinants, and its importance for the parties involved in negotiations, let us now look more closely at the empirical data for the period from 1966 to 1984. As we discuss the trends in the types of negotiating units, we will give specific examples of each of the types and show how important some types have been for the structure of negotiating units during particular years. Following that, we will then go on to discuss other aspects of the negotiation process.

Types of Negotiating Units

Table 7.1 includes the percentage of different types of negotiating units which concluded negotiations for each year cited, while Table 7.2 gives the percentage of workers covered by each type. These tables cover negotiating units of 500 or more workers (excluding those in the construction industry) for the period from 1966 to 1984. An eight-type typology is used to differentiate among the types of negotiating units in the two tables. It will be noted that the single-union type is much more predominant both in terms of the percent of negotiating units and the percent of workers covered than is the multi-union type, and accounts for more than 90% of the negotiating units and workers in most years. Most of the multi-union types occur in the

Table 7.1　Percentage Distribution of Negotiating Units Covering 500 or More Employees by Type for Negotiations Concluded Each Year, Excluding Construction, 1966-1984

Type of Negotiating Unit	1966	1967	1968	1969	1970	1971	1972	1973	1974	1975	1976	1977	1978	1979	1980	1981	1982	1983	1984
Single Employer																			
Single Establishment, Single Union	55	51	49	47	45	45	43	44	40	48	51	43	48	51	49	48	43	49	45
Single Establishment, Multi-Union	1	3	5	a	4	2	1	2	1	a	2	5	2	1	4	2	1	3	1
Multi-Establishment, Single Union	30	25	30	40	34	39	38	39	43	39	30	38	35	36	30	40	46	39	35
Multi-Establishment, Multi-Union	a	1	2	1	2	1	a	3	a	1	2	1	1	a	2	1	a	a	1
Multi-Employer																			
Single Union	4	6	3	4	4	6	4	4	6	4	4	4	4	3	3	3	1	3	2
Multi-Union	a	2	1	1	1	1	1	1	1	1	1	a	a	1	1	a	a	a	a
Employer Association																			
Single Union	8	13	8	6	9	7	11	8	7	7	9	9	9	8	9	6	5	4	14
Multi-Union	a	a	a	a	1	a	1	1	1	1	1	a	a	a	1	a	1	1	2
n	181	175	283	328	295	322	325	327	403	391	525	544	578	484	485	410	412	487	455

[a]Less than .5%.

Source: Labour Data Branch, Labour Canada, *Collective Bargaining Review*, 1966-1984. The Labour Canada data deal with major collective agreements, and not negotiating units. Hence, in coding the information according to the concept of the negotiating unit, many judgment calls had to be made and my role in supervising the data compiled for the study published in 1968 was extremely useful. See Alton W. J. Craig and Harry J. Waisglass, "Collective Bargaining Perspectives," Vol. 23, No. 4, *Industrial Relations/Relations Industrielles* (1968), pp. 570-90, Tables 1 and 2. The term *n* refers to the number of negotiating units each year. Our figures are lower than those reported in the *Collective Bargaining Review* since we deal with negotiating units and not collective agreements. The construction industry is included for the first time in 1984.

Table 7.2 Percentage Distribution of Employees in Types of Negotiating Units Covering 500 or More Employees During Negotiations Concluded Each Year, Excluding Construction, 1966–1984

Type of Negotiating Unit	1966	1967	1968	1969	1970	1971	1972	1973	1974	1975	1976	1977	1978	1979	1980	1981	1982	1983	1984
Single Employer																			
Single Establishment, Single Union	23	23	19	15	18	17	15	16	13	21	18	20	22	19	18	19	12	15	15
Single Establishment, Multi-Union	[a]	1	2	3	2	1	[a]	1	1	[a]	1	4	2	1	2	1	[a]	2	1
Multi-Establishment, Single Union	45	30	47	64	54	57	56	65	55	62	49	62	52	57	51	62	63	61	45
Multi-Establishment, Multi-Union	[a]	[a]	[a]	[a]	7	1	[a]	7	[a]	[a]	2	1	1	[a]	2	1	[a]	[a]	[a]
Multi-Employer																			
Single Union	11	12	2	3	2	5	5	2	4	4	4	4	6	6	10	6	1	8	4
Multi-Union	1	20	11	4	1	12	[a]	1	1	[a]	6	[a]	5	1	[a]	[a]	[a]	[a]	2
Employer Association																			
Single Union	19	13	13	13	14	8	24	8	12	12	13	11	13	11	13	10	9	7	16
Multi-Union	2	[a]	[a]	[a]	2	[a]	[a]	1	15	2	7	1	7	[a]	3	2	14	6	17

[a] Less than .5%

Source: Labour Data Branch, Labour Canada, *Collective Bargaining Review*, 1966–1984. The Labour Canada data deal with major collective agreements, and not negotiating units (see source to Table 7.1). The total employee figures in our study are very close to those reported in *Collective Bargaining Review* except for the year 1977.

railway and pulp and paper industries, as well as in the Federal Government drydocks.

On the employer side, a different pattern occurs. Single-employer negotiating units generally comprise over 85% of negotiating units (Tables 7.1, columns 1 to 4), covering from 54% of workers in 1967 to 87% in 1977 (Table 7.2, columns 1 to 4). Within the single-employer level, an interesting contrast appears between single-establishment and multi-establishment negotiating units. Although single-establishment negotiating units comprise around 40% to 50% of all negotiating units (Table 7.1, columns 1 and 2), they generally cover only about 20% of workers (Table 7.2, columns 1 and 2). The proportion of negotiating units that fall into the single-establishment category is relatively high in comparison with the others, partly because 500 workers is the cut-off point for inclusion. Many negotiating units just barely attain this level. School board and teacher negotiating units in some provinces, especially Ontario, are very decentralized. Negotiations in this sector take place at the local rather than provincial level.

Multi-establishment negotiating units, on the other hand, cover only about one-third of all negotiating units that bargain each year. Nevertheless, multi-establishment negotiating units have accounted for from 36% (1967) to 72% (1973) of workers because of the inclusion of federal and provincial public-sector workers in this category. A number of larger companies in the private sector, such as Stelco and Canada Packers, and members of the auto industry, negotiate on a multi-establishment basis. Allowing for differences in calculations, it is still evident that the multi-establishment, single-employer category covers a higher proportion of workers[16] now than it did prior to 1967.

Multi-employer negotiating units comprise about 4% to 8% of the negotiating units that bargain each year. The percentage of workers covered varies considerably from year to year depending upon the size of the negotiating units. For example, railway agreements in 1967, 1971, and 1979 account for a fairly large proportion of the workers whose agreements were concluded in those years, while the 6% in 1976 includes province-wide negotiations among Quebec hospitals and their unions.

Employer-association bargaining (Tables 7.1 and 7.2, columns 7 and 8) ranges from a low of 6% of negotiating units in 1969 to highs of 13% and 16% in 1967 and 1984 respectively. More dramatic, however, is the variation in the percentage of workers covered by this type of negotiating unit which ranges from a low of 8% in 1971 to highs of 27% in 1974, 10% in 1976 and 1978 and 33% in 1984. In 1974, a railway association negotiated on behalf of more than 70,000 railway workers that year.

The year 1978 witnessed negotiations by the Railway Association of Canada, the Newfoundland Hospital Association, the Alberta Hospital Association, the Saskatchewan Health Care Association, the Health Labour Relations Association of British Columbia, the Quebec Motor Transport Industrial Relations Bureau, and the Fisheries Association of British Columbia. Also included were employer associations in the pulp and paper and food industries in British Columbia, and in the printing and clothing industries in British Columbia, Ontario and Quebec. The construction industry was represented for the first time in 1984. Most of the negotiations in this industry are conducted with employers' associations.

Although insufficient data exist to show an increase in association bargaining, the figures for the past fifteen years give the general sense that such a development is underway, although likely at the provincial level since few industries fall under federal jurisdiction. The extent of association bargaining is much higher in 1984, since the data collected and analyzed by Labour Canada that year included the construction industry for the first time. An increase in association bargaining has occurred in this industry with the advent of accreditation of employer associations in the late 1960's.[17]

The Preparation of Demands

Virtually all North American collective agreements have a specified term of duration. This term may range from less than a year to five years. A study of Canadian collective agreements, excluding those in the construction industry, for the period from 1953 to 1966 covering negotiating units of 500 or more workers showed that the average length of agreements increased from 18.1 months in 1953 to 28.5 months in 1966.[18] The significance of a fixed-duration agreement is that the parties prepare for, and engage in, negotiations some time before it expires in the hope of replacing it with a new agreement. This is what Carl Stevens called the deadline rule. The deadline rule refers to the threat or actual use of a strike or lockout at the end of an agreement. The deadline rule has a significant impact on how negotiations proceed,[19] particularly during the latter stages when the parties may hastily agree to trade-offs so as to avoid a work stoppage.

Long before the two parties begin actual talks, they start preparing demands and counter-demands which form the agenda items for the negotiations. The preparation of demands has at least two dimensions, namely the structural process on each side in formulating demands and the actual sources from which demands emerge. The structural aspect will be discussed first.

Structures for the Determination of Demands

To my knowledge, there has been no systematic study of the ways in which bargaining demands are prepared in the industrial relations systems of Canada or the United States. This is probably due to the fact that the large number of unions and highly decentralized nature of negotiations in each country create a variety of negotiation structures. However, in the absence of systematic study, it is still possible by using examples, to indicate some of the ways in which demands are prepared.

Since unions are not homogeneous organizations, there is a possibility that divergent demands may emerge even within a small negotiating unit. For example, workers nearing retirement may be interested in improving the pension plan whereas young workers may be concerned more with immediate take-home pay. The negotiating committee's job of reconciling these competing claims is what Walton and McKersie call intraorganizational bargaining.[20] Similarly, within the management group, the marketing manager may wish to avoid a strike in order to meet commitments to customers while the finance officer may wish to keep labour costs to a minimum.

If bargaining is conducted largely on a local basis between a local union and a single plant, the demands of the union are likely to be prepared by local members. In these cases, a negotiating committee is usually formed. This committee normally canvasses members of the local to see what items they would like to have negotiated. After receiving suggestions, the negotiating committee will sometimes try to reconcile competing demands from various sub-groups before proposing a negotiation package to the entire membership for approval. If representatives of the national branch or Canadian branch of an international union are members of the negotiating committee, they may wish to include items that the union has included in collective agreements with other employers. This situation characterizes the formulation of demands in many Ontario homes for the aged.

In a multi-establishment negotiation structure, the preparation of demands may be somewhat more complex. The members of the various locals may hold meetings or policy conferences to formulate a package of demands.

This package may be sent to representatives of the head office who will then sift through the demands and sort out, where possible, the conflicting ones. Prior to the commencement of negotiations, a meeting of all members of the negotiating committee may take place to finalize the package.

In the Meat-Packing Industry The history of preparing demands in the meat-packing industry has been characterized by a number of methods. In the 1940's, the Canadian Division of the United Packinghouse Workers Union sometimes sent letters to the locals seeking their demands. This approach usually met with indifference and it was left to the National Office of the Canadian District to form demands which were then discussed by delegates from the various locals on the negotiating committee prior to talks with management. The officers of the Canadian District had a fair amount of say in preparing the demands, particularly since they usually tried to get uniform benefits for union members in the Big Three — Canada Packers, Swift's and Burns. Since the plants of the three companies were often in close proximity, the workers could meet to compare notes on their respective wage-benefit packages. As the union evolved and international conventions were held more frequently, the members of the Canadian District started to meet separately from their American counterparts at these gatherings to formulate a package of demands to be served on the Big Three in Canada and on smaller companies.[21] Advantage was taken of this occasion since most, if not all, Canadian locals would have delegates at the international conventions.

In the Pulp and Paper Industry The pulp and paper industry in the Western, Eastern, and Central parts of Canada has represented two very distinct ways in which demands may be prepared by the companies and the unions. At least this was true prior to the establishment of the Canadian Paperworkers Union in 1974.[22]

While bargaining in the pulp and paper industry on the West Coast has occurred industry-wide, a decentralized format has existed in Central and Eastern Canada. Until 1968, pre-bargaining conferences of Central and Eastern Canadian unions involved three policy groups: one for primary mills in Ontario and Manitoba, the second for primary mills in Quebec and Eastern Canada, and the third for the fine- and speciality-paper mills.

Union representatives at each of these conferences, including members from the locals and the Canadian representatives of the international unions, usually met about six months prior to negotiations. Each local union brought a list of proposals. On the basis of these proposals, a final agenda was drawn up. The Canadian directors were usually successful in ensuring consistency of demands, particularly in the primary sector of the industry. On the West Coast where two unions bargained jointly, a union conference would take place only two or three days prior to negotiations. The locals would bring their proposals which were then combined to form a common agenda.

On the corporate side of the pulp and paper industry, there has existed a great difference between management strategy in the East and West. In Eastern Canada, the majority of negotiating units represent single companies, with the exception of the Canada Newsprint Group. If bargaining agendas were drawn up at all, it was at the level of each company. A few months before negotiations, one of the companies usually organized the bargaining and spoke for the group.

The major newsprint companies in British Columbia, by contrast, in 1952, organized the Pulp and Paper Industrial Relations Bureau (PPIRB) to act as the negotiating agent. B.C. companies usually presented written proposals indicating those provisions they wanted modified. Several weeks before negotiations, the member companies would send suggestions to the Bureau for contract changes. A technical advisory committee to the PPIRB, made up of industrial relations managers from member firms, would meet to consider the companies' suggestions and incorporate these into a draft which was then reviewed and possibly altered by the executive committee of the Bureau, consisting largely of presidents or vice-presidents. This draft became the Bureau's proposals. This formalized structure on the company side in British Columbia contrasted sharply with the very decentralized structure in the East. This contrast may have been due to the greater influence of pattern bargaining in Eastern Canadian negotiations.

In the Steel Industry In the steel industry in Ontario and Quebec, the main negotiations usually take place between the United Steelworkers Union and the Steel Company of Canada (Stelco) in Hamilton or sometimes with the Algoma Steel Company. Representatives from other local unions in Stelco plants usually play an active part in preparing the demands to be served on Stelco. This is primarily because the agreement at Stelco in Hamilton serves as a pattern for other Stelco basic steel and fabricating plants in Ontario and Quebec. While the Canadian director for the district would have a substantial input in the formulation of demands, so would workers from the Notre Dame Works in Montreal, since the final settlement at Stelco in Hamilton would serve as a pattern for the Montreal plants and to some degree for the fabricating plants. In fact, differences in the demands of the Hamilton and Montreal workers caused problems in negotiations during the Summer of 1980.

In the Railways Negotiations in CN and CP, the two major Canadian railways, provide a very complex structure for determining demands, particularly since the unions sometimes negotiate as two major groups — one for the operating personnel (those who run the trains) and another for the non-operating personnel

(repair and maintenance workers, etc.). On some occasions, as many as seventeen unions have been involved.

Let us take one union as an example: the Canadian Brotherhood of Railway, Transport and General Workers (CBRT & GW) which is one of the major non-operating unions. In preparation for the 1977 negotiations with the railways, the national office of the union asked the locals to send in their demands by January 21, 1977. Some 500 to 600 demands were received from the locals, many of which were similar in content. A five-man resolutions committee was set up to study, correlate, amalgamate, and reword the demands. This committee worked six days in February 1977 to accomplish this task.

In addition, proposals were submitted by the National Executive Board of the Brotherhood following its meeting before the local chairman's conference. There was then a three-day meeting of the Brotherhood's Railway Local Chairman's Conference. This conference adopted more than 100 major and addendum demands, the latter covering local work practices. The addendum proposals were to be submitted to the railways at the end of March 1977. The major demands were to be processed by the National Executive Board of the union and were to be presented to the railways in October 1977. To further complicate the picture, if the Brotherhood were to remain as part of the non-operating unions in joint negotiations, their demands had to become part of the overall demands adopted by all unions involved.[23]

In the Automobile Industry Until recent negotiations, particularly in the Canadian automobile industry wherein the Canadian UAW settled with Chrysler before an agreement was reached in the United States, bargaining has been closely tied in with that in the United States. In some cases, this is explained by the fact that the same unions and companies operate on both sides of the border. The 1965 auto pact agreement between the Canadian and

American governments, for example, was designed to rationalize production facilities and narrow the gap between automobile prices in Canada and the United States. John Crispo pointed out that in the auto industry, the Canadian negotiators in the Big Three always attended the pre-negotiation sessions held in the United States:

> The bargaining tie-in between the two countries is so close in some industries that Canadian negotiations are not seriously begun until the appropriate settlements have been wrapped up in the United States. This is usually a reflection of corporate as well as trade-union practice.[24]

In most of these industries, however, local union members' desires are often taken into account by the use of local supplements to the master agreements which allow for variations in contract terms among different plants of the same company, as long as these are consistent with the terms of the master agreement between the company and the union. Since the Canadian section of the UAW broke away from the international union to form the Canadian UAW, the Canadian union will likely formulate demands and establish priorities on its own terms. However, as the wounds from the split heal, informal links between the two unions are likely to emerge, particularly since the two unions deal with the same automobile companies on both sides of the Canadian-American border.

In Public and Parapublic Sectors The unions and associations in the public and parapublic sectors formulate demands in a wide variety of ways because of the recent advent of unionism in these sectors and the different legislative provisions that govern collective bargaining for public-service workers. In the federal public service, a large number of negotiating units are grouped into specific occupational categories. Each of these groups formulates its own demands, although the bargaining agent (whether it be the Public Service Alliance of Canada, the Professional Institute of Public Service (PIPS), or some other union) will have specific proposals that it would like to see incorporated into all agreements which it negotiates. In 1985, PSAC negotiations began to be sector-wide on many issues, with each subgroup negotiating issues unique to it.

Public-sector bargaining is more centralized in Quebec than in Ottawa: management and workers have much less input into the negotiations in Quebec than in Ottawa. In 1972, the Common Front (the CNTU, QFL, and the Teachers' Corporation) representing provincial public servants and parapublic workers negotiated with the Quebec government at a common table over such items as wages and salaries, job security, and social insurance. Issues peculiar to specific groups such as hospital workers, teachers, and professional and nonprofessional public servants, were negotiated at sector tables.[25]

Some Comparisons The few examples cited above do not cover all the ways in which union demands are prepared, but they do indicate some of the typical procedures. They also serve to demonstrate the varying degrees of influence exerted by the leading officials of national unions, Canadian directors of international unions, and trade-union and corporate links between Canada and the United States.

Employers, like unions, use a variety of methods to develop their proposals and counterproposals. In a single-plant company, bargaining proposals are likely to be developed by the company's management, possibly with the aid of industrial relations specialists. In a multi-plant company, proposals and counter-proposals may be developed by the chief personnel officer or designated negotiator, who receives inputs from responsible officials of the various plants that form part of the negotiating unit.

In a number of cases, employer associations may be responsible for developing proposals and counter-proposals. Many suggestions come from the companies themselves, and are submitted to the association membership for acceptance. CN and CP establish an informal negotiating unit, sometimes with other smaller railways, for the purpose of bargaining jointly with unions representing operating and non-operating personnel. Although no formal structure exists for preparing joint proposals and counter-proposals, there is a good deal of discussion between the two companies in developing their agenda items.

In the public sector, bureaucrats are often faced with a different problem: that of reconciling the need for autonomy in bargaining with the explicit requirement of public accountability. Often conflict manifests itself in a wrangle with the union over who the real employer is. This situation is true not only for the public service but also for such institutions as hospitals and school boards. Simply put, the important question is this: Is the designated employer the real employer, or is the government the real employer?

Under the *Public Service Staff Relations Act*, the Treasury Board is the official employer for government departments and a number of agencies. But on a number of occasions, the federal cabinet has seemed to have been the real power behind management. Jean Boivin's study of three rounds of negotiations in the Quebec public and parapublic sectors underlines the question of who the real employer is.[26]

The government, being both legislator and employer, is sometimes placed in an awkward position in negotiations. While private employers are profit-oriented, a government is a collector of revenue, mainly taxes, which it is presumed to spend for the common good. Ultimate responsibility to the taxpayer, therefore, creates a political problem when it comes to satisfying union demands.

In times of recession, cabinet may be forced with the choice of deficit financing: the choice of cutting back on spending because of the large deficit and, thus, cutting back employment and denying requests for salary increases, creating resentment, confrontation, and low morale. The restraint programs in effect from 1982 to 1984 had devastating effects in some jurisdictions, particularly in British Columbia where the possibility of a province-wide strike loomed large. In 1985, the Federal Government cut back spending in agencies such as the CBC, Canada Council, and National Research Council, and encouraged early retirement among government departments to reduce employment costs. These actions provoked bitter attacks by a number of unions. Little remedy is available to unions in such circumstances, however, as will become apparent in our discussion of American events during the depths of the recession, under the heading "Concession Bargaining."

Parapublic entities such as hospitals and schools boards derive their revenue from provincial funds. By the time fixed expenditures are allocated and other facilities provided for, there may not be too much room for manoeuvering in the negotiation of wage increases. This is particularly true where the government pays the full cost of hospital and other services.

Sources for the Determination of Demands

In the present context, the term *source* refers to that which motivates union or management to propose an item for negotiations. Union demands are sometimes referred to as proposals and management responses as counter-proposals.

If the parties are bargaining for the first time, the union may occasionally take an existing agreement with which it is satisfied and present the provisions contained therein as its set of proposals. This situation has arisen in the construction industry and a number of parapublic organizations (hospitals and nursing homes). These model agreements are sometimes presented by the union as the ideal wage and benefit package.

In most cases, however, union leaders and members will also include in their proposals some kind of a union security clause and a dues check-off provision. These are important for the strength and continuity of the union, and provide its leaders with the security to concentrate more on the workers' needs and less on political concerns.

Even after it concludes its first agreement, a union may look to the bargaining positions of unions in the same industry as the basis for its own demands in subsequent rounds. This leader-follower tactic, referred to as pattern bargaining, was discussed previously in the section on the structure of negotiating units. In a union-management relationship that has existed for some time, one of the prime sources for determining demands on both sides is experience with the present collective agreement. If certain clauses cause many grievances, it is in the interest of the two parties to try to have those clauses changed, even though disagreement may exist over what needs changing. Supervisors and shop stewards are good sources of information and advice in this respect.

The economic climate and prospects for the future may spur some union leaders to make demands for which there are no precedents. For example, it was the fear of unemployment due to technological change that prompted the late Walter Reuther, former President of the UAW, to seek a form of guaranteed annual wage in the mid-1950's. More recently, unions have been seeking provisions to protect those who lose their jobs due to technological change. Such attempts have been a difficult item in negotiations since the demands of unions for some measure of control over the introduction of technological change challenge what management perceives to be its traditional prerogative.

A company may use its poor financial performance as a reason for offering a smaller wage increase than that given by companies in the same industry. In February 1977, negotiators for the American Motors Corporation of Detroit and

the UAW reached an agreement on terms below those negotiated with Ford, Chrysler, and General Motors. American Motors suffered a loss of $46 million during the fiscal year of 1976. Union representatives were reported to have said that the settlement would permit the company to stay afloat financially.[27] Early in 1982, American workers at both Ford and General Motors also agreed to give up previously won concessions to help their companies out of serious financial difficulties.

As indicated in Chapter 2, however, the 1984 settlements with GM and Ford restored many of the 1982 concessions: benefits such as paid holidays, lump-sum payments, and profit-sharing plans. Moreover, the agreements contained provisions to help avoid situations such as those which occurred prior to the 1982 negotiations. At the present time, concession bargaining is sufficiently prevalent to merit a separate discussion later in this chapter.

The rate of inflation is a key factor in the preparation of wage demands. The high rate of inflation in Canada during the 1970's led many unions to seek high wage settlements. Changes in productivity, ability to pay, and other factors are also relevant in the formulation of proposals and counter-proposals by unions and companies respectively. A company's competitive position with respect to domestic or international markets may determine to some degree the benefit package that it will be prepared to offer as a counter-proposal.

Unions use factors such as increased inflation and higher productivity to justify the demands that they put forward. Employers use factors such as lack of profits and the loss of a share of the market to support their opening offers. However, non-monetary issues, such as a union's demand that all new workers become members of the union, may be supported by highly developed philosophical arguments. Likewise, an employer's opposition to such a proposal may also have strong ideological underpinnings. These issues are some of the more difficult ones to resolve in negotiations since they represent well-entrenched philosophical extremes.

The Composition of Negotiating Committees

The composition of negotiating committees may be as diverse as the various ways in which demands are prepared. To negotiate on a plant-by-plant basis, a negotiating committee for the union will probably be elected by the local membership. Such a committee usually represents the many interest groups in the local. Generally, there is also a field officer from the larger union of which the local is a part. The field officer often acts as the union's main spokesperson, and is constantly kept informed of the members' wishes by the elected local representatives on the negotiating committee.

In complex bargaining structures involving a number of plants and locations, a senior officer of the national union or a Canadian director of the international union will probably be involved. In the meat-packing industry, for example, the Canadian director of the international union leads the negotiating committee, but there are usually representatives of the various locals involved, as well as plant superintendents on the management side. This arrangement is helpful inasmuch as the local individuals speak to the issues that apply to the particular plants they represent. These individuals also act as information sources to the union members and plant management when it comes to explaining the provisions of the agreement and are useful in processing grievances since they know the original intent of certain clauses. Sometimes, however, negotiating committees become unwieldy. In these cases, a small number of delegates may be elected to form a negotiating committee, while the other members act as observers or take part in sub-committees set up to study particularly difficult issues.

Top union officials are sometimes accused of making too many decisions without ascertaining the wishes of members of their locals. For this reason, the appointment of representatives from the various locals and special interest groups helps to bring a greater sense of democratic decision-making to the bargaining table. However, if the representatives of the various locals have different views on similar problems it may become difficult for negotiations to proceed effectively. Large negotiating committees run into the problem of maintaining democracy at the local level while preserving enough centralized control to keep negotiations on track. Forming a small negotiating committee with side members serving on sub-committees helps to alleviate this problem to some extent.

The employer is usually represented by one or more senior members of management who in turn may be aided by an expert from personnel or industrial relations staff, if the company is large enough to have a well-developed personnel component. The company president, however, is usually the chief management spokesperson and must assume responsibility for the final management offer. The president may also be co-chairman of the negotiating committee, with the chief union negotiator as the other co-chairman.

Negotiation Strategy

In the ordinary course of events, it is the union which initially presents its set of demands to the employer, either before or at the initial meeting between the two negotiating teams. Management is then usually given some time to study the union's demands or proposals, and to develop its counter-proposals. The employer may initiate demands of its own, of course, on items that may or may not be among the union's demands. After this initial exchange, the bargaining agenda begins to become clear to each side and serious negotiations begin. Usually the parties will have more demands than they expect to obtain. This is what Stevens calls the large-demand rule of the negotiating game.

Although the negotiation process involves a relationship between two interdependent organizations, this relationship is mediated by the principal representative or negotiator for each side, whose job it is to try to find the true settlement position of the other party. Initially, each side puts forward a large number of demands, some of which are considered essential and others tradeable or indicative of what 'will become serious issues in the future. The large agenda gives both sides room to manoeuvre.

Contract Zone   Through the negotiation process, the initial number of demands may be gradually narrowed down as each party gains a better understanding of the other's true position. Eventually, this will lead to the discovery of a contract zone — that is, some intermediary area between the two sets of demands wherein both parties will settle rather than undertake a strike or lockout.

Carl Stevens describes the first steps in negotiations in the following terms:

> The initial bargaining proposal is an information-seeking device. During the early stages of negotiations, each party, in addition to giving information about (and concealing) his own preferences, is attempting to discover the true preference of his opponent. In part, the negotiator will infer these preferences from his opponent's bargaining position. He will also infer them from his opponent's reaction to his own bargaining position. The parties at this stage are attempting to demarcate the limits of the contract zone. The movement from initial bargaining positions to some fairly clear perception of the range within which (if any) an outcome by agreement can lie is devious. There is reliance upon ceremonial and semi-ritual modes and upon sign language as each side attempts to estimate the meaning of what is said by the other side.[28]

The following figure depicts two situations which may characterize negotiations as they are perceived during the stage when the parties are trying to map out a contract zone.

In Situation A, there is no overlap between the management's upper limit and the union's lower limit. Therefore, no contract zone exists since the union is not prepared to agree to management's highest offer. The only way a contract zone could come into being is if the parties are prepared to shift their positions so an overlap could occur. In Situation B, the employer's upper limit is above the union's lower limit and, hence, a contract zone exists.

When the parties start negotiations, each begins with a position it knows is inflated (in the case of the union) or deflated (in the case of management). The union has a lower limit below which it would rather strike than settle and management has an upper limit beyond which it would rather tolerate such a strike. Each negotiator should estimate the real limits of the other side's position.

As mentioned previously, the aim of both parties is to find the contract zone and a specific point within that zone; in other words, to discover the other party's bottom line. As a general rule, it is useful to separate monetary

Table 7.3	Determination of the Contract Zone

Situation A	Situation B
⌈UUL ⌊ULL	UUL ⌈ ULL ⌊ ▩ ⌈ MUL ⌊ MLL
MUL⌉ MLL⌋	

UUL = Union's upper limit (the initial demand of the union).
ULL = Union's lower limit (the lowest increase the union will accept).
MUL = Management's upper limit (the highest offer management is prepared to make).
MLL = Management's lower limit (the initial offer by management).
▩   = Contract zone.

from non-monetary items and to settle the easy issues first. This helps to create a climate that is conducive to settlement of the difficult issues. As each issue is settled, an agreement on the issue is drafted and initialled. Such specific agreements are tentative until a final, comprehensive settlement has been reached.

Negotiation Tactics

As Carl Stevens points out, the tactics used in the negotiation process are those of competition and conflict in the early stages and those of cooperation and coordination in the later stages.[29] The first set of tactics are designed to help map out a contract zone, while the latter are instrumental in helping to find a settlement point within the contract zone.

Competition and Conflict　Among the tactics of competition and conflict available to the parties are those of bluff, not-bluff, commitment, persuasion, and rationalization. A party using the bluff tactic attempts to convince his opponent that he or she will do something when, in fact, he or she will not do it. This tactic is a delicate one and could inadvertently lead to a strike. Not-bluff, on the other hand, is a frank statement by a party that he or she will do what he or she threatens to do. Commitment involves taking a position and sticking to it. This may be done by tying an issue to a principle, or by going public on it. However, there are problems with such a strategy, especially when one party takes a firm stand early in the negotiations and finds it difficult to retreat at a later date.[30] Generally, it is preferable to take a flexible, step-by-step approach rather than commit oneself too early in the game and thus risk an unwanted and unnecessary strike. Persuasion is simply an attempt by one party to convince the other of the reasonableness of his or her own position. Rationalization, however, is used primarily to give the other negotiator the material with which to develop: (1) a reason which allows him to retreat from his current negotiating position and

(2) a justification of the retreat which will satisfy his constituents.

Coordination and Cooperation　Once a contract zone is estimated by the parties, tactics of coordination and cooperation are used to reach agreement within the contract zone. Although the chief negotiators may perceive a contract zone, other participants in negotiations may not. In a mature bargaining relationship the chief negotiators may hold off-the-record discussions, wherein they reveal their true position without prejudice. It is understood that they may withdraw any statement which is publically imputed to them.

Often, caucuses are used by negotiators at this stage to persuade constituents that the best possible deal has been negotiated for them. Sometimes, too, a negotiator may have to grandstand (revert to an adversarial role) for the benefit of his constituents, but he knows that the other negotiator will correctly perceive this as putting on a show with the full knowledge that a better settlement is unlikely.

In fact, the ability to prevent the opposing negotiator from losing face with his constituents is often extremely important when the two negotiators realize that a mutually acceptable agreement is in sight, especially if a strike deadline is approaching. If the two chief negotiators agree, for example, that a demand by the union should be dropped, the union's chief negotiator may let a delegate from the local argue the case and have the management spokesperson effectively refute it. This is quite often done when one local delegate feels very strongly about a demand which is not important to the others.

One party may also aid the other by providing the means for the other to become decommitted from an earlier demand. When the chief negotiators see, for example, that a settlement is in sight, they may resort to sign language to communicate their flexibility about certain outstanding items. This may pave the way for both sides to retreat from earlier demands without losing face. The retreat, however, must be made in such a way that it does not convey a sign of weakness to one's own constituents. Neither must too great a concession be made, lest it be interpreted by the other side as weakness.

As Stevens states,

> By the use of sign language a party signals the direction in which it wants to go, and then waits for some answering signal. Either the parties go arm-in-arm, as it were, or do not go at all.... To communicate successfully by means of signs and symbols, the negotiator must be willing to take some chances.[31]

There is also a general convention that when one party makes a move, the other party is expected to respond with a move. The signs and symbols to which Stevens refers include voice intonations, facial expressions, and other subtle body gestures.

The tactics of cooperation and coordination, including sign language, should bring the parties to an agreement if a contract zone has been established and if the negotiators have done a good job. However, if no contract zone exists or can be brought into existence, a strike is likely to occur unless some form of third-party assistance is successfully employed. Such assistance may involve the kind of eleventh-hour marathon bargaining sessions that constitute the most dramatic form of contract negotiations.

Multidimensional Demands

It is useful to view bargaining demands as falling into the two categories proposed by Carl Stevens. First, there are those which seek to alter the terms of trade (rewards or conditions of employment) within a given collective-bargaining game. A change in the wage rate is a good example of this type of category. Second, there are those which seek to alter the basic ground rules of collective bargaining or the definition of the role relationships of the parties.

According to Stevens, "[d]emands which are perceived as a union's challenge to management's control are of this variety."[32]

Non-monetary demands such as job security and management's right to contract out pose a problem owing to their multidimensional character; that is, it is difficult to achieve a trade-off on such demands because their objective value cannot be fixed precisely in monetary terms. This is one reason that some of the models which portray a point of determinacy (single point of settlement) are of little use in the development of a theory of negotiations involving a mixed package of monetary and non-monetary items. How, for example, can a monetary value be placed on the demand for a union shop security provision which requires all members of the bargaining unit to be union members?

For this reason, bargaining models, such as the one proposed by Stevens, do not seem very useful since they make some rather unrealistic assumptions. For example, Stevens argues that there are both necessary and sufficient conditions for a settlement. The necessary condition is that the equilibrium position of the two parties be consonant: that the two parties are willing to settle for exactly the same thing. The sufficient condition requires mutual awareness of this consonance.[33] Thus, it is assumed that each negotiator knows precisely what the other negotiator's settlement position is.

These are rather severe assumptions to impose on a bargaining model for, although each party has its perceptions of the other's settlement position, this perception may not in fact correspond to reality. Moreover, even after agreement has been reached, a negotiator may feel that he could have obtained a better settlement had he held out a little longer. Hence, rather than assume a predetermined settlement point, it is preferable to think of negotiations as a process whereby each negotiator first tries to find the contract zone, and then uses whatever leverage is available to him to arrive at a determinate resolution within that zone. This is in line with the discussion of inputs in Chapter 1 wherein it was stated that the ultimate source for determining a specific point of settlement in contract negotiations is through the use of bargaining power.

Bargaining Power

In Chapter 1, bargaining power was defined as the ability of an actor to obtain objectives despite the resistance of others. It consists of two components: (1) strong attachment to something that is desired or to the possession of something that is threatened; and (2) the ability to impose sanctions.

Chamberlain The most widely used definition of bargaining power is that of Neil Chamberlain who defines it as:

> the ability to secure another's agreement on one's own terms. A union's bargaining power at any point in time *is* for example, management's willingness to agree on the union's terms. Management's willingness in turn depends upon the cost of disagreeing with the union's terms, relative to the cost of agreeing to them.[34]

Management's bargaining power may be defined in a similar way. The bargaining power of the parties may thus be summarized in the following equations:

Union's bargaining power =

Cost to management of disagreeing to union terms

Cost to management of agreeing to union terms

Management's bargaining power =

Cost to union of disagreeing to management terms

Cost to union of agreeing to management terms

Chamberlain uses the term *cost* in the broad sense of *disadvantage* and includes both monetary and non-monetary items. While other models deal only with the issue of wages, Chamberlain is concerned that issues of a non-

monetary nature be incorporated in the concept of bargaining power. He states that:

> The sort of balancing of costs which is contemplated in the definition of bargaining power just given does not require measurement of costs in an arithmetical sense.... What these costs of agreement and disagreement may be to the bargainers cannot be known precisely enough to permit balancing, except through the exploratory process of negotiations.[35]

Chamberlain further states that it is through negotiations that feasible or infeasible combinations are revealed which form the basis of a settlement. He does not proceed, however, to explain the mechanics of such a process. Rather, he discusses overt tactics such as strikes, picketing, and lockouts which influence the cost to management and to the union of disagreement.

Bargaining power depends on the skills of the negotiators and on various external factors surrounding negotiation. Bargaining power cannot be precisely measured. The most one can do is indicate the factors that affect the bargaining power of the union and the employer, and show how the actors' perceptions of bargaining power derives from their assessments of these factors. Such perceptions may be faulty: it is all too easy for a negotiator — especially an inexperienced one — to overestimate or underestimate the influence of different factors in a negotiation situation. During the 1981 Stelco strike, for example, the union believed it had a strong bargaining position. After the strike began, however, the bottom fell out of the steel market, thereby reducing the union's leverage considerably.

Hicks J. R. Hicks's diagram of a determinate wage outcome and his concept of the employer's concession curve and the union's resistance curve is helpful in explaining how various factors affect bargaining power.[36] In Hicks's model, an employer originally offers a wage rate at level E and the union initially demands a wage rate at level U. According to Hicks, the parties are likely to settle at level P where the curves EE'

Table 7.4	Hicks' Bargaining Schedules

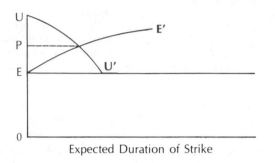

Expected Duration of Strike

Source: J. R. Hicks, Ch. 7, *Theory of Wages* (London and Basingstoke: Macmillan, 1932).
EE′ = Employer's concession curve
UU′ = Union's resistance curve
P = Wage

Note: After a certain period, time is on the side of the employer; hence the slower climb of EE′ versus the steeper descent of UU′. Employers are usually the winners of long strikes whereas workers are usually the winners of short ones. One reason for this is that unions can maintain a strike only as long as its strike fund lasts. Once this is depleted, it may have to settle at or near point E. It should be added that both curved configurations may change daily during negotiations.

and UU′ intersect. Hicks made a number of assumptions in this model, the first of which was that the parties had perfect knowledge of the two curves. This assumption, like those of Carl Stevens, is ambitious. Hicks also assumes that anything below the union's resistance curve (UU′) would be more costly to it than a strike. The same would hold true, in the case of management, for anything above the employer's concession curve. Hence rational behaviour, according to Hicks's model, would dictate a settlement at point P. While this model makes for a nice determinate solution, the assumptions are too great to even approximate the real world.

The reason for including Table 7.4 in this chapter is to indicate that the employer's bargaining power — his concession curve — and the union's bargaining power — its resistance curve — are not static and may be influenced by many different factors. These will be discussed in the following section.[37]

Factors that Affect Management Bargaining Power

The following are some of the more important factors affecting an employer's concession curve or bargaining power:

Size of Inventory   A large inventory allows more bargaining power than a low inventory, since in the former case, customers can be supplied from accumulated stocks. A rough estimate as to how long any employer could endure a strike without serious damage to sales can be calculated by dividing the accumulated inventory by an average week's shipment.

Structure of Business   The question here is whether the company is an integrated operation, in which production units depend on inputs from feeder plants, or whether it is composed of autonomous units which can meet market demands should a part of the operation be closed down. A good example of an autonomous-unit company is a meat-packing company which has a number of plants operating autonomously in different locations. If a strike is conducted against one plant, it is possible to supply the market area affected with meat processed at other plants, assuming that these other plants are operating at less than full capacity. By contrast, an employer with an integrated operation may find that a strike at one feeder plant could affect all other plants after the inventory is used up.

Competitiveness of Company   In a tight product market, especially where the product is a fairly common one, there is always the possibility that customers may be lost permanently to competitors, as they discover substitute products or alternate sources of supply. This fear of loss to competitors may weaken an employer's bargaining power.

Seasonal Nature of Business Generally employers find that their bargaining power is least at the peak period of the season. Canners of fresh vegetables, obviously, are more vulnerable at canning time than any other time of the year. Also, shipping companies which operate on the Great Lakes or the St. Lawrence River are weaker at the beginning of the shipping season. In these and other seasonal industries, unions will try to bring negotiations to a head near the beginning of the seasonal period, knowing that time constraints on management will expedite a settlement and increase union gains.

Strike Insurance An employer's bargaining power will be enhanced by such insurance. A number of airlines in the United States have devised a scheme whereby if one company is struck, any extra profits made by the other airlines are given to the airline whose workers are on strike. A similar provision is found among major railroads in the United States. Deregulation of American airlines may inhibit this practice in the future.

The factors which weaken a company's bargaining power increase a union's bargaining power. There are, however, a number of other factors that have an important bearing on the union's power.

Factors That Affect Union Bargaining Power

Strength of Commitment to Issues If the union is fighting for some cause with which the workers have little immediate concern, then it may not be in a strong bargaining position. For example, a number of surveys that preceded the 116-day strike in the United States steel industry in 1959 showed that the workers were not strongly committed initially to striking over pay and fringe benefits. It was only when management introduced proposed changes in local work rules that the workers got strongly behind the union. Since changes in local work rules would affect them directly and immediately, the workers became very militant in opposing them.

Access to Liquid Assets Walter Reuther, former head of the UAW, always made it a point to build up a large strike fund when he wanted to obtain a major concession from the automobile companies. Also, the Canadian Airline Pilots Association's (CALPA) line of credit with a major American bank in its 1968 negotiations gave it much more power than it otherwise would have had. Another component of a union's financial strength is its ability to obtain grants or loans from other unions if its strike funds run out. Anyone who reads union newspapers will be aware of how often interest-free loans or outright grants are made to striking unions.

Strike Timing There would be little point in workers who operate ships on the Great Lakes going on strike during the winter when the shipping season is closed. Generally, unions will time negotiations to coincide with the period when workers' services are most needed, the employer's inventory is low, or both.

Strike Effectiveness If the workers of a large company with many skilled workers should strike, it would then be difficult for the employer to recruit strike-breakers with sufficient skills to keep the company operating. By contrast, a small local employer with a few workers might be able to recruit enough extra workers to keep his operations going. It was a strike of this nature — with associated violence — that prompted the Quebec government to pass its anti-scab provision in 1977. Under the present Quebec Labour Code, a struck employer is prohibited from hiring replacement workers during a strike. Employers are also prohibited from producing at non-striking plants goods that would normally be produced at the struck plant. They

Figure 7.5   Power and Settlement Level

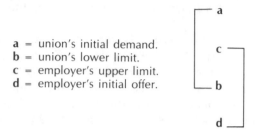

a = union's initial demand.
b = union's lower limit.
c = employer's upper limit.
d = employer's initial offer.

are further prohibited from contracting out work done by the striking workers. The Quebec law is the only legislation of its kind in North America.

Picketing   Primary picketing is aimed at the employer against whom the strike is called. Workers usually assemble at the site of the dispute carrying placards which announce that they are on strike and which may outline one or two demands. Picketers may also try to prevent other workers from crossing their lines. Unions have every right in law to picket peacefully during a strike and the more the picket lines are respected, the more their (the union's) power will increase. Sometimes, however, it may be a violation of a contract for members of another union working in the same establishment to refuse to cross a picket line. In these cases, the workers cannot legally respect the picket line of the other union.

Another form of picketing is the secondary boycott whereby a union, either through its own organization or in conjunction with another union, will try to put pressure on a third party to influence the struck company. The third party maybe a supplier of materials to, or a purchaser of goods from, the struck employer. One may see, for example, workers in front of furriers asking consumers not to purchase from that store because the workers who produced the fur coats are on strike against the suppliers of that company.

Unemployment Insurance   While striking workers in Canada do not qualify for unemployment insurance until production again reaches 80%, workers in New York State do qualify for such benefits after a certain waiting period. During the 1960's, workers on strike against some of the New York newspapers were receiving a high proportion of their regular pay, when both their strike benefits and unemployment insurance were combined.

Relative Power   If the components affecting the union's bargaining power are favourable to it, it may through skillful negotiations obtain something at or near the employer's upper limit (point c in Table 7.5). On the other hand, if the employer's bargaining power is greater, the settlement will probably be nearer the union's lower limit (point b).

If bargaining power is relatively equal, the settlement will fall about half-way between b and c. However, given the present state of knowledge about these variables, it is futile to suggest a determinate solution at a specific point. Bargaining power helps determine the specific settlement point, but this cannot be determined *a priori*, unless some very great assumptions are introduced into a model of contract negotiations. A realistic model with a determinate solution must, in our view, await a better formulation of the variables in the negotiation process and a more accurate measurement of the concepts.

Thomas Kochan, a well known American author, indicates a troubling contradiction between a conceptual discussion of the determinants of bargaining outcomes and empirical analysis. The conceptual argument is cast in terms of a whole range of bargaining outcomes, whereas the empirical testing is limited to wage determination only. Kochan further observes ,

This contradiction mirrors the general state of empirical research on private-sector bargaining outcomes. The study of nonwage outcomes is still in a very primitive stage of development. The central difficulty in studying nonwage outcomes lies in constructing measures of nonwage outcomes that are amenable to quantitative analysis.[38]

Walton and McKersie: A Non-Deterministic Approach to Negotiations

A Behavioural Theory of Labour Negotiations[39] by Walton and McKersie breaks the negotiation process down into four subprocesses: (1) distributive bargaining which represents a set of activities the results of which are viewed as gains for one and losses for the other; (2) integrative bargaining which represents a set of activities whereby a gain for one party is a gain for the other; (3) attitudinal structuring which represents those activities that promote the attainment of the desired patterns of relationship between the parties; (4) intraorganizational bargaining which are those activities which bring the expectations of constituents into alignment with those of the chief negotiator.[40]

After describing each of the subprocesses, these two writers then develop the tactics appropriate to each. Under distributive bargaining, for example, they emphasize the notion of utility function (what an actor considers an item or service to be worth) and indicate that for the negotiator the utility function increases up to a certain point and then begins to drop off. For example, if the going rate for a service in a community is $10.00 an hour, then a negotiator's utility is highest when he obtains this wage for his constituents, since anything beyond that might seriously increase costs to the employer and result in layoffs. Walton and McKersie indicate the types of commitment strategy appropriate to various situations and identify, under various conditions, the point in the sequence of bargaining moves when the maximum commitment should be made. Walton and McKersie have also developed nine hypotheses regarding commitment strategy, the first of which reads as follows: *"The more knowledge Party has about the resistance point of Opponent, the fewer the bargaining moves before Party commits himself to a final position."*[41]

This principle applies well in the case of distributive bargaining. An early commitment pattern under distributive bargaining, however, might seriously hamper the benefits to be achieved under the integrative bargaining subprocess. Similarly, attitudinal structuring suggests that there be a fairly high degree of trust between the parties. A high degree of trust, however, conflicts to some extent with an early take-it-or-leave-it approach.

The tactic appropriate to intraorganizational bargaining raises the question of what degree of control a chief negotiator should try to exercise over his constituents. The question for the chief negotiator here is whether to try for an internal consensus actively or passively. Adopting an active role will likely make it easier to persuade constituents to adopt the negotiator's views. Whether the chief negotiator takes an active or a passive role, his actions will affect the tactics appropriate to the other three subprocesses of bargaining.[42]

The framework presented by Walton and McKersie is a very useful one for analyzing the negotiation process. It does not, however, lead to a determinant solution nor does it suggest how a solution may be obtained.

Ratification of New Agreement Clauses

Once a collective agreement is reached on the items in dispute, these must then be put in the form of a collective agreement. In the case of a new bargaining relationship, this will mean the preparation of a new agreement containing all the clauses agreed upon in the negotiation process. For a renewal of an existing collective agreement, the issues finally agreed upon in negotiation take the form of a "memorandum of understanding," which is usually signed by all the union and management negotiators. The new clauses agreed upon must then be incorporated into the existing collective agreement. This may mean modifying existing provisions or adding new ones.

Although neither the law nor the constitutions of most unions in North America require negotiators to present newly negotiated contracts to union members for ratification, the tradition of most unions is to do so. In recent years, many negotiators who have presented their proposed agreement for membership approval have found that a majority of the members refuse to ratify the collective agreement.

Summers Clyde W. Summers[43] and other labour writers have done some excellent work on this topic. In some instances, it appears that agreements were not accepted by the members because the terms of settlement were not clearly presented — particularly true where job security is concerned. Rejection may also occur because initially inflated union demands have raised the expectations of the membership beyond what any negotiator could be reasonably expected to deliver. Management may also contribute to the rejection of an agreement by dragging its heels during negotiations and only slowly and grudgingly consenting to some of the union's important demands. One must conclude that if negotiators on both sides were to be more realistic than they have been and were to try to conclude their negotiations without long delays, there might be a greater rate of acceptance of settlement terms by union members.

Summers points out, however, that the ratification problem is basically a result of the separation of the responsibility to negotiate an agreement and the authority to make it binding. This partly explains why two schools of thought exist on this subject — a subject of major concern to union leaders, management, and government. Some eminent people in labour relations feel strongly that negotiators should have the authority to make agreements binding. According to Summers, some negotiators do have this power. However, a recent survey of union leaders and members in the United States indicates that about 90% of union leaders and members agree that union members should have the right to ratify the proposed collective agreement, since it is the members who must live with its terms.

There is some agreement, however, that delegates one step removed from the negotiators could be granted the authority by the general

membership to make the agreement binding. The major function of the ratification process, as Summers suggests, is to test the acceptability of the terms of settlement by those who have to work under its provisions. If workers say yes to the agreement, it becomes *their* agreement and not merely that of the union's negotiating committee or the union executive. Also, dissenters will feel bound by the majority's vote. As Summers states, "The democratic character of the union and its statutory role as representative make acceptability the primary test of the legitimacy of a collective agreement."[44] And an agreement, to be accepted, must contain provisions which satisfy, at least to a minimum degree, the competing interests of the diverse groups within a union.

As stated earlier, one of the functions of the union negotiator is to try to establish the priorities of the various groups which make up the union membership. Effective two-way communications between the negotiator and the members are essential to this purpose. As a first step, intraorganizational negotiations within the union and management must precede the negotiations between the two parties. If these internal negotiations are carried out effectively, it is more likely that the settlement finally reached at the negotiating table will be acceptable to the constituents of both negotiating teams. In the final analysis, it is the constituents of both the union and management negotiators who decide the content of a negotiated settlement.

Compulsory Provisions

All jurisdictions in Canada require that collective agreements contain no-strike and no-lockout clauses which prohibit strike and lockout action during the life of a collective agreement. The intent of this provision[45] is to guarantee some degree of stability in the employment relationship during the life of the agreement. As a *quid pro quo* for this provision, all jurisdictions also require that collective agreements contain a provision for final and binding arbitration of disputes arising over the interpretation and application of the clauses in the collective agreement. In some jurisdictions, the legislation spells out the applicable clause where collective agreements fail to include one.

Another legal requirement is that collective agreements operate for a minimum period of one year. Most jurisdictions also require collective agreements to contain a provision which recognizes the union as the exclusive bargaining agent for the group of workers it represents. In addition, as discussed in the previous chapter, five jurisdictions now require that the collective agreement contain a compulsory dues check-off if the bargaining agent so requests. Finally, B.C. legislation requires collective agreements to contain provisions for assisting workers affected by technological change. H. W. Arthurs et al. claim that "These mandatory provisions have the effect of reducing the scope of bargaining to the extent that they establish a minimum below which the parties cannot bargain."[46]

The Duty to Bargain in Good Faith

While there is a tremendous amount of jurisprudence on the duty to bargain in good faith in the United States, there is surprisingly little on this subject in Canada. Legal scholar Michael Bendel said in 1980 that only one article had been published on the subject up to that time.[47] There are two reasons for this dearth. First, labour relations boards in Canada have only recently been given the authority to issue remedial orders in cases where good faith bargaining was found to be lacking.[48] Prior to this, a party who felt that the other had failed to bargain in good faith was obliged to obtain consent from Canadian labour relations boards to prosecute the other party in court. In order to obtain such consent, the aggrieved party had to demonstrate a prima facie case (one which seemed justifiable from the evidence presented) before the boards.

The second reason for the lack of a large body of jurisprudence on the duty to bargain in good faith in Canada is that the compulsory conciliation procedure operates "to escort [the union's negotiating team] to the door of the employer and say, 'Here they are, the legal representatives of your employees.'"[49] If the parties in Canada fail to meet and negotiate, conciliation officers or mediators are appointed to assist the parties. A strike or lockout becomes legal only after this procedure is complied with.

The late Professor H. D. Woods of McGill University, Chairman of the Prime Minister's Task Force on Labour Relations from 1966 to 1968, was a strong critic of the conciliation process in Canada before 1968. During his interviews with the parties over the two-year period from 1966 to 1968, however, he came to believe that there was some merit to compulsory conciliation, particularly where only one conciliation officer was used. According to Woods, the major reason for the lack of bad faith bargaining charges in Canada was the obligation of conciliation officers to get the parties together in the same room to begin negotiations. No such obligation exists in American law. Professor Woods thought that this lack was part of the reason for the large number of unfair practice cases in the United States involving the failure to bargain in good faith.

Actions Deemed to Indicate Bad Faith

Now that most labour relations boards in Canada have the authority to issue remedies in situations where either party fails to bargain in good faith, a body of jurisprudence is emerging. Let us now turn to that jurisprudence. A brief summary follows of some of the actions which constitute a failure to bargain in good faith.

Failure to Meet and Threats First, since collective bargaining is viewed not only as an exercise of economic strength but also as an exercise in human relations, Canadian labour relations boards have placed far greater emphasis on the manner in which negotiations are conducted than on the content of negotiations.[50] The right of bargaining agents to bargain for a collective agreement imposes a duty on the employer to bargain in good faith with a view to concluding a collective agreement: the serving of notice to bargain by one party requires that the other meet with it. A refusal to meet at the commencement of negotiations constitutes a refusal to bargain in good faith. Unlawful strike threats by a union before negotiations begin also constitute refusals to bargain in good faith. However, where the parties have discussed the issues at numerous meetings, a refusal to meet further until some condition is altered does not constitute a failure to bargain in good faith. Labour relations boards have even held that, since workers are entitled to negotiate through their chosen representatives, "an employer's objection to the composition of the union bargaining committee (even when it contains an employee of a business competitor) cannot justify a refusal to meet with the union."[51]

Circumvention of Bargaining Agent   Second, an employer may not circumvent the union which is the exclusive bargaining agent by negotiating with the workers directly or through another union. Employers who have attempted to change unilaterally the conditions of employment after the statutory freeze* has expired have been found, in some circumstances, to have violated the duty to bargain in good faith.

Suppression of Information   Third, full, informed discussion during negotiations is required for good faith bargaining. An explanation of the rationale underlying a wage offer must be included in such discussion. The union representative, is not obliged to accept the rationale, but the management representative, nevertheless, must give one. The offer does not necessarily have to be reasonable, but it must be an honest one, according to American jurisprudence. If the parties, having negotiated in good faith, feel that further discussions are useless, then a take-it-or-leave-it position does not con-

*The statutory freeze upholds the existing agreement during the negotiation and conciliation periods.

stitute a failure to bargain in good faith. Another aspect of a full and informed discussion concerns the extent to which the employer must supply data to the bargaining agent:

> While it has been recognized that there is some duty upon the employer to supply information, the full extent of that duty has never been defined. In one case a refusal by an employer to supply existing wage and classification data was taken into account in determining that a failure to bargain in good faith had occurred.[52]

Failure to Use Prescribed Form of Third Party Assistance   Fourth, as we discussed in the previous chapter, the parties in all jurisdictions in Canada must go through certain forms of third-party assistance before the right to strike or lockout accrues. Untimely strikes and lockouts are clearly illegal. Remedial legislation may be invoked to stop untimely strikes and lockouts. A failure to bargain in good faith exists also in the refusal of one of the parties to comply with a method previously agreed upon by both parties to resolve disputes. Illustrating this situation is an Ontario case in which the parties signed a collective agreement requiring arbitration to be used in the next round of negotiations should the parties be unable to resolve the dispute themselves. In this case, the employer refused to proceed to arbitration, was found guilty of bargaining in bad faith, and was ordered to submit to arbitration.

Contradiction   Five, attempts to renege on committments previously made constitutes a failure to bargain in good faith. Conversely, the introduction of additional demands by a party after the agenda has been clearly established is considered to be a failure to bargain in good faith. The parameters of the negotiations are set in the early exchange of proposals and the introduction of new matters near the end of the negotiations has been held to "effectively destroy the decision-making framework."[53] Labour boards have ordered employers to execute a formal agreement where a mutual understanding has been reached on all issues.

Infraction Six, while Canadian labour law does not distinguish between mandatory demands (those which the parties must negotiate) and voluntary demands (those which a party may refuse to negotiate), Canadian boards have considered demands that are tainted with illegality as a failure to bargain in good faith.[54] For example, a party which attempts to bargain for a national agreement in an industry which falls under provincial jurisdiction may be found to be bargaining in bad faith. Attempts by employers to restrict the scope of the bargaining unit, rearrange the assignment of work between competing unions, or interfere with the internal operation of unions are all illegal. A demand that a union not discipline workers who have crossed picket lines during a strike is one example of illegal interference with the internal operation of unions.[55] Demands which are illegal under other statutes, such as human rights statutes, constitute bad faith bargaining. Hard bargaining, even if it is accompanied by harsh words and insults, does not constitute a failure to bargain in good faith. This is one reason why many employers and unions probably take a very tough stance during the conduct of negotiations.

Attrition Seven, some negotiations seem to drag on for a long period of time. The duty to bargain in good faith does not diminish with the passage of time, but may take different forms where extensive negotiations have already taken place.

Surface Bargaining Eight, a smooth operator may respect all legal procedures associated with the duty to bargain in good faith, but have no intention whatsoever of entering into a collective agreement. This practice is called surface bargaining. An example of surface bargaining is the tabling of unreasonable and predictably unacceptable proposals while refraining from any conduct which is noticeably inconsistent with a desire to enter into a collective agreement.

What remedy, if any, does a bargaining agent have against surface bargaining? Labour relations boards refuse to deal with this kind of situation since it revolves around the concept of motives, and motives are extremely difficult to prove. Bendel suggests that labour relations boards "should be prepared to hold that an employer whose contract proposals it considers unreasonable by reference to a particular objective standard is *prima facie* guilty of failing to bargain in good faith."[56] The problem with this suggestion is in developing an objective standard: Who will establish the standard and its objectivity? What will be the criteria for objectivity? All things being equal, however, it is likely that Mr. Bendel will recommend, in his new capacity as a member of the Public Service Staff Relations Board,* the adoption of an objective standard for determining the good faith of bargaining agents.

Remedies for Failure to Bargain in Good Faith

The measure usually put forward as a remedy for the failure to bargain in good faith is a directive that future negotiations be conducted in good faith. Such a directive, however, is by definition not a remedy. Boards, furthermore, do not supervise such directives. The proposed remedies of imposing the terms which might have been reached had good faith bargaining occurred and postponing a pending decertification vote have been expressly rejected by labour boards on "the basis that they would interfere unduly with the existing balance of bargaining power."[57] In the *Radio Shack* case mentioned in the preceeding chapter, however, the Ontario Labour Relations Board ordered the employer to reimburse United Steelworkers negotiators for extra costs resulting from the failure of management negotiators to bargain in good faith. The OLRB also ordered the company to reimburse the workers for the earnings they lost as a result of the bad faith bargaining.

The OLRB went as far as a board should go, mainly because it is extremely difficult, if not impossible, to determine how much the union and

*Michael Bendel was appointed to the Public Service Staff Relations Board in 1984.

the workers lost as a result of the failure of the employer to bargain in good faith. The major problem is that of determining what the appropriate remedy should be since it is so difficult to determine what the union might have obtained by way of a settlement if the employer had not engaged in bad faith bargaining. It will be some time yet before boards develop remedies, if indeed they ever will.

Concession Bargaining

Just prior to and during the time of the writing of the second edition of this chapter, a new term had been added to the lexicon of industrial relations literature: *concession bargaining.* E. M. Kassalow suggests that many aspects of this phenomenon are not new.[58] T. A. Kochan et al., however, suggest that concession bargaining represents a fundamental change in the negotiation process, at least in the United States.[59] Some writers regard concession bargaining as an outcome of negotiation while others see it as both an outcome and a process of negotiation. Some writers wonder whether this new phenomenon is a passing thing or here to stay.[60] This section will summarize the mainstream of thought which characterizes concession bargaining.

P. Capelli argues that it is impossible to regard concession bargaining as only an outcome, or rollbacks, since negotiations are necessary for outcomes to occur.[61] D. Q. Mills, though, views concession bargaining as an outcome only, where the concessions involve rollbacks by unions with corresponding concessions by management or without them.[62] A. Freedman and W. E. Fulmer view concession bargaining as a breakdown in the process of pattern bargaining which we discussed in the early part of this chapter.[63] The major emphasis in most of the literature, however, is concerned primarily with outcomes.

The general consensus on the history of concession bargaining in the United States is as follows: For years, major bargaining patterns and

new breakthroughs in collective bargaining came about mainly through the leadership of the United Auto Workers and the United Steelworkers. The pension, health, and hospital insurance plans which were first negotiated by these two powerful unions in 1949 and 1950 subsequently spread to other industries. Supplemental unemployment benefits, which were first negotiated in the auto industry in the mid-1950's by the UAW, also soon spread to other industries, but were successfully resisted by the major electrical companies. Cost-of-living allowances (COLA's), which were first negotiated in the auto industry, have gradually found their way to large segments of the unionized labour force. It was the United Steelworkers Union which first introduced the idea of expedited arbitration of contract interpretation disputes in 1971; this idea has spread to a number of unionized employment situations in both Canada and the United States.

If the auto and steel unions cease to be the pace settlers that they have been, no other unions would be in a position to perform this leadership role.[64] Pattern bargaining has been one of the major mechanisms through which the provisions gained by the auto and steel unions has permeated much of the unionized segments of the American and Canadian economies. The auto industry has been the best example of a pattern leader in the United States. In 1950, the UAW and General Motors signed a five-year agreement which included an annual improvement factor of 3% — a figure presumed to represent the average improvement in productivity for the economy as a whole. This improvement factor was accompanied by cost-of-living protection against inflation. These two provisions were incorporated into other auto company agreements. From 1950 until recently, three-year agreements signed between the UAW and either GM or Ford set the pattern for the automobile industry and other industries. Pattern bargaining has also prevailed in the rubber, aerospace, airlines, copper, and farm equipment industries. In 1964, the Teamsters Union and representatives of 9,800 employers negotiated a

National Master Freight agreement which covered most major over-the-road unionized carriers.[65] Many of these patterns, however, are now crumbling because of the uneven developments in the American economy, as we shall indicate later.

Until the onset of the recession, substantial settlements were obtained in most industries against a fairly stable economic background in which increased costs could easily be passed on to consumers in the form of higher prices. Beginning in the late 1970's and continuing into the early 1980's, however, the economic situation changed rather dramatically in the United States where the degree of unionization had dropped from a high of about 33% or more in the 1950's to around 20% in 1980. While the large decline in union membership is difficult to explain, for the first time since the 1920's it has become fashionable for employers to pronounce publically that they wish to keep their companies union free.[66] Recently, moreover, there has been intense competition in the auto and steel industries resulting primarily from the importation of foreign cars, particularly Japanese cars.

In addition, intense competition from non-unionized segments of the American economy have caused many high-cost companies severe setbacks. In particular, much to the surprise of established airline companies, deregulation has enabled many small companies to compete in that market — particularly in the short-haul routes — with the purchase of second-hand aircraft and the hiring of non-unionized pilots and other personnel.[67] Deregulation in the trucking industry has seen similar results with small, non-unionized companies. Also, the rubber industry has recently been confronted by keen competition from foreign companies operating in the United States.[68] These dramatic changes in the economic framework threatened many American companies with cost structures which made it impossible for them to compete with foreign or domestic non-unionized firms.

In an effort to try to turn their companies around, management in many companies pleaded with the unions which represented their workers for concessions which would lower their cost structures and stimulate the competitiveness of their companies. D. Q. Mills claims that "Lowering a company's labor costs… [is] what concession bargaining is all about."[69] In many cases, agreements were reopened before their expiration date. This measure was instigated by both management and unions. Bargaining goals changed as management sought reductions in contract levels and unions focused on employment security.

The concessions have been of two types. First, workers may agree to accept reductions in wages, benefits, or work rules. Second, workers may agree to forego future benefits. In most situations, however, it is not clear what kinds of concessions a company should seek: whether they should be in the form of lower wages, decreased benefits or the elimination of work practices. While reductions in wages have the most immediate impact, workers may be reluctant to concede wages due to the erosion of their real incomes during recent inflationary periods. Yet a cut in benefits, while probably more acceptable to workers, lacks immediate impact. And work rules exist because workers obviously enjoy some benefits from them. Sometimes, work rules vary between plants and, thus, work-rule concessions are usually impossible to obtain in company-wide negotiations. However, work-rule concessions may exist in informal understandings between workers and supervisors, or they may be negotiated at the local level.

In most cases where unions have made concessions, quid pro quo's have been attempted for them. The extent of future benefits depends on how badly companies need concessions at the time. Capelli comments that "industrial unions have been better able to win improvements because they represent a large proportion of a firm's workforce and can therefore deliver large cost savings in the form of concessions."[70]

Benefits of Concession Bargaining

The kinds of improvements achieved by unions through concessions can be summarized as follows:[71] (1) *Symbolic improvements:* These require that management take a cut in benefits along with production workers. (2) *Job security:* For example, Xerox agreed to employment security and no-layoff clauses at one plant in return for concessions over work rules. United Airlines made a similar deal with its pilots. The most common example of job security, however, is embodied in agreements by employers not to proceed with planned closures or layoffs. (3) *Implicit job security:* This includes guarantees of plant investments as occurred in the rubber industry. (4) *Contingent compensation:* Promises are made for improvements in future compensation. These improvements include stock-ownership plans, profit sharing as in some airlines, and arrangements which tie future benefits to improvements in the company's performance. However, when companies enter into stock-ownership or profit-sharing plans, they may have to open up their books to workers later on. These plans represent a latent benefit to workers since companies would not normally open up their books for worker scrutiny. (5) *Formal arrangements to involve the union in business decisions:* These arrangements have been the most publicized, but probably the least common form of quid pro quo. Sometimes, union leaders sit on company boards as in Pan American, Eastern Airlines, and Chrysler. There are also shop-floor participation plans which are often limited to specific issues. Decisions about equipment purchases and manning crews fall into this category. (6) *Union bargaining gains:* These include the supplying by the company of continuous information about its performance and its future plans, such as a number of meatpacking companies are providing to the union at the plant level. It is suggested that these arrangements meet current union needs and may also improve their bargaining power in negotiations. Furthermore, these improvements are weighted heavily in favour of gain-sharing and job security.

"Perhaps the most important point about these quid pro quo's," according to Capelli, "is that they have allowed unions to salvage some gains from the otherwise disastrous cir-

cumstances associated with concession bargaining."[72] In virtually all cases, quid pro quo's expand the range of issues over which the unions have gained some degree of influence.

Problems of Concession Bargaining

Concession bargaining poses some problems for relations between union leaders and members. In small companies, it is relatively easy for both union leaders and members to see the problems which the companies are experiencing. In large companies, however, union leaders perceive the problems better than the workers. In the instances involving Chrysler and General Motors, top union officials were much more sensitive to the problems of the companies than were local union leaders and members.

E. M. Kassalow believes that concession bargaining has not been a one-way street, particularly in the cases of large companies. In some cases unions have been able to obtain bargaining rights in new areas in return for granting some economic concessions. Kassalow points out that

> in auto and meatpacking new rights have been gained on the matter of plant closings or outsourcing to nonunion companies. These new rights are by no means comprehensive, but they represent an important breakthrough in an area where companies in those industries have not yielded ground in the past.[73]

Some management spokespersons have argued that companies through concession bargaining may have given away too much: the gains have been short-term, the cost has been a long-term intrusion of unions into the prerogatives of management. On the other hand, concessions may be asked for and extracted from unions even though such concessions are not necessary to the continued operation of companies.

In light of what we have pointed out above with respect to the gains which unions and management appear to have received from concession bargaining, why are American writers so patently pessimistic about concession bargaining? First, there is great concern in the United States about the low level of unionization there, and it is expected that the drive by employers for union-free shops and the location of new plants in nonunion areas may cause a weak union movement to become even weaker.[74] Second, pattern bargaining has been decimated during the past few years. Chrysler broke away from pattern bargaining in 1979 because of a dire financial situation.

In the rubber industry, the United Rubber Workers for many years negotiated company-wide agreements which set the pattern for the rest of the industry. Since 1979, however, these patterns have been fragmented to respond to specific company and plant situations. In the trucking industry, the *Master Freight* agreement proved to be quite flexible: many companies were given concessions under this agreement. Little pattern bargaining occurred in airlines during 1983. Long-time observer of the American scene G. Strauss has commented that "it is hard to imagine that wages in airlines, meatpacking, and trucking will be restored to their pre-1980 relationships in the near or immediate future. Company ability to pay is partially replacing coercive comparisons as the basis for setting wages."[75]

Three researchers at MIT are attempting to develop a better theory of industrial relations by using the concept of strategic choice at three levels of the union-management relationship. The objective of these researchers is to explain what has happened in the past and also to explain more fully what has happened recently. One intent of their theory is to fully inform policy makers. Thus far, however, these researchers have published only one paper in which the strategic choices of management have been their major concern. One conclusion of the research is that the recent competitive pressures in the United States has accelerated the movement of investments and jobs to nonunion plants.[76] However, this strategy has been successful under fairly restrictive conditions, none of which prevails in the auto and steel industries.

Canada has had little experience with concession bargaining partly because the labour movement in Canada, which is about 40% of the non-agricultural labour force, has taken a strong stand against granting concessions. This stand has been taken despite the fact that the unemployment rate is higher in Canada than it is in the United States. Pattern bargaining, to the extent that it prevails in Canada, has not undergone the major disruptions which have occurred in the United States. This is due in part to the fact that Canadian industries have not been deregulated. In addition, the strong support given to unionization and collective bargaining in Canada has made it difficult for employers to keep their enterprises union-free.

Our tentative conclusion to this section is that concession bargaining may represent a new trend in industrial relations whereby unions and management cooperate at every organizational level to make North American companies competitive with companies anywhere in the world. The entrepreneurial spirit seems, from recent popular accounts in the press, to be alive and well in both countries.[77] The recent turbulent times, particularly in the United States, while not making philosophical partners of unions and management, may make them partners of necessity.

Conclusion

This chapter defined the negotiation process as a periodic event concerned with changing the reward which workers receive for their services. An eight-type typology of negotiating units, through which the periodic negotiaions take place, was discussed along with the determinants of negotiating unit structures. The single-establishment, -single-union type has been the most predominent type in Canada since the mid 1960's due mainly to the emergence of collective bargaining in the federal and provincial public sectors. The implications of Canada's decentralized political system for multi-provincial negotiations were also emphasized. The ways in which employers and unions formulate their demands prior to their bipartite negotiations were examined, and illustrations were given by way of specific examples.

The negotiation process was conceived as constituting two major phases: (1) the mapping out of a contract zone and (2) the reaching of a settlement within the contract zone. The strategies and tactics appropriate to each phase were examined with emphasis on the gradual movement from original positions to one which both parties prefer to a work stoppage. The pivotal role that bargaining power plays in determining bargaining outcomes was discussed, as were the factors that influence the bargaining power of both unions and employers.

The ratification of negotiated settlements is a crucial matter for both negotiators and workers, with the latter contending that they should have the final say since they are the ones who live with the terms of the agreement. The duty to bargain in good faith, which has recently become a matter of great concern to labour relations boards as well as to unions and employers, was discussed insofar as jurisprudence on this subject has developed in Canada.

Since concession bargaining has become a new term in the lexicon of negotiations in North America in recent years, some attention was given to the kinds of concessions which unions have given in the short term and the potential gains they may receive ain the long term. Whether concession bargaining is a phenomenon strictly associated with the recent recession or whether it will become a permanent part of North American collective bargaining remains problematic. What is might do, however, is to make unions and management partners of necessity rather than of choice as they periodically negotiate rewards for workers and at the same time try to keep costs down in order to compete effectively with imported goods in international markets.

questions

1 Differentiate between the negotiation process and collective bargaining. Why is it important to make this distinction?
2 By comparing and contrasting periodic events with day-to-day relationships, describe the components of the bargaining structure. Use conventional terminology.
3 Is the concept of the negotiating unit important? Why?
4 What are the major determinants of the negotiating unit? Explain why each component is important to each party.
5 Discuss how unions and employers prepare for contract negotiations. At what point should the parties start preparing for the next round of negotiations?

6 What is the major function of the chief negotiators on each side of the bargaining table?
7 According to Carl Stevens, what are the major phases of the negotiation cycle; which strategies and tactics are appropriate to each phase?
8 What is the role of bargaining power in the negotiation process? What are the major factors that affect the bargaining power of each party?
9 Do you think it is possible to develop a model that will give a determinate solution to a particular set of negotiations? Justify your opinion.
10 Discuss fully the factors which constitute good faith bargaining. Do they play a significant role in the negotiation process? Elaborate.

notes

1 Neil W. Chamberlain and James W. Kuhn, *Collective Bargaining,* 2nd ed. (New York: McGraw-Hill Book Company, 1965), p. 141.
2 J. R. Hicks, *The Theory of Wages* (London: MacMillan Co., 1932); J. Pen, "A General Theory of Bargaining," *American Economic Review* (March 1952), pp. 24-42; C. M. Stevens, *Strategy and Collective Bargaining Negotiations* (New York: McGraw-Hill Book Company, 1963); R. E. Walton and R. B. McKersie, *A Behavioral Theory of Labor Negotiations* (New York: McGraw-Hill Book Company, 1965); B. M. Mabry, Chs. 8-10,

Labor Relations and Collective Bargaining (New York: The Ronald Press, 1966); Pao Lun Cheng, "Wage Negotiations and Bargaining Power," Vol. 21, No. 2 *Industrial and Labor Relations Review* (January 1968), pp. 163-82, and comments and replies in subsequent issues of the same journal; *Essays in Industrial Relations Theory,* ed. G. G. Sommers (Ames: The Iowa State University Press, 1969); S. M. Bacharach and Edward J. Lawler, *Bargaining: Power, Tactics and Outcomes* (San Francisco: Jossey-Bass Publishers, 1981); Jack Barbash, "Collective Bargaining and the Theory of Conflict," Vol. XVIII, No. 1, *British Journal of Industrial Relations* (March, 1980), pp. 82-90; and Syed A. Hameed, "A Critique of Industrial Relations Theory," Vol. 37, No. 1, *Industrial Relations/Relations Industrielles* (1982), pp. 15-31.

3 Arnold R. Weber, "Stability and Change in the Structure of Collective Bargaining," *Challenges to Collective Bargaining,* ed. Lloyd Ulman (Englewood Cliffs: Prentice-Hall Inc., 1967), p. 23.

4 *Ibid.,* p. 14.

5 Labour Canada, No. 6, *Collective Bargaining Review* (Ottawa. Supply and Services Canada, June 1982), p. 61.

6 Weber, "Stability and Change," p. 14.

7 1977, di 319; 1977 2 Can LRBR 99; and 77 CLLC 16,089.

8 P. Weiler, *Reconcilable Differences* (Toronto: The Carswell Co. Ltd., 1980), pp. 154-55.

9 *Ibid.,* p. 162.

10 Weber, "Stability and Change," p. 15.

11 Labour Canada, No. 2, *Collective Bargaining Review* (February 1982), p. 35.

12 Weber, "Stability and Change," p. 23.

13 W. E. Hendricks and L. M. Kahn, "The Determinants of Bargaining Structure in U.S. Manufacturing Industries," Vol. 35, No. 2, *Industrial and Labor Relations Review* (January 1982), pp. 181-95.

14 D. A. L. Auld et al, *The Determinants of Negotiated Wage Settlements in Canada (1966-1975)* (Hull: Supply and Services Canada, 1979), p. 157.

15 J. C. Anderson, "The Structure of Collective Bargaining," eds. J. Anderson and M. Gunderson, *Union-Management Relations in Canada* (Don Mills: Addison-Wesley Publishers, 1982), p. 176.

16 A. W. J. Craig and H. J. Waisglass, "Collective Bargaining Perspectives," Vol. 23, No. 4, *Relations Industrielles/Relations,* Table 2, p. 583.

17 J. B. Rose, Ch. 3, *Public Policy, Bargaining Structure and the Construction Industry* (Toronto: Butterworth & Co. Ltd., 1980), pp. 35-51.

18 Craig and Waisglass, "Collective Bargaining Perspectives," p. 585. With the introduction in October 1975 of the anti-inflation program, the parties started negotiating short-term agreements, since the duration of the anti-inflation program was somewhat uncertain at the beginning. Since the end of the program, the parties have been returning to long-term agreements.

19 Stevens, *Strategy and Collective Bargaining Negotiations,* pp. 46-47.

20 Walton and McKersie, *A Behavioral Theory.*

21 For a history of bargaining in the Big Three of the packinghouse industry, see Alton W. Craig, "The Consequences of Provincial Jurisdiction for the Process of Company-Wide Collective Bargaining in Canada: A Study of the Packinghouse Industry" (unpublished Ph.D. dissertation, Cornell University, 1964).

22 For a brief description of collective bargaining in the Canadian pulp and paper industry, see Donald V. Brazier, "Collective Bargaining in the Pulp and Paper Industry: A Summary" (A report prepared for the Task Force on Labour Relations, August, 1968).

23 Vol. 63, Nos. 2-3, *Canadian Transport* (February and March 1977).

24 John Crispo, *International Unions* (Toronto: McGraw-Hill Co. of Canada Ltd., 1967), p. 182.

25 For a very good analysis of the first three rounds of negotiations in the Quebec Public Service, see Jean Boivin, *The Evolution of Bargaining Power in the Province of Quebec Public Sector (1964-1972)* (Quebec: Département des relations industrielles, Université Laval, January 1975, micrographed). This study has since been published as a book by the Laval University Press.

26 *Ibid.*

27 "AMC, Union Reach Pact on Contract," *Globe and Mail* (February 17, 1977), p. 5.

28 Stevens, *Strategy and Collective Bargaining Negotiations,* p. 63.

29 *Ibid.,* p. 10.

30 For a good discussion of commitment tactics, see Walton and McKersie, *A Behavioral Theory of Labor Negotiations,* pp. 82-125.

31 Stevens, *Strategy and Collective Bargaining Negotiations,* p. 106.

32 *Ibid.,* p. 120.

33 *Ibid.,* p. 12.

34 Chamberlain and Kuhn, *Collective Bargaining,* p. 170.

35 *Ibid.,* pp. 171-72.

36 J. R. Hicks, ch. 7, *the Theory of Wages.*

37 Hicks and Chamberlain continue to be influen-

tial. Bacharach and Lawler, for example, rely heavily on them in developing their theory of contract negotiations. See Bacharach and Lawler, *Bargaining: Power, Tactics and Outcomes,* pp. 43-44.

38 Thomas A. Kochan, *Collective Bargaining and Industrial Relations: From Theory to Policy and Practice* (Homewood, Ill.: Richard D. Irwin, Inc., 1980), p. 324.

39 Walton and McKersie, *A Behavioral Theory.*

40 *Ibid.,* pp. 4-5.

41 *Ibid.,* p. 123.

42 For a more extensive discussion of the problems associated with adopting various tactics, see Walton and McKersie, Ch. X, *A Behavioral Theory.*

43 For an excellent treatment of this subject, see Clyde W. Summers, "Ratification of Agreements," *Frontiers of Collective Bargaining,* eds. J. T. Dunlop and N. W. Chamberlain (New York: Harper and Row Publishers, 1967), pp. 75-102. Some of the ideas in the following section are taken from this article.

44 *Ibid.,* p. 83.

45 Sources for the material in this and the next section are H. W. Arthurs, D. D. Carter and H. J. Glasbeek, *Labour Law and Industrial Relations in Canada* (Toronto: Butterworths and Co. Ltd., 1981), pp. 200-07 (originally published as a monograph in *The International Encyclopedia for Labour Law and Industrial Relations* (Deventer, The Netherlands: Kluwer, 1981); M. Bendel, "A Rational Process of Persuasion: Good Faith Bargaining in Canada," *University of Toronto Law Journal,* 30 (1980), pp. 1-45.

46 Arthurs *et al., Labour Law and Industrial Relations in Canada,* p. 206.

47 Bendel, "A Rational Process of Persuasion," pp. 1-2.

48 *Ibid.,* p. 2.

49 Quoted, *ibid.,* p. 13.

50 Arthurs *et al, Labour Law and Industrial Relations in Canada,* p. 201.

51 *Ibid.,* p. 202.

52 *Ibid.,* p. 204.

53 Bendel, "A Rational Process of Persuasion," p. 19.

54 Arthurs *et al, Labour Law and Industrial Relations in Canada,* p. 205.

55 *Ibid.*

56 Bendel, "A Rational process of Persuasion," p. 32.

57 Arthurs *et al, Labour Law and Industrial Relations in Canada,* p. 207.

58 E. M. Kassalow, "Concession Bargaining—Something Old, But Also Something Quite New," *Proceedings,* Thirty-Fifth Annual Meeting of the IRRA. (Madison: IRRA, 1982), 372-82.

59 T. A. Kochan, R. B. McKersie, and P. Cappelli, "Strategic Choice and Industrial Relations Theory," Vol. 23, No. 1, *Industrial Relations* (Winter 1984), pp. 16-39.

60 P. Cappelli, "Union Gains Under Concession Bargaining," *Proceedings,* Thirty-Sixth Annual Meeting of the IRRA (Madison: IRRA, 1984), p. 297.

61 P. Cappelli, "Concession Bargaining and the National Economy," *Proceedings,* Thirty-Fifth Annual Meeting of the IRRA (Madison: 1983), pp. 362-63.

62 D. Q. Mills, "When Employees Make Concessions," *Harvard Business Review* (May-June, 1983), pp. 103-13.

63 A. Freedman and W. E. Fulmer, "Last Rites for Pattern Bargaining," *Harvard Business Review* (March-April, 1982), pp. 30-48.

64 Kassalow, "Concession Bargaining," pp. 373, 379-80.

65 Freedman and Fulmer, "Last Rites for Pattern Bargaining," p. 31; and Kochan *et al,* "Strategic Choice and Industrial Relations Theory," p. 28.

66 Kochan *et al, ibid.,* pp. 17-18.

67 H. R. Northup, "The New Employee Relations in Airlines," Vol. 36, No. 1, *Industrial & Labor Relations Review* (January 1983), pp. 169-70.

68 Freedman and Fulmer, "Last Rites for Pattern Bargaining," p. 40; and Kochan *et al,* "Strategic Choice and Industrial Relations Theory," pp. 32-33.

69 Mills, "When Employees Make Concessions," p. 105.

70 Cappelli, "Union Gains Under Concession Bargaining," p. 300.

71 *Ibid.,* pp. 300-04.

72 *Ibid.,* p. 304.

73 Kassalow, "Concession Bargaining," p. 376.

74 G. Strauss, "Industrial Relations: Time of Change," Vol. 23, No. 1, *Industrial Relations* (Winter 1984), pp. 5-8.

75 *Ibid.,* p. 9.

76 Kochan *et al,* "Strategic Choice and Industrial Relations Theory," pp. 16-39.

77 See, for example, "How Unions Are Helping to Run the Business," *Businessweek* (December 24, 1984), pp. 69-70; and "The GM-Toyota Linkup Could Change the Industry," *Businessweek* (December 24, 1984), p. 71.

J. Chris Christiansen, *The Financial Post*

8

Forms of Third-Party Assistance in the Negotiation Process

Introduction

The basic objective of this chapter is to describe and analyze the utility of different types of third-party assistance and their potential impact on the negotiation process. While it would be highly desirable to have clear-cut and specified criteria by which to judge the utility of all forms of third-party assistance, insufficient empirical evidence exists to make this assessment. However, there is a rapidly growing body of empirical literature assessing a number of forms of third-party assistance in the public sector. We will draw upon this literature where appropriate.

If the two parties to the negotiation process are unable to reach an agreement by themselves, various types of third-party assistance may help them to settle. As indicated in the chapter, "Legislation Governing Collective Bargaining In The Private Sector," conciliation is compulsory in most jurisdictions in Canada before a strike or lockout can be deemed legal. Conciliation as prescribed by legislation is a one- or two-stage process, involving first a conciliation officer and then, if necessary, a conciliation board. Legislation in some jurisdictions provides for the appointment of a mediator whose services either supplement or replace those of a conciliation officer or board or both. In addition to conciliation and mediation, there is another type of third-party assistance, namely arbitration, which is used primarily in the public sector. Arbitration may take many forms, the most important of which will be discussed later in this chapter. There are other types of third-party assistance prescribed either by legislation (fact-finding) or available on a voluntary basis (mediation *cum* arbitration, often shortened to "med-arb").

In the previous chapter on labour legislation, we differentiated between interest disputes and rights disputes. The types of assistance with which this chapter is concerned are those utilized in interest disputes, where contract negotiations become deadlocked.

The Stages at Which Agreements Are Reached

Labour Canada publishes reports monthly and annually[1] on the stages at which agreements are reached in negotiations affecting 500 or more workers, excluding those in the construction industry. Constructed from final reports of *The Collective Bargaining Review,* Table 8.1 shows that, except in 1977 and 1980, less than 45% of settlements were reached through direct bargaining between the parties. Hence, at least 55% of the settlements were achieved through some form of third-party assistance. This table, however, understates the extent of such assistance, since Labour Canada's figures do not show how many stages disputes may have gone through prior to an agreement. For example, the conciliation officer stage accounts for less than 20% of agreements reported since 1973, while only 2% of settlements in recent years have been reached at the conciliation board stage. The figures reflect the declining use of conciliation boards. The extent to which conciliation officers have been used before resorting to conciliation boards, however, is understated. Ignored are the times conciliation officers may have unsuccessfully intervened following work stoppages.

This is not the only example of under-reporting third-party activity. Implicit in Labour Canada records of settlements reached at the work stoppage stage is the idea that mediators have assisted in the resolution of disputes. However, in coding this information, Labour Canada does not identify this or any other type of third-party assistance unless special legislation is passed or an inquiry commission is convened. Hence, the figures ignore much mediation (and post-mediation) bargaining. It is clear, then, that Table 8.1 must be read with a great deal of caution. It can be calculated, however, that a mediator was involved in about 20% of the settlements reached between 1967 and 1981. This figure includes mediation during work stoppages. The figures for the years from 1982 to 1984 reflect the effects of wage restraint legislation in the public sector.

The same table indicates the increasing use of mediation in recent years, particularly in the private sector. More importantly, it points to increased mediation in public- and parapublic-sector disputes prior to compulsory arbitration or strikes. It is interesting to note that the use of arbitration has increased somewhat since the late 1960's. This increase results in large part from the trend to unionization and collective bargaining in the public sector, particularly at the provincial level where arbitration is often the final stage of dispute resolution.

Although the press generally gives wide coverage to work stoppages—thereby exaggerating their overall importance—Table 8.1 shows that only 10% to 15% of negotiations actually result in strikes or lockouts. The remaining 85% to 90% are settled without such measures and are thus not the subject of intensive journalistic interest.

The Compulsory Conciliation Process

As indicated above, conciliation is required in most jurisdictions in Canada where the parties reach an impasse in negotiations or wish to engage in a legal strike or lockout or both. The origin of compulsory conciliation began with the

Table 8.1 Stages at Which Settlements Were Reached per Calendar Year from 1965 to 1981 for Collective Agreements Covering 500 or More Employees, Excluding the Construction Industry, by Percentage of Total Agreements for Canada as a Whole

Stages of Settlement	1965	1966	1967	1968	1969	1970	1971	1972	1973	1974	1975	1976	1977	1978	1979	1980	1981	1982	1983	1984
Direct Bargaining	40.2	40.3	37.2	34.7	44.6	36.0	35.0	41.3	39.1	41.7	39.9	42.2	50.1	42.2	43.9	45.8	41.6	40.8	22.4	41.0
Conciliation Officer	28.5	24.1	25.1	38.4	26.1	29.7	20.7	26.8	18.3	19.0	19.5	18.4	19.8	15.7	16.9	14.4	18.2	12.1	9.0	12.0
Conciliation Board	10.0	11.0	6.0	8.2	4.7	2.0	5.1	2.3	3.4	1.7	4.0	1.2	1.4	2.4	2.1	1.5	1.0	2.0	—	0.1
Post-Conciliation Bargaining	7.3	7.3	5.5	2.4	6.7	9.3	9.3	5.7	9.4	6.1	7.5	8.0	8.6	9.6	7.1	4.9	6.7	5.7	2.4	4.7
Mediation	—	—	6.0	—	1.2	5.3	5.7	4.8	4.9	9.3	8.0	10.4	8.8	15.6	7.8	11.9	7.3	11.9	6.1	8.3
Post-Mediation Bargaining	—	—	—	—	.6	.7	.6	.6	1.1	—	—	—	—	.2	.9	1.3	1.5	1.2	.6	4.2
Mediation after Work Stoppage	—	—	—	—	—	—	—	—	—	—	—	—	—	—	—	—	—	—	—	—
Arbitration	2.8	1.6	4.3	2.4	3.8	5.0	9.0	5.4	6.1	6.6	8.2	5.8	5.6	7.6	9.3	7.7	9.0	7.4	2.7	5.4
Post-Arbitration Bargaining	—	—	—	—	.6	.7	—	—	—	—	—	—	—	.2	.2	.6	—	—	—	—
Work Stoppages	10.4	12.0	12.5	14.0	11.7	10.7	13.2	9.0	16.9	15.4	11.7	11.2	5.3	5.3	10.5	8.6	14.6	3.7	6.4	6.5
Bargaining after Work Stoppages	—	—	—	—	—	—	.6	4.0	1.4	.2	1.0	2.3	.2	.5	.5	3.1	.2	2.9	—	—
Other	.8	3.7	3.3	—	—	.3	.6	.5	.3	—	.3	.5	.2	.3	.7	.2	.2	12.1*	50.3*	17.7
Total Percentage	100	100	100.6	100.1	100	100	100.1	100.2	99.9	100	100.1	100	100	100	99.9	100	100	99.9	99.9	99.9
Number of Agreements	249	191	183	294	341	300	334	354	350	410	401	599	567	656	561	547	479	488	595	552

*The high percentage under *Other* in 1982 and 1983 represent a pass-through of the public-sector wage (income) restraint program at the federal and provincial levels.

Source: Data for the period 1965-1969 and 1981 were obtained from *Collective Bargaining Review,* Labour Canada, Ottawa. Data for the period 1970-1980 were obtained from *Wage Developments Resulting from Major Collective Bargaining Settlements,* Labour Canada, Ottawa. The original data are in absolute terms. Agreements in the construction industry covering 500 or more workers are included for the first time in 1984. The total is given in last row.

Industrial Disputes Investigation Act of 1907 which was drafted by Mr. MacKenzie King, then the Deputy Minister of Labour. Previously, King had successfully intervened in the 1906 strike of coal miners in Lethbridge, Alberta and thus enjoyed Prime Minister Laurier's confidence in labour matters. Public opinion, according to King, would support the recommendations of conciliation boards and, thus, create strong pressure on the parties to settle on the terms recommended by the boards.

King felt the *Conciliation Act* of 1900 was too weak. His drafting of the *IDI Act* reflected both his intention to give the new legislation more bite and his very definite ideas about conciliation, investigation (which was a precursor of fact-finding), and the role of public opinion in implementing recommendations issuing from investigations. With respect to investigations, King made the following observations:

> The benefits of Compulsory Investigation do not lie in its coercive features, but in the opportunities it guarantees for conciliation at the outset, and for continuous efforts at conciliation throughout the entire course of an investigation.[2]

King recognized investigation as secondary in importance to conciliation, but essential when the latter did not function well. Although he may have been right in his original assessment of public opinion as a factor in the resolution of labour-management disputes, it became apparent with the increasing use of conciliation boards after World War II that public pressure did not play the important role that he assigned it, particularly when conciliation boards were appointed with little regard for the nature of the dispute.

At present, in Canada, there is a universal conciliation system. Furthermore, although conciliation officers and boards under most statutes are required to attempt to mediate a settlement between the parties when an impasse has been reached (the accommodative approach), more often than not they also play a fact-finding role, and are required to make recommendations (the

normative approach).

The late H. D. Woods contended that these two approaches reflect most Canadian legislation dealing with state assistance in union-management conflicts. According to Woods, the accommodative approach is intended to

> provide a catalytic influence and make it easier for the parties to concede, compromise and agree... [The normative approach is used where] one or both of the parties are believed to be unreasonable or ill-informed, and this condition may be corrected by third-party appraisal and evaluation, which will lead to recommendations.[3]

We will deal first with conciliation and mediation and then with fact-finding with recommendation.

Conciliation Officers

It is necessary to differentiate between conciliation officers and mediators. Usually, a conciliation officer is the person first appointed when the parties, having reached an impasse in negotiations, request government assistance. In most jurisdictions, the conciliation officer attempts to keep the parties together in a joint conference and may act as a catalyst in resolving outstanding issues. If within a short period of time, the conciliation officer is unable to help the parties resolve their differences, he or she will file a report with the Minister of Labour, or another appropriate authority such as the PSSRB, on the items agreed upon and in dispute. When filing the report, the conciliation officer may recommend the appointment of a board.

Since conciliation officers are members of a government department, they may have to deal repeatedly with the same parties. One conciliation officer interviewed during research for this book said he could not "hammer heads" under the *Act* he administered, but could be quite forceful as a mediator under another statute in the same province. This is partly because the parties may perceive the conciliation officer's appointment as the first of a potential two-part process and may not be willing to compromise at that stage. Also, the work of a conciliation officer is not as long and intensive as that of a mediator and is carried out in accordance with a requirement for strict neutrality. A mediator is free, however, to point out unreasonable demands, particularly when these are proposed by or presented to inexperienced negotiators.

Conciliation officers and mediators are used in the private sector, and in many parts of the public sector, including the federal, provincial, and municipal public services. Most statutes giving collective bargaining rights to provincial public-sector workers contain a provision which requires conciliation or mediation before the appointment of an arbitration board and before a strike or lockout. The same is true for many parapublic-sector workers (hospital workers, teachers, etc.).

The Mediation Process

In order to gain some appreciation of the mediation process, it is first necessary to understand that negotiations do not stop once a mediator enters a dispute, but are, or should be, facilitated. For a brief discussion of the two major stages of the negotiation process, the reader is referred to the chapter "The Negotiation Process" which sets out in some detail the various strategies and tactics used by the parties in each stage. If a mediator is to function effectively, he should know which of the two phases of the negotiation process is in progress when he comes upon the scene.

The major objective of the mediation process is to assist the parties to arrive at an agreement that is acceptable to both of them. This, of course, is the most visible form of successful mediation. However, if a mediator is able to reduce the number of unresolved issues in a dispute, then mediation is at least partially successful. Similarly, if a mediator is able to get the parties to narrow the differences on outstanding issues, then also is mediation partially

successful, even though no one issue may be resolved. Finally, if a mediator is able to prevent the parties from delaying concessions until later in the dispute-resolution process, then mediation is partially successful.[4]

As pointed out in the chapter "The Negotiating Process," one objective of negotiation is to establish a contract zone within which a settlement may be reached. Common sense would suggest that it is easier for a mediator to bring the parties to a settlement if they have already mapped out a contract zone. If the parties are unable to establish a contract zone because of inexperience or inflexibility, a mediator may be able to bring one into existence. This, however, is a more difficult task than getting a settlement within a contract zone, although much depends on the nature of the issues.

If both sides come to the bargaining table with a large number of demands but no priorities for them, then part of the function of the mediator will be to assist the parties in establishing priorities. The mediator thus performs an important educational function. Once the parties have a clear sense of the relative importance of their demands, they can begin to trade off low priority items and reactivate the negotiation process.

Another major function of the mediator is to discover the final position of each party. If the mediator does not have this information, it is very difficult for him to establish the parameters of his role. This knowledge is particularly important in the later stages of the process, since at that point the mediator may be offering suggestions of his own for the parties to consider. In most cases, however, the parties are reluctant to reveal their final positions to the mediator. The mediator, therefore, must be adept at reading between the lines and willing to exert a great deal of effort.

Another important duty of the mediator is to maintain control over the mediation process. This person should be the only source of public information on the progress of the negotiations since the parties cannot negotiate freely in a public forum. The mediator should also be alert to and avoid being manipulated by either party; for, once compromised, the influence of the mediator is reduced to nil.

Mediator Experience

Unions and management prefer to deal with mediators[5] who have had some previous experience. This poses a paradox: it is very hard to break into mediation unless one has experience, yet one needs experience to get involved in mediation. Probably, the best way for a person to enter this field is to take on fairly simple situations, then more involved ones in order to gain a higher profile among management and union negotiators. Prior experience as a negotiator may be very helpful. Many of Canada's top mediators, however, have never negotiated an agreement themselves.

Impartiality and Acceptability A major characteristic of the mediator is impartiality and acceptability to both parties in the dispute. Mediators with a reputation for favouritism generally have brief careers. Another important characteristic is the ability to gain the trust and confidence of the parties. A mediator who is not well known normally encounters exceptional difficulties early in the process, prior to any discussion of the issues.

The mediator's ability and willingness to give a sympathetic hearing to the positions of both sides and deal with the technical issues at hand win him or her the confidence of the parties. A mediator, however, should not try to fake an ability to understand technical issues, as such efforts soon become quite transparent, but should seek clarification of such technical issues from the parties so as to gain a thorough understanding of them. This is one area in which the mediator has to be perfectly honest with the parties. Asking to be fully informed on at least a few issues should not destroy his credibility or the parties' trust in him.

Discretion A mediator must also be able to demonstrate a capacity for treating matters in confidence. One of the first things that a party may do is entrust the mediator with confidential information on a minor issue in order to assess his ability to act with discretion. David Kuechle cites an example of this tactic:

> One union negotiator described his recent experience with such a [test of the confidentiality of the mediator]. He told the mediator that he could not proceed unless he gained one point: an additional $50 a month on full-benefit pensions, knowing that the company was willing to give that amount. But he said 'I would like to explore $75 first to see how the company is thinking on this line.' The mediator said 'O.K.' and went to the company. Soon after that he called the parties together and announced that he had been successful in getting a $50 pension increase: now he saw no reason why the parties could not proceed to other points. When that happened, the union's chief negotiator met privately with the company's negotiator and told him what had happened. The two then agreed that they should dismiss the mediator and proceed alone, that he could not be trusted.[6]

A mediator should never share any information that one side gives, unless advised by that party that it is permissible to reveal it to the other party. The mediator mentioned in Kuechle's example revealed confidential information without permission to do so and, therefore, lost the confidence of both union and management negotiators.

Timing In addition to discretion, a mediator must also possess a sense of timing. Union members know generally how long contract negotiations and the mediation process take from past experience. If the mediator tries to settle prematurely, before either the negotiators or their constituencies are ready, his attempts are unlikely to be successful.

A mediator should also know that certain times during the day are more favourable to announcing an agreement than others. For example, if the parties have been negotiating for a lengthy period of time and have been involved in prolonged and intensive mediation, it would be inappropriate to announce an agreement at four o'clock in the afternoon. Four o'clock in the morning would be a better time, since an early-morning announcement creates the impression that the mediation process was a difficult one and that the settlement came only after some very hard bargaining on all sides. Such an impression is likely to leave members with the feeling that their interests have been well represented, fought for, and incorporated as much as humanly possible into the new agreement. Feeling this way about an agreement, members will likely accept it, and such easy acceptance will likely facilitate labour peace.

The mediator must also know whether or not the parties are relating their settlement to another benchmark agreement. If such is the case, it would obviously be unwise to try to force an agreement before the decison in the benchmark case is announced, since the chief negotiators will probably want to read the decision.

A mediator must also pace the negotiations and help to maintain momentum once the parties have started compromising and agreeing on certain items. And it is crucial to sense the precise moment when an agreement is possible. This moment could be when the union has announced a strike or just hours prior to the commencement of a work stoppage. The mediator must be able to sense which of a series of key moments is the most critical for getting the parties to come to an agreement. Should this moment be missed, the future chances of success are diminished.

Sometimes the mediator may have to create a critical moment. If the time for agreement is near, the mediator may inform the parties of other impending cases and of the difficulties and delays likely to be encountered in booking further mediation time. Should the parties at this point be relying fairly heavily on the mediator to reach a settlement, the imposition of a time-limit may be sufficient to achieve it. An astute mediator employs such a stratagem, however, only if convinced that it will work.

Bulking of Items Another important aspect of the mediator's job is what Kressel refers to as the "bulking of items." Through this process, problems are identified and handled as a unit. For example, all the major monetary issues may be grouped together and a subcommittee created to handle these items. Using bulking, it may be easier to get the parties to compromise on bread-and-butter issues. Multidimensional issues, however, are more difficult to bulk since there may not be enough of them in the union's or management's demands to permit the necessary concessions and compromises.

Power Figures An effective mediator is able to determine the real power figures among the negotiators. Quite often, leaders may be discerned in caucuses. During these meetings, the mediator should be looking for the individual who has veto power and whose ideas seem to serve as a basis for group consensus. It is also during these caucuses that one may discover who the important constituents are.

Usually, within unions there are important subgroups who feel strongly about the inclusion of certain items in the collective agreement. The same is true for management. For example, a negotiator representing a school board may be accountable to the school trustees who have given the negotiator his or her mandate and parameters. The more the mediator knows about the constituents, the more effective the mediator's efforts are in helping the parties frame an agreement acceptable to the constituents. Sometimes, in fact, the mediator may help negotiators sell an agreement to their constituents.

As pointed out above, in the early stages of the mediation process, the mediator is concerned with establishing his or her credibility and gaining the trust and confidence of the parties. Upon meeting the two parties for the first time, the mediator will hear a great deal of grandstanding, arguments, and counter-arguments. Each party starts out striving for the better negotiating position, the more sympathetic treatment by the mediator. As the talks proceed and the mediator comes to understand the parties, wins their confidence, and gains some appreciation of the issues, he or she assumes a more active role than during the initial stages. At this point, an attempt might be made either to establish a framework or to arrange the bargaining agenda so as to encourage the parties to negotiate and make compromises on their own. During this stage, suggestions might also be put forward concerning tentative compromise positions.

The final stages of the mediation process may be characterized by a frantic exchange of proposals between the parties in order to reach a settlement before a strike deadline or some other critical time. This is normally the time that parties ask for suggestions to resolve outstanding issues. A mediator will make proposals only if confident of the "bottom-line" positions of the parties and of his or her ability to satisfy these minimum requirements.

It is usually easier to assess the positions of experienced negotiators than those of novices. For one thing, experienced negotiators know that at some point the mediator may have to come up with his own proposals for settlement and, with that expectation, they may in confidence offer suggestions or hints to help him in formulating an acceptable compromise. The mediator may then have off-the-record sessions with the two chief negotiators who, at that point, might be as anxious as the mediator to reach a settlement. The greatest difficulty for a mediator during this crucial stage of mediation is in working with inexperienced negotiators who often do not realize that they themselves are expected to be of some help to the mediator in forming his final proposals.

At the point where a mediator feels that a mutually acceptable agreement is imminent, the negotiating teams may be called together and asked to give their views on the proposed settlement terms. Sometimes these views take the form of general statements which then have to be spelled out in detail so that the parties will have a clear understanding of the meaning of the final agreement clauses. At this time, a good mediator will avoid taking credit for the success of the mediation, but give credit instead to the two negotiating teams. This is in keeping with the purpose of mediators: to serve the two parties and not to enhance a professional reputation.

Effectiveness of Mediation

The foregoing discussion has attempted to elaborate at least some of the characteristics of the mediation process. While it is true that many mediators consider their profession to be an art rather than a science, some degree of scientific analysis is useful. Fortunately, the development of collective bargaining in the public and parapublic sectors has encouraged a good deal of research on various forms of third-party assistance in those sectors. This is particularly true in the United States, although most of the American research has been devoted to fact-finding and compulsory arbitration. Some of the American research, however, may also apply to the private sector.

A few fairly recent empirical studies exist on the effectiveness of the mediation process. One study found that the larger the number of issues at the impasse stage and the greater their severity, the less effective the mediation.[7] Three sources of impasse were found to be particularly difficult to mediate: (1) low motivation by the parties to settle, (2) the inability of the employer to pay, and (3) unrealistic expectations by both parties.

None of these sources is surprising, particularly since the data used were from negotiations involving police and firefighters. In recent years, local governments have been having difficulties in raising funds. Inability to pay, therefore, has been a common complaint at the local level. Low motivation may reflect the fact that there were further stages in the dispute resolution process. The sources of impasse most conducive to mediation were "(1) lack of experience on the part of the negotiators (especially the union negotiators), and (2) disputes involving what the parties viewed as issues of 'principle.'"[8] Perhaps success with inexperienced parties represents the educational aspects of mediation mentioned previously in which the parties learn that compromise is an essential aspect of negotiations. It is surprising, however, that issues of principle were amenable to mediation since these issues have normally culminated in bitter disputes between the parties. One is left wondering, therefore, how the participants in the research project interpreted "principle at stake." It could be that issues of principle such as union security and dues checkoff are specified in the statutes governing collective bargaining in the public sector.

Quality Mediator quality as perceived by the participants was positively related to mediator effectiveness, particularly with respect to the facilitation of progress in bargaining and making concessions. No significant relationship existed, however, between the parties' perceptions of the quality of the mediator and the probability of reaching a settlement in mediation.[9] This finding is somewhat surprising inasmuch as the mediation agency assigned its best mediators to these cases. The inability of the employer to pay might have contributed to this finding.

A number of personal and occupational characteristics of the mediators was also examined. The experience of a mediator correlated strongly with the effectiveness of mediation, including the probability of settlement. It was also found that no consistent relationship existed between the educational background of the mediators and whether or not they were full- or part-time members of the appointing agency.[10]

Strategy As far as the strategies of the mediators were concerned, it was found that aggressive strategies correlated strongly with progress in bargaining and making concessions, but not with the probability of settlement. Also, it was found that mediators were more successful in resolving nonsalary disputes than salary ones, with the exception of complex fringe benefits such as pension plans. An aggressive strategy was more effective in winning concessions from unions than from management, probably because union demands, many of which are inflated for the purpose of being subsequently traded off, are easier to concede than those of management.[11]

Intensity Another study based on data drawn from recent negotiations in twenty-four municipal blue-collar bargaining units among six states found that the intensity of mediation (which was measured somewhat differently from the aggressiveness of strategies) was positively related to the effectiveness of mediation. Intensity of mediation was "characterized by complete immersion in a dispute and full concentration on resolution of the issues. An intense mediator will try new substantive and procedural approaches to identify issues or individuals who will help to resolve the dispute."[12] The major conclusion of this study was that "[w]here disputes are difficult or subject to extended impasse procedures beyond mediation, intense mediator behavior is critical for mediation to be effective."[13] *Effective* in this study was defined as getting a settlement. The study also found that not only might intensive mediation be able to control or eliminate the chilling effect, but that the lack of intensive mediation is likely to result in a chilling effect (the failure of a weak party to make concessions while negotiating, in the expectation that an arbitrator will order a desirable settlement). The authors conclude that mediation *per se* is not the answer in public-sector disputes. "However, intense mediator behavior does appear to be effective in difficult negotiations or ones subject to impasse procedure beyond mediation."[14]

Flexibility and Face-Saving Another study which attempted to assess the effectiveness of mediation was conducted with 1980 data from teacher negotiations in Iowa. The results of mediation in these negotiations were classified as settlement or nonsettlement. A. Karam and R. Pegnetter, the authors of this study, attempted to determine if there were differences between the reactions of unions and management to various types of mediation strategies and qualities. The conclusion was that, for unions, the most important factors in mediation were devising a framework for negotiations, changing expectations during the mediation process, and maintaining the neutrality and confidentiality of the mediators. Management negotiators found mediation to be most effective where the mediators engaged in face-saving activities, where there was discussion of the cost of disagreement and where they respected the mediator's expertise, trust, and impartiality. The authors found no evidence that the testing of proposals or the emphasizing of other settlement patterns bore any relation to settlement in public-sector mediation.[15] These findings support most of the points raised earlier in the discussion of the characteristics of mediators.

The Conciliation Board Procedure (Fact-Finding with Recommendations)

Specific reference in Canadian legislation to fact-finding with or without recommendations is very rare, although this type of third-party assistance is well-established in the United States. Nonetheless, since conciliation boards function in an analogous way to fact-finding and recommendations, we will consider the use of conciliation boards as equivalent to fact-finding with recommendations.

Under Canadian legislation, the mandate of a conciliation board is to try to mediate settlements between unions and management. If the board is not successful in its mediation efforts, it must make its recommendations public. Only after a certain number of days following the release of the conciliation board's report may a union go on strike or an employer initiate a lockout. In preparing its report, the members of

a conciliation board must adopt what the late H. D. Woods referred to as a normative approach to third-party intervention; that is, the board members must investigate the matters in dispute and make pertinent recommendations.

Private-sector legislation in Canada provides no guidelines for conciliation boards. Consequently, board members must develop their own criteria for determining the kinds of recommendations they will make. This freedom sometimes serves to delay the collective bargaining process. Ill-conceived recommendations may also "heat up" rather than "cool off" a dispute. Thus, the overall success rate for conciliation boards is low. For these and other reasons, the compulsory aspect of conciliation boards has come in for a fair degree of criticism and public scrutiny.

As pointed out earlier, conciliation boards originated with the *IDI Act* of 1907. While most writers see the *IDI Act* and the boards established under it as dealing only with contract negotiations or interest disputes, H. D. Woods has enlarged its scope to include recognition disputes.[16] One purpose of the *IDI Act*, according to MacKenzie King, was to bring employers and unions together at the bargaining table. The effect of the statement was, in some cases, to give *de facto* recognition to the union, although of admittedly short duration. Once machinery was set up under P.C. 1003 in 1944 to deal with recognition disputes by means of special tribunals (labour relations boards) and the duty to bargain in good faith became part of that legislation, conciliation boards began to restrict themselves to the consideration of contract negotiation or interest disputes.

As indicated in Chapter 6, conciliation boards continued to be used as one of the major forms of third-party assistance in contract negotiation disputes until well into the 1960's. Boards have been voluntary in Saskatchewan until recently and are now partly voluntary in Manitoba. They were eliminated completely in Quebec in 1961, and at a later date in British Columbia. Other jurisdictions still retain provisions for the establishment of conciliation boards in private-sector disputes. However, as indicated earlier, very few of these jurisdictions now establish conciliation boards and when they do, it is mainly in cases that have a serious public-interest component.

Although not widely used at present, conciliation boards have historically been a significant form of third-party assistance in Canada. For this reason, it might be appropriate to consider their original objectives, how they were set up, and the factors that have led to their gradual decline.

Original Objectives of Conciliation Boards

Conciliation boards are tripartite in nature. This form originated with the *IDI Act* and is still used today. The three board members are chosen as follows: Upon request of either party, or on his own initiative, the Minister of Labour may direct each party to select its nominee to the board. The two nominees are then required to name a mutually acceptable chairman, but if they are unable to do so, the Minister then appoints one. Each of the above procedures has certain time constraints. If a party fails to name its representative within a given time, the Minister, in most jurisdictions, may appoint a nominee on its behalf.

At one time the report of the board consisted of a majority of its members; that is, the report would be signed by the chairman and either one of the other nominees. However, as we indicated in Chapter 6, the legislation in some jurisdictions now provides that, if there is no majority report, the chairman's report becomes the official report of the board. This change has made it easier for conciliation board chairmen since they are now able to draw up reports without having to worry about obtaining a nominee's signature. Even though the chairman's report is the official one, either or both nominees may present reports, and the resulting plurality of reports may hamper rather than aid negotiations.

Despite all that has been written on conciliation boards, very few writers have attempted to define what constitutes the success of a concilia-tion board. In an excellent study, W. B. Cunningham, a leading authority on Canadian conciliation, attempted such a definition:

> It [success] is used in a restricted and narrow sense. A board is credited with a 'success' if the parties reached an agreement on the immediate issues which separated them, and if this agreement was reached after the intervention of a board of conciliation but before the reporting of its recommendations to the Minister.[17]

Using this definition, Cunningham found that most of the New Brunswick conciliation boards that he studied were unsuccessful. While sixty-seven boards were appointed in New Brunswick during the period of Cunningham's research, only twelve boards or 17.9% were able to report that all matters in dispute had been settled.[18]

Another study carried out by Allan Porter covering the year 1952 in Ontario indicated that 36.5% of the disputes involving conciliation-boards were fully settled. While no studies have been done measuring the success of conciliation boards on a national basis, it would not be surprising if such research showed the success rate to be very low.

Disadvantages of Conciliation Boards

As mentioned previously, the compulsory conciliation procedure in Canada, and particularly the compulsory conciliation-board stage, has been the subject of severe criticism by leading academics, labour leaders, and even some employers. One of the major criticisms is the long delay inherent in the process. Another major objection to compulsory conciliation is that it hampers direct negotiations between the parties. For example, if the two sides feel in their private negotiations that their dispute may go to a conciliation officer, they are inclined to withhold concessions until later in the process. If the dispute should proceed to the conciliation board stage, there is an inclination to withhold the last offer until the conciliation board has reported. Only after the report do both parties really begin serious negotiations.

While the elimination of work stoppages

(strikes and lockouts), which is one of the major objectives of the compulsory conciliation process, is a laudable objective, one may question whether delaying the work stoppage until after the issuance of the conciliation board report is conducive to genuine collective bargaining, since the more time there is to settle over the table, the less pressure there is to settle. Furthermore, a conciliation board report may make a recommendation which strongly favours one party over the other. In that event, the favoured party may use the board's recommendation as an argument in and thus prolong subsequent negotiations.

In addition, as H. D. Woods says:

> [T]he fallacy in the Canadian compulsory conciliation procedure is that it ignores the role of the work stoppage as a catalytic agent in bringing about agreement. When the parties are confronted with the possibility of a strike or lockout, each is brought face to face with a choice between (a) the losses to be incurred by the strike and (b) the price that may have to be paid to avoid these losses. But the delay on resort to work stoppages suspends the need to face these alternatives.[19]

In fact, a conciliation report favourable to one side may actually prolong a subsequent work stoppage, should the favoured side persist in seeking to obtain what the report recommended.

Declining Use of Conciliation Boards

Faced with mounting criticism by unions and academics, governments now appoint very few conciliation boards. This decline in appointments is apparent at the federal level. Until recently, the federal jurisdiction relied most on conciliation boards, especially in disputes with a fairly heavy public interest component. When Part V of the Canada Labour Code was amended in 1972, provision was made for the use of conciliation commissioners as well as conciliation officers and boards. In addition, section 195 of Part V of the Canada Labour Code empowers the Minister of Labour to appoint a mediator, either upon request or on his own initiative. This gives the federal Minister of Labour a great deal of discretion in the choice of conciliation strategies.

Over the years, this change has meant a decline in two-stage conciliation: cut-backs on the appointment of conciliation boards and commissioners in private-sector disputes. The 1978 Annual Report of Labour Canada includes the following statement regarding conciliation and mediation activity:

> Over the past several years, the Branch has followed a course of fewer Conciliation Commissioner appointments where disputes have not been settled at the conciliation officer stage. Instead of Conciliation Commissioner appointments, the formal conciliation process has been shortened by resorting to the 'no-action process.' In other words, where settlements are not reached at the conciliation officer stage, the Branch, with ministerial approval, advises the parties that no further form of conciliation procedures (i.e., appointment of a Conciliation Commissioner *or* the establishment of a Conciliation Board) will be applied. This decision gives the parties the right to initiate strike and/or lockout action at the end of seven days. Thus, considerable pressure is immediately brought to bear on the parties to engage in meaningful negotiations.[20]

While we are seeing fewer and fewer boards appointed in the private sector, the *Public Service Staff Relations Act*, which covers workers in the Federal Government, still contains a mandatory provision whereby a bargaining agent choosing to exercise its strike option must first go through a two-stage conciliation process. In light of what has been happening in the private sector it will be interesting to see what, if anything, will be done with respect to the establishment of conciliation boards in the federal and provincial public sectors.

An interesting case under the *Public Service Staff Relations Act* involved the Canadian Union of Postal Workers (CUPW). In negotiations up to 1981, lengthy conciliation board reports were not at all instrumental in bringing about agreements between CUPW and the Treasury Board, which is the employer for the Federal Government. In fact, in the 1978 and 1981 negotiations, three separate (and lengthy) board reports were written, one by each of the nominees and one by the chairman. It is true that, in an intervening round of negotiations in the Spring of 1980, a settlement was reached between the postal workers and Treasury Board on the basis of a conciliation board report. However, in that particular case, the conciliation board recommended favourably on almost every item that the union wanted. In fact, in the post-conciliation negotiations, CUPW made it very clear that it would settle without a strike only if the government gave substantially what was contained in the conciliation board report. An added factor in these post-conciliation negotiations was the presence of the President of the Canadian Labour Congress — the first time that such a high-ranking official in the labour movement had ever taken part in negotiations between a union and an employer. CUPW and Canada Post now came under the jurisdiction of Part V of the Canada Labour Code.

Multiprovincial Bargaining As pointed out in Chapter 6, it is extremely difficult to get effective conciliation or mediation in those negotiations where the parties bargain on a multiprovincial basis but fall under provincial rather than federal jurisdiction. The decreasing use of conciliation boards, the procedures of which vary from province to province, should facilitate collective bargaining in those situations and bring pressure to bear more quickly on the parties concerned. During the Summer of 1980, for example, the Canadian Paperworkers Union, which bargains on a multi-provincial basis with Abitibi-Price Incorporated in Ontario, Quebec, and Newfoundland, took a strike vote among twelve mills in these three provinces. The union indicated that it would begin a staggered shutdown of the twelve mills if an agreement was not reached by a specified date. Assistance was provided in this case mostly by a mediator from the Ontario Ministry of Labour.[21] Less reliance on conciliation boards should also facilitate the pattern of national bargaining between the United Food and Commercial Workers Union and the major meat-packing companies. Overall, it should be easier for those parties who bargain interprovincially to conduct their negotiations without conciliation boards.

Effects of Declining Use of Conciliation Boards If all the criticisms directed at conciliation boards in the past are true, the decreasing use of conciliation boards should mean that the negotiation process takes less time. This conclusion has yet to be verified. Furthermore, as the 1968 Task Force Report on Labour Relations pointed out, if the activities of conciliation boards were curtailed or eliminated, the role of the conciliation officer would become more effective in achieving contract settlements. Again, however, no studies have been conducted to determine whether the use of conciliation officers has in fact increased.

One thing that the reduction of conciliation boards has achieved is the extension of the role and function of mediation. Not too many years ago, the appointment of mediators in contract negotiation disputes was something of a rarity in Canadian industrial relations. In recent years, however, increasing references have been made to the appointment of mediators in such disputes in the public, parapublic, and private sectors. It is expected that mediators will gradually replace conciliation boards and possibly conciliation officers.

Effectiveness of Conciliation

Conciliation appears to be less effective than mediation. Table 8.1 indicates that only a small proportion of settlements are reached at the conciliation board stage. Whether this is due to the declining use of conciliation boards or their ineffectiveness is difficult to say. Certainly, strong criticism of the board stage has existed for many years, largely because of the long periods of time expended at this stage. In addition, the conciliation board has often been viewed as an interim step to be endured before hard bargaining can take place. In this sense, conciliation boards are considered to have a chilling effect on negotiations. Figure 8.1 also indicates that the conciliation-officer stage is less effective than mediation in terms of the number of settlements reached.

A study of conciliation in New Brunswick some years ago and the results of conciliation efforts in the 1981 negotiations between the federal Treasury Board and CUPW confirm these observations. In the 1981 CUPW negotiations, the conciliation report led to a hardening of positions and an eventual postal strike. Veteran labour columnist Wilfred List was especially critical of the report issued by the conciliation board in the postal negotiations:

> [T]he conflict over the report's contentious recommendations brings into question the advisability of continuing the current practice at the federal level of appointing conciliation boards or commissioners to report and to make recommendations for the settlement of disputes.[22]

He suggests that a conciliation board may be more useful if its members are perceived as mediators, with the union and management nominess playing a mediation role with the parties they represent. This arrangement would enhance the possibility of obtaining informal agreements which could then be set down officially in the conciliation report issued by the board. This tactic has been used by one conciliation chairman in disputes in the meat-packing industry.

This form of conciliation-mediation would certainly be preferable to fact-finding with recommendations, activities which sometimes widen rather than narrow the differences between the parties' positions, and which may also undermine third-party credibility. An example of unsuccessful fact-finding is the 1982 doctors' dispute in Ontario. A fact-finder charged with recommending a new fee schedule for medical services came up with a figure which the On-

tario Medical Association claimed was less than the original government offer. The OMA further alleged that the fact-finder's report seemed to be based entirely on his personal concern with inflation and did not seriously examine the legitimacy of the doctors' demands.[23] The result was a temporary disruption of medical services in the province.

While the compulsory conciliation process has been seriously criticized in the private sector for many years, it has recently found some support in a study which deals with impasse disputes in the federal public sector of Canada.[24] The *Public Service Staff Relations Act (PSSRA)* governs collective bargaining between federal public servants and the Federal Government. While the most salient features of the *Act* will be discussed in Chapter 9, it is sufficient to indicate here that where two parties are unable to reach an agreement through the negotiation process, the *Act* provides for two dispute settlement routes: (1) conciliation with the right to strike, (2) binding arbitration. The bargaining agent for each group of workers chooses a route before each round of negotiations begins. An agent may change routes at the beginning of each round of negotiations but never during the course of negotiations.

The data used for this study consist of the results of the first four rounds of negotiations for the period from 1968 to 1975. The results show that a higher proportion of disputes were settled in the intermediate stages (conciliation and mediation) of the conciliation and strike route than by the arbitration route. The authors state that the "data suggest that the costs of disagreement associated with a strike provide much higher pressure or motivation for the parties to settle in mediation or conciliation than the associated costs of going to arbitration."[25] In the public sector, therefore, the incentive to use the conciliation route with a strike as its final step appears to be much greater than that for the route with arbitration as its final step.

The Arbitration Process

Before analyzing the arbitration of interest disputes, it would be useful to distinguish between binding and non-binding forms of third-party assistance. Mediators, fact-finders and conciliation boards may recommend the terms of a settlement, but these are not binding on the parties to the dispute. The results of arbitration, on the other hand, are binding.

Arbitration of Contract Negotiation Or Interest Disputes

While arbitration has been practised in the private sector to a very limited extent, it is only with the recent, widespread adoption of collective bargaining in the public sector that this method has become a major form of third-party assistance in Canada. This is because public servants in Ontario, Alberta, and several other provinces have the right to bargain collectively, but not to strike. Hence, arbitration becomes an important means of resolving impasses in negotiations. In some parapublic sectors, too, arbitration is the final form of settlement. For example, under the Ontario *Hospital Disputes Arbitration Act*, workers in hospitals and other health-care facilities do not have the right to strike (nor can management undertake a lockout). Instead, the parties must submit any unresolved issues in negotiations to binding arbitration. Close to twenty states in the United States have granted collective bargaining rights to their public-sector workers at the state and municipal levels, but most states make compulsory arbitration the final step in the dispute settlement procedure.

A conceptual distinction exists in the types of arbitration currently employed in Canada. First of all, there is compulsory arbitration which is mandated or required by law as the final stage in the contract-negotiation dispute. The examples cited in the previous paragraph are forms of compulsory arbitration since the parties are unable legally to conduct strikes or

lockouts in the situations mentioned. There is also voluntary arbitration which involves a mutual agreement between the two parties to be bound by third-party recommendations. The parties may, for example, decide before or during the proceedings of a conciliation board, that they will be bound by the recommendations of that board.

Generally speaking, employers in the private sector are very strongly opposed to any form of compulsory arbitration. Although many private employers recommend compulsory arbitration as a method of resolving contract negotiation disputes in the public and parapublic sectors, they have made it quite clear that they themselves do not wish to be bound by such a measure. Unions are also generally opposed to compulsory arbitration in both the private and public sectors. The major exception to this statement occurs with weak unions which prefer to have their disputes settled by arbitration rather than deal directly with powerful employers. These unions are not capable of conducting effective strikes and it is, therefore, to their advantage to invoke arbitration rather than use the strike weapon. Weak employers may also prefer arbitration to enduring a strike or initiating a lockout.

Experimental Negotiating Agreement (ENA) Although management and unions in the private sector generally do not like compulsory arbitration to settle unresolved contract negotiation issues, a bold experiment was initiated in 1972 between the United Steelworkers Union and the ten major steel companies in the United States. This bargaining procedure is officially known as the Experimental Negotiating Agreement (ENA) and is an example of voluntary arbitration. Under ENA, one bargaining procedure exists to resolve national issues and another to resolve local issues. (Since, however, no provision exists for binding arbitration to settle local issues, the strike option remains.) If a national agreement cannot be reached by a specified date, either party may then submit the unresolved issues to an impartial arbitration panel which has the authority to render a final and binding decision on the outstanding issues. The arbitration panel is made up of one union representative, one management representative, and three impartial arbitrators selected by both parties. At least two of the three arbitrators are thoroughly familiar with collective bargaining agreements in the steel industry.[26]

This procedure was used in negotiations in 1974, 1977, and 1980. During these negotiations, the parties were able to reach agreement without having recourse to the arbitration panel stage. It was expected that a large number of companies and unions might follow the example of the steel experiment, but to date only a few have chosen voluntary, binding arbitration.

The major impetus to the Experimental Negotiating Agreement was the boom and bust phenomenon which provided the background for negotiations between 1959 and 1974. During each round of negotiation prior to 1974, the steel companies stockpiled extensively in anticipation of a strike. Conversely, the workers made a good deal of money in overtime building up this large inventory. However, in each case following 1959, a settlement was reached without a strike. Consequently, union members were laid off and company production was more or less halted until stockpiled steel had been sold. The desire to prevent this boom and bust kind of situation led the union and the companies to try out the Experimental Negotiating Agreement. Both parties were also determined to avoid the slight increase in imports of steel which had taken place during the 1959 strike.

There were some incentives for each party to enter into an ENA. For example, each member of the union having employee status as of August 1, 1974 received a bonus of $150, a price which the companies agreed to pay in recognition of the savings in production costs anticipated from not stockpiling. Also, there were certain fundamental safeguards in the existing collective agreements that each side wanted to pro-

tect and preserve. These pertained to local working conditions, past practices, union-shop and check-off guarantees, no-strike/no-lockout provisions, and a management rights clause. The 1974 agreement also assured the union that the cost-of-living clause won in 1971 would continue to operate to 1977.

The Experimental Negotiating Agreement was intended, as well, to force the parties to reach settlement terms of their own, rather than having terms imposed by outside third parties. Mr. Abel, President of the union at that time, claimed that

> A third party dictating the terms of a settlement might not be aware of technical problems that may, unwittingly, stem from an imposed settlement.
>
> The need to formulate contract conditions that are workable and acceptable to both sides will serve as an additional pressure to resolve issues independent of the arbitration machinery that has been established.[27]

Mr. Abel predicted accurately that the parties would make every attempt to reach an agreement on their own. It should also be pointed out, however, that part of the agreement allowed strikes over local issues. Strikes over local issues had always been a very thorny problem in steel industry negotiations. Since the companies bargain on a multi-company basis, it was extremely difficult to deal with local issues at the national level.

Only a few industries and services have attempted an ENA. Voluntary, final-offer-selection arbitration occurs in American major league baseball, as well as in a number of Canadian universities, including the University of Ottawa where the author teaches.[28] The agreement between the University of Ottawa and the Association of Professors of the University of Ottawa (APUO) provides for a three-member panel of selectors. This instrument was invoked in the Summer of 1985.

Compulsory Arbitration

Most writers who analyze compulsory arbitration enter immediately into discussions of *its labour relations aspects*, without specifying the criteria by which its effectiveness may be assessed and without providing a framework for their discussions. What we wish to do here, then, is to provide a framework for discussing the fundamental aspects of compulsory arbitration and to indicate the difficulty of assessing its effectiveness.

Strike Prevention One of the presumed benefits of compulsory arbitration (which is used primarily in the public and parapublic sectors) is that it protects the public interest (however that may be defined) from the adverse consequences of strikes. From this perspective, then, compulsory arbitration has a strike-prevention function. The prevention of strikes assures the delivery of goods to the public and the maintenance of labour peace. However, to date not one study has surveyed the public to ascertain if it wishes its interests to be protected by the use of compulsory arbitration.[29] It is quite possible that the public has not suffered sufficient hardship or inconvenience to favour compulsory arbitration as the preferred way of resolving public-sector disputes. Furthermore, rather than thinking in terms of a unitary public interest, perhaps we should be thinking in terms of multiple public interests. For example, an individual who always drives a car to and from work may not find a transit strike inconvenient, except that traffic congestion may make driving a little slower at times.

Protection of Public-Sector Workers Compulsory arbitration is a dispute settlement procedure which protects the interests of public-sector workers. Collective bargaining without the right to strike or without an arbitrated settlement may not be sufficient to bring a public-sector employer to the negotiation table. In the absence of the strike weapon or compulsory arbitration, an employer may have little or no incentive to negotiate in good faith with a view to concluding a collective agreement covering the terms and conditions of employment. In fact, it is quite possible that the employer would unilaterally impose the terms and conditions of employment. The evidence supports the propo-

sition that arbitration has worked effectively in promoting good faith bargaining, although much depends on the type of arbitration procedure used. Also, the fact that arbitrators use the same labour market data in making their awards suggests that arbitration may provide roughly even results, particularly concerning wages, for groups of workers across bargaining units in the same labour market areas.[30] Hence, arbitration appears to protect the interests of public-sector workers quite well.

Regulation of Conflict It has been suggested that collective bargaining with arbitration has become a regulator of interest-group conflict.[31] That is, collective bargaining has brought into the open the fact that a set of group interests exists among public-sector workers which is potentially costly and which has made overt the potential conflicts between public-sector workers and the public sector as an employer.

Public-sector workers have as much interest in protecting their wages and working conditions as private-sector workers do. One public-policy response to collective bargaining in the public sector has been the provision of procedures for third parties to resolve impasses. These procedures include arbitration. Arbitration not only resolves impasses between the public-sector employer and union, but may also resolve disputes among members of either or both groups. It is argued that arbitration "performs this regulatory function primarily through the finality, impartiality, compromising and face-saving features of the process."[32] Arbitration can help both union leaders and management spokespersons in dealing with their constituents inasmuch as the parties can save face by blaming the arbitrator for unfavourable outcomes.

Inhibition of Representative Government The critics of compulsory arbitration argue that it inhibits representative government. This argument is based on the premise that the political system should reflect the will of the governed by holding publically elected officials accountable for allocative decisions and by allowing interest groups to be heard during public decision-making processes.[33] Arbitration, however, lacks accountability. The determination of wages and working conditions by arbitrators has led to a high degree of bureaucratization in the decision-making process. This bureaucratization has been perpetrated by labour relations professionals who concern themselves most about how their decisions will affect the union and management representatives with whom they deal. Little concern is shown about how other groups, such as taxpayers, are affected by the decisions. It is suggested that this criticism of compulsory arbitration may be largely overcome by legislative bodies through a reformulation of the arbitration process. It has been stated, for example, that

> legislative bodies may restrict the scope of arbitrable subjects, limit the coverage of the arbitration legislation, specify exceedingly tight decision criteria, require that the decisions be made by tripartite panels instead of single arbitrators, and mandate final-offer selection rather than conventional decision making.[34]

It is questionable whether or not the measures suggested above will be sufficient to control arbitrators' decisions. A number of Canadian jurisdictions which give collective bargaining rights to their workers specify criteria which arbitrators must follow, but these criteria are not precise enough to ensure specific arbitration outcomes. This topic has been of concern to elected political leaders in Canada, including the Premier of Alberta who mused several years ago about ways in which arbitrators could be mandated to be less generous in rendering their awards. The Government of Quebec, regardless of the party in power, refuses to have wages and working conditions in the public and parapublic sectors arbitrated. They claim that to do so is to lose control over their budget, about one-half of which comprises the cost of wages and other benefits. The problem is even more accute in Quebec since negotiations for all public and para-public workers take place about the same time every three years. Hence, settlement terms have an immediate and substantial impact over the distribution of government revenues.

Inhibition of Genuine Bargaining It is alleged that compulsory arbitration, and particularly compromise arbitration in which the arbitrator more or less splits the differences between the parties, acts to inhibit genuine bargaining. Of all the research done on arbitration, this one aspect has received the lion's share of attention. Research findings suggest that compromise arbitration has a chilling effect on negotiations since one or both of the parties may withhold concessions during bipartite negotiations in the hope of gaining a better settlement if the dispute goes to arbitration. This practice prevails among weak unions or weak employers. Research findings also suggest that compromise arbitration has a narcotic effect on bipartite negotiations since the parties may build up a dependence on it during consecutive rounds of negotiations.

As we pointed out in the preceeding chapter, periodic negotiations over the terms and conditions of employment involve three sets of negotiations. First, internal negotiations or trade-offs take place within the union in order to finalize a bargaining agenda. Similar negotiations take place among members of the management team. This is what Walton and McKersie refer to as intraorganizational bargaining.[35] Only after these intraorganizational negotiations have been completed do the parties engage in genuine bilateral negotiations with a view to obtaining a negotiated settlement. Each of these sets of negotiations have costs and benefits:

> As a result of this cost-benefit calculus, the availability of arbitration may have a 'chilling effect' upon the parties' efforts to negotiate an agreement, and over time there may be a 'narcotic effect' as the parties become arbitration addicts who habitually rely upon arbitrators to write their labour contracts."[36]

Reliance on Impasse Procedures While the empirical research literature on the subject of the chilling and narcotic effects is abundant, there is no concensus on the extent to which the parties rely on the step beyond the bilateral negotiation process. Two recent articles debate the appropriateness of statistical techniques used to determine if a narcotic effect exists.[37] One article claims that the definition generally fitting the popular usage of the concept is "repeated or heavy reliance on an impasse procedure."[38] Precisely what *repeated* or *heavy reliance* means is still open to conjecture.

A study of collective bargaining among British Columbia school teachers under a system of compulsory arbitration between 1938 and 1973 concluded that "compulsory arbitration can avert strikes without causing collective bargaining to disappear and without leading to wage awards far above or below negotiated settlements."[39] Another writer subsequently analyzed the same data, manipulated it in different ways, and concluded that "arbitration has significantly reduced the incentive to bargain among British Columbia teachers' unions and school districts during the period studied, and the authors therefore overstate their case when they refer to the 'success' of the B.C. teachers' arbitration system."[40]

Choice of Settlement Routes In the section on mediation, we stated that the federal *Public Service Staff Relations Act* provides for two types of impasse settlement procedures: (1) conciliation and strike, and (2) arbitration. The bargaining agent must choose a route before negotiations begin. One study compared the results of the two dispute settlement routes for the first four round of negotiations between 1968 and 1975 and found an increasing trend for disputes to be settled at the arbitration stage over the four rounds of negotiations. The percent of cases going all the way to arbitration in each of the four rounds was as follows: 5%, 32%, 33%, and 54%.[41] The authors of this study concluded that

> the overall pattern of results supports the existence of a chilling effect. Over time the proportion of units settling on their own, with no third-party assistance, steadily decreased. Furthermore, the chilling effect appeared to be greater under the arbitration route than under the conciliation-board strike route.[42]

This study also found that there was preliminary evidence of a narcotic effect: "a history of experience with the impasse procedure increases the probability of relying on third parties in the subsequent rounds of bargaining."[43] While this study concluded that both a chilling and a narcotic effect existed under the compulsory arbitration route, it did not specify the criteria used to determine the existence of these effects.

Experience with compulsory arbitration between the Ontario government and its workers shows that, since 1963, about 30% of settlements were reached at the arbitration stage. An examination of some of the awards revealed that, by the time they went to arbitration, the parties were often very far apart.[44]

In addition to the Canadian studies cited above, numerous American studies exist, particularly of police officers, firefighters, and teachers. Most of these studies confirm that the chilling effect and narcotic effect result from the use of compromise settlements handed down under compulsory arbitration. A prominent writer recently concluded that, ultimately, the line between an acceptable and an unacceptable rate of impasse under any system is subjective. Judgment must be balanced against other policy objectives as well as the effectiveness of the impasse resolution procedure.[45]

Compromise Arbitration Compromise arbitration has been criticized on the grounds that it is not an innovative process. If one looks at the major innovations in collective agreements over the years, one will find that very few of these have come about through arbitration.

One exception to this rule, at least in Canada, was the union-security clause which was established following a strike by the United Automobile Workers against the Ford Motor Company in 1946. In that particular dispute, the union wanted a union-shop provision whereby all members of the bargaining unit would be required to become union members. The Ford Motor Company of Canada refused to accept this proposition and, after about a six-month work stoppage, the issue was submitted to arbitration. The arbitrator in that case was the late Ivan C. Rand, the Chief Justice of the Supreme

Court of Canada. His decision, later called the "Rand Formula," did not require workers within a bargaining unit to become union members, but did require that they pay union dues. This was, however, one of the few major innovations under the compromise or conventional form of arbitration in Canada.

Another major criticism of the conventional form of arbitration is that arbitrators act in what Woods has referred to as a normative context; that is, in handing down their awards, they generally use their own criteria as the basis for such decisions. Usually the arbitrator or arbitration board in an interest or contract negotiation dispute will hear evidence by each of the parties in which each party tries to justify its own position. It is only by selecting criteria presented by the parties, or in some cases adopting criteria of their own, that the arbitrators or arbitration tribunals are able to provide a rationale behind the award which they hand down.

Thus far in Canada, only the *Public Service Staff Relations Act,* and a few provincial public sector statutes which specify arbitration as the final stage of dispute resolution, provide guidelines for arbitrators in those situations in which the bargaining agent selects the arbitration process. These acts still permit, however, the introduction of any other factors that the arbitrators deem relevant.

In an effort to eliminate the detrimental effects of compromise arbitration on the negotiation process, a number of variants of compulsory arbitration have been introduced in a number of American states and in at least one important Canadian parapublic sector. The most prominent of these is final-offer selection (FOS) — sometimes referred to as final-offer arbitration (FOA).

Final-Offer Selection (FOS)

Because of the criticism of conventional or compromise arbitration, demand has grown for alternatives to this method. The first person to give some attention to the problem of providing alternatives was Carl M. Stevens, an innovative thinker in the fields of contract negotiations and

third-party assistance. In his article "Is Compulsory Arbitration Compatible With Bargaining?"[46] Stevens proposed what he called a type of either-or arbitration which was later dubbed "final-offer selection."

What Stevens suggested was that, if the parties could not reach an agreement through negotiations, they could appeal to an arbitrator or arbitration tribunal which would select the bargaining package of one party or the other. This would introduce a high degree of uncertainty in the outcome of the arbitration award, and would encourage the parties to negotiate a settlement. A major hypothesis running through Stevens' article is that the greater the degree of uncertainty of the arbitration award, the more likely the parties are to negotiate to finality. What Stevens was suggesting essentially is that the threat of an either-or type of arbitration award was almost equivalent to the threat of a strike:

> Compulsory arbitration of this type provides an instrument through which each party may impose a cost of disagreement upon his opposite number. Generally speaking, it seems quite possible that a threat to arbitrate, much like a threat to strike, might invoke the negotiatory process of concession and compromise which are characteristic of normal collective bargaining.[47]

An idea implicit in this type of arbitration is that even if each side is unsure as to which party's position the arbitrator will select, incentive will exist for both sides to continue negotiating. Thus, if a final-offer selector is appointed, his decision would not be of major concern to either party. In effect, the objective of final-offer selection (FOS) is to make the parties agree on their own or to at least cut down the number of contentious issues and reduce the distance between bargaining positions.

Ideally, FOS should roughly approximate what both sides would expect to gain from a negotiated settlement. Since Stevens made his original proposal, a number of states in the United States have adopted final-offer selection as a form of third-party assistance of last resort. A few Canadian statutes, such as The Ontario *School Boards and Teachers Collective Negotiations Act* of 1975, also include it.

Three types of final-offer selection exist. One is the *total-package type,* in which the arbitrator or arbitration panel chooses either the final package of the union or the final package of the employer. The selector or arbitrator under this system has to select *in toto* the final offer of either side and cannot take items from both packages.

The second type is *final-offer-by-item.* This form enables the arbitrator or arbitration tribunal to select specific positions from either union's or management's final offers, and comes somewhat closer to compromise arbitration; that is, the award is based on both sides' offers and according to what the arbitrator perceives as a fair settlement, given the final positions of the two parties.

The third type is *tri-offer.* Under this system, the arbitrator may choose the last offer of the union or management or the recommendations of a fact-finder who is usually involved in tri-offer arbitration. These recommendations are made known to the parties before the arbitrator arrives on the scene. Tri-offer arbitration has been utilized in Massachusetts for public-safety workers, but was recently introduced into Iowa as well for all categories of public-sector workers. In Iowa, the arbitrator selects on an issue-by-issue basis.[48]

Total-Package FOS   Although conventional arbitration may rightly be considered one of the least effective forms of third-party assistance, there is still some reason for optimism with respect to the use of the newer forms of arbitration, particularly total-package, final-offer selection.

Let us suppose, for example, that at time X a union is demanding a 30% salary increase and a company is offering 5%. Settlements in the industry are averaging 10% to 12%. Final-offer arbitration is available to both sides and may be invoked at any time. Neither party, at this point,

Table 8.2 — **Total-Package, Final-Offer Selection**

would want an arbitrator to choose from the two packages since an adverse decision would represent a significant loss to one side. Hence, there is an incentive to negotiate further. By time X_1, the union's demand has declined to 20% and management's offer has risen to 7%. Since the two sides are still far apart — neither is in the 10% to 12% range — there is continued reason to negotiate for further concessions. At time X_2, the union demand is for 12.5% and the management offer is 9.5%. Neither side stands to lose too much if the final-offer arbitrator accepts the other side's offer. It is logical to assume that arbitration might now be invoked to bring the negotiations to a close.

The above scenario portrays an ideal situation for the use of final-offer selection and demonstrates how its use may encourage parties to remain at the bargaining table. Total-package FOS thus seems an effective third-party procedure in cases where well-defined monetary issues are being negotiated. It is less well-suited, however, to negotiations involving non-monetary matters or questions of principle. Nonetheless, this form of arbitration is vastly superior to traditional methods which rarely give the parties any incentive to continue bargaining.

Effectiveness of FOS   The theoretical scenario of total-package FOS depicted graphically in Figure 8.2 applies neither to issue-by-issue FOS nor to tri-offer selection, since these two do not have the immediacy of an imposed settlement. Because the available empirical research often assesses any one or a combination of the various forms of FOS, we shall assess all three types in the following discussion. In order to assess the effectiveness of FOS, however, we shall first indicate the criteria to be used in our analysis.

The following criteria will be used in our assessment: first, the proportion of cases which have gone to the terminal step in the procedure; second, the number of issues which have gone to the terminal step; third, the extent to which the parties tend to converge towards a settlement before reaching the final step; and fourth, the extent to which wages and benefits have been affected by the process. In addition, other less frequently used criteria may be used where appropriate. These criteria should be used with caution, however, because of procedural, economic, organizational, and interpersonal differences among jurisdictions.

Iowa Tri-Offer Selection Since tri-offer selection in Iowa has some unique features, perhaps we should discuss the steps in that procedure before attempting to assess the effectiveness of FOS. The Iowa statute requires (1) mediation, (2) factfinding with recommendations, and (3) arbitration on an issue-by-issue basis in the sequence noted here. An additional and unique feature of the Iowa statute is that the arbitrator may select from three sets of proposed settlements: namely, the offers of the union and management, and the recommendations of the factfinder. Furthermore, each one of the consecutive steps has fairly tight time-limits in order to impose pressure points on the parties to compromise and come to agreement.[49] It should also be noted, however, that the parties may negotiate a procedure of their own, which replaces the statutory procedure. The most common of such procedures is negotiation, followed by mediation with arbitration as the final step. Let us now return to our assessment of FOS.

Reduction of Chilling and Narcotic Effects
The decrease in the number of cases which go to the terminal stage is a rough measure of the effectiveness of the procedure in reducing or

eliminating chilling and narcotic effects associated with compromise arbitration. Experience for the first six years under the Iowa procedure shows that arbitration awards have ranged from 4.5% to 7.1% of all negotiations. The experience in Michigan shows that about 10% to 15% of police and firefighter (public-safety) negotiations resulted in arbitration awards. In Wisconsin, the evidence shows that nine out of eighteen public-safety negotiations resulted in the issuance of total-package FOS awards, while about 5.4% of nonessential worker impasses were settled by arbitration during 1978 and 1979. The Minnesota experience between 1973 and 1980 indicated that about 30% of all negotiations for essential service disputes in which mediation was requested resulted in arbitration awards.[50] Another source, however, shows that arbitrated settlements as a percent of all negotiations for Wisconsin during the years from 1973 to 1977 varied from a low of 10% in 1973 to a high of 28% in 1976. The level dropped to 14% in 1977. It could be that the year 1977 marked a turning point in Wisconsin as parties became more familiar with the procedures.[51] With the possible exception of Minnesota, these figures appear to indicate that FOS does eliminate the chilling effect associated with compromise arbitration. The figures across jurisdictions, however, should be interpreted with caution for the reasons suggested earlier.

Deterrent Effect A second criterion for assessing the effectiveness of FOS is the number of issues which end up at the terminal stage of the process. The fragmentary evidence on this criteria indicates that the number of issues submitted to arbitration was three under the Iowa tri-offer system, three also under the Wisconsin total-package FOS, seven under conventional arbitration in Minnesota, and eight or more under Michigan issue-by-issue FOS.[52] The number of issues taken to factfinding preceeding arbitration was 6.7 in Iowa, nine for New York States teachers according to a 1971 study, and thirteen for police and firefighters in New York State. The average was 5.7 for Michigan between

1966 and 1973, and 14.7 for Massachusetts police and firefighters between 1974 and 1975.[53] A good deal of variability exists among jurisdictions, but the evidence, in conjunction with other variables, does not permit us to assert with any degree of confidence that one system is superior to another.

Convergence Effect The third criterion we suggested above was the degree to which the parties tended to converge or narrow the differences before the final step in the procedure. The Iowa experience suggests that the degree of convergence varies considerably depending on the factfinder's report. If the factfinder's recommendation was between the positions of the parties, there was a tendency for both parties to modify their positions, although the modification was slightly higher for the union than for management. However, if the factfinder report endorsed one party's position, there was little movement on the part of the other party. Much may depend, though, on the nature of the issues. In the Iowa experience, most situations in which there was little movement were characterized by either-or issues. To modify one's position in such a case was tantamount to supporting the other's position, while maintaining one's position might result in a win at the arbitration stage. When either-or issues were removed or reformulated, slightly more movement occurred, particularly on the part of the union.[54]

Consensus-Building Effect It has been suggested that final-offer selection has a consensus-building function similar to that of convergence discussed above. The consensus-building function is said to exist in Massachusetts, Michigan, Oregon, and Wisconsin where FOS encourages continued negotiations. This is particularly true in states such as Michigan, where the arbitrator plays a mediation role.[55] A number of states use panels which include two adversaries and a neutral chairman. The adversaries not only mediate with their constituents, but give clues to the neutral chairman concerning what they perceive constitutes a fair settlement.

Equitable-Award Effect It has also been suggested that an arbitrator enters into any arbitration system with some idea of what constitutes an equitable award rather than an intention to merely split the differences between the parties. It is claimed that under FOS the parties manipulate their positions around the equitable award by submitting less extreme offers than they would if the equitable award concept did not exist. While an interesting theory has been built around this concept, it has not been tested empirically.[56]

Intertemporal Compromise (ITC) One major criticism of final-offer selection is that it may lead to intertemporal compromise, or the issuance of arbitration awards which attempt to achieve a balance between arbitration winners and losers over time. This proposition was first put forward by Gene Swimmer:

> Final offer arbitration substitutes intertemporal compromise for static compromise.... We believe substituting final offer arbitration for regular arbitration in any of these jurisdictions would not increase the likelihood of real collective bargaining between management and union. Indeed, without a possibility of static compromise the likelihood of going to the final step might be higher than under regular arbitration.[57]

What Swimmer is suggesting is that the loser in the first arbitration round would be declared the winner in the second (when the contract is renewed), the second-round loser, the winner in the third round and so forth. Feuille and Dworkin point out, however, that

> The final element of the ITC [intertemporal compromise] theory is that the parties involved expect such flipflopping to occur and base their behavior upon such expectations. Consequently, the loser in the first arbitration round will press for arbitration in round two because of that party's expectation that it will win the second time around, and so on for each subsequent round.[58]

After analyzing the results of final offer selection in major league baseball, and certain public sector bargaining (e.g. state workers in Massachusetts), the authors conclude that, on the basis of their data, the intertemporal compromise concept has three substantial flaws. First the theory does not encourage the winners of one round of arbitration to compromise in the second round. Second, the theory does not account for the fact that in most arbitration cases one side (the union) invokes the arbitration procedure more often than the other. Third, it does not accept that outcomes may have to be determined on merit rather than because of any desire on the part of arbitrators to balance winners and losers over time.[59] Keeping in mind that this article was based on a limited number of studies, I suggest that the effectiveness and benefits of intertemporal compromise have yet to be proven.

Levelling Effect The final criterion by which we wish to assess FOS is the extent to which settlements reached through this procedure approximate those attained through negotiations with strike action as the last resort. While there is very little research on this subject, D. G. Gallagher indicates that

> the results of regression studies generally show a slight or nonsignificant relationship between arbitration and wage levels except where comparatively lower wage-rate units were brought closer to the wage settlement in similarly situated situations.[60]

This supports the point made earlier in this chapter that arbitration may have a levelling effect in labour market situations.

In most jurisdictions, only a relatively small proportion of the cases have gone to the final stage in the procedure. The number of issues which have gone to the last stage is relatively small. In addition, there is a possibility that the parties might converge towards a settlement before the final step, and this seems to be more likely where factfinding is part of the procedure. Finally, there is the possibility that FOS might have a levelling effect, particularly in bargaining units in the same labour markets.

Concluding Observations on FOS To what extent, if any, does FOS alter the conclusions reached earlier on the compromise form of com-

pulsory arbitration? First, FOS seems to protect the public interest by acting to prevent strikes. While there is very little discussion of FOS and strikes, one can be sure that if FOS was correlated with the incidence of strikes, there would have been some evidence of it in the research. We can take the lack of research, evidence, and concern as a positive sign that FOS prevents strikes. However, there is no evidence that the public prefers FOS to strikes. Hence, FOS is more or less taken as an article of faith on the part of the politicians who have introduced it.

Second, insofar as there is no negative correlation between public-sector wages and FOS, FOS probably protects the interests of public-sector workers since it appears to have a levelling effect in the same labour markets. I make this general statement with great caution, for I am far from fully informed of the issues covered by FOS.

Third, FOS appears to act as a regulator of interest-group conflict since it protects public-sector workers vis-à-vis the government as employer. It acknowledges that public-sector workers have a right to protect themselves against arbitratory or capricious action by the government, since the last step in the procedure is impartial third-party arbitration.

Fourth, FOS is perhaps as much an inhibitor of representative government as compromise arbitration is. Decisions about government allocation of scarce financial resources are not made by elected politicians, but by industrial relations specialists whose main preoccupation is the prevention of strikes and the promotion of harmonious relations between the government as employer and the unions. Professional arbitrators seldom show much concern for the citizenry at large.

Fifth, FOS seems to promote rather than inhibit genuine bargaining. A number of FOS procedures have pressure points built into them which are designed to facilitate rather than inhibit bargaining: parties are pressured to make concessions at points where they feel that more might be lost by forcing an award through inflexibility than by ceding ground on an issue.

The tri-offer method used in Iowa not only has critical pressure points built into it, but an additional decision to be considered by the arbitrator — namely, the recommendation of the factfinder as well as the offers of the two parties. Theoretically, tri-offer FOS seems to be the most desirable method, and according to the empirical evidence to date, it appears to be working well.

In summary, FOS appears to contribute greater benefits than costs as contrasted with compromise arbitration. The one function that it does not appear to perform well is representation, except in cases where public policy establishes tight criteria to guide arbitrators in the selection of their awards. The available evidence suggests that FOS performs much better than conventional or compromise arbitation.

Fact-Finding, Mediation, and Voluntary Arbitration

As far as we know, there is only one piece of legislation in Canada which provides for fact-finding, mediation, and arbitration, whether voluntary or in the form of total-package, final-offer selection. This statute, the Ontario *School Boards and Teachers Collective Negotiations Act* (1975),[61] provides that a fact-finder may be appointed at the request of the parties or on the initiative of the Ontario Education Relations Commission, the body that administers the statute. The fact-finder is given thirty days within which to make a report. This report may or may not contain recommendations for settlement. Upon receipt of this report, the parties are given fifteen days to settle, after which time it is made available to local news media, in order to bring public pressure to bear on school board and teacher negotiators.

Section 14 of the statute gives the Commission, in the exercise of its own discretion, the right to assign a person to assist the parties to make or renew an agreement. This had been usually interpreted as the right to appoint mediators following fact-finding efforts. A union may legally strike only after mediation has been attempted. There is also provision in the statute whereby the parties may submit their outstanding issues to voluntary binding arbitration of the compromise form, or they may refer their unresolved issues to a third party for final-offer selection of the total-package variety. To date the FOS method has been used in a very small percentage of cases.

It probably should be noted here also that the Ontario Education Relations Commission has a very extensive data bank upon which the parties to the negotiations or a fact-finder, mediator or selector may draw. Moreover, the Commission has a program for training fact-finders and mediators involved in school negotiations, and has recently embarked upon a program to improve long-term union-management relationships in those cases where the two sides have been unable to develop some measure of mutual trust.

Assessments

A study[62] which assessed the first two years under the *Act* criticized the way in which various aspects of the *Act* have functioned, particularly the factfinding process. In the first round of negotiations, ninety-seven factfinders were assigned over approximately 200 sets of negotiations. This means that factfinders were appointed in nearly 50% of the cases in the first year, and over 40% in the second.[63] The response to a questionnaire sent to the parties indicated that in only 36.4% of the cases did the parties claim that an impasse had been reached, and that only slightly over 50% of the parties felt the appointment of a factfinder to be necessary.[64] Also, teacher negotiators felt more strongly about the need to appoint factfinders than school board negotiators did. This disparity indicates that very few meaningful negotiations had taken place prior to the appointment of factfinders, a conclusion supported by the fact that "the forty-eight fact finders reports written in the first round of negotiations listed 590 items in dispute, or more than 12 items per fact finder."[65]

Despite this gloomy picture, the author of the report, B. M. Downie, concluded that factfinding has the potential to encourage bargaining. Part of the problem with the factfinding process in the first two rounds was that factfinders made recommendations on only about 45% of the issues. In addition, factfinders often failed to give a rationale for their recommendations. In about 45% of the cases, moreover, the recommendations made were of a compromise or nondirectional nature. Downie sums up the factfinding process by suggesting that

[a] possible conclusion, then, is that fact finders are not making, or not able to make, the hard choices that would give a report some strategic or therapeutic importance. It may be in the future that we will see stronger language, more recommendations, and more presentation of rationale by fact finders.[66]

Little mention of mediation was made in the study since mediation had been used only sparingly in the first two years. Only in thirty-five of the approximately 200 sets of negotiations during the first round — about 18% of the cases — was mediation used. On some occasions, mediators were appointed for training or strategic purposes. Mediators were appointed in only 35 cases during the second round.[67]

Effects

A more recent study of the results of teacher and school board negotiations in Ontario indicates that the duration of negotiations has increased dramatically. In each round of negotiations from 1976 to 1982, the average length of negotiations exceeded eight months.[68] In an effort to decrease the time spent in negotiations and to increase the effectiveness of the procedures under the legislation, particularly the factfinding process, the Education Relations Commission adopted a number of changes in the use of factfinding and mediation. First, the parties were encouraged to use factfinding only if absolutely necessary and to continue their negotiations after the agreement expired. The Commis-

sion, instead of appointing factfinders when the contract expired as required by the legislation, delayed making appointments until much later than it had in the past. In 1980 and 1981, the Commission also recruited highly qualified individuals who were very familiar with both industrial relations and school board negotiations. As a result of these changes, the factfinders produced reports with recommendations, rationales, and data which were more acceptable to the parties.[69]

While the Commission had earlier followed the practice of releasing factfinders' reports only if the parties had not done so, it adopted a new policy of releasing these reports to the local media in every case. Factfinders were required to provide a summary of their reports so that more accurate reporting could be made by the media. Starting in 1980, the Commission also started recruiting and training individuals as intensive mediators. Also, from 1980 to 1982, there was much greater use of pre-factfinding mediation. Concurrent with this change, a dramatic drop occurred in the use of factfinders: from 61% to 37% of all negotiations. Factfinding had been used in only 25% of the cases in the 1980 to 1982 rounds.[70] Downie, who is also Chairman of the Commission, makes the following comment about the factfinding process:

fact-finding and the procedures of Bill 100 have been a conspicuous success and a model to which industrial relations specialists should pay heed. Certainly, one of the key factors of this success is reports that include specific recommendations on substantive terms.[71]

Downie concludes that if a public-disputes tribunal such as the Ontario Education Relations Commission is to be successful, it must have a variety of tools at its disposal and the discretion to implement new and different proposals.[72] Since arbitration of either the compromise form or final-offer selection type were included in the strike category, one may safely assume from the figures that compromise and FOS had been used very sparingly.

Mediation-Arbitration (Med-Arb)

Mediation-arbitration is another form of third-party assistance sometimes used to help resolve contract negotiation disputes. Med-arb, like FOS, has both its advocates and its detractors. There are some people who argue that it is very difficult for any one person to play both the role of mediator and arbitrator. It is suggested that, if a person plays both roles, the negotiating parties are not likely to reveal their final positions to that individual as mediator.

On the other hand, a number of people contend that a good mediator is able to detect the final settlement positions of the two parties and the mere fact that he may become an arbitrator should not prevent him from detecting what these final positions are. It should be pointed out, however, that these commentators have had many years of experience as negotiators or mediators or both. As a consequence, they are able to detect the nuances of the parties' declarations during the negotiation and mediation processes. Overall, there does not seem to be any clear-cut consensus among industrial relations specialists concerning the effectiveness of med-arb. This does not mean, however, that the topic is being ignored.[73]

Judge J. C. Anderson has proposed a type of med-arb with a number of unique characteristics. The process would substitute for the right to strike or lockout in the public sector, with an agreement between the parties to continue direct negotiations, using mediation, if required, until a specified date. The mediator/arbitrator would be completely independent and fully experienced in the labour field, and would only function as an arbitrator if mediation failed. The report of the arbitrator would become final and binding on the parties. However, a procedure would be added to the med-arb process whereby either party could appeal to a special tribunal against the arbitration decision.

Judge Anderson sees the following advantage to his proposal: (1) it would allow the parties to obtain an agreement between themselves; (2) if agreement does not occur, it would give the parties the opportunity of negotiating with the assistance of a mediator; and (3) if mediation were not successful, the arbitrator, while acting as a mediator, would be able to establish the priorities which each party places upon outstanding issues.[74] Judge Anderson also suggests that any arbitrator's report will not differ too much from the kind of agreement that the parties might fashion for themselves.

There are, however, admitted drawbacks to this form of med-arb: the hesitation on the part of the parties to submit their dispute to a third party; the lack of skilled mediators/arbitrators; and the fact that acting as mediator may prejudice a person's decision as arbitrator. Since the publication of Judge Anderson's article in 1975, there has been no great rush in Ontario or any of the other provinces for the parties to adopt this new med-arb procedure.

A Proposed Labour Peace Commission

Ed Finn, the former Publications and Information Director of the Canadian Brotherhood of Railway, Transport and General Workers Union, proposed that a Labour Peace Commission be set up to handle disputes in the public sector.[75] Finn suggests that governments have erred by applying the adversary concept, which was devised for private-sector collective bargaining, to public-sector negotiations. Governments, unlike companies, are not concerned with maintaining a competitive edge and no profits exist to be fought over, as is the case in the private sector. The traditional criteria of productivity and the company's ability to pay are therefore not available to negotiators, and it is difficult to objectively determine what constitutes a just settlement.

Finn proposes the establishment in each jurisdiction of an effective, impartial agency for determining the fairness and adequacy of salary levels and working conditions for public-sector workers. The objective of the Labour Peace Commissions would be "to monitor working agreements in the essential industries and services and to propose equitable terms of settlement in each set of negotiations."[76]

The selection of commission members of high calibre would be of critical importance in making such a commission function effectively. A major function would be to avoid strikes and to determine what is adequate and equitable. If these terms could be appropriately defined then unions and employers in the public sector should be able to resolve most of their disputes without the use of strikes. However, it is not recommended that the commission have powers of binding arbitration, but rather that it be made up of people with such prestige and stature that their recommendations would be practically always acceptable to the negotiating parties. Any out-of-hand rejections, by either side, of the commission's recommendation would doubtless adversely affect the image of the dissenter, be it union or government. This fear of bad public relations would thus oblige both parties to examine all recommendations carefully.

In addition, such a commission would probably be more consistent in its application of criteria for determining wages and working conditions in the public sector than is the present system of *ad hoc* boards of arbitration. After a certain period of time, the proposed Labour Peace Commission would not only gather a substantial body of objective empirical data, but would also be able to define terms and conditions of settlement that would be almost identical to those received by workers in comparable occupations in the private sector.

It is somewhat regrettable that no government, either federal or provincial, has as yet seen fit to experiment with such a plan. As is becoming more evident, public servants are growing restive in many parts of Canada because many of them feel that their wages and benefits are not keeping pace with those in the private sector. A Labour Peace Commission might help to establish a rough parity between public and private sector wage/benefit packages and would at least allay the suspicion that government is prepared to sacrifice the interests of its workers in the pursuit of economic (or electoral) advantage. In fact, the Conservative government of Joe Clark from 1979 to 1980 seriously considered the establishment of such a commission.

Finn's proposal goes further than that of Harry Arthurs for the Prime Minister's Task Force On Labour Relations, although the Task Force report applied to both the private and public sectors. Arthurs suggested the establishment of a three-man Public Interest Disputes Commission, independent of any government department, reporting directly to the Prime Minister, and composed of public members only. Acknowledging that it might be hard to obtain highly qualified personnel on a full-time basis, Arthurs envisaged commissioners serving on a part-time basis, supported by a full-time secretariat of high-calibre bureaucrats. In the Task Force Report, the two major functions of the commission are outlined as follows:

> The first relates to determining special procedures for resolving industrial disputes in industries in the federal jurisdiction which, because of their record of industrial relations, are prone to disputes which are likely to jeopardize the public interest. The second function relates to the handling of actual disputes in any industry under federal jurisdiction where the public interest is threatened. The Public Interest Disputes Commission will be charged with assisting the parties, in industries whose record of labour relations has been such as to make them prone to work stoppages likely to jeopardize the public interest, to negotiate special procedures for settling their disputes. In the event of a failure to agree to a procedure, or if the agreed procedure is deemed inadequate by the Commission, the Commission would have power to prescribe a procedure short of seizure, trusteeship, partial operation, statutory strike (full operation with complete or partial impounding of incomes and profits), or compulsory arbitration. Such a procedure would be subject to a three-year limitation in the first instance.[77]

In proposing a Public Interest Disputes Commission, the Task Force was responding to a perceived need to monitor industries which were characterized by a bad record of industrial relations. If a particular industry was found to generate a climate of bad industrial relations, or a series of strikes that inconvenienced the public, then the Commission would attempt to help the parties to work out some kind of on-going mechanisms for resolving the difficulties between them. Furthermore, if union and management could not develop their own procedures to improve the functioning of their industrial relations system, the Commission itself would be in a position to recommend such corrective procedures. Presumably, this would require a mandate to restructure the relationship between the parties, as the Commission saw fit.

The Federal Government did not, however, establish the Commission proposed by the Task Force on Industrial Relations. Whether or not these suggestions are worth trying is a matter of some speculation. Given our decentralized structure of bargaining, however, an argument might be made that at least one of the eleven jurisdictions should take some initiative in establishing some sort of commission to avert frequent or unnecessary strikes in the public sector and, thus, bring about a greater degree of peace and harmony between unions and management. And if a commission is possible in the public sector, then it is conceivable that a similar initiative could be attempted in the private sector.

Industrial Inquiry Commissions

Legislation in most jurisdictions provides for the appointment of industrial inquiry commissions. These commissions may be composed of one or several persons who are experts in those particular fields of industrial relations. On many occasions, the Federal Government or the provinces have set up special inquiry commissions to look into particularly difficult labour-management situations.

One notable inquiry examined the so-called "run throughs" on Canadian National Railways.

Before the diesel engine came into being, railway cars were pulled by coal engines. Because these coal engines were unable to make very long runs, many small towns grew up around railway terminal stations; that is, places where the trains would stop to pick up enough fuel to take them to their next destination. When the diesel motor came along, trains were able to travel longer distances without refueling. Former terminal stations were bypassed or "run through" and in effect became ghost towns.

In 1964, the Federal Government appointed a one-person commission[78] to look into the effects of run-throughs on the towns and railway workers involved. The commissioner found that run-throughs were indeed creating major adjustment problems for the railway workers and unions, as well as for the communities affected. He made some very strong recommendations to the Federal Government on this problem, as it applied to the railway workers. These recommendations are reflected in Part V of the Canada Labour Code which requires employers to give 120 days advance notice to the unions of technological change which may have serious impact on a substantial number of workers.

Arsenal of Weapons

Thus far we have discussed practically all types of third-party assistance that have been proposed or utilized in the North American setting. It has often been suggested that all of these mechanisms be included in statutes governing labour-management relations. This "arsenal of weapons," as it is sometimes called, would be available to a government or government agency at any time during a labour-management dispute. The idea behind including a variety of techniques is to enable the administrators of legislation to select the procedures which, to the administrative agency, seem most appropriate at that time and for that particular kind of dispute. An arsenal of weapons has considerable appeal since it avoids building-in a predetermined sequence of forms of third-party assistance. With a predetermined scheme, serious negotiations often do not begin until a very late stage.

When, by contrast, the parties do not know in advance which form of third-party assistance they will receive, strong incentive may exist for them to reach agreements themselves. Since unions and management generally dislike arbitration, they are likely to engage in any negotiations which minimize the chances of compulsory arbitration. One unknown factor in this proposal, however, is how feasible it is to keep track of the various forms of third-party assistance in use at any given moment.

Conclusion

In this chapter, we have discussed a variety of forms of third-party assistance in the negotiation process. The major conclusion that has emerged from this discussion is that there is no one best form. In fact, it is still unclear which

instruments measure most appropriately the effectiveness of different forms of third-party assistance. Totally different conclusions may be drawn from the same body of evidence depending on the statistical tools used.[79] In addition, personal preferences often dictate the method used.

From a policy point of view, it seems clear that provision should be made for a number of types of third-party assistance, and that the administrative agencies charged with implementing the policies should, hopefully with some degree of sophistication, use procedures appropriate to each type of dispute. It would be useful for future studies to include not only procedures as independent variables, but also environmental, organizational, and interpersonal characteristics. Inclusion of these additional variables will make rigorous research more difficult, but it should not detract from our attempts to develop more effective forms of third-party assistance under given conditions.

questions

1 What does Table 8.1 tell you about the use of various forms of third-party assistance in contract negotiations in the Canadian industrial relations system?

2 Distinguish among the types of third-party assistance with binding recommendations and those with non-binding recommendations.

3 Discuss the major types of third-party assistance prescribed by law in the various Canadian jurisdictions. What is your assessment of the prescribed procedures? Elaborate.

4 You have been involved recently as a mediator in several small-scale contract negotiations. Tomorrow you are to begin as a mediator in a major high-profile dispute. How will you proceed as a mediator and what are some of the things you will do and not do to get a settlement in this dispute? Elaborate.

5 Given the criticisms of conventional arbitration

in interest disputes and the strong case for FOS, how do you account for the continued reliance on conventional arbitration?

6 What is your assessment of the arsenal-of-weapons approach as a form of third-party assistance?

7 How do you assess the framework for judging the effectiveness of compromise arbitration? Do you agree that all five factors are relevant? Elaborate.

8 What is your assessment of Iowa tri-offer arbitration? Elaborate. How do you account for the disuse of a comparable form in the educational sector in Ontario? Elaborate.

9 Which third-party dispute settlement procedure would you prefer in the private sector? Would you suggest the use of the same procedure for public-sector disputes? Elaborate.

notes

1 Labour Canada, *Collective Bargaining Review,* (Ottawa: Supply and Services Canada). Each

year, the No. 12 December issue contains a table giving the number of collective agreements and the workers covered for the various stages where negotiations were completed each year.

2 Hon. W. L. MacKenzie King, *Industry and Humanity* (New York: Houghton Mifflin Company, 1918), p. 219.

3 H. D. Woods, *Labour Policy in Canada,* 2nd ed. (Toronto: Macmillan of Canada, 1973), p. 158.

4 T. A. Kochan and J. Jick, "The Public Sector Mediation Process," Vol. 22, No. 2, *Journal of Conflict Resolution* (June 1978), pp. 211-12.

5 For an excellent discussion of the strategies to be used by a mediator see Kenneth K. Kressel, *Mediation: An Exploratory Survey* (Albany: Association of Labour Mediation Agencies, 1972). See also Carl M. Stevens, "Mediation and The Role Of The Neutral," *Frontiers of Collective Bargaining,* eds. John T. Dunlop and Neil W. Chamberlain (New York: Harper & Row, Publishers, 1967), pp. 252-90; A. Karim and R. Pegnetter, "Mediation Strategies and Qualities and Mediation Effectiveness," Vol. 22, No. 1, *Industrial Relations* (1983), pp. 105-14.

6 David Kuechle, "How To Prepare For Mediation," *Labour Gazette* (February 1974), p. 128.

7 Kochan and Jick, "The Public Sector Mediation Process," pp. 213, 221.

8 *Ibid.,* p. 221.

9 *Ibid.*

10 *Ibid.,* pp. 223-24.

11 *Ibid.,* p. 225.

12 P. F. Gerhard and J. E. Drotning, "Dispute Settlement and the Intensity of Mediation," Vol. 19, No. 3, *Industrial Relations* (Fall 1980), p. 354.

13 *Ibid.,* p. 352.

14 *Ibid.,* p. 358.

15 Karam and Pegnetter, "Mediator Strategies and Qualities and Mediator Effectiveness," p. 112.

16 H. D. Woods, "Canadian Collective Bargaining and Dispute Settlement Policy: An Appraisal," *Readings In Canadian Labour Economics,* ed. A. E. Kovacs (Toronto: McGraw-Hill Company of Canada Limited, 1961), pp. 248-51. This article was first published in Vol. XXI, No. 4, *The Canadian Journal of Economics and Political Science* (Nov. 1955).

17 W. B. Cunningham, *Compulsory Conciliation and Collective Bargaining: The New Brunswick Experience* (published jointly by The New Brunswick Department of Labour, Frederickton, N.B., and The Industrial Relations Centre, McGill University, Montreal, c. 1958), p. 43. Cunningham's study covered the period from 1947 to 1956.

18 *Ibid.,* p. 43.

19 H. D. Woods, *Labour Policy In Canada,* p. 201.

20 Labour Canada, *Annual Report* (for the fiscal year ended March 31, 1978), p. 9.

21 "CPU to Begin Staggered Closing of Abitibi-Price Mills," *Globe and Mail* (June 28, 1980), p. B16.

22 Wilfred List, "Skilled Mediation Preferable to Conciliation Board Efforts," *Globe and Mail* (July 18, 1981), p. 35.

23 Geoffrey York, "MDs Livid Over Weiler Report Calling for 14% Fee Increase," *Globe and Mail* (April 2, 1982). For a good discussion on the possibility of the OMA becoming a formalized union, see Geoffrey York, "OMA May Seek Union Powers if MDs Lose Fee Fight," *Globe and Mail* (April 12, 1982), p. 8.

24 J. C. Anderson and T. A. Kochan, "Impasse Procedures in the Canadian Federal Service: Effects on the Bargaining Process," Vol. 30, No. 3, *Industrial and Labor Relations Review* (April 1977), pp. 283-301.

25 *Ibid.,* p. 291.

26 I. W. Abel, "Basic Steel's Experimental Negotiating Agreement," *Monthly Labor Review* (September 1973), pp. 39-42.

27 *Ibid.,* p. 42.

28 J. D. Dworkin, "The Impact of Final-Offer Interest Arbitration On Bargaining: The Case of Major League Baseball," Twenty-Ninth Annual Winter Meeting of the IRRA, *Proceedings* (Madison: 1977), pp. 161-69; J. R. Chelius and J. B. Dworkin, "Arbitration and Salary Determination in Baseball," Thirty-Third Annual Meeting of the IRRA, *Proceedings* (Madison: 1981), pp. 105-12.

29 P. Feuille, "Selected Benefits and Costs of Compulsory Arbitration," Vol. 33, No. 1, *Industrial and Labor Relations Review* (October 1979), pp. 66-67.

30 *Ibid.,* p. 69; J. Delaney, P. Feuille, and W. Hendricks, "Police Salaries, Interest Arbitration, & the Leveling Effect," Vol. 23, No. 3, *Industrial Relations* (Fall 1984), p. 423.

31 Feuille, "Selected Benefits and Costs of Compulsory Arbitration," p. 70.

32 *Ibid.*

33 *Ibid.,* p. 71; R. D. Horton, "Arbitration, Arbitrators, and the Public Interest," Vol. 28, No. 4, *Industrial and Labor Relations Review* (July 1975), p. 499.

34 Feuille, "Selected Benefits and Costs of Compulsory Arbitration," p. 72.

35 R. E. Walton and R. B. McKersie, *A Behavioral Theory of Labor Negotiations* (New York: McGraw-Hill Book Co., 1965), p. 4.

36 Feuille, "Selected Benefits and Costs of Compulsory Arbitration," p. 72.

37 R. J. Butler and R. G. Ehrenberg, "Estimating the Narcotic Effect of Public Sector Impasse Procedures," Vol. 35, No. 1, *Industrial and Labor Relations Review* (October 1981), pp. 3-20; T. A. Kochan and J. Baderschneider, "Estimating the Narcotic Effect," Vol. 35, No. 1, *Industrial and Labor Relations Review* (October 1981), pp. 21-28.

38 Kochan and Baderschneider, "Estimating the Narcotic Effect," p. 27.

39 M. Thompson and J. Cairnie, "Compulsory Arbitration: The Case of British Columbia Teachers," Vol. 27, No. 1, *Industrial and Labor Relations Review* (October 1973), p. 14.

40 P. Feuille, "Analyzing Compulsory Arbitration Experiences: The Role of Personal Preferences," Vol. 28, No. 3, *Industrial and Labor Relations Review* (April 1975), pp. 432-35; M. Thompson and J. Cairnie, "Reply," Vol. 28, No. 3, *Industrial and Labor Relations Review* (April 1975), pp. 435-38.

41 Anderson and Kochan, "Impasse Procedures in the Canadian Federal Service," p. 291.

42 *Ibid.*

43 *Ibid.*

44 G. W. Adams, "The Ontario Experience with Interest Arbitration," Vol. 36, No. 1, *Relations Industrielles/Relations* (1981), p. 245.

45 T. A. Kochan and J. Baderschneider, "Dependence on Impasse Procedures: Police and Firefighters in New York State," Vol. 31, No. 4, *Industrial and Labor Relations Review* (July 1978), p. 432. For an excellent treatment of compulsory arbitration in the public sector, see B. M. Downie, *The Behavioural, Economic and Institutional Effects of Compulsory Interest Arbitration* (Ottawa: Economic Council of Canada, December 1979).

46 Carl M. Stevens, "Is Compulsory Arbitration Compatible With Bargaining?" Vol. 5, No. 2, *Industrial Relations* (Calif.) (Feb. 1966), pp. 38-52.

47 *Ibid.*, p. 42.

48 D. G. Gallagher and M. D. Chaubey, "Impasse Behavior and Tri-Offer Arbitration in Iowa," Vol. 21, No. 2, *Industrial Relations* (Spring 1982), p. 129.

49 D. G. Gallagher and R. Pegnetter, "Impasse Procedure Under the Iowa Multistep Procedure," Vol. 32, No. 3, *Industrial and Labor Relations Review* (April 1979), pp. 328-29.

50 D. G. Gallagher, "The Use of Interest Arbitration In the Public Sector," 1982 Spring Meeting of the IRRA, *Proceedings*; rpt. *Labor Law Journal* (August, 1982), pp. 502-03.

51 C. A. Olson, "Final-Offer Arbitration in Wisconsin After Five Years," Thirty-First Annual Meeting of the IRRA, *Proceedings* (Madison: 1979), p. 115.

52 Gallagher, "The Use of Interest Arbitration in the Public Sector," p. 504.

53 Gallagher and Pegnetter, "Impasse Procedure Under the Iowa Multistep Procedure," pp. 335-36.

54 *Ibid.*, p. 338.

55 G. T. Sulzner, "The Political Functions of Impasse Procedures," Vol. 16, No. 3, *Industrial Relations* pp. 293-94.

56 H. S. Faber, "Does Final-Offer Arbitration Encourage Bargaining?" Thirty-Third Annual Meeting of the IRRA, *Proceedings* (Madison: 1981), pp. 219-26; H. S. Faber, "Splitting-the-Difference in Interest Arbitration," Vol. 35, No. 1, *Industrial and Labor Relations Review* (October 1981), pp. 70-77.

57 Gene Swimmer, "Final Position Arbitration and Intertemporal Compromise: The University of Alberta Compromise," Vol. 30, No. 3, *Industrial Relations/Relations Industrielles* (August 1975), p. 536.

58 Peter Feuille and James B. Dworkin, "Final-Offer Arbitration and Intertemporal Compromise or It's My Turn to Win," Thirty-First Annual Meeting, Industrial Relations Research Association, *Proceedings* (Chicago, Aug. 29-31, 1978), p. 89.

59 *Ibid.*, pp. 92-95.

60 Gallagher, "The Use of Interest Arbitration in the Public Sector," p. 504.

61 *Statutes of Ontario*, 1975, c. 72.

62 B. M. Downie, *Collective Bargaining and Conflict Resolution in Education: the Evolution of Public Policy in Ontario* (Kingston: Industrial Relations Centre, Queen's University, 1978).

63 *Ibid.*, p. 11.

64 *Ibid.*

65 *Ibid.*, p. 112.

66 *Ibid.*, p. 115.

67 *Ibid.*, p. 101.

68 B. M. Downie, "Collective Bargaining Under an Essential Services Commission," *Conflict or Compromise: The Future of Public Sector Industrial Relations*, eds. M. Thompson and G. Swimmer (Montreal: The Institute for Research on Public Policy, 1984), p. 283.

69 *Ibid.*, pp. 393-96.

70 *Ibid.*, pp. 395-96.

71 *Ibid.*, p. 396.

72 *Ibid.*, p. 397.

73 Judge J. C. Anderson, "Labour Relations — Changing Concepts — New Techniques." *Vuepoints* (Society of Professionals in Dispute Resolution, Summer 1975), pp. 13-15.

74 *Ibid.*, p. 14.

75 Ed Finn, "A Proposal for Labour-Management Peace in the Public Sector," *The Labour Gazette* (November 1974), pp. 762-72.

76 *Ibid.*, p. 770.

77 *Canadian Industrial Relations: Report of the Task force on Labour Relations* (Ottawa: Privy Council Office, December 1968), p. 171.

78 The Honourable Mr. Justice Samuel Freedman, *Report of Industrial Inquiry Commission on Canadian National Railways "Run-Throughs"* (Ottawa: Queen's Printer, 1965).

79 Butler and Ehrenberg, "Estimating the Narcotic Effect of Public Sector Impasse Procedures," pp. 3-20; Kochan and Baderschneider, "Estimating the Narcotic Effect," pp. 21-28.

9

Administration of the Collective Agreement

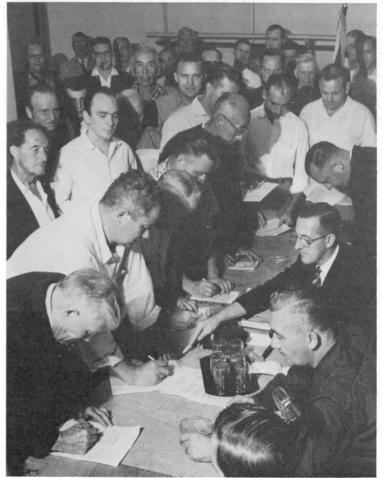

The Financial Post

Introduction

The purpose of this chapter is to define the objectives and procedures of the grievance process, particularly arbitration. We will discuss the steps involved and some substantive issues emerging in jurisprudence as a result of arbitration decisions. Judicial review and enforcement of arbitration awards, criticisms of conventional arbitration, the emergence of expedited arbitration in a number of industries, and some recent innovations to improve the ongoing relationship between unions and management will be discussed also.

The Grievance Process

In Canada, grievances and contract interpretation disputes have long characterized the relationship between unions and management. If collective agreements do not contain clauses that deal with grievances, then clauses are set out by the labour relations boards or statutes.

Grievances do not merely constitute the voicing of worker complaints. Their processing is an essential part of collective bargaining. Grievance procedures are necessary for three reasons: First, the parties must settle any differences of opinion which arise concerning the meaning, application, and interpretation of the various clauses of the collective agreement. Second, the parties must agree on how to apply the general terms contained in a collective agreement to specific situations. Third, since the duration of agreements has been increasing, unions and managers must deal realistically with worker and management demands for local adjustments during the life of the agreement.[1]

Negotiators who agree upon the clauses to be included in collective agreements cannot spell them out in such detail as to cover every concrete situation which may arise during the life of the agreement. The potential for grievances arises from ambiguous collective agreements. Sometimes, ambiguities have been condoned so as to expedite settlement. Grievances may also arise where two or more provisions of a collective agreement appear contradictory, and a complaint is lodged by a worker under the provision most favourable to him or her. If both parties know that some ambiguity or contentious point exists in a provision, then both parties should anticipate the need for arbitration at some point during the life of the collective agreement. Nevertheless, only when a provision is allegedly violated may a grievance be lodged.

Formal Aspects of Grievance Handling

All statutes in the private, public, and parapublic sectors prohibit strikes and lockouts while an agreement is in force. This is intended to provide stability during the life of the agreement. To compensate for this restriction on strikes and lockouts, the statutes further stipulate that collective agreements provide for the resolution of disputes concerning the interpretation, application, or alleged violation of the agreement's provisions. In most jurisdictions, the grievance procedure specifies binding arbitration by outside neutrals as the last step in the process. It is generally agreed that using such a procedure is preferable to seeking judicial action through the regular court system.

The grievance procedure varies widely from one organization to another and may have as few as two or as many as five separate steps. Most grievance procedures contain time limits on each step in the process. For example, a worker may have a certain number of days within which to present a grievance from the time that the alleged infraction occurred. Management, upon receiving the grievance, has a certain number of days within which to reply at each stage of the grievance process. The union also is allotted specified periods of time within which to appeal management's decision, if it so wishes, to higher levels. Failure to file an appeal or submit a response on time or in the correct order may invalidate the whole grievance procedure, particularly if the matter is later referred to arbitration.

In the first step of the grievance procedure, an important party may be the shop steward. Practically all collective agreements provide for the election of shop stewards by the members. There may be as many as fifteen or twenty shop stewards in a large organization. The main functions of this official are to hear the grievance as it is presented by the worker and to take part in processing it through the lower levels of the grievance procedure. Most collective agreements contain provisions which permit shop stewards to go from their places of work, usually with the permission of their supervisor, to handle the grievances of other workers within the same working unit. The shop steward has *superseniority* — the highest seniority in the unit. Shop stewards are usually the last ones to be laid off even though their ordinary seniority may be much less than that of other workers whose employment is temporarily or permanently terminated. The superseniority clause ensures availability of a steward for the immediate handling of grievances.

Generally, a worker with a grievance first takes it up with the supervisor of the work group, either with or without the presence of the shop steward. The supervisor is required to respond positively or negatively to the worker's complaint within a given time-frame. If the supervisor disagrees with the worker, the worker may at that point discuss it with the shop steward and the two of them may then decide whether or not the matter should be pursued to the next level in the grievance procedure.

In one sense, shop stewards often perform an important managerial function by pre-screening potential grievances. This is usually done by informal discussion with the aggrieved worker, during the course of which the shop steward may advise the worker whether or not a legitimate grievance exists. Undoubtedly, many complaints do not go to grievance because the shop steward has advised the worker that the case is not well founded. A low incidence of grievance is not necessarily a good indication of the quality of a union-management relationship. It may indicate, for example, that the supervisor is "giving the shop away." In such a case, management may instruct that individual to get tougher with the union or, failing that, may arrange for the supervisor's transfer.

As previously noted, when the worker files a grievance it must relate to a specific provision in a collective agreement. An argument can be made, however, that anything which bothers a worker at the place of work automatically interferes with his performance. He should, therefore, be given a thorough hearing by management. The collective agreement of National Capital Commission workers provides for complaints to be heard at all stages of the grievance process except the adjudication stage.

The grievance procedure gives a worker who feels unjustly treated by management an opportunity to present his case before those in managerial and supervisory positions and ultimately to an outside third party. Thus, it helps the worker to relieve frustration and preserve a sense of personal dignity. One problematic aspect of the grievance process, however, is the fact that workers may grieve only after management has given an improper order. Some critics have argued that it would be desirable if workers were given a chance to make their formal objection before management required them to obey an offensive instruction, since

> workers are, perhaps, as interested in assurance of justice *before* the act as in justice through the grievance procedure *after* the act. They want a manager to hear and explicitly to consider their interest before he acts, as well as afterward.[2]

It is interesting to note that some of the recent legislation concerning health and safety permits workers to refuse to do a job if they feel that the job poses a significant threat to their health. Previously, they had no recourse but to perform the work and subsequently file a grievance.

Informal Aspects of Grievance Handling

James W. Kuhn, a long-time student of the grievance process, has discussed the various ways in which workers may use bargaining power daily in the workplace.[3] He discusses, for example, the informal shop-floor tradeoffs that take place between supervisors and shop stewards. Generally, if shop stewards and the particular work group they represent are fairly strategic to any operation within an organization, they will have a high degree of bargaining power which may be used to win concessions from the supervisor. In the same way, adept supervisors may win concessions from shop stewards and the informal work group by offering certain benefits in exchange for a faster rate of production to meet a particular daily or weekly standard. These informal tradeoffs work very well as long as both sides live up to mutual expectations. The tradeoffs also forestall grievances resulting from unilateral changes to the conditions of employment.

However, should one party make a commitment to give concessions and subsequently renege on that promise, the informal understandings or expectations between the parties might very well be destroyed. This is one reason that those higher up in their respective organizations should not tamper with the way that people at the local level work out their own accommodative arrangements. Kuhn claims that

A major problem of industrial relations arises if either union or management tries to resolve issues arising out of negotiations at the place of work between foremen and stewards with no regard for the complexity of the activities that brought them about.[4]

These local shop arrangements can best be worked out by those who initially formulated them.

The grievance procedure is also a communication device for both unions and management to obtain information on the operation of the collective agreement. They may then use this knowledge to amend provisions in the collective agreement during subsequent negotiations. Since management is usually the one to initiate communication in the workplace, it bears the major responsibility for advising managers and also shop stewards of decisions significantly affecting working conditions. These decisions may not only trigger individual grievances but generalized union demands.

Not all items can be resolved informally. For example, discipline and discharge cases should always be adjudicated by higher authorities who are far removed from the scene of the initial action. Also, special committees may have to be set up to deal with complex issues such as job evaluation, job classification, and apprenticeship. Some agreements also provide for special procedures and personnel to deal with highly technical matters such as supplemental unemployment benefits, pension plans, and health and welfare plans. Grievances arising out of the administration of these fringe benefits require expert handling.

The Requirement for Arbitration

Where informal bargaining has proved ineffective and the steps in the grievance process involving different levels in the union and management hierarchies have been systematically followed without satisfying the grievor, arbitration is prescribed in all Canadian jurisdictions as the final step in the grievance process.

The award of the arbitrator or arbitration tribunal is binding on union, management, and the worker or workers affected. Although grievance arbitration is voluntary in the United States, about 90% of collective agreements in that country provide for the final and binding arbitration of grievances. Much of the impetus for the use of arbitration in the United States came with the National War Labor Board during World War II.[5] The Board required arbitration of disputes over the interpretation or application of collective agreements. This policy laid the foundation for the subsequent widespread practice of terminating contract interpretation disputes by arbitration.[6] In Canada, the use of binding arbitration at the federal level was made compulsory under P.C. 1003 of 1944, and all provincial jurisdictions now require its use in the grievance process.

Arbitration Tribunals

Several types of arbitration tribunals are available to the parties in the grievance process, including a single *ad hoc* arbitrator, a tripartite arbitration board, and what is often referred to as a permanent umpire. (A permanent umpire is an arbitrator named by the parties either in the contract or by mutual agreement to serve for a specified period of time.) The usual practice, however, is to employ *ad hoc* arbitrators or arbitration boards which are appointed every time a new arbitration case arises. Sometimes, the parties name a number of arbitrators to serve on a rotating basis as grievance disputes arise.

Every form of arbitration tribunal has its advantages and disadvantages. A permanent umpire, for example, usually gets to know the parties and the industry very well and quite often makes decisions that become part of the jurisprudence of the parties involved in that particular collective-bargaining relationship. In other words, these decisions or awards may set precedents which may be invoked in similar disputes, thus obviating the need for the umpire's services. In addition, the permanent umpire has the advantage of being readily accessible to the parties, and this helps cut down on time delays which are often characteristic of the arbitration process.

However, a possible disadvantage for the parties is that they may rely too heavily on the permanent umpire to help resolve their problems for them. It is generally conceded that it is much better for the parties to reconcile their differences over the interpretation and application of the terms of a collective agreement rather than having a neutral party do so. This is particularly true where a deliberately vague clause has been included in a collective agreement. In such a case, it is better for the parties who negotiated it to give meaning to the clause rather than to have a neutral party guess its intent.

If the parties choose to employ a tripartite board rather than a permanent umpire, they benefit from the experience of the union and management nominees. These nominees generally have a fairly sophisticated understanding of the industry in question and are thus able to advise the chairman of the board on relevant technical problems. This is particularly important in the case of *ad hoc* arbitration boards where the chairman may not be fully familiar with the technical aspects of the question being arbitrated.

However, tripartite arbitration boards also have their disadvantages. First, it may be more time consuming to hear an arbitration case since meetings must be scheduled to accommodate

the three members of the board as well as the management and union personnel who must appear before it. Second, the decisions of arbitration boards, until recently, had to be majority decisions. This requirement meant that the chairman of the board, in preparing an award, had to ensure that either or both union and management nominees concurred.

These shortcomings caused the late Bora Laskin, Chief Justice of the Supreme Court of Canada and professor at the University of Toronto, to observe: "The conclusion is inescapable, and is amply fortified by experience, that a three-man board of arbitration is a waste of manpower and time."[7] He further maintained that the use of a single arbitrator would raise the status of arbitration by freeing him from the post-hearing pressure usually exerted by the union and management members of a tripartite board. As we indicated in a previous chapter, present legislation covering contract interpretation disputes in the private sector in all jurisdictions in Canada states that, where there is no majority decision of an arbitration board, the decision of the chairman rules.

The advantage of using a single arbitrator is that the parties have to rely only on the availability of one person. This may substantially reduce both the time and cost involved in the arbitration. In addition, if the same arbitrator is selected by the parties each time, he or she then becomes familiar with the technical details of the industry. The decisions of these arbitrators are thus more likely to be appropriate to the given circumstances of the parties than if repeated consultation had not occurred. Appointing a different arbitrator each time around, however, may be preferable to the establishment of a permanent umpire, since the parties might learn to settle their disputes among themselves and thus avoid overdependence on the decisions of third-parties.[8]

At one time, the majority of cases in Canada was handled by tripartite arbitration boards. In Ontario, the use of arbitration boards is still almost double that of single arbitrators. However, adjudication of disputes in the public sector is performed much more by single arbitrators than by arbitration boards. For example, the *Public Service Staff Relations Act* of 1967, which governs Federal Government workers, does not provide for a tripartite arbitration board. Rather, either full-time or part-time members of the Public Service Staff Relations Board are used as adjudicators. (The term adjudication rather than arbitration is used in the *Public Service Staff Relations Act.*) The same appears to be true for many of the provincial governments that have given their workers the right to collective bargaining. The prevalence of arbitration boards in the private sector possibly reflects the fact that, when arbitration was made compulsory in 1944, the concept of tripartite conciliation boards may have been used as a model.

Selection of Arbitration Tribunals The method for selecting a type of arbitration tribunal is usually contained in the collective agreement itself. However, if the parties are unable or unwilling to select the members or the chairman of an arbitration board, then the ministers of labour in practically all jurisdictions have the right to nominate members to the board. In those provinces which make a list of arbitrators available to the parties, an arbitrator or chairman of an arbitration board is appointed when both parties have selected the same name. The American Arbitration Association, which has chapters in Canada, has a similar list and will help the parties to select arbitrators or chairmen of arbitration boards.

Often the parties make use of what is known as the "box score" in selections. If a union or management finds that an individual has fairly consistently ruled in favour of the other side, it will probably not want him as an arbitrator. Making selections using this method is not always the best way to judge an arbitrator's impartiality, since it fails to take into account the rationales for previous decisions, which make up the box score.

Once it is decided who is to be the arbitrator, either the union or management will contact the person chosen. At this point, the prospective arbitrator does not seek, nor should he seek, any further information about the case but merely accepts or declines the appointment. Once the arbitrator is seized of a case, however, it is up to him to arrange for the arbitration hearings, to see that they are conducted properly, that all interested parties are given their chance to present evidence, and that appropriate awards are determined.

Arbitrator's Fees and Expenses When a case is heard by a single arbitrator, the two parties share the cost of the arbitration proceedings, including the arbitrator's fees and any fees for hotel rooms where the arbitration proceedings take place. In addition, the parties jointly share the cost of any verbatim transcript. C. H. Curtis, after having done a study of arbitration in Ontario some years ago, indicated that, in some Ontario cases, arbitrators have experienced difficulty in collecting their fees and expenses: "From the arbitrator's point of view, it is probably sound practice to have an understanding with the parties about fees before the arbitration is undertaken. The American Arbitration Association follows that procedure with the arbitrations it conducts in Canada."[9]

As a rule of thumb, arbitrators are generally permitted two days' fees for each day of hearing to cover the time of going through the submissions of the parties, the collective agreement, the material obtained during the hearing, analyzing the information, and writing the award. In Ontario, the most frequently used arbitrators charge about $800 to $900. This assumes that a case takes one day of hearings, and includes the time taken to write the award.[10] In addition to the fees mentioned above, if either or both parties engage legal or other counsel in assisting with their presentation, each party bears its own costs for such counsel.

Arbitration Process: Two Interpretations

Most writers on arbitration of contract interpretation disputes refer to it as an adjudication process. D. J. M. Brown and D. M. Beatty define this kind of arbitration as

> the primary, if not the exclusive, process for the final and authoritative settlement of disputes arising out of the application of collective agreements …The arbitrator…adjudicates upon specific, concrete disputes which he resolves by applying the legal regime established by the collective agreement to the facts which he finds on the basis of the evidence and argument presented to him.[11]

In earlier days, however, some analysts, including Selekman of Harvard and Shulman of Yale, believed that arbitration was more of a clinical than an adjudicative process. Those who adopted the clinical approach emphasized the importance of getting at the problem behind the stated grievance, since it was their contention that very often the stated grievance did not reflect the real complaint of the worker. James W. Kuhn takes a somewhat similar position and indicates that it takes a sophisticated ear to read between the lines of a stated grievance: "Written grievances and answers may be purely formal, describing problems in conventional terms that hide or distort more than they reveal."[12] Notwithstanding the clinical approach to grievances, it appears that the adjudicative interpretation prevails in Canada and the United States.

Arbitration Hearings One of the principle responsibilities of an arbitrator or chairman of an arbitration board is to ensure that hearings are conducted properly. To accomplish this task requires that certain rules be followed: (1) all interested parties must receive notice of the time and place of the arbitration hearings and they must be given an opportunity to attend; (2) the parties must be permitted without unreasonable restrictions to introduce evidence; (3) the parties must be permitted to present witnesses and there must be ample opportunity for cross-examination of witnesses; (4) the parties must be allowed to make concluding oral arguments which, in effect, summarize the major thrust of their evidence during the arbitration proceedings; (5) if the parties so desire, they must be allowed

to file written, post-hearing briefs; and (6) witnesses should not be permitted in the hearing room until called upon. The assumption behind this practice is that if the presence of more than one witness is permitted in the hearing room, individual testimonies may be tainted.

Such ground rules are important since

> a refusal to permit cross-examination, a refusal to compel the attendance of a witness at the instance of a party, or the exclusion of admissible and relevant evidence will provide grounds for review and may result in an order quashing the award if a substantial injustice has resulted therefrom.[13]

Defining Issues and Making Awards It is extremely important for an arbitrator or an arbitration board to have a very clear statement of the issue under consideration. Such a statement sometimes takes the form of what is called a "submission to arbitrate" in which the parties make a joint submission to the arbitrator indicating the precise basis of the grievance. On other occasions, however, the parties come to an arbitration hearing without a clear statement or submission of the issue, and it is up to an arbitrator or an arbitration board to obtain a concise expression of the grievance as it was stated towards the latter part of the grievance procedure. If such a statement is not available, the arbitrator, after hearing from both parties, may try to formulate a statement of the issue by using phraseology upon which the two parties agree. A statement of the issue is important to the arbitrator because an award may be overturned by a legal decision if a court finds that the arbitrator has gone beyond his jurisdiction.

The statement of the issue or the submission to arbitrate plus the provisions of the collective agreement may greatly inhibit the arbitrator's manoeuvreability. In addition, an arbitrator must be very careful that any submission is not phrased in such a way that the provisions of the collective agreement will not allow him to deal with it. For this reason, it is in the interest of both parties to state the submission to arbitrate in fairly general terms.[14] In making an award, the arbitrator must account for the record of the arbitration hearing and any other data both generated by the arbitrator and known to the parties. To summarize, then, the collective agreement, the submission agreement, and the record or evidence produced at the hearing or deposited with the arbitrator form the sole basis for the arbitration decision.

Objections to the Arbitrator's Jurisdiction At the beginning of the hearings, an arbitrator or the chairman of an arbitration board usually will try to get the parties to agree that (1) if he or she is the sole arbitrator, the appointment has been duly made and accepted by the parties; or (2) if he or she is a chairman of an arbitration board, that the board is appropriately constituted. At this point, either of the parties may object that the arbitrator or board does not have jurisdiction over the case and will provide evidence to support this contention.

There are a number of grounds on which the parties may challenge jurisdiction. They may, for example, claim that the time allowed between the day on which the last reply was given and a request for arbitration was made has expired. This is usually referred to as a procedural irregularity. Alternatively, one of the parties may challenge the arbitrator's appointment when, for instance, it is suspected that the appointee has discussed the case with one of the parties before the hearing, or allege that the arbitration board is not properly constituted because one of the board members appears to have a financial interest in the arbitration award. In addition, since arbitration deals with the interpretation, application, or alleged violation of a collective agreement, one of the parties may argue that the subject matter before the arbitrator does not fall under the terms of the collective agreement. Whatever the objection to the arbitrator's jurisdiction, it is usually a matter to be disposed of before beginning the hearing. However, an arbitrator may take the objection under advisement and proceed with the hearing since, in many instances, arbitrability is inextricably bound up with the merits of the case itself.[15]

Burden of Proof When an arbitration hearing begins, the side bearing the burden of proof must give a general opening statement setting forth the issue in dispute, an outline of the pertinent facts, and the conclusion that the party expects the arbitrator to reach. When the moving party has finished speaking, the opposing party must make its opening statement along similar lines.

In most arbitration cases, the burden of proof is on the party bringing the grievance. The main exception to this general rule is in cases involving discipline and discharge. In such cases, the grieving party is obliged only to establish that there is a collective agreement, that the person was employed by the organization, and that the person has either been disciplined or discharged.[16] Beyond that point, the burden of proof then shifts to the employer who must prove why the discipline or discharge should be upheld. However, once the employer has shown a *prima facie* case of just cause for his action, the burden of proof shifts to the worker who must then present a defence or indicate mitigating circumstances.

The reason why the burden of proof in discharge cases falls upon the employer is that discharge in the industrial relations system is the equivalent of capital punishment in the legal subsystem: Just as the Crown Attorney in prosecuting homicide cases in some American states must prove that the person charged with the crime is guilty, the employer in justifying to an arbitrator the dismissal of a worker must bear the burden of proof. The assumption in both situations is that the individual is innocent until proven guilty. The same reasoning applies to discipline, since an accumulation of upheld discipline grievances on a worker's record may be used at some point in time as a basis for discharge under the doctrine of culminating incident. One school of thought argues that, if a worker has spent some time on a job, a kind of property right accrues to that worker with respect to the job. Also, as workers age (older workers have sometimes been defined as those over forty years of age), it becomes more and more difficult for them to find other jobs due to anti-age discrimination. The burden of proof in discharge and discipline cases, therefore, is also a kind of insurance discouraging employers from acting in an arbitrary or capricious manner against older workers and other minority-group workers.

Examination of Witnesses In an arbitration case, the party with the right to lead off the discussion also has the right to call witnesses first. After the moving party has adduced evidence from a witness, the opposing party may cross-examine. Following cross-examination, the initiating party may re-examine the witness but only to fortify or clarify the original evidence. No new evidence may be introduced during the re-examination of a witness.

Before a party calls a person to testify, the party should be sure that the witness is very knowledgeable on the subject matter on which he or she is to be examined and cross-examined. When giving evidence, there should be no hesitation in responding to a question in either the original presentation of evidence or on cross-examination. A weak witness or one who appears to be uncertain of the facts can do more damage than good to the party presenting evidence, particularly when subjected to cross-examination by the opposing side. As is the case in courtroom procedure, the person questioning the witness should ask direct questions, should avoid leading questions or putting words in the mouth of the witness and, where possible, should let the witness relate the facts in his or her own words with little or no interruption.

The purposes of cross-examination are to weaken or destroy an opponent's case, to adduce evidence to support one's own position, and to discredit a witness.[17] The examiner in cross-examination should be careful to avoid asking leading questions or badgering a witness. Too many questions of the latter type may be ob-

jected to by the moving party and those objections, if upheld by the arbitrator, may harm the cross-examiner's case. Since arbitrators have a fair amount of discretion in controlling cross-examinations, they may on occasion forbid questions that do not appear to be relevant to the case or that are meant to deliberately put the witness off-guard. The arbitrator may also ask questions of the witness, but such questions should appear neutral in tone with the intent of clarifying matters for the arbitrator himself, without appearing to support one party or the other.

At the end of the arbitration proceedings, the arbitrator should give the parties time to present closing arguments which allow them to summarize succinctly the issue in dispute and the points they have made in support of their case. A further objective of the final summation is to give the parties a last chance to impress upon the arbitrator or the members of an arbitration board the importance of the matter in question and the merits of the case.

Standard of Proof In legal proceedings before the courts, there are two standards of proof which are required. One of these is the *balance of probabilities* which relates to civil law proceedings and which, in effect, means that if, on the basis of the evidence presented, the balance of probabilities appears to lie against one side then that side is found guilty. In criminal cases, courts usually require proof *beyond a reasonable doubt*. Two recent outstanding Canadian books suggest that arbitrators generally follow the civil law standard of proof. At one time, some arbitrators argued that something approaching the criminal law burden of proof should apply in discharge cases. However, this view is no longer generally accepted.[18]

Making the Award Once the arbitrator has heard the issue in dispute, looked at all the relevant provisions in the collective agreement, and examined all the evidence on record, the award must be made. Sometimes the submission to the arbitrator or arbitration board may be in two parts. For example, a discharged worker may ask both to be reinstated and to be compensated. If the arbitrator or arbitration board finds that a dismissal has been unjust, the employer may be ordered to reinstate the worker with compensation for the period since he or she was fired. In such cases, the arbitrator will usually retain jurisdiction over the case until the parties have resolved the financial problem; and, should they be unable to agree upon the amount of compensation, the arbitrator may make that determination.

Ambiguity in Contract Language

As pointed out at the beginning of this chapter, one problem often faced in arbitration is that of applying ambiguous language to a specific and concrete situation. Brown and Beatty observe differences of opinion among arbitrators as to what constitutes ambiguity:

> One view holds that more than the arguability of different constructions of the collective agreement [is] necessary to constitute an ambiguity. Another view is that an ambiguity exists if there is no clear preponderance of meaning stemming from the words and structure of the agreement.[19]

One way of dealing with the problem of ambiguity is to invoke past practice, as it "has occurred during the life of the collective agreement and ...has come to be relied on by one of the parties,"[20] since this implies a tacit understanding between union and management regarding their mutual obligations. Another method is to look at the negotiating history of the parties, so as to determine what meaning the parties attributed to the ambiguity in the original collective agreement. A transcript of the record of the negotiations or the notes kept by the parties greatly assist such an investigation. Where research discloses that the parties have always attributed different meanings to a particular phrase, past practice may be the only method invoked to resolve the ambiguity.

Just Cause for Discipline and Discharge

There are very few topics involving arbitration which have received so much attention as discipline and discharge. In particular, the concept of "just cause" has become the subject of a great deal of arbitral jurisprudence. Prior to the introduction of just-cause clauses into collective agreements, common law permitted employers to sever the employment relationship for cause, or, in the absence of cause, upon proper and reasonable notice.[21] Today, even in those collective agreements that do not contain a just-cause provision, both arbitrators and courts appear to take the view that an employer's right to discharge depends upon his ability to prove "cause" or "just cause."[22]

Dealing with the concept of just cause for discharge has posed problems for some arbitrators. Some feel that, since workers in these situations have very much more at stake than employers do, there must be certainty that the evidence adduced constitutes just cause for discharge. American arbitrator S. J. Rosen claimed that arbitrators "ultimately must feel comfortable with the decision. Perhaps, just cause eventually becomes a matter of being able to retire at night with an untroubled feeling."[23]

In preparing the worker's case, it is wise for the union advocate to grill the worker and his or her witnesses thoroughly with the kinds of difficult questions likely to be posed by the management advocate during the arbitration hearing. This preparation is extremely important for, should the management advocate find the grievor or the grievor's witnesses hesitant in responding to a question or should either volunteer information which may potentially damage the grievor's case, then the management advocate will be presented with an opportunity to discredit the grievor. Good preparation will help the grievor and the grievor's witnesses to give quick, crisp, and credible replies, and also greatly help the arbitrator, for the arbitrator cannot take on the task of representing the grievor in the absence of adequate preparation on the part of the grievor.

Cases involving discipline or discharge pose two questions: Are there sufficient grounds for discipline or discharge, and if so, is the penalty imposed appropriate in the given situation? While there are many factors which justify an employer's using suspension and discharge against workers to punish certain types of behaviour, there are other factors which would mitigate the severity of the penalty:

1 The previous good (and unblemished) record of the grievor;
2 The long service of the grievor;
3 Whether or not the offence was an isolated incident in the employment history of the grievor;
4 Provocation (which may have been initiated by an agent of the employer);
5 Whether the offence was committed on the spur of the moment as a momentary aberration, due to strong emotional impulses, or whether the offence was premeditated;
6 Whether the penalty imposed has created a special economic hardship for the grievor in the light of his particular circumstances;
7 Evidence that the company rules of conduct, either written or posted, have not been uniformly enforced, thus constituting a form of discrimination; [This, in effect, means that if breaking a rule results in discipline, it is up to the employer to ensure that the rule is well known and consistently enforced.]
8 Circumstances negating intent, e.g., likelihood that the grievor misunderstood the nature or intent of an order given to him, and as a result disobeyed it;
9 The seriousness of the offence in terms of company policy and company obligations;
10 Any other circumstances which the board should properly take into consideration, e.g., failure of the grievor to apologize and settle the matter after being given an opportunity to do so.[24]

Only one of the conditions noted above need be established in order for an arbitrator or an arbitration board to mitigate the severity of the penalty imposed by the employer.

Arbitral Authority Versus Managerial Authority

The original view of arbitration generally excluded an arbitrator from modifying a judgement imposed by management on a worker. For example, if an employer discharged a worker, an arbitrator did not have the authority to substitute a lesser penalty. By 1965, however, arbitrators

were taking the view that they could indeed change the penalty imposed by management even if just cause were established by the employer. In other words, employers were obligated not only to prove the worker's wrongdoing, but also to justify the severity of their own response.

The *Port Arthur Shipbuilding* case, however, deprived arbitrators of this discretionary power. In that case, Harry Arthurs substituted suspension for discharge in the case of three workers, all of whom had many years of seniority with the company. This decision was eventually quashed by the Supreme Court of Canada. Mr. Justice Judson, who delivered the Supreme Court decision, observed:

> The sole issue in this case was whether the three employees left their jobs to work for someone and whether this fact was a proper cause for discipline. Once the board had found that there were facts justifying discipline, the particular form chosen was not subject to review on arbitration.[25]

Following this decision, a group of Ontario arbitrators successfully appealed to the provincial Minister of Labour to pass legislation confirming their authority in arbitration cases and making court intervention more difficult. The Ontario *Labour Relations Act* was amended in 1966 to include Section 44(9):

> Where an arbitrator or arbitration board determines that an employee has been discharged or otherwise disciplined by an employer for cause and the collective agreement does not contain a specific penalty for the infraction that is the subject-matter of the arbitration, the arbitrator or arbitration board may substitute such other penalty for the discharge or discipline as to the arbitrator or arbitration board seems just and reasonable in all the circumstances.[26]

Since Ontario passed this amendment, practically all other provinces in Canada have enacted similar legislation, which confirms an arbitrator's power to amend an excessive penalty imposed by an employer, assuming that there is no explicit provision made for such a penalty in the collective agreement.

Enforcement of Arbitration Awards

Section 44(11) of the Ontario *Labour Relations Act* states that:

> Where a party, employer, trade union or employee has failed to comply with any of the terms of the decision of an arbitrator or an arbitration board, any party, employer, trade union or employee affected by the decision may file in the office of the Registrar of the Supreme Court a copy of the decision, ...whereupon the decision shall be entered in the same way as a judgement or order of that court and is enforceable as such.[27]

Other jurisdictions in Canada have legislation somewhat similar to that of the Ontario provision. Once a decision is filed with the court it then becomes a court order. Parties who fail to comply with the award leave themselves open to contempt of court proceedings.

Judicial Review of Arbitration Awards

All jurisdictions require the use of arbitration as the last step in the grievance procedure. Hence, the courts tend to look upon arbitration as a quasi-judicial process, and, therefore, subject to judicial review. There are a number of grounds upon which the judiciary may review arbitration decisions and, while this area is a fairly complicated one, a simplified analysis yields four grounds for court intervention: (1) belief that the arbitrator has exceeded his jurisdiction; (2) alleged lack of impartiality on the part of the arbitrator; (3) procedural defects in the arbitration hearing and in rendering the award; and (4) an alleged error of law on the face of the award.

An arbitrator will have exceeded his jurisdiction by answering a question not under consideration, by failing to respond to the question to be considered, or by amending, altering, or varying the collective agreement. It is important, therefore, to ensure that the question submitted is dealt with according to the terms of the collective agreement.

Generally, it is conceded that bias, or interest on the part of the arbitrator in the outcome of the case, or reasonable fear thereof, may justify a court either in prohibiting an arbitrator from proceeding or in setting aside an award which has been rendered. Bribery, fraud, and corruption would also be grounds for questioning impartiality.

Procedural defects encompass a number of irregularities. For example, an arbitrator who does not permit all interested parties to participate in the arbitration process may be found guilty of denying the parties natural justice. In addition, such rulings as the refusal to permit cross-examination or the exclusion of admissible and relevant evidence, may result in the decision being reviewed and quashed if a substantial injustice has resulted therefrom. *Ex parte* fact-finding by an arbitrator (i.e., the taking of evidence in the absence of one of the parties of interest) may also result in the quashing of an award.

An error of law on the face of the award is somewhat difficult to explain. The legal definition of an error of law is an error in the application or interpretation of some legal standard, statutory or otherwise. Since questions of interpretation of collective agreements have always been viewed as questions of law in most jurisdictions in Canada, a court will review an arbitrator's interpretation of provisions in a collective agreement with a view to assuring itself that is is a plausible construction (understanding) of the document. The court itself may not agree with the arbitrator's interpretation but, if it finds that the construction is a "reasonable one" (i.e., one that would be made by a reasonable person), it will not necessarily quash the award.

An arbitrator may also commit an error of law if he or she misconceives that law. For example, if the Ontario *Labour Relations Act* indicates the applicability of a directive to both union and workers, the arbitrator who applies such a directive to only one of the parties will be committing an error of law.[28]The term *on the face of the award (or record)* is a time-honoured formulation which conveys no precise legal meaning in grievance proceedings, but is merely a way of referring to the documentation upon which an arbitrator bases his decision. A court upon finding that an award is defective may quash it, set it aside, or send it back to the arbitrator for reconsideration. Wherever possible, the latter course is followed.

Criticisms of the Traditional Form of Arbitration

The conventional form of grievance handling and arbitration has been severely criticized by unions, management, academics, and many practitioners as a time-consuming process that may require the parties to wait years for a final arbitration award. In addition, the traditional arbitration process tends to be a very expensive proposition, particularly for small companies and unions with limited financial resources. The process has also been criticized on the grounds that many arbitrators write lengthy dissertations in formulating their awards and rationales. This not only increases costs, but also deprives the grievor of a swift determination of the case.

One of the major reasons for the long delay and expense occasioned by arbitration is that about 10% of the arbitrators do about 90% of the work. This means that cases must be booked for arbitration hearings many months in advance because the arbitrator whom the parties want is not available until that time. Another major difficulty is to get more and younger arbitrators into the field. Parties generally prefer an experienced individual, well-versed in the arbitration process and familiar with the jurisprudence. Novices to the arbitration field may have neither the technical qualifications and expertise to rule on many of the issues that come up during an arbitration hearing, nor the background necessary to understand the kind of award that would

be appropriate to the collective agreement and industry.

Despite these criticisms, conventional arbitration is certainly much better than using the courts as a vehicle for resolving problems between unions and management; for, although the courts should review arbitration awards to safeguard the system, they are no substitute for the grievance procedure and arbitration as it is practised on the North American continent.

Expedited Arbitration

In 1971, the ten major American steel companies and the United Steelworkers Union adopted an expedited arbitration procedure on an experimental basis. This procedure is designed to deal with routine grievances and ordinary discipline cases. Grievance cases are presented by local union people and companies are usually represented by industrial relations personnel. High-echelon personnel who normally present arbitration cases do not participate in the expedited arbitration process. Furthermore, it is well understood by the parties to expedited arbitration that any decisions resulting therefrom do not form precedents for the normal arbitration process.

Workers and management in the American steel industry were so impressed with the expedited arbitration procedure that they have included it in all agreements since 1971. Now, some 200 panel members are assigned to various local centres. Each panel has an administrator who assigns panel members to cases in alphabetical rotation depending on their availability for the time and place designated by the local union and management people — the people who decide which cases go through this procedure and who handle the cases at the hearing. Hearings are kept informal, no briefs are presented and no transcripts made. Arbitrators present awards within forty-eight hours after completion of the hearing.

This new procedure has not only resulted in prompter decisions, but has allowed arbitrators to examine *in situ* the particular conditions under which the grievance was submitted. Costs have been reduced substantially. Most importantly, more grievances can be settled at the lower levels, thereby decreasing the number of cases reaching the regular arbitration stage.[29]

Lawrence Stessin, writing in 1977, stated that more than 500 companies and unions use expedited arbitration. He observed that it is rare for a case channelled through the expedited route to stay on the books for more than sixty days. In addition, in most expedited procedures, the arbitrators are formally charged with the duty of rendering their opinions by the next day.[30]

Examples of Expedited Arbitration in Canada[31] The United Steelworkers of America and the International Nickel Company of Canada Limited have a form of expedited arbitration, called the Grievance Commissioner's procedure, which is in effect at both the Sudbury and Port Colborne operations. Two Grievance Commissioners act as sole arbitrators and serve alternatively on a monthly basis. Hearings are held on the third Thursday of each month, but are only convened if there are at least four cases outstanding. Once a grievance has been processed through the regular procedure without being resolved, the union's general grievance committee and the company's industrial relations supervisors meet to determine if it should be heard by a regular tripartite arbitration board or if expedited arbitration will be used. Expedited arbitration may be chosen only by mutual consent of the parties. Failing such consent the grievance must undergo regular arbitration.

The Grievance Commissioner procedure is a very informal one. Not less than ten days prior to the hearing, the Commissioner is provided with a copy of the grievance, a written summary of the stage-two grievance meeting which outlines the facts agreed to, the facts in dispute, the union's position, and the company's position, and a copy of the written decision of the management representative at stages two and three of the grievance procedure. In addition, the parties supply brief written arguments supporting their position.

The purpose of the hearing is solely to clarify issues or facts in dispute. Usually, no witnesses are called; the written material generally serves as the basis of a decision, although the parties may make further representations or present such evidence as the Commissioner may permit or require. There is, however, no obligation to conform to strict rules of evidence. A written decision must be rendered within seven days of the hearing. Brief reasons for the award accompany but do not form part of the award. The parties understand that decisions in the Grievance Commissioner procedure establish no legal precedents.

In 1977, the cost of the Grievance Commissioner procedure averaged $242 per case which meant that it cost each party $121 for each case. The Commissioner's cost is based on a sliding-scale cost structure which includes $400 for a fixed hearing on which no cases are heard. However, when cases are heard, the charge in 1977 was $650 for the first case, $150 for the second and third cases, and $100 for the fourth and subsequent cases. Six grievances were presented during the first Commission hearing which took place on February 1, 1973. During the next thirty-seven hearings, a total of 192 grievances were heard.[32]

Another example of expedited arbitration in Canada is that of the British Columbia Maritime Employers' Association and the International Longshoremen's and Warehousemen's Union procedure for handling urgent grievances. These involve safety on the job, handling of damaged cargo, or situations where a work slowdown or stoppage is in effect. These cases are referred to a job arbitrator for a summary disposition. The job arbitrator serves on a full-time basis and possesses practical waterfront experience. He is empowered, when requested by either party, to render oral dispositions on the spot. The oral award is immediately effective and binding on the parties, but is confirmed in writing as soon as practical thereafter, usually within forty-eight hours.

The summary disposition is generally a short award that takes into account the background of the case, the positions of both parties and the appropriate clauses of the collective agreement. The job arbitrator is paid a retainer of approximately $2000 per month, the cost of which is shared equally by the parties. This stipend is modest considering that the job arbitrator must be available twenty-four hours a day and may be called at any time by either of the parties. An alternate job arbitrator may be called in when the full-time job arbitrator is on vacation or not available.

Should either of the parties request a rehearing of a matter on which the job arbitrator has rendered a decision, the question is referred to the Joint Industry Labour Relations Committee on which both labour and management representatives sit in equal numbers. Such rehearings are rare. The Committee, moreover, has set aside only a small number of decisions rendered by the job arbitrator.[33]

Expedited arbitration can be tailored to each industry in which it is used and is eminently well-suited for handling relatively routine types of grievances. It may also be used for handling discipline and discharge cases in which quick decisions are usually desirable. In complex discharge cases, which involve the testimony of witnesses, the regular arbitration process may be more appropriate than the expedited form. It also appears that the regular arbitration process will continue to play an important role in resolving major disputes between the parties over the interpretation, application, or alleged violations of collective agreements. Policy issues, such as contracting out, should not be dealt with in expedited arbitration proceedings.

One benefit of the expedited arbitration process is that it encourages people interested in arbitration to become active in this field and thereby gain the experience required to handle more complex cases. The resulting increase in the availability of arbitrators might serve to reduce the cost and delays currently associated with regular arbitration.

Expedited Arbitration in Ontario and Manitoba During the Summer of 1979, the Ontario government passed legislation which provides for a form of expedited arbitration. Bill 25 amended the Ontario *Labour Relations Act* by adding Section 45. Under the new section, a party to a collective agreement may request the Minister to appoint a single arbitrator. This individual may then attempt to resolve a dispute regarding the interpretation, application, administration or alleged violation of an agreement. A request may be made for the appointment of a single arbitrator after the grievance procedure under the collective agreement has been exhausted or after thirty days have elapsed from the time the grievance was first brought to the attention of the other party, whichever occurs first. In the case of a grievance concerning discharge, an application may be made after the grievance procedure set out in the agreement has been exhausted or after fourteen days have elapsed from the time at which the grievance was first brought to the attention of the other party, whichever occurs first.

Under subsection 6, the Minister may appoint a settlement officer to confer with the parties and endeavour to bring about an agreement prior to the hearing of an arbitrator. An extremely important provision of the amendment is subsection 7 under which an arbitrator shall commence to hear the matter referred to him within twenty-one days after the receipt of the request for an arbitrator to be appointed by the Minister. Furthermore, subsection 8 provides that upon agreement of the parties, the arbitrator shall deliver an oral decision forthwith, or as soon as practicable, without giving his reasons in writing for the decision.

During the Summer of 1984, Manitoba added

to its *Labour Relations Act* a form of expedited arbitration based largely on Section 45 of the Ontario *Labour Relations Act*. Manitoba, however, also makes provision for the appointment of a grievance mediator on the joint application of the parties. The function of the grievance mediator is to assist the parties in resolving their differences over the meaning, application or alleged violation of a collective agreement. The Manitoba statute also provides for a grievance mediator to be named in the collective agreement.

Under the expedited form of arbitration provided for in the Manitoba *Labour Relations Act*, a bargaining agent or an employer may apply to the Labour Relations Board for the appointment of an arbitrator. Where a worker has been suspended for a period of over thirty days or dismissed, the bargaining agent may apply to the Board for the appointment of an arbitrator when the grievance procedure has been exhausted or when fourteen days have elapsed from the time that the grievance was first brought to the party's attention. In other cases, an application may be made when the grievance procedure is exhausted or thirty days from the date on which the party heard of the grievance. The Board shall then appoint an arbitrator within twenty-eight days from the date the grievance was referred.

The Board may also appoint a grievance mediator to assist the parties prior to the appointment of an arbitrator. The grievance mediator under the Manitoba legislation is similar to the settlement officer under the Ontario legislation. The arbitrator appointed under the Manitoba legislation must render a decision within fourteen days after the conclusion of the hearing in the case of dismissal or suspension of over thirty days, and within twenty-eight days in other cases.[34]

When jointly requested to do so, the arbitrator shall issue an oral decision within one day after concluding the arbitration hearing. Written reasons shall be issued within fourteen days in cases of discharge or suspension of over thirty days, and within twenty-eight days in other cases.

Since Ontario passed its expedited form of arbitration, many cases have gone that route. The same is expected to occur in Manitoba. And, while no big rush is evident among the other jurisdictions to enact a form of expedited arbitration, one may speculate that they will follow the examples of Ontario and Manitoba.

A further incentive for the use of quicker forms of arbitration was revealed in a major study of arbitration in Ontario discharge cases. This study found that, the sooner the case was heard after a discharge, the more likely the discharged worker was to be reinstated:

> [W]here the hearing was held within three months, 42 percent of the grievors were reinstated with a lesser penalty; 29 percent were completely exonerated; and 29 percent were not reinstated. However, where the hearing was held more than nine months after the discharge, 74 percent of the grievors were not reinstated; 21 percent received a lesser penalty; and 5 percent were completely exonerated.[35]

Relations-by-Objectives

In 1975, the Federal Mediation and Conciliation Service (FMCS) in the United States adopted "Relations-by-Objectives" (RBO), a new voluntary approach designed to improve poor union-management relations by involving key labour and management leaders in resolving problems at all organizational levels. The FMCS first seeks a commitment from both sides to attempt to resolve lingering divisive issues. In return for this commitment, the FMCS agrees to work with the parties on a long-term basis.

Members from management and unions formulate objectives relevant to what they consider mutual problems. The members are split up into joint groups or teams. Each group is given a specific set of problems to solve with an agreed-upon timetable. Periodic checks on progress are made by FMCS mediators. If necessary, additional counselling services are offered.

The key to the RBO process is its focus. The process enlists the support not only of senior union and management people, but also of participants at the plant level where the actual problems occur. Hence, the FMCS mediators can aim to improve communication at all levels from senior echelons to shop floor. A number of groups from a variety of industries and services have successfully used this new approach.[36]

The FMCS is very active in helping to establish labour-management committees to deal with problems on an ongoing basis. Training programs are provided for shop stewards and supervisors to help improve day-to-day working relationships. The success of such programs is evidenced by the fact that, in 1979, the FMCS mediators were involved with 1,591 technical assistance programs, the largest number for any year since these programs were started.[37]

Through the use of labour-management committees and RBO programs, FMCS mediators in hundreds of cases have helped labour and management to bring a cooperative and problem-solving attitude to the workplace. The efforts have included organizations in the private sector as well as in the public and parapublic sectors, such as health care and education. Many positive results have been attributed to RBO, including declines in the number of grievances, arbitration cases, and wildcat strikes, as well as the early and amiable settlement of contracts and general improvement in labour-management relations.[38]

Following the lead of the FMCS, a number of Canadian agencies are now designing programs to encourage the parties, during the term of the collective agreement, to adopt more cooperative attitudes and to tackle problems of a long-standing nature.

Grievances and Arbitration of Rights Disputes in the Public Sector

Although there have been various types of appeal procedures for public servants for many years under the auspices of public service commissions, it was only with the advent of collective bargaining in the public sector that arbitration (often referred to as adjudication which is the term that will be used in this section) of rights disputes became available to public-sector workers. Adjudication has not done away entirely with various types of appeals still subject to public service commissions, such as the protection of the merit principle in some matters including appointments, promotions, transfers, and termination of employment for lack of competence. Since the phenomenon of a collective bargaining regime for public-sector workers is relatively new, there is a paucity of information on the subject.[39]

What we shall attempt to do in the next few pages, therefore, is to outline the types of adjudication tribunals which exist in a few jurisdictions, some aspects of public-sector adjudication unique to that sector, an example of one of the challenges with which adjudicators have had to contend, and the development of grievance mediation which had its origin in the public sector.

The various jurisdictions in Canada have taken different approaches for handling grievances in the public sector. The private-sector model of appointing *ad hoc* arbitrators has been adopted in the public sector of Nova Scotia. Here, the Civil Service Employee Relations Board appoints an adjudicator where the parties have agreed on one, or if the parties cannot agree upon one. In British Columbia, the Labour Relations Board makes appointments from a panel whose members are selected by the parties. In Alberta, the parties have made provision in their collective agreement for a Public Service Grievance Board with a chairman and a number of vice-chairmen. The federal, Ontario and New Brunswick statutes provide for panels of adjudicators. Under the federal *Public Service Staff Relations Act (PSSRA)*, adjudication is usually carried out by a single adjudicator who is either a full- or part-time member of the Public Service Staff Relations Board (PSSRB). One of its three deputy chairmen administers the adjudication system. The parties may use a tripartite board of adjudication under the federal *Act*, but so far they have not elected to do so. The Ontario *Crown Employees Collective Bargaining Act* provides for a Crown Employees Grievance Settlement Board which is made up of a panel of neutral adjudicators, plus panels of employer and union nominees.[40]

K. Swinton points out several advantages to the use of a panel of adjudicators. These advantages include the speedier handling of cases, since no time is lost in searching for chairmen, and a greater consistency between decisions. This consistency may be jeopardized, however, if the panels become too large. Also, during the early phase of a collective bargaining regime, the adjudicators may play an educational role for inexperienced parties.[41] Part-time Federal and Ontario adjudicators operate in both the private and public sectors.

In some ways, adjudication in the public sector is different from arbitration in the private sector. One major difference is that, in the public sector, a statute may confer a right on an individual to have a grievance taken all the way to adjudication. No such legislative right exists in the private sector. Private-sector grievances relate solely to the interpretation, application, or alleged violation of the terms of a collective agreement.

One example of a situation where a statute confers a right to the grievance process and adjudication in the public sector is contained in sections 90 and 91 of the *PSSRA*—which will be discussed in detail in Chapter 10. In effect, these provisions say that if a person feels aggrieved by the application of a statute, regulation, provision of a collective agreement, or arbitral award, the grievance may be addressed to all levels of the grievance procedure, including adjudication if there is no other administrative procedure for redress. If the case involves the interpretation of a collective agreement or arbitral award, the worker must have the support of the bargaining agent. All workers who have been subject to disciplinary action resulting in discharge, suspension, or financial penalty may take their cases all the way to adjudication, and

may be represented by a bargaining agent, irrespective of whether or not the worker is a member of a bargaining unit.

When a person accepts a position in a public service, that person is on probation for a specified period of time, which may range from six months to two years in the federal public service. The same applies if a person is promoted to a higher level in the same classification. Workers are seldom aware of this fact, however. Let us assume that, before the end of the probationary period, the person is discharged on the ground of incompetence. The worker, however, may feel that he or she is being disciplined rather than dismissed. In this situation, the individual may take the case to arbitration, with or without the assistance of a bargaining agent. There are similar provisions, or what is referred to as "critical job interests," in the Ontario and other statutes.[42]

The employer will often argue that an adjudicator has no jurisdiction to hear such cases. Writers J. Finkelman and S. Goldenberg, however, disagree:

> [F]rom the outset adjudicators [under the *PSSRA*] have taken the position that they are entitled to entertain a grievance by an employee who has been rejected by a deputy head during the probationary period in order to ascertain whether the termination of employment really constituted disciplinary action resulting in discharge.[43]

Where adjudicators have found that the person was discharged, they have ordered reinstatement, sometimes with an extension of the probationary period. In other cases, financial compensation has been awarded.[44] The courts have generally upheld such action by public-sector adjudicators.

Another important difference between arbitration in the private and public sectors is that the concept of public interest may arise in public-sector cases. For example, if a worker in a home for retarded persons should spontaneously hit a patient, should that worker be dismissed or given a lesser penalty? Such cases are likely to attract media attention. In addition, not only the public interest but also employer interests may be involved. A competing concern exists in such cases, particularly when workers have records of long and competent service. While arbitrators are acutely aware of the delicate nature of such cases, "they have adopted the jurisprudence of progressive discipline from the private sector, even where that has been controversial."[45] Apart from the type of legislated right discussed above, which is rather unique to the public sector, jurisprudence in the public sector is very much the same as that in the private sector.

As indicated earlier, one of the things found in the public sector is the use of mediation in grievance cases. Between 1980 and 1981, there was quite a backlog of cases in the Post Office. Two special tripartite committees, each chaired by a mediator/adjudicator, were appointed on a one-time basis to resolve the outstanding cases. In Ontario, there has been continuous grievance mediation since 1979 when one vice-chairman was appointed specifically for that purpose. While he hears no cases, he meets regularly with the parties in an attempt to settle and consolidate cases of the same nature. While his success is difficult to measure, a substantial number of cases has been withdrawn in recent years, and this reduction is attributable in large measure to his efforts.[46]

Grievance mediation, while not used in the Canadian private sector, is used fairly extensively in the United States in both the private and public sectors.[47] The reason for its more widespread use in the public sector is because of the large number of grievances to be processed, and also because it is a speedier and less costly way of dealing with large numbers of grievances. An informal poll conducted in Michigan in 1978 showed that mediators from the

Federal Conciliation and Mediation Service and from the state agency had very high success rates—well over 80%![48] In the United States, widespread use of grievance mediation occurs on an *ad hoc* basis, and some parties are including it as a part of their regular grievance procedures. Grievance mediation is not perceived as a substitute for arbitration, but as an important step in the grievance procedure. It is quite possible, moreover, that grievance mediation will help remove some of the high degree of legalism from the grievance process, and perhaps result in a more clinical approach to grievance handling.

Conclusion

In this chapter, the pros and cons of the grievance process have been discussed as well as those of formal arbitration. Also outlined were the steps in an expedited form of arbitration which seems to be gaining acceptance in the labour-management field. Examples of this form of arbitration are found in recent amendments to the Ontario and Manitoba *Labour Relations Acts*. These amendments provide for expedited arbitration, not only of discharge cases, but of any type of grievance. The techniques of the Relations-by-Objectives program were examined to illustrate another approach to improving difficult union-management relations. Finally, there was a discussion of arbitration (adjudication) in the public sector, distinguishing it from private-sector arbitration. In addition, we looked at grievance mediation in the public sector and saw that this kind of mediation might foreshadow things to come in both the public and private sectors.

questions

1 What is the major objective of the grievance process?
2 What is the nature of clauses in collective agreements that lead to the filing of grievances, some of which go all the way to arbitration as the final stage?
3 What are the pros and cons of the legalistic vs. the clinical approach to resolving grievances?

4 Arbitration as the final step in the grievance procedure is the *quid pro quo* for no-strike and no-lockout provisions during the life of collective agreements as required by the statutes in all Canadian jurisdictions. What is your assessment of this arrangement?

5 What is meant by the "submission to arbitrate" and the nature of the burden of proof in arbitration decisions?

6 Assume that you will be conducting your first arbitration hearing tomorrow. What factors will you take into account in conducting the hearing and the rendering of your award to assure that it will not be overturned by a court?

7 What is your assessment of expedited arbitration as an alternative to the traditional arbitration process? What kinds of grievances lend themselves best to this procedure?

8 Do you think that the differences between arbitration in the private sector and adjudication in the public sector are significant? Do those things which are unique to the public sector pose problems for adjudicators in that sector? Elaborate on both questions.

9 Do you think that there should be a total ban on strikes and lockouts during the life of collective agreements, or are there some issues on which the parties should have the right to strike or lockout? Elaborate.

10 There were a number of references in the chapter to "judicial review" of arbitration cases. Do you think that courts, which often lack members with expertise in industrial relations, should have the right to review decisions made by experts? Elaborate.

notes

1 N. W. Chamberlain and James W. Kuhn, *Collective Bargaining,* 2nd ed. (New York: McGraw-Hill Book Company, 1965), p. 141.

2 James W. Kuhn, "The Grievance Process," *Frontiers of Collective Bargaining,* eds. J. T. Dunlop and N. W. Chamberlain (New York: Harper & Row, Publishers, 1967), p. 257.

3 *Ibid.,* pp. 252-70.

4 *Ibid.,* p. 256.

5 F. Elkouri and E. A. Elkouri, *How Arbitration Works,* 3rd. ed. (Washington: The Bureau of National Affairs, Incorporated, 1973), p. 15.

6 *Ibid.*

7 Bora Laskin, "Legal Issues in Labour Relations: Some Problems of Arbitration," *Labour Relations Trends: Retrospect and Prospect,* ed. H. D. Woods, Proceedings of the Tenth Annual Conference of the McGill Industrial Relations Centre (Sept. 11-12, 1958), p. 27.

8 For those wishing to see a more complete statement on the advantages and disadvantages of different types of arbitration tribunals, see Elkouri and Elkouri, Ch. 4, *How Arbitration Works.*

9 C. H. Curtis, *Labour Arbitration Procedures* (Kingston: Industrial Relations Centre, Queen's University, 1957), p. 45.

10 Wilfred List, "Ontario Grievance Bill Touches Raw Nerve," *The Globe and Mail* (May 14, 1979), p. B5.

11 D. J. M. Brown and D. M. Beatty, *Canadian Labour Arbitration,* 2nd ed. (Aurora: Canada Law Book Limited, 1984), pp. 9-10. For the second

of the two excellent books referred to in the text, see E. E. Palmer, *Collective Agreement Arbitration,* 2nd ed. (Toronto: Butterworth & Co. (Canada) Ltd., 1983).

12 James W. Kuhn, "The Grievance Procedure," p. 259.

13 Brown and Beatty, *Canadian Labour Arbitration,* pp. 29-30. For an excellent discussion on the procedures of arbitration, see A. W. R. Carrothers, Ch. 4, *Labour Arbitration in Canada* (Toronto: Butterworths, 1961). This book is the first major book on arbitration in Canada.

14 For a more detailed analysis, see Brown and Beatty, *Canadian Labour Arbitration,* pp. 58-59; Palmer, *Collective Agreement Arbitration in Canada,* pp. 28-34; Paul Praslow and Edward Peters, *Arbitration and Collective Bargaining: Conflict Resolution and Labor Relations* (New York: McGraw-Hill Book Company, 1970), pp. 17-28.

15 Palmer, *Collective Agreement Arbitration in Canada,* pp. 22-28; and John P. Sanderson, Q.C., *Labour Arbitration and All That* (Toronto: Richard De Boo Limited, 1976), pp. 45-50.

16 Brown and Beatty, *Canadian Labour Arbitration,* pp. 129-30.

17 *Ibid.,* p. 142.

18 Palmer, *Collective Agreement Arbitration in Canada,* pp. 268-71; Brown and Beatty, *Canadian Labour Arbitration,* p. 133.

19 Brown and Beatty, *Canadian Labour Arbitration,* p. 154. Brown and Beatty also differentiate between latent or patent ambiguity. Basically, a patent ambiguity is one that appears on the

face of the agreement, whereas a latent ambiguity exists where it is not apparent on the face of the agreement.

20 Palmer, *Collective Agreement Arbitration in Canada,* p. 83.

21 Brown and Beatty, *Canadian Labour Arbitration,* pp. 330-31.

22 Palmer, *Collective Agreement Arbitration in Canada,* pp. 234-35.

23 S. J. Rosen, "How Arbitrators View Just Cause," Twenty-Fifty Annual Meeting of the IRRA, *Proceedings* (Madison: 1983), p. 133.

24 *Re: United Steelworkers of America, Local 3257 and the Steel Equipment Co. Ltd. (1964), 14 L.A.C. 356,* quoted in Labour Relations Law Casebook Group, *Labour Relations Law: Cases, Material and Commentary* (Kingston: Industrial Relations Centre, Queen's University, 1970), pp. 262-63. For a much more complete discussion of the above mentioned topics, see Palmer, pp. 215-34, and Brown and Beatty, pp. 361-84.

25 *Port Arthur Shipbuilding Co. v. Arthurs* (1968), D.L.R. (2d) 693, quoted in Labour Relations Law Casebook Group, *Labour Relations Law,* p. 293.

26 *Ontario Labour Relations Act,* R.S.O., 1980, c. 228, s. 44(9).

27 *Ontario Labour Relations Act,* R.S.O., 1980, c. 228, s. 44(11).

28 Brown and Beatty, *Canadian Labour Arbitration,* pp. 31-42.

29 For more details on this procedure, see "Expedited Arbitration Breaks Grievance Log Jam," *Steel Labour* (April 1973); Ben Fischer, "The Steel Industry's Expedited Arbitration: A Judgement After Two Years," *Arbitration Journal* (September 1973), pp. 185-90.

30 Lawrence Stessin, "Expedited Arbitration: Less Grief Over Grievances," *Harvard Business Review* (January-February 1977), pp. 128-34.

31 Those who wish to study the Canadian industries which have some form of expedited arbitration should refer to the following two documents: Federal Mediation and Conciliation Service, Labour Canada, *Industry and Expedited Arbitration: Alternatives to Traditional Methods* (Ottawa: Supply and Services Canada, 1978); *Expedited Arbitration — An Alternative* (Mon-treal: McGill University, Industrial Relations Centre, 1977).

32 *Industry and Expedited Arbitration,* pp. 18-21; *Expedited Arbitration — An Alternative,* pp. 101-05.

33 *Ibid.,* pp. 14-18; pp. 96-100.

34 *Manitoba Labour Relations Act,* s. 113.5(10).

35 George W. Adams, *Grievance Arbitration of Discharge Cases: A Study of the Concepts of Industrial Discipline and Their Results* (Kingston: Industrial Relations Centre, Queen's University, Research and Current Issues Series, No. 38, 1978) p. 50.

36 For a brief description of how RBO works, see Vol. 1, No. 7, *World of Work Report* (September 1976). Also for a brief summary of the results of these and other FMCS programs, see U.S. Federal Mediation and Conciliation Service, *Annual Report* (1975-1979), in particular the chapters on technical assistance.

37 U.S. Federal Mediation and Conciliation Service, *Annual Report* (1979), p. 28.

38 *Ibid.,* p. 19.

39 For two good Canadian articles, see K. Swinton, "Grievance Arbitration in the Public Sector," *Conflict or Compromise: The Future of Public Sector Industrial Relations,* eds. M. Thompson and G. Swimmer (Montreal: The Institute for Research on Public Policy, 1984), pp. 343-71; and J. Finkelman and S. Goldenberg, Chs. 11, 12, *Collective Bargaining in the Public Sector: The Federal Experience in Canada* (Montreal: The Institute for Research on Public Policy, 1983).

40 Swinton, "Grievance Arbitration in the Public Sector," pp. 344-45.

41 *Ibid.,* pp. 345-48.

42 *Ibid.,* p. 350.

43 Finkelman and Goldenberg, *Collective Bargaining in the Public Sector,* p. 589.

44 *Ibid.,* 590.

45 Swinton, "Grievance Arbitration in the Public Sector," p. 359.

46 *Ibid.,* p. 348.

47 G. A. Gregory and R. E. Rooney, Jr., "Grievance Mediation: A Trend in the Cost-Conscious Eighties," Spring Meeting of the IRRA, *Proceedings* (Madison: 1980), pp. 502-08.

48 *Ibid.,* p. 507.

10

Collective Bargaining in the Public and Parapublic Sectors

Peter Redman, *The Financial Post*

Introduction

In recent years, collective bargaining for workers in the public and parapublic sectors has become a major topic in the field of industrial relations in both Canada and the United States. It is of great concern to policy-makers, administrators, academics, journalists and, perhaps most importantly, to the public at large. In this chapter, collective bargaining in the public and parapublic sectors is treated as two separate but related topics. The term *parapublic sector* includes such groups as teachers, health-care workers, firefighters, and police officers. These groups are considered parapublic workers since they are not directly employed by governments, but by organizations which are extensively supported by government funding.

Our discussion of collective bargaining in the public sector will begin with an analysis of the provisions governing federal and provincial government workers. This analysis will be followed by a consideration of collective bargaining among municipal workers. The chapter will conclude with a comparison of collective bargaining among teachers and health-care workers in several provinces.

After a brief discussion of the history of

federal and provincial public-sector collective bargaining and the federal sovereignty issue, we will proceed to discuss the actors. The legislative provisions governing federal and provincial workers may be discussed most usefully in terms of the three types of classical disputes covered in Chapter 6: recognition, contract negotiation, and contract interpretation disputes. Table 10.4 provides a "road map" for our discussion of federal and provincial bargaining.

The Historical Development of Collective Bargaining Among Federal and Provincial Workers

With the exception of Saskatchewan which, in 1944, granted collective bargaining rights to both government and private-sector workers, no other Canadian government gave collective bargaining rights to provincial or federal workers until the mid-1960's. At present, the Federal Government and all provincial governments grant collective bargaining rights to their workers. This contrasts with the American situation where many states still do not permit collective bargaining in their public or parapublic sectors or both.

Apart from Saskatchewan, the first jurisdiction in Canada to accord collective bargaining rights was the province of Quebec which amended its Labour Code in 1964 to include professional and other government workers. However, what has been termed the "boldest experiment" occurred in 1967 when the Federal Government passed the *Public Service Staff Relations Act*. This *Act* gave collective bargaining rights to workers in federal departments and a number of federal agencies. Following the passage of this legislation, the remaining provincial jurisdictions have given public-service workers the right to collective bargaining, including right-to-strike or arbitration provisions. With the exception of

Manitoba, Quebec, and Prince Edward Island, all provinces have special public-sector labour statutes. Manitoba and Prince Edward Island have given their workers the right to collective bargaining but have done so through their respective civil service statutes. In Quebec, workers in the public and parapublic sectors come under the Quebec Labour Code. Some provisions in this code are unique.

Sovereignty Issue

The historical resistance to collective bargaining in the federal public service was based largely on the principle of the sovereignty of the state. Collective bargaining and the right to strike were considered incompatible with this principle and with the essential nature of many government services.[1] W. B. Cunningham, writing in 1966, contended that conventional wisdom in the United States and Canada viewed the advent of collective bargaining in the public service as unnecessary, impractical, illegal, and supportive of the notion that the sovereign state "cannot be compelled by lesser bodies to do anything that it chooses not to do, and it cannot enter into contract arrangements that bind its freedom to exercise its sovereign power in the future."[2] American writer R. W. Fleming recently asserted that the original debate over whether public-sector workers should be permitted to organize and bargain is over. He went on to say that "Remnants of it [the sovereignty issue] persist, and there are jurisdictions where there is no such right, but in the overall the battle is now on a different front."[3]

Another important aspect of the whole question of public-sector collective bargaining is the delegation to arbitration boards of the power to make binding decisions. Canadian scholar Kenneth P. Swan, aware of both American and Canadian jurisprudence, claims that "[a] clear majority of judicial pronouncements [in the United States] have rejected constitutional objections to the validity of compulsory binding interest arbitration statutes, but the opposition is not entirely routed, and ammunition for further assaults is readily available."[4] Overall, however, it would now appear that the sovereignty argument carries little weight and that public-sector collective bargaining, at least in Canada, is likely to continue.

The Actors in Public Sector Bargaining

In every industrial relations system in which workers are unionized, there are three major actors: (1) the union or unions, (2) those bodies designated to represent the government as employer, and (3) the administrative tribunals which help to regulate the relations between the first two.

Unionism at the Federal Level

Worker organizations in the Federal Government existed long before the emergence of collective bargaining in the late 1960's. Many of these organizations acted as consultative bodies through the National Joint Council created in 1944, in which employer and worker organizations were represented equally. The Council dealt with several matters, one of which was salary. In the late 1950's and early 1960's, worker organizations and the Public Service Commission often consulted and agreed on salary increases. Their recommendations, however, were frequently ignored by the Treasury Board.[5] The *Public Service Staff Relations Act (PSSRA)* in 1967 encouraged an increase in unionism and collective bargaining. It is claimed that worker organizations in the federal public sector now bargain on behalf of more than 95% of eligible federal public servants.[6]

Union membership at the federal level increased by 200% between 1966 and 1970, doubling in 1967. However, the rate of growth from 1970 to 1981 increased an average of less than 4% each year, levelling off in 1977.[7] This growth resulted for the most part in the certification of existing units. Some recruiting took place also among unorganized groups. Clerical and stenographic groups were particularly difficult to organize. Union organizers felt that, because clerical and stenographic workers at that time were mostly young married women whose involvement with the industrial relations system tended to be limited to those years preceding periods of full-time childrearing, unions appeared low on the scale of needs experienced by members of this group.

Many of the present unions arose out of earlier worker associations—for example, the Civil Service Federation of Canada (CSFC), which had its origin in 1909. The original CSFC membership of 5,223 grew to 80,000 in 1958. The Civil Service Association of Canada (CSAC), which resulted from a breakaway from the CSFC, had a membership of 33,000 in 1966.[8] These two associations are singled out because it was their merger in 1967 which resulted in the formation of the Public Service Alliance of Canada (PSAC) with a membership of over 181,460 in 1985.[9] The PSAC, now the third largest union in the Canadian Labour Congress, represents a very large majority of all federal public servants. Its structure is complex with seventeen components, each with its own elected officers. While the components are organized along departmental lines[10], the bargaining units in the federal public service are organized along occupational lines. Hence, a number of departmental components may have a keen interest in negotiations for occupational units. The components perform an important function by helping their members to handle grievances. Some PSAC components are strong; others are weak—and the fair management of these unequal components is difficult.

Seventeen unions represent federal public servants. The Professional Institute of the Public Service of Canada (PIPS) was established to represent professional workers. PIPS has shrunk in recent years with the establishment of The Economists', Sociologists' and Statisticians' Association (ESSA) and several other groups which formerly belonged to PIPS. One of the more militant federal unions is the Canadian Union of Postal Workers (CUPW). This union now operates under Part V of the Canada Labour Code since Canada Post is now a crown corporation. The Canadian Air Traffic Control Association, with a membership of about 2,300, will likely have a lot of clout unless all air traffic controllers are designated as essential workers in future disputes as they were during the last round.

Unionism at the Provincial Level

The organization of provincial workers is similar to that at the federal level. Most provincial government workers had associations which were concerned mainly with social and recreational activities, although they sometimes acted as pressure groups to improve general welfare and working conditions. By 1966, membership in these associations was over 90,000.[11] Membership increased steadily during the 1970's and, by 1978, there were more workers in unions at the provincial level than at the federal level.[12]

In the early stages of the CLC, some provincial associations, such as the British Columbia Employees' Association (BCEA), were affiliated directly with the CLC. This caused strained relations between the PSAC and CUPE, each of which wanted to incorporate these provincial associations. To circumvent this problem, the National Union of Provincial Government Employees (NUPGE) was formed in 1976, thus removing these workers from the realm of competition between the PSAC and CUPE. All provincial associations, including those which had been directly affiliated with the CLC but excluding those of New Brunswick and Quebec, are now affiliated through this umbrella union.[13] In 1985, NUPGE was the second largest union in Canada with a membership of close to 245,000—a figure considerably higher than that

for the PSAC with its more than 181,460 members.[14]

It is interesting to note that bargaining rights were acquired by statutory recognition in six provinces.[15] When bargaining rights were granted to public servants in Quebec in 1964, the Quebec Government Employees' Union was designated by statute as the bargaining agent for clerical and blue-collar employees.[16] The apparent unevenness in the growth of unions at the provincial level has been due in part to the practice whereby union members are included in the statistics only when collective bargaining rights have been accorded these members.

In concluding this section, it seems fair to say that favourable government legislation was the major catalyst in the phenomenal growth of unionization in the federal and provincial public sectors. In fact, it is quite possible that the saturation point in union growth may now have been reached in these sectors.

Public-Sector Employers

When a government gives collective bargaining rights to its public servants, one major problem is that of determining which government agency is the employer. A number of options exist, the most notable of which have been to vest authority with the Treasury Board or the Public Service Commission. In the cases of the Federal Government and New Brunswick, authority is vested in the treasury boards of the two governments. The Ontario statute designates "the management board of cabinet" as the employer. Newfoundland defines the government negotiator as the president of the Treasury Board, or such other person authorized by him to bargain under his control and supervision on behalf of the employer. Prince Edward Island regulations specify that Her Majesty the Queen in right of the province shall be represented by such person as may be designated by the Treasury Board. Nova Scotia designates its Public Service Commission as the employer.

All public-sector negotiations at the provincial level in Quebec are conducted with the government as the major actor on one side of the bargaining table and a common front of public-service unions on the other side.[17] The Alberta, Saskatchewan, and Manitoba statutes make no specific reference to the body responsible for negotiations on behalf of public servants. However, as pointed out by a number of authors, the Public Service Commission is the negotiating authority in the province of Saskatchewan.[18]

A major problem with negotiations in the public sector is to name a negotiating body and to make it very clear to the union and other interested parties that it has full authority to conclude a collective agreement. If the negotiating committee is not given full authority to do so, the parties of interest are likely to appeal to politicians to influence the outcome of negotiations—a practice which is now referred to as "making an end run."

Saskatchewan has been very successful in avoiding end runs. Its Public Service Commission, which is fully in charge of negotiations, keeps in close touch with cabinet. The bargaining parameters within which the Public Service Commission negotiators must operate are approved by the Cabinet Committee on Collective Bargaining, with final authority residing in cabinet. Wetzel and Gallagher have pointed out that

> The government has found little need to become directly involved in negotiations since it can safely assume that the PSC comprehends its interests and will see that they are protected. The level of trust and comfort which the government feels with this relationship is manifested by the fact that it does not feel the need to have a non-PSC government representative to report on the pulse and direction of talks as it does where the immediate employer is outside of government, e.g. hospitals and nursing homes. Aside from an occasional direct communication between the Minister-In-Charge and the unions, the unions expect to deal with the PSC, as the government's spokesman.[19]

Other governments might do well to follow the example set by the Saskatchewan government

by delegating sufficient authority to experienced negotiators to both make deals and inspire confidence in union negotiators that they have the authority to do so. If such is not the case, cabinet ministers may very well have to come to the bargaining table.[20]

Tribunals Which Administer Public-Sector Statutes

Politicians are for many reasons very interested in the processes and outcomes of collective bargaining in the public sector. This interest may sometimes result in political interference in collective bargaining. One example of political interference occurred in the Spring of 1981 when the President of the federal Treasury Board requested the Public Service Staff Relations Board to designate all air-traffic controllers as essential in case of a strike in the aviation industry. The Board refused to comply. However, an appeal to the Federal Court of Appeal overturned the Board's decision and the Supreme Court, in turn, upheld the Appeal Court ruling. Commenting on the Appeal Court decision, first and long-time PSSRB Chairman Jacob Finkelman observed that such changes to labour relations policy are better made in Parliament.[21] It is surely arbitrary in the extreme for government to modify criteria for designation while neither consulting the unions concerned nor proceeding duly through Parliament.

In order to lessen political interference, it is generally accepted that independent machinery be established to administer the provisions of the public-sector statutes. For this reason, the Federal Government, when it passed the *Public Service Staff Relations Act,* set up the Public Service Staff Relations Board (PSSRB), a body entirely independent of the Federal Government. Practically all other jurisdictions have established similar separate administrative tribunals to administer the provisions of their public-sector legislation. In some cases, the functions of these tribunals are related to those of the labour relations boards which administer the legislation in the private sector. In fact, three provinces—

British Columbia, Newfoundland, and Saskatchewan—use the labour relations boards under the private sector to administer their public sector statutes. Quebec no longer has a labour relations board but uses certification officers, certification commissioners, certification commissioners general, and a labour court. These functionaries administer the Quebec statute for the public and parapublic sectors and are sometimes aided in their task by advisory bodies to the provincial government. Under the Prince Edward Island regulations, the tribunal or authorizing body for the public sector is a group of three persons: the Minister responsible for the *Civil Service Act* acts as Chairman and two additional members are appointed by the Lieutenant-Governor-in-Council.[22]

These tribunals have a number of important functions. First, they act as agencies which define bargaining units and certify bargaining agents—functions performed in the private sector by labour relations boards. Second, since most statutes list a whole series of unfair labour practices, these tribunals must hear charges or complaints about such activities and make decisions with respect to them. Third, if a government department such as the Treasury Board wishes to designate (deny the right to strike to) all workers in a specific category as the president of the Treasury Board did to the air traffic controllers in the Spring of 1981, the tribunals must hear and interpret these requests.

While appointments of conciliation officers, mediators, and conciliation boards are usually made through ministers of labour in the private sector, the same appointments in the public sector are made by the separate tribunals. The tribunals use either full-time members or part-time members as adjudicators in contract interpretation disputes. Hence, the administrative tribunals perform the combined functions of labour relations boards and ministers of labour and are thus extremely important to the collective bargaining process in the public sector.

Table 10.1	Collective Bargaining in the Public Sector

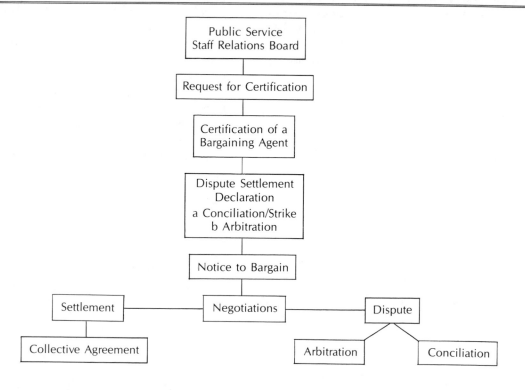

Statutes Covering Collective Bargaining for Public-Sector Workers

Having discussed the three actors, let us now turn to a discussion of the nature and coverage of statutes in the public sector. As indicated in Chapter 6, eleven statutes govern bargaining in the Canadian private sector. While the Quebec Labour Code and the Saskatchewan *Trade Union Act* apply equally to public and private sectors, all other jurisdictions have separate statutes to govern public-sector workers. Some of these statutes, such as that in New Brunswick, also cover hospitals, schools, and public utilities. Hence, in Canada we have a variety of statutes governing workers in the public and parapublic sectors, ranging from one statute covering all groups in Quebec to seven in Ontario, including those for police and firefighters. What has developed is a "crazy quilt" of legislative provisions.

In every jurisdiction, with the exception of Saskatchewan and Quebec, there are at least two relevant statutes—one for employers and workers in the private sector and at least one other for workers in the public (and in some cases parapublic) sector. For example, the Federal Government has both Part V of the Canada Labour Code which applies to workers in transportation, communications, banking, and radio and television broadcasting and the *Public Service Staff Relations Act* which covers workers in all federal departments and a number of federal agencies. The *PSSRA*, to be examined in the next section, will serve as a basis for a comparison of federal and provincial collective-bargaining legislation for public-sector workers.

Coverage of the Statutes The federal *Public Service Staff Relations Act* applies to all government departments and a lengthy list of commissions and agencies for which the Treasury Board acts as the employer. The statute also mentions separate employers or agencies which negotiate for themselves, such as the Atomic Energy Control Board, the Economic Council of Canada, the Medical Research Council, and the National Film Board.[23] Public-sector statutes in most provinces also refer to a number of other agencies and crown corporations.

While the Quebec Labour Code at one time listed a host of organizations and services under the definition of the public sector, it now includes the following under the public and parapublic sectors:

> "public and parapublic sectors" means the Government and the governmental departments, and those government agencies whose personnel is appointed and remunerated in accordance with the Civil Service Act, as well as the colleges, school boards and establishments contemplated in the Act respecting management and union in party organization collective bargaining in the sectors of education, social affairs and government agencies.[24]

The Ontario *Crown Employees Collective Bargaining Act,* 1972 covers not only all public servants *per se* but also workers in the Liquor Control Board, Workers' Compensation Board, Niagara Parks Commission, and the Ontario Housing Corporation within the Municipality of Metropolitan Toronto.[25]

The *Public Service Staff Relations Act* does not cover certain essential workers such as members of The Royal Canadian Mounted Police and the Canadian Armed Forces. There have been some rumblings, however, that one or both of these groups should fall within the purview of the *Act.* Most other jurisdictions exclude police and firefighters, since they are covered by separate statutes. Notable exceptions are in British Columbia, where police and firefighters are covered by the *Essential Services Disputes Act* of 1977,[26] and in Nova Scotia and New Brunswick where these workers are covered by the *Trade Union Act* and *Industrial Relations Act* respectively.

As with private sector statutes, most of the statutes governing workers in the public sector exclude persons who act in a confidential capacity in matters relating to industrial relations and who take an active part in policy development and implementation. In general, the cut-off mark for management people is higher in the public sector than it is in the private sector. But in the federal jurisdiction, more managerial exclusions exist than in most of the provinces.

At this point, it will be helpful to recall the three major types of classical labour relations disputes utilized in discussing the legislation covering collective bargaining in the private sector. First, a discussion of *recognition disputes* will deal with the determination of bargaining units and the certification of bargaining agents. Second, a discussion of *contract negotiation disputes* will deal with negotiable issues and impasse resolution. Third, a discussion of *contract interpretation disputes* will deal with grievance handling, arbitration procedures, and matters subject to arbitration.

Determination of Bargaining Units

In some jurisdictions, the composition of bargaining units is determined by the statutes which give collective bargaining rights to public-sector workers. In other jurisdictions, labour relations boards, or special tribunals for the public sector, review union submissions in order to determine the appropriateness of proposed bargaining units. In making such decisions, the boards may refer to existing regulations, if any, respecting the original composition of bargaining units.

In the federal public service, literally hundreds of occupational groups existed within the service before the *Public Service Staff Relations Act* was passed in 1967. As part of the new regime under collective bargaining, the Public Service Commission was charged with the responsibility of defining occupational groups within five broad occupational categories.

This arrangement made for a total of seventy-two occupational groups, each generally equivalent to a bargaining unit. Bargaining units may consist of workers plus supervisors, workers only, or supervisors only. Two years after the *Act* came into effect, 98% of workers belonged to bargaining units for which bargaining agents had been certified. As of September 1981, nineteen worker associations had been certified as bargaining agents in the federal public service. These agents represented 122 bargaining units, of which eighty-one were in the central administration and forty-one comprised separate employers.[27] (Separate employers do their own negotiating. In other cases, the Treasury Board is the employer.)

The New Brunswick statute contains the same occupational categories as the federal statute, but exactly what percentage of workers now comprise bargaining units is unknown. In addition, the New Brunswick statute also recognizes the distinction between supervisory and non-supervisory bargaining units.[28] The B.C. Statute defines bargaining units for nurses, other licensed professionals, and public servants other than those described in the first two classes above.[29] According to the Alberta statute, workers for the Crown in right of Alberta constitute a single bargaining unit.[30] However, the statute mentions that a number of professions

Table 10.2 Occupational Categories and Groups Under the Federal *Public Service Staff Relations Act*

Occupational categories	Number of groups
Scientific and Professional	28
Technical	13
Administrative and Foreign Service	13
Administrative Support	6
Operational	12

Source: Alton W. J. Craig, "Collective Bargaining in the Federal Public Service of Canada," Vol. 5, No. 2, *Optimum* (1974), p. 28.

including doctors, dentists, architects, engineers, and lawyers should not be included in the bargaining unit unless the board is satisfied that a majority of such workers wish to be included.[31]

Although the Ontario statute does not name the bargaining units in the statute, it does indicate that those designated in the regulations under the *Crown Employees Collective Bargaining Act* are appropriate for collective bargaining purposes.[32] The following groups also comprise separate bargaining units: social services, operational services, scientific and technical services, administrative services, general services, law enforcement, and correctional officers. While the Registrar of the Ontario tribunal refers to these as salary units, it is our contention that they are more appropriately entitled bargaining units.[33] Only the Liquor Control Board of Ontario, the Workers' Compensation Board, the Niagara Parks Commission, and the Ontario Housing Corporation are listed in the regulations, but it would appear that the theory underlying the selection of these organizations resembles the separate employer concept under the federal *Public Service Staff Relations Act.*

An interesting case arose in Ontario when the correctional officers, who were formerly part of a larger group, went on strike several years ago to carve out for themselves a separate bargaining unit. The correctional officers claimed not to belong to the occupational group containing social workers. The President of the Ontario Public Service Employees Union was jailed because he advised these workers to strike, in contravention of the Ontario statute. The issue was resolved by arbitration—an unusual way for determining a bargaining unit, since the tribunal responsible for administering the *Act* usually makes this decision.

The Quebec Labour Code provides for three types of bargaining units for public-sector workers: professional bargaining units, white-collar units, and blue-collar units.[34] The Nova Scotia statute identifies eight different bargaining units, some of which apply to the health services and education areas.[35] The statutes of Manitoba, Saskatchewan, Prince Edward Island,

and Newfoundland do not define bargaining units.

Determination of Bargaining Agents

A number of provinces list in their statutes the unions or associations which are to represent their public-sector workers. The following is a partial list of the associations that are named in the different provincial statutes: The P.E.I. Public Service Association, The Nova Scotia Government Employees Association, The Ontario Civil Service Association (since renamed The Ontario Public Service Employees Union), and The Manitoba Government Employees Association.[36] Although the British Columbia Government Employees Union is not named as the bargaining agent in the British Columbia *Public Service Labour Relations Act*, this union represents a large proportion of workers in the public sector in that province.

As we stated earlier in this chapter, the Quebec Government Employees' Union was designated the bargaining agent by statute for clerical and blue-collar workers when Quebec gave its workers the right to collective bargaining in 1964. In 1985, this union represented the vast majority of public servants, with a membership of over 55,000.[37] In practically all other provinces, the provincial associations or unions still represent a substantial number of public servants.

Even those statutes which name the bargaining agent in the statute provide for a replacement of the bargaining agents should a majority of workers become dissatisfied with them. In addition, practically every statute provides for bargaining agents to represent new groups of workers not previously certified. Most of the statutes also provide for special tribunals, rather than the existing labour relations boards, to certify unions.

A Comparison of Provisions Dealing with the Certification of Bargaining Agents Only the statutes of British Columbia, Alberta, Saskatchewan, Ontario, Newfoundland, and Quebec specify the proportion of workers in the bargaining units necessary to make application for certification and the proportion of support that is needed in order for a bargaining agent to become certified. As Table 10.3 indicates, the British Columbia statute permits an application for certification if a bargaining agent claims between 35% and 51% support. The bargaining agent may be certified if 50% of those voting approve. The Alberta statute indicates that a majority of workers in the bargaining unit is necessary in order both to make an application for certification and to be officially certified. The Saskatchewan statute provides for the making of an application for certification if the bargaining agent has 25% support of members in the bargaining unit. The bargaining agent may then be certified if it gets 50% support from those voting. Both the Ontario and Quebec statutes provide that the bargaining agent needs at least 35% support in order to make an application for certification. However, in Ontario, a bargaining agent may be certified if it receives the support of 50% of those voting, while in Quebec certification requires 50% support from the entire membership of the bargaining unit. The Newfoundland statute requires the support of a majority of members in the bargaining unit both to make an application for certification and, if a vote is conducted, to certify the bargaining agent. Manitoba, New

Brunswick, Nova Scotia, and Prince Edward Island in their statutes do not specify any precise figures relating to the certification process, but do name the bargaining agents.[38]

As can be seen from Table 10.3, three statutes require 50% of those voting to support bargaining agents before these bargaining agents may be certified. Another four, including the federal statute, require that the bargaining agent must obtain the approval of 50% or more of those in the bargaining unit. Former Chairman of the federal Public Service Staff Relations Board Jacob Finkelman did an exhaustive analysis of the federal statute and recommended that the *Public Service Staff Relations Act* be amended to allow a bargaining agent to apply for certification where it claims to have the support of 35% of those in the proposed bargaining unit, and that it be certified if it is supported by a majority of workers voting, provided that not less than 35% of eligible voters cast ballots.[39] If the study's proposals were implemented, they would bring the federal law more into line with most of the statutes governing workers in the private sector.

The growing tendency in Canadian statutes to adopt the principle of a simple voting majority would require those who oppose certification for a particular union or association actually to cast

Table 10.3 — A Comparison of Provisions Dealing with Certification

Jurisdiction	% support needed to apply for certification	% support necessary for a union to be certified when a vote is taken	
		50% + of those in the bargaining unit	50% + of those voting
Federal	Not specified	X	
British Columbia	35-51%		X
Alberta	50% +	X	
Saskatchewan	25%		X
Manitoba	Not specified	Not specified	
Ontario	35%		X
Quebec	35%	X	
New Brunswick	Not specified	Not specified	
Nova Scotia	Not specified	Not specified	
Prince Edward Island	Not specified	Not specified	
Newfoundland	50% +	X	

a vote rather than allow them to stay at home and expect their abstention to count as a "no" vote. Following the will of the active voting membership corresponds with established democratic practice in the political sphere.

This completes our discussion of the ways in which recognition disputes are handled in the different jurisdictions. The following sections deal with the contract negotiation dispute.

The Scope of Bargainable Issues

From looking at the definition of a collective agreement in the statutes in the various jurisdictions, it would appear that almost anything is negotiable, except those items which would require the enactment or amendment of a statute or the amendment of pension legislation. Under the federal *Public Service Staff Relations Act*, the following matters are *not* subject to arbitration:

the standards, procedures or processes governing the appointment, appraisal, promotion, demotion, transfer, lay-off or release of employees, or with any term or condition of employment of employees that was not a subject of negotiation between the parties during the period before arbitration was requested in respect thereof.[40]

This provision is designed to protect the merit principle in the appointment, promotion, etc. of public-sector workers. Such staffing regulations are to be found in a separate law: the *Public Service Employment Act*.

While the federal statute contains what is probably the most exhaustive statement of subjects which are not subject to arbitration, the statutes of Alberta and Ontario contain clauses almost as comprehensive as those of the federal statute.[41] The B.C. statute prohibits collective agreements from containing clauses relating to the merit principle and its application in the appointment and promotion of workers. This statute also prohibits negotiation over all matters included under such *Acts* as the *Public Service Act* and the *Pension Act*.[42]

The number of items negotiable under most statutes governing collective bargaining in the public sector is relatively small in relation to the number of items negotiable in the private sector. In some jurisdictions, the fact that so few issues are subject to arbitration is cause for considerable concern and frustration among bargaining agents. While the parties may jointly negotiate over a substantial number of issues, it sometimes happens that if government negotiators do not wish to deal with a particular item, they may threaten to go to arbitration where the issue may not be discussed. This kind of tactic is hardly conducive to genuine collective bargaining.

In some jurisdictions, two-tier bargaining exists. The British Columbia *Public Service Labour Relations Act* contains the following provision:

Two collective agreements shall apply to each bargaining unit, as follows: (a) a master agreement including all the terms and conditions of employment common to all employees in the bargaining unit, or to two or more occupational groups in the bargaining unit, and (b) a subsidiary agreement for each occupational group, including the terms and conditions of employment that apply only to employees in a specific occupational group in the bargaining unit.[43]

The specific occupational groups mentioned in *(b)* above are determined by negotiation between the parties.

This form of bargaining would seem to be close to ideal, for those items which are common to all workers in the public sector may be covered by one major or master collective agreement. In addition, subsidiary collective agreements containing provisions that are unique to each occupational group may be negotiated by the groups concerned.

The Ontario Government has three types of collective agreements. The first relates to each of the eight or ten specific occupational groups or bargaining units discussed earlier in this chapter. Under this type of negotiation, each group may negotiate salary scales peculiar to its own occupational group. In addition to these multiple salary agreements, there is another general agreement for the entire civil service relating solely to working conditions and terms of employment such as overtime, hours of work, and grievance procedures. Finally there is a service-wide collective agreement negotiated at two- or three-year intervals on fringe benefits for the entire Ontario public service. As with the two-tier structure in British Columbia, the Ontario system makes a good deal of sense by providing for one set of negotiations on items that are common to all public-sector workers and at the same time enabling particular groups of workers to negotiate salaries for their specific occupations.

Dispute Settlement Procedures Under Federal and New Brunswick Statutes

Public Service Staff Relations Act

To summarize thus far, we have dealt with those workers covered by the public-sector statutes, the determination of bargaining units and bargaining agents (unions), the scope of bargainable issues, and who the employer is in the various jurisdictions.

When a bargaining agent is certified, it is entitled — as are bargaining agents in the private sector — to serve notice to negotiate for a new collective agreement, or for the renewal of an existing one. The negotiation process in the public sector is very much the same as it is in the private sector, and the processes explained in the chapter "The Negotiating Process" apply to the private, public, and parapublic sectors. If the parties are successful in reaching an agreement, the provisions agreed upon will be written into the collective agreement just as they are in the private sector.

Should an impasse occur in negotiations and the parties are unable to reach an agreement, various forms of third-party assistance are available to them. The effectiveness of these different forms is currently one of the "hottest" topics in the field of industrial relations, both from research and practical points of view. In the private sector, a strike or lockout usually follows if conciliation or mediation or both are unsuc-

cessful in resolving contract negotiation or interest disputes. Public-sector disputes generally contain more of a public interest component than do those in the private sector. There are also many more ways in which public-sector disputes may be handled. It is to a discussion of these procedures that we now turn our attention. We will focus on the federal *Public Service Staff Relations Act* and, where appropriate, compare its provisions with procedures used in different provinces.

Prior to the introduction of collective bargaining for federal workers in Canada, a committee, headed by A. D. P. Heeney, was set up to study a proposed system of collective bargaining for the Federal Government which included arbitration as the final form of dispute resolution if the parties could not reach a settlement on their own. Arbitration was part of the mandate of the Heeney Committee.[44]

In keeping within its mandate, the Heeney Committee recommended arbitration as the impasse resolution procedure. However, during the Summer of 1965, a week-long wildcat strike took place among postal workers in some provinces. A commissioner was appointed to look into the problems in the Post Office; his report was released in October, 1966. Bill C-170, first introduced in the House of Commons on April 25, 1966, provided for a choice of impasse resolution procedures: arbitration or conciliation with the right to strike. Whether the postal strike in 1965 had anything to do with the two options is a matter for speculation. Bill 170 also required the bargaining agent to specify its choice of procedure before it could be certified. The Bill, passed in February 1967 as the *Public Service Staff Relations Act*, contained a provision whereby a bargaining agent could be certified without specifying its choice of procedure. However, the agent was required to specify its choice before giving notice to bargain.[45]

One of the unique features of the *Public Service Staff Relations Act* is that it does provide for these two methods of dispute resolution. At the present time, the bargaining agent must make its choice before a specific round of negotiations and may not change the procedure once the negotiations have begun. The New Brunswick statute is similar in this respect to the federal statute, except that the bargaining agent must decide between the conciliation-and-strike route or the arbitration route only when an impasse is reached in negotiations. These are the only two jurisdictions in Canada where such a choice is available.

An interesting question with respect to the federal and New Brunswick statutes is why one should require the bargaining agent to determine its route prior to the commencement of negotiations and the other at the stage of impasse. A partial answer to this question is found in a report prepared for the government of New Brunswick:

> The choice [under the *PSSRA*], however, must be indicated *after* a group has been certified as a bargaining agent and *before* negotiations begin. Both sides are thus committed in advance to the method that could be used ultimately to resolve a deadlock. Yet, it may be argued that this very element of certainty about the final method of settling differences has serious disadvantages. Students of collective bargaining have noted on the basis of many empirical studies that a degree of uncertainty about how far either of the parties is prepared to go in pressing its case encourages the give-and-take and flexibility that are necessary for successful negotiation. Bargaining tends to be inhibited or ritualized when the parties know they must go through predetermined procedures at given stages of their negotiations. The procedural steps proposed by this Commission are designed to avoid some of this difficulty. They seek to maintain the atmosphere of uncertainty that is considered conducive to effective negotiations by delaying the choice between the strike or arbitration to the end of the bargaining exercise.[46]

Students of industrial relations would agree that a degree of uncertainty about the procedural steps involved may encourage the parties to reach an agreement on their own.

Both statutes specify that an arbitrable award may deal only with "rates of pay, hours of work, leave entitlements, standards of discipline and other terms and conditions of employment

directly related thereto."[47] Hiring and firing practices are not bargainable.

Arbitration in the Federal Jurisdiction and New Brunswick

The federal *Public Service Staff Relations Act* provides for the appointment by the Public Service Staff Relations Board (PSSRB) of two panels, one consisting of at least three persons representing the interest of the employer and the other consisting of at least three persons representing the interest of the workers. If a dispute reaches the arbitration stage, the PSSRB appoints one of its own members and selects one other person from each panel discussed above. It should be noted that a number of boards may be sitting at the same time to handle different disputes as long as there are enough members on the panels representing the employers and workers and enough members of the board to act as chairmen. Under the federal statute, the arbitration board, in conducting its proceedings and in formulating its award, is required to take into consideration the following factors:

1 the needs of the Public Service for qualified employees;
2 the conditions of employment in similar occupations outside the Public Service, including such geographic, industrial, or other variations as the Board may consider relevant;
3 the need to maintain appropriate relationships in the conditions of employment as between different grade levels within an occupation and as between occupations within the Public Service;
4 the need to establish terms and conditions of employment that are fair and reasonable in relation to the qualifications required, the work performed, the responsibility assumed and the nature of the services rendered; and
5 any other factor that to it appears to be relevant to the matter in dispute.[48]

The New Brunswick statute is identical but for the addition of the term *the interest of the public*.

While Mr. Finkelman was not responsible for the two-route system, it is quite obvious from his report that he prefers the arbitration route to that of conciliation with the right to strike. He states in his report that, "if an impasse is reached, every possible step should be taken to encourage resort to arbitration, a technique whose time appears to have come."[49] This preference no doubt reflects Mr. Finkelman's experience as an arbitrator for over thirty years in the men's clothing industry in Toronto with a union whose philosophy has been traditionally to submit interest disputes to binding arbitration.[50] With obvious reservations, he suggests that the parties should have the right, by mutual consent, to use final-offer selection in whatever form they may deem appropriate to the situation. This last recommendation should be studied carefully before it is included in any revision of the *Act*, for American experience indicates that it takes experienced and professional negotiators to make effective use of final-offer selection.

There has been some criticism of the arbitration route, especially if it can be instituted only at the request of the bargaining agent, as is presently the situation under the *Public Service Staff Relations Act*. One argument for the use of arbitration is that only through the present arbitration system can weak groups achieve equity. This assumption is open to question since little consideration has been given to other alternatives. For example, leaders of weak unions could use pattern-setting as a vehicle for strengthening their bargaining position. Similarly, coalition bargaining could be instituted to permit weak groups to join with the stronger ones to increase their bargaining power.

If Finkelman downplays the desirability of using the strike route as a norm in negotiations, neither does he fully develop all the drawbacks of the arbitration procedure. According to Crispo, some of these drawbacks include: the difficulty in appointing an arbitrator acceptable to both sides and determining a suitable tenure for the person chosen; the potentially detrimental effects of compulsory arbitration on the process of collective bargaining itself; the fact that union leaders may use the arbitrator or arbitration tribunal as a scapegoat in the event that they do not make a proper internal trade-off among the conflicting interests of their own members;

and the potential for the haphazard determination of criteria by arbitrators in interest disputes. Furthermore, strikes sometimes provide a release for worker frustration and are therefore helpful in restoring morale and self-respect.[51] While the federal *Public Service Staff Relations Act* does provide certain criteria as indicated above for arbitration boards, the final section — "any other factor that to it [the arbitration board] appears to be relevant in the dispute" — gives just about as much flexibility as would exist were no criteria specified.

It would seem, therefore, that discussions leading to any future legislative amendments to the *Act* might well take the strike norm into serious consideration. It is generally accepted that arbitration of interest disputes is not an instrument for innovation — this has been demonstrated in the federal public sector. In addition, if it had not been for the use of the strike or the threat thereof in the private sector, there would be less creative provisions in private-sector agreements than there are today.

The New Brunswick arbitration procedure differs from that of the Federal Government. Under the New Brunswick statute, the maximum period for collective bargaining is forty-five days unless otherwise agreed to by the parties. Where the parties have bargained in good faith with a view to concluding a collective agreement but have failed to reach one, they may, by mutual written agreement, submit their differences to binding arbitration. The New Brunswick statute makes provision for a Public Service Arbitration Tribunal consisting of a chairman responsible for the administration of the system of arbitration, and two panels of three persons each, representing the respective interests of employer and worker. The Lieutenant Governor-in-Council may authorize the Board to designate one or more persons to be alternative chairmen of the Arbitration Tribunal. This provision is obviously meant to allow for the simultaneous sitting of two or more arbitration boards. If the two parties agree jointly to submit their dispute to arbitration, the arbitration board would be guided by the same criteria as the Federal Government except that in New Brunswick "the interest of the public" would be an additional factor.

Conciliation and Strikes in the Federal and New Brunswick Public Sectors

The other option open to parties under both the federal and New Brunswick statutes is the conciliation/strike option. Both statutes empower the chairmen of the respective boards to appoint a conciliation officer at the request of either party or as a matter of personal initiative. A conciliation officer may also be appointed as part of the arbitration route. If, however, a conciliation officer is unable to bring the parties to an agreement, a conciliation board may be established, again at the request of either party, or on the initiative of the chairman of the Board.[52]

A provision introduced as part of the federal *Public Service Staff Relations Act* and now adopted by a number of provincial jurisdictions specifies that no conciliation board may be established until the parties have agreed or the board has determined the workers or class of workers, the performance of whose duties are considered *essential to the safety or security of the public*. These "designated workers" may not legally take part in a strike. Under the federal statute there are two occasions on which a list of designated workers must be furnished by the employer. The first occurs before a bargaining agent specifies the dispute resolution process. This list cannot be challenged by the bargaining agent. The second arises if the bargaining agent has chosen the conciliation route as the dispute resolution procedure. In this case, the employer is required to provide a list to the bargaining agent and to the board within twenty days after the notice of bargaining has been given. The bargaining agent is then given twenty days to file an objection to the employer's list. If the two parties cannot resolve their differences, the board holds hearings and makes a final determination. The New Brunswick statute, which also has a method of designation, differs from the federal statute in-

asmuch as the designation of essential workers takes place only when an impasse in negotiations is encountered.

When a federal conciliation board is established, the Chairman of the PSSRB presents the board with a statement setting forth the matters on which the board shall report its findings and recommendations. The original statement of issues may be amended at any time in the interest of assisting the parties to reach an agreement. Conciliation boards are established in the same way as they are in the private sector. It is interesting to note, however, that a federal conciliation board may not make recommendations concerning "the standards, procedures or processes governing the appointment, appraisal, promotion, demotion, transfer, lay-off or release of employees."[53]

Under both the federal and New Brunswick statutes a majority of the members of a conciliation board speak for the board in deciding upon any matter referred to it. In addition, the New Brunswick statute provides that, where there is no majority decision by the conciliation board, the Chairman of the Board shall report his own findings and recommendations but in no case shall the findings and recommendations of the minority be reported.[54] Both statutes contain a clause providing for voluntary arbitration in the sense that before a conciliation board has made its report the parties may agree in writing to accepts its recommendations as binding. Under the federal statute, if the workers reject the recommendations of the conciliation board and the bargaining agent is authorized to call a strike, it may do so seven days after the receipt of the conciliation board report by the Chairman of the PSSRB.

The New Brunswick statute is more complex. In principle, a strike vote may take place after seven days have elapsed from the publication of any conciliation board report. One of the parties, however, must first ask the Chairman of the Public Service Labour Relations Board (PSLRB) to declare that a deadlock exists, and the Chairman must subsequently make an offer to union and management of voluntary binding arbitration. Only when the latter offer is refused by at least one of the parties is the union finally free to ask for a strike mandate which must be sanctioned by a majority vote of the bargaining unit's membership.

If the union does not obtain a strike mandate, the Chairman of the PSLRB can order both sides back to the bargaining table for twenty-one days, at the end of which time the union may take another strike vote, if no settlement has been reached. This procedure offers the possibility of a prolonged stalemate which can be ended only by a successful strike vote or by the conclusion of a negotiated agreement. In the event that a strike is authorized, it may take place only after seven days have elapsed from the date on which the bargaining agent has notified the Chairman and the employer that the workers in the relevant bargaining unit have authorized strike action.[55]

Dispute Settlement Procedures in Other Jurisdictions

Compulsory Arbitration

Five provinces — Alberta, Ontario, Manitoba, Nova Scotia, and Prince Edward Island — do not allow public servants to go on strike but require that arbitration be the final step in the dispute resolution procedure. Most of the pertinent statutes also provide for the use of conciliation services prior to the imposition of arbitration, and voluntary arbitration if the parties agree in advance to abide by the terms of a conciliation board report. Each of the statutes also contains criteria to guide arbitrators in formulating their awards, including an item with respect to the interests of the public. The Nova Scotia statute includes an interesting provision to the effect that the Governor-in-Council and the Civil Service Commission are not bound to implement an arbitration award which would result in any department exceeding its appropriation unless the Minister of Finance includes in the estimates for the next ending fiscal year an amount sufficient to implement the arbitration award retroactive to the date on which the arbitration award was to be effective.[56] Also, no arbitration award may require the government to amend a statute for its implementation.

Conciliation and Strikes

The province of Saskatchewan has allowed strikes among its public servants since 1944, but very few strikes have taken place in that province. The B.C. statute makes provision for the parties to seek the assistance of a mediator should they fail to reach a collective agreement on their own. If mediation fails, the parties are asked to agree to have any issues in dispute submitted to arbitration for a final and binding decision. Should either side refuse, the union is free to exercise its strike option. A majority of the members of the union must vote in favour of a work stoppage and the strike must begin within the three-month period following the taking of the vote. In addition, the bargaining agent must notify the government negotiators at least three days before any strike begins.

British Columbia strike votes reflect the two-tier bargaining system in that province. If the issues in dispute are those in a master agreement covering various occupational groups, then a strike vote must be taken among all members covered by the agreement. However, if the matters in dispute refer to a subsidiary agreement covering the members of an occupational group, then the strike vote must be taken among these members only. In either case, a majority of the members must vote in order for a strike to be deemed legal.[57]

In 1977, the B.C. Government passed the *Essential Services Disputes Act* which applies to a number of agencies, including provincial public servants. Part 3 of the *Act* provides for the Lieutenant-Governor-in-Council to designate those facilities, productions, and services which he considers necessary or essential to prevent immediate and serious damage to life, health, safety, or an immediate and substantial threat to the economy and welfare of the province and its citizens. In other words, this statute enables the B.C. Government to prevent certain essential workers in both the private and public sectors from going on strike.

The Newfoundland statute makes provision for the appointment of conciliation officers and conciliation boards if the parties are unable to reach agreements on their own. The findings of the conciliation board, however, are not binding on the parties, and workers in the Province of Newfoundland have the right to strike.

In 1983, Newfoundland amended its legislation to make it possible for the Minister of Manpower and Industrial Relations to appoint a mediator from within the public service or outside either on his own initiative or by the request of the parties. A mediator may also be appointed when a request is made for the appointment of a conciliation board. Furthermore, a conciliation board may be appointed if the efforts of a mediator prove unsuccessful.[58]

The Newfoundland statute has always provided for the designation of essential workers in the event of a strike. In 1983, however, the provisions of the statute were changed with respect to the designation process. Under the amendment, the bargaining agent or the Board may seek, any time after the certification of the bargaining agent, a statement from the employer regarding the number and names of essential workers in each classification.[59] This amendment could very well be the result of a decision of the Federal Court of Appeal, subsequently upheld by the Supreme Court of Canada, regarding the designation of all air traffic controllers in 1981. If so, the Newfoundland Government is to be commended for its responsiveness in legislating provincially a policy change which had failed to be legislated federally.

A strike may be undertaken when a majority of the workers in the unit *actually vote by secret ballot* in favour of such action. There is, however, a waiting period of seven days between the time the bargaining agent gives notice in writing to the Minister of Labour of the workers' intentions and the beginning of the work stoppage. The *Act* also provides that, where less than a majority of the workers in the unit vote in favour of a strike, either party may by notice in writing request the resumption of collective bargaining. Also, where the provincial assembly resolves that a strike of workers is or would be injurious to the health or safety of persons or any group or class of persons or the security of the province, it may declare that a state of emergency exists and forbid the strike of all workers in the unit or units specified in the resolution. The assembly may, in addition, order the workers of such unit or units to return to duty if they have already gone on strike. In the event that a state of emergency has been declared, any dispute concerning outstanding issues is referred to adjudication, which is equivalent to compulsory arbitration. The adjudication board is guided by criteria similar to those contained in those statutes which make arbitration the norm for settlement.

When the Quebec Government revised its Labour Code in 1964, it gave the right to strike to all public- and private-sector workers, with the exception of police and firefighters. In addition, both Liberal and Péquiste governments have come out against arbitration, since they prefer to retain control over how their budget is allocated and spent rather than delegate any part of that responsibility to an arbitrator.

In 1978, the Quebec National Assembly passed Bill 59, a complicated piece of legislation which outlined provisions for negotiations and dispute settlement in the public and parapublic sectors, including education and social affairs. The Bill created a Committee of Information on Negotiations which is responsible for informing the public on the state of negotiations. The intended effect undoubtedly is to bring public opinion to bear on public- and parapublic-sector disputes. The Bill also provides that the negotiation stage begin 180 days before the date of expiration of a collective agreement, and that every certified association in the public and parapublic sectors must, through its bargaining agent, present in writing to the other party its proposals on all the matters that are to be negotiated at the national and regional levels no later than 150 days before the date of expiration of a collective agreement.

In turn, the management negotiating committee in these sectors must, within sixty days following receipt of these proposals, present in writing to the other party and to the Committee of Information on Negotiations their proposals on all the matters that are to be negotiated. The Bill also sets out procedures for designating essential workers to whom the right to strike is denied. This designation process is a matter of negotiation between both sides, with the union having the final say in the case of any disagreement about the designation of specific workers. The Bill states furthermore that, if the Lieutenant Governor-in-Council is of the opinion that a strike (whether proposed or in progress) endangers the public health or public safety, he or she may suspend the exercise of the right to strike for a period not exceeding thirty days. (This provision now constitutes sections 111.5 to 111.12 of the Quebec Labour Code).

In June, 1982, the Quebec Government passed Bill 72 to ensure the continuance of essential services at all times in the health and social service sectors. The Bill applies also to telephone services, subways, buses, ferries, agencies responsible for the production, transmission, distribution or sale of gas, water and electricity, garbage removal services, ambulance services, the Canadian Red Cross Association, and unspecified government agencies. In addition, the government on the recommendtion of the Minister of Labour may require the employer and union to maintain essential services in the event of a strike if the government believes that a strike in the public service might endanger public health and safety. Such an order must be made not later than fifteen days before the union acquires the right to strike.

A similar action may be undertaken after a strike has already begun if the government believes that essential services are insufficiently covered and that there is therefore a danger to public health and safety. The suspension of strike activity is effective until it is proved to the government that adequate essential services will be rendered. In order to ensure the maintenance of essential services, the parties are required to reach agreement on the essential services to be maintained. If they are unable to reach agreement, the union must establish a list of the services which, in its view, must be maintained in the event of a strike.

An important part of the Bill is the establishment of an Essential Services Council composed of eight members — a chairman, two persons chosen after consultation with management and two after consultation with labour, and three other members. The Council has the responsibility of assessing whether an agreement by the parties on essential services, or the list supplied by the union, is adequate to maintain the necessary level of essential services. If the Council finds the proposed services inadequate, it may propose amendments to the joint agreement of the parties or the list supplied by the union — the Council is not empowered, however, to impose amendments. The Council must report every case to the Minister of Labour where essential services provided for in a joint agreement or a union list are inadequate, or where they are not rendered during a strike. It must also indicate the extent to which this constitutes a danger to the public. The Council must inform the public of the contents of any such report made to the Minister.

The Bill prohibits lockouts by employers in establishments deemed to be providing essential services. It also imposes heavy fines for workers, union leaders and managers, and unions and employers who declare or instigate a strike or lockout contrary to the provision of the Labour Code.

By establishing a mechanism for determining and requiring the provision of essential services during a strike, and by giving the Cabinet the power to prohibit or suspend a strike for an indefinite period, the Quebec government is moving away from the frequent use of special back-to-work legislation which has characterized labour relations in the public sector in that province for years. The Bill also contains provisions which facilitate class-action suits. (The provisions of this Bill now comprise sections 111.0.1 to 111.0.22 and 111.10.1 to 111.10.6 of the Quebec Labour Code.)

The Essential Services Council (Conseil des services essentiels) was established on December 1, 1982 and now has a full complement of members, a support staff, and a Professional Services Branch which includes several mediators. From the time the Council was established until December 31, 1984, it handled well over 500 essential services cases. These cases included the maintenance of essential transportation services in the City of Montreal during the morning and evening rush hours. Transportation services were maintained in other communities as well. The Council has also dealt with such services as snow removal (in order for ambulances and police vehicles to operate), garbage removal, radio communications in police departments, telephones, and sanitation. Ninety-five percent of the cases were resolved without recommendations by the Council. Most of the other 5% were settled on the basis of recommendations made by the Council after consultation with the parties involved.

One of the strengths of the Council is that it tries to mediate with the parties when it believes that insufficient services are being supplied. Council mediators work with the parties to try to obtain negotiated settlements, and sometimes engage in bench mediation where the parties appear before the full membership of the Council. In difficult cases, the Council conducts public hearings: publicity brings pressure to bear on the parties to make concessions and thus to agree on the number of people needed to provide essential services. Thus far, only one of the Council's recommendations has been refused. In that case, the workers went back to work, however, one day after the recommendation was made. To date, the Council has held about sixty hearings and has been involved in about forty strikes which, as the above evidence indicates, did not result in a lack of essential services.[60]

Ever since collective bargaining was granted to public and parapublic workers in Quebec, many serious confrontations have occurred between unions and the Quebec Government. The use of special back-to-work legislation has become almost commonplace in practically every round of negotiations. It is to be hoped that the Essential Services Council will continue to play an effective role. Since no government has lasted more than two sets of negotiations, some correlation may exist between the incidence of public-sector negotiations and changes in government.[61] In June 1985, the Quebec Government passed Bill 37 relating to collective bargaining in the public and parapublic sectors. A summary of this Bill is included in the instructor's manual to this text.

Summary on Dispute Resolution

In studying the literature on public-sector bargaining, it becomes clear that Canada has been bolder than the United States in experimenting with different forms of dispute resolution. "[O]ne of the more apparent differences between the two countries is the relative toleration displayed by Canadians toward public-sector strikes and strike rights compared to the *de jure* strike paranoia which exists in many parts of the United States."[62] In order to complete an already complex picture, we should indicate that, if a group of workers in any jurisdiction should go on strike and the government has used any or all of the means mentioned above, special back-to-work legislation may be used as a last resort.

There have been many cases, in both the federal and provincial sectors, where governments have enacted special back-to-work legislation in order to terminate a strike when it was felt that the public would no longer tolerate the strike. This might happen in a province where arbitration is the final form of dispute resolution, or in the federal jurisdiction should an arbitration decision be considered so meager that the workers affected would rather strike than accept the award. In some critical public-sector disputes, the final judgement concerning the

Table 10.4

Actors
—Employer: TB, PSC
—Unions
—Administrative Tribunals

Recognition Dispute

• **Bargaining units determined in statutes**

Federal (72 groups)
—workers
—supervisors } 122 negotiating units
—both   81 in central administration
                          41 separate employers

Quebec (3 negotiating units)
—professionals
—white collar
—blue collar

Some other jurisdictions
—master agreements
—negotiation units for 8-10 groups

• **Certification of bargaining agents**
—no voluntary recognition
—no quickie vote

Federal
—if 52%, then certify
—if less than 52%, then vote

Provinces which determine bargaining agents
P.E.I. Public Service Association
Nova Scotia Government Employees Association
Ontario: OPSEU
Manitoba Government Employees Association
Quebec Government Employees Union
British Columbia Employees Association[1]

Interest Dispute

•**Negotiations**
—all jurisdictions
—Federal chooses route
  and designates at this
  stage

**Issues (Federal and
New Brunswick)**
—rates of pay
—hours of work
—leave entitlement
—standards of
  discipline
—other

•**Impasse**
—further negotiations
—appointment of
  conciliation officer
—mediation in some
  jurisdictions
—conciliation in some
  jurisdictions
—strike or lockout
—New Brunswick
  chooses route and
  designates at this
  stage
—Federal: conciliation
  and strike route or
  arbitration route

[1]The British Columbia statute does not name a bargaining agent,
but the statutes of the other provinces do.

Dispute Settlement Provisions Under Federal and Provincial Public-Sector Statutes

Rights Dispute

•**Essential Service
Methods**
—designation
—compulsory
arbitration
—court injunction if
above two are not
conformed with
—special *ad hoc*
back-to-work
legislation

Designation	**Compulsory Arbitration**
—Federal	—Alberta
—New Brunswick	—Ontario
—Quebec	—Manitoba
—British Columbia	—Nova Scotia
—Newfoundland	—P.E.I.

•**Collective agreement**
•**Grievance procedure**
—last step is adjudication

—Federal: The grievance is in the name
of the worker, but the bargaining agent
must approve and usually supports the
worker. Disciplinary action consists of
discharge, suspension, or financial penalty.
Membership in bargaining unit unnecessary to have discipline cases adjudicated.
Only single adjudicators.

Ontario: adjudication is broader in
scope than federal one. Grievance Settlement Board interprets, classifies,
appraises performance and decides on
cases of discipline or dismissal without
just cause.

prevention or ending of a strike must be exercised by our elected politicians. This measure has occurred fairly frequently in Canada. In many situations, special back-to-work legislation is merited, but it should not be employed too frequently, nor should it be invoked as a political expedient.

Since we have discussed in some detail the contract negotiation dispute at the federal and provincial levels, we shall now briefly discuss contract interpretation disputes at these levels. Wages and strikes in the public and parapublic sectors will be discussed in the following chapter which deals with the outputs of the Canadian industrial relations system.

The Grievance Process and Adjudication of Rights Disputes at the Federal Level

All collective agreements covering federal public-sector workers contain a provision requiring arbitration or adjudication of contract interpretation or rights disputes. Some statutes contain the words *by arbitration or otherwise*, but do not specify what *otherwise* means. Since the federal *Public Service Staff Relations Act* contains a fairly elaborate statement on the grievance procedure, we shall discuss this legislation in some detail and then look briefly at a few provisions in some of the other jurisdictions.

Section 90(1) of the *Public Service Staff Relations Act* provides that a worker who feels aggrieved by the interpretation or application of "a provision of a statute, or of a regulation, bylaw, direction or other instrument made or issued by the employer, dealing with terms and conditions of employment, or a provision of a collective agreement or arbitral award" or as a result of any occurrence or matter affecting the terms or conditions of employment, may carry a complaint through the various steps of the grievance procedure from the level of the direct supervisor up to that of the department's deputy minister.

However, a worker is not entitled to present a grievance relating to the interpretation or application of a provision of a collective agreement or an arbitrable award without the approval and participation of the responsible bargaining agent. The only kinds of grievances that may go to adjudication are those relating to the interpretation or application of a provision of a collective agreement or an arbitral award, or those relating to disciplinary action resulting in discharge, suspension, or financial penalty. Otherwise, the final step is at the deputy-minister level.

In the case of discharge, suspension, or disciplinary action, any worker, whether a member of a bargaining unit or not, may seek the help of a bargaining agent in presenting the case to adjudication. In the federal public sector, the worker initiates and pursues the grievance, not only through the grievance procedure, but also to adjudication, although the case may be prepared with the support and active assistance of the bargaining agent. This differs somewhat from arbitration in the private sector where the arbitration of rights disputes is in the name of the union and not in the name of the worker.

In his report, a former PSSRB chairman recommended that the federal *Act* be amended to allow a bargaining agent and the employer to include in a collective agreement a provision that the bargaining agent be entitled to present grievances on behalf of a worker with certain safeguards built in to protect the worker if he or she does not wish to pursue a grievance.[63] This recommendation seems valid since the bargaining agent, for example, may want to have a clause in a collective agreement brought to arbitration in order to obtain a clear and definitive interpretation of its meanings.

Mr. Finkelman makes a number of suggestions for changes in matters subject to adjudication. Among these are that classification grievances be made adjudicable and that a provision be included in any revision of the *Act* which would give an adjudicator the right to substitute his judgement for that of management in cases involving suspension or discharge, which in most cases, result in lesser penalties. It would seem reasonable that any revision of the *Public Service Staff Relations Act* should incorporate the latter provision since it is now fairly widespread in the private sector and is also part of the Ontario *Crown Employees Collective Bargaining Act*.[64]

Grievance Procedures in Provincial Jurisdictions

Only the Manitoba *Civil Service Act* makes no reference to a grievance procedure. The B.C. statute contains provisions relating to arbitration of grievances under the *Public Service Act* and also refers to grievances regarding dismissal, discipline, or suspension in addition to the traditional interpretation, application or alleged violation of a collective agreement. The Ontario statute provides for a Grievance Settlement Board regarding the interpretation, application, or alleged violation of a collective agreement. The Ontario statute also states that, in addition to these kinds of grievances under a collective agreement, a worker claiming (1) that his position has been improperly classified, (2) that he has been appraised contrary to the governing principles and standards, or (3) that he has been disciplined or dismissed or suspended from his employment without just cause, may process such matters in accordance with the grievance procedure. Failing settlement at that stage, the worker may apply for arbitration of the case by the Grievance Settlement Board.[65]

The Ontario provision appears to have a broader application than any other statute in Canada governing public-sector workers. Other jurisdictions might very well think about following the lead of Ontario in giving the adjudicator the right to substitute his judgement for that of management in cases regarding discipline and discharge. Finally, other jurisdictions might consider adopting a provision similar to that in the federal statute whereby a worker who is not a member of the bargaining unit but who is discharged, suspended, or disciplined may seek the help of a bargaining agent in presenting his case to adjudication.

Collective Bargaining at the Municipal Level[66]

Collective bargaining for municipal government workers was introduced at the same time that the provinces passed legislation allowing collective bargaining rights in the private sector. The main reason for this is that municipal governments and members of municipal services were defined as "employers" and "employees" respectively under the labour relations legislation enacted in each province. However, in the case of firefighters and police, separate legislation has modified the application of collective bargaining. In most jurisdictions, firefighters and police come under separate statutes and collective bargaining for the latter group usually ends in binding arbitration. Only a few provinces have given their police the right to strike. Nowhere in Canada do firefighters have the strike option.

Most municipal governments with a population of 10,000 or more are now involved in a collective bargaining relationship. At least two or three hundred municipal corporations exist in this category.[67] Apart from police and firefighters, municipal workers are usually divided into two groups, outside and inside workers. Outside workers are defined in the following terms:

> employees engaged in maintenance and operational activities relative to municipal services and facilities, e.g. water and sewage services, road and street maintenance, refuse collection and disposal, maintenance of parks, recreational facilities, and public buildings.[68]

Inside workers are defined as:

> Employees engaged in clerical, accounting and stenographic duties.... Also, ...many...employees engaged in technical duties relative to engineer-

ing, building inspection, property valuation, etc.[69]

In addition, some municipal corporations have to negotiate with other bargaining units. For example, in some provinces municipal governments must deal with unions of public health nurses and technicians.

The largest union in the municipal field in Canada is the Canadian Union of Public Employees (CUPE). In 1985, CUPE had 1,864 local unions across the country with a total membership of 295,960.[70] The major groups represented by CUPE in the municipal field are the inside and outside workers and in most of the medium to large cities there are usually two locals of this union. Quebec is the only province which has developed a sizeable union for municipal workers other than CUPE. This is the Fédération canadienne des employés de services publics (Canadian Federation of Public-Service Employees) which is affiliated with the CNTU.[71]

In municipal bargaining, one of the most serious problems is who will represent the municipal corporation as an employer in bargaining with its unions. In this respect, practice varies widely among municipalities of various sizes within and among provinces. In some municipalities, particularly the smaller ones, negotiations frequently are conducted by a committee of the municipal council assisted by a senior officer who provides staff support. In such cases, the governing body may be reluctant to delegate this responsibility or there may not be a person with sufficient skills to negotiate. Furthermore, where collective bargaining is conducted in this manner, it generally suffers from a lack of continuity since municipal officials are subject to periodic elections.

In many medium to large municipal corporations, the management structure is uncoordinated (i.e., there is no chief executive officer) and comprises a number of departments which report to a committee or council. Such municipalities usually have personnel departments. Responsibility for negotiations may be delegated to the personnel manager. Problems arise, however, when the personnel manager's mandate is not clearly defined: the result may be that union negotiators will undertake direct contact with the council where negotiations are normally concluded.

In a municipal jurisdiction which has a chief executive officer or agency such as a city manager or city administrator, the responsibility for conducting negotiations is generally assigned to such a person. Under this kind of situation, negotiations may be delegated further to a personnel director or labour relations officer operating under a clear mandate concerning the limits within which he may negotiate. Under this kind of an arrangement, the municipal council as such is not usually directly involved in the negotiations.

A 1977 study of twenty-six large Canadian cities showed that twenty-one had a labour relations director or city manager responsible for negotiations, three had elected negotiation officials, and two hired labour lawyers as needed. The study also indicated "that professional and formally trained labour relations specialists had more discretion and authority, less trouble obtaining a mandate from the political officials, and less interference in bargaining than their nonspecialist peers."[72]

In major metropolitan areas, municipal collective bargaining may present special difficulties. For example, a union involved in negotiations in one municipality may be very reluctant to settle until it has a good idea of what the terms of settlement will be in an adjacent municipality. This is a pattern-leader, pattern-follower situation. While the municipalities in these situations may try to coordinate their negotiations, the unions may whip-saw in order to use an increase obtained from one municipality as a precedent to obtain the same or a larger increase from another municipality.

Other considerations are associated with collective bargaining at the municipal level. The revenues received by municipalities vary. This variation implies much in collective bargaining.

Since approximately 60% to 70% of the annual operating budget of a municipality is devoted to salaries, wages, and fringe benefits for its workers, the effect of negotiated salary and wage increases clearly has a direct effect on the real property tax rate.[73] Although growing municipalities with an increasing tax base may be able to cushion the impact of wage and salary increases, municipalities in decline or stasis may find themselves in very serious financial difficulties if they have to raise the tax base substantially in order to meet new wage and salary commitments. A problem is also inherent in the determination of wages and salaries for non-unionized workers. Most municipalities usually pay their nonunion people, including their managerial and supervisory personnel, increases which are relatively in line with those increases paid to other groups.

While this description of collective bargaining among municipal workers is somewhat abbreviated, it at least provides a basis for understanding what goes on at that level. In these days of high inflation and property tax increases, managers and negotiators at the municipal level have difficulty in offering fair wage increases on the one hand, without raising taxes beyond what is economically or politically acceptable to local citizens.

Collective Bargaining in the Fields of Education and Health Services

Rather than discussing the legislation governing collective bargaining in education and health services in each of the ten provinces, we shall deal here only with the provinces of Quebec, Ontario, and Saskatchewan. A study of these jurisdictions offers an insight into contrasting parapublic systems.

Quebec Education and Health Care

In June, 1978, the Quebec National Assembly passed Bill 55 which deals with the organization of management and union parties for collective bargaining in the sectors of education, social affairs, and government agencies. Under this Bill, the Government of Quebec contemplated a highly centralized form of bargaining in education and social affairs, the latter of which would include hospitals. The result has been to put in statute form what has been taking place informally for a number of years (i.e., a two-tiered system of negotiations).

Both worker groups (such as local teachers' associations and hospital workers' unions) and management teams are organized into national negotiating committees which wrestle with most of the substantive wage and policy issues in collective bargaining. A national negotiating committee is established for each sector: education, health care, and the public sector, for example. Usually, these committees will negotiate separately but, in some years (like 1972 and 1982), they may form a common front of all unions in the education, health care, and public sectors. The national committees may allow certain subjects to be negotiated at a lower (local or regional) level, thus permitting the insertion or replacement of clauses in the national contract which reflect specific regional concerns. In general, however, the contract negotiated by the national committees is binding on all affiliated worker and management groups.

Management negotiators are directly responsible to the Ministers of Social Affairs and Education. In fact, these ministers must personally sign any contract approved for the educational sector. The Quebec Treasury Board is responsible for ensuring the orderly progress of talks and for authorizing the management committee's negotiation positions where these represent a particular concern to the provincial government.

Politicians play a very prominent role in education and social affairs in Quebec. This role is important because both Liberal and Péquiste governments in Quebec have totally opposed the use of compulsory arbitration in public and parapublic sectors. The government allocates a certain amount of money to the educational sector and a certain amount to the social affairs sector which includes health care. It is then up to the minister concerned to engineer an agreement which respects as closely as possible these budget estimates.

It is not known what effect highly centralized negotiations have on parties at the local level. However, it is reasonable to assume that parties may feel greatly frustrated in being obliged to live with agreements negotiated with little of their own input. Nonetheless, Jean Boivin contends that centralized bargaining in the public health and educational sectors reflects and is generally supported by the cultural situation of French Canadians:

> Each successive government since 1960 has clearly affirmed the necessity to build a strong and centralized administration in order to preserve and maintain the peculiar cultural distinction of Quebec in North America. Such need for a centralized form of government in Quebec contrasts singularly with the home rule or local community syndrome which is typical of the rest of North America.[74]

Ontario Education and Health Care

Prior to the passage of the *School Boards and Teachers Collective Negotiations Act* of 1975, the province of Ontario permitted school board and teacher associations to bargain independently of government. However, with the passage of the *Act* in 1975, a more elaborate scheme was put into place. The *Act*, now administered by a special body designated as the Education Relations Commission, provides for negotiations between local school boards and teachers' association branches, although representatives from national teacher associations may attend the local negotiations. Bargaining takes place separately for elementary and secondary school teachers, but nothing in the *Act* prohibits the parties from negotiating jointly for both levels.

With respect to third-party assistance, the *Act* provides for the appointment of a fact-finder who, in the event of stalled negotiations, may make recommendations on any items in dispute. The report of a fact-finder is meant to serve as a basis for further negotiations towards the attainment of a settlement, but may be made public if an agreement is not reached within fifteen days. The underlying assumption is that making the report public in the local community will put pressure on both schoolboard and teacher negotiators to come to a settlement. Should negotiations drag on, the statute provides for the appointment of a mediator who may become more actively involved than a fact-finder in the actual negotiations. The statute also provides for arbitration which allows for final-offer selection of the total-package type. This provision, however, is seldom used.

Unlike the situation in Quebec where school board and teacher negotiations are very centralized, Ontario negotiations are very decentralized. So far, it does not appear as if there is any trend towards greater centralization of school board and teacher negotiations.[75] Hospitals and nursing homes in Ontario operate under the *Ontario Hospital Arbitration Disputes Act* of 1965 which provides for binding arbitration of contract negotiation disputes in hospitals and nursing homes. Until relatively recently, the hospitals bargained on a decentralized basis, each hospital negotiating its own agreement with nurses and other groups. In recent years, however, and particularly in 1981, a dramatic move has occurred toward centralized negotiations. During the Winter of 1981, a large number of hospitals attempted to negotiate a settlement with CUPE which bargains for many hospital workers. A negotiating team was drawn from a representative number of hospitals.

When negotiations broke down, CUPE negotiators disobeyed the provision of the Ontario statute requiring the appointment of a member to an arbitration board. In fact, CUPE leaders recommended a strike in protest against the arbitration proceedings since the union felt that it would not catch up or get a settlement large enough to bring its workers into line with other groups. CUPE, furthermore, advised workers to disobey a court injunction ordering striking workers to return to work.

It is generally conceded by observers that the strike was badly organized. Not surprisingly, therefore, the strike failed after a couple of weeks. A number of CUPE leaders were sentenced to prison or were fined for encouraging the workers to defy the court injunction.[76] Even when an arbitration board was set up under the chairmanship of the highly respected Paul Weiler, a former Chairman of the B.C. Labour Relations Board, CUPE refused to name its representative to the arbitration board, and the government was obliged to name a person to represent the union. When the arbitration decision was handed down, many workers and union leaders felt the decision to be slanted totally in favour of management.

The trend towards centralization of collective bargaining among hospitals in Ontario is, as we mentioned before, a fairly recent phenomenon. However, it is significant that over 100 hospitals joined together to bargain on a provincial basis during the round of negotiations in the Winter of 1981. What will take place in the future cannot be known for certain, but developments in recent years point to increasing centralization.

With respect to nursing homes, the picture in Ontario is a very different one. Practically all the nursing homes in the province negotiate on an individual basis. Few, if any, signs exist that coordinated or province-wide bargaining among nursing homes is likely to begin. This indication may be because some of the nursing homes are government owned and operated while others are private concerns. In addition, nursing homes do not rely solely on provincial funds as hospitals do: they receive money from both residents and government.

In summary then, one may identify a developing trend towards more centralized bargaining among hospital workers in Ontario which has yet to make itself felt among nursing home staff. Also, there is a growing disenchantment with the arbitration process in the health care field.

Saskatchewan Education and Health Care

Negotiations for teachers in Saskatchewan are conducted under the *Teacher Collective Bargaining Act* (1973) which is administered by the Education Relations Board. The *Act* provides for two-tier bargaining with one set of clauses negotiated at the provincial level and another at the local level. The Saskatchewan Teachers' Federation is the bargaining agent in provincial negotiations. The employers' association is the Saskatchewan School Trustees Association.

The statute provides that the Federation shall, prior to the commencement of negotiations and in any case no later than 101 days prior to the date on which an agreement negotiated pursuant to the *Act* expires, prepare written notice specifying the process for resolution, whether mediation, conciliation, or arbitration. The Saskatchewan statute does not allow teachers to strike. Stewardship of the employers' interests is shared by the Saskatchewan School Trustees Association (SSTA) and by government representatives.[77] The management negotiating team consists of nine members, four appointed by the SSTA and five by the government. Of the five government representatives, four are from the Department of Education and one from the Department of Finance.

Under this hybrid structure, the government contingent has a controlling vote in policy and position formulation. The government's main concern is with the high cost of settlements. Currently it pays in the range of 30% to 85% of the local operating costs of school districts. Hence any significant concessions would likely require a substantial increase in public spending. Although the SSTA wants to become the major negotiator for management, the government is reluctant to give up the control it now exercises.

A recent study by Wetzel and Gallagher concludes that

> To varying degrees, the Saskatchewan government has managed to divest itself of direct bargaining roles, assured that its legitimate interests will be adequately protected. Having been reasonably satisfied with the system during the recent bargaining round, there are no signs that the government wants any drastic change.[78]

Negotiations have become centralized not only in the Saskatchewan educational sector but also in the Saskatchewan health care sector. The government has encouraged hospitals and nursing homes to sign their bargaining rights to two non-governmental provincial industry associations. The Saskatchewan Health-Care Association (SHA) represents the province's 107 organized hospitals in bargaining, a responsibility it has carried since 1973. The Saskatchewan Association of Special Care Homes (SASCH) negotiates for thirty-eight of its 110 member nursing homes, a function begun in 1975. A government observer is present at negotiations for both hospitals and nursing homes.

The government seems anxious to avoid direct participation in these bargaining relationships. Wetzel and Gallagher point out that, "by placing distance between itself and the negotiations, the government endeavours to reduce its vulnerability to direct pressure from unions for bargaining concessions."[79] The SHA and SASCH both believe that maximum freedom from government interference can be attained by demonstrating trustworthiness in evolving reasonably stable relationships with the unions and in producing prudent settlements. Hence,

in Saskatchewan, the highly centralized structure of bargaining in the educational and health care fields parallels the centralized structure of negotiations in the province of Quebec, except that Quebec politicians appear to play a more active role.[80]

Conclusion

It is difficult to undertake a comprehensive discussion of collective bargaining among public servants in eleven jurisdictions as well as among teachers and municipal and health care workers. Nonetheless, it is possible to treat this subject adequately by elaborating on some of the statutory provisions and by giving some pertinent examples of their application. Students are encouraged to investigate more fully the specific provisions of the statutes for the province in which they live in order to fully appreciate the complexities of public-sector bargaining within a given jurisdiction.

questions

1 What kinds of workers are usually referred to as public and parapublic workers?
2 Do most jurisdictions in Canada have one statute governing both private and public-sector workers, or do most have at least two statutes?
3 Do you think that public-sector workers should have the right to collective bargaining? Should they have the right to strike?
4 How does the collective bargaining regime for public-sector workers, especially those covered by the federal *Public Service Staff Relations Act,* differ from the regime for workers in the private sector?
5 How have the various jurisdictions in Canada attempted to cope with strikes in essential services in the public sector? What is your assessment of these attempts?
6 How does collective bargaining apply to the educational and health care sectors in the provinces of Ontario, Quebec, and Saskatchewan?
7 If you were an advisor to a government contemplating the establishment of collective bargaining for its public servants, what would be the essential components of the scheme that you would suggest?
8 Prepare a list of services which are so essential that workers who perform them should not have the right to strike. Elaborate on the rationale for the inclusion of each service.
9 Are there goods or services in the private sector which are so essential that workers involved in them should not have the right to strike? Elaborate.
10 Do you feel that you have suffered personally as a result of an essential-service strike? Elaborate.

notes

1 S. B. Goldenberg, "Collective Bargaining in the Provincial Public Services," *Collective Bargaining in the Public Sector* (Toronto: Institute of Public Administration of Canada, 1973), p. 11; "Public Sector Labour Relations in Canada," *Public-Sector Bargaining*, eds. B. Aaron, R. Grodin, and J. L. Stern, Industrial Relations Research Association Series (Washington: The Bureau of National Affairs, Inc., 1979), p. 256.

2 W. B. Cunningham, "Public Employment, Collective Bargaining and the Conventional Wisdom: U.S.A. and Canada," Vol. 21, No. 3, *Relations Industrielles/Industrial Relations* (July, 1966), pp. 408-09. Cunningham provides an excellent critique of the conventional wisdom regarding the sovereignty of a state.

3 R. W. Flemming, "Public-Employee Bargaining: Problems and Prospects," Thirty-First Annual Meeting of the IRRA, *Proceedings* (Wisconsin: 1979), p. 6.

4 K. P. Swan, "Public Bargaining in Canada and the U.S.: A Legal View," Vol. 19, No. 3, *Industrial Relations* (Fall 1980), p. 278.

5 C. A. Edwards, "The Public Service Alliance of Canada," Vol. 23, No. 4, *Relations Industrielles/Industrial Relations* (1968), p. 636.

6 J. Finkelman and S. Goldenberg, *Collective Bargaining in the Public Service: The Federal Experience in Canada* (Montreal: The Institute for Research on Public Policy, 1983), p. 3. This comprehensive study of collective bargaining under the federal *Public Service Staff Relations Act* will go down as a classic piece of analysis in the annals of industrial relations research in Canada.

7 J. B. Rose, "Growth Patterns of Public Sector Unions," *Conflict or Compromise: The Future of Public Sector Industrial Relations*, eds. M. Thompson and G. Swimmer (Montreal: The Institute for Research on Public Policy, 1984), p. 97.

8 Edwards, "The Public Service Alliance of Canada," p. 635.

9 Labour Canada, *Directory of Labour Organizations in Canada* (Ottawa: Supply and Services Canada, 1985), p. 150.

10 *Ibid.*, pp. 152-53.

11 Rose, "Growth Patterns of Public Sector Unions," p. 100.

12 *Ibid.*

13 Finkelman and Goldenberg, *Collective Bargaining in the Public Sector: The Federal Experience in Canada*, p. 4.

14 Labour Canada, *Directory of Labour Organizations in Canada*, p. xxii.

15 Rose, "Growth Patterns of Public Sector Unions," p. 100.

16 *Ibid.*

17 S. Goldenberg, "Collective Bargaining in the Provincial Public Sector," p. 29.

18 *Ibid.*, p. 37; K. Wetzel and D. G. Gallagher, "The Saskatchewan Government's Internal Arrangements to Accommodate Collective Bargaining," Vol. 34, No. 3, *Relations Industrielles/Industrial Relations* (1979), pp. 452-70.

19 Wetzel and Gallagher, "The Saskatchewan Government's Internal Arrangements to Accommodate Collective Bargaining," pp. 455-56.

20 Goldenberg, "Collective Bargaining in the Provincial Public Sector," p. 37.

21 See T. Wills, "Ottawa Goes Nose-to-Nose with Civil Service," *Montreal Gazette* (June 5, 1982).

22 P.E.I. *Regulations*, Part XV, 66(d).

23 *Public Service Staff Relations Act*, R.S.C., c. P-35 with amendments up to 1978-79, Schedule I, Parts 1 and 2.

24 Quebec Labour Code, R.S.Q., C-27 with amendments up to April 1, 1984, s. 111.2.

25 Ontario Regulations 577/72 under the *Crown Employees Collective Bargaining Act*, 1972, ss. 1-10.

26 *British Columbia Essential Services Disputes Act*, 1979, c. 113, s. 1.

27 Finkelman and Goldenberg, *Collective Bargaining in the Public Service: The Federal Experience in Canada*, p. xxxii.

28 S.N.B., 1968, c. 88, s. 24(6) (a).

29 S.B.C., 1979, c. 346, s. 4.

30 R.S.A., 1980, c. P-33, s. 18.

31 R.S.A., 1980, c. P-33, s. 22.

32 R.S.O., 1980, c. 108, s. 56(a).

33 The information contained herein was derived, at least in part, from a telephone conversation with the Registrar of the Ontario Public Service Labour Relations Tribunal, June 19, 1981.

34 Goldenberg, "Collective Bargaining in the Provincial Public Services," p. 26.

35 S.N.S., 1978, c. 3, Schedule "A."

36 The *Regulations* of the P.E.I. *Civil Service Act*, Part XVI, 113(c); S.N.S., 1978, c. 3, s. 2(c); *Regulations* 577/72 made under the Ontario *Crown Employees Collective Bargaining Act*, 1972,

O. Reg. 577/72, ss. 7-11.

37 Labour Canada, *Directory of Labour Organizations in Canada, 1985*, p. 172.

38 R.S.C., c. P-35 with amendments up to 1978-79, s. 34(c); R.S.B.C., 1979, Ch. 346, s. 5(b); R.S.A., 1980, c. P-33, as amended up to January 18, 1984, ss. 25 and 29; S.S. as of October 1983, c. T-17, ss. 6(2) (b) and 8; R.S.O., 1980, c. 108, s. 4; R.S.Q., c. C-27 with amendments up to April 1, 1984, ss. 21 and 28; S.N. 1973, No. 123, ss. 6 and 7. The Ontario statute also makes provision for prehearing votes which are conducted in the same way as they are conducted in the private sector.

39 J. Finkelman, Q.C., Pt. 1, *Employer-Employee Relations in the Public Service of Canada: Proposals for Legislative Change*, (Ottawa: Information Canada, 1974), p. 232.

40 R.S.C., c. P-35 with amendments up to 1978-79, s. 70(3).

41 R.S.A., 1980, c. P-33, s. 48(2); R.S.O., 1980, C. 108, s. 18.

42 R.S.B.C., 1979, Ch. 346, s. 13.

43 R.S.B.C., 1979, Ch. 346, s. 11(1) (a) (b).

44 *Report of the Preparatory Committee on Collective Bargaining in the Public Service*, (Ottawa: Queen's Printer, 1965), pp. 34-39.

45 I am very grateful to my good friend, G. Plant, Secretary-Registrar of the Public Service Staff Relations Board, for correcting the mistakes on this subject in the first edition of the book.

46 *Report of the Royal Commission on Employer-Employee Relations in the Public Service of New Brunswick* (1967), p. 34.

47 R.S.C., c. P-35 with amendments up to 1978-79, s. 70(1); S.N.B., 1968, c. P-25, s. 84(1).

48 R.S.C., c. P-35 with amendments up to 1978-79, s. 68.

49 Finkelman, Pt. 1, *Employer-Employee Relations in the Public Service*, p. 125.

50 Finkelman, "Voluntary Arbitration," (an address prepared for delivery to the Electrical Contractors Association of Ottawa, May 5, 1972; mimeographed and unpublished).

51 John Crispo, "Collective Bargaining in the Public Sector: Seminar Report," *Collective Bargaining in the Public Sector*, pp. 95-105, particularly pp. 101-05.

52 R.S.C., c. P-35 with amendments up to 1978-79, s. 78; and S.N.B., 1968, c. 88, s. 49.

53 R.S.C., c. P-35 with amendments up to 1978-79, s. 86(3).

54 S.N.B., 1968, c. 88, s. 57(1).

55 Much of the material on the federal statute is taken from the author's own study which is cited as the source for Table 10.2.

56 S.N.S., 1978, c. 3, s. 33(2).

57 R.S.B.C., 1979, Ch. 346, s. 17(7)-(10).

58 S.N., 1983, c. 24, s. 3. This became section 17.1 of the *Public Service (Collective Bargaining) Act, 1973*.

59 S.N., 1983, c. 24, s. 2. This section replaces section 10 of the *Act, ibid*.

60 The author is deeply indebted to Mr. B. Bastien, Chairman, and Mr. A. Gagnon, Member, of the Quebec Essential Services Council for the information which they so freely supplied on the operations of the Council.

61 G. Hebert, "Public Sector Bargaining in Quebec: A Case of Hypercentralization," *Conflict or Compromise: The Future of Public Sector Industrial Relations*, eds. Thompson and Swimmer, pp. 229-81.

62 P. Feuille and J. C. Anderson, "Public Sector Bargaining: Policy and Practice," Vol. 19, No. 3, *Industrial Relations*, (Calif.) (Fall, 1980), p. 316.

63 Finkelman, Pt. 1, *Employer-Employee Relations in the Public Service of Canada*, pp. 179-80.

64 R.S.O., 1980, c. 108, s. 18(3).

65 R.S.O., 1980, c. 108, s. 18(2).

66 T. J. Plunkett, "Municipal Collective Bargaining," *Collective Bargaining in the Public Service*, pp. 1-10.

67 *Ibid.*, p. 4.

68 *Ibid.*

69 *Ibid.*

70 Labour Data Branch, Labour Canada, *Directory of Labour Organizations in Canada 1985*, p. 55.

71 Plunkett, "Municipal Collective Bargaining," p. 6.

72 Feuille and Anderson, "Public Sector Bargaining: Policy and Practice," p. 313.

73 Plunkett, "Municipal Collective Bargaining," p. 9.

74 J. Boivin, *The Evolution of Bargaining Power in the Province of Quebec's Public Sector (1964-1972)*, (Quebec City: Département des relations industrielles, Université Laval, January 1975), p. 313.

75 For a recent discussion of negotiations in the Ontario grade school system, see B. M. Downie, "Collective Bargaining Under an Essential Services Disputes Commision," *Conflict or Compromise: The Future of Public Sector Industrial Relations*, eds. Thompson and Swimmer, pp. 373-401.

76 W. List, "Hartman Sentenced to Forty-Five Days in Prison," *Globe and Mail* (June 12, 1981), p. 1.

77 Wetzel and Gallagher, "The Saskatchewan Government's Internal Arrangements to Accommodate Collective Bargaining," p. 464.

78 *Ibid.*, p. 468.

79 *Ibid.*, p. 459.

80 For an interesting comparison of the approaches of Canada's three western provinces in hospital negotiations, see K. Wetzel and D. B. Gallagher, "Management Structures to Accommodate Multi-Employer Hospital Bargaining in Western Canada," *Conflict or Compromise: The Future of Public Sector Industrial Relations*, eds. Thompson and Swimmer, pp. 282-313.

11

The Outputs of the Canadian Industrial Relations System

The Financial Post

Introduction

In the chapter "Framework for Analyzing Industrial Relations Systems," the field of industrial relations was defined as a complex of private and public activities, operating in a specified environment and concerned with the allocation of rewards to workers for their services and the conditions under which the services are rendered. So far, our discussion has centered primarily on the actors, the environment, and the complex of private and public activities under which we include the labour movement, the legislative provisions, the negotiation pro-

cess, the forms of third-party assistance, the grievance procedure, and the arbitration of contract interpretation disputes. It is now time to turn our attention to a discussion of the outputs of industrial relations systems since, by definition, the outputs are the most important part of real-world industrial relations systems. The outputs or rewards to workers for their services are at the very core of and constitute the dependent variables of our framework. The outputs are the raison d'être of industrial relations systems.

We will discuss two kinds of outputs — *organizational* and *worker-oriented* — and will follow the breakdown given by Beal, Wickersham, and

Kienast in the *Practice of Collective Bargaining.*[1] Among the organizational outputs, we will examine *management rights, union recognition, union security,* and *dues check-off.* Three types of worker-oriented outputs will be considered: (1) the *wage and effort bargain* including wage rates, hours, and pay for time not worked, such as holidays and paid vacations; (2) *job rights* and *due process* which will involve items such as seniority, just cause in cases of discipline and discharge, some aspects of the grievance process, and the establishment of reasonable rules and fair treatment; and (3) *contingency benefits,* including compensation for layoffs, permanent separation from a job, illness, accidents, or untimely death; provisions to ensure safety in the workplace and to protect worker health; and superannuation, pensions, and insurance plans for workers. In addition to organizational and worker-related outputs, this chapter will also deal with a third output of the industrial relations system: industrial conflict, be it in the form of strikes or lockouts.

When collective bargaining first started in North America, collective agreements were basically one page in length. Workers would post a new wage schedule on the employer's door and await the employer's approval. Over the years many items other than wages have become the subject of negotiations. Present-day collective agreements are, as a result, very complex. A quick glance at Table 11.1, which sets out a table of contents from a Canadian collective agreement, shows the tremendous amount of detail now involved.

Since it is impossible to discuss all clauses in collective agreements, a select number will be analyzed in the remainder of this chapter. Before beginning the discussion of these outputs, however, we should first comment on the statistics which we will be using. The tables in this chapter are based on collective agreements covering 500 or more workers, excluding those in the construction industry. The tables in the first edition of this book were based on an analysis of collective agreements covering 200 or more workers in 1981, the only year for which 200 workers served as the basis for the annual publication. Due to constraints in the federal public sector and possibly a change in the priorities given to different activities, the data in the 1985 publication are based on collective agreements covering 500 or more workers.

While the figures included in most of the tables are averages, the tables may be broken down by twenty major groupings in the manufacturing industry: three primary industries such as forestry, fishing, and mining and thirteen additional non-manufacturing industries such as transportation, communications, trade, services, and public administration. Construction is excluded in all of the tables since Labour Canada has only recently included construction in its data bank.

Organizational Outputs

Management Rights Clauses

Management rights clauses usually refer to the prerogatives of management to operate the enterprise subject to the terms of a collective agreement. The following is an example of these clauses:

> Nothing in this agreement shall be deemed to restrict the management in any way in the performance of all functions of management except those specifically abridged or modified by this agreement.[2]

Table 11.2[3] shows that the vast majority of agreements covering about three-quarters of workers provide for management rights.

A major controversy exists over the so-called residual rights theory. Management claims to have unilateral control over all decision-making unless otherwise stated in the collective agreement. Management further contends that, if there is no clause in a collective agreement with respect to a particular issue, it has the right to make unilateral decisions on that issue. Most trade-union leaders would argue, on the other hand, that no such thing as residual manage-

Figure 11.1

Sample Table of Contents of a Collective Agreement: Index

Article	Page	Section
1. Scope	1	1.01-1.04
2. Recognition	1	2.01-2.03
Contracting Out	2	2.04
3. No Discrimination	3	3.01-3.03
4. Management	4	4.01
5. Union Security	4	5.01-5.03
6. No Cessation of Work	5	6.01
7. Adjustment of Grievances		
Differences Between the Company and Workers	5	7.01-7.07
Differences Between Company and Union	9	7.08
Time Limit Extensions	10	7.09
General Grievance Committee—Grievance Stewards and Plant Committeemen	10	7.10-7.22
8. Third Party Determination	14	8.01
Grievance Commissioner	14	8.02-8.05
Arbitration Board	15	8.06-8.13
9. Discharge and Discipline	18	9.01-9.04
10. Workers in Armed Forces	19	10.01
11. Seniority		
Definitions	20	11.01
Applications of Seniority on Layoff	21	11.02-11.07
Application of Seniority in a Department	24	11.08-11.09
Application of Seniority—Curtailment in Operations	25	11.10
Temporary Promotions, Demotions, and Transfers	26	11.11
Job Posting	26	11.12-11.20
Transfers General	31	11.21-11.23
Leaves of Absence	32	11.24-11.31
General (Designated Individuals, Summer Workers, Seniority List)	36	11.32-11.36
12. Establishment of New Department, Transfers, and Special Seniority Provisions	37	12.01-12.05

Article	Page	Section
Stationary Engineers, Refrigeration Operators, and Compressor Operators	69	20.12-20.15
Incentive for Study Courses	70	20.16
21. General Training	71	21.01-21.06
22. Incentives	73	22.01-22.07
23. Pensions	75	23.01-23.02
24. Insurances, Health, and Hospital Services	76	24.01-24.05
25. Cost of Living Allowance	77	25.01
26. Authority	79	26.01
27. Further Conferences	79	27.01-27.02
28. Termination	80	28.01
Signatures	81	
Schedules		
"A" Classifications of Workers Excluded from the Bargaining Unit	82	
"B" Rules Governing Proceedings of Grievance Commissioner	89	
"C" Rules of Arbitration	90	
"D" Departments	91	
"E" Classifications Entitled to Preferential Recall	92	
"F" Wages Rates	93	
"G" Apprentice Wage Rates	94	
"H" Plant Committeeman Areas	96	
"J" S.H.E. Committee Areas	98	
Worker Benefit Plans		
Group Term Life Insurance Plan	100	
Group Non-Occupational Accidental Death and Dismemberment Insurance Plan	103	
Prescription Drug Plan	105	
Non-Occupational Sickness and Accident Insurance Plan	106	
Dental Plan	107	
Letters of Agreement		

ment rights exists since the mere ownership and operation of capital does not give management the authority to rule on all matters concerning workers. Some labour leaders also argue that unions have the right to bargain not only over personnel matters, but also investment policy, pricing policy, and a variety of other areas in which management has traditionally had sole discretion.

Irrespective of the merits of either school of thought, there is no question that unions have, through collective bargaining, acquired a much broader role in decision-making than was previously true. For example, management at one time claimed that pension plans were not negotiable and that the administration of such plans was a management prerogative. Following a lengthy strike in the United States in 1947, however, pension plans became negotiable in the steel industry. This decision soon affected practically all other industries on the North American continent. Hence, if one were to look at management rights from a historical standpoint, one notes that as unions have gained the right to bargain over more and more issues, the area of management discretion or residual rights has narrowed considerably. This trend has not, however, eliminated the major philosophical difference between union and management spokesmen over the whole issue.

Union Recognition Clauses

Provisions to recognize a union as the sole bargaining agent for a group of workers resemble management rights clauses since both serve to define the relationship between two organizational entities. Usually, specific reference is made to the group of workers represented; for example, all the production and maintenance workers at Plant X located in City Y. The practice of including such clauses in collective agreements is, in some cases, a holdover from the days of voluntary recognition, when there were no laws requiring employers to negotiate in good faith with a certified bargaining agent. Today, most certificates issued by labour relations boards also name the bargaining agent and the group of workers for which it is the exclusive representative. This sometimes creates difficulties at a later stage when occupations in the original certificate begin to disappear and new ones evolve. Unless unions and management can agree to define the term "employee" in the certificate to include individuals in jobs not explicitly mentioned in the certificate, those individuals who logically should be part of the bargaining unit may be technically excluded. (The B.C. Telephone Case in Appendix 1 deals with this problem.)

Generally, union recognition clauses are helpful in dealing with this sort of difficulty which may, in part, account for their survival. In addition, such clauses may also be invoked in filing grievances over matters not explicitly covered in collective agreements.

Table 11.2 The Incidence of Management Rights Clauses in Collective Agreements Covering 500 or More Workers

	Agreements	Workers
	%	%
General statement of management rights	30.0	36.0
Enumerated list of management rights, residual with management	24.5	18.3
Enumerated list of management rights, residual rights silent	22.7	19.2
No provision	22.7	26.3
Total	100.0	100.0

Source: A special computer printout from Labour Canada as of February 1985. The universe for this analysis is 963 collective agreements in force covering 2,044,660 workers.

Union Security Clauses[4]

Union security clauses define the relationship between the union, as an organization, and its members. The different types of union security clauses include the closed shop, the maintenance of membership, the union shop, the modified union shop and the Rand formula. These are defined in the following terms:

Closed Shop Under the closed-shop form of union security, the company agrees to hire and retain in its employ union members only. The terms *closed shop* and *hiring hall* have been defined to include recruitment by or through the union. In a closed shop, however, it is customary for agreements to state that, if the union is unable to provide workers to the employer, the latter is free to hire workers of his own choice, providing these workers immediately become union members. Closed shops are very frequently found in the construction and longshore industries and are often associated with hiring halls which represent an arrangement between the union and employer(s) whereby the union agrees to supply the number of workers required.

Maintenance of Membership Under maintenance of membership clauses, workers are under no obligation to join the union; however, those who do must, as a condition of employment, maintain their union membership throughout the life of the contract.

Union Shop A union shop agreement requires all workers to become union members. No direction is given to the employer, however, as to whom should be hired. The employer is entirely free to employ non-union members, but they must join the union within a specified period after being hired and the employer must discharge any who fail to do so.

Modified Union Shop A modified form of union shop exempts from compulsory membership all workers who are not union members at the time the agreement comes into force but requires all those taken on subsequently to join the union. Maintenance of membership for those who are already union members may or may not be mentioned.

Rand Formula This formula requires that all workers within the bargaining unit, that is, union members and non-union members alike, must pay the equivalent of union dues as a condition of retaining employment. Table 11.3 shows that about 50% of agreements covering close to 50% of workers have union security clauses, the most prevalent of which are the union shop and the modified union shop. The Rand Formula is not contained in this table and hence the figure 51% for workers not covered by a provision is somewhat misleading.

Table 11.3	Union Security Clauses	
	Agreements	Workers
	%	%
Closed Shop	2.8	2.0
Union Shop	22.8	15.7
Modified union shop	19.2	27.7
Maintenance of membership for present and/or future workers	4.4	3.5
Other	0.1	0.0
No provision	50.7	51.0
Total	100.0	100.0

Source: Labour Data Branch, Labour Canada, *Provisions in Collective Agreements in Canada Covering 500 and More Employees: All Industries (Excluding Construction)* (Ottawa: Supply and Services Canada, July 1985), pp. 4-5. Reproduced by permission of the Minister of Supply and Services Canada.

Use of Union Security Clauses   The whole issue of union security clauses, and particularly those which require compulsory union membership, is a very controversial one between unions and management. Some employers take the view that they should not require workers to join unions as a condition of employment. They argue instead that it is the union's job to convince the workers of the merits of union membership and that only those who favour joining unions should be made to do so. Unions respond that membership is a means of making for greater solidarity of workers in the bargaining unit and also enables a larger number of workers in the bargaining unit to take part in union affairs, to run for union office, etc.

Employers also argue that the closed shop is a means of enabling unions to restrict the supply of workers by having control over the number of people admitted to a trade. Unions, however, contend that the closed shop, in conjunction with a hiring hall, is a real advantage to employers since the union acts more-or-less as the employers' recruiting agency. Many heated debates have taken place over compulsory unionism in the past and these still continue today. Among the general public, there is also much disagreement over the appropriateness of union security clauses, a fact which doubtless reflects the divergence in opinion of people coming from union and non-union backgrounds. The decisions which will emerge from cases now before the courts under the Charter of Rights and Freedoms may have a serious impact on compulsory unionism.

Check-off Clauses

A check-off clause refers to the practice whereby the employer, by agreement with the union, regularly withholds union dues from workers' wages and transfers these funds to the union. The check-off is a common practice in organized establishments and is not dependent upon the existence of a formal union security clause. The arrangement may also provide for deductions of related initiation fees, assessments and fines.

There are various types of check-off clauses: (1) *compulsory check-off* whereby the worker has no option but to have the dues deducted; (2) *voluntary revocable check-off* whereby the worker may sign dues over to the union but may subsequently revoke such assignment; and (3) *voluntary irrevocable check-off* whereby the worker, having once authorized the deduction of union dues, may not revoke such authorization. An additional form of check-off clause is one that is compulsory for union members only. Below are sample clauses relating to dues check-off:

Compulsory for all Workers

In the case of an employee covered by this agreement who is not a member of the union and who is not required to become a member of the union, the employer agrees to deduct and forward to the union, monthly, the regular weekly union dues in accordance with the Rand formula.

Compulsory for Union Members Only

The employer agrees to deduct at such intervals, as may be agreed upon by the parties, from the wages of each of its employees, who are members of the union and who have authorized the same, the prescribed dues and to remit the same once each month to the union. Each authorization shall be in writing, signed by the employee, and shall be delivered by the union to the employer.

Voluntary Revocable

The company shall remit to the union not less often than once each calendar month, amounts deducted from employees' wages in respect of initiation fees, regular monthly dues and duly authorized union assessments, pursuant to an assignment by individual employees in the following form:

To: (Company)
Until this assignment is revoked by me in writing, I, _____, hereby authorize you to deduct from wages earned by me the sum of $_____ for the month of _____ and thereafter the regular monthly dues and such assessments as may be generally levied by the local union in accordance with the constitution and by-laws thereof, and to forward these amounts to said union.

(Employee's Signature)

The local union hereby agrees that the company shall be saved harmless with respect to all deductions made and paid to the said Union in respect of provisions herein.

Use of Check-off Clauses Table 11.4 shows that compulsory dues check-off clauses are by far the most predominant. Hence, unions have been very successful in negotiating these clauses into their collective agreements. This success has enabled union officers and shop stewards to devote their time to more important matters such as handling grievances. During the early days of unions, union officers would collect dues from members as they entered their places of employment — a time-consuming method.

Dues check-off clauses, like union security clauses, have fairly serious philosophical implications for both unions and management. During the Winters of 1979 and 1980, a number of major strikes occurred over compulsory dues check-off. The problem had become so serious in Ontario during the Spring of 1980 that the government of that province passed legislation requiring that, if a union made a request for a dues check-off clause, the employer was compelled to include such a clause in the collective agreement. This measure effectively took the compulsory dues check-off out of the strike area in Ontario. In 1977, the Quebec Government revised its legislation to make dues check-off compulsory. Other provinces have taken similar action.

As indicated in Chapter 6, certain jurisdictions also provide for the payment of an amount of money comparable to the amount of the union dues to be paid to a charitable organization if a worker, because of religious beliefs, objects to the payment of union dues to the union.

Worker-Oriented Outputs

In the preceding section, we have discussed the organizationally oriented outputs or clauses of

Table 11.4	Check-Off Clauses	
	Agreements	Workers
	%	%
Voluntary (whether revocable or irrevocable)	5.4	3.6
Compulsory check-off for all workers	59.3	70.6
Voluntary for old workers, compulsory for new	1.5	2.6
Compulsory only for union members	24.7	17.3
Other	0.3	0.1
No provision	8.9	5.8
Total	100.0	100.0

Source: Labour Data Branch, Labour Canada, *Provisions in Collective Agreements in Canada Covering 500 and More Employees: All Industries (Excluding Construction)*, (Ottawa: Supply and Services Canada, July 1985), pp. 6-7. Reproduced by permission of the Minister of Supply and Services Canada.

collective agreements. We will now turn our attention to worker-oriented outputs, beginning with the wage and effort bargain.

Wage and Effort Bargain

As we noted in the chapter "Theories of the Labour Movement," most theorists believe that workers join unions to improve their wages, working conditions, job security, protection from arbitrary management action — and, in general, their lot in life. It should come as no surprise, then, that the vast majority of provisions in collective agreements are worker-oriented clauses which define workers' incomes and conditions of work. In discussing worker-oriented outputs, it is necessary to be quite selective since many modern-day collective agreements are over 100 pages in length, comprise some 100 or more sections, and include clauses on wages, COLA, hours, and various types of time paid for but not worked, all of which come under the heading of "wage and effort bargain."

In discussing the wage and effort bargain, we are looking at two sides of a coin. Workers are compensated for the services they perform. This compensation is a cost for the employer — a cost which must be justified by the productivity of the workers. During periods of inflation, workers are likely to demand large wage increases so as to maintain real income. If this occurs, the balancing of wage costs and productivity becomes both critical and difficult.

Wage Increases   Very few provisions in collective agreements are more important to workers than those covering the wages they receive in the performance of their duties. Table 11.5 gives an indication of percentage wage increases for the commercial and non-commercial sectors and an all-industry average for the years

1972 to 1984. The percentage changes in the tables are increases in base rates for new settlements during the year in question. These percentage increases for Canadian workers, which are based on the lowest or "sweeper" rate, are inflated in comparison with the figures published by the Bureau of Labour Statistics (BLS) in the United States which uses *average* rather than *base* rates. Also, American settlements are based on major agreements covering 1,000 or more workers while the Canadian data are restricted to major agreements covering 500 or more workers — the only negotiated wage data now available. This distinction should be kept in mind when readers see Canada-U.S. comparisons in the press, since the press does not differentiate the bases on which the data are computed in the two countries.

Table 11.5   **Average Effective Annual Percentage Changes in Base Rates for New Settlements Covering All Collective Bargaining Units of 500 or More Workers by Year, Construction Industry Excluded**

Year	Commercial	Non-Commercial[6]	All Industry
1972	9.2	7.7	8.0
1973	10.9	10.0	10.4
1974	14.9	14.8	14.8
1975	15.1	19.6	17.4
1976	9.6	11.0	10.4
1977	7.4	7.8	7.6
1978	8.2	7.0	7.6
1979	10.8	8.5	9.8
1980	11.6	10.8	11.1
1981	12.9	13.0	13.0
1982	10.1	10.5	10.2
1983	5.5	4.5	4.9
1984	3.4	3.8	3.6

Source: Collective Bargaining Division, Labour Data Branch, Central Analytical Services, Labour Canada for the year 1972 to 1977. Effective increases were calculated starting in 1978. The figures for the years 1978 to 1983 are taken from Collective Bargaining Division, Labour Data Branch, Central Analytical Services, Labour Canada, *Major Wage Settlements — Fourth Quarter and Annual Summary 1983,* Table F-1, p. 16. The figures for 1984 are taken from Labour Canada, *Major Wage Settlements:* Second Quarter, 1985 p. 1. The effective rates are based on an assumed CPI figure as a proxy for the inflation rate, the figure is applied to agreements with COLA clauses, and adjustments are made if the actual CPI is different from the assumed level.

Table 11.5 shows that the average annual percentage increases[5] in the commercial sector are slightly higher for the years from 1972 to 1974 than they are for the non-commercial sector, which includes the public sector. However, the average annual percentage increases in the non-commercial sectors for the years from 1975 to 1977 are somewhat higher than the increases in the commercial sector; this is particularly significant for the year 1975. As we shall see later, this may be explained in part by the spread of unions and by the great demand for labour in the public sector during this period. The increases for the years 1978 and 1979 again show that increases in the commercial sector are slightly higher than increases in the non-commercial sector, whereas 1980 and 1981 reverse this two-year pattern and show the negotiated average annual increases to be slightly higher in the non-commercial sector.[6] The figures for 1983 and 1984 are dramatically lower than those for any year since the 1950's. The figures are slightly lower in the non-commercial sector, resulting at least in part from the various public-sector restraint programs for these two years and from the serious recession of the past few years.

These figures stand out in sharp contrast to average annual percentage increases during the early 1950's when they were in the neighbourhood of 3.5% and, in 1956, slightly under 5%.[7] While the negotiated increases in Table 11.5 are somewhat high — especially for the years 1974, 1975, 1976, and 1980 — the figures alone tell us little, if anything, about workers' real income. The figures, in nominal dollars, need to be depreciated by increases in the consumer price index to arrive at real negotiated increases. (See Chapter 2 for tables on the CPI and the indexes of real income. The latter also include real average weekly wages and salaries.)

In recent years, there have been a substantial number of studies on the wage determination process both under collective bargaining and in the non-union sector. These studies adopt different methodologies and produce, to varying degrees, varying results.[8] While we will not examine their findings in detail, we will show what some of these studies have concluded with respect to the wage determination process in both the union and non-unionized sectors.

Effects of Inflation One study presents a model of wage determination which includes an analysis of the impact of price increases, labour market developments, and wage spillovers or pattern bargaining. The authors also compare the effects of direct bargaining, mediation, and work stoppages on wage determination in the negotiating process. Inflation is seen to affect wage outcomes in two respects: (1) as an anticipated factor which is built into a negotiated wage increase and (2) as a past reality that has not been compensated for. The researchers summarize their findings on these points in the following terms:

> The empirical results indicate that in the private sector approximately 40 percent of expected future inflation is built into the wage rate at the time the contract is signed and approximately 60 percent of past uncompensated inflation is corrected for at the next contract negotiation. Under a steady, fully-anticipated inflation, the combined price effects suggest that approximately 75 percent of the movement in consumer prices will be incorporated into wage rates.[9]

Thus, inflation, which we discussed in Chapter 2, has a significant impact on wage outcomes.

Labour Market Effects As far as the labour market is concerned, this study used various measures of unemployment and job vacancy rates in order to determine whether or not a relationship exists between unemployment and wage increases. The authors conclude that "Negotiated wage changes are remarkably insensitive to changing labour market conditions."[10] In fact, negotiated wages seldom decline at all but move up, level off, and then move up again — a phenomenon called the ratchet effect.

Pattern Bargaining Effects What seems of most importance is the impact of pattern bargaining. Four types of spillover or pattern bargaining, all mentioned in the study, include regional, industry, and combinations of the two. The strongest type was industry-related for a particular region. National patterns seem to be very weak and have very little if any impact on wage settlements, whereas patterns for a given industry within the same region do have pronounced effects on the outcome of negotiated wage settlements.[11] The pulp-and-paper settlements discussed in Chapter 2 thus had a pattern-setting effect, particularly in Eastern Canada.

In assessing the negotiating process on wage outcomes, these researchers used three stages at which settlements are reached: direct bargaining, mediation-conciliation, and work stoppages. While the three processes show significant differences among each other, the differences may be attributed principally to price considerations and spillover effects. By themselves, these three processes have very moderate influences.[12] These researchers found no evidence that settlements in the public sector spill over into the private sector.

Another study was concerned with a comparison of wage changes in major collective agreements in the private and public sectors, with more emphasis on the public sector than on the private sector. Like the previous study, it is based on the average annual percentage wage increases in base rates for major collective bargaining agreements covering 500 or more workers in Canada, excluding those in construction, and deals with approximately the same period (1967 to 1975). While the major dependent variable in this study is changes in wage rates, the major independent or explanatory variables are excess demand for labour and anticipated inflation. The authors assert that the economic environment creates an upper limit and a lower limit within which a wage settlement will take place. In addition, they indicate that the power of unions and management will indicate where the minimum and maximum wage levels fall within the range determined by

the market.[13] This supports our own assertion in the chapter "The Negotiation Process" that bargaining power is very significant in determining a specific settlement point.

Public-Sector Effects In a chapter on wages in the public sector, Cousineau and Lacroix suggest that government production of goods and services responds relatively little to typical variations in economic activity. In the early phases of public-sector unionization, wages increased markedly — a circumstance also noted for initial unionization in the private sector. This substantial wage increase could be absorbed, in part, because government derives its revenues from taxes and borrowings, rather than from the marketplace. The main beneficiaries of these initial wage increases were workers at the bottom end of the pay scale. Over the survey period, rates of increase in wages were found to be consistently higher for workers at the bottom of the wage scale than for those with moderate or high wages. This phenomenon was not, however, found in the private sector. Another difference between the private and public sectors was that labour market conditions (e.g. high unemployment) affect public servants' wage rates less than those of workers in the private sector. On the other hand, wage rates are more responsive to inflation in the public sector than in the private sector.[14]

The authors of this study suggest that, should Canada find itself in a situation with recession and high inflation occurring simultaneously, wages in the public sector could act as a factor in causing an economic slowdown:

> Indeed, wages in the public sector will increase even though they would decrease during a recession in the private sector. Business will then be faced with excessive wage demands even when it finds itself in serious financial difficulty.[15]

Furthermore, in an open economy such as Canada's, the pressure of public-sector wage increases on private-sector settlements results in a weakness in the competitive ability of Canada's economy, especially those sectors which are exposed to international competition.[16] To the extent that these findings are accurate, they support the contention in Chapter 2 concerning the impact of unions and collective bargaining on the export sector of our economy.

The picture painted in this study was dismal, and as a consequence the study received considerable attention when it was first released. However, the first study found no evidence to support the hypothesis that settlements in the public sector significantly spilled over into settlements in the private sector.[17]

Catch-up Effects One study which analyzed the bargaining outcomes (both wage and nonwage) of forty-nine of the seventy-two occupational groups in the federal public service for the first four rounds of negotiations found that the first three rounds were characterized by a high degree of pattern bargaining in which the clerical and manual occupations gained in relation to the professional occupations, thus narrowing the wage differentials. This is explained at least in part by the fact that the first three rounds of negotiations were characterized by a catch-up phase, in comparison to private-sector occupations and internal comparisons. A large proportion of the nonwage outcomes appear to have occurred during the first round. During the fourth round of negotiations, many bargaining units switched from arbitration to the conciliation board and strike route. The resulting strikes affected wage and nonwage outcomes significantly. This round-ended the catch-up phase and resulted in greater wage dispersion.[18]

Human Capital Effects Gunderson, one of the most prolific writers on comparisons between wage increases in the private and public sectors, has come to several conclusions. One conclusion — based on 1971 census data and human capital variables (human resource endowments) such as education, experience and training, along with other independent variables of wage determination — was that public-sector workers have greater human capital endowments than do their private-sector counterparts. Another conclusion was that male and female public-sector workers with human capital endowments equivalent to their private-sector counterparts earned 6.2% and 8.6% more respectively than their private-sector equivalents.[19]

A subsequent study by the same author in which the data used were all industry averages for various occupations in various cities during 1977 showed that the public-sector advantage was about 1% for male blue-collar occupations and about 3% for predominantly female white-collar jobs. The author concluded that, since the private-public wage differentials are very volatile, the public-sector advantage which appeared in his earlier study had probably dissipated by 1977.[20] Using more recent data, the same author's most recent conclusion is that

> although there was a rising trend from a public sector wage disadvantage to a wage advantage over the period from 1952 to 1980, that advantage peaked sometime in the latter part of the period. In addition, the advantage, even at its greatest, was not very large.[21]

The author concludes that, with the maturation of unions in the public sector, the new taxpayer militancy, and the fiscal crises of many governments, the public sector may not be the place to be in the future.[22] And this writer's consistent conclusions have not yet been disproven.

Effects of Unionization A study undertaken by G. F. Starr dealt with the general effect of unionization on wages, and concluded that the "union-nonunion wage differential for production workers in manufacturing lies in the range of 10 to 17 percent."[23] This study concluded that, while spillover effects between unionized and nonunionized sectors may be important, it would be difficult to indicate with any degree of accuracy the difference between wage increases in the unionized sector and wage increases in the nonunionized sector.[24]

Johnson's study of non-union wage changes in Canada listed the factors which are taken into account when decisions are made regarding wage adjustments.[25] Johnson differentiated between primary and secondary factors, primary factors being those which had the greatest impact on a given wage change and secondary factors being those which contributed in a less significant way to a wage change. The primary and secondary factors were then summed for each item to show its overall impact on wage settlements. Outside wages, inside wages and turnover (number of workers who quit relative to number of workers hired) headed the list as having the most influence on wages, followed by profits, cost-of-living, minimum wages, market conditions, employment changes, and arbitrary (miscellaneous) items.[26]

Overall, outside wages (the going rate for this type of work in the same industry or area or

both) far outstripped other items in determining wage adjustments, including inside wages (a rate of pay for other jobs within the same company or institution). Many of the factors noted in these studies were discussed in Chapter 2. These factors demonstrate how important the environment of an industrial relations system can be on the outcomes of the system, even in the non-union sector.

It should be noted that, in recent years, other writers have attempted to develop and test general models of industrial relations systems to explain bargaining outcomes and, in particular, wage settlements. Many of these studies show very low correlations between the variables in these models and the outputs of the industrial relations system.[27]

It may be some time yet before we will be able to quantify the variables in industrial relations in order to adequately explain and predict the increases and the levels of the outputs of the industrial relations system, because there are far too many variables in our frameworks to quantify and too many outputs to explain. What seems to be needed is the development of proxy variables for a number of the more detailed variables in the frameworks in order to develop an explanatory — and more importantly — predictive model.

Table 11.6   Cost of Living Allowance Provisions in Force at the End of Each Year Covering 500 or More Workers, Excluding Construction 1975-1984

Year	% Agreements	% Workers
1975	38.1	43.7
1976	45.5	49.0
1977	33.2	45.3
1978	36.9	43.0
1979	34.2	42.3
1980	32.8	46.1
1981	39.4	49.7
1984	28.1	35.4

Source: The data for the years 1975 to 1978 are taken from Collective Bargaining Division, Labour Data Branch, Labour Canada, "Cost-of-Living Allowance Provisions in Major Collective Agreements, 1977, 1978 and the first half of 1979," December, 1979. The data for the years 1979-1981 were provided by the Collective Bargaining Division, Labour Data Branch, Labour Canada. The data for these years are preliminary and subject to revision. No data were available for 1982-83, and that for 1984 is based on only 802 agreements covering 1,769,953 workers, including the construction industry. The data for 1984 are for agreements that have an expiry date greater than or equal to December 31, 1984 and result from a special computer printout from Labour Canada, February 26, 1985.

Cost-of-Living Allowance Cost-of-living allowances are regular cents-per-hour or percentage increases made to workers through the operation of escalator clauses or other types of cost-of-living adjustments. In Canada, the rate is determined in accordance with changes measured by Statistics Canada's Consumer Price Index for the whole country. A sample clause of a cost-of-living allowance is the following:

In addition to the wage rates set out in the Schedule, any increase or decrease in the cost of living, during the period of this agreement, shall be based on changes in the Consumer Price Index as published by Statistics Canada and pegged on the figure of 126.8. Adjustment either upward or downward will be made on the basis of 1 cent per hour for each 0.6 change in the CPI but in no event will a decline in the CPI below 126.8 provide a basis for reduction in the negotiated wage schedule.

Table 11.6 summarizes the major collective agreements on file (covering 500 or more workers in all industries, except construction) which have COLA clauses and the percentage of workers covered by such clauses. The figures indicate that COLA clauses became more important during periods of high inflation because it was a means whereby workers could try to maintain real income. COLA clauses reached a peak of 49% in 1976 when the CPI was still above 10%, declined somewhat when inflation fell below 10%, but reached an all-time peak in 1981 when the CPI hit 12.5%. Hence, the incidence of COLA clauses appears to follow the inflation rate fairly consistently. Note that only about 45% of workers were covered by COLA clauses during 1984, a year of low inflation.

Table 11.7 shows that for the year 1985 less than one-third of agreements covering about 45% of workers had COLA clauses: with inflation running relatively low for two years, the incidence of COLA clauses could be expected to decline also. The table also shows that only about one-third of workers were covered by immediately effective COLA clauses. In the public sector of Quebec, COLA clauses were more prevalent than in any other jurisdiction in Canada.

From a worker's point of view, COLA clauses are particularly important in multi-year collective agreements when the rate of inflation is very difficult, if not impossible, to predict. There is a serious disagreement as to whether or not COLA clauses are inflationary in nature and the evidence is so mixed that it is impossible to reach a definite conclusion on this issue. What studies on this matter do indicate, however, is that, contrary to what many economists refer to as the "money illusion," i.e. that people tend to judge wage raises in absolute rather than relative terms, workers are very much aware that their actual negotiated increases could be substantially eroded if they were not protected by some kind of COLA provision in the case of increasing or sustained inflation.

The evidence shows that quarterly and annual adjustments are the most frequent provisions in COLA clauses. One of the more

Table 11.7	Cost of Living Allowance	
	Agreements	Workers
	%	%
Provision is effective immediately	26.7	33.7
Provision exists but to be implemented at a later date	3.6	4.4
Provision inoperative	3.6	5.5
Other	—	—
No provision	66.0	56.3
Total	100.0	100.0

Source: Labour Data Branch, Collective Bargaining Division, Labour Canada, *Provisions in Collective Agreements in Canada Covering 500 and More Employees: All Industries (Excluding Construction)* (Ottawa: Supply and Services Canada, July 1985), p. 79. Reproduced by permission of the Minister of Supply and Services Canada.

Table 11.8	Method of Calculating COLA Rate of Payment for Agreements with COLA	
	Agreements	Workers
	%	%
Cents per point increase in index	52.9	26.4
Percent increase in wages per percent increase in index	36.4	62.0
Cents per percent increase in index	2.2	0.7
Other	8.4	11.0

Source: The data for this table are based on 255 collective agreements covering 626,603 workers, including construction. The agreements have an expiry date greater than or equal to December 31, 1984 and result from a computer printout from Labour Canada, February 26, 1985.

Table 11.9	Triggering Formula Used for Payment of COLA for Agreements with COLA	
	Agreements	Workers
	%	%
Minimum percent increase in CPI	48.9	63.8
Minimum points increase in CPI	0.4	0.2
After specified level in CPI	1.3	0.6
Minimum cents for cents and percent increase in CPI	4.0	1.5
No trigger mechanism specified	45.3	34.0

Source: The data for this table are based on 255 collective agreements covering 626,603 workers, including construction. The agreements have an expiry date greater than or equal to December 31, 1984 and result from a computer printout from Labour Canada, February 26, 1985.

Table 11.10	Eligibility Requirements for Paid Statutory Holidays	
	Agreements	Workers
	%	%
Must have worked the last scheduled working day before	0.4	0.3
Must have worked the next scheduled working day after	0.0	0.0
Must have worked both working days immediately before and after	41.4	34.9
Must have worked either working day immediately before or after	10.4	16.8
Must have worked a specified length of time prior to the holiday	9.6	10.2
Other	0.2	0.1
No provision	38.0	37.8
Total	100.0	100.0

Source: Agreement Analysis Section, Labour Data Branch, Labour Canada, *Provisions in Collective Agreements in Canada Covering 500 and More Employees: All Industries (Excluding Construction),* (Ottawa: Supply and Services Canada, July 1985), pp. 88-89. Reproduced by permission of the Minister of Supply and Services Canada.

interesting aspects of the COLA phenomenon is the different methods used in making adjustments for increases in the cost-of-living.

As can be seen from Table 11.8, the two most important methods used for calculating COLA adjustments are the *cents-per-point increase* in the consumer price index and the *percent increase in wages per percent increase in the consumer price index*. The first accounts for over 50% of agreements covering over one-quarter of workers. The second accounts for 36% of agreements covering about two-thirds of workers. The percent increase in CPI is the prevalent method of triggering COLA clause adjustments, but close to 50% of agreements with COLA clauses specify no triggering mechanism — past practice or common understanding, however, probably governs the implementation of these COLA clauses.

Hours of Work According to the most recent statistics on hours of work per day, less than 50% of agreements covering about 40% of workers specify eight-hour days. Seven and a half hours, the next most prevalent length of workday, is required of over one-third of workers. Unions have been making slow but steady gains in reducing the length of the workday. Now, less than 2% of workers are required to work more than eight hours per day.[28]

Labour Canada data indicate that 47% of collective agreements require 38% of workers to put in forty hours of work per week. The next most prevalent length of workweek is thirty-seven and a half hours which is required by 11% of collective agreements covering 14% of workers.[29]

Overtime Compensation Usually, workers who put in time beyond normal hours are compensated for overtime by a rate of pay much greater than normal hourly wages. The available evidence indicates that about 45% of the collective agreements covering over 49% of the workers make provision for time-and-a-half. Another 29% of the agreements covering more than 30% of workers provide for time-and-a-half to be followed by double time. Over 17% of agreements covering about 15% of workers make no provision for overtime.[30] An interesting thing about these figures is the provision for double time — a fairly recent development. Now, 7% of agreements covering over 4% of workers makes provision for double time only, and it is likely that demands for double time will increase in the future.

Paid Holidays A substantial proportion of collective agreements stipulate that workers must be paid for statutory holidays. In order to be eligible for this payment, however, workers must meet certain conditions with respect to days worked before and after the statutory holiday. The following is a sample clause setting out the most common requirement:

> In order to be eligible for pay for a statutory holiday, an employee should work his scheduled hours the day *immediately preceding* and *immediately succeeding* the holiday unless he has received permission in writing to be absent.

Table 11.10 indicates that the most prevalent provision (34.9%) requires workers to work both the day before and the day after the holiday. A significant proportion (16.8%) of workers are paid for statutory holidays if they work either the day before or the day after the statutory holiday.

Paid Vacations In addition to the provisions shown in Table 11.11, there is often some arrangement for unused vacation time to be car-

Table 11.11	Selected Data for Paid Vacation Clauses in Collective Agreements Covering 500 or More Workers			
		Minimum years of service	% Agreements	% Workers
3 weeks:	most common provision	1 year	31.3	38.0
	2nd most common provision	5 years	19.2	12.5
	no provision		19.7	24.0
4 weeks:	most common provision	10 years	27.3	32.0
	2nd most common provision	6-9 years	27.5	23.7[a]
	no provision		15.6	11.2
5 weeks:	most common provision	20 years	26.9	30.3
	2nd most common provision	16-19 years	21.8	17.7
	no provision		22.6	18.0
6 weeks:	most common provision	30 years	9.3	13.0
	2nd most common provision	25 years	11.9	8.8
	no provision		56.7	59.6

[a]These workers are concentrated in the Community, Business and Personal Services sector which includes such fields as education, health and retail trade.

Source: Labour Data Branch, Labour Canada, *Provisions in Collective Agreements in Canada Covering 500 and More Employees: All Industries (Excluding Construction)* (Ottawa: Supply and Services Canada, July 1985), pp. 95-103. Reproduced by permission of the Minister of Supply and Services Canada.

ried over from year to year. About 30% of workers are covered by such a provision in their collective agreement. Only 16% of collective agreements covering 12% of workers prohibit such a carry-over. For the remaining 51% of workers, there is no specific provision in their contracts in this regard. In some instances, however, an informal arrangement with management might hold.[31] Five- and six-week vacations, a fairly recent phenomenon, may become more prevalent in the future as a means of sharing available work.

Job Rights and Due Process

This category of benefits relates to job rights such as the use of seniority in promotion, lay-off and recall, and the procedures set out to handle workers' grievances.

Seniority Seniority may be defined broadly as a worker's total length of continuous service with the employer. Seniority is based upon the principle that priority or preference is accorded to the worker with longer service. The term is used to fix a worker's status relative to other workers as a criterion to be used in determining promotions, layoffs, vacations, etc. Seniority may be on a departmental basis, plant-wide basis, or some combination of these.

Super- or special seniority is a position higher than what the worker would acquire solely on the basis of length of service or other general seniority factors. Usually such treatment is reserved for union stewards who are entitled to special consideration in connection with layoff and recall to work, since it is they who help workers in the handling of their grievances and they who have the most experience in the shop and in the grievance procedure. The following is a sample clause relating to the use of seniority in promotions:

> The company agrees to recognize the principle of departmental and plant seniority in job progression and in the layoff and rehiring of employees in a fair and equitable manner having regard not only to the length of service, but as well to the knowledge, training, skill, efficiency and physical fitness of the employee or employees concerned to do the work assigned.

It will be observed in the sample clause that although seniority is one of the major factors taken into account in promotion, skill, efficiency, and physical fitness are also considered.

Seniority is one criterion for determining layoff priority. A layoff is an involuntary separation from employment for a temporary or indefinite period that results from no fault of the workers. Although layoff usually implies eventual recall, or at least an intent to recall workers to their former jobs, the term is occasionally used for separations plainly signifying permanent loss of jobs, as, for example, in plant shutdowns. A sample clause relating to the use of seniority in layoffs is as follows:

> In cases of transfer to avoid layoff, other than those of a temporary nature, and layoff due to lack of work, the company agrees that seniority in the classifications and in the classes within the classifications shall be the prime consideration, but the union recognizes the company's right to have

Table 11.12	Seniority on Promotion	
	Agreements	Workers
	%	%
Straight seniority	0.6	0.3
Seniority with other factors such as ability, skill, knowledge, and physical fitness	34.3	30.7
Straight seniority if other factors are equal or sufficient	39.3	33.4
No provision	25.8	35.6
Total	100.0	100.0

Source: Agreement Analysis Section, Labour Data Branch, Labour Canada, *Provisions in Collective Agreements in Canada Covering 500 and More Employees: All Industries (Excluding Construction)* (Ottawa: Supply and Services Canada, July 1985), p. 11. Reproduced by permission of the Minister of Supply and Services Canada.

regard for ability and to retain a limited number of employees of lesser seniority who, because of special training or ability, are essential to the efficient operation of the plant, provided such employees are placed in jobs making use of such special training or ability.

Interesting contrasts appear when one analyzes the use of seniority in promotion and in layoff. While provision is made in 17.8% of agreements covering 17.9% of workers for layoff on the basis of straight seniority, only 0.6% of agreements covering 0.3% of workers make provision for promotion on this basis. Also, while straight seniority is the most common provision respecting promotion, *ceteris paribis*, such is not the case with layoffs, where seniority is given more weight compared with other factors such as ability, skill, knowledge, and physical fitness. This possibly reflects employers' desires to bring back workers with skill levels above the minimum required, in case promotional opportunities occur before the end of the layoff.

Seniority is also a criterion for determining recall. Recall is the process of bringing laid-off workers back to work, usually based on the same principles that governed the order of layoff but in reverse order (e.g., the last worker laid off is the first to be recalled.) A sample clause dealing with the use of seniority in recall is the following:

> When the working force is increased after a layoff...employees will be recalled according to seniority, providing the greater seniority employees are able to perform the available work.

While numerous strikes were conducted in the past over the role of seniority in promotions, layoffs and recalls, there have been very few within recent memory. Unions argued that the longer workers remained with an employer, the more rights they acquired to available jobs. Employers, on the other hand, wanted as much flexibility as possible in dealing with their workers. Over the years, the parties seem to have resolved the dilemma by recognizing the validity of both the seniority criterion and

Table 11.13	The Use of Seniority on Lay-Off	
	Agreements	Workers
	%	%
Straight seniority	17.8	17.9
Seniority with other factors such as ability, skills, knowledge and physical fitness	40.6	40.9
Straight seniority if other factors are equal or sufficient	21.4	15.5
No provision	20.2	25.8
Total	100.0	100.0

Source: Labour Data Branch, Labour Canada, *Provisions in Collective Agreements in Canada Covering 500 and More Employees: All Industries (Excluding Construction)* (Ottawa: Supply and Services Canada, July 1985), p. 12. Reproduced by permission of the Minister of Supply and Services Canada.

Table 11.14	The Use of Seniority in Cases of Recall	
	Agreements	Workers
	%	%
Straight seniority	13.5	12.9
Seniority with other factors such as ability, skills, knowledge, and physical fitness	43.1	38.2
Straight seniority if other factors are equal or sufficient	17.3	13.3
No provision	26.0	35.6
Total	100.0	100.0

Source: Agreement Analysis Section, Labour Data Branch, Labour Canada, *Provisions in Collective Agreements in Canada Covering 500 and More Employees: All Industries (Excluding Construction)* (Ottawa: Supply and Services Canada, July 1985), p. 14. Reproduced by permission of the Minister of Supply and Services Canada.

criteria of ability, suitability, etc. in determining promotions, layoffs, and recall. Tables 11.12 to 11.14 demonstrate this resolution.

Worker Grievances — Initial Presentation As indicated in the chapter "The Administration of the Collective Agreement," a worker may take a grievance to the supervisor alone or in the company of a shop steward. The following sample clause is one which makes provision for both cases:

> An employee may make a complaint to his foreman or other immediate supervisor either individually or accompanied by a shop steward. Such complaint shall be submitted within 30 calendar days of the occurrence or cause thereof.

The latest available evidence indicates that in about 73% of agreements covering 70% of workers, grievances may be submitted to supervisors with or without union representatives.

Table 11.15 Special Grievance Procedure in Disciplinary or Dismissal Cases

	Agreements	Workers
	%	%
Number of steps in the grievance is reduced	46.4	45.1
Duration of delays between steps is reduced	4.0	5.3
Reduced number of steps in grievance & reduced duration of delays between steps	7.5	6.4
Other	—	—
No provision	42.2	43.2
Total	100.0	100.0

Source: Agreement Analysis Section, Labour Data Branch, Labour Canada, *Provisions in Collective Agreements in Canada Covering 500 and More Employees: All Industries (Excluding Construction)* (Ottawa: Supply and Services Canada, July 1985), p. 28. Reproduced by permission of the Minister of Supply and Services Canada.

The next most frequent provision requires that workers alone submit grievances to supervisors. The submission of grievances by union representatives alone is less frequent still.[32]

Special Grievance Procedures in Disciplinary or Dismissal Cases Discipline and discharge cases are initiated at higher levels of the grievance procedure than other cases. A sample clause providing for a special procedure in the case of dismissal is as follows:

> A claim by an employee that he has been unjustly discharged shall be treated as a grievance if a written statement of such grievance is lodged at Step No. 3 of the Grievance Procedure within three working days after the discharge, or within three working days after the union has been notified of the discharge, whichever is the later.

Table 11.15 indicates that 46% of the agreements covering about the same percentage of workers provide for a reduction in the number of steps in the grievance procedure in disciplinary or dismissal cases. The relatively high incidence of such provisions indicates how seriously disciplinary and dismissal cases are taken.

Contingency Benefits

Contingency benefits are intended to cover situations that cannot be anticipated precisely for any individual worker. Such benefits may be activated in response to a number of unforeseen events including layoff, bereavement, or illness. It is to some of these items that we now turn our attention.

Severance Pay and Supplemental Unemployment Benefits (SUB) Severance pay is defined in general terms as monetary payments made by employers to displaced workers, generally upon permanent termination of employment with no chance of recall. Sometimes, however, severance pay is given upon indefinite layoff with recall rights intact. The plans usually provide for lump-sum payments but may allow several payments over a period of time. Plans normally calculate such payments in accordance with length of service. Severance pay is also sometimes termed termination pay, dismissal allowance, separation benefit, or layoff allowance (where layoff implies permanent layoff.) The following is a sample clause of the use of severance pay on retirement:

> An employee who has ten or more years, continuous service in the employ of the employer is entitled to be paid on resignation or retirement severance pay equal to the amount obtained by multiplying the number of completed years of continuous employment by his weekly salary to a maximum of twenty weeks pay.

Supplemental unemployment benefit plans (SUB) provide regular weekly payments to laid-off workers. Usually SUB plans are funded by an employer contribution to the fund in terms of so many cents per hour worked and are used primarily in cases where workers are laid off owing to cyclical downturns in the industry or, sometimes, in cases of major seasonal variations. A sample supplemental unemployment benefit plan is as follows:

> The regular benefit payable to an eligible employee for any week beginning on or after December 31, 1973 shall be an amount which, when added to his unemployment insurance benefit and other compensation, will equal 95% of his weekly after-tax pay.

The use of averages masks a great deal of disaggregated information. For example, while close to 43% of the total agreements covering 30% of workers have no provision for severance pay and supplemental unemployment plans, wide variation exists among industry classifications. There is no such provision in fishing because of the extremely seasonal nature of the industry. In mining, which is a year-round operation, 34% of agreements covering 27% of workers have no provisions. Hence, the environment of the industry is an important factor influencing the outputs of industrial relations systems. Within the manufacturing sector, the presence of such provisions range from a high of about 100% in agreements covering 100% of workers in tobacco

products to no agreements in knitting mills.[33] The latter industry in Canada must compete with cheaper foreign-made imported goods. The fact that many of them are barely able to exist could be the major reason the incidence of severance pay and supplemental unemployment insurance is so low.

Paid Leave of Absence for Death in the Immediate Family The vast majority of collective agreements make provision for paid leave of absence in cases of death in the immediate family. What one has to watch for in examining these kinds of clauses is how the collective agreement defines *immediate family*. The following sample clause indicates the provisions contained in one particular agreement:

> In the event of death in the family of an employee with three months or more service, the employee will be granted a leave of absence for a reasonable period of time to attend the funeral and will be reimbursed for wages lost by reason of time lost, provided, however, that the amount reimbursed will not exceed three days' wages at average earnings or hourly rate. The term *member of an employee's*

Table 11.16	Paid Leave of Absence — Death in Immediate Family	
	Agreements	Workers
	%	%
1 day	0.4	0.5
2 days	0.2	0.1
3 days	51.9	45.0
4 days	10.5	15.7
5 days	26.0	28.4
More than 5 days	1.4	2.2
Other	2.9	3.1
No provision	6.7	5.0
Total	100.0	100.0

Source: Agreement Analysis Section, Labour Data Branch, Labour Canada, *Provisions in Collective Agreements in Canada Covering 500 and More Employees: All Industries (Excluding Construction)* (Ottawa: Supply and Services Canada, July 1985), p. 108-09. Reproduced by permission of the Minister of Supply and Services Canada.

family means a husband or wife, son or daughter, brother or sister, mother or father and mother-in-law or father-in-law.

Table 11.16 indicates the provisions in collective agreements which require paid leave of absence in case of death in the immediate family. Most collective agreements contain a provision allowing at least three days of paid leave of absence in the case of a death in the immediate family. Four and five days are the two next most prevalent provisons.

Paid Maternity Leave An increasing number of collective agreements provide for leave of absence with or without pay in maternity cases. A sample clause reads as follows:

Maternity leave of not more than six months shall be granted, with pay for four weeks.

Maternity leave with pay, a relatively new phenomenon, is provided for in agreements

Table 11.17	Maternity Leave With Pay	
	Agreements	Workers
	%	%
With pay	4.4	11.9
Without pay	42.5	37.0
With and without pay	9.8	19.2
Use of sick leave (with or without specified maximum)	3.2	2.9
Weekly indemnity or group insurance plan	0.6	0.3
Other	0.6	0.6
No provision	38.9	28.1
Total	100.0	100.0

Source: Agreement Analysis Section, Labour Data Branch, Labour Canada, *Provisions in Collective Agreements in Canada Covering 500 and More Employees: All Industries (Excluding Construction)* (Ottawa: Supply and Services Canada, July 1985), pp. 140-41. Reproduced by permission of the Minister of Supply and Services Canada.

covering about 12% of workers. About 43% of agreements covering 37% of workers provide for maternity leave without pay. In some cases, sick leave may be used as maternity leave.

These figures, taken by themselves, would appear to indicate that unions still have much to do in order to provide paid leave for maternity cases. The maternity leave provisions negotiated in the Post Office Agreement during the Summer of 1981 and by Bell Canada in 1982 will no doubt be a target which many unions will seek to achieve in the future. Nonetheless, the figures used here grossly underestimate the coverage given to women since the percentages apply to all workers under collective agreements covering 500 or more workers, and such agreements, in many cases, cover bargaining units which are predominantly or exclusively composed of male workers. (Thus far, paternity and adoption leave is somewhat of a rarity and usually does not extend beyond a few days.)

Labour standards legislation, which covers such things as minimum wages, hours, paid holidays, vacations, and maternity leave, usually follows well behind provisions found in collective agreements. An examination of all eleven labour standards acts revealed that none of them requires an employer to grant paid maternity leave. While every act requires employers to grant maternity leave, some specify that such leave will be without pay. As more workers gain paid maternity leave under collective agreements, eventually most jurisdictions will probably require a minimum period of paid maternity leave.

Medical, Dental, and Disability Coverage Among the other important contingency benefits that are contained in collective agreements, basic medicare, dental, and long-term disability coverage are among the most important. Employer-paid medicare premiums have been of concern to unions ever since medicare was first introduced into Canada. Contributions by employers vary between 100% (in

33% of agreements) and 75% (in 9% of agreements). Nevertheless, 50% of workers still must pay 100% of their medicare premiums — a situation which may soon change in the workers' favour.[34]

About one-third of workers are covered by dental plans for which premiums are fully paid by the employer. A number of other arrangements exist for the payment of dental care premiums by employers, but over 50% of workers are still not covered by dental plans. This situation, too, may soon change in the worker's favour.[35] Long-term disability coverage is a recent development. Sixty percent of workers are not yet covered by such plans. A small percentage (16%) have their premiums paid in full by their employers. A smaller proportion still (5.5%) have their premiums partially (75% to 99%) paid by their employers.[36] With respect to sick leave, the most common provision is for fifteen days a year.[37]

Contracting-Out

Contracting-out refers to a practice of having certain steps in a manufacturing process, plant maintenance, or other functions performed by outside contractors using their own work forces. The following clause is a sample of a contracting-out clause in a collective agreement:

> It shall be the policy and intention of the company to use its workers as much as practicable for work at the plant. The company has the right to contract out work as required when such action does not result in a regular qualified employee of the bargaining unit being replaced.

Quite a controversy exists over the right of management to contract out work. A majority of collective agreements do not contain a provision regarding contracting-out, since employers are averse to concessions that challenge the management residual rights theory. The unions, for their part, wish to safeguard the jobs of their members from encroachment by contract workers.

But, despite the general aversion of actors in the industrial relations system to contracting-out, agreements covering 21% of workers specifically permit it. It is interesting to compare this figure to the 25% of workers covered by agreements which prohibit contracting-out that leads to layoffs or failure to recall. It is surprising that employers have made such concessions concerning layoffs and recall, particularly since the jurisprudence on this issue has been unclear for some time: "it is now universally accepted that bargaining unit work may be subcontracted to non-employees, provided that the subcontrac-

Table 11.18	Provisions in Collective Agreements Regarding the Contracting-Out of Work	
	Agreements	Workers
	%	%
Permitted	16.9	21.0
Prohibited	1.5	0.6
No contracting-out if it leads to layoffs or failure to recall members of bargaining unit	26.1	25.8
No contracting-out to non-union employer	1.3	1.4
No contracting-out if it leads to layoffs or failure to recall members of bargaining unit & if it is to a non-union employer	1.1	0.6
Other	0.1	0.2
No provision	53.0	50.3
Total	100.0	100.0

Source: Agreement Analysis Section, Labour Data Branch, Labour Canada, *Provisions in Collective Agreements in Canada Covering 500 and More Employees: All Industries (Excluding Construction)* (Ottawa: Supply and Services Canada, July 1985), pp. 152-53. Reproduced by permission of the Minister of Supply and Services Canada.

ting is genuine and not done in bad faith."[38] *Legitimate* in this context means that the work must be performed by independent contractors or the workers of independent contractors.[39]

Some Concluding Comments on Worker-Oriented Outputs

This section on worker-related outputs has tried to cover some of the major provisions in collective agreements dealing with remuneration for work and the conditions under which work is performed. Outputs are determined by the general management philosophy or personnel policies of the employer and by workers' attempts, through their unions, to have an impact on the terms and conditions that govern their employment. The latter is quite obviously one of the most important aspects of an industrial relations system, for without the desire of workers to have some control over the conditions under which they work and over the compensation and other benefits they receive, neither unions nor collective bargaining would be necessary.

Industrial Conflict as an Output of the Industrial Relations System

A collective agreement reached between union and management without a strike may have a positive feedback to the participants in the industrial relations system. For example, if a settlement satisfies the vast majority of workers, then they are likely to be happy with their work, working conditions, and benefits. Consequently, there may be a decline in absenteeism or staff turnover and, possibly, higher output or productivity. While there is certainly no hard evidence to support the statements we have made here, there are some indications that these kinds of results will likely take place if a collective agreement is reached peacefully and if the provisions of that agreement are acceptable to the vast majority of workers.

Should union and management not be able

to reach an agreement on their own, or with third-party assistance, then they may resort to strikes or lockouts. Should a work stoppage occur, another type of output from the industrial relations system results. Strikes may have a beneficial effect insofar as they enable workers to relieve frustrations. Strikes also act as catalysts — as lockouts do — in the negotiation process. Nonetheless, strikes and lockouts may have potentially detrimental consequences for other aspects of the economy and society. We shall deal more fully with this topic when we deal with the concept of the feedback loop.

Strikes may be defined as a cessation of work or a refusal to work by workers in combination, in concert, or in accordance with a common understanding which is directed at getting the employer to agree to terms and conditions of employment. Strikes are also defined in a number of statutes as a slow-down or other concerted activity on the part of workers to restrict or limit output. Strikes are legal during the negotiation or renegotiation of collective agreements only after certain conditions have been met. Strikes are illegal if conducted during the life of a collective agreement. A wildcat strike is one which is conducted without the approval of union officers. A lockout may be defined as the closing of the place of employment or the suspension or refusal of work by an employer to compel his workers, or to aid another employer to compel his workers, to agree to proposed terms or conditions of employment.

There are a number of ways of measuring the incidence of strikes: a major problem, however, is finding an appropriate way. This is true particularly in comparing strikes among jurisdictions or countries. The number of strikes occurring during a specified period of time is one measure, but this tells us little since some countries may have a large number of very short strikes while others may have a small number of very long ones. The number of person-days lost is another measure sometimes used, but this too tells us little unless we know something about the size of the labour forces, particularly for purposes of comparison. The number of workers involved in strikes during a specified period is another measure, but this too tells us little unless we know something about the size of the labour forces being compared.

Time lost due to strikes and lockouts as a percent of estimated working time is another way of measuring the incidence of strikes — this is the most widely used method. By giving a percentage or relative measure, this method makes comparisons much easier. However, one must be careful in comparing strikes among countries since the reporting of strikes may vary from one country to another. For example, one-day walkouts in protest against government policies may be counted as strikes in some countries, but not in others.

Strikes and Lockouts in Canada from 1901 to 1984

The most important element in Table 11.19 is the last column which shows the percentage of estimated time lost due to strikes and lockouts. This table reveals a high number of man-days lost following both World Wars (.6% in 1919 and .54% in 1946). More recently, the percentage of estimated working time lost began to increase in 1966 when it jumped to 0.34% from 0.17% in 1965. The figures continued to be high during the late 1960's, throughout the 1970's with the exception of 1971 and 1977, and throughout the early 1980's with the exception of 1983. An examination of this data will reveal the cyclical nature of increases and decreases in the frequency of work stoppages.

Before proceeding to attempt an explanation for this cycle, we should first put strikes in their proper perspective. If we look at the number of person-days lost in 1980 due to unemployment (217 million) or due to accidents or illness for which money was claimed through workers' compensation (13.4 million), the figures for strikes and lockouts (approximately 9 million) fade into pale insignificance.[40] In recent years, absenteeism has become an increasingly important phenomenon among workers and, if allowed to grow, will become a much more important

cause of person-hours lost. Furthermore, as pointed out previously, about 90% of collective agreements in Canada are settled without strikes.

Major Causes of Strikes

The continued high incidence of strikes in Canada relative to other countries in recent years has led to an increased interest in this topic. One of the better studies which attempts to analyze industrial conflict in Canada is that of S. M. Jamieson, a long-time commentator on this subject.[41] Jamieson indicates that, for the period from 1966 to 1975, Canada has experienced the highest incidence of strikes (as measured by person-days lost per 1,000 workers) of any nation except Italy. He contends that this high level of conflict seems to have been caused by two particular features of Canada's political economy and industrial relations system:

> (1) the unique pattern of economic instability in Canada, arising from the high degree of specialization of her export trade and highly unstable and capital-intensive resource industries. These have exerted a strong and destabilizing 'multiplier effect' on other sectors of the economy, particularly the construction and 'heavy' capital goods industries; and (2) the highly decentralized trade union movement, and its political weakness and inability to exert any significant influence over the economic policies of business and governments.[42]

He goes on to point out that economic instability generates high levels of industrial conflict for a variety of reasons. These include:

> the rapid increase in profits as compared to wages during boom periods; the widespread feelings of insecurity created by periodic labour shortages and over-expansion, by mass layoffs and unemployment; and, most important perhaps, the widely unequal gains in wages and fringe benefits for workers in different industries.[43]

In addition, Jamieson claims that six industries which employ less than 15% of all workers accounted for more than 50% of all person-days lost due to strikes during the period from 1966 to 1975. These six industries are construction, mining and smelting, transportation, primary

Table 11.19   **Strikes and Lockouts in Canada,**
                                                                    1901-1980

Year	Number beginning during year	Number	Workers involved	Man-days	% of estimated working time
1901	97	99	24,089	737,808	—
1902	124	125	12,709	203,301	—
1903	171	175	38,408	858,959	—
1904	103	103	11,420	192,890	—
1905	95	96	12,513	246,138	—
1906	149	150	23,382	378,276	—
1907	183	188	34,060	520,142	—
1908	72	76	26,071	703,571	—
1909	88	90	18,114	880,663	—
1910	94	101	22,203	731,324	—
1911	99	100	29,285	1,821,084	—
1912	179	181	42,860	1,135,786	—
1913	143	152	40,519	1,036,254	—
1914	58	63	9,717	490,850	—
1915	62	63	11,395	95,042	—
1916	118	120	26,538	236,814	—
1917	158	160	50,255	1,123,515	—
1918	228	230	79,743	647,942	—
1919	332	336	148,915	3,400,942	0.60
1920	310	322	60,327	799,524	0.14
1921	159	168	28,257	1,048,914	0.22
1922	89	104	43,775	1,528,661	0.32
1923	77	86	34,261	671,750	0.13
1924	64	70	34,310	1,295,054	0.26
1925	86	87	28,949	1,193,281	0.23
1926	75	77	23,834	266,601	0.05
1927	72	74	22,299	152,570	0.03
1928	96	98	17,581	224,212	0.04
1929	88	90	12,946	152,080	0.02
1930	67	67	13,766	91,797	0.01
1931	86	88	10,736	204,238	0.04
1932	111	116	23,390	255,000	0.05
1933	122	125	26,558	317,547	0.07
1934	189	191	45,800	574,519	0.11
1935	120	120	33,269	288,703	0.05
1936	155	156	34,812	276,997	0.05
1937	274	278	71,905	886,393	0.15
1938	142	147	20,395	148,678	0.02
1939	120	122	41,038	224,588	0.04
1940	166	168	60,619	266,318	0.04
1941	229	231	87,091	433,914	0.06
1942	352	354	113,916	450,202	0.05
1943	401	402	218,404	1,041,198	0.12
1944	195	199	75,290	490,139	0.06
1945	196	197	96,068	1,457,420	0.19

Table 11.19 continued

Strikes and Lockouts in Canada,
1901-1980

Year	Number beginning during year	Number	Workers involved	Man-days	% of estimated working time
1946	223	226	138,914	4,515,030	0.54
1947	231	234	103,370	2,366,340	0.27
1948	147	154	42,820	885,790	0.10
1949	130	135	46,867	1,036,820	0.11
1950	158	160	192,083	1,387,500	0.15
1951	256	258	102,793	901,620	0.09
1952	213	219	112,273	2,765,510	0.29
1953	166	173	54,488	1,312,720	0.14
1954	155	173	56,630	1,430,300	0.15
1955	149	159	60,090	1,875,400	0.19
1956	221	229	88,680	1,246,000	0.11
1957	238	245	80,695	1,477,100	0.13
1958	251	259	111,475	2,816,850	0.25
1959	201	216	95,120	2,226,890	0.19
1960	268	274	49,408	738,700	0.06
1961	272	287	97,959	1,335,080	0.11
1962	290	311	74,332	1,417,900	0.11
1963	318	332	83,428	917,140	0.07
1964	327	343	100,535	1,500,550	0.11
1965	478	501	171,870	2,349,870	0.17
1966	582	617	411,459	5,178,170	0.34
1967	498	522	252,418	3,974,760	0.25
1968	559	582	223,562	5,082,732	0.32
1969	566	595	306,799	7,751,880	0.46
1970	503	542	261,706	6,539,560	0.39
1971	547	569	239,631	2,866,590	0.16
1972	556	598	706,474	7,753,530	0.43
1973	677	724	348,470	5,776,080	0.30
1974	1,173	1,218	580,912	9,221,890	0.46
1975	1,103	1,171	506,443	10,908,810	0.53
1976	921	1,039	1,570,940	11,609,890	0.55
1977	739	803	217,557	3,307,880	0.15
1978	1,004	1,058	401,688	7,392,820	0.34
1979	987	1,050	462,504	7,834,230	0.34
1980	952	1,028	441,025	8,975,390	0.38
1981	943	1,048	338,548	8,878,490	0.37
1982	608	677	444,302	5,795,420	0.25
1983	576	645	329,309	4,443,960	0.19
1984	655	718	186,767	3,871,830	0.16

Source: For the figures 1901 to 1973, *Strikes and Lockouts in Canada,* Information Canada, 1975, pp. 7-8; and the figures for the years 1974 to 1980 are taken from Labour Data, Labour Canada, *Strikes and Lockouts in Canada* (Ottawa: Supply and Services Canada), p. 9. Reproduced by permission of the Minister of Supply and Services Canada. The figures for 1981-1983 are taken from Labour Data, Labour Canada, *Strikes and Lockouts in Canada* (Ottawa: Supply and Services Canada, 1983), Table 1, p. 13. Reproduced by permission of the Minister of Supply and Services Canada. The figures for 1984 are taken from Labour Canada, *Collective Bargaining Review,* October 1985, p. 78.

metals, pulp and paper, and wood products. Between 1966 and 1970, these industries accounted for 53.5% of person-days lost. The addition of transportation, communication, and public utilities raised the total to 73.4%.[44] Construction is the leader in person-days lost due to strikes. Jamieson has been claiming for some time that economic instability is one of the major factors in the high incidence of strikes in Canada. In his more recent study, he contends that this factor has accounted for a disproportionate share of all strike activity in Canada during the 1960's and 1970's. With respect to the period from 1966 to 1975, he observes that:

> the half-dozen or so goods-producing industries which accounted for more than one half of all man-days lost in strikes during 1966-75 were also among the most cyclically sensitive, and enjoyed among the largest wage increases during the 1960's. These, in turn, appeared to have a pattern-setting role, stimulating workers in other major sectors such as transportation, public utility and public sectors generally to demand and strike for larger gains in the 1970's.[45]

In keeping with his earlier analysis, Jamieson also claims that more than three-quarters of all person-days lost due to strikes during the period from 1966 to 1975 were concentrated in the three main industrial provinces of Ontario, Quebec and British Columbia. He suggests that if the person-days lost due to strikes under federal jurisdiction were estimated for each province in proportion to its share of workers in the industries or occupation involved, these three provinces would account for more than 90% of all person-days lost. However, he indicates that the timing of strikes, the different percentages of person-days lost, and the uneven strike record for these three provinces in the 1960's and 1970's may be attributed to different provincial responses to the same broad economic forces.

One may also attribute the high percentage of person-days lost in Canada to the long duration of strikes. From 1960 to 1976, the percentage of strikes in Canada which lasted over twenty-five days increased from 19% to 40%. In 1977,

Canada experienced 100 strikes, 10% of which lasted between fifty and ninety-nine days and accounted for 30% of all time lost that year. In addition, about 4% of the strikes lasted from 100 to 199 days and accounted for 17% of the time lost. Thus 14% of the strikes in 1977 accounted for approximately 47% of the time lost, a fact which confirms the view that Canada's problem is not the number of strikes, but their duration.[46]

Public- and Private-Sector Strikes

As indicated in the previous chapter, we will now discuss strikes in the public sector. The analysis here is based on a recent study of strikes in the Canadian public sector.[47] The basic issue explored in this study is which sector — the public or private — is more strike-prone. D. A. Smith, the author of the study, compared the frequency, size, and duration of strikes between the two sectors.

Using the frequency of strikes as a measure of strike activity, it was concluded that there was a slight upward trend in the proportion of public-sector strikes. However, when allowances were made for the degree of employment and unionism in the public sector, Smith concluded that "[s]ince public employees constitute approximately 25 per cent of the Canadian labour force and approximately 45 per cent of union members, it is clear that in terms of frequency the public sector is less strike prone than is the private sector."[48]

Using time lost due to strikes for the period from 1972 to 1981 as a measure of strike activity, Smith found that in only two of the ten years studied did time lost exceed the employment rate in the public sector. However, for the entire period from 1972 to 1981, "the average share of the public sector in the total number of workdays lost is just over 20 per cent, a figure which is below the employment share of the public sector."[49]

On a sectoral basis, strikes were found to be more frequent in the education and health care sectors. Over 61% of public-sector strikes occurred in these two sectors in 1980, compared with just over 30% in 1972.[50] In attempting to discover explanatory variables for the frequency of public-sector strikes, Smith found that when inflation, unemployment, and other variables were controlled for, the number of strikes continued to increase in the public sector.[51] In addition, strikes in the public sector were found to be less responsive to labour market conditions than were strikes in the private sector. The author concluded that strikes in the public sector are motivated more by politics than by economics.[52]

Some Consequences of the Outputs of the Canadian Industrial Relations System

In keeping with the framework set out in the first chapter, it is appropriate, at this point, to discuss the outputs of the industrial relations system as they feed back into the system itself and into the environmental subsystems. Among the organizationally oriented outcomes of the industrial relations system, union security clauses and union dues check-off clauses have aroused the most controversy and have generated a fair amount of industrial conflict in a number of jurisdictions. The degree of conflict was so great in Ontario that the Ontario government felt it necessary to legislate compulsory dues check-off so as to avoid strikes over the issue.

Union recognition clauses in collective agreements have served to legitimize unions not only in the workplace, but also at higher societal levels. Many public and parapublic white collar workers now belong to unions because of union security clauses, and pay union dues according to dues check-off provisions. This fact has been responsible in part for the widespread acceptance of unions in Canada as the legitimate voice for the aspirations of practically all categories of Canadians.

With respect to worker-related outputs, wages and other items which have a cost component to them are sometimes seen as causes of the in-flationary spiral. It can be argued that at the micro or plant level a high increase in wages in any one year, if not offset by a substantial increase in productivity, could cause an increase in costs and eventually an increase in prices. Yet, while most economists agree that unions may have some "wage push" effects on inflation, no one has yet been able to specify precisely what impact negotiated wage increases and other cost items have in the inflationary process. Nevertheless, it is the real or perceived effects of wage increases on cost, prices, and hence inflation which prompt governments to introduce wage and price controls (sometimes called incomes policies) in an effort to reduce the rate of inflation. The high wage settlements in Canada in 1975 led the government of the day to legislate wage and price controls effective as of October 15 of that year.

Unions have a long history of lobbying governments and trying to negotiate shorter working hours. Shorter hours of work, negotiated holidays, and the increasing length of vacations are now giving workers more leisure time in a highly-paced and stressful society. In addition, the forty-hour work week in most collective agreements has also had an impact on governments setting standard hours per week and establishing regulations concerning overtime for non-unionized workers.

Negotiated group medical and dental plans give workers a sense of security should they become ill, and retirement plans, including early retirement, allow workers a good deal of flexibility in deciding how to spend their later years. The recent emergence of negotiated maternity leave should also add to this sense of security, especially among those working women who are important contributors to family incomes or who are primary wage-earners. In addition, such measures in collective agreements may eventually serve as a model for legislation governing the provision of maternity leave.

On the general question of job security, unions have been instrumental in establishing seniority as an important factor in matters of promotion, lay-off, and recall. Here, too, there is evidence that clauses in collective agreements have served as models for legislation covering both unionized and non-unionized workers. Another output of the industrial relations system — the work stoppage — also has important societal implications. This will be discussed in more detail in the following section concerning industrial disputes and their political consequences.

Industrial Conflict and Back-to-Work Legislation

A strike in one industry may very well have serious detrimental effects on other industries in our economic system or may affect the well-being of citizens nationally or in a given province. If it seems clear that the public strongly objects to such work stoppages and if the politicians are convinced that hardships are occurring, they will likely pass back-to-work legislation. This is a good example of a feedback loop.

Some governments monitor the effects of a strike and pass special back-to-work legislation only when a strike begins to have serious consequences. In 1966, for example, when railway workers struck, the federal Department of Labour watched the impact of the strike on the movement of grain and other goods. It was only when the movement of goods came close to a halt that special legislation was enacted. Department officials knew from experience that railway workers do not undertake strike action lightly and that, in this case, there were many pent up frustrations that a short strike might alleviate.

Governments are not always sensitive to the need to relieve worker tension resulting over stalled bargaining talks. In the 1978 postal strike, for example, where postal workers had been working for a year or more without a renewed agreement and there was much hostility on both sides, the Federal Government passed special back-to-work legislation very soon after the strike was called. This seemed a puzzling deci-

sion since two previous postal strikes of a month or more were settled without back-to-work orders. It was later revealed that the Postmaster-General had been erroneously advised by informed sources that the workers would not obey a strike call by the president of the union. It was only the day that special legislation was introduced in Parliament that the Postmaster-General discovered that the workers were in fact prepared to strike.

In the above case, the government may be criticized for basing the decision to invoke back-to-work legislation on the anticipated outcome of a strike vote rather than on any clear-cut notion of a strike's detrimental effects. As such, the decision was potentially damaging to respect for the rule of law because it invited defiance of the back-to-work order.

As may be seen from the above examples, the problem of strikes is particularly acute in public-sector bargaining. Laval University professor Jean Boivin observed that, while there seems to be no superior alternative to collective bargaining in determining the working conditions of public-sector workers, there is also no universal solution to problems in public-sector labour relations.[53] "What should be recognized in the end," he claimed, "is that the final solution to labour relations conflict in the public sector will always be a political one."[54]

I concur with this view, inasmuch as there seems to be no final answer as to what the most appropriate form of action should be with respect to disputes in the public sector and in essential areas of the private sector. Arbitration as a method of resolving interest disputes is often violated, as was demonstrated in the Ontario hospitals case in the Winter of 1981. Back-to-work legislation tends to be habit-forming because governments, as well as the parties, often look to it as a face-saving device. Fines and imprisonment do not seem to be effective remedies to collective bargaining problems, particularly in the public and essential-service sectors. Generally speaking, "The openness of the Canadian economy," according to the *Report of the Royal Commission on the Economic Union and Development Prospects for Canada,*

the importance of cyclically unstable industries, such as mining, which have high strike/lock-out rates, the large number of items covered by North American collective agreements, the decentralized nature of collective bargaining, and the absence of institutional mechanisms for the exchange of information among employers, employees, and the union leadership all contribute to a high level of work stoppages compared to that of other countries, which generally do not share all...these characteristics.[55]

One must finally conclude that the ultimate responsibility for resolving industrial disputes resides with the elected Members of Parliament or the provincial legislators who are there to act on behalf of society as a whole. This principle implies, however, a respect both for the parties involved in an industrial dispute and for the public good.

questions

1 Do you see any relationship between the outputs (particularly the wage settlements and COLA clauses) contained in this chapter and some of the environmental factors discussed in Chapter 2? Elaborate.
2 What are the major organization-oriented outputs? Elaborate.
3 Is the three-fold conceptual distinction of worker-oriented outputs a useful one? Why or why not?
4 What is the significance of each of the three types of worker-oriented outputs? In which category do you expect to see the most changes in the next five years?
5 Discuss the incidence of industrial conflict as an output of the industrial relations system. What are the major causes for its high incidence and how may it be reduced?
6 What significance do the outputs of the Canadian industrial relations system have for other subsystems of Canadian society?

Elaborate.
7 Do the sample clauses and tables in this chapter give you a better understanding of collective bargaining than you had when you began the course? Elaborate.
8 Do you now see why increases in wages, if not offset by increases in productivity, might account for increases in prices? Through what process might this occur for a small company operating in the community from which you come?
9 Does the evidence presented in this chapter on the incidence of strikes in the private and public sectors accord with what the public generally thinks? Elaborate.
10 Do you agree with the assessment of back-to-work legislation presented in this chapter? Do you see any alternatives to it? Do you consider an essential-services council, such as that in Quebec, to be a good solution to essential-service disputes? Elaborate.

notes

1 E. F. Beal, E. D. Wickersham, and P. K. Kienast, *The Practice of Collective Bargaining*, 5th ed. (Homewood Ill: Richard D. Irwin, Inc., 1976) in particular Pt. 3, Chs. 9-13.
2 The sample clauses contained in this and other sections are taken from Labour Data Branch, Labour Canada, *Sample Clauses for the Analysis of Collective Agreements*, Annex to the Coding Manual for the Analysis of Collective Agreements (1974).
3 All tables, with the exception of this one and a few others which are the result of special computer print-outs, are based on an analysis of 972 collective agreements covering 2,060,486 workers.
4 Definitions of union security clauses have been modified from those provided by Labour Canada in the publication cited above.
5 The annual figures were obtained by taking all negotiations settled in any given calendar year and calculating the average annual percentage increase over the life of the agreement. These figures were then weighted by the total number of workers covered by the agreements,

summed, and the weighted mean for the calendar year was obtained. The effective wage increase is arrived at by assuming an estimated inflation rate based on the CPI and used as a proxy for the rate of inflation. The CPI is applied to those agreements which contain COLA clauses. Adjustments are made subsequently if the increase in the CPI is different from the assumed increase.

6 The non-commercial industries consist of highway and bridge maintenance, water systems and other utilities, hospitals, welfare organizations, religious organizations, private households, education and related services, public administration, and defence. Commercial industries consist of all industries except the non-commercial industries.

7 See Alton W. J. Craig and Harry J. Waisglass, "Collective Bargaining Perspective," Vol. 23, No. 4, *Industrial Relations/Relations Industrielles*, (1968), p. 587.

8 Jean-Michel Cousineau and Robert Lacroix, *Wage Determination in Major Collective Agreements in the Private and Public Sectors* (Ottawa: Supply and Services Canada, 1977); D. A. L. Auld, L. N. Christofides, R. Swidinsky, and D. A. Wilton, *The Determinants of Negotiated Wage Settlements in Canada* (1966-1975) (Hull: Supply and Services Canada, 1979); G. G. Johnson, *Non-Union Wage Changes in Canada: Theory and Survey Evidence* (Hull: Supply and Services Canada, 1979); A. A. Porter *et al.*, *Wages in Canada and the United States: An Analytical Comparison* (Ottawa: Queen's Printer, 1969); G. F. Starr, *Union-Nonunion Wage Differentials: A Cross Sectional Analysis* (Toronto: Research Branch, Ontario Ministry of Labour, March 1973); N. M. Meltz and D. Stager, *The Occupational Structure of Earnings in Canada, 1931-1975* (Hull: Supply and Services Canada, 1979); J. C. Anderson, "Determinants of Bargaining Outcomes in the Federal Government of Canada," Vol. 32, No. 2, *Industrial and Labour Relations Review* (January 1979), pp. 224-41; M. Gunderson, "Earnings Differential Between the Public and Private Sectors," Vol. XII, No. 2, *Canadian Journal of Economics* (May 1979), pp. 228-42; M. Gunderson,"Public Sector Compensation in Canada and the U.S." Vol. 19, No. 3, *Industrial Relations* (Fall 1980), pp. 257-71; M. Gunderson, "The Public/Private Sector Compensation Controversy," *Conflict or Compromise: The Future of Public Sector Industrial Relations*, eds. M. Thompson and G. Swimmer (Montreal: The

Institute for Research on Public Policy, 1984), pp. 5-43.

9 Auld *et al.*, *The Determinants of Negotiated Wage Settlements in Canada*, p. 8.

10 *Ibid.*, p. 118.

11 *Ibid.*, pp. 131-52.

12 *Ibid.*, pp. 183-84.

13 Cousineau and Lacroix, *Wage Determination in Major Collective Agreements in the Private and Public Sectors*, p. 25.

14 *Ibid.*, p. 63.

15 *Ibid.*, p. 66.

16 *Ibid.*, p. 67.

17 Auld *et al.*, *The Determinants of Negotiated Wage Settlements in Canada*, p. 157.

18 Anderson, "Determinants of Bargaining Outcomes in the Federal Government in Canada," pp. 232-33.

19 Gunderson, "Earnings Differentials Between the Private and Public Sectors," p. 238.

20 Gunderson, "Public Sector Compensation in Canada and the U.S.A.," p. 264.

21 Gunderson, "The Public/Private Sector Compensation Controversy," p. 19.

22 *Ibid.*, p. 33.

23 Starr, *Union-Nonunion Wage Differentials: A Cross-Sectional Analysis*, p. 115.

24 *Ibid.*, p. 115.

25 Johnson, *Non-Union Wage Changes in Canada: Theory and Survey Evidence*, pp. 124-25.

26 *Ibid.*, p. 125.

27 For an example of one such study see John C. Anderson, "Bargaining Outcomes: an IR System Approach," Vol. 18, No. 2, *Industrial Relations* (Calif.) (Spring 1979), pp: 127-43.

28 Labour Data Branch, Labour Canada, *Provisions in Major Collective Agreements in Canada Covering 500 and More Employees, All Industries (Excluding Construction)* (Ottawa: Supply and Services Canada, 1985), pp. 37-39.

29 *Ibid.*, pp. 40-42.

30 *Ibid.*, pp. 43-45.

31 *Ibid.*, p. 104.

32 *Ibid.*, pp. 26-27.

33 *Ibid.*, p. 23.

34 *Ibid.*, pp. 157-58.

35 *Ibid.*, pp. 161-62.

36 *Ibid.*, pp. 175-76.

37 *Ibid.*, pp. 167-68.

38 D. J. M. Brown and D. M. Beatty, *Canadian Labour Arbitration* (Aurora: Canada Law Book Limited, 1984), pp. 215-16.

39 *Ibid.*, pp. 216-17.

40 From preliminary figures of the Occupational

Safety and Health Branch, Labour Canada, and *Historical Labour Statistics,* Catalogue #77-201 (Annual), p. 128.

41 S. M. Jamieson, *Industrial Conflict in Canada 1966-1975,* (Discussion Paper No. 142, Centre for the Study of Inflation and Productivity, Economic Council of Canada (December 1979). See also the large number of studies cited in the footnotes to Jamieson's paper.

42 *Ibid.,* Summary, p. 1.

43 *Ibid.*

44 *Ibid.,* p. 13.

45 *Ibid.,* p. 30.

46 Alton W. J. Craig, "Canada's Industrial Relations in International Perspective," Vol. 3, No. 1, *Foreign Investment Review* (Autumn 1979), p. 9.

47 D. A. Smith, "Strikes in the Canadian Public Sector," *Conflict or Compromise: The Future of Public Sector Industrial Relations,* eds. Thompson and Swimmer, pp. 197-228.

48 *Ibid.,* p. 204.

49 *Ibid.,* p. 206.

50 *Ibid.*

51 *Ibid.,* p. 215.

52 *Ibid.,* p. 222.

53 J. Boivin, "Collective Bargaining in the Public Sector: Some Propositions on the Causes of Public Employee Unrest," *Collective Bargaining in the Essential and Public Services Sectors,* ed. M. Gunderson (Toronto: University of Toronto Press, 1975), p. 13.

54 *Ibid.,* p. 15.

55 Vol. 2, *Report of the Royal Commission on the Economic Union and Development Prospects for Canada* (Ottawa: Supply and Services Canada, 1985), p. 697.

postscript
Some Concluding Observations

The Financial Post

Industrial Relations — A Limited Purpose Instrument

The practice of industrial relations, or more narrowly collective bargaining, should be looked upon as a limited purpose instrument and not as a panacea for all problems in the workplace. This book has defined industrial relations systems as *complexes of private and public activities operating in specific environments and concerned with the allocation of rewards to workers for their services and the conditions under which work is performed.* By definition, then, industrial relations systems are not designed to handle major social and economic problems such as unemployment, technological change, and inflation. Industrial relations systems may be of partial assistance in helping workers to adjust to technological change. But they can neither assume the entire responsibility for the consequences of technological change nor amend the difficulties arising from such change. Similarly, while industrial relations systems may assist in alleviating inflation, they cannot solve it.

Even the best efforts of economists and politicians seem insufficient when applied to resolving these major problems in highly industrialized countries. Yet, some observers of the industrial relations scene, particularly socialist writers, seem to think that industrial relations should be able to succeed where politics and economics have failed. A good example of writing which has been critical of industrial relations systems for its failure to cure social ills is a book by Paul Jacobs: *Old Before Its Time: Collective Bargaining at 28.* Jacobs, a long-time socialist and supporter of unionism in the 1930's, concluded that unions had become too conservative. He accused them of failing society by failing to end inflation, unemployment, and maladaptation to technological change — all of which were subjects of great concern during the early 1960's.[1] Such a view lacks a genuine appreciation of the limited but important objectives that an industrial relations system serves. Moreover, it may be dangerous to ask a system to perform functions for which it was not intended since this could very well inhibit or destroy its capacity to carry out its intended role.

Dunlop's assessment of industrial relations systems is very much more pertinent than Jacobs':

> it is a system to establish, revise and administer many of the rules of the workplace; ...it is a procedure to determine the compensation of employees and to influence the distribution of the economic pie; ...it is a method for dispute settlement during the life of agreements and on their expiration or reopening, before or after resort to the strike or lockout.[2]

According to Dunlop, three forces competed to perform these functions: unilateral management action, unilateral union action, and government fiat. Various combinations were possible among the three. Again, fundamental social issues such as poverty, civil rights, and unemployment were not amenable to solution by means of actions undertaken by industrial relations systems. Any assessment of industrial relations systems, Dunlop claimed, must be made against their intents.

In this respect, it is interesting to consider the response of the PSAC to layoffs in the federal public sector during 1985: the PSAC ran adver-

tisements in newspapers and conducted demonstrations across Canada on January 21, 1986.[3] The president of the PSAC claimed that job security was the union's number one priority in the 1985-1986 negotiations. And, while the government had committed itself to eliminating 5,000 jobs during 1986, it claimed that only 500 public servants would lose their jobs. The PSAC refuted this claim, suggesting that, on the basis of past experience with having had to find jobs for surplus workers, it expected 3,500 of its members to be laid off.

A work-to-rule campaign, according to the PSAC president, was not out of the question, and could be implemented as early as March 1986. Strike action was also a possibility.[4] The effectiveness of such a strike, however, was dubious — especially since the government appeared determined to reduce its deficit in part by reducing overall employment. Rather than imposing new and impossible demands on the industrial relations system, what we should have been thinking about is what other social institutions can be deployed to tackle the economic, social, and political difficulties that we are currently facing.[5]

Critical Issues for Labour, Management, and Government During the 1980's

Critical Issues for Labour

Nationalism and Consolidation There has already been a number of mergers among sizable unions and several Canadian branches of international unions have formed autonomous Canadian unions. Although one may predict that this trend will continue in the years ahead, the major question is how much consolidation will in fact take place. The answer probably lies in the degree to which existing unions adequately serve their membership. If it is perceived by a substantial number of people that the present structure of unions is not doing the job in this respect, then the degree of consolidation may be substantial. On the other hand, if workers are satisfied with the service which the present union structure gives them, then the trend to consolidation may be insignificant.

Should the high level of nationalistic sentiment continue in Canada, there are likely to be a number of break-away movements, especially among larger Canadian branches. Conversely, if nationalism subsides, so will the desire for autonomous organizations. International unions cannot count on such a development, however, and would be wise to review past disaffections of Canadian branches from international unions in order to determine how to better serve their Canadian members. Such concern on the part of international unions would, doubtless, inhibit further breakaway movements.

The breakaway of the Canadian section of the United Auto Workers in 1984 to form a strictly Canadian union in 1985 exemplifies what may happen if the head office of an international union tries to dictate what Canadian workers should do, particularly if the Canadian section is headed by dynamic leaders. A sense of nationalism may have been involved, since Canadian unions in general refrained from concession bargaining to the extent that American unions did in the early 1980's.

A major policy decision that will confront a number of independent unions that do not now belong to the mainstream of the Canadian labour movement is whether or not to join the Canadian Labour Congress, the Canadian Federation of Labour, or some other national body. Groups such as engineers in private industry, nurses, and teachers, among others, may decide to remain independent. Most teachers' and nurses' associations, for example, have been independent for a long time at the provincial level and are unlikely to join a national federation. The recent formation of a national union among nurses may, however, serve as a model for similar groups. Engineers not employed in the public sector have only recently formed associa-

tions. These associations are isolated and local in nature and it may be some time before they form bargaining entities at the provincial and national levels.

If the teachers and engineers do join the CLC, they will add to the growing presence of public and parapublic workers within the Congress. The PSAC, representing federal workers, has long been affiliated with the CLC and is, indeed, one of the largest components within that body. The largest union in the CLC (and in Canada) is the Canadian Union of Public Employees (CUPE) which represents municipal workers, non-professional workers in hospital and hydro-electric companies (Ontario Hydro, for example), and school board and university workers.

Since 1975, an umbrella association, the National Union of Provincial Government Employees, representing public servants in provincial associations, has also been a member of the CLC. Although some problems in leadership had emerged in the past, NUPGE now seems ready to maintain its position as another important member of the Congress.

Duty of Fair Representation   Another critical issue which unions are going to have to face in an increasing number of jurisdictions is that of the duty to represent workers fairly in grievance cases. Three jurisdictions in Canada now have a legislative requirement that unions represent their members fairly. In a recent case, the Ontario Labour Relations Board stated that a union must act in a manner that is not arbitrary, discriminatory, or in bad faith. In the case before the Board, a worker had alleged that she had been fired for union activities but that her union had refused to file a complaint with the OLRB. The Board found the union guilty of not representing the worker fairly, had her reinstated, and ordered the union to pay the woman's legal costs since she took the case to the Board at her own expense.[6] As more jurisdictions are likely to pass legislation requiring unions to represent their members fairly, union leaders are going to have to be very careful in dealing with members' complaints about the quality of union representation.

Women have been steadily assuming more and more leadership in Canadian unions. The Ontario Federation of Labour and the CLC have now increased the number of women on their executive councils. With Shirley Carr as the new CLC President, it is likely that women will feel encouraged to run for executive office in their unions. A twenty-three year old woman, for example, was elected in late 1985 as President of the Winnipeg Labour Council which represents 33,000 workers.[7] Since women now constitute 43% of the labour force and about 33% of unionized workers, moreover, many women will be seeking not only a greater role in union leadership, but improvements in benefits, such as paid maternity leave and day care.[8]

Legislative Protection At common law, workers had few rights attached to their jobs. Their employment could be terminated upon the employer giving reasonable notice, a concept which has caused a great deal of controversy.[9] However, as we indicated in Chapter 1, one close observer[10] of the Canadian labour scene has argued that unorganized workers are becoming a force to be reckoned with. Under the legal model in the nonunioned sectors, a host of laws govern all workers in matters such as unemployment insurance, minimum wages, maximum hours, statutory holidays, equal pay for work of equal value, and human rights or equality under the law irrespective of colour, creed, race, national ancestry and, in some cases, age. Some human rights legislation prohibits sexual harrassment at the work place. Also, in some jurisdictions, workers may refuse to do work which they consider a serious threat to health and safety. Most of these provisions apply to both the unionized and nonunionized sectors of the economy, and are usually found in what is referred to as labour standards legislation.

Federal legislation and legislation in Nova Scotia and Quebec gives nonunionized workers the right of appeal in cases where they feel that they have been dismissed (and in some cases disciplined) without just cause. These cases may go all the way to binding arbitration by an impartial arbitrator. Many cases have been reported where arbitrators have ordered workers reinstated with compensation from the time of their dismissal. While much labour standards legislation lags behind practices in the unionized sector, procedural rights are at the leading edge of labour-management relations.

Group Action In addition to extensive and growing individual protections, support is building for group action, particularly in the area of health and safety. Joint union-management and worker-management committees functioned very effectively in Saskatchewan in the health and safety field during the 1970's. In these committees, workers and management were able to resolve issues quite successfully on their own. One major reason for their success is that both workers and management knew that government administrators were committed to making the actors in the industrial relations system the prime agents for ensuring compliance.[11] The Ontario *Occupational Health and Safety Act* requires the establishment of committees consisting of at least two people. Worker members are selected by the workers where no unions exist, and by unions where they do exist.

The universal-committee idea in nonunion as well as union organizations was recently introduced under the federal *Labour Adjustment Benefits Act* of 1982, and deals with redundancies. When an employer plans to terminate the employment of fifty or more workers within a four-week period, a joint planning committee of not less than four members must be established. In nonunionized organizations, the workers are entitled to select members to the committee, just as a union is in unionized organizations. The joint committees are charged with the development of adjustment programs to eliminate the necessity for termination or to minimize its impact on redundant workers by assisting them in finding other employment. In attempting to reach their objectives, joint planning committees may, unless the members agree otherwise, deal only with matters normally addressed in collective agreements with respect to termination of employment. "The members shall cooperate and make every reasonable effort to develop an adjustment program as expeditiously as possible."[12] These very strong words are similar to those which impose an obligation on the parties to bargain in good faith.

It is possible that this type of government-sponsored procedure may encourage the formation of unions, particularly when workers experience what it is like to deal with employers on a united rather than individual basis. One observer sees the possibility of committees undertaking a multitude of tasks such as redundancy, technological change, health and safety, training, and possibly the joint management of pension plans. Instead of having a committee to deal with each of these issues, he foresees one general-purpose committee emerging which would be responsible for coordinating all these different programs, particularly since the boundaries of some programs overlap. "Should collective employment decision making become as widespread as the current trend suggests it might," he claims, "the term [*unorganized*] will cease to have any real meaning. Everyone will be organized."[13] Another writer, however, sees these government initiatives as obstacles to the formation of unions since, as he argues, governments seem to be doing so much that there is little need for unions in many instances.[14]

We need hardly take sides with one or the other of these predictions. Workers in nonunionized organizations in some jurisdictions already have some input into the ways in which their rewards and the conditions under which they work are established. A central question is whether they will be satisfied with what they have now or whether they will attempt to gain more by unionizing.

Human Rights Legislation The advent of the Canadian *Charter of Rights and Freedoms* will affect unions, workers, and employers greatly in the immediate future. The provisions of the *Charter* apply to Parliament, the legislatures, and federal and provincial governments. Any action which contravenes guaranteed rights and freedoms may be challenged.[15] Section 1 of the *Charter* guarantees rights and freedoms "subject only to such reasonable limits prescribed by law as can be demonstrably justified in a free and democratic society."[16] Every time a court invokes one of the rights or freedoms, it must determine if the infringement is justified under the words quoted above. *Reasonable limits* and *demonstrably justified* could mean different things to different judges. Thus, contradictory judgments will likely be handed down.

Freedom of association is guaranteed under section 2(d) of the *Charter*. An important question is whether freedom of association carries with it the right to collective bargaining and the right to strike. In the few decisions handed down to date involving wage restraints in three public sector jurisdictions, the judges in one case concluded that the right to collective bargaining and strike action are part of the freedom of association while the judges in the other two cases disagreed.[17] The courts view the restraint programs as temporary or exceptional. One writer, after citing legislation such as the restraint programs in the various Canadian jurisdictions and various back-to-work statutes, concludes that the courts failed to see the restructuring which is taking place in Canada and which is denying rights to trade unions—rights attained at great cost, rights which should be protected.[18]

Section 15(1) which came into effect on April 17, 1985 states:

> Every individual is equal before and under the law and has the right to the equal protection and benefit of the law without discrimination and, in particular, without discrimination based on race, national or ethnic origin, colour, religion, sex, age or mental or physical disability.[19]

This section is expected to usher in a flood of cases which may take years to resolve. One such case is that initiated by the CLC which filed an action in the Supreme Court of Nova Scotia to have section 24A of the Nova Scotia *Trade Union Act* declared illegal.[20] This section, a 1979 amendment euphemistically known as the Michelin Bill, requires that for a union to be certified as the bargaining agent of a manufacturing company with interdependent plants, the bargaining unit shall constitute workers at all interdependent locations and must win over a majority of them in order to be certified. This means, in effect, that a union cannot apply for certification at one plant only. This is the only legislation of its kind in North America.

In addition to these two examples, numerous cases arising from the Charter of Rights and Freedoms have been brought before the courts. Some noteworthy issues have been challenged: the use of compulsory union dues for political causes, the use of closed shop union security provisions whereby workers must be members of a union in order to be hired, the imposition of first collective agreements designed to help weak unions, the use of union shop arrangements whereby workers must become union members within specified time periods after they are hired, and the use of accreditation in the construction industry whereby employer associations bargain on behalf of employers. In fact, the very rights to bargain collectively and to strike are being challenged.[21]

Since judges tend to interpret statute law conservatively, it is quite possible that some of these issues may be ruled invalid. Imagine what would happen if the courts were to find that compulsory union dues checkoff clauses are illegal: much of a union officer's time would be spent trying to collect union dues! This would set us back to a situation typical of the period prior to 1944 when there was very little legislative support for unions and collective bargaining. The decisions of the courts on these issues could very well change the nature of unionism and collective bargaining as we have come to know them and even wreck what constructive arrangements have been worked out between employers and unions over the years—a bleak scenario, and hopefully one that will not come about.

Social Partners The above issues are a few of the many that the labour movement in Canada will have to confront in the very near future. In addition to these kinds of issues, there are the larger concerns about the joint relationship between unions and management or the three-way relationship between unions, management, and government. Such matters as humanizing the workplace (whatever that may come to mean in the North American context) and worker participation in management may also be very fundamental issues that labour may wish to consider in the future. In addition, if the labour movement wants greater input into the formulation of national policy, it may have to consider, along with management and government, the possibility of some kind of forum in which consultation among the three social partners may take place. At the very least, such a forum would allow both unions and management to air their views with respect to proposed government policies.[22]

The creation in 1984 of the Canadian Labour Market and Productivity Centre might be the beginning of more effective cooperation between unions, management, and government in the years to come. Such cooperation may be critical to Canada's competitiveness in international markets in the future, particularly if it improves Canada's low rate of productivity during the 1970's and 1980's.[23]

With respect to worker participation in management, trade unions in North America have long taken the view that they do not wish to take part in managerial decision-making outside the framework of collective bargaining. However, with the problems that many companies are now facing with respect to productivity, absenteeism, turnover, and increasing foreign competition, unions in Canada and in North America generally may have to rethink their position. Canadian unions in particular may have to formulate demands more in line with those proposed by their counterparts in the United States. Canadian unions may also have to consider policy options such as representatives on the boards of directors of companies, profit-sharing schemes, and greater worker participation in management decision-making. Worker-safety and product-safety may be improved by greater worker participation if Canadian workers are willing and able to face these challenges.

Critical Issues Facing Management

Union Acceptance Many employers accept unions as an integral part of today's industrial society, while others merely tolerate their existence. In addition, a significant number of employers would prefer to fight unionism to the bitter end, as has been demonstrated by a number of labour relations board decisions in recent years. Management in the latter category may very well have to rethink their positions with respect to unions, particularly in light of the fact that the federal and all ten provincial governments have given collective bargaining rights to their own workers.

Canadian employers as a whole, however, have been more receptive to unions, even during the recession, than their counterparts in the United States. It has become fashionable in the United States for employers to attempt to keep their companies union-free. The same has not been true of employers in Canada. The approaches of Canadian governments generally and that of the United States under President Reagan have stood in very sharp contrast.

Human Rights Legislation With the recent enactment of human rights legislation which bars discrimination on the basis of colour, race, creed, and age, employers are going to have to become much more sophisticated in the development of their personnel policies so that they may justify their decisions before administrative tribunals under various types of legislation. In the past few years, there has been a substantial number of cases in which employers, found guilty of violating these laws, have embarrassed themselves before administrative tribunals or courts or both by trying to justify out-moded personnel policies. What emerges from these cases is the fact that some employers have neither done a very sophisticated analysis when determining the types of qualifications necessary to fill their personnel positions nor confronted other issues such as discrimination against the handicapped worker and the problem of sexual harassment.

Group Action Another issue deals more specifically with union-management relations. Traditionally, employers in North America have withheld important information from unions when it comes to negotiating collective agreements. As one observer has pointed out, all Western European unions receive more relevant data at the enterprise level than North American unions do. He predicts that sooner or later employers in Canada and the United States will have to start sharing information in order to make our collective bargaining system more effective.[24] It will probably take some time for this to happen, and it may occur initially only in those cases where companies are in dire financial conditions and plead with unions to help them remain solvent.

The experience of the Chrysler Corporation in 1980 and 1981, and of General Motors and Ford in the United States in 1981 and 1982, is typical of what some companies will do when their financial positions become precarious. The question that many employers are going to have to face is whether to share information with unions only during hard times or on an ongoing basis so that unions will understand the financial positions of companies during negotiations. Even companies that make excess profits may wish to disclose this information to unions. A few companies in Canada disclosed information several years ago while giving increases to workers during the closed period of the contract but just prior to the release of quarterly or annual financial reports which showed record-breaking profits.

Issues of the *World of Work Report*, which is published monthly by the Work in America Institute Inc., show that a substantial number of companies in the United States are developing programs to increase job satisfaction, worker participation, and quality of work life. Most of these have as their primary objective an increase in productivity. In some cases, these programs are initiated unilaterally by the employer, but often they are undertaken jointly by employers and unions. Such experiments have generally resulted in lower rates of absenteeism, higher morale, and better union-management relations —all of which have contributed to higher productivity. In some cases, these programs have also led to greater community involvement on the part of both workers and management.

Critical Issues Facing Governments

In recent years, most governments in Canada have amended their legislation to make it easier for unions to become certified bargaining agents, to require workers to pay union dues, and to require employers to engage in good faith bargaining.

Redundancy A problem that has received a good deal of attention on the part of governments has been that of plant closures which render redundant substantial numbers of workers. The Ontario government has already initiated legislation to help cope with these redundancies. In 1982, the Federal Government passed the *Labour Adjustment Benefits Act* based on the report of an inquiry commission.[25] The provisions in the *Act* went further than the Commissioner's recommendations, however, in providing benefits to workers affected by plant closures and industrial restructuring, including some aspects of technological change. It is to be hoped that other jurisdictions will enact similar legislation.

The Royal Commission on the Economic Union and Development Prospects for Canada (also known as the Macdonald Commission) has recommended that "increased consultation and cooperation between labour and management should be an objective of Canada's labour rela-

tions policy, as well as of employers and employees generally."[26] In the Commission's view, increased cooperation would improve personal relationships, reduce the incidence of strikes and lockouts, provide more enjoyable work environments for workers, involve workers in more planning and decision making, improve productivity, product quality, and competitiveness, and produce higher profits and wages.[27] These themes have been familiar ones from time to time ever since I first started studying labour-management relations in Canada some twenty years ago. I doubt that the Commission's recommendations will have any more impact on employers and unions now than such exhortations have had in the past, for the adversarial nature of the Canadian industrial relations system is still very firmly embedded in the thinking of both employers and unions.

The Macdonald Commission has also recommended arbitration as a viable alternative to strikes or lockouts in sectors where the cost of workstoppages are deemed by the public to be excessive.[28] It may be very difficult to withdraw the right to strike from those who already have had it.

Group Action Another issue which governments, and the Federal Government in particular, must face is whether or not they wish to consult with labour and management before passing legislation relating to industrial relations and social and economic policies. Both the Quebec and Manitoba governments have joint labour-management committees which examine proposed changes in labour legislation. The same thing was true in Nova Scotia until the passage of the infamous Michelin Bill in 1979. The Federal Government has no permanent consultative machinery, but it usually consults major union and management groups before it passes legislation in the industrial relations field, at least until recently. With respect to the larger problem of developing macro-economic and social policies, however, the question is whether or not the Federal Government is willing to set up consultative machinery and use it in a meaningful way so as to pass the most appropriate forms of legislation.

Essential Services Another major issue or policy with which governments are going to have to deal is the increasing use of special back-to-work legislation when strikes develop in the so-called essential services or industries. There has been a trend in recent years in some jurisdictions to use special back-to-work legislation. This legislation is adding, in effect, a predetermined step to the procedure used in handling contract negotiation or interest disputes. Too frequent recourse to back-to-work legislation not only invites defiance of the law, but also diminishes the possibility of the parties to the dispute developing a satisfactory collective bargaining relationship. For this reason, governments may be better advised, in some cases, to allow strikes to continue and let both parties suffer until they come to an agreement by themselves. Granted, this laissez-faire attitude may mean inconvenience and even hardship in some cases. The benefits would, however, outweigh these short-term considerations, since any movement toward restoring bargaining in good faith in specific situations has the effect of engendering greater trust among the participants, especially between government negotiators and union leaders and members.

During the Winter of 1985, the Mulroney government invited labour, management and other groups to Ottawa for a two-day session which was televised nationally. Labour took part in the exercise, but with some scepticism. Since the CLC thought that none of its recommendations were taken into account when the government's budget was prepared, it convened a two-day conference in early 1986 to discuss the proposals it put forward last year along with some new ones. Although government and management were invited to take part in the conference, neither accepted the invitation. Hence, it seems

that any joint union, management, and government action which may have been expected with the election of the Mulroney Government will not be forthcoming, unless the new leader of the CLC is able to acquire greater access to the corridors of power in Ottawa or the Mulroney Government changes its mind and accepts a greater role for the union movement in the formulation of national policy. It seems questionable, however, that either of these will come about.

Human Rights It is imperative that governments at the federal and provincial levels enact adequate legislation in the areas of human rights, employment standards and sexual harassment. A reading of some of the cases examined by special tribunals and human rights commissions reveals some deplorable practices by some employers. Undoubtedly, the cases investigated represent a small fraction of the actual cases in which such harassment takes place. Many occurrences are not investigated since no complains are lodged. The 1984 Federal Government legislation requiring all employers in the federal jurisdiction to develop and inform employees of such policies is one to be emulated by other jurisdictions.

Conclusion

The history of union-management relations in Canada, as in most other countries, has traditionally been characterized by a certain amount of conflict. One may believe this to be inherent in union-management relations, since there will always be some disagreement as to how the profits of organizations should be shared by the owners of capital and the workers. This is not to suggest, however, that a certain degree of cooperation does not exist between unions and employers, for their relationship is a symbiotic one—each side needs the other. Many innovations mentioned in this book, in fact, tend to

Table 12.1

A Framework for Analyzing Industrial Relations Systems (A Structural-Functional Approach)

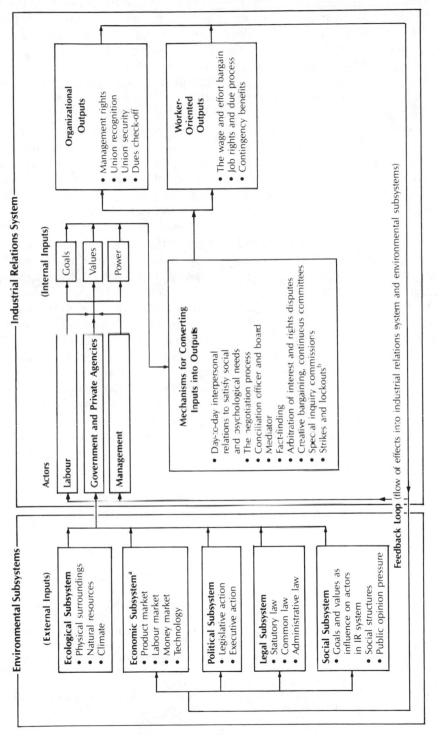

Environmental Subsystems

(External Inputs)

Ecological Subsystem
• Physical surroundings
• Natural resources
• Climate

Economic Subsystem[a]
• Product market
• Labour market
• Money market
• Technology

Political Subsystem
• Legislative action
• Executive action

Legal Subsystem
• Statutory law
• Common law
• Administrative law

Social Subsystem
• Goals and values as influence on actors in IR system
• Social structures
• Public opinion pressure

Industrial Relations System

(Internal Inputs)

Actors

Labour

Government and Private Agencies

Management

Goals

Values

Power

Mechanisms for Converting Inputs into Outputs
• Day-to-day interpersonal relations to satisfy social and psychological needs
• The negotiation process
• Conciliation officer and board
• Mediator
• Fact-finding
• Arbitration of interest and rights disputes
• Creative bargaining, continuous committees
• Special inquiry commissions
• Strikes and lockouts[b]

Organizational Outputs
• Management rights
• Union recognition
• Union security
• Dues check-off

Worker-Oriented Outputs
• The wage and effort bargain
• Job rights and due process
• Contingency benefits

Feedback Loop (flow of effects into industrial relations system and environmental subsystems)

[a] This model presupposes but does not explicitly show the interrelationship between the various societal subsystems.
[b] A work stoppage may also be considered an outcome or output of the industral relations system.

stress the cooperative as opposed to the adversarial approach, having as their aim the reduction of labour strife, the delivery of fair and swift justice to aggrieved parties, and the overall improvement of the working environment for both employers and workers.

The systems approach adopted in this book is valuable since it allows for a sophisticated analysis of the motivations of the parties, their tactics and rewards, which goes beyond that usually associated with industrial relations. For example, basic philosophical questions have been raised in this book about the different ways in which various jurisdictions treat the same policy issues.

In addition, the systems approach employed in this text is an appropriate analytical tool by which to gauge a maturing relationship between unions and management, a relationship in which both sides may recognize destructive patterns and seek to replace them with more pragmatic and productive alternatives.

Throughout this book we have emphasized the decentralized and atomistic nature of the Canadian industrial relations system. With eleven political jurisdictions in Canada, no one voice can speak on behalf of any one of the major actors. As a result, many of our trade-union, employer, and government structures seem geared towards parochial interests. There is a serious void at the national level—a crying out for strong and courageous leadership from unions, management, and government to develop integrated policies and programs. In fact a greater degree of real centralized decision-making by unions, management, government—and possibly other interest groups—is now critical in Canada.

It is well recognized that leaders must satisfy their constituents' aspirations and, perhaps more importantly, allay their fears especially in the face of possibly losing some previously hard-won gains. In the long run, however, leaders can influence, as well as be influenced by, their constituents' opinions. It is in the best interest of management to involve our highly educated work force in some of the day-to-day decision-making. It is equally advantageous that trade union members be persuaded to voluntarily forego their strike option in given situations.

Adoption of these ideas, however, requires an awareness and courage not normally associated with the kind of political expediency seen during the past few years, but present in the long-term creative relationships between organizations and individuals. These qualities have characterized the leaders of union-management relationships at various times in the past. Will they continue to do so in the precarious years which we now face?

---

questions

1 What scenario do you see for Canadian industrial relations in the near future? Elaborate.
2 Do you foresee more or less cooperation among unions, management, and government in the near future? Give a rationale for your answer.
3 Do you consider unions to be limited-purpose instruments? Elaborate.
4 Do you think that nonunion group action will prove to be as effective as union action? Do you think that nonunion group action will lead to unionization in those situations in which workers are not yet unionized? Elaborate.

5 Discuss some of the recent court decisions arising from the Charter of Rights and Freedoms and their impact on unions, management, and governments.
6 Do you consider the Macdonald Commission's suggestion that arbitration of interest disputes is a viable alternative to strikes in those situations in which society deems the cost of strikes to be excessive? Who do you propose should decide whether or not the cost of strikes in certain sectors is excessive? What reaction do you expect from those sectors which will lose the right to strike? Elaborate.

notes

1 P. Jacobs, *Old Before Its Time: Collective Bargaining at 28* (Santa Barbara: Center for the Study of Democratic Institutions, 1963).

2 J. T. Dunlop, "The Social Utility of Collective Bargaining," *Challenges to Collective Bargaining,* ed. L. Ulman (Englewood Cliffs: Prentice-Hall Inc., 1967), p. 169.

3 "PSAC Presses on with Ad Campaign Against Layoffs," *Ottawa Citizen* (January 18, 1986), p. A19.

4 B. Hill, "PSAC Threatens Work Slowdown over Job Security," *Ottawa Citizen* (January 21, 1986) pp. A1, A20.

5 For a more developed statement of the views expressed above, see A. H. Raskin and J. T. Dunlop, "Two Views of Collective Bargaining," *Challenges to Collective Bargaining,* pp. 155-80.

6 W. List, "Labour Board Attacks CUPE Failure to Aid Woman Fired Over Union Role," *Globe and Mail* (June 15, 1981), p. 1.

7 B. Gory, "Woman, 23, Is New Head of Labour Body," *Globe and Mail* (January 2, 1986), p. A10.

8 I. Hossie, "Union Women Are Revving Up and Moving Up," *Globe and Mail* (January 2, 1986).

9 H. J. Glasbeek, "The Contract of Employment at Common Law," *Union-Management Relations in Canada,* eds. J. Anderson and M. Gunderson (Don Mills: Addison-Wesley (Canada) Ltd., 1982), p. 69.

10 R. J. Adams, "The Unorganized: A Rising Force," a paper presented to the 31st annual McGill Industrial Relations Conference (Montreal, April 6, 1983); also as Research and Paper Series No. 201, Faculty of Business, McMaster University (Hamilton: April 1983).

11 *Ibid.,* p. 11.

12 *Labour Adjustment Benefits Act* (Bill C-78, 1982), s. 60. 13(3).

13 Adams, "The Unorganized: A Rising Force," p. 19.

14 C. R. Brookbank, "The Adversary System in Canadian Industrial Relations: Blight or Blessing?" Vol. 35, No. 1, *Relations Industrielles/Industrial Relations* (1980), p. 34.

15 Joel Fichaud, "Analysis of The Charter and Its Application to Labour Law," Vol. 11, 20th Annual Meeting of the Canadian Industrial Relations Association, Vancouver, B.C., pp. 599-600.

16 *Ibid.,* p. 603.

17 Amy Bartholomew, "The Guarantee of Freedom of Association in *Canada's Charter of Rights and Freedoms:* A Double-Edged Sword for Labour?" A paper presented to the 26th Annual International Studies Association Conference, (Washington: March 5-9, 1985) p. 21.

18 *Ibid.,* pp. 12-29.

19 Quoted in Fichaud, "Analysis of The Charter and Its Application to Labour Law," p. 599.

20 "CLC Files Suit Challenging Michelin Bill," *Globe and Mail* (May 9, 1985), p. 8.

21 Lorne Slotnick, "Charter Cases Major Challenge Facing Unions," *Globe and Mail* (January 13, 1986), pp. A1, A23.

22 J. Crispo, *Industrial Democracy in Western Europe: A North American Perspective* (Toronto: McGraw Hill Ryerson Limited, 1978), C. J. Connaghan, *The Japanese Way: Contemporary Industrial Relations* (Ottawa: Supply and Services Canada, 1982).

23 B. J. C. Smith, "Canada Falling Behind in Productivity," *Globe and Mail* (February 25, 1985), p. B8.

24 J. Crispo, *Industrial Democracy in Western Europe: A North American Pespective,* pp. 150 ff.

25 *Report of the Commission of Inquiry into Redundancies and Lay-Offs,* A. W. R. Carrothers, Chairman (Ottawa: Supply and Services Canada, 1979).

26 Vol. 2, *Report of the Royal Commission on Economic Union and Development Prospects for Canada* (Ottawa: Supply and Services Canada, 1985), p. 707.

27 *Ibid.,* pp. 698-707.

28 *Ibid.,* p. 705.

appendix one

Certification

The Agnew Lake Mines Case* — A Question of Jurisdiction

Reasons for Judgment in Applications for certification affecting
Labourers' International Union of North America
(Applicant No. One)
United Steelworkers of America
(Applicant No. Two)
and
Agnew Lake Mines Limited (Respondent)

1   These are two counter applications for certification of the Applicant therein, each being a trade union, as bargaining agent for substantially the same unit of employees of the Respondent therein, namely a unit of employees employed by the Respondent in the development and operation of a uranium mine at the Respondent's mine site in Hyman Township in the province of Ontario, excluding office and clerical employees employed in a confidential capacity in matters relating to labour relations. Application No. One was dated March 24, 1969, and Application No. Two was dated April 3, 1969.

2   The classifications of employees of the respondent appearing on the respondent's payroll as at the dates of the applications and comprising the proposed bargaining units were those of trades leader, hoistman (with compressor papers), tradesman-group 1- "A" tradesman-group 1- "B", tradesman-group 2- "A", heavy equipment operator "A", journeyman helper-group "1", general labour, light truck driver, dryman, general miner, and skiptender, excluding the classifications of manager, secretary, engineering supervisor, lay out engineer, surveyor, mine accountant, chief warehouseman, paymaster, clerk-

*Permission to use this case was granted by the Canada Labour Relations Board. Minor deletions were made by the author for the purposes of this book.

typist, surface foreman, mechanical foreman, electrical foreman, mine captain, and shift boss.

Based upon the report of the Board's investigating Officer following upon his check of the payroll records of the Respondent and the membership and attendant records of each of Applicant No. One and Applicant No. Two, the Board finds that at the date of application No. One there were 24 employees in the proposed bargaining unit of whom 15 were claimed by Applicant No. One to be members in good standing of the said Applicant, and finds that at the date of application No. Two there were 31 employees in the proposed bargaining unit of whom 18 were claimed by applicant No. Two to be members in good standing of the said applicant.

3   The Respondent submits that both applications are premature as its uranium mining operation is still in the process of underground development, no ore has as yet been taken out of the mine, and the mill which the Respondent has decided to build at the mining site to process the mined ore into the form of uranium concentrate for marketing purposes, is not in operation as yet. The Respondent's evidence is that the 12 classifications of employees in the proposed bargaining unit on the payroll at the time of the making of the applications constitute only 30 per cent of the number of classifications of employees who will be employed and who would be covered in the proposed bargaining unit when the mine comes into full production and the build-up of employees is completed. Based upon its presently planned production and its progress estimates, the Respondent anticipates that the build-up of employees in the proposed bargaining unit will result in an increase to 100 by the end of 1969, to 200 by the end of 1970, and to a minimum of 400 at full production by the end of 1971.

The Respondent submits that any application for determination of the wishes of the employees in the proposed unit as to their choice of a bargaining agent would be premature until the build-up has reached at least roughly 50 per cent of the ultimate build-up total. It considers this percentage would constitute a representative group of employees for such purpose. The Respondent made representations also in relation to an appropriate description of the proposed bargaining unit in the event the applications are further processed at this time. Counsel for Applicant No. One submits that in view of the uncertainties of the future build-up in the Respondent's mining development and production operation, there is no reason why at least the employees in the categories now employed should be denied bargaining rights at this time. Counsel for applicant No. Two concurs in this view.

Counsel for Applicant No. Two and Counsel for the Respondent cited also for the Board's consideration the practice followed by the Ontario Labour Relations Board in dealing with applications for certification in the mining industry in Ontario of tying the certification granted to the currently appropriate stage of mining operation then being carried on at the mining site designated as either the construction, development, or production stage as an alternate to a deferral of certification pending further anticipated build-up (see O.L.R.B. judgment in International Union of Mine, Mill & Smelter Workers (Canada), vs. Surlaga Gold Mines Ltd. dated July 13, 1967, for an outline of this policy).

questions

1 Does this case fall under the jurisdiction of the Canada Labour Relations Board? If not, why not? If so, under what authority?
2 Do you see any discrepancy in the figures claimed by the two applicants and the total number of workers on the job?
3 How is the proposed bargaining unit defined?
4 As a member of the Board, would you consider the unit proposed to be appropriate?
5 If you do consider the unit appropriate, for what stage of operations do you consider it appropriate?
6 What would happen when that stage of the mine was completed?
7 How would you define the next stage of operations?
8 Which union, if either, do you think will be certified in this case? Why?

The Eastern Provincial Airways (1963) Case* — Two Unions Attempt to Represent Security Guards

Canadian Air Line Employees Association, applicant,
and
Eastern Provincial Airways (1963) Limited,
Gander, Newfoundland,
employer
International Association of Machinists
and Aerospace Workers, applicant,
and
Eastern Provincial Airways (1963) Limited,
Gander, Newfoundland,
employer

1   These cases involve two competing applications to represent the same group of employees, namely, a group of security guards of the respondent, Eastern Provincial Airways (1963) Limited. The first is an application for review presented pursuant to Section 119 of the *Canada Labour Code* (Part V — Industrial Relations) by CALEA seeking to have its existing certificate for a

*Permission to use this case was granted by the Canada Labour Relations Board. Minor deletions were made by the author for the purposes of this book.

unit of employees of the employer amended in order to include said security guards therein. The second is an application for certification made pursuant to Section 124 of the Code by the IAM for the same group of security guards. The first application was filed on August 1, 1978, and CALEA claimed to represent all of the security guards. The second application was filed on August 18, 1978, and the IAM claimed to represent all of the same employees.

2 The Board first wishes to state that it will decide whether or not both applications are receivable in the light of the provisions of Sections 119, 124 and 126 of the Code. The first aspect is whether or not the Board can entertain, at the same time, an application filed under section 119 and another application made under section 124. Let us first state that the Board, as a matter of policy, is not formalistic as to the procedure in which applications are made to the Board. In the present instance, both unions wish to represent a group of employees who were not formerly represented by any union. According to section 124, an application for certification can be presented for such a group at any time. Whether or not such a group would be made part of an existing certificate or would form a distinct unit is a decision that the Board will take after the filing of the applications and after having completed its investigation. It seems to us that whether an application to represent a group of employees filed at an appropriate time, be presented by way of section 119 or 124, is not essential to its admissibility. The goal pursued in each case is to be declared the certified bargaining agent for a group of employees. The Board will not, as a matter of policy, dismiss an application for revision under section 119 to include a group of employees in an existing unit on the sole basis that the application should have been made under section 124 when such application is otherwise timely and satisfies the prerequisites of other pertinent sections of the Code relating to certification and more precisely, the provisions regarding the wishes of the employees. In short, the Board finds that the application for review under section 119 in this case will be considered both as an application for review under section 119 in the event the Board decides that the security guards are to be included in the existent certificate, or as an application for certification if the Board decides that the security guards must form a distinct bargaining unit and the employees wish to be represented by the applicant, CALEA.

The next question the Board must ask itself is whether or not it will consider the application for certification presented by the IAM in the light of section 126(c) which reads as follows:

> 126. Where the Board
>   (c) is satisfied that, as of the date of the filing of the application, or of such other date as the Board considers appropriate, a majority of the employees in the unit wish to have the trade union represent them as their bargaining agent, the Board shall, subject to this Part, certify the trade union making the application as the bargaining agent for the bargaining unit.

At the time of the filing of the application for revision by CALEA, the Board's investigation revealed that all of the security guards had signed membership cards with CALEA. Normally, since the coming into force on June 1, 1978, of the revised subsection (c) of section 126, the Board, as a policy, will consider the wishes of the employees at the date of the application. Before the amendment to the Code, the Board had to follow the interpretation of the original subsection (c) as given by the Federal Court of Appeal in the case CKOY Limited [1972] 2 F.C. 412, and as a result the Board had to consider the wishes of the employees at the time it was making its decision. Because of this decision, the Board had to change its policy, as stated in the case of Swan River The Pas 1 di 10 [1974] 1 Can LRBR 254, and in which decision the Board had explained why it wanted to consider the wishes of the employees as of the date of application. As stated above, the Board can now resume the policy it had developed in 1974 and consider the wishes of the employees at the date of application. In this case, however, the other applicant, IAM, filed an application for certification 17 days later and our investigation revealed that all of the security guards had expressed their wish to be represented by IAM. The Board was then confronted by the situation in which a group of employees had indicated to the Board that they wished to be represented but by different unions. In such circumstances, the Board cannot ignore this conflicting situation as to the wishes of the employees. We are in a situation similar to the one in which more than one union applies to represent the same group of employees, each union claiming to represent a majority. In such cases, Labour Relations Boards when given reasonable grounds to doubt the true wishes of the employees, have normally ordered a vote and considered as valid both applications, even though they were not presented at the same time. This is not a situation where the employees are trying to get out of union representation but a situation where the employees have clearly expressed their wishes to be represented by a union, and the question to decide is which union will represent them. Because of the above given reasons, the Board is of the opinion that we are in a situation where we must consider the wishes of the employees at another date than the dates of the filing of the applications. The Board has, on August 25, 1978, directed that a vote be held among the security guards covered by both applications, giving them the choice to express their wishes as whether they would like to be represented by CALEA, the IAM or not to be represented by a union at all. This vote was ordered according to the provisions of section 118(i), which gives the Board power to order a vote in a precautionary way, as a matter of speaking, in order that the wishes of the employees be expressed and the ballots sealed until such time as the Board decides if the vote is to be considered or not.

The employer has contested both applications on the following grounds. First of all, it contends that the security guards are not employees as defined by the Code, as they are employed in a confidential capacity in matters relating to industrial relations. This is based on the interpretation of the employer as regards the work performed by the security guards and mainly because their duties consist of:

1 screening passengers emplaning on the employer's aircraft in accordance with section 5.1 of the Aeronautics Act;
2 protecting the employer's property and prevention of fire;
3 prevention of public intrusion upon the employer's property and theft of the employer's property by the public;
4 monitoring all the employer's employees in relation to theft in this connection, security guards have authority to check and search the person and possessions of employees while on the employer's premises;
5 inspecting all aircraft that terminate their flight plans at Gander and to check for shortage of inventory;
6 inspecting commissary supplies;
7 conducting special investigations of cases of observed theft or alleged theft committed by either employees or the public; and
8 other investigations relating to industrial relations.

The Board, in its decision Canadian Union of Bank Employees v. Bank of Nova Scotia 21 di 439; 1977 CLLC ¶16090, has reviewed the jurisprudence and restated the threefold test under which a person will not be considered an employee because he is performing functions in a confidential capacity related to industrial relations. The Board at page 16,625,21 di 460 said

> To this end this Board and other Boards have developed a threefold test for the confidential exclusion. The confidential matters must be in relation to industrial relations, not general industrial secrets such as products formulae (e.g. Calona Wines Ltd. [1974] 1 Can LRDR 471, headnote only (BCLRB decision 90/74). This does not include matters the union or its members know, such as salaries, performance assessments discussed with them or which they must sign or initial (e.g. Exhibit E-21). It does not include personal history or family information that is available from other sources or persons. The second test is that the disclosure of that information would adversely affect the employer. Finally, the person must be involved with this information as a regular part of his duties. It is not sufficient that he occasionally comes in contact with it or that through employer laxity he can gain access to it. (See Greyhound Lines of Canada Ltd. 1974 CLLC ¶[16,112] 4 di 22, and Hayes Trucks Ltd. [1974] 1 Can LRBR 284).

After having reviewed the results of its investigation, the evidence and the submissions of the employer, the Board is of the opinion that none of the security guards perform work in a confidential capacity in matters relating to industrial relations.

The employer also contended that certification should not be extended so as to include the subject employees within a trade union which has an existing collective bargaining relationship with the employer. Further, the employer stated that certification should not be granted nor extended so as to include the subject employees within a unit for which a trade union already has a collective agreement with the employer.

The Board, being of opinion that the security guards are employees within the meaning of section 107 of the Code, must decide if they are appropriate for inclusion in an existing unit or should form a separate unit, and in this second alternative whether they can be represented by a union which already has ties with the employer. It is to be noted that both CALEA and IAM have ties with the employer as they hold certificates and have bargained collective agreements with the employer for its operations at Gander.

The Board is convinced that even though the security guards are working in the same premises and in close relation with members of the applicant CALEA, this fact is also true of their relation with the members of IAM. The whole question is whether or not the security guards should form a distinct bargaining unit or be included in a general unit. In Ontario, section 11 of the Ontario Labour Relations Act reads as follows:

> The Board shall not include in a bargaining unit with other employees, a person employed as a guard to protect the property of his employer and no trade union shall be certified as bargaining agent for a bargaining unit of such guards and no employer or employer's organization shall be required to bargain with a trade union on behalf of any person who is a guard if, in either case, the trade union admits to membership or is chartered by, or is affiliated, directly or indirectly, with an organization that admits to membership persons other than guards.

As we see it, this section expressly forbids the Ontario Board from certifying a union for a unit of security guards if that union does not exclusively represent security guards. We have no such provision in our Code. In British Columbia, where there are no provisions such as in the Ontario Labour Relations Act, the Board, in the case of The Hospital Employees Union Local 180 and St. Vincents Hospital, [1974] 1 Can LRBR 363, has taken the following view at page 367:

> This Board has no firmly determined policy on security guard units. The question of whether security guards should be placed in separate units or in general employee units has received considerable attention elsewhere (e.g., Ontario Labour Relations Act, s. 11). Any policy development will focus its attention on conflicts of interests between employees who have authority over fellow employees and their fellow employees. The nature of this authority will have to be examined to determine whether the employees designated as guards are employed to monitor the actions of their fellow employees and perhaps to admonish or report employees for actions tainted with illegality. Where persons are employed principally to exercise this sort of surveillance over fellow employees, the Board may find it inappropriate to include them in the same unit as their fellow employees. Central to a policy developed on the appropriateness of the unit for guards will be concern as to whether the guards and the employer are placed in a position where the guard's duties conflict with his interests as a member of a bargaining unit.

This Board adopts the approach of the B.C. Labour Relations Board.

In order to decide, this Board must then look at the functions of the security guards and it becomes a question of facts whether or not they perform security functions or surveillance over fellow employees. In the present instance, the security guards perform a dual role. Fifty percent (50%) of their time consists of screening passengers emplaning on the employer's aircraft and the other 50% consists of surveillance of the company premises, and this includes, as stated above, the monitoring of all the employer's employees in relation to theft, conducting special investigations of cases of observed theft or alleged theft committed by either employees or the public. The Board's investigation revealed that, in numerous cases, the security guards had to report and investigate thefts by fellow employees. It is also important to mention that the security guards are on a rotating shift so that they are all performing the dual functions described above.

. . .

As to the argument raised by the employer that the Board should not certify a group of security guards with a union which already negotiates with the employer for different groups, the Board, in United Steelworkers of America v Denison Mines Limited case, 8 di 13,75 CLLC¶16,150, has already decided that security guards, such as those in the present instance, are not private constables and as such are not covered by section 135 of the Code, which reads as follows:

> The Board shall not certify a trade union as, and a trade union shall not act as, the bargaining agent for both a bargaining unit comprised of private constables and a bargaining unit comprised of employees other than private constables if any or all of the employees in both such bargaining units are employed by the same employer.

However, it must be pointed out that the limitation expressed in Section 135 of the Code is restricted by the definition of *"private constable"* given in Section 107 of the Code which reads:

> 'private constable' means a person appointed as a constable under the Railway Act or the National Harbours Board Act;

The Board, 8 di 14, of the Denison Mines decision, said:

> There was no evidence that the security guards under study were appointed private constables under the 'dominium' of either of these two Statutes. Therefore, the provisions of section 135 do not avail to the Respondent in the circumstances and this Board is not directed to deny certification to a bargaining agent seeking to represent these security guards although it already represents other bargaining units of employees of the same employer.

questions

1 What is (are) the major issue(s) that the Board has to decide in this case?
2 How could both applicant unions claim support of all of the workers at the same time?
3 What is the operative date on which the Board will determine the wishes of the workers in this case?
4 On what date did the Board conduct a vote among the workers? Is this the regular certification procedure or is it a prehearing vote? Elaborate.
5 Should the security guards form a separate bargaining unit or should they be included with other workers all in one unit? Elaborate.
6 Can only one of the unions or both or neither be considered as a bargaining agent for these workers? Elaborate.
7 Assume that a vote has been conducted on ballots which show the names of both unions and a designation of "no union," and that neither union gets 50% support of the members voting. What happens then? Elaborate. Should legislation make provision for such an outcome? If so, what form should the provision take?

The B.C. Telephone Co. (1977) Case*— The Impact of Changing Technology and Public Policy

Society of Telephone Engineers and Managers, applicant,
and
British Columbia Telephone Company, Vancouver, B.C., employer,
and
Telecommunication Workers' Union
(Formerly: Federation of Telephone Workers
of British Columbia),
Intervenor,
and
G. Fred Pearson, et al,
employee intervenor

The Society of Telephone Engineers and Managers has filed with the Board an application for certification as bargaining agent for a unit comprising all persons employed in the first four levels of management of the Marketing Department of the British Columbia Telephone Company.

Because of a number of special circumstances surrounding this application and the existence of similar or related applications filed with the Board, the Board determined that it would be appropriate to conduct a hearing and issue a decision in order to determine whether all or some of the persons employed in the proposed bargaining unit were *"employees"* within the meaning of the *Canada Labour Code* (Part V — Industrial Relations). The relevant facts are fully outlined in the interim decision issued by the Board on February 26, 1976.[1]

In its interim decision, the Board ruled that *"all persons employed as managers in the Marketing Department of the British Columbia Telephone Company with the exception of the Vice-President — Marketing and the Marketing Operations Manager are 'employees,' within the meaning of section 107(1) of the Canadian Labour Code (Part V — Industrial Relations)."* Accordingly, the Board advised the parties that it intended to convene further hearings in order to allow the parties to lead evidence and present arguments with regard to the issues raised by the instant application for certification and particularly with regard to the appropriateness of the bargaining unit proposed by the applicant. In view of the conflicting positions of the applicant and of the intervenor, the Board raised the following question:

Should these employees be included in a separate bargaining unit for which

---

*Permission to use this case was granted by the Canada Labour Relations Board. Minor deletions were made by the author for the purposes of this book.

STEM wishes to be certified or should all or some of them be included in the bargaining unit which is already represented by the Federation of Telephone Workers of British Columbia.

The parties were subsequently convened to further hearings. All parties were also requested to file further written evidence and submissions on the issue.

The Society of Telephone Engineers and Managers is a relatively new organization which, as its name indicates, wishes to represent the engineers and managers employed by the British Columbia Telephone Company. In support of its application, it has provided the Board with the usual documentation in order to establish that it is a trade union within the meaning of the *Canada Labour Code* (Part V — Industrial Relations). After having reviewed that evidence, the Board is satisfied that the Society of Telephone Engineers and Managers is a trade union within the meaning of section 107(1) of the *Canada Labour Code* (Part V — Industrial Relations).

In 1949, the Federation of Telephone Workers of British Columbia was certified as bargaining agent by the Canada Labour Relations Board to represent all employees of the employer except the incumbents of certain classifications, specified in the Certification Order, which were to be excluded from the bargaining unit.

On March 13, 1975, the intervenor applied to the Board for a revision of its certificate of bargaining authority which would have the effect of substantially increasing the number of persons included in the bargaining unit which it represents. Many of the persons employed in the Marketing Department and included in the bargaining unit which the applicant wishes to represent are included in this application for revision.

Since then, the Federation of Telephone Workers of British Columbia has revised its constitution and changed its name to Telecommunication Workers' Union. It will be referred to hereinafter by its new name.

Because of the overlap between the application for certification filed by the applicant and the application for review filed by the Telecommunication Workers' Union with regard to persons employed in the managerial ranks in the Marketing Department, the Board allowed the intervenor to file evidence and submissions with regard to that group of employees in the course of the hearing on the application for certification filed by the Society of Telephone Engineers and Managers.

Circumstances of Instant Case

This case is unusual in a number of respects. The position of the applicant is, to say the least, somewhat unusual since it wishes to be certified as bargaining agent to represent a group of employees employed in the first four levels of management of the Marketing Department. The instant application is only one of a number of similar or related applications filed with the Board. The applicant itself, the Society of Telephone Engineers and Managers, has filed two other applications for certification to represent a unit of employees in the Finance Department and to represent a group of engineering employees. In all cases, the persons who it wishes to represent have been considered by the employer to be Level I to Level IV managers who heretofore have been excluded from the existing bargaining unit of classified employees. The Board has also received an application for certification from the Telephone Supervisors' Association in which it seeks to be certified as bargaining agent for a unit comprising first level plant supervisors. Finally, on March 13, 1975, the Telecommunication Workers' Union filed an application for review made pursuant to section 119 of the *Canada Labour Code* (Part V — Industrial Relations) asking the Board to decide that some 600 additional persons, employed at different levels of the management structure of the employer, were and should be included in the bargaining unit which it represents. Although there is no overlap between the application for review filed by the Telecommunication Workers' Union and the application for certification filed by the Telephone Supervisors' Association, there is a substantial measure of conflict between the application filed by the Society of Telephone Engineers and Managers and the Telecommunication Workers' Union.

The employer has reacted to these various applications in a similar fashion. B.C. Tel. has intervened to oppose each application asking that it be dismissed because the persons proposed for inclusion in the various bargaining units were not *"employees"* within the meaning of section 107(1) of the *Canada Labour Code* (Part V — Industrial Relations) as they performed management functions or, in some cases, were employed in a confidential capacity in matters relating to labour relations. In no case has the employer disputed the appropriateness of the bargaining unit proposed by the applicant. In some cases, the employer has deliberately and continuously refrained from taking a position on the apropriateness of the bargaining units. In other cases, after being expressly invited to do so by the Board, it has contested the appropriateness of the proposed unit suggesting instead that the appropriate unit be company wide and include only persons employed at one level of management. It is worth noting that, at this stage, none of the applicants has proposed such a bargaining unit.

When a trade union files an application for certification, it must, in order to be certified by the Board, meet the requirements outlined in section 126 of the *Canada Labour Code* (Part V — Industrial Relations). Therefore, the application of the normal rules of procedure and evidence require the applicant to satisfy the Board that it meets the requirements prescribed in section 126 of the Code. Of course, the Board is not bound by the rules of procedure and evidence normally applied in the common law courts. Often, an application for certification can be disposed of without a hearing. Information and evidence elicited by the Board in the course of its investigation of an application will often make it unnecessary for the Board to require an applicant to establish that it meets one or the other of the requirements outlined in section 126 of the Code. In the instant case, prior to the resumption of the hearing, the Board notified the parties as follows:

> Following a review of the file for the purpose of determining an appropriate procedure, the Board finds there is at least a prima facie case to suggest that the proposed bargaining unit may be appropriate for collective bargaining. Accordingly, any party disputing the appropriateness of the proposed unit or objecting to the inclusion of certain classifications in that unit will be invited to lead evidence first.

When the hearing resumed on the instant application for certification, the employer, although expressly invited to do so by the Board, declined to take any position with regard to the appropriateness of the bargaining unit proposed by the applicant or by the intervenor in its application for review. It also declined to lead further evidence although it did provide the Board with information and submissions expressly requested by it. The employer also informed the Board that a reorganization had taken place within the Computer Communications Group of the Marketing Department which had the effect of substantially increasing the number of persons employed at levels I to IV in the managerial ranks of the Marketing Department of the British Columbia Telephone Company. It indicated that it felt that the incumbents of these various classifications were not employees under the provisions of the *Canada Labour Code*. However, the employer has until now provided the Board with no further information or submissions regarding the duties and responsibilities of these persons.

There can be little doubt that the procedure outlined above, which was designed to facilitate and speed up the determination of the various issues raised by the applications now before the Board, has caused a number of problems. Certainly, it was well designed to assist in the determination of the *"employee"* status of the various persons proposed for inclusion in the bargaining units. It was not, however, particularly well designed to allow the Board to familiarize itself with the overall organization of the British Columbia Telephone Company particularly as regards the relationship between the various departments or branches and the possible community of interest existing among the managerial employees of the company. Accordingly, in a letter dated April 15, 1976, the Board requested from the parties to the various cases further information and submissions on this point. It is worth noting, however, that these were requested and obtained following the conclusion of the hearing on the instant application for certification. It is only in the documentation thus requested by the Board that the British Columbia Telephone Company eventually let the Board know its position on the appropriateness of the bargaining units proposed by the various applicants.

It is clear that there is a marked conflict between the position of the applicant and the intervenor with regard to the right of representation of quite a number of managerial employees in the Marketing Department of the B.C. Tel. In many respects, the position of the intervenor and that of the applicant are incompatible and diametrically opposed.

The Evidence

In view of the circumstances of the case and in the light of the evidence submitted during the preliminary hearing conducted by the Board with regard to the *"employee status"* of the marketing managers employed by B.C. Tel., the position of the applicant with regard to the appropriateness of the bargaining unit for which it seeks to be certified is fairly clear and straight-forward.

Briefly, the applicant contends that the marketing managers are a distinct group sharing a particular community of interest and, in view of the circumstances, a departmental unit is appropriate for collective bargaining. In so arguing, it does not dispute that a single all-inclusive bargaining unit comprising all the managerial employees of B.C. Tel. would also be appropriate for collective bargaining. In fact, it has stated quite bluntly that its overall objective was the creation of such an all-inclusive unit.

Since the employer had taken the position that it declined to lead further evidence, the Telecommunication Workers' Union was invited to lead evidence. In rebuttal, the applicant led further evidence in support of its contention that the Telecommunication Workers' Union's position should not be upheld and that the applicant should be certified as bargaining agent to represent the unit described in its application for certification. The position of the intervenor is fairly simple. On February 23, 1949 it was certified by order of the Canada Labour Relations Board as bargaining agent for a unit described as follows:

> A unit of employees of the British Columbia Telephone Company, *comprising all employees of the Company* save and except those employed in the following occupational classifications.

Therefore, the intervenor contends that it is the certified bargaining agent for a unit comprising all the employees of the British Columbia Telephone Company save for the classifications specifically excluded in the Certification Order issued by the Board.

Over the years, however, this relatively simple definition of the bargaining unit represented by the union has become a source of problems. In particular, a practice has developed of describing the bargaining unit in a manner completely opposite to the terms of the Certification Order. This has its origins in a practice or understanding which apparently developed quite early in the negotiations between the employer and the intervenor.

Therefore, over the years, the Telecommunication Workers' Union, which was the certified bargaining agent for a unit comprising all employees of the employer excluding certain named classifications, has negotiated collective agreements applicable to a unit comprising only certain listed classifications. The Board has received no evidence as to when this practice originated but it is understood to go back to the early 50's.

The intervenor contends that, over the years, the employer has engaged in various practices which have had the effect of eroding the bargaining unit which it represents. In some cases, new job titles or job descriptions have been assigned to existing classifications which have then been unilaterally declared by the employer to be excluded from the bargaining unit because the incumbents allegedly performed management functions or were employed in a confidential capacity in matters relating to industrial relations. Alternatively, new positions or classifications have been created and the employer has refused to recognize that they were properly included in the bargaining unit represented by the Union.

The evidence discloses that since 1967 the intervenor has attempted to assert its jurisdiction over a number of disputed classifications. In particular it protested decisions of the employer to create *"management trainee"* and other allegedly managerial positions which were then deemed to be excluded from the bargaining unit. It was, and still is, the contention of the intervenor that these positions were properly included in the bargaining unit which it is certified to represent.

In an attempt to resolve this issue, the intervenor first resorted to the grievance and arbitration provisions of its collective agreement with the employer. This occurred as a result of the creation of five new positions designated as *"Communications Consultants — Data."* The Telecommunication Workers' Union sought a ruling that these employees whom the employer contended were performing management functions and thus were not subject to the terms of the collective agreement were, in fact, employees subject to the collective agreement and particularly to the dues check off provisions of the agreement. The arbitration board ruled in favour of the intervenor. Shortly thereafter, these classifications were abolished and the employees affected by the arbitral award were assigned to new duties. The intervenor soon concluded that the problem could not be satisfactorily resolved in this manner since each instance would have to be the subject of a new grievance and of a new arbitral award and nothing precluded the employer from abolishing the classifications which had been the subject of an arbitral award and creating new ones.

The intervenor then filed various applications with the Canada Labour Relations Board pursuant to section 61 of the Industrial Relations and Disputes Investigation Act which reads as follows:

> 61(1) If in any proceeding before the Board a question arises under this Act as to whether a person is an employer or employee;.... a group of employees is a unit appropriate for collective bargaining;....
>
> (2) A decision or order of the Board is final and conclusive and not open to question, or review, but the Board may, if it considers it advisable so to do, reconsider any decision or order made by it under this Act, and may vary or revoke any decision or order made by it under this Act.

The intervenor sought a determination that persons employed in 14 different classifications were employees within the meaning of the *Canada Labour Code* and included in the bargaining unit under the certification order issued in 1949. The classifications in question were the following: Programmer, Programmer Analyst, Programmer Assistant, Programmer Trainee,

Temporary Programmer, Associate Programmer, Computer Input-Output Analyst, Computer Scheduling Assistant, Systems Design Coordinator, Technical Services Coordinator, Data Processing Training Coordinator, Computer Shift Supervisor, Accounting Machine Supervisor and Home Consultant. The Telecommunication Workers' Union was then advised by the Board that *"while this is an application to have the Board vary the existing certificate, it will be processed in accordance with the Board's established practice for the investigation of applications for certification."* Accordingly, the Union was advised that an investigating officer had been appointed. It was further advised that it would be required to provide to the Board's investigation officer its membership and financial records in order to determine whether the employees in the additional classifications were members in good standing of the Union. At all times, the position of the Union was that it was simply requesting the Board to make a ruling pursuant to section 61(1) of the Code to determine that the persons affected were employees within the meaning of the Code and were included in the bargaining unit for which it was already certified. The position of the Board, as expressed in correspondence under the signature of its then Chief Executive Officer, was that the matter could only be dealt with pursuant to section 61(2) of the IRDI Act and that the applicant union was required to establish to the satisfaction of the Board that it had *"a mandate from the employees in the classifications listed in the request for review".* The position of the Board was apprently that it was without authority to make the decisions requested by the Union. It may be useful to quote from a letter addressed by the Chief Executive Officer of the Board to the Telecommunication Workers' Union and dated June 29, 1971:

> It is quite right, as stated in your application of May 12, 1971, that the wording of the Board's certificate issued on February 23, 1949 is sufficiently broad to include additional classifications initiated by the company after the date of the said Order of certification providing both parties are in mutual agreement regarding such inclusion. Where the parties fail to agree that the incumbents of newly created classifications are employees within the meaning of the Act and hence within the meaning of the order of certification, the bargaining agent has two options opened to it, namely (a) the filing of a new application for certification under Section 7 or Section 8 of the Act, and (b) the filing of a request for review pursuant to the provisions of subsection (2) of Section 61 of the Act.

> Under either option, the Board's policy is to ascertain whether the applicant trade union has as members in good standing a majority of the employees comprising the group which it wishes added to the unit and in respect of whom it seeks the right to bind them by collective agreement.

Shortly afterwards, the Union withdrew its application for review.

A similar application filed on behalf of the Plant Division of the intervenor met with a similar fate.

At that time, proposals for amending Part V of the *Canada Labour Code* were being considered by the Parliament of Canada. Therefore, the Telecommunication Workers' Union wrote to the then Minister of Labour suggesting that suitable provisions should be incorporated in the new Code to obviate the defects of the existing legislation which had the effect of *"enabling Companies under Federal jurisdiction to rape initially established certifications."* They received a reply which suggested that their suggestion was ill-founded.

Eventually, the Telecommunication Workers' Union sought to resolve this problem in its negotiations with the employer over the renewal of the collective agreement. A Conciliation Board report issued on May 4, 1973 recognized that there was a serious problem arising out of *"a long out-dated Certificate of Bargaining Authority and the apparent lack of appropriate machinery to update it as becomes necessary from time to time."* The Conciliation Board felt that it could not adequately deal with the issue but recommended that the parties resume negotiations with a view to reaching agreement. In the event of a failure to reach agreement by November 1, 1973, the parties would receive the assistance of an officer of the Department of Labour. If the parties came to an agreement, a joint application would be made to the Canada Labour Relations Board for appropriate amendments to the certificate of bargaining authority. Failing agreement prior to January 1, 1974, the matter would be referred to an arbitrator for binding decision. The parties would be required to file a joint application with the Canada Labour Relations Board to amend the certificate of bargaining authority in accordance with the award. The arbitrator or board should deliver its award by March 1, 1974 or some later date agreed to by the parties. The employer and the Union eventually concluded a collective agreement embodying the recommendations contained in the report of the Conciliation Board. Shortly thereafter, negotiations commenced. On May 10, 1974, the Union applied to the Department of Labour for the appointment of a mediation officer to assist the parties in their negotiations. On May 16, 1974, the Department of Labour appointed one of its officers as mediator pursuant to the provisions of section 195 of the *Canada Labour Code* (Part V — Industrial Relations) to deal with the jurisdictional dispute between the Telecommunication Workers' Union and British Columbia Telephone Company.

It is while this process was under way that the supervisory or managerial employees of the British Columbia Telephone Company began to organize into associations of their own. Shortly thereafter, applications for certification were filed by the Society of Telephone Engineers and Managers and by the Telephone Supervisors' Association of British Columbia. By filing these applications for certification, these associations sought bargaining rights for many of the employees in the classifications which the intervenor was itself seeking to represent. These applications for certification clearly had the support of the employees affected as shown by the evidence of membership tendered to the Board in the course of its investigations, whereas the intervenor could not claim any significant support from these employees. Therefore, in March 1975, the intervenor filed with the Board an application for review made pursuant to section 119 of the *Canada Labour Code* (Part V — Industrial Relations) seeking a determination that a number of disputed classifications were and should remain included in the bargaining unit which the Union already represents.

Position of the Parties

1 The Applicant

The evidence demonstrates that the managerial employees of the Marketing Department are a cohesive group, generally working as a team and sharing a distinct community of interest. Although they have much in common with other managerial employees of the British Columbia Telephone Company, those in the Marketing Department constitute, by themselves, a separate unit which is appropriate for collective bargaining.

The intervenor does not now and has never in the past represented the employees in the proposed bargaining unit. Therefore, any expansion of the bargaining unit represented by the intervenor to include additional positions or classifications not now represented by it amounts to an application for certification for the additional group. Whether the application is filed pursuant to section 124 of the Code or pursuant to section 119, the Board cannot and should not ignore the wishes of the employees involved. Therefore, the fact that the intervenor has made no attempt to organize these employees, and does not even claim that a majority of the employees in the additional group wish to be represented by it, can only lead the Board to reject the contention of the intervenor.

This evidence becomes even more significant in view of the fact that a majority of the employees affected have clearly indicated their wish not to be represented by the intervenor but have opted instead to be represented by the applicant union.

2 The Intervenor

Pursuant to the Certification Order issued in February 1949, all employees of the employer who are not clearly and primarily supervisors are included in the bargaining unit which the intervenor was certified to represent. Therefore, these employees cannot and should not be included by the Board in a separate unit represented by a different bargaining agent.

Accordingly, the Telecommunication Workers' Union contends that a number of the classifications proposed for inclusion in the bargaining unit for which STEM seeks to be certified should really be included in the existing bargaining unit which it represents. It claims jurisdiction over the following classifications because the persons involved do not supervise anybody: Marketing Services Administrator, Product Analyst, Liaison Assistant, Sales Promotions Supervisor, Phone Mart Coordinator, Market Methods Analyst, Operations Research Coordinator, Methods Analyst, Pricing Practices Administrator, Market Research Supervisor, Market Training Supervisor, Market Research Analyst, Market Support Analyst, and Systems Development Analyst. They further wish to represent some employees who have only very limited supervisory duties such as: Product Manager, Product Coordinator, Communications Companies' Relations Supervisor, Marketing Methods Supervisor, Phone Power Supervisor, Product Manager, Computer Communications Group, Computer Communications Consultant, Computer

Communications Group — Market Support Supervisor, Systems Development Supervisor and Communications Consultant. Finally the intervenor also contends that the classifications of Pricing Assistant, Marketing Training Assistant, Marketing Operations Analyst Supervisor and Inter Company Services Coordinator should be included in the same unit as the classified employees because they devote only a very small proportion of their time to the supervision of other employees. -1

Since the application for review filed by the intervenor simply involves a clarification and an updating of the original Certification Order issued in 1949, the Board does not need to and should not consider the wishes of the employees in the additional classifications which are proposed for inclusion in the existing unit.

In any event, in view of the nature of the operations of B.C. Tel. and in view of its operational and organizational structure, the bargaining unit proposed by the applicant is not appropriate for collective bargaining. It would be absurd to fragment bargaining units along departmental lines since the evidence discloses that the activities of the Marketing Department and of its managerial employees are closely integrated with the overall operations of B.C. Tel.

3   The Employer

Because of the stance it took following the issuance of the Board's interim decision in this case, the employer has not taken a position as such. However, it has already indicated that it felt that the Board should be governed in its decision by the wishes of the employees affected.

Subsequently, the employer has indicated that the bargaining units proposed by both the applicant and the intervenor were not appropriate for collective bargaining and has suggested that the Board should find appropriate company wide units comprising all managerial employees at the same level of management.

Reasons for Decision

In its earlier decision in the instant case, the Board found that all persons employed as managers in the Marketing Department of the British Columbia Telephone Company, with the exception of the Vice-President — Marketing and the Marketing Operations Manager, were *"employees"* within the meaning of section 107(1) of the *Canada Labour Code* (Part V — Industrial Relations). This decision affected at the time approximately 100 employees. The intervenor contends that, under the terms of the Certification Order issued in its favour in February 1949, it is entitled to represent some 70 of these employees and that these employees cannot and therefore should not be included in the separate bargaining unit for which the applicant seeks to be certified. It is necessary to deal with this contention before we consider the appropriateness of the bargaining unit proposed by the applicant.

It is reasonable to first consider and discuss the merits of the application for review filed by the Telecommunication Workers' Union, insofar as it affects managerial employees in the Marketing Department, before dealing with the issues raised by the application for certification.

1 The Application for Review Filed by the Telecommunications Workers' Union

The position of the intervenor is quite understandable and, in view of the circumstances, it deserves some sympathy. For nearly ten years, the Telecommunication Workers' Union has sought a binding ruling on its contention that the employer had acted illegally in failing to recognize that a number of classifications were properly included in the bargaining unit which the intervenor represented pursuant to the Certification Order issued in February 1949. When this proved to be of no avail, it sought to resolve its dispute with the employer at the bargaining table. When some progress was achieved in the negotiations on this issue, new associations or trade unions were created which applied to the Board to be certified as bargaining agent for many of the classifications which it felt it was entitled to represent.

Because of the importance of the issues raised by the intervenor's contention, we feel that it is appropriate to discuss the general principles involved, before considering the merits of the application for review as it affects employees of the Marketing Department.

a General principles

Pursuant to the provisions of the *Canada Labour Code* (Part V — Industrial Relations), a trade union which wishes to become the bargaining agent for a unit of employees has two avenues open to it. It may apply to the Board for certification but it may also attempt to obtain recognition from the employer. This possibility is recognized in a number of provisions of the Code but is particularly reflected in the definition of *"bargaining agent"* found in section 107(1).

'bargaining agent' means
1 a trade union that has been certified by the Board as the bargaining agent for the employees in a bargaining unit and the certification of which has not been revoked, or
2 any other trade union that has entered into a collective agreement on behalf of the employees in a bargaining unit
  a the term of which has not expired, or
  b in respect of which the trade union has, by notice given pursuant to subsection 147(1) required the employer to commence collective bargaining.

Therefore, a trade union that has concluded a collective agreement with an employer which is applicable to a group of employees is the bargaining agent for this group of employees, and as such enjoys basically the same rights and privileges as a trade union that has been certified by the Board.

Should the employer refuse to *"recognize"* the trade union as bargaining agent or should the trade union prefer to avail itself of the certification procedure provided by the Code, it may file with the Board an application for certification. When the Board is seized with an application for certification and when it finds that the applicant trade union meets the requirements of the Code, section 126 provides that:

the Board shall, subject to this Part, certify the trade union making the application as bargaining agent for the bargaining unit.

Section 136 of the Code further provides that:

1 Where a trade union is certified as the bargaining agent for a bargaining unit,
   a the trade union so certified has exclusive authority to bargain collectively on behalf of the employees in the bargaining unit....

Therefore, pursuant to section 146 of the Code, the bargaining agent may, by notice, require the employer to commence collective bargaining. When notice to bargain collectively has been given, the bargaining agent and the employer are required, pursuant to section 148 of the Code, to *"bargain collectively in good faith, and make every reasonable effort to enter into a collective agreement."*

There is, however, a fundamental difference between the two processes. Recognition depends entirely on the agreement of the employer and becomes effective only upon the execution of a collective agreement between the employer and the trade union concerning the group of employees to which the collective agreement is applicable. A certification order is an *"order or decision of the Board"* which is *"final"* pursuant to section 122(1) of the Code. Therefore, once a certification order has been issued by the Board, the employer is no longer free to recognize or refuse to recognize the trade union as the bargaining agent for the group described in the order.

When a collective agreement is entered into, section 154 of the Code provides that it is binding not only on the bargaining agent and the employer but also on *"every employee in the bargaining unit".* Section 107(1) of the Code contains the following definition:

'bargaining unit' means a unit
a determined by the Board to be appropriate for collective bargaining or
b to which a collective agreement applies

This would appear to indicate that, at least when the Board has certified a trade union as bargaining agent for the employees in a bargaining unit, the parties to the collective agreement are no longer free to exclude from the application of the collective agreement any employee included in the unit *"determined by the Board to be appropriate for collective bargaining".*

Of course, a bargaining relationship need not for that reason remain forever static. In bargaining collectively with a certified trade union, an employer may recognize the trade union for a unit larger than the one to which the certification order originally applied and, in such a case, the execution of a collective agreement amounts to the recognition of the trade union as bargaining agent for the additional group of employees. Therefore, once a bargaining relationship has been established, the bargaining unit originally defined by the Board in the certification order may expand and may, by this process of incremental recognition, extend to cover a larger group of employees. When an application is filed with it pursuant to section 119 of the Code, the Board may sanction such arrangements and grant a corresponding amendment to the original certification order issued by the Board. Should such recognition not be achieved in this fashion, a trade union may only become the bargaining agent for such an additional group of employees by filing an application for certification or for review with the Board in order to obtain additional bargaining rights. In such a case, it will of course be required to satisfy the Board that it enjoys the necessary membership support among the new group of employees which it wishes to represent, as would any trade union wishing to be certified to represent a group of employees for which it does not already have bargaining rights.

If a bargaining unit originally defined by the Board in a certification order can thus be expanded, the possibility that it can be contracted must also be considered.

Situations where this occurs inadvertently are not particularly bothersome. However general the language used by the Board in a certification order, the parties may by their behaviour demonstrate that they understand the bargaining unit to be smaller than the one apparently originally determined. A typical example of this might be a situation where a union is certified as bargaining agent for a unit comprising *"all employees"* but where, over the years, the parties clearly show by their behaviour that they consider the sales staff or the office employees to be excluded from the unit. In such a case, little more can be done but to give effect to the *"new"* description of the bargaining unit, as evidenced by the behaviour of the parties over a long period of time. Thereafter, should the trade union wish to acquire bargaining rights for the *"forgotten employees"*, it will be required to proceed by way of application as if, in fact and in law, it had never had any right to represent these employees.

A more serious problem arises if the employer and the certified bargaining agent deliberately enter into a collective agreement which is expressly made applicable to a bargaining unit which is smaller than that described in the certification order. In such a situation employees included in a bargaining unit for which a trade union has been certified by the Board are effectively deprived of the benefits of the collective agreement and of their right to be represented by the bargaining agent in collective bargaining with their employer. As between the employee and the bargaining agent, such an agreement appears to involve a breach of the duty of fair representation which is owed by the bargaining agent to every employee in the unit.

In such a case, the Board should at the very least be extremely cautious against endorsing or otherwise giving effect to an agreement between the employer and the bargaining agent which is in contravention of the Board's certification order and which further has the effect of infringing on the rights of the employees affected. Since an agreement has been concluded between the employer and the bargaining agent, the Board must also be wary of undermining the very collective bargaining system which the Code was designed to uphold by making it possible for a party to a bargain to renege on its part of the deal.

Certainly, and whether such agreements between the employer and the bargaining agent are valid or not, an employer may not lawfully compel or seek to compel the bargaining agent to conclude a collective agreement which is expressly made applicable to a group which is smaller than the unit that the trade union has been certified to represent as bargaining agent pursuant to a certification order issued by the Board. As the Board has already indicated a party may be in breach of its duty to bargain collectively in good faith under the provisions of section 148(a) of the Code if it seeks to compel the other party to include in a collective agreement a provision which is illegal or otherwise contrary to public policy. Therefore, an attempt to compel the inclusion in a collective agreement of a *"scope clause"* under which the collective agreement would not be applicable to *"every employee in the bargaining unit"*, despite the clear language of section 154 of the Code, might very well amount to a failure to comply with section 148(a) of the Code. Furthermore, since a certified bargaining agent has, pursuant to section 136(1)(a) of the Code, the *"exclusive authority to bargain collectively on behalf of the employees in the unit"*, an employer may not evade its obligation under the Code by refusing to recognize a trade unit [sic] duly certified as the bargaining agent for all or part of the unit described in the certification order.

In any event, and whether we like it or not, it is a well-known fact of industrial relations in this country that, over the years, employers and trade unions have bargained over the application of a collective agreement and have concluded agreements which may be incompatible with the terms of a certification order issued by the Board. We have already expressed serious reservations as regards the validity of such agreements, which appear to contravene both the language and the policies of the *Canada Labour Code*. While such agreements certainly cannot allow either party to the contract to evade their legal obligations *vis-à-vis* the employees affected, it would be equally unacceptable to allow a party to renege on its agreement, because it is no longer convenient or acceptable to it. In the name of preserving the effectiveness and continuous validity of a certification order issued by it, the Board will not use the discretion vested in it by section 119 of the Code to rescue a trade union from *"poor deals"* made at the bargaining table, particularly when a union later seeks to invoke bargaining rights against the very employees which it has abandoned or ignored over a long period of time. Although a certification order issued pursuant to the provisions of the Code normally continues to have full force and effect until such time as it is revoked whether expressly pursuant to section 138(1) or implicitly pursuant to section 136(1)(b) of the Code, the bargaining rights which it confers may lapse as a result of the failure of the bargaining agent to exercise them over a long period of time. Whether or not a trade union can be allowed to invoke its own dereliction as regards the employees affected by it, it should not be able to invoke it against those very employees or against the employer who is entitled to rely on the agreement reached with the union and implemented over a period of time.

Therefore, a certified bargaining agent who has, over the years, voluntarily relinquished its bargaining rights with regard to some employees who were originally included in the bargaining unit for which it was certified should be in no better position than a trade union which has done so inadvertently or one which has entirely failed to exercise its bargaining rights over a long period of time. In such a situation, if the certified bargaining agent wishes to obtain anew the bargaining rights which it has relinquished, it is entirely normal and appropriate that the Board should take into account in reaching its decision the wishes of the employees affected, as if a new application for certification were involved.

We must nevertheless recognize that, over the years, problems may arise over the interpretation or application of a certification order issued by the Board. The language used in the description of the bargaining unit may become out-of-date. New positions or classifications may be created or the duties and responsibilities of certain positions may vary. Often, the parties may be able to resolve such disputes themselves by agreeing that the newly-created classifications were meant to be covered under the terms of the original certification order or that certain persons clearly do or do not perform management functions or are or are not employed in a confidential capacity in matters relating to industrial relations. Of course such an agreement does not bind the Canada Labour Relations Board which, pursuant to section 118(p) of the Code, is expressly empowered to make such a determination. Nevertheless, it is only reasonable that the Board should, as a general rule, give effect to such agreements unless they appear to it to directly contravene the policies or provisions of the Code.

Direct negotiations between the employer and the bargaining agent are not, however, the sole means of resolving such disputes. Pursuant to section 119 of the *Canada Labour Code* (Part V — Industrial Relations):

> the Board may review, rescind, amend, alter or vary any order or decision made by it, and may rehear any application before making an order in the [sic] respect of the application....

In the course of determining such an application, the Board may certainly invoke the powers given to it by section 118(p) of the Code to determine whether a person is an employee or whether a person performs management functions or is employed in a confidential capacity in matters relating to industrial relations. Only after such a determination has been made, can the Board determine whether it is appropriate to review or vary an existing certification order so that the description of the bargaining unit properly reflects the existing situation.

The Board has already indicated that the powers conferred upon it by section 119 of the Code could and would be used to update or otherwise clarify an order or decision of the Board having a continuing effect.

> Whenever an order or decision of the Board has a continuing effect, and this is typically the case where a Certification Order has been issued, various circumstances may change which may require corresponding amendments or clarifications of the Board's original decision. For example, the name of the bargaining agent or that of the employer may have changed or the classification titles referred to in the Board's order may be replaced by new ones. Alternatively, new classifications may have been created and it may be unclear whether they are dealt with by the Board's original decision. In such a case, an application may be filed under section 119 asking the Board to review and alter its decision or to clarify it. Here, an eventual decision on the application for review will not change the nature and effect of the original Board's order. It will simply up-date or clarify the wording of the decision and accordingly, the Board must simply be satisfied that these changes are in order.

In this way, the parties can seek and obtain from the Board a ruling with regard to the scope of the bargaining unit described in a certification order issued by the Board. The Board can determine whether the incumbent of a new classification is an employee who was meant to be included in the bargaining unit originally defined by the Board or whether the person in question performs management functions or is employed in a confidential capacity in matters relating to labour relations, in which case it may be appropriate to vary the existing certification order so as to add the new classification to the list of exclusions.

Furthermore, for the purpose of making that determination, it should matter little whether the person or persons whose status is raised in the application wish the trade union to represent them as their bargaining agent. Obviously, in order to be certified as bargaining agent for a bargaining unit, a trade union must enjoy the support of a majority of the employees in the unit found appropriate by the Board. However, in order to make the determination required by section 126(c) of the Code, the Board does not and must not consider the wishes of individual employees or of employees in given positions or classifications but the overall wishes of all the employees included in the unit which it has found appropriate. It is a basic principle of our labour relations legislation that the wishes of the majority of the employees in an appropriate bargaining unit must prevail with regard to the question of whether a trade union will be certified as bargaining agent for the whole unit, and which trade union must be so certified. In such a context it is unavoidable that some employees or groups of employees may disagree with the majority and that their wishes may have to be subjected to those of the majority. There appears to be no valid justification to depart from this principle in the context of an application for review made pursuant to section 119 of the Code simply because an employer may have created a new position or classification and may contend that the incumbent is not an employee within the meaning of the Code or because the employer contends that the duties and responsibilities of a particular individual have changed in such a manner that that individual is no longer an *"employee"* under the Code.

The Board cannot and should not ignore the *"facts of life"*. When an employee is hired or promoted into a position by an employer and is led to understand by that employer's representatives that he is now a *"manager"* and entitled to receive the *"privileges"* normally accruing to the managerial ranks, it is not very likely that this person will be inclined to obtain or retain membership in the trade union representing the *"ordinary"* employees of that employer. If, as a result of his alleged promotion from the bargaining unit, the employer stops deducting union dues from that employee's salary, as required under the collective agreement, only a very determined and exceptional individual will take the necessary steps to maintain his membership by directly forwarding to the trade union the requisite financial contribution. It is clear that a union attempting to recruit a member under these conditions is at least severely handicapped. Furthermore, it is equally clear to us that, normally, a trade union should not be required to do so. An employer may not, by creating a new classification and labelling the incumbent a *"manager"*, vary or alter a bargaining unit defined by the Board in a certification order. If the nature of the duties and responsibilities of that person are such that the position is clearly included in the bargaining unit for which the Board has certified a trade union, only the Board can determine whether that person performs management functions or is employed in a confidential capacity in matters related to industrial relations so that the position should, accordingly, be expressly excluded from the bargaining unit for which the trade union is certified. In making that determination, it is clear that the Board must focus on the nature of the duties and responsibilities of the person involved and not on the subjective beliefs of that person or of the employer as to the importance of his alleged managerial function.

It is clear, however, that in order to secure a determination from the Board on the basis of these principles, a trade union must act without delay. At the very least, it must not acquiesce in the contention of the employer that persons employed in *"disputed classifications"* are excluded from the bargaining unit. Failing that, the Board may very well find that the parties have, by their agreement or by their behaviour, interpreted the certification order issued by the Board in a manner that is binding on both the employer and the bargaining agent. In such a case, it would not be proper for the Board to invoke the discretion conferred upon it by the provisions of section 119 of the Code to disturb a long established relationship, without regard for the wishes of the employees involved.

b The instant application for review

The contention of the intervenor is that, pursuant to the Certification Order issued in its favour in February 1949, it is entitled to represent all the employees of the British Columbia Telephone Company except those who devote a major portion of their time to the supervision of other employees. Therefore, the Board should refuse to give effect to the unilateral actions of the employer which have eroded the bargaining unit over the years, and review the 1949 order so as to restore the bargaining unit which it had originally certified. Since what is at stake is a simple up-dating and clarification of the Certification Order originally issued by the Board, the wishes of the approximately 600 employees which it claims should be added to the unit are irrelevant.

The facts are not quite as simple and straightforward. The Certification Order at issue in this application for review was issued by the Board on February 23, 1949. A review of the Board's files with regard to the original application for certification is singularly uninformative. The file contains little or no information with regard to the employer's organizational structure or with regard to the reasons which warranted the exclusion of certain classifications from the unit and it is therefore difficult to ascertain the intended scope of the bargaining unit described by the Board in the Certification Order. In fact, the file makes it clear that the Certification Order which was issued by the Board in February 1949 simply reflected and endorsed an agreement reached between the employer and the Federation of Telephone Workers of British Columbia with regard to the scope of the bargaining unit. Certainly, it is not possible to conclude, as does the intervenor, that the unit originally defined by the Board included all employees except those who were involved in the supervision of other employees. The list of exclusions outlined in the Certification Order is now rather useless. Some job titles can still be related to existing ones which are supervisory in nature. The basis for a number of the exclusions can still be fairly easily ascertained when the job title is that of *"manager"* or indicates that the incumbent must have been a *"professional"* and, as such, was not an employee under the legislation as it then existed. Unfortunately, the justification for a large number of exclusions is not all that clear. The original unit description can be interpreted as the intervenor proposed but it is equally consistent with the interpretation proposed by the applicant, according to which only *"ordinary"* employees were originally included and all positions with important managerial, supervisory, professional or technical functions were excluded. According to this latter interpretation, the employees whom the applicant now wishes to represent comprise the very group which was originally excluded, for one reason or another, from the unit represented by the intervenor. In view of this, it is neither possible nor desirable to attempt to interpret or clarify the Certification Order issued in 1949, without considering the changes which have taken place in the organization of the employer over a period of twenty-five years. We are far from satisfied that it is possible, as the intervenor contends, to restore the bargaining unit originally determined by the Board to be appropriate in view of the fact that the evidence is far from conclusive.

Furthermore, even if it were possible to do so, it is far from clear that it would be appropriate to do so in this case. The intervenor was certified in 1949. Since then, it has negotiated several collective agreements with the employer. It now protests the fact that these collective agreements have not been applicable to the entire bargaining unit for which it had originally been certified. We recognize of course that, for a period of close to ten years, the intervenor has been trying to obtain a resolution of its dispute with the employer over this issue and to counteract what it considers to be an erosion of the bargaining unit which it represents. It is extremely regrettable that its efforts in this regard have proven to be of no avail and that various circumstances have deprived it of the opportunity to obtain a final decision on the validity of its claim. The fact remains, however, that, from 1949 to 1967, the intervenor did little or nothing to remedy the situation. In view of this, the Board can only conclude that, if the intervenor ever did have the authority to bargain on behalf of a group of employees wider than that which is now covered by its collective agreement with the employer, these bargaining rights have now lapsed.

Since 1949, the telecommunications industry has undergone major transformations. The nature of the operations of B.C. Tel. has changed as well as have the skills and qualifications required of its employees. Over the years, the number of employees employed in supervisory positions or in highly specialized staff positions has grown dramatically and these employees have, in fact, been excluded from the bargaining unit represented by the union. Although the bargaining unit represented by the union may to some extent have been eroded by this phenomenon, we are not prepared at this stage to rule that this occurred solely or mainly as a result of the employer's determination to restrict the bargaining rights of the intervenor. In fact, this seems to be due in large part to the development of the industry and of this enterprise over a period of many years.

It is now clear, from the earlier decisions of this Board in this or in related cases, that a number of persons employed in the managerial ranks of the British Columbia Telephone Company do not in fact perform management functions and are indeed *"employees"* within the meaning of the Code. Whatever the reasons for this, these employees are not now and have not for many years been represented by a trade union. The Telecommunication Workers' Union has not seriously attempted to recruit these employees and does not claim that they wish to be represented by it.

2 The Application for Certification

In the instant case, the Board has already ruled that the employees proposed for inclusion in the bargaining unit were *"employees"* as that term is defined in section 107(1) of the *Canada Labour Code* (Part V — Industrial Relations).

We also find on the basis of the documentary evidence filed with the Board that the applicant is a trade union within the meaning of section 107(1) of the *Canada Labour Code*. In this regard, we note that the employer had contested the trade union status of the applicant on the grounds that its members were not *"employees"* but managers. This assertion has been disposed of, at least in part, by the interim decision of the Board in the instant case. We recognize, however, that many managerial employees of B.C. Tel. are members of the Society and that, at this stage, it would be premature for the Board to rule that these persons are all *"employees"*. Nevertheless, we find that the applicant is an *"organization of employees...the purposes of which include the regulation of relations between employers and employees".* We are confident that, should some of the members or leaders of the Society be found not to be *"employees",* the applicant will nevertheless be able to continue to operate as a trade union and will take whatever steps are necessary to remove any possible inference of *"managerial interference".*

Therefore, there remains for us to determine, pursuant to section 126(b) of the Code, *"the unit that constitutes a unit appropriate for collective bargaining"* and pursuant to section 126(c), whether the applicant enjoys the support of a majority of the employees in that unit. In so doing, we are aware that it is up to the applicant to establish to the satisfaction of the Board that it meets the requirements outlined in section 126 of the Code.

The position taken by the other parties to the application has been of little assistance to the Board in reaching a determination on that issue. The employer has not contested the appropriateness of the bargaining unit proposed by the applicant. It has also refused to take any position with regard to this issue although it has provided the Board with the written information and submissions which it had expressly requested. The intervenor has indeed disputed the appropriateness of the bargaining unit proposed by the applicant. It is clear, however, that its position has been largely influenced by its concern to protect and promote its own claim that it is entitled to represent more than two-thirds of the employees in the proposed bargaining unit. The intervenor does not dispute the right of the applicant to represent those managerial employees of the Marketing Department who are involved, to a considerable extent, in the supervision of other employees. It has however questioned the appropriateness of a supervisory unit which would comprise only the employees of that department.

To some extent, the applicant itself may have been hampered in presenting evidence and submissions to the Board on the issue of appropriateness. It may have been led to rely unduly on the Board's statement that at least a *prima facie* case has been established with regard to the appropriateness of the bargaining unit which it proposes. It may also have been handicapped by its own frankness as to its goals and ideals. It is the clearly avowed goal of the Society to eventually secure bargaining rights for a single bargaining unit comprising all the employees of B.C. Tel. in the managerial ranks. It recognizes that such a bargaining unit would be appropriate, indeed would be the most appropriate and desirable from the point of view of the effective representation of the employees involved. In view of the circumstances of this case, however, it nevertheless requests that, for the time being, the Board find appropriate the bargaining unit which it proposes and which would include only employees in the managerial ranks of the Marketing Department.

Section 125(4) of the Code provides that:

> Where a trade union applies for certification as the bargaining agent for a unit comprised of or including employees whose duties include the supervision of other employees, the Board may, subject to subsection (2) determine that the unit proposed in the application is appropriate for collective bargaining.

It is obvious that the unit proposed here is not one that comprises only supervisory employees but one that includes both supervisory and non-supervisory employees. Subsection 125(4) of the Code makes it clear that the Board may find appropriate either type of unit.

In support of its position, the applicant has relied to quite an extent on modern management theory. Counsel for the applicant has quoted in argument Galbraith and Drucker. It contends that, in the modern enterprise, it is neither possible nor desirable to draw a line between managers and ordinary employees. Because of the explosion of knowledge and of the ever increasing complexity of the modern enterprise, a *"technostructure"* has developed in larger corporations. It is composed of *"knowledge workers"* who, by the nature of their work which often involves the supervision of other employees, by the nature of their skills and by their working conditions, are different from *"ordinary"* employees although they are *"employees"* themselves, as that term is defined in section 107(1) of the *Canada Labour Code*. According to the applicant, these persons share a distinct community of interest which warrants the creation of separate bargaining units.

On the other hand, it is clear that this application for certification applies only to those employees of the Marketing Department who are not already represented by the intervenor. In this regard, the applicant contends that, because the Marketing Department is organized as a team and because of the unique function of the Marketing Department in the employer's operation, a unit comprising only the employees of the Marketing Department would be appropriate for collective bargaining. In support of this contention, the applicant invokes the difficulty of organizing persons who have until very recently, been considered not to be *"employees"* and deprived of the right to bargain collectively under the provisions of the *Canada Labour Code*. It further indicates that it intends and hopes to continue to organize the managerial employees of the employer and to file subsequent applications for certification. In this respect, it is prepared to concede that the granting of additional bargaining rights to this applicant should not lead to the creation of numerous additional units. Instead, all the various units for which the applicant may become certified should be merged into a single unit.

The British Columbia Telephone Company employed, as of December 31, 1975, more than 10,500 persons. Of this number, 1,902 persons were considered to be *"management"*. In October 1976, the number of *"managerial"* employees had grown to 1,983. Of this number, some 100 persons were employed in the Marketing Department as of the date of the instant application for certification. Following a reorganization which has since been implemented, new services and groups were brought into the Marketing Department, particularly in the Computer Communications Group. Accordingly, in the Fall of 1976, there were more than 140 employees in the managerial ranks of the Marketing Department.

In earlier decisions, particularly in the decision of the Board in *Trade of Locomotive Engineers and Canadian Pacific Limited and Brotherhood of Locomotive Engineers*, the Board has already indicated that, in most circumstances, a bargaining unit comprising all the employees of a given employer is appropriate for collective bargaining. Indeed, in most cases, such a bargaining structure is best designed to ensure the effective representation of the interests of the employees, while promoting *"effective industrial relations"* and the *"constructive settlement of disputes".* The *Canada Labour Code,* however, has not mandated the Canada Labour Relations Board to determine in any given case the *"most appropriate"* bargaining unit. It is a well known fact of industrial relations that, in most situations, more than one unit may be appropriate for collective bargaining. The Board should not, however, endorse the creation of a number of small bargaining units unless it is satisfied that there exist valid considerations for departing from the concept of a broad overall unit.

Within the British Columbia Telephone Company, there already exists one bargaining unit represented by a certified bargaining agent. This unit of *"classified employees"* comprises office and clerical employees, telephone operators and other traffic personnel as well as tradesmen, technicians, installers, construction or maintenance employees and other blue collar workers. In order to effectively represent these rather diverse groups of employees, the intervenor is organized as a federation comprising three relatively autonomous divisions: clerical, traffic and plant. The success of the Telecommunication Workers' Union in negotiating a single collective agreement on behalf of some 9,000 employees testifies to the fact that it is possible to accommodate diverse and varied interests within a single unified bargaining structure. There can be little doubt that the intervenor could further adapt its structures to include in its ranks and to effectively represent other employees of the employer, even if they are employed in a supervisory or managerial capacity or perform highly skilled work. It is however clear that, at this stage, these employees do not wish to be represented by the Union and many of them have expressed a wish to be represented by another trade union.

In view of the circumstances of this case, the Board is not prepared to find that the only unit appropriate for collective bargaining is one which would include all employees of the British Columbia Telephone Company, or all the employees of the British Columbia Telephone Company except those who perform supervisory functions. To so rule would amount to a finding that all those employees who are not already represented by the intervenor could only exercise the rights which are granted to them by section 110(1) of the Code by becoming members of the intervenor in such numbers that the Board would be justified to review the existing Certification Order so as to expand the existing bargaining unit to include these additional classifications. Under this reasoning, these employees could only avail themselves of the provisions of the Code with regard to certification and collective bargaining by opting to be represented by the Telecommunication Workers' Union. While we recognize that such an outcome may be unavoidable in some cases, we feel strongly that such a conclusion should be avoided if at all possible, since it severely restricts the freedom of employees to select the bargaining agent of their choice.

Therefore, in this case, while reiterating our opinion that a single all-inclusive unit would be appropriate for collective bargaining, we are prepared to find appropriate for collective bargaining a separate unit comprising only those employees who are not presently represented by the Telecommunication Workers' Union. The concept of the *"technostructure"* proposed by the applicant is certainly novel in industrial relations terms. Yet, we feel that it is a useful concept. The modern enterprise does employ large numbers of *"knowledge workers"*. Whether they perform a staff or a line function, these employees will often share a distinct community of interest. In many circumstances, such as in the instant case, it may be appropriate to recognize this fact by sanctioning the creation of a separate bargaining unit comprising only these employees. Accordingly, as we have indicated in our decision on the application for certification filed by the Telephone Supervisors' Association, the Board is prepared to find appropriate for collective bargaining a separate unit of *"supervisory"* or managerial employees of the British Columbia Telephone Company. It may even be that more than one *"supervisory"* unit could be found to be appropriate for collective bargaining.

The Board is fully aware of the difficulty of organizing into a trade union employees who have, at least until recently, been led to believe that they are *"managers"* and that belonging to a trade union is somehow incompatible with their status as *"managers"*. As a result, it is not entirely surprising that these employees, when they choose to organize pursuant to the provisions of the Code, should be inclined to do so through organizations created specifically for that purpose and should favor the creation of separate *"supervisory"* bargaining units. In this context, it is clear that any decision on the appropriateness of such supervisory or quasi-supervisory units may have a tremendous impact. If the right of these employees to join a trade union and bargain collectively with their employer through the bargaining agent of their own choice is not to remain a dead letter, it may well be that the Board should, at least for the time being, adopt a fairly sympathetic approach as regards proposals for the creation of such units, where they are not otherwise inappropriate. Nevertheless, the wishes of the employees involved or the extent of a union's organizing campaign cannot by themselves establish the appropriateness of a bargaining unit for collective bargaining.

questions

1 Why would the Society of Telephone Engineers and Managers (STEM) have filed separate applications for certification of workers in the marketing and finance departments and for a group of engineers? Elaborate.
2 What is the difference between certification by the Canada Labour Relations Board (CLRB) and voluntary recognition? Elaborate.
3 Why did the intervenor not try to get support from the workers whom it wished to have included in its bargaining unit?
4 The CLRB refers to the possibility that the intervenor and the employer may not have been bargaining for workers who may technically have been covered by the collective agreement. How could the parties have known this in an industry where occupational changes and job duties were changing so quickly?

5 How would you assess the intervenor's arguments? Would you find it appropriate to represent the group it sought to represent?

6 What does the intervenor's experience with its 1949 certificate tell you about the dynamics of bargaining units and how they might be kept up to date?

7 What order, if any, would you make for the intervenor?

8 Why did STEM make its application for workers in separate departments when it eventually wanted to represent all levels of management in the company?

9 a) Why did STEM raise the issue of knowledge workers and technostructure?
  b) Did this issue increase or decrease its chances of becoming certified as the bargaining agent for the first four levels of management in the marketing department? Elaborate.

10 If you were writing the decision for the Board, would you find the unit proposed by STEM appropriate for collective bargaining? Elaborate.

11 a) This case lends itself beautifully to role-playing. Have the three members of the class act as members of the Board with your professor as chairman and the other two as representatives of employer and union interests. Have other class members play the roles of the chief spokesmen for the two unions involved, the president of the company, and Fred Pearson, *et al*. Role-play the case as if it were a real-life one and assume that all of the players would like to take on cases of a similar nature in the future.
  b) What is the assessment of each actor with respect to the roles played by the others?
  c) How does the class as a whole assess each of your roles?
  d) If you have audio-visual equipment, tape this case, replay it, and critique it
  e) Did you find the exercise worthwhile?

The Amok Ltd. and M. Tabouret Case* — An Employer's Freedom of Speech or an Unfair Labour Practice?

Reasons for Decision in

United Steelworkers of America,
complainant,
and

Amok Ltd. and M. Tabouret,
respondents

Reasons for Decision

1 The United Steelworkers of American complained on December 2, 1980 that Amok Ltd. and its managing director, M. Tabouret, contravened sections 184(1)(a) and (3)(e) by distributing memoranda dated September 25, 1980 and

*Permission to use this case was granted by the Canada Labour Relations Board. Minor deletions were made by the author for the purposes of this book.

October 31, 1980 to its employees. The union was seeking to organize the employees at the time and, although it was aware of these memoranda one or two days after they were issued, delayed complaining until December.

The complaint was heard in Saskatoon on April 30, 1981 in conjunction with one other complaint which was withdrawn and a third complaint arising from the dismissal of an employee on September 15, 1980 which was not complained about until December.

On February 25, 1981 the union applied for certification for a unit of 104 employees at the employer's Cluff Lake mining site. The union has as members a majority of this number. The employer submits that the appropriate bargaining unit should include over sixty more employees who are employed at the mill at Cluff Lake which operates in conjunction with the mine. About sixty percent of the mill employees are northern residents. The union represents over thirty-five percent of the unit proposed by the employer. The employees who are members of the union joined between August 26 and December 10, 1980. The August 26 to February 25 period is the full extent of the time allowed for membership evidence in the Board's regulations.

> 27.(2) On any application for certification made after June 1, 1979, the Board may accept as evidence of membership in a trade union evidence that a person
> a has signed an application for membership in the trade union; and
> b has paid to the trade union a sum of at least five dollars for or within the six-month period immediately preceding the date of the filing of the application for certification by the trade union.

The Board heard representations by the parties and determined that it would postpone making any decision on the certification application until the conclusion of these proceedings and the parties have had an opportunity to make representations on the affect, if any, the findings in these proceedings should have on the certification proceedings.

2 To those aware of public debate in Saskatchewan Cluff Lake is a familiar name. It is north of 58 degrees latitude in the northeast corner of the province at the end of an improved road called the Semchuk Trail. It is on Canada's frontier. It is also rich in uranium.

Amok Ltd., owned by three French companies, discovered the Cluff Lake deposit in 1971. It is labeled the "D" ore body. Before 1971 uranium was mined from an open-pit mine at Rabbit Lake and underground mines at Uranium City. The community reaction to Cluff Lake mining was not as subdued or passive as in the past.

On February 1, 1977 the Government of Saskatchewan appointed the Cluff Lake Board of Inquiry....

The Board filed a report on May 31, 1978 (The Cluff Lake Board of Inquiry Final Report). [It] made many recommendations on each subject it addressed. It was concerned about the social effects of development on northern residents and businesses. Among them were the following:

. . .

4 Northerners should be appointed to most, if not all, existing boards and agencies that now fashion policies closely affecting the North.
5 The provincial government should establish a Board (Northern Development Board) composed primarily of Northerners.

. . .

8 The Board should be assigned the task of keeping Northerners informed about development in the North generally and uranium mining/milling specifically.
9 If the Board is not established or if there is a time lag in establishing it, Amok should be obligated legally to undertake its proposed program for employing Northerners and that obligation is perhaps best contained in the surface leases to be granted to Amok.

. . .

The recommendations were an outgrowth of principal conclusions arrived at on each subject. Two relevant ones for these proceedings were the following:

15 Trade unions, along with employers and the government, have a responsibility to ensure the well-being of the northern workers and they should be given the opportunity to exercise that responsibility.
16 If, given the opportunity, trade unions fail to exercise their responsibility and as a result their practices tend to inhibit the employment of northern workers for northern projects, existing legislation should be amended to ensure that union practices do not stand in the way of northern workers having the first chance of developing the North (p. 207).

The background discussion to these conclusions is reproduced in full.

8.102 The intrusion into the North of technology, industrialization and modernity in the form of uranium development will inevitably result in the introduction to the North of such concomitants as trade unions. Whether the Development Board we suggest does or does not come into existence, an important issue is likely to arise in the future concerning the involvement of a trade union at the Cluff Lake development and other developments. Part of that issue is the extent to which the certification of a union may retard the hiring of Northerners as workers in the mine/mill, or in the construction of the mine/mill or of the road leading to it, and other similar works. It cannot be disputed that if the introduction to trade unions retards the hiring of Northerners as workers in these complexes and these construction jobs then it will be causing the Northerners to bear social costs they would otherwise not have to bear.

8.103 We make three points in this regard:
  i   We recognize that there most certainly is room for unionizing the workers in the mine/mill, the construction company building the mine/mill, the company building the road, etc., to the same extent and for the same reasons as exist with respect of any group of Saskatchewan employees. In other words, simply because the employer's operations are situated in northern Saskatchewan does not somehow disqualify unionization as a beneficial step for the workers.
  ii As noted, the present unofficial attitude of the Saskatchewan Federation of Labour (which may or may not reflect the attitude of individual unions) is favourable from the standpoint of employing Northerners as workers.
  iii We hope and expect that the unions of Saskatchewan will recognize (if they have not already done so) that they, as well as the employers and government, have a responsibility to ensure the well-being of the northern worker (as one of the primary factors in the development of the North);

and to that end will take whatever steps may be necessary to modify any practices in the labour movement which may tend to inhibit the hiring of northern workers for northern projects. These modifications may involve a special type of membership in the case of northern workers. They may involve the unions going out of their way to educate Northerners in unionism. It will be up to the unions to devise their own methods to enhance the hiring of northern workers. In view of the manner in which we expect the unions to act, we do not recommend any legislation in this respect.

iv If, given the opportunity, the unions fail to discharge the responsibility referred to in (iii) above we regard a failure of that nature of sufficient importance and magnitude to warrant an amendment to existing legislation to provide for the curbing of practices by unions which tend to inhibit the employment of northern workers for northern projects, and to further provide for legal sanctions including where appropriate an order of decertification by the appropriate Labour Relations Board. The application for such sanctions should be available to the Development Board, if one is established or to some representative of northern workers if there is no Development Board. In short, we regard the concept of unionism as most laudable, but where a conflict arises, union practices must be altered so that they do not stand in the way of northern workers having the first chance at developing the North (pp. 205-6).

The Board of Inquiry's ultimate recommendation was that the Cluff Lake mine/mill proceed subject to the conclusions and recommendations it reached and made.

The Saskatchewan Government responded to the Board of Inquiry's report in June, 1978 and published its decision.

1 That Phase I of the Cluff Lake project may proceed provided that suitable agreement is reached with Amok under which the company will agree to implement the additional measures recommended by the Board to safeguard health and safety of workers and to ensure the participation of northerners in the construction and operation of the project. The government will proceed, in consultation with the federal government and the company, to an immediate review of those recommendations directed at governments and specifically related to the Cluff Lake project. The objective will be early implementation.

. . .

In the summer of 1978 the Government of Saskatchewan through the Minister of Northern Saskatchewan negotiated a surface lease agreement with Amok Ltd. It was concluded on September 29, 1978. The lease obliges Amok Ltd. to meet certain employment levels for northern residents during the operation of the mine and mill.

13 EMPLOYMENT DURING THE OPERATION OF THE MINE AND MILL

. . .

2 The Lessee and the Minister agree to co-operate to ensure that the greatest possible number of northern residents are employed at the mine and mill.

3 The Lessee agrees to make reasonable progress toward meeting the employment ratio of northern residents to total employees set out in subparagraph (4) during the years prior to 1982.

4 The Lessee shall, during the 1982 calendar year and each year thereafter, employ not less than that number of northern residents necessary to result in the said northern residents performing at least 50% of the man years of

> work required in the normal operation of the mine and mill for one calendar year.
>
> 5 The Lessee agrees that, to the extent possible northern residents shall be distributed throughout the widest possible range of job classifications with the Lessee's operations at the mine and mill.
>
> . . .
>
> 7 Northern residents employed by the Lessee shall receive the same rates of pay that any other person would receive in the same position or in an equivalent classification.
>
> . . .

Articles 16 to 19 of the lease contain conditions of employment and controls on Amok Ltd. Article 16 establishes seven day shifts and eleven hour days that cannot be altered except with approval of a majority of the employees. It also deals with such items as free air transportation, training northern residents, apprenticeship, scholarship funds, and native speaking employees to communicate directly with senior management. Article 17 deals with recruitment. A monitoring committee is to be established pursuant to Article 18 to review and evaluate recruitment, employment and training in accordance with the agreement. That committee is to consist of three to five members appointed by the Minister of Northern Saskatchewan of whom one shall be nominated by Amok Ltd. and one by the northern resident employees. The committee must meet regularly and publish reports. Article 19 requires the Minister at a future date to determine a final employment plan and provides for arbitration of differences.

Article 20 is entitled "Trade Unions" and states as follows:

> If any of the employees of the Lessee shall be or become members of a trade union, then, notwithstanding anything contained in paragraphs 16 and 17 of this Agreement, the terms and conditions of employment of such employees shall be governed by the terms of any collective bargaining agreement entered into between the Lessee and any such trade union, and in the event of any conflict between the terms of any such collective bargaining agreement and this Agreement, the terms of the collective bargaining agreement shall prevail.

The background of public inquiry and debate resulted in governmental decisions that benefit northern residents. The Board of Inquiry recognized this may mean modification of some union practices. The government negotiated into the lease certain protections for northern residents. Tabouret, who attended all lease negotiations for Amok Ltd., testified the government suggested the inclusion of Article 20. He was not aware of any federal government involvement on this subject and had no recall of any mention that collective bargaining would be under federal government law. (For a discussion of the federal government's jurisdiction in the exploration and mining of uranium see this Board's decision in another case involving uranium mining in Northern Saskatchewan: *Uranerz Exploration and Mining Limited* 27 di 728; [1978] 2 Can LRBR 193; and 78 CLLC ¶16,135).

The consequences of the potential loss of the benefits of Articles 16 and 17 by a choice to engage in collective bargaining could easily be perceived as undesirable by northern residents unfamiliar with industrial development and the role of trade unions. The government, not trade unions, is the familiar organization for protection of their rights. On the other hand, for many southern workers and particularly skilled tradesmen union membership is an integral part of their working life. The resulting employee mixture is industrial and pre-industrial society, informed and uninformed, northern resident (with preferred treatment protected by government) and southern worker, and those aware of the rule and function of collective bargaining and trade unions and those who are not and have no experience with southern institutions. The mixture is in a bowl cast by public inquiry and necessary governmental regulation.

3 Against this overview of the background we skip ahead to September 1980. The events of this month and the employer's actions must be seen in the light of the events of the preceding month which are recounted in our companion decision *Amok Ltd.*, 43 di 282.

After the work stoppage in August and the settlement terms, a labour-management committee was established. The employer gave notice of the procedure for electing representatives in a memorandum to employees dated September 24, 1980. Meetings were to be held monthly.

After the events of August there was much discussion among the employees about unions and on-site supervisory employees received inquiries about unions. The employee complement of northern residents targeted for 50% by 1982 was met earlier than expected. In 1979 it was 57%. In 1980 it was 51 to 52% and in 1981 it was 50% exactly. Tabouret heard about these inquiries and decided to communicate to the employees. He did so in a memorandum dated September 25. Its text is as follows:

TO ALL EMPLOYEES

It has been brought to our attention that a trade union has been asking our employees to sign cards indicating support for the union. This has resulted in a number of questions being asked of us by employees, and we have decided to state the company's position as clearly as we can for all concerned. The company's views are:

1 Our company would prefer not to have a trade union representing its employees and it is our sincere belief that our employees do not need a trade union.
2 However, according to law, you are free to organize or join a trade union or association of your own choice, and you are equally free not to join any such union or association. Whether you do or do not join a trade union will not prejudice your position with the company.
3 If the majority of our employees sign support cards for a union then that union will likely apply to the labour relations board to be certified as the bargaining agent for our employees. If the union is certified as your bargaining agent, then the company must deal and negotiate with that union on all matters relating to our employees, such as promotions, training, whether seniority or skill should determine advancement, and virtually all other conditions of employment. The company will then also have to negotiate with the union as to wages, but we feel that a union will make little or no difference as to wages because we are constantly reviewing our wage schedule to ascertain that our wages are at least as high as wages paid by other

companies in the mining industry, whether they are paid to union or non-union employees. The company would prefer to deal with all these matters directly with our employees.

4 If a union becomes the bargaining agent for our employees, then you will have to pay union dues to the union, and these dues will likely amount to about 2 hours of pay per month. We do not believe that having a trade union or paying union dues will improve your conditions of employment or wages.

5 We would like to point out that our employment policies are under constant review and evaluation by the Monitoring Committee as established under the terms of our Surface Lease Agreement.

In any event, if you have any concerns regarding your employment or other matters, please feel free to discuss them with your supervisor or persons in our Human Resources Department.

M. Tabouret,
Managing Director

During the month of October it was reported to Tabouret that northern resident employees were concerned about the effect trade union representation would have on their special status. He responded by issuing a second memorandum on October 31, which reads:

TO ALL EMPLOYEES

In order to establish regular communication between the company and its employees, elections were held in the four main working areas of Cluff Lake to designate representatives to the Labour Management Committee.

The selected employees were:

Group A

Mine	Frank Park
Mill	Murray Gordon
Maintenance	John Holman
Camp	Alex Kenny

Group B

Mine	Harold Aubichon
Mill	Roger Morin
Maintenance	Hank Von Niessen
Camp	Don Rayburn

Preliminary and introductory meetings were held with Group A and B on October 22 and October 29 in order to prepare for a first formal meeting scheduled November 19, 1980. At that time the eight above employees will meet with an equal number of management representatives to review matters of common interest. Those among the selected employees who have to stay at Cluff Lake over their normal week in to attend the meeting will be compensated at overtime rate by the Company.

A number of northerners employed by our Company have expressed concern regarding the maintenance of their special status (as guaranteed by the Surface Lease Agreement) should a union be certified to represent the Company's employees.

Paragraphs 12-19 of the Surface Lease Agreement require the Company to give preference to Northern residents with respect to hiring, training, apprenticeship, promotions, and many other important matters with the intention of obligating the Company to provide Northern residents the maximum direct economic benefits that may be achieved during the construction and operation of the mine and mill.

There is, however, another clause in the Agreement that would come into force should a union be certified.

At the request of those employees who have contacted us and for the information of all employees, we quote the following relevant section:

Paragraph 20 TRADE UNIONS

If any of the employees of the Lessee shall be or become members of a trade union, then, notwithstanding anything contained in paragraphs 16 and 17 of this Agreement, the terms and conditions of employment of such employees shall be governed by the terms of any collective bargaining agreement entered into between the Lessee and any such trade union, and in the event of any conflict between the terms of any such collective bargaining agreement and this Agreement, the terms of the collective bargaining agreement shall prevail.

More information on this important matter can be obtained from our Personnel people at Cluff Lake.

> M. Tabouret,
> Managing Director, Amok Ltd.
> as Manager for Cluff Mining.

The only testimony the Board heard was from Tabouret and Norman McCallum, a former employee of the employer employed as a native co-ordinator and personnel assistant for 2½ to 3 years. He is a northern Metis who lived in Buffalo Narrows and now resides in Prince Albert. He was a union witness whose professed lack of knowledge about trade unions we accept as reflective of most northern residents.

The testimony is clear that the employer is vigilant for every ripple of activity affecting this highly public and sensitive enterprise being undertaken in experimental and pioneer social, economic and managerial circumstances.

The union submits these memoranda and employer behaviour contravene sections 184(1)(a) and (3)(e) of the Code. These read as follows:

184.(1) No employer and no person acting on behalf of an employer shall
    a participate in or interfere with the formation or administration of a trade union or the representation of employees by a trade union;

. . .

184.(3) No employer and no person acting on behalf of an employer shall
    e seek, by intimidation, threat of dismissal or any other kind of threat, by the imposition of a pecuniary or other penalty or by any other means, to compel a person to refrain from becoming or to cease to be a member, officer or representative of a trade union or to refrain from
      i testifying or otherwise participating in a proceeding under this Part,
      ii making a disclosure that he may be required to make in a proceeding under this Part, or
      iii making an application or filing a complaint under this Part;

4 The Board has had many occasions on which it has had to determine whether employer communications to employees contravene these sections of the Code. The most recent review of the Board's interpretation of these sections in the context of employer communications is *American Airlines Incorporated* 43 di 156, [1981]3 Can LRBR 90, where the Board said as follows:

> We cannot stress enough the unique relationship that exists between an employer and his employees and the privileged position that puts the employer in to influence those employees.
>
> . . .
>
> The Board, in *General Aviation Services Ltd.*, 34 di 791 and [1979]2 Can LRBR 98, referred to that privileged position:
>
>> In judging the actions of an employer during a union organizing campaign among its employees, the test is to what extent if any, the employer departs from a stance of strict neutrality. *What is prohibited by the Code is the employer's exercise of its privileged position in relation to its employees in attempting to influence their free exercise of their right to be represented by a bargaining agent of their choice* (pp. 795 and 102: emphasis added).
>
> Any statement, action, comportment that indicates to employees the employer's desire not to have them join a union, further impresses on them that their action clearly goes against his wish, he who is ultimately responsible for their job security.
>
> . . .
>
> Any involvement by the employer in the exercise by the employee of his/her basic right to join a union puts unfair pressure on the employees. An employee joining a union must not be put in a situation of a second class citizen who is adhering to a secret society and being ashamed of it. Either the right is recognized or it is not; if it is, it must be exercised in full light and without fear.
>
> The employer's right to communicate with its employees must be strictly limited to the conduct of the business. The employer is only permitted to respond to unequivocal and identifiable, adversarial or libellous statements; by this we do not consider as being adversarial the fact that an employee wishes or does not wish to join a union.
>
> In the light of this background, the employer's communications are to be permitted inasmuch as they are related to the efficient operation of the business. If they are not, then they must be viewed as a participation or interference in the representation of employees by a trade union and thus in contravention of Section 184(1)(a)(pp. 28-30).

The Board has had to contend with determining on the facts of each case the limits of permissible employer speech about matters that are not properly within its domain of concern.

. . .

The objective assessment is not dependent upon a finding of improper motive by the employer.... The same may not necessarily be said in criminal proceedings as opposed to the processes before this Board....

The policy objective for which the legislation is intended and must be administered was expressed In *Bank of Montreal, Tweed and Northbrook Branch, supra,* as follows:

> Each [employee] is given the freedom 'to join a trade union of his choice and to participate in its lawful activities' (section 110(1). To give that freedom meaning 'no employer and no person acting on behalf of an employer shall...interfere with...the representation of employees by a trade union' (section 184(1)(a) or 'seek...by any other means, to compel a person to refrain from becoming or cease

to be a member...of a trade union' (section 185(3)(e)). These are wide prohibitions and they reflect a policy that an employee's choice of the exercise of his freedom is not to be the subject of any employer pressure (pp. 612 and 140).

The interference in representation prohibited by section 184(1)(a) is not confined to post-certification representation and the interference with union formation is not confined to events relating to the creation of the status of the union as an entity. The concern is also exercise of employee rights to gain representation by a union....

---

questions

1 Why do you think the union would file an unfair labour practice case against both the employer and Mr. Tabouret, Managing Director? Elaborate.
2 Do you think that the Board of Inquiry's discussion of union activity among workers in well established industrial communities and its discussion of workers in frontier northern development communities served any useful purpose? Elaborate.
3 Do you think that the surface lease agreement accepted by Amok adequately protected the interests of northern workers? Elaborate.
4 What do you think of the line of argument which the CLRB developed on its case-by-case basis in implementing sections 184.(1) and 184.(3) of Part V of the Canada Labour Code? Elaborate.
5 Do you think that it is important for employers to be aware of the jurisprudence developed by the labour relations boards in the jurisdictions in which they operate? Elaborate.
6 Do you deem the letters addressed to workers by Mr. Tabouret to have reflected a genuine concern for northern workers or did they represent a desire to avoid unionization of Amok's workers? Elaborate.
7 If you had been assigned the duty of writing the Board's decision, would you have found the company or Mr. Tabouret or both guilty of an unfair labour practice? Give the rationale for your decision.
8 If you did find either or both guilty of an unfair practice, what remedy, if any, would you order? Elaborate.

appendix two

Negotiation

The Bridgetown Manufacturing Company Case*
— A Question of Strategy

Prepared by:
Mr. E. L. Roach,
Department of Management
Studies, Algonquin College,
Ottawa

Bridgetown Manufacturing Company is located in a city in Eastern Ontario with a population of about 100,000. It is a medium size manufacturer of home and office furniture, with a smaller plant in a suburban city located 30 miles outside of Montreal.

Bridgetown Manufacturing employs 250 employees, many of whom have been with the company for over 15 years. The employees are represented by the Canadian Brotherhood of Cabinet and Furniture Workers, Local 555. Two hundred of the employees are hourly wage employees and the contract provides for a union shop.

Bridgetown Manufacturing has been in operation for fifty years and has always had a healthy profit. In recent years, however, the margin of profit has gradually declined in the face of competition from other furniture manufacturers, and the general slump in the economy.

The relationship between the company and the union has been cordial and most of the contracts were negotiated without any third party assistance.

During the 1975 contract which expired in June 1978, some cracks began to appear in the cosy relationship which hitherto existed between the company and its employees. The rank and file were unhappy about the impact of inflation on their wages and their inadequate fringe benefits package. The

*Permission to use this case was granted by Mr. Roach. Minor deletions were made by the author for the purposes of this book.

union had fought for a COLA clause in the last agreement, but management was adamant in its refusal to discuss this demand.

The 1975 settlement was ratified by only 60 percent of the membership after a bitter and acrimonious ratification meeting. A small but militant faction in the union voted for rejection and called for strike action. Management was dissatisfied with the way that union stewards were performing. They conducted most union business on company time and, while the company allowed this practice to continue, it expressed a desire to impose limits on it.

In an attempt to improve its profit position, the company recently subcontracted work to a private contractor which would normally have been done by the workers in the plant. This reduced the overtime available to the workers and caused a great deal of resentment and frustration.

Three months before the contract was to expire, the company dismissed a shop steward for drinking on company premises during his lunch period. Another employee, with 10 years' service, was suspended one week without pay for excessive tardiness and absenteeism.

In the union elections conducted in January 1978, a young, aggressive and militant executive was elected on the platform of "increased democratic control over production," a better pension plan and greater job security. Jim Trimble, a member of the Marxist-Leninist Party and leader of the militant faction, was elected president of Local 555.

Negotiations

Week 1

Negotiations in past years were based on "a cooperative bargaining" concept. Two months prior to negotiations both sides submitted to each other proposals for changes in the existing contract and their initial bargaining positions. Because relationships between the union and the company had deteriorated, this practice was not followed in 1978, and the union waited for the first formal negotiation session to submit its demands.

They included the usual demand for changes in vague and ambiguous wording in the hundred paragraphs of the old agreement. Since some recent arbitration decisions supported management's position, some amendments were requested to the relevant clauses to nullify management's advantage. The union also presented an impressive list of new demands, some of them obviously "fillers" to be traded away later in the negotiation sessions.

The company's negotiation team accepted the new demands without comment and agreed to meet within a week. This would give them time to study the demands and prepare counterproposals.

It was agreed that the next session would start with a revision of the contractual language of the existing contract, and then proceed with the new demands. There was an air of cautious optimism at the bargaining table and each party left the initial session with renewed confidence that a settlement would not be difficult. They agreed in advance that they would try to conclude negotiations within 4 weeks. The union set a strike deadline four weeks from the commencement of negotiations.

Representing the union were:

1 Jim Trimble — newly elected president of Local 555, Chairman;
2 Peter Tull — representative of the Canadian Cabinet and Furniture Workers Union;
3 Rick Kennedy — Secretary Treasurer, Local 555;
4 Peter Hermann, Don Lindsay, Lloyd Campbell — shop stewards;
5 Arthur Black — representing the membership at large.

Representing the management were:

1 Lance Gibbs — General Manager, Chairman;
2 Andy Jacobs — Director of Personnel and Industrial Relations;
3 Dale Andrews — Production Manager.

Week 2 (Monday)

There were very few disagreements over the revision of the contractual language in the existing contract and the management team was anxious to begin discussing the list of forty-two union demands. It was confident that the union was serious about twelve of them, and that the others were mere bargaining tools to gain concessions later in the negotiations.

Its strategy, therefore, was to determine which of these demands had "top priority" status and to focus the negotiations on them. The quicker this was done, the easier it would be to reach an early settlement.

Peter Tull, the union's national representative, was not interested, however, in discussing specific demands, but preferred to review in great detail job titles, job descriptions and classifications which had already been discussed and revised by the Joint Management-Union Evaluation Committee. A recent evaluation resulted in 8 job classes being upgraded and 4 job classes being down graded.

The next two days were spent on this exercise much to the annoyance of the management team. Management perceived the analyzing and questioning of the judgment of the Joint Committee as an obvious "go slow" tactic on the part of the union.

Week 2 (Wednesday)

Lance Gibbs, Chairman of the management's negotiation team, attempted to counter the union's delaying tactics at the start of the meeting.

Mr. Gibbs:	Let's get on with the job at hand. Your strategy is clear. You are trying to stall, and force us into a strike to squeeze the last dollar out of us, but it won't work. The decisions of the Joint Evaluation Committee are not topics for negotiations.
Mr. Trimble:	We have a responsibility to our membership to look after their welfare to the best of our ability. We feel that it is the duty of the negotiation team to review the deliberations of the Committee.
Mr. Gibbs:	You have that right, but not at the negotiating table. When you

are ready to enter into serious negotiations let us know." (Mr. Gibbs and his team stormed out of the room, muttering that the union was not bargaining in good faith.)

Later, an agreement was finally reached on this contentious issue, and the decision of the Joint Committee, by agreement, was considered as binding on both parties.

Mr. Gibbs was convinced that the union's strategy was to extend negotiations to the strike deadline, and to coerce management into accepting their demands under the threat of strike action. "Crisis bargaining" was clearly their game plan. He, therefore, reported his suspicions to John Chapman, plant manager, and advised him to make the necessary preparations for a strike. Extra overtime was scheduled and instructions were sent to their suppliers of raw materials to "hold off" on deliveries. The services of a security guard firm were also secured.

Week 3 (Monday)

No serious negotiations took place since the management team abruptly left the last session. Attempts to resume serious bargaining were rebuffed by the union. Mr. Gibbs was prepared to begin serious negotiations, but he was no longer willing to be taken in by the union's games.

Mr. Gibbs: Are you ready to tell us what exact wage increases you are demanding?

Mr. Trimble: For the past three years our workers have been receiving wages much less than the average for this region, and the high cost of living is making it difficult to feed our families and meet our mortgage payments. The company is making substantial profits, and we are expecting a substantial increase.

Mr. Gibbs: What I want to hear from you is an exact amount. What is a substantial increase?

Mr. Trimble: First we want to hear what the company is prepared to offer.

Mr. Gibbs: O.K., can we have a half-hour coffee break?

The parties returned to their respective hotel suites to plan strategy. Each side wanted the other to take the initiative and put an exact wage increase on the table. The company representatives did not want to take the initiative since they wanted to start well below the union's initial demand. The union team was in no hurry to state a precise wage demand with the hope that, as the deadline approached, management would be forced to offer a higher wage increase.

After the recess, Mr. Gibbs revealed the company's offer to make the union tip its hand.

Mr. Gibbs: I will give you the total package amount by which the company is willing to increase its overall labour costs. You can break up the amount any way your membership wishes for all your economic demands. You can allocate the total dollar package between wages and the usual fringe benefits. The company cannot afford any more and remain in business. If you press for more, we might have to consider shifting some production to our non-unionized Quebec plant.

Mr. Trimble: How are we to determine how this total amount should be broken down? We have no way of determining the cost of each of our demands, such as the cost of O.H.I.P., shift premiums, etc., to the company. We will, however, discuss your offer over the weekend and meet with you again next Monday.

During the weekend there was considerable activity on both sides. The company was busy preparing for a strike and managers were told to prepare for a three or four week work stoppage. On the union side, the word went out to the membership to refuse overtime. Union officers and stewards began to condition the membership for strike activity. "We have been shafted long enough" became somewhat of a slogan. Strike signs were hastily prepared and picket captains were being instructed as to their conduct and responsibilities on the picket lines. Letters went out to the District Labour Council enlisting moral and monetary support from the locals of the Council.

Week 4 (Monday)

This was the final week of negotiations, and Friday at 12 midnight was the strike deadline set earlier by the union. The company persisted in negotiating a package deal while the union preferred to negotiate on an item-by-item basis.

The company offered a package totalling $200,000 to cover a three year contract. The union promptly turned down this offer and countered with its proposal.

Mr. Trimble: We have decided to negotiate for a one year contract.
Mr. Gibbs: Forget it.
Mr. Trimble: Then we shall not give you any proposals at all.
Mr. Gibbs: Sure you can — just adjust them to a three-year contract.

At this point in the negotiations Mr. Trimble gave the company the union's detailed demands based on a one-year contract.

The list consisted of ten major demands including a 25 cent an hour general wage increase — the first time that a precise wage increase was put on the table. In addition, there were some non-economic items; e.g. plant-wide, instead of departmental, seniority governing lay-offs, a sub-contracting clause, and a job security clause.

The company's negotiating team left the room to discuss the union's demands. On returning, Mr. Gibbs said that he was willing to negotiate a one-year contract, but that the cost of the union's demands was far beyond what the company was capable of paying. The 25 cent an hour wage increase was absolutely ridiculous. Uncertain economic conditions, declining sales and lower profit margins made the union's wage demands a joke.

Mr. Gibbs: Do you want to drive us into bankruptcy? The most we can afford — and I am being generous — is a 10 cent general wage increase. I am very upset over the conduct of these negotiations. In the past we had a good working relationship and negotiations were

> conducted with very little rancour. We compromised, made concessions, and signed contracts that were fair and realistic. I am very dissatisfied with the slow pace of negotiations, and I am not going to be "sucked in."
>
> Mr. Trimble: The union will adjust its demands if you allow our accountants to inspect your financial statements. Our membership helped to make your company a success over the years, and we are entitled to a fair share of its wealth.

Mr. Gibbs did not reply to the union's request to examine the company's financial statements, but reiterated, "that if the union persisted in making unreasonable demands, and if the company could not be assured of labour stability in the plant, management would postpone plans for further expansion. It would seriously consider moving the plant to their other location. Ten cents increase per hour is all the company could afford."

Week 4 (Wednesday)

The union resumed negotiations with some significant changes in its demands. It would accept a two-year agreement calling for fifteen cents an hour in each year of the agreement, 4 weeks vacation after 10 years of service instead of 8 as set out in the demands, and 12 paid holidays instead of 14.

> Mr. Gibbs: I thought as much. You come to the negotiations with a large shopping list and you expect me to raise my offer a couple of cents each time you drop a demand.

It was decided to postpone negotiations on the wage issue and discuss some of the non-economic demands. The session lasted until midnight, and agreement was reached on most of the clauses. The parties agreed to take another look at "job security" the following morning.

Week 4 (Thursday)

With the strike deadline only 24 hours away, the pressure was on. Both sides wanted to avert a strike, but each side was waiting for the other side to make concessions. The union picket leaders had met to plan the final strike strategy, but the membership was having second thoughts although by an overwhelming majority it had given the negotiation team a strike mandate earlier. Most of them could not survive a strike of more than two weeks, and the union's strike fund would last for only about three weeks.

Little was achieved in the first hour of negotiations, since both sides merely traded insults. After lunch, however, the company submitted its final offer — 12 cents an hour general wage increase for each year of a three-year contract together with an improved life and health benefits package.

The union assessed its position. It would agree to a three-year contract as proposed by management with the addition of COLA and sub-contracting clauses. The company's representatives agreed to discuss the union's latest position with senior management and meet the following day. The union negotiators reminded Mr. Gibbs that the strike deadline was only hours away.

Week 4 (Friday) (Contract expires midnight)
The management team disagreed as to what should be done about the union's latest proposal.

Mr. Jacobs
(Personnel Director):
Our relations with the union have not been very stable lately, and I think that a compromise now would be a great help in improving relationships. Further, I think we should consult more with the union committee before bringing about changes in the plant — anything to restore our workers' morale and confidence in the company. I do not think that they can afford to strike, but we should offer them a few more cents, or at least try to negotiate a COLA clause.

Mr. Andrews
(Production Manager):
With the new executive in charge and the present mood of the workers, a strike is a distinct possibility, if only for a couple of weeks. We have a backlog of production orders and I am afraid that we could lose some of our customers if there is a strike. Let's 'sweeten the pot.' We can find ways of increasing production and we can still be competitive with a moderate increase in prices.

Mr. Gibbs
(General Manager):
The union is bluffing. They are in no position to withstand a lengthy strike. If they do strike, they will be begging us to take them back when their credit has dried up. They are behind in their mortgage payments, and their wives are beginning to get on their backs. We should show the new executive who runs the plant. If we stand up to the union, its influence with the membership would be somewhat weakened. We should 'hang tough.'

The management team, unable to reach an agreement, decided to let Jack Anderson, the company president, review the situation and resolve the impasse. The president, after a thorough analysis of the situation, agreed with Mr. Gibbs, and directed the management team to reject the union's proposal.

Mr. Gibbs met with Mr. Trimble at 10:00 p.m. and informed him that the company was not prepared to accept the union's latest proposal. The company, however, would now pay 70% of O.H.I.P., and 100% of the premiums for the employees' group insurance package. The company's right to subcontract was not negotiable. It would not consider a COLA clause.

Mr. Trimble hastily convened a meeting of the union executive. They decided to submit the company's latest offer to the membership with a recommendation that it be rejected.

---

questions

1 Why did the union want to bring the issue of job evaluation to the negotiating table?
2 Evaluate the negotiation strategies employed by:
   a the management team
   b the union's bargaining team.

3 Why is the package approach particularly important to bargaining on economic issues?

4 Did the presence of a strike deadline force the negotiating teams to engage in "good faith" collective bargaining?

5 Is the exchange of demands and other proposals for change prior to negotiations preferable to the submission of demands at the first negotiating session? Elaborate.

6 Which party seems to have the advantage?

7 Do you think the union membership will accept the company's final offer or opt for the strike? Elaborate.

8 If you had been called in to mediate, what would you have done to head off a strike? Elaborate.

A Canadian Collective Bargaining Simulation*
A Role-Playing Exercise in Collective Bargaining Negotiations

By:
Gene Swimmer
School of Public Administration
Carleton University

And:
Jamie Wyllie
Student, Faculty of Law,
University of Ottawa

1 Introduction and Ground Rules

The following exercise is designed to give the student some feel for the process of union-management negotiations.

The periodic negotiation of the terms of reference of employment is a fundamental part of the Canadian industrial relations system. To simplify the scope of this exercise, the negotiations will involve amending an existing collective agreement.

1 Students will be divided into groups of approximately twelve members. These groups will be subdivided equally into management and union negotiation teams. Team members will be assigned roles which will help clarify their tasks and special concerns in the coming negotiations. For instance, the personnel manager of the company is concerned with management's unrestricted right to hire and fire workers. It may be his task

*Permission to use this simulation was granted by Professor Swimmer. Minor deletions were made by the author for the purposes of this book.

to answer union charges of management abuse of this right. It is important that *all team members adhere to their roles* during the entire simulation.

2 Once the teams are formed, each team will hold sessions to determine their negotiation positions.

3 The preliminary strategy sessions will develop a "Bargaining Book" which will be presented to the instructor in advance of the actual negotiations. The book should include your team's initial position (or demands), your true or fall-back position and an evaluation of the opposing team's true position. If your team is considering any specific strategy for the negotiations you should summarize it in the book. Finally, all documentary evidence which will be used to strengthen the union's or management's case in the coming negotiations should be included. Each team is free to obtain whatever evidence from outside sources it wishes. *Half*...the grade on this exercise will depend upon this paper.

4 All wage demands may be defined in terms of a *cents (¢) per hour* or *percentage across the board* increase. A cost-of-living clause, if any, should be considered in terms of the *cents per hour increase per worker* which would result from a one percentage point increase in the consumer price index. Pension demands should be expressed in terms of the employer's and employees' *contributions* rather than in terms of anticipated benefits. For example, the union might demand that management contribute a sum to the pension plan equal to 1% of all workers' wages. Framing demands in this way will enable both sides to establish the monetary implications of the various demands made during negotiations.

5 The legal environment for the simulation is determined by the provincial Labour Act and/or Labour Standards selected by the Instructor.

6 The teams will meet twice to negotiate a new contract (in a room designated by the Instructor). Prior to the first session of negotiations, teams will hand in their "Bargaining Books" (to the Instructor) *and* exchange their initial positions containing demands for new clauses or changes to existing clauses in the collective agreement.

7 Total time in negotiations is limited to 6 hours (two 3-hour sessions). At this time the teams have either decided to go to conciliation or have settled upon a new contract. Neither team may stop negotiating before the conclusion of Session 2. In the event of an impasse, both teams involved must submit final reports to the Instructor analyzing why and on which issues the bargaining failed. Those teams which reach agreement must submit a copy of all changes and additions included in the new contract.

8 All strategy and negotiation sessions are in the STRICTEST CONFIDENCE.

9 All teams will present a 3-5 minute oral report to the entire class summarizing the strategies and results of their negotiations.

10 *Half*...the grade on this exercise will depend on the team's/student's conduct of the negotiation sessions and on the presentation of the oral report to the class.

2 The Company

J. A. Atchinson is a manufacturing company with a 10,000 square foot plant located in the industrial area of your city. The company manufactures housetrailers and portable buildings for construction, oilfield and survey crews.

The company was started in 1957 by J. A. Atchinson who is the president of the company. In order to expand in 1960 common shares were offered at a par value of $15.00 each. J. A. Atchinson retains control of the company. The expansion plan has led to the formation of branch plants in Alberta and the recent acquisition of a metal fabrication firm in Sudbury.

Atchinson realized that the market for portable buildings would be strong with increased energy exploration in the north. During the 1970's Atchinson's local and Alberta plants were major suppliers to the James Bay and the Tar Sands construction projects. In the fiscal year prior to this round of negotiations, two-thirds (2/3) of the local plant's sales came from specialized portable buildings and the other third from residential mobile home sales.

The company enjoys a good reputation for quality with its customers. Few changes have been initiated in the production process and the company can still be described as labour intensive.

With the recent downturn in mobile home demand, the company has encountered stiff competition from new modern entries into the manufacturing field. It has maintained its leadership position due largely to the president's personal dynamism and charisma. Nonetheless, the need for more automation and prefabrication in the company's production process has become clear to management. The local plant was only working at 75% capacity, during this past year.

3 The Union

The workers of J. A. Atchinson Enterprises' plant in this city formed Local 122 of the Canadian Constructionists Union in May of 1962. The local negotiates its own contract, with the help of the national union. The national union is a member of the Canadian Labour Congress. The Alberta plant is organized by another local of this union. The Sudbury fabrication plant is represented by an international union.

In the entire bargaining history of the company, the union has never called a strike. In the seven times the union has gone to grievance arbitration in the past two years, the decision has been in favour of the company; this is largely due to the fact that the contract is not comprehensive in defining many areas of labour activity.

At the present time, there are 150 employees in the bargaining unit. There are an additional 20 non-union office workers (who are not part of the bargaining unit). Ten percent (10%) of the workers are female; one hundred percent (100%) of the office staff is female. Sixty percent (60%) of the members of the bargaining unit are married.

Union-management relations have been good in the past. This had led to charges of "coziness" between management and top local officials by many in the rank and file. Recently, three old time shop stewards were rejected in an election in favour of younger, more militant candidates. A concerted attempt is being made to get rid of the President and Vice-President of the Union.

Elections are to be held in six months' time. In a response to these efforts, the President and Vice-President have pledged to take a much harder line towards management in the next negotiations. Specifically, they have vowed to introduce a jointly-sponsored pension plan into the next contract. The younger stewards also want to see more statutory holidays, higher wages, sick leave, and paid maternity leave.

The present contract is considered to have good grievance and arbitration procedures, but many other clauses are considered inadequate by the rank and file. It is felt that many of the residual powers not spelled out in the contract or granted to management leave important areas to management's sole discretion. Some shop stewards believe that "management discretion" has allowed the personnel manager to fire militant unionists.

Perhaps the most important issue to the workers is job security. With the plant working below capacity during the life of the contract, the workforce was reduced by 10% — all the reductions were accomplished by attrition. In its last shareholders' annual report, management announced its intention to begin buying prefabricated sheet metal from its new Sudbury subsidiary. This decision, coupled with the precarious position of the northern consumer market, could result in extensive layoffs.

60% of the workers have less than five years' seniority with the company. Only 25% of the workers have over 10 years' seniority; 50% of this latter group have been with the company since 1957.

The union is very adamant about a pension plan. The company has operated a pension plan for its office staff for the past fifteen years.

4   Aspects of the Mobile Home Industry

1   In September 1977, a Joint Study Team on Mobile Homes released a report prepared for the Minister of State for Urban Affairs. Portions of that report appear below.

The following definition was developed to identify the product which is the subject of this report and is believed to be the most pertinent:

> A mobile home is a housing unit designed, built and certified in a factory to a nationally recognized mobile home standard for use as a principal residence. It is constructed complete with the necessary plumbing, heating and electrical systems. It is designed to be transported on its own undercarriage or by other means to a prepared site, and becomes suitable for permanent occupancy after proper installation on foundation supports and connection to utility services.

State of the Industry   The use of factories in the production of this form of housing makes fixed overhead a significant component of the cost of a mobile home. In order to operate profitably and compete effectively in the housing market, a manufacturer must operate his factory on a more   constant   production   basis   than   is   required   for   site-built construction. Due to the decline in the mobile home market, most manufacturers are suffering from excessively high fixed overhead costs resulting in decreased profits and increased prices. Industry estimates are that its fixed overhead will reach about 15% this year but would drop to around 7.5% at full capacity. In this event the reduction in cost of a mobile home could be as much as $1,500.

Unit Description	Single-Wide Mobile Home In Park
Square Feet of Living Area	**896**
Construction Cost	$ 14,244
Site Amenities	819
Dealer Markup	3,766
Land	—
Retail Selling Price	18,829

Affordable housing has always been one of the nation's greatest needs, and the Canadian mobile home manufacturing industry has demonstrated a capability of building affordable housing units without federal government assistance to consumers. Mobile homes have satisfied the requirements of many home owners over the years.

The result of this led to a dynamic growth rate for the mobile home industry that began in the 1960's, and between 1968 and 1974 was increasing at over 25% annually. In 1974 domestic and imported mobile homes accounted for approximately 13% of all new housing starts in Canada, and 21% of single family housing starts. In that peak year the Canadian industry built over 28,000 mobile homes and employed more than 5,000 workers in 43 plants.

Later in 1974 the growth rate of the industry reversed and has been declining ever since. In 1976 mobile homes accounted for only 7% of the new housing market and this downward trend is continuing. While no predominant single factor precipitated this decline, several likely causes have been responsible:

1 A slowdown of the economy.
2 The fact that most mobile homes do not quality for AHOP because many are built to C.S.A. Z240 standards instead of the Residential Standards and because 50% are located on rented sites in parks and therefore are automatically excluded from the programme.
3 An increase in the supply of affordable site-built housing due to the success of the federal government AHOP programme.
4 Financing for mobile homes is available only at higher interest rates and shorter amortization periods than those available for site-built housing.
5 A decrease in the availability of land on which to place mobile homes, due in part to municipal resistance to such developments.

Figures indicate that the mobile home industry is operating at only 40% of its potential capacity, and this situation is deteriorating. If the industry's full production capacity to produce affordable housing could be utilized, the net effect would include:

Canadian Mobile Home Manufacturing Capacity

	June/75	Dec./75	June/76	Oct./76	Est. June/77
No. of plants operating	41	43	41	36	33
Approx. no. direct labour employment per plant	118	109	103	78	103
Total direct labour	4870	4695	4238	2816	3388
Est. employment, incl. related services	14,610	14,085	12,714	8,448	10,164
Approx. daily production rate	111	107	97	64	77
Approx. annualized production rate	26,640	25,755	23,237	15,447	18,586
% of capacity	58%	56%	51%	34%	41%

---

1 the creation of up to 16,000 additional jobs for Canadians, (5,000 direct labour);
2 the production of more than 25,000 additional low cost housing units per year;
3 a reduction in the already low cost of mobile homes.

Furthermore the overhead costs would drop to around 7.5% at full capacity resulting in the reduction of the cost of a mobile home of about $1,500.

This could be accomplished without significant capital expenditure since factories and management teams are in place.

The Industry's Ability to Produce Affordable Housing It is the team's opinion that the mobile home industry is producing a safe, sanitary and satisfactory housing unit at a lower cost than the site-built housing industry. In the case of a single-wide mobile home, the difference in cost at present is estimated to be about 20% less per square foot than the site-built single family dwelling. Even for a unit built to Residential Standards, the cost per square foot is significantly lower.

For a variety of reasons, however, this saving to the consumer is being lost under present circumstances. The primary cause is the financing disadvantages which afflict the mobile home purchaser. Most purchasers must finance their units with short-amortization, high-interest chattel mortgages or personal loans. Consequently a factory-built product that may be produced for less than a site-built house may cost the consumer more and the mobile home industry has lost its ability, in large part, to compete effectively in the low-cost housing market.

. . .

2 Aside from the extensive 1977 Joint Study Team Report, statistics on the mobile home industry are virtually non-existent. When interpreting the 1977 data provided above, it is essential to bear in mind that:

1 The retail selling price of mobile homes is rising sharply. For instance, a $25,000 price tag is not unusual on a new, 1982 mobile home.
2 It is no longer accurate to speak of a "declining growth rate" when describing

the mobile home industry — the industry may well be shrinking in size. Since 1977, three of the 10 largest employers have ceased operations.

3 The only assistance CMHC offers to mobile home purchasers (in 1982) is in the form of mortgage insurance (thereby making it easier for mobile home owners to obtain mortgages). Where the mobile home is to be located on a park lot, the park must be CMHC approved if assistance is to be given — few parks receive such approval.

3 It is general practice for Canadian manufacturers to produce within one of three quality or price ranges, i.e. low line, medium, high line or custom in order to limit the variety and increase effective repetition. Within a particular price range a manufacturer may produce several series, each series having models of varying lengths, floor plans and accessories. Because of the variety of models required to suit the tastes of the relatively small Canadian market, it is difficult for a firm to achieve long production runs and exploit fully the principles and economies of assembly line production.

4 The long Canadian winter tends to discourage sales and the movement of mobile homes between the months of November and April. Since production closely follows sales with limited stockpiling of the finished product, manufacturers slow down production during this period. The result is reserve production capacity in most plants, together with disruption of labour supplies. Plants often use this slack season to develop new models, retool, or extend their manufacturing facilities.

5 While a cost study has not been undertaken in Canada it appears to be the experience of Canadian manufacturers that cost advantages from the use of assembly line techniques are not significant with production running under 3 units per day. At this rate and faster, benefits begin to accrue. Considerable cost savings can be realized by having as many components as possible prefabricated elsewhere in the plant or purchased from outside sources and brought to the assembly line at appropriate stages. With this development manufacturing becomes a true assembly line operation. To avoid costly cutting and fitting, such components must be dimensionally coordinated, and accurately scheduled to meet the production plan.

6 Most plants in Canada are either unionized or have employee associations. The nature of work involved precludes labour organization on a craft basis. Therefore, one industrial union may represent workers performing the tasks of carpenters, welders, electricians and so on. Any union capable of gaining the required support can represent a plant. Companies with more than one plant frequently deal with more than one union.

5   List of Union and Management Representatives

Detailed role profiles will be distributed by the Instructor

Management
1 Director of Production.
2 Personnel Manager.
3 Vice-President in charge of Finance.
4 Assistant General Manager.
5 Director of Salary Administration.
6 Assistant Director, All Operations.

Union
1 Local Union President.
2 Vice-President.
3 Secretary-Treasurer.
4 Shop Steward — Construction.
5 Shop Steward — Shipping and Receiving.
6 National Union Representative.

6 The Collective Agreement

1 Article: Intent and Purpose

1.01   The purpose of this agreement is to maintain a harmonious relationship between the Company and its employees; to provide an amicable method of settling any grievances or differences which might possibly arise; to promote the mutual interests of the employer and the employees.

2 Article: Recognition

2.01   The Company recognizes Local 122 of the Union as exclusive bargaining agent for its plant in this city, save and except all office staff, salesmen, salaried foremen and those above salaried foremen, security guards and salaried inspectors.

2.02   The Union recognizes the sole right of the Company to manage the plant and direct the work of the employees including the right to hire, promote, demote, suspend, discharge for cause, lay-off, assign to jobs and shifts, transfer employees from department to department; increase or decrease the working forces; determine the products to be handled, processed or manufactured, the schedule of production and methods, processes and means of production and the handling of same.

2.03   The Union will elect or appoint sufficient Steward(s) not to exceed one Steward to twenty (20) employees on the average, the said Stewards shall not be discriminated against. The Union shall give notice to the Company, in writing, of the names of the Shop Stewards selected within seven (7) days from the date of selection.

2.04   The Shop Steward shall act for the employee or employees in respect of his duties. Shop Stewards, after obtaining permission from his own foreman, which permission shall not be unreasonably withheld, may be permitted to leave his work for a reasonable time without loss of pay in order to carry out his duties.

3   Article: Union Security

3.01   All employees who come within the terms of this Agreement shall become members of the Union within fifteen (15) working days from the date of their first employment.

3.02   All members of the Union employed by the Company shall maintain their Union membership in good standing as a condition of employment.

4   Article: Checkoff

4.01   The Company agrees to deduct the monthly Union dues from each employee's pay on his first pay-day in each calendar month during the term of this agreement and in the case of a newly-hired employee, on the first pay-day in the month next following date of hire. The total so deducted with an itemized statement of same, in duplicate, shall be forwarded to the Union prior to the end of the month in which said deductions apply.

4.02   It is agreed that the President of the Union will be allowed reasonable time to interview new employees at the beginning of their first shifts.

5   Article: Hours of Work and Overtime

5.01   This article is intended to define the normal hours of work and shall not be construed as any guarantee of work or pay, or of hours of work per day or per week or of days of work per week.

5.02   The normal work week shall be Monday to Friday except in cases of breakdown, emergencies and holidays.

5.03   There shall be two shifts: the day shift and the evening shift. The normal work day is eight (8) paid hours, broken only by coffee breaks and lunch period.

5.04   The starting and quitting times shall be from:
a 7:30 a.m. to 4:00 p.m. for the day shift.
b 4:00 p.m. to 12:30 a.m. for the night shift.
The coffee break period shall be 10 minutes away from work with pay during the third hour of each half shift. The wash up period shall be 5 minutes with pay at the end of each half shift.

5.05   The lunch period shall be thirty (30) minutes without pay between the hours of 12:00 noon and 12:30 p.m., on the day shift, and between the hours of 8:30 p.m. and 9:00 p.m. on the night shift.

5.06   Schedules of work shall be posted or otherwise made known to employees by 2:00 p.m. Thursday of the preceding week. Schedules of work shall not be changed to avoid the payment of overtime.

5.07   The Company and the Union recognize that it may be necessary for employees to work in excess of their regular number of hours. The company will limit the hours of work beyond such regular number of hours to what is reasonable.

5.08   For all hours worked in excess of eight (8) hours per day, an hourly employee shall be paid overtime at one and one-half (1½) times his regular hourly rate or temporary rate (whichever is being paid when overtime commences). For all hours worked in excess of twelve (12) per day, an hourly employee shall be paid overtime at twice (2) times his regular hourly rate or temporary rate.

After twelve (12) hours of continuous work a meal will be furnished by the Company to be eaten on Company time not to exceed 30 minutes.

5.09   An employee who has left the Company's premises, and who is called outside his scheduled hours for emergency work, shall be paid four (4) hours at his job rate or the hours actually worked at the overtime rate, whichever is greater.

5.10   Double the regular hourly rate shall be paid to hourly-paid employees for work performed on Saturday or Sunday.

5.11   All employees working on the night shift shall be paid an additional 45¢ per hour.

6   Article: Seniority

6.01   The Company recognizes the principle of seniority, ability to perform the work and other pertinent factors being considered.

6.02   Seniority of each employee in the Company as covered by this Agreement shall be established after a probation period of thirty (30) days and shall count from date of employment. Seniority shall be maintained and accumulated through:

    1 absence due to lay-off

    2 sickness or accident up to a maximum of nine (9) months and then frozen until return to work

    3 authorized leave of absence

    4 an employee transferred by one plant and accepted by another plant.

6.03   Maternity leave shall be granted upon application provided an employee presents proof of pregnancy. The employee shall notify the employer as soon as the pregnancy becomes known. The employer may require an employee to provide a doctor's statement that she is physically able to continue working or to return to work. Length of such leave shall be determined by mutual agreement in each individual case, but generally such leave shall start ninety (90) days prior to the expected birth and continue until sixty (60) days after termination of pregnancy.

6.04   An employee shall lose his seniority standing and his name shall be removed from all seniority lists for any of the following reasons:

    1 voluntary quitting of employment

2 discharge for cause

3 nine months absence due to lay-off, sickness or accident

4 failure to report to work within two (2) working days after he has been notified to do so by the Company by telegram or registered mail at his last known address

5 failure to return from an authorized leave of absence when due

6 acceptance of employment during a leave of absence.

6.05   The Company shall maintain a seniority list for this Shop; a copy of such list shall be submitted to the Union on January 1 and July 1 of each year.

7   Article: Layoff and Recall

7.01   In cases of layoffs, employees will be laid off in the following order:

1 Probationary employees;

2 Employees with less than 18 months' seniority in the classifications affected;

3 And thereafter, employees on a plant-wide seniority basis, provided, however, that in the selection of employees on the basis of (1), (2) and (3) above, the senior employee is qualified and willing to do the work which is available.

7.02   Recalls shall be made in reverse order to that in which the employees were laid off and the Union will be given a list of employees to be recalled. Employees shall be recalled from layoff to the same classification as when laid off.

7.03   The Company will make available to the Union a list of employees to be laid off at least three working days prior to the lay-off becoming effective, except in circumstances where the Company has no control.

7.04   Notwithstanding the provisions of the Agreement, Stewards and committeemen shall head the seniority lists for purpose of lay-offs and recalls.

8   Article: Posting of Job

8.01   New jobs and/or vacancies shall be posted on the bulletin board for three working days. Employees wishing to bid on these jobs may do so in writing on forms supplied by the Company, within the three (3) working days. The job shall be awarded to the most senior applicant who can satisfactorily perform the normal requirements of the job classification. If there are no applicants, the Company may fill the job as it sees fit. It is understood the Company may fill the job without regard to seniority on a temporary basis of five (5) working days during the period of posting.

9   Article: Paid Holidays

9.01   Nine (9) paid holidays shall be recognized as follows:

New Year's Day	Labour Day
Christmas Day	Canada Day

Boxing Day   Thanksgiving Day
Civic Holiday   Victoria Day
Good Friday

9.02   For each paid holiday, eight (8) hours holiday pay at regular rate shall be paid to employees:

1 who have completed the probationary period; and,

2 who work their regular scheduled shift immediately before and immediately after the holiday.

10 Article: Vacations

10.01   The vacation year is the period from June 1 to May 31, inclusive.

10.02   An employee shall be entitled to an annual vacation with pay in accordance with the following schedule, on the basis of his service at June 1 in each year.

Length of Seniority	Length of Vacation
Less than 1 year	4% gross salary payment
1 year and less than 3 years	2 weeks
3 years and less than 10 years	3 weeks
10 years and less than 20 years	4 weeks
20 years and over	5 weeks

11 Article: Wages

11.01   Each job shall be described and classified and a rate of pay applied to each employee on such job in accordance with the provisions of the agreement.

11.02   Job Description Classification is the joint responsibility of the Plant Foreman acting on behalf of the Company and the Union Vice-President acting on behalf of the employees.

11.03   The Job Classification and Standard Hourly Wage Scale are incorporated into this agreement as Exhibit "A" and govern the wage schedule and dates of implementation of changes in the wage scale.

11.04   As of the date each Standard Hourly Wage Scale becomes effective, the standard hourly rate for each job class shall be the standard hourly rate for all jobs classified within such job classes.

12 Article: Grievance Procedure

12.01   In case a grievance arises in the plant, an honest effort shall be made to settle the difference in the following manner:

1 There shall be a grievance committee consisting of four (4) employees selected by the Union, who have at least eighteen (18) months' service with the Company. The Union agrees to advise the Company of the names of the members of the grievance committee, in writing, and also of any change which may occur.

2 In addition to any special meetings of the grievance committee and the Company, there shall be a regular meeting of the grievance committee and the Company to be held on the third Thursday of each month.

12.02   Members of the grievance committee will not suffer any loss of pay for attending regular meetings or for processing grievances through steps 1 to 3, provided that the total number of hours lost does not exceed six (6) hours per committee member attending such meetings in any calendar month. No remuneration shall be paid for lost time exceeding six (6) hours per committee member in any calendar month.

12.03   A representative of the Union shall obtain the permission of his Foreman before leaving his work to deal with a grievance. Such permission shall not be unreasonably withheld.

12.04   *Step No. 1* Any employee who believes that he has a justifiable grievance shall take up the matter with his Foreman with or without his grievance committeeman being present, or the grievance committeeman may take up the matter with the Foreman as the employee may elect. Grievances not adjusted in this way within one (1) full working day are eligible to be brought forward to Step No. 2.

Step No. 2 The grievance will be put in writing and shall be submitted to the Superintendent by the grievance committeeman within six (6) full working days after the employee has received the verbal decision of the Foreman. The written grievance will contain particulars of the incident giving rise to the grievance and shall be signed by the aggrieved employee and dated as of the date of its submission. The superintendent shall give his answer in writing to the grievance committeeman within six (6) full working days after the date of the presentation. Grievances not adjusted in Step No. 2 are eligible to be brought forward to Step No. 3.

Step No. 3 In case of appeal from such decision, notice of the appeal must be given in writing to the Personnel Manager or his representative within seven (7) working days from date of the written decision of the Superintendent or his representative. The Personnel Manager or his representative shall meet with the grievance committee and a representative of the National Union within ten (10) working days in an attempt to arrive at a settlement. The Personnel Manager or his representative shall submit his answer in writing within five (5) working days.

12.05   A grievance must be presented within fifteen (15) days of occurrence unless it be a grievance concerning discharge to which paragraph below is applicable. Grievances not presented within the time provided will not normally be considered and, in any event, are not subject to arbitration.

12.06   A grievance not referred to the next step within the time allowed will be considered settled.

12.07   When an employee has been discharged, the Company will notify the grievance committeeman concerned within forty-eight (48) hours. A discharged employee may appeal the discharge to the Superintendent within three (3) working days. If a settlement is not reached, a grievance may be presented at Step No. 3 within five (5) working days....

1 In the event that more than one employee is directly affected by one specific incident and each such employee would be entitled to process a grievance, the Chief Steward may sign the statement of the grievance on behalf of the aggrieved employees and shall identify the grievance as a "Group Grievance." Where retroactive wages are claimed, the names of such employees shall be attached to the grievance.

2 If the Company is alleged to have violated any provisions of this agreement and such violation affects the interests of the Union as a party to the agreement, the Union may file a grievance, beginning at Step No. 2, which shall be signed on behalf of the Union by the Chairman of the Grievance Committee and shall be identified as a "Union Policy Grievance."

13 Article: Arbitration

13.01   Grievances concerning the interpretation, application, operation, or alleged violation of this agreement which are not settled in Step No. 3 of the Grievance Procedure, may be referred to an Arbitration Board by notice in writing to the Company within fifteen (15) days from expiry of the time limits for settlement under Step No. 3. Such notice shall indicate the agreement clauses relied upon.

13.02   The Union shall, within five (5) days thereafter, appoint its representative to the Arbitration Board and the Company within the same five (5) days thereafter shall appoint its representative.

13.03   If the two (2) representatives fail to settle the grievance within a further period of seven (7) days, they shall jointly appoint a third impartial member who shall be Chairman of the Arbitration Board. If the representatives fail to agree upon a Chairman, then he shall be appointed by the Minister of Labour upon the request of either party.

13.04   The decision of a majority of the Board shall be final and binding upon both parties but the Board shall not have jurisdiction to change, amend, add to or subtract from any of the provisions of this agreement. However, if the agreement has been violated by the Company and disciplinary action resulting in loss of wages is involved, the Board may decide whether the disciplinary action should be modified if, in the opinion of the Board, the extent of the discipline is unreasonable in relation to the offence. Where there is no majority decision, the decision of the Chairman shall be the decision of the Board.

13.05   The parties will each bear one-half of the expenses and remuneration of the Chairman and his secretarial expenses and rent, but all other expenses shall be borne by the party incurring them.

14 Article: Leave of Absence

14.01   The Company may grant leave of absence without pay (retroactive when justified by the circumstances) to any employee for legitimate personal reasons or for assuming a Union office. Any person who is absent with written permission for such reasons shall continue to accumulate seniority during his absence. It is agreed that the Company will provide the Union with a copy of each such Leave of Absence authorization.

15 Article: Health Insurance

15.01 The Company agrees to pay 75 percent of the cost of provincial health insurance premiums.

15.02 The Company agrees to carry and pay for 75 percent of a "Supplemental Medical Benefits" plan incorporated into this agreement as Exhibit "B".

16 Article: Bereavement Pay

16.01 In the event of one or several simultaneous deaths occurring in an employee's family, the employee will be allowed three (3) consecutive days, if working days, of paid leave, one of which shall be the date of the funeral service providing the purpose is either to attend the funeral or make arrangements for the funeral. For purposes of this clause the family is considered to be the employee's father, mother, husband, wife, children, brother, or sister.

16.02 In the event of the death of a grandfather, grandmother, father or mother-in-law, brother or sister-in-law, the employee shall be entitled to one (1) day with pay at his/her regular rate, if a working day and for the purpose of attending the funeral.

17 Article: Jury and Crown Witness Pay

17.01 The Company shall pay to all employees who are required to perform jury duty or act as a witness for the Crown, the difference between their remuneration for the above functions and their normal salary. The employee shall present proof of service and amount of remuneration received.

18 Article: Safety and Health

18.01 The Company and the Union agree that they mutually desire to maintain high standards of safety and health in the plant to prevent accidents, injury and/or illness.

18.02 The Company shall furnish the equipment and supplies necessary to protect employees from injury to a minimum of Workers' Compensation Board regulations. The Union will assist the Company in carrying out any reasonable accident prevention program.

18.03 The Company and the Union agree to name a Safety and Health Committee comprising of an equal number of Company and Union members each to a maximum of six (6) on the Committee.

18.04 Both parties agree that the accident prevention regulations of the Workers' Compensation Board will be adhered to in all sections of the Plant. The Company will not request employees to perform work under unsafe conditions. At the same time, refusal on the part of an employee to abide by the Workers' Compensation Regulations or other safety rules after having been warned, will be grounds for dismissal.

18.05   The Committee will:

1 Function primarily to promote safety and industrial hygiene in the plant.
2 Make regular monthly inspections of the plant and equipment.
3 Hold regular monthly meetings and maintain minutes.
4 Review accident records together with minutes of previous meetings.
5 Forward recommendations regarding safety and health to the management committee and the union.

18.06   The regular monthly meetings are to be held during regular working hours without loss of pay to the employees involved.

18.07   An employee hurt in an industrial accident shall be remunerated for the remainder of his regular day at his regular hourly rate.

18.08   It is expressly understood and agreed that the Safety and Health Committee has no power or authority by unanimous decision or otherwise to bind either party to any decision made by it. The sole right of this Committee is limited to making their recommendations to the parties hereto for their consideration and any disagreement among Committee members shall not be subject to the Grievance Procedure as provided for in this Agreement.

19   Article: Duration of Agreement

19.01   This agreement shall be effective from February 1, 198__ until January 31, 198__ and shall continue in force after January 31, 198__ on a yearly basis, which in each instance of renewal shall be regarded as the term of the agreement, until terminated by either party giving the other party not more than sixty (60) days, and not less than thirty (30) days, notice in writing prior to the expiration date. If amendments are contemplated by either party to become effective in the ensuing term, the party proposing such amendments shall give notice in writing thereof to the other party not more than ninety (90) days, and not less than sixty (60) days, prior to the expiry date. During the period of negotiations, this agreement shall continue in full force and effect.

19.02   No provision of this agreement shall be applied retroactively from the date of signing except as specifically provided.

Exhibit A

JOB CLASSIFICATION

1 Janitor
2 General Labourer

7 Welder
  Steelcutter

Shipping and Receiving Labourer	8 Millwright
3 Fabrication Helper	Machinist
Yard Labourer	9 Carpenter
4 Furniture Assembler	Electrician
Carpet Layer	Plumber
5 Mill Utility Man	10 Groupleader, Maintenance
6 Forklift Operator	
Crane Operator	

STANDARD HOURLY WAGE SCALE
(figures provided by the instructor)

Job Class	Effective Last Year	Effective This Year (until contract expires)
1		
2		
3		
4		
5		
6		
7		
8		
9		
10		

Exhibit B: Supplementary Medical Benefits

Supplemental Medical Benefits cover the following necessary services and supplies:

1 Services of a graduate registered nurse (licensed vocational nurse acceptable where an RN is not available).
2 Limited services of a licensed chiropractor, podiatrist or osteopath (operating within the scope of his licence).
3 Drugs and medicines purchased on the prescription of a doctor.
4 Professional ambulance service.
5 Physiotherapy.
6 Prosthetic appliances, crutches, splints, oxygen, as well as the rental of durable equipment for therapeutic treatment.
7 Dental treatment necessary as the result of an accident.
8 Hospital charges for the difference between the ward cost and semi-private, or where necessary private accommodations.

The plan provides 90% reimbursement of the above covered expenses that are reasonable and necessary.

Except for prescription drugs, there is no deductible. For prescription drugs, the deductible is $25 per individual per calendar year with a family deductible each calendar year of no more than $50.

The Supplemental Medical Benefits Plan has a maximum of $10,000 with an automatic restoration of benefits of up to $1,500 each January 1.

The maximum payment on account of the services of a chiropractor, podiatrist or osteopath is limited to $100 per calendar year.

7 Financial Data

Excerpts from J. A. Atchinson Enterprises Annual Report to Shareholders
(Local Plant)
(figures provided by instructor)

Fiscal Year	Sales ('000s)	After Tax Income ('000s)
198___(last 2 yrs.)		
198___		
198___(this year)		
198___(projected for		
198___next 2 years)		

Note: The projected figures assume substantial subcontracting and, as well, no change in current input/output prices. The forecast for next year includes a confirmed order with the federal government for 60 specialty trailers to be delivered in four months — this is the only major order expected for quite some time into the future. The fiscal year is January 1 to December 31. The present contract with Local 122 expires January 31, 198___(this year).

For the Purposes of the Simulation, the First Session of Negotiations is Deemed to Take Place on (date provided by instructor).

Dividends: In the last three years, the Company has paid no dividends, preferring to re-invest its earnings in new projects. However, the Company had decided on a dividend payment in the current fiscal year (198___) which will amount to twenty percent (20%) of the after tax income being distributed as dividends.

Economic Strategy: The Company has been investigating the use of the Sudbury acquisition to fabricate some of the standard components in its trailers. A consultant has estimated that prefabrication would reduce labour force requirements by twenty percent (20%), distributed proportionately through all job classes, in the presnt plant and reduce total production costs by two percent (2%) per unit on average. This cost reduction would be passed on to consumers to support demand.

J. A. Atchinson Enterprises Ltd. — Local Plant Income Statement for the Year Ended December 31, 198___ (Last 12 Months)
(figures provided by instructor)

(All figures in '000s)

Net Sales

Cost of Goods Sold[1]

Material and Overhead
Labour[2]

Selling and Administrative Expenses _____

Income before taxes _____ _____

Taxes

Income after Taxes _____

_____

[1]Based on production of _____ mobile homes (standard and specialized mobile homes included).
[2]Includes overtime of $_____ spread proportionately among job classes 1-10 and employer contributions to UIC, CPP, OHIP etc. amounting to $0.51/hour.

J. A. Atchinson Enterprises Ltd. — Local Plant Balance Sheet: January 1, 198___(This Year)
(figures provided by instructor)   (All figures in '000s)

Assets
 Cash
 Accounts Receivable
 Inventories of Goods[1]
 Prepaid Expenses

  Total Current Assets _____
 **Building and Equipment
 (net of depreciation)**

TOTAL ASSETS _____

_____

Liabilities and Shareholder's Equity
 Accounts Payable
 Short Term Debt

  Total Current Liabilities _____
  Long Term Debt

 TOTAL LIABILITIES _____
 Common Stock
(100,000 shares, $15 par)

 Retained Earnings _____

_____

[1]Includes finished inventories with retail value of $150,000.

Payroll of the Local Plant of J. A. Atchinson

Job Class	No. of Workers in Each Class
1	5
2	15
3	30
4	15
5	20
6	15
7	15
8	15
9	15
10	5

8 Costs of Various Contract Changes: Sample Calculations

1 Annual cost of a one cent per hour across the board wage increase:

(40 Hours) x (52 weeks) x (150 workers) x ($.01) = $3120

2 Annual cost of a 1% across the board wage increase:

(.01) x (40 Hours) x (52 weeks) x (150 workers) x (average hourly wage) =

3 Annual cost of a 1% employer contribution to the pension fund:

(.01) x (150 workers) x (average hourly wage) x (40 hours) x (52 weeks) =

4 Annual cost of one extra holiday:
(150 workers) x (8 hours) x (average hourly wage) =

5 Annual cost of a 1¢ per hour increase in the shift premium:

$$\frac{\text{Annual Cost of a 1¢ per hour wage increase}}{2} = \$1560$$

appendix three

Arbitration

The Kenneth Cameron Case* — Extent of Union Responsibility

Kenneth Cameron,
complainant,
and
Canadian Brotherhood
of Railway, Transport and
General Workers, CBRT,
respondent,

and
Via Rail, Montreal, Quebec
employer.

. . .

1 On April 18, 1980, Mr. Kenneth Cameron filed a complaint with the Canada Labour Relations Board, alleging that his union, CBRT, breached its duty of fair representation by its refusal to refer to arbitration his grievance against his discharge. The section of the Code alleged to have been contravened is section 136.1.

> 136.1 Where a trade union is the bargaining agent for a bargaining unit, the trade union and every representative of the trade union shall represent, fairly and without discrimination, all employees in the bargaining unit.

Efforts by the Board's officer to assist the parties to reach a settlement were unsuccessful. A hearing was held in Montreal on October 6, 1980.
Although Via Rail was made a party, it chose not to appear at the hearing.

2 The complainant was, at the time of his discharge, a dining car steward. He

---

*Permission to use this case was granted by the Canada Labour Relations Board. Minor deletions were made by the author for the purposes of this book.

had been assigned to that position two and a half years previously. His length of service for CN and Via Rail, its successor, totalled five years and a half. He had an untarnished work record.

The events giving rise to the dismissal concern a trip made on July 18, 1979, between Montreal and Winnipeg on a skyline car.

The salient facts can be summarized as follows.

The complainant worked on two types of cars — the skyline car and the café car. Both wagons are for dining, bar and take-out services. However, their layout is different. On the café car, a closed area exists for each kind of service whereas on the skyline car, the services are provided for in an open area.

The teams assigned to these cars differ in their composition as well as in their responsibilities. For the café car, the staff comprises a take-out attendant, a bar attendant, a chef and a steward, whereas on the skyline car, there is a chef, an assistant chef, two waiters and a steward. On the café car, each employee is accountable for his/her work area, whereas on the skyline car, the steward is accountable for the quality of service as well as the money involved in the total operation. Furthermore, detailed instructions and forms exist for the café car whereas for the skyline car, few directives on how to operate had been issued at the time of the run in July 1979.

It was also established that when the skyline cars were acquired in June 1978, by Via Rail, its employees were not given the opportunity to familiarize themselves with the new equipment whereas the employees of CP used to the skyline car were provided training on the café cars.

The evidence also showed that a written complaint from a client to Via Rail on July 31, 1979 prompted the employer to investigate the matter. The quality of the food, the filthy condition of the skyline car and the poor service on the train en route from Winnipeg to Thunder Bay were concerns of the client. The complainant was the steward on duty for that trip. In the preliminary inquiry made by the employer some discrepancies in reporting funds were discovered and statements of employees were gathered. With these elements on hand, the employer charged the complainant with gross dereliction of duty, unbecoming action for a supervisor contrary to sanitary and hygiene regulations and misreporting revenue for saleable take out items on trains 1 and 2, ex. Montreal, July 18, 1979. As required by article 24.7 of the collective agreement (No. 2) in cases of major offences, the employer held a hearing on August 30, 1979. The purpose of such a hearing is to establish and determine the facts upon which action may be taken.

Mr. Cameron was notified by telephone, on August 28, by Mr. Durand, his supervisor, that he was being held out of service and that he had to appear at a hearing and be interrogated. The complainant declared that he was never served the written notice which spells out the charges.

Following his telephone conversation with his supervisor, Mr. Cameron contacted Mr. Kiley, member of the local grievance committee in order to obtain his assistance. The union did inquire to find out the charges generally. Mr. Kiley was present at the investigation hearing. At the end of the hearing, Mr. Cameron stated:

> I think the treatment I have received from Mr. de Cotret has been fair and civil. But I do feel that it is not right that I received no specifics regarding the accusation before coming to the hearing. Also I wish to reserve my right to have the Brotherhood Regional V.P. cross-examine witnesses who have testified against me. (article 24.9).

The hearing was recorded and each party revised the copy and signed it.

When Mr. Cameron was informed of his dismissal, he went to Ottawa with his Local Chairman, Mr. Rouleau, to meet Mr. Thivierge, the Regional Vice-Chairman. Mr. Rouleau, acting under the instructions of Mr. Thivierge, filed a grievance at Step 1 of the procedure against the discharge. Later on, Mr. Thivierge pursued the procedure at Step 2. Following the employer's reply not to amend its decision, Mr. Thivierge turned the matter to Mr. J. D. Hunter, National Vice-President of CBRT, and recommended a referral to arbitration as he felt the penalty was too severe. In his correspondence, he also raised the possible collusion of the employees who had filed statements against Mr. Cameron. All along, Mr. Cameron had requested verification of the employees' statements.

In view of Mr. Thivierge's concern of possible collusion between the employees who accused the complainant, Mr. Hunter proceeded to Step 3 of the grievance procedure. At the meeting with Via Rail, he raised the possibility of collusion and requested the employer to verify it. In reply, the employer rejected the suggestion of collusion and turned down the grievance.

Mr. Hunter, after reviewing the file which contained the investigation report, the statements of the employees, the letter of the client and the remittance form from Cameron for commodities sold, decided against a referral to arbitration.

3   As the duty of fair representation under the Quebec legislation was raised in argumentation as a basis for establishing the extent of the obligation of a bargaining agent under the *Canada Labour Code,* it is appropriate to examine extensively the Quebec system.

Section 38b of the Quebec Labour Code statutorily expresses the duty of fair representation in the following terms:

> a certified association shall not act in bad faith or in an arbitrary or discriminatory manner or show serious negligence in respect of employees comprised in a bargaining unit represented by it, whether or not they are members.

There exists a rigorous procedure for this type of complaint. It is initiated by the filing of a written complaint to the Minister within six months from the circumstances giving rise to the complaint. On receipt of a complaint, the Minister appoints an investigator who shall endeavour to settle the dispute in fifteen (15) days. Within the fifteen (15) ensuing days if no settlement is reached or if the association does not honour the agreement, the employee shall apply to the Labour Court for authorization to submit the claim to arbitration. The Court, before granting it, must determine if the association has contravened Section 38b. Following a positive ruling, the claim is heard by an arbitrator and judged on its merits.

Since the duty of fair representation has been included in the Code, the Quebec Labour Court has rendered a number of decisions. It emerges from its jurisprudence that the section has a very limited coverage. It was ruled that section 38e, which establishes the procedure, restricted the scope of section 38b. Consequently, the legislation envisages complainant relating strictly to disciplinary measures including all forms of dismissals....

It also flows from the jurisprudence that the onus of proof rests on the complainant, the reasoning being... that the legislator presumed that unions represent fairly all employees of a bargaining unit.

The complainant, therefore, has to demonstrate that a serious prejudice would result if denied a recourse to arbitration.... To evaluate the seriousness of the prejudice, the reasonable success of a claim in arbitration is taken into consideration.... The consequences of the dismissal are used in determining the extent of the prejudice. The complainant had demonstrated a violation of seniority rights as well as a loss in earnings that an extra year of employment would have granted. Furthermore, the cooperative behavior of a complaint is also taken into account....

The most important factor in the evidence is the alleged violation of the duty of fair representation. The union and the complainant share the burden to establish, for the complainant, the union's violation: for the union, its compliance to the requirements of section 38b....

> If the union enjoys such discretion shielding it from the tribunal's intervention, it must still demonstrate that it took steps in order to have been able to take a decision with full knowledge of the facts (page 96) (Our translation).

The extent of the obligation for a bargaining agent...as stated in another case is

> The duty stipulated in Section 38b of the Labour Code cannot be qualified as being the best authority to exercise nor is it the most advantageous. It is negative in the sense that in representing an employee a certified association must not act in bad faith or in an arbitrary or discriminatory manner or show gross negligence.... That is a far cry from a duty unconditionally imposed upon a certified association...not to lack proficiency or to take the part of any employee who believes he is in difficulty or declares he is dissatisfied (page 158) (Our translation).

Therefore, the conduct of an association, to be declared in contravention to the Code, has to be arbitrary, discriminatory, of bad faith or gross negligence. Of all these qualifications, only the latter seems to cause a difficulty. Two schools of thought have emerged.... The concept of gross negligence could include a simple error but which resulted in serious damage.

> In my view, here the legislator did not wish, in spite of the ambiguity of the text which seems in fact to require proof of gross negligence, to limit this remedy to the point where an employee would, for example, be absolutely deprived

of his right to have his grievance taken to arbitration if he could establish merely simple negligence on the part of his union.

The concept of negligence which can be more or less serious, of great or minor consequence or of another type is always difficult to deal with. On the one hand, a simple negligence can result in serious damage, on the other hand, a gross one can have no consequences. The law must be appreciated by taking into account the whole of the facts and their effects, the negligence and its consequences, the cause and the resulting prejudice. That is why I do not hesitate to say that a simple negligence (for example, a simple oversight) which results in an employee being deprived of his recourse to arbitration where that recourse would prevent him from losing his position, truly constitutes gross negligence (page 335) (Our translation).

However, ...only blatant errors would be considered gross negligence:

Sometimes the grievance can first appear to be without any merit where there is however evidence of gross negligence. Sometimes also, the association may have acted in a satisfactory manner but simply erred by wrongly refusing to defend an employee's dismissal.

Unless there is a clear and obvious situation where it appears that the discretion was not manifestly exercised in a judicious manner, the remedy provided for in Sections 38b. et seq. of the Code will not be available to the employee. The legislator certainly did not intend, through the actions of union officers, to deprive an association of employees existing within the concrete reality of a business of the choice and the appropriateness to act or not in view of rectifying a situation which an employee covered by the certificate judges to be prejudicial towards him. That is why an employee does not have an absolute right to arbitration, nor an absolute right to have his association act according to his instructions. He does, however, possess a clearly established right — and that is where the law affords him protection — that his association not abuse its discretion by acting in bad faith, or in an arbitrary or discriminatory manner or showing gross negligence, when the employee asks it to file a grievance on his behalf (pages 326 and 327) (Our translation).

...it is further elaborated:

Section 38b. of the Code has the effect of slightly broadening the parameters of fair representation. Not only must a union take a malevolent attitude, but it must not demonstrate gross negligence. In taking a grossly negligent attitude, the union will therefore not be able to rely on its good faith and lack of intention to prejudice the employee in order to escape any judgement condemning its attitude (page 235) (Our translation).

and:

Serious negligence involving an association of employees must therefore be related to an attitude characterized by gross negligence, by a negligence of great consequence attributable to its representatives, by an unpardonable oversight of the required precautions, by an undisguised or obvious lack of ability or by a manifest lack of concern revealing the association's inability to look after the interests of the employees in its bargaining unit seriously and efficiently (page 236) (Our translation).

Failure to appoint representatives to a meeting with the employer before any decision on a grievance can be made...to investigate, file a grievance and call a grievance committee...withdrawal of a grievance based on the record and word of the employer...failure to request from a complainant her vision of the facts... refusal to file a grievance based on the employer's opinion...were all ruled gross negligence.

To qualify a union's behaviour as being arbitrary, discriminatory, of bad faith or gross negligence, various tests are adopted. Thus borrowed from civil law, the concept of a prudent administrator (conduite du bon père de famille) is a norm applied to the actions of an association.... The merits of a grievance are also considered for the same reason with the proviso that they be examined strictly in relation to an association's actions to assess the nature and extent of inquiry made by a union.... Other criteria of evaluation are also proposed....

> Our labour law affords little room to individual rights. It could certainly have been otherwise, but there was a clear desire to favour collective organization in the work place over any other type of employer-employee relationship which would have allowed individual rights more latitude.
>
> Since, on an individual basis, employees have access to grievance and arbitration procedures with respect to the application of the collective agreement only to the extent which that agreement permits, the duty of a union regarding individual grievances must be appreciated in this light. The duty of the union is that much more vital as, only it, is empowered to enforce these rights.
>
> Furthermore, the union's discretion can be appreciated in a different light according to the nature of the grievance (general, group or individual).
>
> Finally, the possible divergent interests between the union and the employee who may be concerned, must be taken into account.
>
> The more the interests diverge, even to the point of being contradictory, or the more individual interests are pronounced, then the union will have to be more cautious in exercising its discretion and in fulfilling its duty of fair representation.
>
> Otherwise, the union runs the risk of playing the twofold role of judging and being judged, or simply violating the rules of natural justice which require that all interested parties be heard (Our translation).

It should be mentioned that the Quebec Labour Court, on a petition under section 38 of the Code, sees its mandate as being:

> In exercising its jurisdiction in accordance with section 38d., the Court's role is not per se one to assess the quality of the decisions taken by a certified association and, finding it appropriate, to substitute its own assessment of a case to that of the said assocation; in order to intervene, the Court must have proof of violation of section 38b (Our translation)....

Having perused the jurisprudence on the duty of fair representation under the Quebec Labour Code, the question to turn to now is how does it relate to the federal legislation?

4   Section 136.1 states the duty of fair representation under the *Canada Labour Code*. The section was proclaimed in force on June 1, 1978.

As in Quebec, the procedure in the federal jurisdiction is initiated by a written complaint. It must be filed not later than ninety days (90) from the date on which the complainant knew, or in the opinion of the Board ought to have known, of the action or circumstances giving rise to the complaint.

It should be stressed that the delay of ninety days is strict. The Board has not the power to extend the time limit under any circumstances....

Contrary to Quebec legislation where the person who alleges unfair representation must apply to the Labour Court when dissatisfied with the investigator's efforts, under the federal legislation, once a person has initiated the procedure, the Board remains seized of the complaint and retains total jurisdiction. It uses mediative techniques to seek early resolution of complaints. On failure of settlement the Board adjudicates the complaint and may exercise remedial authority under Sections 189 and 121.

The recourse under the federal legislation is available to all employees comprised in a bargaining unit, the bargaining agent being certified or not. Even though it would seem that the accessibility is greater under our jurisdiction (member of certified or recognized bargaining union being covered) than in Quebec where it is specifically referred to members of certified union, in reality, it is not so, as only certified unions have legal status to enter into collective bargaining with an employer under the Quebec legislation.

Although the federal text is positive and broad, contrary to the Quebec legislation, the Board has been cautious in delineating its coverage. Until recently, the Board has made a distinction between complaints relating to collective agreement administration and those concerning collective bargaining. It has recognized that both types of complaints were envisaged by section 136.1. The Board has also expressed its intention not to fetter the wide latitude of discretion an exclusive bargaining agent must have in collective bargaining.... It also stated that section 136.1 did not cover the internal appeal procedure of a union relating to grievance which was accessible strictly to members of the union, precluding therefore, its recourse to non-members....

The burden of proof under the federal regime, like in Quebec, rests on the complainant. The onus can be overturned by a preponderance of evidence.

The legislated standards imposed in the federal jurisdiction are for a union to act "fairly and without discrimination". In provincial legislations, the test is negative and states that a union's conduct should not be arbitrary, discriminatory or of bad faith (see B.C. and Ontario legislations) and includes gross negligence in Quebec. Although aware of these provincial standards, the Board has expressed several times its preference for a prudent attitude in the imposition of any standard.... It has voiced its difficulty in combining the provisions of the Code, the intentions of Parliament and the need to protect the individual.... However, it rejected an allegation made that the words "fairly and without discrimination" should be read conjunctively and as requiring an element of bad faith....

As far as tests are used in the evaluation of a union's conduct, the furthest the Board went, was to adopt the seriousness of a grievance as a factor to be considered in assessing the quality of an association's behaviour....

In summary, the federal and the Quebec systems appear similar in many respects. The scope of the duty to represent fairly under section 136.1 of the federal Code encompasses the subjects covered by the Quebec legislation. However, in view of the federal text being affirmative and broad, the Board opted for a case by case approach and refrained from adopting any specific criteria.

5   With this understanding of the Quebec and federal concepts of fair representation, we now turn to the task of assessing the conduct of CBRT in the handling of the complainant's grievance.

On the one hand, it must be kept in mind that the union is the bargaining agent, and as such, has an exclusive bargaining authority pursuant to section 136(1) of the Code. On the other hand, its authority must be exercised fairly and without discrimination in the representation of employees.

Therefore, it must be recognized that in the processing of a grievance and its control, a union has the exclusive right to make a decision at any step of the procedure, be it to proceed with the grievance, to settle it or to abandon it, and the Board should not interfere in this respect. The rationale is analyzed in *Rayonnier Canada (B.C.) Ltd.* [1975] 2 Can LRBR 196 (B.C.L.R.B.) and *Frederick Carl Vincent*, [1979] 2 Can LRBR 139 (O.L.R.B.) and [1979] OLRB Feb. Rep. 144.

However, its conduct can be subject to scrutiny under the duty of fair representation. Consequently, the question to be addressed is "Did CBRT, in processing the grievance of Mr. Cameron, satisfy its obligation under section 136.1?"

The evidence has established that Mr. J. D. Hunter, Vice-President, is the union official with the responsibility of determining whether or not a grievance should be referred to arbitration. When he made his decision, he relied on the grievor's version as taken by the employer, the client's complaint, the employees' statements (chef and assistant chef) as gathered by the employer and their remittance form as prepared jointly by them and the employer as well as the remittance form of Mr. Cameron as submitted to the employer.

From Mr. Hunter's testimony, it was clear that based on those documents, he would also not have proceeded to Step 3 of the procedure if Mr. Thivierge, the Regional Chairman, had not insisted on his suspicion of collusion between the employees accusing Mr. Cameron and on the merit of the grievance.

---

questions

1 On whom does the onus of proof lie in duty of fair representation cases? Why is this so?

2 Why does the Canada Labour Relations Board (CLRB) discuss the duty of fair representation as it exists under the Quebec Labour Code?
3 What is your assessment of the procedure followed in Quebec whereby the Labour Court must find that an association (union) has contravened the relevant section of the Quebec Labour Code and the case is heard by an arbitrator? How does this procedure differ from that of the Canada Labour Relations Board? Elaborate.
4 What are the factors that have been held to constitute gross negligence under the Quebec Labour Code? Do they seem adequate to you?
5 What is the difference between stating the duty of fair representation in a positive sense and in a negative sense? Elaborate.
6 The CLRB, until recently, made a distinction between complaints relating to both the negotiation and administration of collective agreements. Do you see any difficulties with this comprehensive approach, particularly as it applies to the negotiation process?
7 If you had written the reasons for decision in this case, would you have found the union guilty of an unfair labour practice? Elaborate on the rationale for your decision.
8 Assume that you have found the union guilty of an unfair labour practice by virtue of its failure to take Mr. Cameron's case to arbitration. Sections 121 and 189 give the Board remedial powers. What remedies, if any, would you have granted to Mr. Cameron? Which party would bear responsibility for awarding them? Elaborate.
9 In 1984 Part V of the Canada Labour Code was amended to read as follows:

A trade union or representative of a trade union that is the bargaining agent for a bargaining unit shall not act in a manner that is arbitrary, discriminatory, or in bad faith in the representation of any of the employees in the unit with respect to their rights under the collective agreement that is applicable to them.

What are the practical implications of this reworded section, and why do you think the change was made? Elaborate.

A Question of the Timeliness of Arbitration*

In The Matter of an Arbitration

between:

Thibodeau-Finch Express Limited
(Hereinafter referred to as the Company)

and

TEAMSTERS UNION, LOCAL 880
(Hereinafter referred to as the Union)

And in the Matter of the Grievance of R. Legault

*Permission to use this case was granted by Labour Canada. Minor deletions were made by the author for the purposes of this book and all names changed to prevent embarrassment to the individuals involved.

Hearing held at Windsor, Ontario on August 1 and October 1, 1984.

Decision

The grievor alleged in a grievance dated September 9, 1984 that he was unjustly discharged by the Company. Following the second step in the grievance procedure the Company was not notified of the Union's intention of proceeding to an "inside board" until it received the Union's letter dated October 17, 1983. At that time and to this day the Company has objected to the Union's right to have the matter determined on its merits. Without prejudice to its position the Company allowed the matter to be heard by an "inside board" and, following the inability of that board to reach a decision, the matter was referred to this board of arbitration. At the hearing the Company informed the board that it was objecting to its jurisdiction to hear and determine the merits of the grievance because the mandatory time limits of the collective agreement had not been strictly adhered to and, in the alternative, if the time limits were not mandatory was asking the board to decline to relieve the Union against the consequences of its breach of the time limits. This award will only deal with the issues arising out of the timeliness objection pressed by the Company.

The grievor is a member of the Garage and Maintenance Employees bargaining unit. The parties agreed that on or about October 1, 1982 they executed a memorandum of settlement which applied to that bargaining unit and which together with some terms contained in the Ontario General Maintenance Master Agreement comprises the collective agreement between them. That being the case the following provisions of the collective agreement are relevant to the resolution of the matter before us:

Article 7
Grievance Procedure and Arbitration

. . .

Section 7.2 (b) – Step 2 – General Manager or Designate

Failing settlement at the above step, the Branch Manager shall render his decision in writing and shall refer the grievance to and arrange a meeting between the Union and the General Manager or his designate within seven (7) days of the date that the grievance was registered in writing. This meeting shall be held in the locale of the terminal involved unless otherwise agreed. The General Manager or his designate shall render his decision in writing within seven (7) days from the date that the grievance was referred to him.

Section 7.2 (c) – Joint Grievance Committee

Should the parties fail to reach satisfactory settlement in the preceding steps, the final settlement of the grievance may be submitted to an arbitration board as outlined below. Before submitting the grievance to arbitration, the dispute shall, if requested by the grieving party and in accordance with the procedures outlined in this Section, be brought to the attention of a Joint Grievance Committee established for this purpose by the Company and by the Local Unions. The Joint Grievance Committee will render a decision unless it is deadlocked which shall be final and binding and have the same judicial powers as a Board of Arbitration established under the following provisions. The Joint

Grievance Committee shall be comprised of two (2) persons, one (1) of whom shall be selected from Management, and one (1) from the Local Unions.

It is further agreed that the Company and the Local Unions shall name only experienced representatives who are engaged in the day to day administration of this Agreement as nominees to the Joint Grievance Committee as required. It is understood that in the selection of the representatives the Company must name a representative from another Company and the Union must name a representative from another Local Union. It is further agreed that in the event that any Joint Grievance Committee is unable to render a majority decision, the grieving party must within fourteen (14) calendar days of the date the Joint Grievance Committee declares a dead-lock, unless they wish to withdraw the grievance, proceed to Arbitration as outlined in Article 7.5.

. . .

Section 7.4 – Discharge and Suspension Grievances

Grievances dealing with discharges and suspensions shall be registered in writing within seventy-two (72) hours (Saturdays, Sundays and General Holidays excluded) from the time of the discharge or suspension and shall commence with Step 2 of the Grievance Procedure as outlined in Section 7.2 (b).

Section 7.5 – Procedure for Arbitration

It shall be the responsibility of the party desiring Arbitration to so inform the other party in writing in the case of:

1 An employee grievance within fourteen (14) calendar days after the General Manager or his designate has rendered a decision or failed to render a decision as provided for in Section 7.2 (b);

. . .

Section 7.6 – Powers of Board of Arbitration

The Board of Arbitration shall not have the right to alter or change any provisions in this Agreement or substitute any new provisions in lieu thereof, or to give any decision inconsistent with the terms and provisions of this Agreement. The Board, however, shall have the power to vary or set aside, any penalty or discipline imposed relating to the grievance then before the Board.

. . .

As already mentioned above, the objection is based on the delay which occurred between step 2 and the submission to the Joint Grievance Committee or "inside board." On Friday, September 9, 1983 the step 2 meeting was held and the Union was informed orally that the Company was denying the grievance. On Monday, September 12, 1983 Mr. Howard, the Union Business Representative, prepared a letter to the Company informing it that the Union was submitting the grievance to the Joint Grievance Committee. That letter was never sent. The reason why the letter was not sent is attributable solely to the Union and arises out of changes in its internal office practice and a breakdown in communications regarding those changes.

Mr. Howard discovered that the letter was not sent in mid October, 1983 when he was informed by a steward whom he had asked to get some information that the Company was taking the position that the matter was closed. On October 17, 1983 he wrote the following letter to the Company:

> Mr. A. Baldwin
> Assistant Terminal Manager
> Thibodeau-Finch Express
> 7260 Dix Avenue
> Detroit, Michigan 48209
>
>
> Dear Sir:
>
> Enclosed please find a copy of the notice of our intent to proceed to the Windsor Area Joint Grievance Committee.
>
> It appears that as a result of a mix-up in our office this notice was not sent out on September 12, 1983.
>
> Yours truly,
> (signed)
>
>
> John Howard
> Business Representative

On October 21, 1983 the Company replied by letter acknowledging receipt of the Union's letter and setting out its position as follows:

> It is our position that you failed to notify the Company of your intent to proceed to the Windsor Joint Area Grievance Committee within the time period specified in our Collective Agreement, therefore no further action can or should be taken.

There are three separate questions which must be determined by this board of arbitration. Did the Union exceed the time limits as set down in the collective agreement for the submission of the matter to the Joint Grievance Committee? If so, are the time limits in the collective agreement mandatory so as to deprive the board of arbitration of jurisdiction to hear and determine the merits of the grievance? If the time limits are not mandatory, should the board of arbitration hear and determine the merits of the case?

1 Did the Union exceed the time limits as set down in the collective agreement for the submission of the matter to the Joint Grievance Committee?

We recognize that the Union did not receive a written reply from the Company at step 2 of the grievance procedure. It was not argued that the oral reply was insufficient for the purposes of the application of any time limits. It was argued by the Union that there were in fact no time limits set out in the collective agreement for referring the matter to the Joint Grievance Committee.

We recognize that section 7.2(c) of the agreement does not specifically refer to any time limits in connection with the referral of a matter to the Joint Grievance Committee. Section 7.2(c) only specifies a time limit in connection with the step to be taken if the Joint Grievance Committee is unable to render a majority decision. The first sentence of section 7.2(c) speaks of a referral to arbitration "as outlined below." Clearly this must refer to section 7.5 since the rest of section 7.2(c) goes on to deal with the situation when the matter is not referred directly to a board of arbitration. The parties also agreed that "before submitting the grievance to arbitration" they could submit it to a Joint Grievance Committee. That phrase surely refers to a time which must be within the time periods set out in section 7.5 — be they mandatory or directory — because that is the only period when the party wishing to refer the matter on to a next step can do so as of right and without objection being raised. We therefore conclude that section 7.2(c) necessarily incorporates the fourteen day time limit set out in section 7.5 for the period during which the matter can be referred to the Joint Grievance Committee.

It is therefore our conclusion that the Union had fourteen days after the second step reply to notify the Company that it intended to refer the matter to the Joint Grievance Committee and that the Union failed to meet the time limit. We must therefore proceed to answer the second question which we posed.

2 Are the time limits in the collective agreement mandatory so as to deprive the board of arbitration of jurisdiction to hear and determine the merits of the grievance?

The time limits which we are concerned with are those specifically set out in section 7.5 of the collective agreement. We acknowledge that in order to give proper effect to the intent of the provisions we must consider the collective agreement as a whole. In *Re Smith Transport Company Ltd. and Teamsters Union, Local 938* (1978), 20 L.A.C. (2d) 35 (Brunner) the board of arbitration considered virtually identical language and concluded that the time limits as expressed in section 7.5 were directory rather than mandatory. The collective agreement before the board in the *Smith* case (supra) was the "master agreement" between the Motor Transport Industrial Relations Bureau of Ontario (Inc.) and various Teamster Union locals which forms the basis for this collective agreement. The only real difference in language is that section 7.2(c) of the "master agreement" clearly incorporates the procedures of section 7.5 rather than leaving it to be implied.

Counsel for the Union also cited two other cases for our consideration both of which held that time limits using the term "shall" were directory rather than mandatory. Those cases were *Jones Transport Company Limited and Teamsters Local Union No. 879,* [1980] unreported (Brown) and *Thibodeau-Finch Express Ltd. and Teamsters Union, Local 938,* [1983] unreported (Brent). There is no doubt, though, that the most thorough analysis of the language is done in the *Smith* case (supra) and that that is the case which should be given the most consideration.

The reasons for the finding that the time limits are discretionary are found at pages 39 to 48 inclusive of the report of the *Smith* case (supra). Counsel for the Company urged us not to follow or adopt that reasoning because of three weaknesses in the reasoning, namely: (a) its attempt to distinguish the *Union Carbide Canada Ltd. v. Weiler et al.* (1968), 70 D.L.R.(2d) 333 was improper; (b) its ignoring of the sense of responsibility imposed on a party in the opening lines of section 7.5; and (c) its reliance on the absence of a penalty clause in the face of other penalty clauses in the collective agreement.

Without for the moment commenting on those alleged weaknesses, suffice it to say that the use of the word "shall" in section 7.5 does not of itself render the time limits mandatory. In our view that is by now well settled. Further, we accept that the absence of a specific penalty for non-compliance in section 7.5 does not automatically or necessarily render the time limits directory. We accept that we must have regard to the collective agreement provisions as a whole in order to try to determine whether the intent of the language was to make compliance with the time limits fundamental so that a board of arbitration would be without jurisdiction to hear the merits of a case whenever those time limits were breached.

With respect to the language of this agreement, we can see no particular significance to the use of the word "responsibility" in section 7.5. It seems to us to be as equivocal as the use of "shall" in that it can be interpreted as merely stating the obvious. That is, it can be read as simply meaning that the party who wants the matter to proceed to arbitration is the proper party to serve notice of that intent. In a general grievance procedure which contemplates grievances by either party it would seem to be appropriate to introduce the clause setting out the time limits for the various types of grievances with words indicating that the party who wishes the matter heard by arbitration is the proper one to give notice. It was argued that the use of the word "responsibility" denoted a sense of imperative duty or strict obligation which must be met in order to fulfill the requirements of section 7.5. While that is a possible interpretation of "responsibility" it is not the only interpretation possible.

In order to determine the intent of the words in section 7.5 it is necessary to look at the collective agreement as a whole. In doing this, it must be kept in mind that that section deals with procedural rather than substantive matters and that when analyzing the language it is appropriate to do so in the context of other procedural sections. In looking at the grievance procedure as a whole, one must be struck by the fact that the parties have obviously inserted a penalty for non-compliance with time limits in section 7.2(c), where they set out a specific consequence for failing to proceed to arbitration within fourteen days of the declared deadlock of the Joint Grievance Committee. The presence of a specific penalty in one section of the grievance procedure can surely lead to an inference that the absence of a specific penalty in other sections is meaningful. In other words, if time limits were mandatory why would there be a need to address specifically the consequences of failure to meet them in one part of the procedure? Surely silence in all parts of the grievance procedure would speak more eloquently to the mandatory nature of the time limits than would one instance where it was considered to be necessary to insert a penalty.

Having reviewed the other sections of the collective agreement cited to us and the reasoning in the *Smith* case (supra) we are not prepared to come to a different conclusion than that reached in the *Smith* case (supra) and in so doing we adopt the reasoning of the *Smith* case (supra) as our own along with the reasons which we have already set out above. In connection with the alleged weaknesses of the reasoning in that case (a) we do not consider that, even if the *Union Carbide* case (supra) was improperly distinguished, it was a material aspect of the analysis of the language in the collective agreement upon which the *Smith* decision turned; (b) we have dealt with the question of "responsibility" and find that it is not a fatal flaw in the *Smith* reasoning; and (c) we substantially agree that the presence of penalty clauses in procedural sections of the collective agreement is a factor which should be taken into consideration when determining the nature of the time limits. It is therefore our conclusion that the time limits set out in section 7.5 of the collective agreement are directory and not mandatory.

3 Should the board of arbitration hear and determine the merits of the case?

In the *Smith* case (supra) it was apparently not argued that even if the time limits were directory the board should still decline to hear the merits. In this case the company has argued that even if the time limits are discretionary we cannot ignore section 7.6 of the collective agreement and that we must determine whether the Union's breach of the time limits has led to the sort of delay which would justify our refusal to give a decision on the merits.

The Company has conceded that it has not suffered any substantial prejudice by the delay. The evidence is clear that the responsibility for the delay is entirely the Union's and that it arises out of an internal breakdown in procedure. It can be characterized as carelessness on the part of one or more people in the Union office. The evidence gives a reason for the delay but not a justification for it. Given that the Company's second step answer was rendered on September 9, 1983, then the Union's notice of intention to proceed to the Joint Grievance Committee should have been given on or about September 23, 1983. It was in fact given on or about October 17, 1983 — roughly three and one-half weeks late.

This case does not arise under the *Ontario Labour Relations Act*; therefore, there is no statutory provision which allows boards of arbitration to extend time limits. Accordingly, in determining whether or not the merits of the case should be heard we must be guided by the test of reasonableness. In *Re Loblaw Groceterias Co. Ltd. and Union of Canadian Retail Employees C.L.C.* (1973), 3 L.A.C.(2d) 325 (Adams) at pages 331 and 332 [cited in Palmer *Collective Agreement Arbitration in Canada* second edition at page 202] the following was said regarding the duty of the arbitrator in the case of directory procedural provisions:

> ...If the provision is found to be directory in nature, non-compliance is not necessarily fatal. In this latter case, the parties have intended that the arbitrator fashion an appropriate remedy to the circumstances, and typically, arbitrators look to the degree of prejudice suffered by a party due to non-compliance as a guide. Where a procedure is directory only, the parties 'must accept reasonableness as a touchstone' although an arbitrator is free to dismiss irregular

conduct in proper cases. See *Re U.E.W., Local 504, and Canadian Westinghouse Co. Ltd.* (1963), 14 L.A.C. 139 (Laskin); *Re Ottawa Newspaper Guild, Local 205, and Ottawa Citizen* (1965), 55 D.L.R. (2d) 26, [1966] 1 O.R. 669; *Re Int'l Longshoremen's Ass'n, Local 1879, and Hamilton Terminal Operators Ltd.* (1966), 17 L.A.C. 181 (Arthurs).

In applying "reasonableness as a touchstone" in order to dismiss a grievance because of the breach of directory time limits it is in our view necessary to find both unreasonable delay and prejudice to the other party. It is further our view that the prejudice to the other party must be of the sort that cannot be remedied by an adjustment in any compensation which may be awarded but rather must be of the sort that substantially prejudices the right of the innocent victim of the delay to a full and fair hearing of the merits. Where delay has been substantial, and that is a question of fact in each case, then it may be axiomatic that such prejudice has resulted. In this case it is conceded that there has been no substantial prejudice to the Company.

While there has been a reason given for the delay it is not one which absolves the Union of responsibility for the delay. In the instant case, where there has been no substantial prejudice to the Company as a result of the delay and where the subject matter of the grievance is one which involves a discharge, we consider that it would be unreasonable to deprive the grievor of a hearing on the merits — even where the Union was completely at fault in causing the delay. On the other hand, we do not consider that it would be reasonable to hold the Company liable to fully compensate the grievor for all losses in the event that the grievance is successful on its merits. It is therefore our conclusion that the matter should be heard on the merits but that in determining the compensation which should be paid to the grievor, if any compensation is ordered by this board, the Union should bear full responsibility for the consequences of the delay and the award of compensation should be reduced accordingly. We reserve the right to determine what this reduction should be until we hear the submissions of the parties on the appropriate remedy to be ordered when the merits are considered....

---

questions

1 The company and local union in this case are apparently part of the Master General Maintenance Agreement between a number of trucking companies and various locals of the Teamsters' Union. What advantages, if any, do you think that the local company and union acquire as parties to a "master" collective agreement which covers a number of companies and locals of a union or, in some cases, a number of unions? Elaborate.

2 According to the second paragraph of the case, the parties agreed about October 1, 1982 to a memorandum of settlement which applied to the Garage and Maintenance Employees bargaining unit. Do you consider these so-called "supplemental agreements" as advantageous to the parties? Elaborate.

3 What do you think of the idea of having a "Joint Grievance Committee"

composed of one representative of another company and another local union, and of having its decision made equivalent to that of an arbitration board for all legal purposes? Elaborate. Might this kind of arrangement be contemplated by those jurisdictions which prescribe "arbitration or otherwise" as the terminal step in the grievance procedure?

4 What do you make of the arbitration board's discussion of the term "responsibility"? Why do you think it saw fit to discuss this matter? Elaborate.

5 What do you make of the arbitration board's differentiation between "silence" and one specific penalty in one clause of the grievance process? Elaborate.

6 What is the subtle distinction between the concepts of "directory" and "mandatory"? Do you see where "common sense" is applied by the members of the arbitration board in coming to their decision to allow the case to be heard on its merits?

7 Do you think the arbitration board asked itself the right three questions? Are there others which it could have asked? Elaborate.

8 Arbitral jurisprudence plays a vital part in arbitration cases. Has this case served to demonstrate this to you? If so, in what ways? Elaborate.

9 If you had been a member of the arbitration board, would you have gone along with the decision of the chairperson? Elaborate.

A Dispute over New Classifications*

In the Matter of an Arbitration

Between:

Tri-Co Broadcasting Ltd.,

And:

National Association of Broadcast Employees and Technicians

Award

The undersigned was appointed, pursuant to a letter of appointment dated June 27, 1983, by the Minister of Labour as a Sole Arbitrator for the purpose of resolving the within dispute. The arbitration is pursuant to Part V of The Canada Labour Code. A hearing was arranged for October 19th, 1983.... At the conclusion of the evidence and argument my Decision was reserved.

The Grievance —

The grievance was filed under a Collective Agreement between Tri-Co

---

*Permission to use this case was granted by Labour Canada. Minor deletions were made by the author for the purposes of this book and all names changed to prevent embarrassment to the individuals involved.

Broadcasting Ltd. AM & FM Radio, Cornwall, Ontario (Tri-Co) and the National Association of Broadcast Employees and Technicians (NABET). The agreement...covers the period September 1, 1980 to August 31, 1982.

The grievance...is dated July 14th, 1982, and reads as follows:

> Date of Occurrence: Ongoing since Feb/82
>
> Nature of Grievance:
>
> The Company unilaterally expanded the number of classifications of excluded persons described in the CLRB certificate dated December 2, 1973 and outlined in Article 2.2.
>
> The Union has repeatedly suggested that the Company should seek a change from the CLRB but after months of stalling have refused to take any action to solve the dispute.
>
> This grievance is being filed under Article 6.2 and furthermore the Union would suggest that adequate discussion has taken place and that the matter should proceed to Arbitration. – Step 4.
>
> Settlement Desired:
>
> Retroactive to the date of the unilateral action, the Company shall put Mr. Howard Hughes back in the bargaining unit subject to all benefits and provisions of the contract including dues check-off.

Preliminary Matters —

At the outset Tri-Co indicated that some issue might be taken with the timing of the delivery of the grievance and its submission to arbitration. However, during the course of the hearing, this issue was described by Counsel for the employer as "not being seriously pressed." Accordingly, I have not treated timeliness as one of the issues before me. The parties acknowledged my jurisdiction at the opening of the hearing.

It is clear that the complaint of the Union in this grievance relates to a purported unilateral expansion of the number of positions excluded from the bargaining unit. At the hearing the Union conceded that the employer had a perfect right to promote Mr. Howard Hughes out of the bargaining unit and into a managerial position and that this step taken by the employer was not directly related to the issue of expansion of the number of excluded positions. Thus no question of returning Mr. Hughes, as an individual, to the bargaining unit arises. In the circumstances the Union amended its request for relief in the grievance by inviting me to issue a declaration with respect to two issues:

> Whether or not the employer in fact unilaterally expanded the number of classifications of excluded persons contemplated by the Collective Agreement, and
> Whether the employer could do so legally.

The disposition of this grievance by me is confined therefore to the matter of the declarations requested.

Mr. Hughes, who was present at the hearing, was invited, in view of the fact that his position was referred to in the grievance, to seek status before the tribunal. He declined and thus took no independent part in the proceedings. As a precaution Mr. Robert Blackburn, a former occupant of a position at issue, who was also at the hearing, was asked whether he wished to be accorded status and he also declined and took no independent part in the proceedings.

The Facts

By letter dated January 28, 1982...Mr. Robert Blackburn, over the title "Operations Manager" wrote to the representative of the Union advising him that Mr. Howard Hughes had been appointed to the post of Program Director of Radio Station CJSS. This document was accompanied by a memorandum from the Operations Manager to all staff at the station advising of the same appointment.

To understand the significance of this event in the context of the filing of the grievance some history is required. Tri-Co is a Company which operates two separate radio stations through the same corporate vehicle in the City of Cornwall, Ontario. It has an AM facility which has been operating for several years on a 24 hour a day basis using the call sign CJSS. In addition, for some years it has been licensed to operate an FM facility which it has done under the call letters CFLG. Until 1978 CFLG was operating on a 6 hour a day basis as an introductory exercise, in accordance with the requirements of the [CRTC]. My impression of the evidence is that, during the period of time that the FM station was operating at less than full capacity, the staffing was reduced over that which developed once FM became a 24 hour a day on-air station.

The Union was certified on December 2nd, 1975. The description of the bargaining unit as found in Article 2.2 of the Collective Agreement has not changed since then. It reads as follows:

> All employees of Tri-Co Broadcasting Limited, Cornwall, Ontario, *excluding* the President, Vice-President/General Manager, Program Director, salesmen and secretary to the President (bookkeeper) (Emphasis added).

At the time of certification there was only one Program Director who was, for all practical purposes, the Program Director for CJSS (AM) because this was the major business undertaking of Tri-Co. The office was occupied by one John Wayne. In August of the year 1978, the management team consisted of Mr. John Gordon, President, Mr. Thomas Henderson, Vice-President/General Manager, and Mr. Wayne, Program Director. These were the positions occupied and also the line of authority, that is to say, the Vice-President/General Manager was responsible to the President, the Program Director to the Vice-President/General Manager etc.

On September 5, 1978, CFLG (FM) went to a full time 24 hour a day service.

This required some reorganization and addition of staff. While the realignment of people was described in evidence there was some lack of clarity as to the rationale in every case. It is clear that the need was to marry programming as opposed to marketing skills to the various positions in question. According to Mr. Henderson, who gave evidence on behalf of the Employer, this involved moving Mr. John Wayne up to Operations Manager with added responsibility over his continuing responsibility as Program Director. Effectively, he remained Program Director at CJSS (AM) and had added responsibilities in the FM operation. He secured additional assistance from one Terry Brood, a member of the bargaining unit who was Music Director. The "Operations Manager" position was created in July 1978 for this purpose and Wayne was the first to occupy it. Mr. Samuel Gompers, the Union Representative, said that the first time he heard of this "new position" was in January 1982.

In early 1981 John Wayne left Tri-Co. At that time Mr. Robert Blackburn was appointed Operations Manager, and also Program Director at CFLG (FM). In January 1982 Mr. Hughes was appointed Program Director at CJSS (AM).

In January of 1982, therefore, middle management consisted of either an Operations Manager and one Program Director, two Program Directors, or two Program Directors, one of whom also functioned as the Operations Manager. The significant fact is that the office of Operations Manager is not identified as one of the exclusions in the definition of the bargaining unit.

It is clear that as each successive person viz; Wayne, Blackburn and Hughes were appointed to their positions, dues were stopped since they were leaving the bargaining unit and joining the management team.

As above indicated, the position of Operations Manager was created by the President of the Company in July of 1978. The two incumbents have been Mr. Wayne and presently Mr. Blackburn. Mr. Blackburn's duties include programming in the FM operation and, as Operations Manager, coordinating the complete AM/FM operation from an administrative standpoint. He stands, from a hierarchial point of view, between Mr. Henderson, as Vice-President/General Manager, and Mr. Hughes as Program director. It would appear to be clear that, *for the moment at least*, there are two Program Directors and one Operations Manager, but only two people.

Decision

Certain things are clear and beyond dispute. In the first place the Union does not challenge Management's authority to promote people out of the bargaining unit into managerial positions, provided such positions are within the exclusions set out in Article 2.2. Further there is no dispute that at the time that the individuals in question were promoted to the management team their dues were stopped as they had clearly been removed from the bargaining unit.

It is perhaps not without significance that in cross-examination Mr. Hughes said that when Mr. Blackburn took over Mr. Wayne's position in 1981, he only took over the Program Director's role, and not the Operations Manager's role. This would lead one to the conclusion that after Waldruff's departure there was no Operations Manager, and that the true state of affairs was that the promotion of Hughes was to fill the vacancy created by Mr. Blackburn who was in fact being appointed Operations Manager.

The Union argues that when the post of Operations Manager was created there were additional responsibilities associated with the position which went beyond those conventionally borne by a Program Director. It was also pointed out that when Mr. Hughes was appointed Program Director there was then an added managerial person over the situation which pertained at the time of certification. Mr. Porter, in behalf of Tri-Co, describes this added managerial person as a Program Director and urges that the certificate contemplates more than one Program Director. Mr. Gompers suggests that this is not the case and says that, in fact, the added person is an Operations Manager.

The exclusions outlined in Article 2.2 refer to a "Program Director". In my opinion it is unnecessary to deal with the question of whether or not this description entitles the employer to add Program Directors from time to time as the operations expand or whether this exclusion from the bargaining unit is confined to a single Program Director.

The real issue is whether or not there really is a new and separate position, that of Operations Manager. In my opinion there is and I draw this conclusion from two circumstances. The first is that there is indeed an office entitled "Operations Manager." In fact when the Union was advised of the appointment of Mr. Hughes to the position of the Program Director the letter of advice was signed by the Operations Manager, not by another Program Director. Further, and perhaps more important, it is clear that Mr. Blackburn and Mr. Hughes do not share the same position of responsibility. The Program Director reports to the Operations Manager, the Operations Manager reports to the Vice-President/General Manager, and the latter reports to the President. This is a sequential arrangement of authority which is inconsistent with the conclusion that Mr. Blackburn and Mr. Hughes occupy essentially the same position.

While Mr. Blackburn may be performing the functions of a Program Director, it is clear that he is also occupying another office, that of Operations Manager. Little imagination is required to see that in future as the business expands, it is likely that a Program Director (or some such person) would be appointed for CJSS/FM, and Mr. Blackburn's activities would be confined entirely to his role as Operations Manager. This flows logically from the manner in which the managerial hierarchy has been developed to date and would be consistent with the lines of authority. Managerial exclusions could, over time, expand by creating a new position and superimposing it upon an existing excluded position "for the time being".

I therefore conclude that Tri-Co has created a new managerial position with new responsibilities which it regards as being excluded from the bargaining unit, the position being Operations Manager. It is a position which stands between Program Director and Vice-President/General Manager. This answers the first question posed in the grievance, whether or not management has unilaterally expanded the number of classifications of excluded persons. The answer is that it has. It matters not who the "persons" are that are occupying the positions. The issue is whether the positions, in number, have changed over those set out in the exclusion. They clearly have.

There can be no doubt of the practical entitlement of management to proceed as it sees fit in the best interests of the Company in accordance with its management rights as set out in Article 3 of the Collective Agreement. No criticism can be leveled at the Corporation for creating this management position. Indeed the fact of its creation, and its character as a senior management position, has been conceded by the Union in documentation filed before the Canada Labour Relations Board. The legal issue however is whether or not there can be effective creation of such a position without the intervention and approval of the Board. Mr. Gompers, on behalf of the Union, says that the Board must approve any changes in the bargaining unit on the application of the employer and that this has not been done in the present case. Mr. Porter essentially argues that there is no need to secure approval of the Board because no new position has been created, both Mr. Blackburn and Mr. Hughes are said to be Program Directors. I have already disposed of this question. My understanding of Mr. Porter's position is that he is in agreement that if a new position is created (a fact which he does not admit has occurred) it cannot be unilaterally imposed. The Canada Labour Relations Board must approve it by appropriate application to alter the certificate. This has not been done in the present case.

A number of authorities were cited in support of the jurisdiction of the Board in this area. No useful purpose would be served in reviewing them in detail, suffice to say that in the *British Columbia Telephone Moffatt et al* case,[1] the Board, after referring to Section 119 of the Code, dealt with this general subject. Section 119 reads as follows:

> The Board may review, rescind, amend, alter or vary any Order or Decision made by it, and may rehear any application before making an Order in respect of the application.

The Order in question of course is the certificate dated December 2nd, 1975 as referred to in Article 2.2 of the Collective Agreement.

In the *B.C. Telephone* case the [CLRB] observed as follows with respect to its jurisdiction:

> The practice of describing bargaining units by listed classifications is one that was followed for several years by this and provincial boards. Because of the problem that resulted from that mode of describing bargaining units, most labour relations boards have abandoned that approach where possible and described bargaining units in terms of "all employees" excepting certain listed classifications. The practical

---

[1]Telecommunications Workers' Union and British Columbia Telephone Company and Telecommunications Employees Managerial and Professional Organization and Paul L. Moffatt et al and Association of Professional Engineers 1978 CLR BR387 Dec. 140.

effect of this "all employee" description of bargaining units is that the *onus is on the employer* to establish that new classifications created by the employer should be excluded from the bargainIng unit. Failing acceptance of that proposition by the union, *the remedy for the employer* is to bring the matter to the board. (Emphasis added).

The rationale underlying the Board's supervisory role is to prevent the erosion of the unit by the unilateral creation by management of managerial positions and staffing the same with persons within the unit. This of course is not to say that a legitimate reorganization of management's team including the creation of new managerial positions, will not have the full approval of the Board, but it is to say that it is a matter for the Board and not for the unilateral action of management. This, it seems to me is true, even if the managerial character of the position is conceded by the Union. Approval is nonetheless required. This jurisdiction is jealously guarded by the Board as appears from the fact that it will insist on being the instrumentality for change even if the parties consent to management's action.

In answer to the second question therefore the unilateral action of management in creating the positon of Operations Manager, in the absence of the approval of the change by the Canada Labour Relations Board, is illegal and of no force and effect.

Conclusion

In allowing the grievance therefore I declare that indeed Tri-Co created a new position, that of Operations Manager, a position not theretofore contemplated by the exclusions set out in the certificate as reproduced in Article 2.2 of the Collective Agreement and that, absent the approval of the Canada Labour Relations Board, it had no authority to do so.

---

questions

1 Were the two questions posed by the arbitrator the only major issues in the case?
2 What do you think the arbitrator had in mind in inviting Mr. Hughes and Mr. Blackburn to seek status before the arbitration tribunal? Do you think it was necessary to seek status? Elaborate.
3 Do you agree with the arbitrator's decision that a new position had been created?
4 If you so agree, do you agree with his conclusion that the position is illegal and of no force and effect? Elaborate.
5 Do you agree that, even if the union agreed with management on the appropriateness of the position and its exclusion, management would still have to seek approval from the CLRB? Elaborate.
6 Could the parties agree on the exclusion and include it as part of the collective agreement without changing the certificate issued by the Board when the union was certified? Elaborate.
7 Why should an issue which is submitted to arbitration appear to be a matter for a labour relations board? Elaborate.

8 If the arbitrator's award is correct, do you think that there are many illegal exclusions among the many bargaining relationships established by the CLRB? Elaborate.

9 What are the implications of this decision, if it is correct, for the workload of the CLRB? Elaborate.

A Dispute over Manning Requirements*

In the Matter of an Arbitration

Between:

The International Longshoremen's Association,
Local 273, hereinafter referred to
as the "Union"

And:

The Maritime Employers' Association
(Saint John, New Brunswick)
acting for and on behalf of
Ceres Stevedoring Co. Ltd.,
hereinafter referred to
as the "Company"

Hearing: at Saint John, New Brunswick,
on April 22, 1981.

Decision

This case involves the question of whether extra men must be hired by the Company when the work which is being done by a foreman and his gang on the job involves the moving of containers out of one hatch into another hatch of the same ship.

The Facts

The evidence is that members of the Union have the primary duty of loading and unloading ships that dock in the Port of Saint John. They are employed by the various stevedoring companies that do business within the Port. The method of hiring most of the Company's employees is that the Company names its foremen twice each year from among the membership in the Union.

*Permission to use this case was granted by Labour Canada. Minor deletions were made by the author for the purposes of this book and all names changed to prevent embarrassment to the individuals involved.

The foreman, in turn, is responsible to select 12 members from the Union to make up his gang. It is then his responsibility to make sure that the men in his gang have the skills to do the tasks for which the Company may be hired. It is also the foreman's responsibility to make sure that the men in his gang are available for work when they are called out. The basic work gang for the Union in the Port is a foreman and 12 men. A notice by the Company (or any member of the MEA) that men are needed is given to the Union by naming the foreman and indicating the wharf and work for which the Company requires men. If extra men are needed the extra number is noted on the call out to the Union.

On the shifts in question, (on January 16 and January 17, 1981) the gang for which Fraser Cameron was the foreman had been called out to work on the loading of newsprint into the #4 hold (or hatch) of the M.V. Visha Pallov. That operation was being carried on by placing 5 men in the ship's hold to handle the cargo as it was lowered into the hold and stowed, 3 men on the deck of the ship to operate the cranes and to give directions to the crane operator, and 4 men on the wharf, or pier, to feed the cargo from the shed to the area alongside the ship. It is customary in such an operation that 2 of the men on the pier and 2 in the hold operate fork-lifts, or other similar machines, to carry the cargo so that the operation will run smoothly, efficiently and safely.

Mr. Cameron was ordered to bring his wharf crew of 4 men on board the ship and have them work in the #3 hold. The order was given to move containers from the forward section of #3 hold in one continuous movement into the after section of #4 hold. The containers were lifted by using two of the ship's cranes (which were "married" to work in tandem) up out of #3 hold over the top deck, and down into #4 hold, without putting the containers onto the pier.

The Union protested that the operation should not have been done so as to split Mr. Cameron's gang to work on two hatches. They suggested that this was a violation of the Collective Agreement in that Article 7.01-B.3 (see Appendix "A") prohibits splitting a gang between hatches and that not less than 5 men be in the hold. The Union submits that in the past the normal method would have been for the containers to be lifted from the #3 hold onto the pier from where they would be taken into a storage shed. Then the containers would be taken by men from a second gang to a position abreast of the #4 hold from whence the ship's crane would lift them up and into the #4 hold. There would be one gang, of 12 men each, working on each of the holds (or hatches).

It is the Union's submission that all members of a gang remain with its foreman in that it is not split up between holds. In addition, they all move from one hold to another when the foreman moves.

There was evidence that cargo is not shifted from one hold to another on the same ship in one continuous movement in a situation where only one gang is used…in 2 holds. There was additional evidence that on the "Barbour" ships one gang does shift containers from one hold to another so as to maintain the ship's trim in the water.

The alleged violation took place on the evening shift of January 16 from 7:30 to 11:00 P.M. and from 8:00 A.M. to 10:00 A.M. on January 17, 1981. The Union claims that a foreman and 12 men should have been compensated for the lost time when the extra gang was not called out.

Argument for the Union

Mr. Brown suggested that the loading and unloading spoken of in 7:01-B.3 includes the shifting of cargo from one hatch to another. That is clearly in the evidence in this case.

Article 6.11 decrees that the basic gang is to consist of one foreman and 12 men. The onus is on the foreman, and the Union, to make sure that a normal complement of men is selected for each gang, Article 6:10(b). Under Article 7:02(a) the men in each basic gang are required to be flexible and interchangeable in all the work that is required to be done. In fact in Article 7:02(a) loading or unloading a ship includes shifting cargo from ship to ship, hatch to hatch, as well as, ship to and from shed. That is the only article where the concept of hatch to hatch is mentioned in the Collective Agreement.

Reference in Article 2:02(b)(7) concerns shifting cargo in the hold, not from one hatch to another. The work function of shifting from hatch to hatch is included within the recognition article 2:02(b) in "(1) discharging/loading of cargo vessels."

It was the submission of Counsel that the concept that a gang stays together (under Article 7:01-B.3) is reinforced in Article 7:02(b) where it is said that extra men may be shifted from gang to gang.

Further Article 7:01-B.3(c) requires that *at least 5* men be in a hold. Article 13.08 requires 3 men to be on deck working the ship's gear for each hatch.

It was submitted that the Union's position is the only way that the Collective Agreement can be read. Mr. Brown requested that the grievance be allowed and the corrective action be ordered.

Argument for the Employer

It was the submission of Counsel for the Company that there is no violation of Article 7:01-B.3 in that the gang in the instant case was not split between 2 operations. There was just a single flow of material or cargo from one hold to the other. The similarities between the normal movement of cargo from ship to shore are quite evident. A gang is not said to be "split" just because 5 men may be working in a hold, 3 on deck and 4 on a pier.

The Cameron gang was not taking cargo from the pier to 2 hatches.

Article 2:02(b) in defining the local's work jurisdiction does distinguish between loading and unloading as longshoremen's work and shifting cargo in the hold. The very concept of loading signifies that a vessel becomes heavier and in unloading it becomes lighter.

Mr. Christopher, counsel for the company, suggested that the impugned Article 7:01-B deals solely with manning a gang when it is loading or unloading a ship at a pier. Each of the 12 subdivisions of Article 7:01-B refers to a separate operation, loading or unloading ships. And, it is clear in the instant case that the Cameron gang was shifting cargo not loading or unloading it; therefore, there can be no breach of 7:01-B.3 for what was done here.

Instead, the Article that covers this situation is 7:01-C. It was work other than loading/unloading of a cargo vessel. It was not the work of the basic gang under 7:01-B. Accordingly, the rules that pertain to a basic 12-man gang are irrelevant. Rather, it was up to the management of the Company to determine the number of men required in this operation. Article 7:01-C covers those situations that are described elsewhere in the Collective Agreement. Shifting cargo from one hatch to another is not described in 7:01-B.

Mr. Christopher also referred to Article 14:00(n), at page 43; where the concept of loading and unloading cargo is separated from shifting or restowed cargo. There it is clear that the payments to the Union's Pension and Welfare Fund is based on cargo movement onto and from a ship. No payment is made for cargo that is merely shifted.

Company counsel requested that the grievance be dismissed.

Reasons for Decision and Conclusion

Collective Agreement between Maritime Employers' Association and General Longshore Workers of the Port of Saint John, N.B.
Local 273, International Longshoremen's Association
Effective from September 29, 1978 to June 30, 1981

Article II — Recognition

2:02 (a) It is agreed that at container terminal operations, the loading/unloading of containers to/from railcars, the receiving and delivery of cargo to/from truck tailgate including any related terminal work shall be performed by members of the Union.

2:02 (b) It is agreed that the following work, when under the control of the employer shall be performed by members of the Union unless another Union is certified and recognized:
1 discharging/loading of cargo vessels;
7 shifting cargo on deck, in the hold or in the shed.

6:10 (b) each foreman of a gang shall select the normal complement of his gang from among the Union membership and shall at all times be responsible for his gang and have his men available for work when called.

6:11 (a) The basic gang shall consist of a foreman and 12 men.

(b) Where extra men are required in compliance with manning provisions of Article VII and/or employed, they shall be considered as additions to the basic gang or work unit set forth therein.

7:01 — Manning and Deployment

B. The following manning and deployment provisions shall apply for all work performed in the loading or unloading of a cargo vessel when alongside the pier:

3. When loading/unloading heavy lifts, units, pieces, packages, bundles, pre-slung and non-manhandled cargo, not less than a foreman and twelve men. It is understood that (a) the twelve men will not be split between hatches; (b) not more than four of the twelve men will be required to operate ...trucks at any one time; (c) during the actual loading/unloading of cargo in the hold, not less than five men will be in the hold.

10. When loading or unloading containers at other than a container terminal operation, not less than a foreman and twelve (12) men.

C. For work other than the loading/unloading of a cargo vessel, the number of men required shall be determined by Management, except that on a container terminal operation a foreman is to be employed when men are employed on the terminal.

7:02 (a) The men in the basic gang shall be flexible and interchangeable to the extent that during any work period they will perform any and all work as directed by Management in connection with the loading/unloading of the ship, which is the place of rest to the hold and vice versa, except as otherwise provided for in Section 7:02(d) below. It is understood that this shall include shifting from hatch to hatch, from ship to ship, and ship to/from shed within a Company, except as otherwise provided for in Section 7:02(d) below.

(b) Extras or men employed in addition to the basic gang shall work under the same conditions as Paragraph (a), and may be shifted from gang to gang.

Article X — Violation of Agreement

10:01 Should working conditions as set out in the present Agreement be violated by either party to this Agreement or by any person represented by either party, the party affected by such violation may submit a grievance according to Article XI. In such cases, the Arbitrator has the authority to order reimbursement of any payment made or loss suffered by Management, or loss suffered by any employee as a result of said violation.

Article XIII — General

13:08 Any ship loading or discharging using ship's gear (i.e. winches or cranes), three (3) men to be employed on each working hatch, year round.

Health, Welfare and Pension Plans

14:00 (n)

(ii) It is clearly understood that transhipments are paid for only once and that shifted or restowed cargo is exempt.

questions

1 Paragraphs 3 and 4 in the case describe the work to be done. Do you find any inconsistency in what was requested and what was actually done? Are there clauses which cover this situation? If so, identify them.

2 What do you make of the union's argument that the containers should have been unloaded and put into storage by one gang of 12, and later taken from storage and loaded by a gang of 12? Elaborate.

3 Since the gang in question was called out to work on loading newsprint into the #4 hold (or hatch), did the company have the right, as it maintains, under Section 7:01-C to use the gang to move containers from one hold to another in light of the wording of Clause 7:01-B(a)? Elaborate.

4 If you had been the arbitrator in this case, would you have supported the company's position or the union's position? Give the rationale for your decision.

5 Assume that you supported the union's position which claimed that "a foreman and 12 men should have been compensated for the time lost when the extra gang was not called out". To whom and for what period of time would compensation be made? Give the rationale for your award.

Misuse of Organization's Financial System*

Between:

Canadian Broadcasting Corporation

And:

Canadian Union of Public Employees

Grievance of Alfred Keating

The grievor, Mr. A. Keating, was discharged by the CBC for "abusing [his] position of trust" as a Set Designer "by using...*Instaccount* purchase orders to secure money for personal use" (letter of dismissal, Jan. 15, 1979).

There is no substantial dispute as to the facts. As a Set Designer, the grievor was required to procure props to dress sets for television productions. When appropriate props were not available from CBC stores, they were purchased outright or rented for the duration of the production. In order to facilitate procurement, the grievor, and other employees, were provided with serially-numbered purchase orders (called "Instaccount" vouchers) which guaranteed payment to the merchant supplying the props of the amount shown, up to a total value of $300 per order.

The merchant would submit an invoice for the goods to the CBC, either showing the Instaccount number or attaching a copy of the voucher. These

*Permission to use this case was granted by Labour Canada. Minor deletions were made by the author for the purposes of this book and all names changed to prevent embarrassment to the individuals involved.

invoices would be verified by the CBC Accounts Payable department against the voucher copy submitted by the employee. In the event no voucher had yet been submitted, the invoice would be sent along to the employee (identified by his holding of the relevant numbered voucher) for verification, and then returned to Accounts Payable for payment.

The grievor, in brief, arranged by use of his Instaccount, to lease a number of musical instruments, which he subsequently pawned. On several occasions, he prolonged the lease of these instruments by further Instaccount transactions. Finally, in circumstances related below, he redeemed the pawned instruments and paid the rental charges. No loss was actually incurred by the CBC, but this course of action was, nonetheless, serious misconduct warranting serious disciplinary action. The only issue of consequence is whether the misconduct was so extreme as to warrant discharge, or whether there were circumstances which would make a lesser penalty appropriate.

1 The analysis must begin with a consideration of why the misconduct was so extremely serious. Employees permitted to use Instaccount are undoubtedly in a position of trust. They are enabled to pledge the credit of the CBC and are, of course, thereby the custodians of its commercial reputation. If merchants cannot be sure whether they are dealing with the CBC or one of its employees, acting in his personal capacity, the whole Instaccount system may be undermined. Moreover, while as matters turned out, the grievor did pay for all transactions in question (except one legitimately chargeable to the CBC), he was able to do so only because he received two sizeable last-minute loans from a sympathetic supervisor and from his girlfriend. Since he could not, as he testified, borrow from either his bank or his credit union, due to an already excessive burden of debt, it is clear that he was very lucky to be able to pay what he owed. In the circumstances, this means that the CBC was very lucky not to have been saddled with debts by the grievor for his own purposes. Thus it can be seen that the grievor risked both financial and reputational [sic] injury to his employer.

Moreover, his acts were incompatible with the discharge of his fiduciary responsibilities, and approached the border of criminality, if they did not actually cross it. There can be no doubt — he admitted as much — that Mr. Keating would not have been able to obtain the lease of the musical instruments, and the several extensions of the lease period, without elaborate personal identification and a sizeable deposit, if he had not used Instaccount vouchers. But a person in a position of trust is not permitted to make personal gain from that position, whether or not he does so at the expense of the person whose interests he is supposed to serve. Thus, apart from financial loss or reputational [sic] damage to the CBC, the grievor breached his duty to it. And, moreover, he did so by an act which was clearly wrongful *vis-à-vis* the merchants who leased him the instruments. A person who leases the goods of another is under an obligation to return them; he acquires only possession of, and not property in, the goods. Yet by pawning the goods, the greivor put himself in the position of being possibly unable to return them; indeed, for some part of the period, the grievor was in precisely that position. Next, the grievor represented to the merchants that they were dealing with the CBC, when he intended that they should deal with him personally. He thus obtained the rental by a false pretense. And finally, in pawning the goods, Mr. Keating implicitly or explicitly represented to the pawnbroker that they were his to pawn; they obviously were not.

Clearly, it is no part of my function to determine which of these acts, if any, amounted to criminal conduct. Quite apart from the question of the grievor's guilty intention, or lack thereof, it is possible that one or more technical aspects of the relevant crimes were absent. But to accept that conduct may not have transgressed the boundaries of the criminal law is not to concede that it was acceptable in the industrial relation sense. It was not. Each of the matters mentioned betrayed a substantial ignorance of, or indifference to, the obligations of an employee in a position of trust.

2   Is discharge the only possible response to employee misconduct involving such a breach of trust?

Counsel for both parties submitted extensive, but of course not binding, arbitral authority on this point. I have examined all authorities cited, and I believe that the following summary accurately reflects their significance. The older cases generally (but not inevitably) treated theft or dishonesty as an offence which warranted automatic discharge; more recent cases, especially those decided by arbitrators subscribing to the theory of "corrective discipline," do not treat dishonesty as *per se* grounds for discharge; and, various mitigating factors have been identified as justifying the substitution of a lesser penalty for discharge in such cases. Such factors include:

1 *bona fide* confusion or mistake by the grievor as to whether he was entitled to do the act complained of;
2 the grievor's inability, due to drunkenness or emotional problems, to appreciate the wrongfulness of his act;
3 the impulsive or nonpremeditated nature of the act;
4 the relatively trivial nature of the harm done;
5 the frank acknowledgement of his misconduct by the grievor;
6 the existence of a sympathetic, personal motive for dishonesty, such as family need, rather than hardened criminality;
7 the past record of the grievor;
8 the grievor's future prospects for likely good behaviour; and
9 the economic impact of discharge in view of the grievor's age, personal circumstances, etc.

But these factors, while helpful, are not components of a mathematical equation whose computation will yield an easy solution. Rather, they are but special circumstances of general considerations which bear upon the employee's future prospects for acceptable behaviour, which is the essence of the whole corrective approach to discipline. How well or badly the grievor had behaved in the past is some indication of his likely future behaviour.

How aggravated or trivial was the offence is some clue to the risks the employer is being asked to run if the grievor is reinstated in employment. And how seriously the discharge will affect the grievor is at least one (but not the only) measure of whether a reasonable balance is struck between the other two considerations.

3   I accept the reasoning of those arbitrators who hold that breach of trust should not be automatic grounds for discharge. How, then, should I assess Mr. Keating's conduct?

First, it is said that the grievor had redeemed the pawned instruments and paid all rental charges, prior to being confronted by the CBC with this misconduct. If, indeed, he had voluntarily brought his misconduct to an end, the quality of the offence would not have been altered, but such an act might be evidence of contrition going to the question of self-awareness, and hence of his future prospects. In fact, it was virtually admitted that the grievor did what he did because he was warned by his supervisor that an investigation was imminent. In such circumstances "voluntary" rectification of misconduct neither alters the basic nature of the wrong nor diminishes the penalty.

Second, it is said that the grievor did not appreciate the wrongfulness of his conduct, although it may be properly characterized (in the words of union counsel) as "naive, foolish, stupid, or ill-conceived."

This allegedly missing element of guilty intention may be dealt with in one of two ways. The absence of guilty intention may be rejected as inconsistent with any sensible interpretation of the facts; this, in effect, was the CBC's primary position. Or the grievor's naiveté may be treated as evidence of insufficient understanding to warrant his continuation in an employment situation requiring keen awareness of his trust responsibility. Both responses, in my view, are equally plausible, and both have the effect of underlining the seriousness of the offence, rather than the contrary.

As to the facts, it is hard to accept that the grievor believed that he had a "colour of right" to act as he did, or that he acted under the innocent misapprehension that what he was doing was permissible. He knew he had to conceal these transactions from the CBC; that is why he never submitted his Instaccount vouchers. He knew he was misleading the merchants; he conceded expressly that they were relying on Instaccount rather than himself in giving him possession of the instruments in the first place. And he knew he was misleading the pawnbrokers; that is why he took instruments to two different pawnshops rather than arouse suspicion by trying to pawn two instruments in a single visit to one establishment.

As to the fitness of the grievor to continue to occupy a position of trust, if his version of the facts is believed, his equities are not strong. I have already sketched out the several respects in which the grievor proved himself unworthy of trust responsibilities, by conduct which was wrong *vis-à vis* three separate "victims" — the CBC, the merchants, and the pawnbrokers. It is conceivable that a wrong done to any one of these could be described as a lapse of judgment. But repeated wrongs done to all three over a period of several weeks, and as part of an integrated scheme, betray, at least, more than passing insensitivity to basic precepts of honesty.

I, therefore, decline to relieve the grievor of the consequences of his conduct on the basis that he did not believe it to be wrongful.

Third, and most important from the grievor's point of view, is his apparent attempt to ensure that no financial loss was incurred by the CBC. It is relatively clear that the grievor knew that he could intercept all invoices before they were approved for payment by the Accounts Payable department. This he was able to do, and did, by not submitting his Instaccount vouchers, thus forcing all invoices to be sent to him for verification, and by not in fact verifying any such invoices, thus preventing payment from being made.

The grievor also apparently cancelled two of his Instaccount vouchers by marking them "Cancel. Pay Cash on return. Personal." No such marking appeared on the two corresponding invoices submitted by the merchants to whom, however, he had given only Instaccount numbers, and not copies of the vouchers themselves. These two invoices were both addressed to "CBC c/o Alfred Keating" which, perhaps, lends some slight credence to his claim that he had declared his intention to pay for them personally. All other invoices relating to the grievor's personal transactions were similarly addressed, except for one. That one was issued in respect of a transaction which, it is conceded, was initially entered into by the greivor for the CBC and only subsequently converted into a transaction for himself. And, finally, the grievor gave uncontradicted evidence that he had orally advised the merchants involved on several occasions that he would be paying their accounts personally.

The effect of this evidence, however, is equivocal. Even interpreted in the light most favourable to the grievor, it can be read as a scheme on his part to prevent the CBC from discovering that he was using the Instaccount system to his own advantage, and to ensure that no payments were made by the CBC on behalf of himself. It does not convincingly exculpate him from the charge that he was misleading both the merchants who leased him the instruments, and the pawnbrokers who advanced him money. However the invoices were addressed (presumably at the grievor's direction), these facts remain clear: the goods were rented against Instaccount numbers; the invoices were addressed to the CBC, while the grievor's name appears only as that of a reference, not a primary contracting party; and the merchants were looking to the CBC for payment, rather than the grievor.

In all of this, there is the sole redeeming consideration that the grievor intercepted all invoices and thereby prevented the CBC's direct financial loss. But that does not change the basically improper and serious nature and quality of the grievor's conduct. As I have said, even without loss to the CBC, it verged on criminality.

I turn finally to evidence submitted on behalf of the grievor to indicate that he acted "bizarrely," atypically, and in such a way that there is no reason to anticipate any such conduct in the future.

The grievor testified that the motive for his behaviour was the desire to buy Christmas presents, and an expensive ring (worth over $500) for his girlfriend. Because he was already carrying a burden of debt over $12,000, partly as the result of old gambling obligations, he could not borrow money for these concededly altruistic purposes. He, therefore, decided to obtain the money by means of the scheme described above, but at the same time to redeem the pawns and pay the rental charges by earning money driving a taxicab during a period of his annual leave taken just prior to Christmas. The scheme failed; he could not earn enough as a cabdriver; and he had to extend the rental period because he could not redeem the pawned instruments.

I was not given extensive details of the grievor's earlier financial difficulties. However, Mr. Keating did say that he had previously gotten into difficulty by spending more than he earned, and that he was now obliged to pay about $650 per month in respect of his debts, in effect all he was making. In light of his past experience and present obligations, it would seem that the decision which led the grievor into his present difficulty — especially the purchase of an expensive ring — was not at all atypical. Rather, it was part of a continuing history of financial management.

It is true that the grievor conceded at the hearing that his conduct was "foolish," and that he answered "yes, sir" when union counsel asked him whether he had learned from this present experience (although he did not explain what he had learned). But there is nothing in these two, brief statements which would justify the conclusion that the grievor is unlikely to encounter similar financial pressures in the future, or deal with them more sensibly.

Finally, the grievor's work record of some eight years' duration was placed in evidence. It shows him to have been good at his job of set decoration, and it is free from any recorded notation of misconduct. There is no suggestion at all that the grievor has been guilty of breach of trust in the past. In certain circumstances, such a record might argue for a diminished penalty on the grounds that the grievor could be expected, on the basis of past behaviour, to correct the current problem. But such a prediction is difficult to make in the present case because the grievor's financial pressures have not abated; indeed, they have probably increased because he has earned virtually nothing since his discharge, while incurring additional debts of $1,000, and, probably accumulating additional debt charges to be added to his former burden of $12,000.

---

questions

1 If you had been the arbitrator in this case, what decision would you have handed down? Be concise and logically consistent in your reply.
2 What is your assessment of the nine factors suggested as mitigating factors, particularly item 9?

3 What do you think the arbitrator meant by the "theory of 'corrective discipline'"?

4 Does the evidence about the grievor's behaviour suggest that he has any redeeming features? Elaborate.

5 To what extent does a worker's work record "compensate" for the kind of behaviour exhibited by Mr. Keating?

6 Do you see any hope in Mr. Keating changing his behaviour to become a responsible worker? Elaborate.

The Effect of Criminal Conviction on Employment*

In The Matter of an Arbitration

Between:
Telecommunications Workers Union

And:
British Columbia Telephone Company
Re: Grievance of A.S. Gallant

There is little in issue factually in this case. The union questions the propriety of the dismissal of Mr. Gallant from his job by the employer on 20 June, 1978. Mr. Gallant is 26 years of age, married. He had been employed since 15 October, 1975, as an installer repairman. His total service was approximately 4 years. It is of some relevance to note that a strike prevailed between 20 November 1977 and 14 February, 1978.

Mr. Gallant's difficulties began, in sense, when he essayed to traffic in drugs in the Courtenay area on 18 November 1977 (M.D.A.), 3 December, 1977 (cocaine), 4 December, 1977 (cannabis) and 20 December — conspiring to traffic in cocaine in Victoria and on 6 March, 1978, driving with blood alcohol over the maximum permitted.

These activities led to his trial and conviction on the driving offence on 2 June, 1978, which produced a fine and a suspension of his licence to drive, and to his trial and conviction for the Courtenay drug offences on 15, 16, 19 June 1978, resulting in a sentence of 90 days to be served intermittently of which in fact he served 60 days, and to his trial and conviction in Victoria in April 1979 for the Victoria offence which resulted in a sentence of 30 days, of which he in fact served 20 days.

Filed as an exhibit was an item from the Comox Valley paper of 22 August, 1978, which described his conviction by a jury for the Courtenay drug cases, the judge's observations relative to the matter and to the fact adverted to by his counsel that he was employed by B.C. Tel and faced loss of that

---

*Permission to use this case was granted by Labour Canada. Minor deletions were made by the author for the purposes of this book and all names changed to prevent embarrassment to the individuals involved.

employment. It may be noted that the board was constituted on 22 November 1978 and first met on 9 March at which time the matter was by consent, adjourned *sine die* because of the necessity of disposition of the Victoria drug charge then outstanding.

Mr. Gallant's supervisor, Mr. Gillis, testified to calling Gallant in when the strike was over, discussing the pending charges of which he had read in the press, expressing concern about the "public image" of a telephone installer repairman in the circumstances and transferring Gallant to an "inside" job minimizing his public contact. In his view it was a sort of "created" job which in his mind would continue pending disposition of the charges against Mr. Gallant. He had also read of Mr. Gallant's driving charge in the press and was concerned about his licence because he was occasionally required to operate a vehicle in what Mr. Gillis called the "makeshift" job.

When Mr. Gallant was convicted of the Courtenay drug charges and so advised Mr. Gillis, the latter discussed the matter with the personnel department of the employer. There had been apparently some intimation to him that the pending Victoria drug charge might result in a lengthy sentence of imprisonment. In any event considering that Gallant had been convicted of the serious offence of trafficking in so-called "hard drugs" to the prejudice of his and his employer's image in the Courtenay community, the loss of his licence to drive (necessary for his job), a question about his access to Canadian Forces Base Comox by reason of his conviction and the pending criminal prosecution, it was determined to fire him.

Mr. Gallant's stance is that he was a good and competent employee, that he "fell" into these activities which were not in fact profitable and emphasized that though there were separate charges — all arose out of one foolish involvement.

Counsel "zeroed in" on the "Craig" case. In it an employee of B.C. Tel had been convicted of conspiracy to traffic in a large amount of marijuana. He was initially sentenced to a fine of $500.00 and one day's imprisonment. On appeal this was raised to two years less a day. In addition in the course of investigation, tools and materials, the property of the employer of a value of about $300.00 were recovered from Craig's home. He was dismissed from employment on 3 November 1976. Craig was apparently in custody for only six days following the C of A decision and then given a work release. Craig grieved his dismissal and the arbitrator (Professor T.) directed his reinstatement on 7 July, 1978, without compensation.

Employer's counsel says the Craig decision is distinguishable or wrong or both. Union's counsel says the Craig case was right, that Gallant's conduct is not as "bad" as Craig's and hence his dismissal was improper.

It may be invidious but nevertheless useful to make a comparison of the two cases. Craig had a good record of 11 years' service with the company, supporting a wife and three children. He was convicted of conspiracy to traffic in a large amount of marijuana which resulted in a sentence of two years less a day — actual incarceration amounting to 6 days.

Gallant had a good record 4 years with the company and supported a wife. He was convicted of three counts of trafficking (Mar., M.D.A., cocaine) and one of conspiring to traffic in cocaine resulting in a total sentence of 120 days of which he was incarcerated for 80 days on an intermittent basis. These several convictions arose out of basically one involvement. In addition he was convicted of impaired driving resulting in a fine and licence suspension. Professor T. noted that the fact of Craig's being an employee of the company was not publicized, though he suffered "public humiliation." The press in reporting Mr. Gallant's conviction and the judge's comments did advert to his being an employee of the company.

Professor T. adverted at some length to the circumstance of the recovery of tools and materials belonging to the Company from Craig's home. Professor T. went at some length into the prevalance of practices whereby employees contrary to rules might possess and use company tools and equipment for private purposes and concluded that the Company had not met the burden of proof of theft he reckoned applicable in cases of this kind, although he was obviously troubled by

> the installation of the extension telephone and the unexplained possession of chimes, screws, plugs and tool boxes,

he nevertheless concluded,

> When seen in the context of the grievor's long and commendable employment record, the theft and misappropriation of the items referred to earlier (which are of small monetary value) do not warrant a penalty of discharge.

In our view, with respect, this conduct by Craig puts him in a much graver situation than Mr. Gallant on a comparative basis. The question of value of items has to be considered in perspective. At the bottom line, the bulk of what the company sells is the rental of telephone service to individuals. The improper installation of an extension phone is theft of its basic product.

As to the issue of the comparative publicity between the two cases, we are not sure but that the reporting of the sentencing judge's remarks did not, in a sense, ameliorate any adverse effect the company sensed from the disclosure by his counsel (as reported) of his employment relationship with the employer.

Derived from earlier cases, Professor T. set out criteria for judging whether discharge for conduct outside the workplace is justified. These are:

1 The conduct of the grievor harms the Company's reputation or conduct.
2 The grievor's behaviour renders him unable to perform his duties satisfactorily.
3 The grievor's behaviour leads to a refusal, reluctance or inability of the other employees to work with him.
4 The grievor has been guilty of a serious breach of the Criminal Code and thus rendering his conduct injurious to the general reputation of the Company and its employees.
5 The grievor's conduct places difficulty in the way of the Company properly carrying out its function of efficiently managing its works and efficiently directing its working forces, adding that it was not necessary to prove all of these factors in order to sustain discharge.

. . .

questions

1 How serious is a criminal conviction on future employment of a worker? Elaborate.
2 What do you think of the criteria discussed by Professor T. regarding conduct outside the workplace with respect to the justification for discharge? Elaborate.
3 How would you assess Gallant's behaviour against these criteria? Elaborate.
4 By the time the case was heard, the grievor's driving licence had been reinstated. Would this have any effect on your decision? Elaborate.
5 Does the decision in the Craig case have any binding influence on your decision? Elaborate.
6 If you had been chairperson of the arbitration board, what decision would you have handed down? Be concise and logically consistent in your reply.

The Bell Canada Case* — Alcohol and Drug Abuse

IN THE MATTER OF AN ARBITRATION

BETWEEN:

Bell Canada
("the Company")

AND:

Communications Workers of Canada
("the Union")

AND IN THE MATTER OF A GRIEVANCE OF:

Helen Barry

A hearing in this matter was held in Toronto on January 25, 1984.

Award

This is a grievance against discharge. The grievor, Ms. Helen Barry, also grieves a letter of warning dated August 3, 1982. Both the warning and the discharge relate to the grievor's rate of innocent absenteeism. It is on that basis that the grievor was discharged pursuant to the following letter dated January 31, 1983:

Helen Barry

Your health problems continue to prevent you from fulfilling your obligation to

---

*Permission to use this case was granted by Labour Canada. Minor deletions were made by the author for the purposes of this book and all names changed to prevent embarrassment to the individuals involved.

be at work on a regular and consistent basis. This situation was reviewed in our letter dated 1982 08 03.

We regret, that in view of the circumstances, your employment with Bell Canada will terminate effective Monday, 1983 01 31.

"Velma Haire"
Manager Operator Services
Intercept

The foregoing letter of termination followed the earlier warning letter dated August 3, 1982 which is as follows:

Miss Helen Barry

This letter confirms our discussion of 1982 08 03 concerning your complete absence record. As you are aware, we do consider it to be excessive. Your absence record demonstrates that you are unable to report for work on a regular and consistent basis. If this performance continues, we will be obligated to terminate your employment with Bell Canada.

"Velma Haire"
Manager Operator Services
Intercept/SOST
6 Fl. 15 Asquith Ave.
Toronto, Ontario

The grievor maintains that both the warning letter and her termination were without just cause, contrary to the provisions of the collective agreement. She seeks reinstatement without loss of seniority and with full compensation for wages and benefits lost.

The facts are not disputed. The evidence establishes that the grievor is afflicted both by alcoholism and the abuse of prescription drugs. These difficulties caused the grievor chronic absenteeism throughout the entire period of her employment with the Company. The grievor was first employed as an operator for the period of one year in 1969. She voluntarily left the Company at that time to return to school. She was subsequently rehired as an operator in the centralized intercept office of the Company on Asquith Street in Toronto on September 14, 1981. The evidence of Ms. Velma Haire, manager of Operator Services at the time of the grievor's employment, establishes beyond any doubt that Ms. Barry recorded an excessive and unacceptable rate of absenteeism. While the grievor's record was adduced in evidence in some detail, it suffices to say that the Board is satisfied, on the unchallenged evidence before it, that the grievor's rate of absence between the time of her re-employment and the letter of warning of August 3, 1982 was approximately 45 to 50 per cent of her scheduled work time. We are satisfied that that rate of absence was far in excess of the average of other employees in the same division of the Company's operations and that the grievor's recurring and intermittent absences caused substantial inconvenience and disruption to the normal operations of her department.

The evidence also establishes that on a number of occasions the grievor received verbal counselling from Ms. Haire with respect to the rate and causes of her attendance problems. The evidence establishes that Ms. Haire met with the grievor in January, February and May of 1982 with a view both to impressing upon her the seriousness of her ongoing absenteeism and to offering any assistance, including medical assistance, which might help to correct her problem. While Ms. Haire had grounds to suspect that alcohol might be at the root of Ms. Barry's attendance problems, she had no firm evidence to confirm that suspicion. The grievor generally justified her absences in terms of short-term illnesses and family problems, offering explanations which her supervisor was not in a position to challenge. On November 4, 1982 Ms. Haire met with the grievor following another period of absence. Without confronting her or suggesting the nature of her problem, her supervisor did emphasize that, as an employee, she could take advantage of the Company's benefit plan which included some measure of wage protection during an extended leave of absence for illness, including mental illness, alcoholism and drug addiction. The grievor did not pursue that suggestion, and made no further inquiries either of the Company or her Union with respect to the possibility of treatment with the support of the Company's benefits plan.

The grievor's medical absences were monitored by the Company's medical health physician, Dr. Roberta Hall. In the normal course, documentation provided by the grievor in relation to her absences was forwarded to Dr. Hall. The documents were in the nature of confidential memoranda from her own physician which established that she was medically unfit for work and under a doctor's care. Although the Company's physician had as many as six interviews with the grievor relating to her medical absences and her ongoing ability to work, she did not treat Ms. Barry or give her any medical examination. In the course of her encounters with the grievor, Dr. Hall developed a concern that she might be abusing herself chemically. On several occasions she wrote reports to the grievor's supervisors, based on the medical records before her, indicating that in her view there was little or no basis to expect improvement in Ms. Barry's rate of attendance in the future. On four occasions Ms. Haire requested that Dr. Hall do an employee health assessment with respect to the grievor's future employability. Each time the report returned to Ms. Haire expressed a pessimistic prognosis for her future attendance. However, the evidence of Dr. Hall, and a memorandum which she wrote to Ms. Haire, establish that she did not view the grievor's situation as hopeless. In a memorandum dated December 16, 1982 Dr. Hall noted that in light of the grievor's age (30 years) and good physical condition it would be within her ability to end the problems giving rise to her absences, and that she could correct her attendance pattern in a period of three to six months. Unfortunately, Ms. Barry's attendance pattern was not corrected.

The grievor continued to believe that she could solve her own problem without medical assistance or outside help. In the result, her attendance problems continued, and indeed worsened, until the point of her termination.

Evidence was adduced respecting the grievor's change of attitude and her efforts at medical rehabilitation after her discharge. By her own account, following her termination, the grievor's abuse of alcohol increased and was further complicated by her continuing intake of prescription drugs, including a compound of codeine and barbiturates, a sedative and valium. Her own concern increased when she began to have progressively longer memory black-outs; in the earlier stages these were as short as five minutes and eventually lasted as long as a half-day in which she would have no recollection of what she had done. According to the grievor's evidence she first acknowledged that she was an alcoholic and was drug-dependent in the spring of 1983. In June of that year she approached her family physician, Dr. Joseph Tillman, and asked for medical help for her alcohol and drug dependency. Dr. Tillman referred her to the Donwood Institute where she was admitted for seven weeks of treatment on July 15, 1983.

A letter from Dr. J. Cohen, co-ordinator of medical services at the Donwood Institute, was adduced in evidence by agreement. It establishes that the grievor was diagnosed as having no substantial medical or psychiatric problems other than her alcohol and drug dependency. During her treatment she participated in an educational program of lectures and discussion groups and in group therapy. According to Dr. Cohen's letter, Ms. Barry took good advantage of her seven weeks' treatment and made appropriate gains during that time. She appeared positively motivated at the time of her discharge. She was then given a prescription for 50 mgs. Tempacil to be taken twice a day and was scheduled to participate in the Institute's two-year "continuing health services program" for continuing support during her recovery.

Her record of progress and attendance in that program has been less than perfect. She suffered relapses in September, October and November of 1983, although she did re-attend at the Institute on two occasions in December of 1983 and January of 1984 respectively, at which times she is described as appearing "well and chemically clear." Dr. Cohen's letter indicates that maintaining regular contact at the Donwood Institute would provide the grievor with the support necessary to work toward a complete recovery from her illness. Dr. Tillman also indicates, in a letter filed by the agreement of the parties, that the grievor has responded well and is now taking Antabuse, and that he sees "a good progress."

Substantial argument was addressed to the issue of the admissibility and weight to be given to evidence respecting the facts of the grievor's condition as they evolved after her discharge. Counsel for the Company argued that the correct arbitral authority in this regard looks to the date of termination as the appropriate time to determine whether the prognosis for the grievor's attendance was such as to justify her termination. In his submission subsequent events cannot be admitted to alter the merits of the grievor's case or to establish that the Company did not have just cause for her termination. In support of that proposition, reference was made to a number of cases: *Re Corporation of the City of Sudbury and Canadian Union of Public Employees, Local 207* (1981), 2 L.A.C.(3d) 161 (P. Picher), and two unreported decisions involving the parties to this grievance, *Bell Canada and Communications Workers of Canada*, a decision of a board of arbitration chaired by Mr. H. Frumkin, dated August 6, 1982 (Dion grievance) and a subsequent award between the same parties issued by a board of arbitration chaired by Mr. Andre Rousseau, dated November 4, 1982 (Veillet grievance).

Counsel for the Union argued that a board of arbitration is entitled to take into account circumstances arising after the discharge of an employee for innocent absenteeism, particularly as they may have a bearing on the discretion of the arbitrator to fashion a remedy with regard to the future employment of the grievor. Counsel for the Union referred the Board to *Re Canada Post Corporation and Canadian Union of Postal Workers* (1982), 6 L.A.C.(3d) 385 (Burkett) and another case involving the parties to the instant matter, *Re Bell Canada and Communications Workers of Canada* (1983), 10 L.A.C.(3d) 285 (Shime). The decision of the board chaired by Mr. Shime, which was apparently unanimous, plainly rejects the approach taken by arbitrators Rousseau and Frumkin in the cases noted above. In that case, as in the instant case, the grievor was an alcoholic who did not recognize or admit his problem until his dismissal. Between the time of his discharge and the arbitration of his grievance, the employee received treatment, joined Alcoholics Anonymous and became a complete abstainer. Relying in part on the authority of the Divisional Court of Ontario in *Re The Queen in right of Ontario and Grievance Settlement Board* (1980), 107 D.L.R.(3d) 599, and also based upon the provisions of article 15.06 of the collective agreement, which allow the board of arbitration "to modify the penalty in a just and reasonable manner," the board found that it could rely on facts and events occurring subsequent to the grievor's dismissal in considering a modification of the penalty. Taking into account the grievor's work record, his seniority and his rehabilitative steps, the board then reinstated the grievor, without compensation, subject to a number of conditions relating to continued rehabilitative treatment and his record of employment in the next two years.

It is generally accepted that an employer may terminate with justification when it is shown that an employee has a blameless shortcoming which undermines his or her employment relationship and where it is reasonably probable that the conditions giving rise to that shortcoming are not likely to improve. Blameless absenteeism, including absenteeism for alcoholism, can therefore entitle an employer to end the employment relationship if it is established that the employee has been and will continue to be incapable of regular attendance at work. (See *Re U.A.W., Local 458 and Massey-Ferguson Industries Ltd.* (1972), 24 L.A.C. 344 (Shime); *Re U.A.W. and Massey-Ferguson*

Ltd. (1969), 20 L.A.C. 370 (Weiler); *Re Atlas Steels Co. and Canadian Steelworkers' Union, Atlas Division* (1975), 8 L.A.C.(2d) 350 (Weatherill); *Re National Auto Radiator Manufacturing Co. Ltd. and U.A.W., Local 195* (1976), 11 L.A.C.(2d) (Brandt); *Re Niagara Structural Steel (St. Catharines) Ltd. and U.S.W., Local 7012* (1978), 18 L.A.C.(2d) (O'Shea); *Re City of Sudbury and C.U.P.E., Local 207* (*supra*); *Re Crousse-Hinds Canada Ltd. and U.A.W.* (1981), 3 L.A.C.(3d) 230 (Brown), and *Re American Standard, Division of Wabco-Standard Ltd. and Int'l Brotherhood of Pottery & Allied Workers* (1977), 14 L.A.C.(2d) (Burkett).)

The evidence in the instant case establishes that the Company has an enlightened policy with respect to the treatment of employees suffering from alcohol and drug dependencies. Among the materials filed in evidence is a notice distributed by the Company's personnel headquarters establishing a generous and sophisticated plan "for identifying and treating those employees with a health problem caused by alcohol or drug abuse." Without relating the details of that plan, it specifically acknowledges that alcohol and drug abuse are to be treated as an involuntary illness. The plan reflects an offer of assistance to the afflicted employee involving five components: identification, confrontation, referral, treatment and rehabilitation. Unfortunately, in the instant case, the best efforts of Ms. Haire and Dr. Hall did not succeed in bringing the grievor to the critical acknowledgement of her own drug dependence. If the grievor had recognized her own problem, and bearing in mind that the refusal to recognize alcoholism is itself part of the illness, Ms. Barry would in all likelihood have had the advantage of a leave of absence with medical benefits to help her overcome her problem, as well as the ongoing support of her employer in working toward her rehabilitation. We make that observation in full awareness of the similar comment by the unanimous board chaired by Mr. Shime, noted above, at p.287. In that instance the board reinstated the grievor.

. . .

---

questions

1 What do you think is meant by "innocent absenteeism"?
2 Do you think that the "Manager Operator Services" was forceful enough in dealing with the grievor?
3 Do you think that the Company's physician was assertive enough with the grievor?
4 What do you make of the conflicting awards by arbitrators in the other cases cited?
5 How far does an organization's responsibility go in cases such as this one? Elaborate.
6 Do you think that cases such as this should become the subject of an arbitration case when a worker has been discharged and has been away from the company for such an extended period of time? Elaborate.
7 If you had been the chairperson of the arbitration board, what award would you have handed down in this case? Give the rationale for your award.

A Case of Alleged Insubordination*

Public Service Staff Relations Act
Before the Public Service Staff Relations Board

Between:

Paul Potvin, Grievor,

And:

Treasury Board (Department of Veterans' Affairs), Employer.

Decision

This decision concerns a grievance referred to adjudication by Paul Potvin, an orderly, HS-PHS-5, employed at the Ste-Anne-de-Bellevue Hospital. The grievance reads as follows:

On May 25, 1983, I received a letter dated May 25, 1983 and signed by Ms. Audette Meursault, Assistant Director of Nursing, informing me that I was being suspended for three days.... I consider this decision unfair, arbitrary, discriminatory and unfounded.... This action is contrary to article I of my collective agreement. (unofficial translation)

The grievor requests the following corrective action:

1 That the employer delay implementation of the decision to suspend me until the final resolution of this grievance, as a demonstration of its good faith.
2 That the employer rescind the decision it announced in its letter of May 25, 1983 and that no other measures be imposed.
3 That the employer reinstate me in my duties, retroactively.
4 That the employer reimburse me fully for the pay I lost, retroactively and with no loss of benefits.
5 That all documents relating to this matter be removed from my personal file and destroyed in my presence and/or in the presence of my union representative, that these documents not be replaced with any other documents, and that no further use be made of such documents.
6 That the employer issue me a letter of apology exonerating me of all blame or suspicion.
7 That I receive the assurance that no reprisals will be taken against me for filing this grievance.
8 That the employer hold consultations at each and every level of the grievance procedure, subject to any mutual agreement to dispense with one or more levels.
9 That I be present during these consultations, at the employer's expense.
10 That the employer comply with article I of my collective agreement. (unofficial translation)

*Permission to use this case was granted by the Public Service Staff Relations Board. Minor deletions were made by the author for the purposes of this book and all names changed to prevent embarrassment to the individuals involved.

Evidence

Mss. France Joly, Sylvie-Anne Poirier, and Audette Meursault, and Mr. Berthelot Bélanger testified for the employer and filed the following exhibits:

Exhibit 1: Letter of May 25, 1983, signed by Ms. Audette Meursault, suspending the grievor without pay on June 1, 2, and 3, 1983 for insubordination.

Exhibit 2: (filed jointly) Letters of March 22, 1982, May 20, 1982, August 3, 1982, August 6, 1981, February 24, 1982, November 25, 1982, December 7, 1982 and March 17, 1983, constituting the grievor's personal file.

I ordered the witnesses excluded. The grievor did not present any evidence and his representative argued that the employer had not proved the misconduct alleged against the grievor.

Ms. France Joly testified that she has worked at the Ste-Anne-de-Bellevue Hospital for six years. She is a nursing team leader. She works with the grievor, an orderly, whose job it is to provide basic care to the patients at the Hospital. She explained that a team comprises one or two nurses and a number of orderlies. The nurse asks the orderly to provide the care that the patients require. The team leader decides what duties the nurses perform and how many orderlies are needed. The duties are then allocated among the team members.

On May 19, 1983, the team consisted of three nurses and a single orderly, the grievor. Ms. Joly was the grievor's immediate supervisor that day and the grievor was responsible to Ms. Sylvie-Anne Poirier and Ms. Boisvert. Mr. Potvin and the witness worked from 7:30 a.m. until 3:30 p.m. They were entitled to half an hour for lunch, but this half-hour was not always taken at the same time; it varied, depending on the department's needs. In principle, the first lunch break was at 11:15 a.m. The second was around 12:00 noon or 12:10 p.m., depending on how long it took to prepare the patients' lunches. On May 19, Ms. Joly had 34 patients under her care. The majority were bedridden, confused and ambulatory to varying degrees. Mr. Potvin and Ms. Poirier had seated a patient by the name of Sim on the toilet. Mr. Sim was difficult to handle, nervous, hesitant and very stiff, was not co-operating and was confused. He weighed about 150 pounds. He was in the bathroom for some fifteen or twenty minutes.

Ms. Joly explained that it was not part of the nurses' duties to put a patient like Mr. Sim into bed. She knew the technique, but did not do this work routinely, and when she did, she was assisted by an orderly. On May 19, around 11:15 a.m., the witness was some thirty feet away from the grievor. She heard Ms. Poirier twice call out "Paul, Paul." Ms. Poirier was 10 to 15 feet away from Ms. Joly and behind the grievor who was in front of the elevator, opposite Ms. Joly. The witness then said in a rather loud voice, "Paul, come and help us put Mr. Sim to bed." Mr. Potvin answered, "I'm down for the first lunch hour; I'm going down," to which Ms. Joly replied, "I'm asking you to put off your lunch and come and help us put Mr. Sim to bed right now." Mr. Potvin replied, "All you had to do was schedule two orderlies. I'm going to lunch." The grievor then took the elevator and went downstairs.

The witness testified that the three nurses (Sylvie-Anne Poirier, Lyne Boleyn and France Joly) had to put Mr. Sim into bed, and that they had problems doing so. It took five minutes. They had to get him up from the toilet, wipe him, bring him to the bed and put him into it. Once Mr. Sim was in bed, Ms. Joly telephoned Mr. Bélanger, the Co-ordinator, around 11:20 a.m. to inform him of the incident. Around noon, Mr. Bélanger called her back to ask whether Mr. Potvin was back from lunch and asked her to tell him to report to the personnel office. When Mr. Potvin returned from lunch at noon, she told him she was going to make a report to Mr. Berthelot Bélanger, Co-ordinator, on his refusal and attitude. The grievor replied, "Make a report. Anyway, I'm sick. I'm going home." Mr. Potvin went to the personnel office and was away some 30 to 50 minutes.

Sylvie-Anne Poirier testified that she has been a nurse and team leader at the Ste-Anne-de-Bellevue Hospital for six years. She was in charge of a nursing team that included an orderly. On May 19, 1983, she was working with the grievor. Ms. Joly was a fellow nurse. She testified that, on May 19, around 10:50 or 10:55 a.m., she and Mr. Potvin had seated patient Sim on the toilet. Mr. Sim's limbs were stiff and he was a difficult patient. He weighed about 140 pounds.

She described the incident as follows. Mr. Potvin informed nurses France Joly, Lyne Boleyn and Sylvie-Anne Poirier that he was going to lunch. He said, "I'm going to lunch," and no one objected. However, Sylvie-Anne Poirier, who is a quiet person, suddenly exclaimed, "Oh my God, Mr. Sim is still in the bathroom!" and she immediately called out in a normal tone of voice, "Paul, Paul," but the grievor did not answer. She stated that Mr. Potvin may not have heard her. Ms. Joly, who was at the nurses' station, ten feet away from Mr. Potvin, turned around and saw the grievor in front of the elevator. She then asked him to help and said to him, "Will you delay your lunch a little?" Mr. Potvin replied, "You should have scheduled more orderlies. If the elevator had come earlier, I would be gone now," and he got into the elevator. Ms. Joly told him she was going to make a report on the incident and he replied, "Make a report. Anyway, I'm booking off sick. All you had to do was schedule two orderlies."

Nurses France Joly, Lyne Boleyn and Sylvie-Anne Poirier put patient Sim back to bed. France Joly then telephoned Mr. Bélanger and Mr. Potvin returned from lunch around noon. Ms. Poirier testified that she did not discuss the incident with Ms. Joly in any detail because the lunch hour was a very busy time. Ms. Joly said that she was going to make a written report, which she did. The witness also made a report.

Berthelot Bélanger testified that he has worked the Ste-Anne-de-Bellevue Hospital since October 1982. He was co-ordinator of six work units. He was responsible for scheduling, leave applications, patient care and work assignments. He testified that, on May 19, 1983, around 11:25 a.m., he received a first call from Ms. Joly who explained to him that Mr. Potvin had just left. She had asked the grievor repeatedly to help her, but Mr. Potvin took the elevator. Ms. Joly added that she had approached the grievor to make sure that he had heard her. Ms. Joly told Mr. Bélanger that she had said to Mr. Potvin, "Will you put off your lunch a few minutes?", to which Mr. Potvin had replied, "If the elevator had come earlier, I would be gone now."

Ms. Joly explained to Mr. Bélanger that she needed help with Mr. Sim. Mr. Bélanger recalled that Ms. Joly spoke to Mr. Potvin more than once. The first time, she said to him, "Will you come here and help us?" The second time she said, "Will you put off your lunch hour a few minutes?" Ms. Joly also told the witness that another nurse had also asked Mr. Potvin to help her.

Mr. Bélanger discussed the incident with the three nurses involved and noted down the most important facts in a report. He also asked the nurses to make a written report.

Around noon, he called unit 8B back to ask whether Mr. Potvin had returned from lunch and to ask him to come and see him. At noon, the grievor came to the personnel office, and during the afternoon of May 19, he came to the witness's office to discuss the incident in 8B.

Mr. Bélanger asked the grievor three specific questions:

Why did you leave the unit?, to which Mr. Potvin replied that it was 11:15 a.m., his lunchtime, and he was leaving anyway.

Did you hear the nurses' words? and Mr. Bélanger repeated the nurses' words: "Will you put off your lunch? Come and help us get Mr. Sim up right away." Mr. Potvin did not remember the exact words the nurses used.

Did you understand what the nurses said? Mr. Potvin simply replied, "Yes."

Mr. Bélanger then stated that he explained to the grievor that this situation was intolerable and constituted insubordination. The grievor replied that the employer was responsible for assigning the necessary personnel and that he did not want to miss his lunch break to which he was entitled. Mr. Bélanger was angered by this incident. He tried to make the grievor understand the consequences of his action in terms of his responsibilities and those of the unit.

Mr. Bélanger consulted the staff relations officer, Charles Larocque, his immediate superior, and Ms. Audette Meursault regarding the appropriate disciplinary action for this incident.

Audette Meursault has been assistant director of nursing at the Ste-Anne-de-Bellevue Hospital for two years. She wrote the disciplinary letter of May 25, 1983 (Exhibit 1) which imposed a three-day suspension served on June 1, 2 and 3, 1983. She testified that she studied the reports on the incident from the nurses (Mss. Joly, Poirier and Boleyn) and from Mr. Bélanger, the co-ordinator, as well as the grievor's disciplinary record (Exhibit 2), and concluded that he deserved a three-day suspension. He had job responsibilities that consisted in doing the work assigned by the nurses to ensure the care and comfort of the patients. Ms. Meursault testified that the grievor had received a two-day suspension earlier for a similar offence. Ms. Meursault also took into consideration the nature of the assistance requested, the fact that the patient was on the toilet, the kind of patient, and the fact that the patient's care and comfort took precedence. Employee Potvin had no valid reason to refuse to assist the nurse when she asked for help.

The witness did not discuss the incident with the grievor. She left this matter to the nurses and the co-ordinator. She could not say with certainty that she had discussed the incident with Ms. Poirier and Ms. Joly, but said that she probably saw them. She did discuss the incident with Mr. Bélanger.

Arguments

Ms. Roy, counsel for the employer, argued that the grievor's insubordination was serious. She added that the employer proved its allegation according to the balance of probabilities. The evidence established that an order was given, even if the witnesses did not agree on the exact words used by Ms. Joly. It was also clear that the grievor did not obey the order and that he went to have his lunch instead of helping the nurses, as was his duty. He was therefore guilty of insubordination. Ms. Roy cited *Varzeliotis* (166-2-9721) to illustrate the principles that apply in cases of insubordination.

Mr. Potvin worked in a hospital where there was no set lunch hour. This hospital was responsible for the health and care of veterans and it was essential that the obligations to the patients be fulfilled. For this reason, the grievor's insubordination was very serious. Ms. Roy cited *Reiner Busse* (166-2-9535) in which a three-day suspension was imposed, *Collective Agreement Arbitration in Canada* by Palmer, at pages 11 and 12, and *Terrence S. Arnfinson* (166-2-13851), in which Mr. Arnfinson displayed an attitude similar to Mr. Potvin. Mr. Arnfinson had said, "I will be back when I get my laundry done." This attitude therefore constituted insubordination.

Ms. Roy argued that the grievor could easily have obeyed the order, and in support of this argument, she cited *Re International Nickel Co. of Canada Ltd. and United Steelworkers*, 6 L.A.C. (2d) 172. In *Re United Steelworkers and Lake Ontario Steel Co. Ltd.* 19 L.A.C. 103, where the lunch break was also at issue, it was held that the employer could reasonably interrupt an employee's lunch break. In the present case, the employer asked the grievor to perform a necessary duty that would not have taken much time. The employer's request was reasonable.

Citing *Gareau* (166-2-11454) and *Varzeliotis*, (supra), Ms. Roy argued that I should not reduce the three-day suspension because it would deter Mr. Potvin from any further such behaviour.

Mr. Dupuis argued that there was no evidence to substantiate the employer's allegation and referred in this regard to the disciplinary letter that imposed the three-day suspension (Exhibit E-1). The letter stated that Ms. Meursault reported Ms. Joly's statements. The onus of proof was on the employer who must prove that the grievor refused to obey an order. Mr. Dupuis wondered whether Ms. Joly really made the remarks attributed to her in the disciplinary letter. Did Ms. Joly ask Mr. Potvin to delay his lunch a few minutes and help her move a patient? The letter stated that Ms. Joly made her request in a direct manner and, furthermore, that she spoke the following words to him in a clear and polite tone of voice: "Put off your lunch a few minutes and come and help us lift Mr. Sim off the toilet and put him into bed right away." Mr. Dupuis argued that the statements attributed to Ms. Joly were a distortion of the truth and of the actual words she used.

Mr. Dupuis cited the three principles that apply in cases of insubordination as described in *Canadian Labour Arbitration,* by Brown and Beatty, and in *"Les Mesures disciplinaires...",* by Claude Daoût, who stated at page 323 of his work that the order must be clear, unequivocal, and clearly understood by the employee. The order must be given by a person in authority, during working hours.

Reviewing the evidence, Mr. Dupuis noted that the grievor asked the three nurses on his team for permission to go to lunch. They did not object. When Ms. Poirier realized that Mr. Sim was still in the bathroom, she uttered an exclamation and called out "Paul, Paul." Could this exclamation be considered an order? Moreover, Ms. Poirier testified that she heard Ms. Joly say to the grievor, "Will you put off your lunch hour?" This question was a request. It was not a command. This question was not therefore an order. Ms. Poirier further testified that Ms. Joly added, "Will you help us?" Again, this question was not a command, and even if one wanted to argue that Mr. Potvin clearly understood the question, it was not an order. Mr. Dupuis argued that precedent established that the employer must prove that an order was given. However, in this case, the words used were "Will you," and one must ask whether this expression was an order or merely a request that could be refused. In *Emile R. André* (166-2-12239), Mrs. Falardeau-Ramsay showed how this expression could be distorted. The question "Will you" was not an order. The testimony of the employer's witnesses regarding whether Mr. Potvin actually received an order was contradictory and confused.

Mr. Dupuis argued that the employer did not adduce any *prima facie* evidence. Since the letter of May 25, 1983 (Exhibit 1) did not establish the truth about the incident, and since there was no insubordination, the grievor did not have to answer the allegation.

On this point, Mr. Dupuis cited *Adam Butcher* (166-2-13507), a decision rendered by Leon Mitchell, Q.C., in which the grievor did not testify and in which the adjudicator held that the onus was on the employer to establish the facts as they happened. Mr. Dupuis argued that the employer did not prove that the grievor was guilty of the misconduct alleged against him, and in support of this argument, he cited *Gareau,* (supra), at page 23. Moreover, the fact that Mr. Potvin sought permission to go to lunch showed that he was not insubordinate or disrespectful. Furthermore, no proof was adduced that Mr. Potvin's alleged misconduct affected the Hospital's productivity. For these reasons, Mr. Dupuis asked that the three-day suspension be rescinded, that the disciplinary letter be removed from the grievor's file and destroyed, and that all the benefits denied Mr. Potvin as a result of this three-day suspension be restored to him. If a penalty was warranted, Mr. Dupuis asked that the three-day suspension be reduced to a reprimand, as decided in *Emile André, supra*.

In reply, Ms. Roy argued that the employer, with whom the burden of proof rested in this case, had proved insubordination. The evidence revealed that the incident described by the witnesses was not a figment of their imagination or a "distortion," as the grievor's representative claimed. There was uncontradicted evidence that Mr. Potvin told Mr. Bélanger that he understood what was being asked of him. Mr. Dupuis' claim that Mr. Potvin sought permission to go to lunch was not valid. The grievor merely said that he was going to lunch and this statement was not a request for permission. Moreover, there was no evidence that he was granted permission. On the contrary, Ms. Joly testified that she in no way gave Mr. Potvin permission to leave the workplace.

. . .

questions

1 What is the major issue involved in this case? Elaborate.
2 For whom do you think the environment in which this case took place made it easier to prove a point — the grievor or the employer? Elaborate.
3 Do you think that the nurses needed to make such a fuss over putting a 150-pound man into bed? Why did they do so?
4 If you had been counsel for the grievor, what approach would you have taken during the arbitration proceedings? Elaborate.
5 If you had been the arbitrator, what award would you have handed down? Give the full rationale in support of your award.

Falsification of Time Cards*

In The Matter of an Arbitration

Between:
Western Airlines, hereafter referred to as the "Employer"

And:
Brotherhood of Railway and Airline Clerks, Canada
(on behalf of J. Ward and hereafter referred to as the "Union")

This proceeding occurred pursuant to Section 36 of the Collective Agreement

*Permission to use this case was granted by Labour Canada. Minor deletions were made by the author for the purposes of this book and all names changed to prevent embarrassment to the individuals involved.

between the parties. The parties agreed that the Board was properly constituted to hear the case and that the issue before the Board was as follows:

> Was the termination of [the employment of] the grievor, J. Ward, for just cause? If not, what shall be the remedy?

Specifically, the offence for which the grievor was discharged was the alleged falsification of his time card August 28, 1978. The parties agreed to waive the time limits for issuing an award in the collective agreement.

Evidence presented by the Employer indicated that the Grievor arrived late at his work station, the passenger check-in counter in the Vancouver International Airport August 28. His supervisor, Mr. Goodwin, testified that Mr. Ward's starting time that day was 8:00 a.m., and that he arrived between 8:20 and 8:25. Mr. Waugh, who was in operations August 28, saw the Grievor enter the building at 8:10 a.m.; a few minutes later Mr. Ward entered the operations office, and the two talked for 7 or 8 minutes. Because Mr. Ward arrived late, passengers were not checked in at the normal rate. The flight scheduled to depart at 8:50 a.m. was late, although other factors may have caused the delay. Delayed departures are not uncommon in August.

Later that morning, when he was in the operations area, Mr. Goodwin checked Mr. Ward's time card. The card had the single digit "8" in the box for punching in August 28. The time clock normally imprints one or more digits for the hour, followed by a decimal, a digit to indicate tenths of an hour, plus one or more letters corresponding to the day of the week. Mr. Waugh also testified that the time card contained only an "8" later that morning. He notified Mr. Gordon, the Assistant Manager for the station, who made a photocopy of the card, date stamped the copy, and returned the card to its normal position. The next day Mr. Gordon examined the time card and found it contained the notation "8.AM" for August 28, i.e. showing that Mr. Ward had punched in at 8:00 a.m. There was no mark on the card for punching out that day. Again he made a copy of the card and dated the copy. Examples of both copies were presented to the Board as evidence. On August 29 Mr. Gordon commenced disciplinary action that ended in the Grievor's discharge.

According to Mr. Gordon, the Employer regards falsification of time cards as a grave matter. The Employer's publication "You and Your Job," distributed to employees, warns that altering a time card is "a serious offense and is considered cause for dismissal." An excerpt from the publication, plus a management bulletin containing similar language, were posted in the operations area in June 1978. There were marks opposite Mr. Ward's name on the briefing sheet which might have been his initials, indicating that he had read the notice.

The parties recently negotiated their first collective agreement for the Vancouver station, and this case was the first example of an employee having been charged with falsification of a time card. Management witnesses could recall no such incidents prior to certification of the Union. Problems with time cards improperly filled in have arisen from time to time.

The Union based its case on Mr. Ward's testimony, the burden of proof on the Employer, and management's failure to comply with provisions of the grievance procedure.

Mr. Ward stated he arrived on time August 28 and punched in at 8:00 a.m., changed into his uniform in the locker room, and proceeded to his work station. He admitted that he might have arrived at his work station five or ten minutes late. He completed his shift, but forgot to punch out at the end of the day. Mr. Ward denied altering the time card in any way. When he received a disciplinary letter August 29, Mr. Gordon refused to elaborate on the specifics of the charge against him. The letter referred to "falsification of company records — your time card," and the Grievor assumed it referred to his failure to punch out on August 28. On August 29 or soon thereafter, the Union representative assisting him with his grievance explained the specific offense with which he was charged.

The Union pointed to Section 33B of the Collective Agreement which states: "an employee charged with an offense...shall be furnished with a letter...stating the precise charge against him...." According to the Union, the Employer's letter of August 29 failed to meet this requirement, thereby denying the Grievor natural justice in the disciplinary hearing that followed.

In analyzing this case, the Union's procedural argument is an appropriate starting point. The contract requires statement of a "precise charge" against an employee in the Employer's letter. The letter referred to "falsification" of a time card. To have amplified on that statement might have required several paragraphs, given the problem of describing the time card before and after the alleged alteration of the original entry. Such amplification would have contained primarily the facts of the incident leading to the charge. Moreover, the Employer supplied the Union with the full facts of the case shortly after the letter was issued. By the Union's admission, the purpose of Section 33B is to ensure that an employee knows the charges against him when preparing his defense. Mr. Ward had the relevant facts of the charges well before the hearing. Therefore, we rule that the Employer fulfilled the requirements of Section 33B.

The Union also asserted that the Employer had to establish the basic facts on which the action was based. In this category of case, where an employee's morality has been attacked, guilt must be demonstrated beyond reasonable doubt. The Union claim raises the issue of the standard of proof, inevitably a question to be addressed in a case of alleged misconduct. The general principle applied is summarized by Brown and Beatty, *Canadian Labour Arbitration* at pp. 289-291. In general, arbitrators require the employer to prove its case on "the balance of probabilities." They note, "at one time where the alleged misconduct might have involved a criminal offense, some arbitrators required the employer to prove beyond a reasonable doubt, that is clearly no longer the prevailing principle" (*Ibid.* at p. 290). Some arbitrators hold that the balance of probabilities is the appropriate standard, though many others demand a higher standard, but still less than the criminal burden of proof. In the latter case, the standard required is more stringent the more serious the alleged misconduct. "Thus, it is said that an allegation of criminal misconduct must be proven by 'clear evidence' or a standard of 'reasonable probability'" (*Ibid.* at p. 291).

In this case, criminal conduct was not alleged. Many of the decisions cited by Brown and Beatty as justifying a standard of proof substantially higher than the civil burden dealt with employee theft of company property, or similar offenses. Although the Employer asserted that the Grievor's intent was dishonest, there was no allegation of material or monetary loss. Therefore, the appropriate standard of proof in this case is the balance of probabilities.

Using this standard, we find that the Grievor did falsify his time card. The Employer presented documentary evidence that someone altered the time card, an assertion the Union admitted. Both Mr. Goodwin and Mr. Waugh gave testimony consistent with Mr. Ward arriving at his work station between 8:20 and 8:25. Because of their jobs, both witnesses must be aware of the time of day, so their evidence has special weight. We prefer their testimony to that of Mr. Ward when he claimed to have arrived at the time clock by 8:00. While the case against Mr. Ward is circumstantial, his own account of the events of August 28 was confused. We find no other probable explanation for the changes in the time card except action by Mr. Ward.

This finding raises the question of the appropriate penalty. Counsel for each party submitted copies of past arbitration awards by employees of the Employer involving falsification of time cards. All of the cases were from the United States. Clearly, prior decisions within the Employer deserve careful consideration by this Board. But the incident occurred in Canada, and this proceeding was governed by the *Canada Labour Code,* so due consideration must be given to Canadian practice.

A review of the cases heard elsewhere in the Employer's system reveals that discharges for *falsification* of time cards is not the norm. In four cases (Rockey, Letourneau, Anderson, and Orcutt) the arbitrator ruled that the Employer had not demonstrated guilt beyond a reasonable doubt, and the grievors were found guilty of some infraction that warranted discipline. In two cases (Farias and McSwain), discharges were upheld in light of the grievor's past record. In the *Farias* case, the arbitrator stated,

> While this referee would find it difficult to support discharges solely on the issue of questionable falsification of a time card, when it is related to a clear attempt to avoid potential discharge for absence and tardiness and when there is no question the employee did falsify his time card, then just cause for discharge would seem to be well established.

In the *McSwain* case, the grievor's discharge was upheld partly because of three previous offenses.

The Employer's experience seems typical in American arbitral jurisprudence. In a thoroughly researched decision, involving falsification of a time card, Arbitrator Williams in *Park 'N Fly of Texas and International Association of Machinists* (1975) 64 L.A. 1009 at 1013, wrote, "It is clear that arbitrators generally uphold discipline in cases similar to the subject one, but tend to consider discharge, demotion, etc. as too severe." In *National Airlines and International Association of Machinists* (1973) 61 L.D. 681 (Cushman), the arbitrator upheld the discharge of an employee who falsified his time card for 1 hour 45 minutes in light of his very poor work record.

Few similar cases seem to have been decided in Canada. Falsification of time cards is typically related to piece rates, so the offense implies an attempt to secure payment for work not performed. Such cases raise issues of theft and criminal conduct mentioned earlier, but which are absent here (See *United Automobile Workers, Local 127 and Ontario Steel Products Ltd.* (1962) 13 LAC 197 (Beardall). In one case an employee signed his time sheet for a full shift, even though the arbitrator concluded he had arrived late, and the award sustained the penalty of demotion. (*International Chemical Workers, Local 721 and Brockville Chemical Industries* (1971) 23 LAC 336 (Shime).)

In assessing a penalty for such an offense, several criteria seem appropriate. Dishonesty by an employee of any variety is a serious offense and should not be treated lightly. The Employer had taken reasonable action to ensure employees knew the gravity of the offense. But the degree of trust in an employee's job should be considered. The employee's work record, seniority, and possible motive are also important. Finally the magnitude of the offense should be considered.

In this case, the Grievor's job does not involve an unusual amount of trust. His arrival and departures are subject to monitoring. He has approximately 2.5 years of seniority, with no record of previous disciplinary action of any type. Beyond concealing his negligent arrival, he had no motive to deceive the Employer. Finally, his offense did not entail a claim for a substantial amount of money, perhaps $2.00.

. . .

questions

1 What procedural rules did the arbitration board dispose of in the first paragraph of the case?
2 In your view, did the charge "falsification of company records—your time card" meet the requirement of Section 33B of the collective agreement?
3 What standard of proof was the employer required to provide? Elaborate.
4 Would you as the arbitrator, uphold the discharge in this case or would you change the penalty? Be specific and logical in your answer.

A Dispute Over Overtime Rates of Pay*

In The Matter of an Arbitration

Between:
The Halifax Longshoremen's Association, I.L.A. local 269, hereinafter called
"The Union" of the One Part:

And:
The Maritime Employers Association, hereinafter called
"The Employer" of the Other Part:

There were no preliminary objections, and the parties agreed that the Arbitrator was properly seized with jurisdiction.

Exhibits filed by the Union were:
A–1 — Collective Agreement between the parties, dated July 11, 1978.
A–2 — Letter of grievance, dated January 14, 1980, signed by G.W. Crowley, to Mr. R.L. Fenn.

The grievance in issue is amount of pay per hour that four gangs of longshoremen are to receive, for work performed from noon hour, December 24, 1979, to 3:30 p.m. of that day, and six men, for a further period to 4:45 p.m., for line work, pursuant to Article 14.08 of the Agreement, which is as follows:

14.08 The rates of pay for all hours worked on the following holidays or their day of observance shall be as per the appended Schedule of Wages: Sundays, Good Friday, Sovereign's Birthday on day proclaimed, Canada Day, Labour Day, Remembrance Day, Thanksgiving Day and Boxing Day.

Furthermore, with the exceptions of emergency work and lines, there shall be no work during the following periods:

LABOUR DAY: From 8:00 A.M. on Labour Day to 8:00 A.M. the following day.

CHRISTMAS DAY: From noon on December 24th (unless ship can finish in which case work may be performed up to 5:00 P.M.) until 1:00 P.M. on December 26th.

NEW YEAR'S DAY: from 5:00 P.M. on December 31st until 8:00 A.M. on January 2nd.

The rates of pay for emergency work and lines performed during the Christmas and New Year's periods set forth above shall be double the rates shown for Holidays in the appended wage schedules.

On December 23, 1979, the *M.V. Haul Trotter* arrived at Autoport in Dartmouth, N.S. to unload automobiles. Stevco Marine, the stevedoring company engaged to unload the ship, requested four gangs of longshoremen, to work the ship commencing at 8:00 a.m. December 24, 1979, with it being

---

*Permission to use this case was granted by Labour Canada. Minor deletions were made by the author for the purposes of this book and all names changed to prevent embarrassment to the individuals involved.

understood at the time of the request that the work would finish at noon, allowing for the Christmas Day holiday as per Article 14.08, outlined above.

Don Brown, a foreman of one of the gangs, gave evidence that he reported to Autoport on December 24, 1979, at 8:00 a.m., with his gang. He was requested to have a twelve man gang, but only ten men showed up and he requested from the dispatcher a further two men. Shortly after 8:00 a.m. four more men per gang were requested from the dispatcher, M. Lester.

Mr. Brown further indicated that at approximately 10:30 to 11:00 a.m. he was requested by the walking boss to find out how many of his men would be prepared to work beyond noon, to finish unloading of the ship *M.V. Haul Trotter*, because it was decided earlier that morning to work the vessel to finish, in order for it to clear Port, and not incur the expenses of a layover until sometime after 1:00 p.m. on December 26, 1979. Mr. Brown indicated that five men would not work beyond noon, in his gang; and, as a result, a call was made to the dispatcher, M. Lester, to obtain further fill-ins, in order that the unloading could be finished, and the ship clear Port.

The gangs worked through lunch hour, with additional fill-ins arriving, and, in the words of Mr. Brown, everything was in an "uproar," to finish the unloading of the ship.

The other witness for the Union, Mr. M. Lester, was the dispatcher on duty at the Hiring Hall, on both Sunday, December 23, 1979, and December 24th, 1979. In his evidence, he stated that he was requested by the Superintendent of Stevco Marine, on Sunday, December 23, 1979, to have four gangs available for the morning of the 24th, at 8:00 a.m., to work the ship. And his evidence further indicated that it was only until noon that the gangs would be required for work. As a result, he got in touch with four foremen, one of whom was Mr. Brown, to line up their gangs, for the four hours of work on the *M.V. Haul Trotter*, at Autoport, on the 24th of December.

He further indicated that, as the ship docked at 8:15 p.m. on the 23rd of December, the Company, Stevco Marine, could have placed an order for four gangs to commence work at 6:00 p.m. on the 23rd of December, or midnight on the 23rd of December, if it was considered urgent to unload the ship, in order for it to clear Port as soon as possible.

He further indicated that D. Craig, of Stevco Marine, got in touch with him on the morning of December 24th (Christmas Eve) at approximately 10:30 a.m., placing an order for more men to come over, to finish the ship, as it had been decided that the ship had to clear Port as soon as possible.

Throughout the evidence of Brown and Lester, the circumstances of having the ship unloaded as soon as possible, in order to clear the Port, was made by both witnesses, which evidence was not rebutted by the Employer.

The Employer takes the position that in these circumstances, the holiday for Christmas Day does not commence until 5:00 p.m. on December 24th, as outlined in Article 14.08, allowing work to 5:00 p.m. to finish a ship; and, therefore, the men are only entitled to receive $18.50 per hour...for working through lunch hour, from noon on December 24th, until finish, at 3:30 p.m., for all but six men who remained, to let the lines go, until 4:45 p.m.

The Union, in their submission, argued that, in the circumstances the work performed was in the nature of an emergency, in order for the ship *M.V. Haul Trotter* to clear Port, and that the Christmas Holiday commenced at noon, and therefore the Christmas Holiday pay provisions, of double-double time, bringing the rate of $74.00 per hour, is applicable in the circumstances.

questions

1 In your view, is the language of section 14.08 of the collective agreement clear? Elaborate.
2 What do you make of the conflicting claims of the parties on the question of overtime pay?
3 If you had been the arbitrator, would you have granted double-double time as requested by the union? Elaborate and be as concise as possible.
4 If you were acting as a mediator in the next round of negotiations, what changes, if any, would you make in the wording of section 14.08? Elaborate.

Indecisiveness in Applying a Disciplinary Penalty*

Public Service Staff Relations Act
Before the Public Service Staff Relations Board

Between:
T. Smith, Grievor,

And:
Treasury Board (Post Office Department), Employer

Mr. T. Smith filed a grievance under date of September 16, 1978 reading:

I grieve that I am being disciplined without just cause, resulting in my being suspended. Commencing August 28, 1978.
Corrective Action Requested: Full redress.

The grounds relied upon by the employer for the suspension of the grievor are set out in a letter of September 1, 1978 and signed by the Postmaster A. Jones.

The purpose of this letter is to advise you that you are being suspended from duty for a period of twenty (20) working days from 6:35 A.M. August 28th, 1978 to 3:05 P.M. September 25th, 1978.

*Permission to use this case was granted by the Public Service Staff Relations Board. Minor deletions were made by the author for the purposes of this book and all names changed to prevent embarrassment to the individuals involved.

The reason for this suspension is your act of major misconduct on Friday, August 18th, 1978 in that you did physically assault P.O. Sup 1, J. McGough in the Letter Carrier Section.

I have had the opportunity to review the facts and the situation again as well as revised thinking on corrective discipline in this Region. In view of this I have decided that this suspension of twenty (20) days is appropriate.

Further, the intention of this revised suspension is to impress upon you the serious nature of these actions. You chose not to exercise the options open to you when you observed the supervisor activity that you disagreed with. Instead, you chose to physically abuse the supervisor. Such actions cannot and will not be tolerated.

Any further occurrences will result in recommendation to discharge you from the service. You have the right to the grievance process.

Mr. Smith has been employed in the Sarnia Post Office for a period of 18 years and is presently classified as a Letter Carrier (PO-3). He is also president of the Sarnia Local of the Letter Carriers' Union of Canada.

Counsel for the employer called as witnesses J. McGough, a Cell Supervisor (Supervisor 1); P. Jay, a Letter Carrier Coordinator, (Supervisor 3); and T. McKenzie (Operations Supervisor, Days). In addition, counsel called but did not examine J. Burke, a Letter Carrier, who on August 18 was an Acting Supervisor. Mr. Burke was made available for cross-examination by the representative of the grievor but no cross-examination was undertaken.

The representative of the grievor called T. Smith and a witness, W. Clarke, also a Letter Carrier (PO-5). Notwithstanding my having made an order for the exclusion of witnesses at the outset of the hearing, Mr. Clarke did remain in the room during much of Mr. McGough's testimony. His ability to testify was challenged by counsel for the employer. I permitted Mr. Clarke to testify but advised the parties that the weight to be attached to his testimony could be affected by his conduct. As will be noted later, Clarke's testimony was not material to my decision.

At approximately 8:35 a.m. on August 18, 1978, Mr. McGough together with Mr. Burke were at a relay bundle rack (identified as a C 22 rack), situated temporarily in the centre aisle of the letter carrier section of the Sarnia Post Office. Mr. McGough was opening a relay bundle bag on a lower shelf of the C 22 rack when the grievor, in a loud voice spiced with some profanity, challenged Mr. McGough's authority to open relay bags of a letter carrier not under his supervision (Note: but under Mr. Burke's). Following an exchange of opinions, the grievor placed his right hand on the C 22 rack and his right foot on top of the bag, apparently in an attempt to prevent Mr. McGough from continuing his examination. Mr. McGough, in pulling the string that closed the relay bag, jerked the bag out from under the grievor's foot. There is serious disagreement as to what then transpired. The grievor would have me believe that he was momentarily off balance and reached at Mr. McGough for support. Mr. McGough was convinced that the grievor was able to retain his balance and then deliberately seized him. They are, however, in agreement that the grievor did place his arms around Mr. McGough's shoulders and "pushed/pulled" him against the C 22 rack. Mr. McGough may have suffered some contusions as a result of the incident.

The evidence indicates that the grievor was guilty of misconduct in that he was abusive in his remarks and insubordinate in his conduct. On the balance of probabilities I must conclude that the evidence of Mr. McGough as to what occurred with respect to the alleged physical abuse appears more reasonable than the testimony of the grievor. However, I must point out that my decision does not turn on my finding on the conflict of evidence.

Immediately following the incident, in the words of Mr. McGough, "things came to a stop." Asked how he would account for the incident, Mr. McGough testified in cross-examination that "I was the most surprised man in the world."

Mr. Jay, the senior plant supervisor, appeared upon the scene at that point. He testified that he had been in his office when he heard the commotion and had identified the grievor's voice. Upon his arrival he saw Mr. McGough and the grievor facing each other. He demanded, "What the hell is going on" and Mr. McGough replied, "I don't have to take that kind of abuse. I want that man out of the plant." The grievor then interjected to say he wanted Mr. Jay to tell Mr. McGough that it was against procedure for Mr. McGough to touch the relay bags.

Mr. Jay testified that he then told the grievor to "shut up," that he would not tolerate his profane language. The grievor quietened down and Mr. Jay decided to "take the situation from the work floor." He asked the grievor to accompany him to his office and the two left the scene.

In his office Mr. Jay talked with the grievor. The grievor was subdued but still convinced that supervisors could not check relay bags. Mr. Jay stated that he cautioned the grievor as to his "ranting and raving" and suggested to him that he grieve if he felt supervisors could not examine relay bags. Mr. Jay then stated that he told the grievor that, in order to permit him to perform his duties for the day, he would first have to apologize to Mr. McGough. The grievor agreed to apologize.

Mr. McGough, in his evidence, stated that the grievor returned after approximately 15 minutes, with Mr. Jay behind him. The grievor apologized, stating he was sorry "it" had happened. Mr. McGough accepted the apology, the two men shook hands and Mr. McGough said to the grievor, "Okay, Tom, go on and get your work done." Mr. McGough testified that he had looked at Mr. Jay as the two men had approached and had concluded from the look on Mr. Jay's face that "that was what he wanted me to do."

It may be observed that there was no effort on Mr. Jay's part to secure any explanation from Mr. McGough as to what had transpired. For reasons best known to Mr. Jay himself, he elected to make the decision without communicating with Mr. McGough. He was well aware of the latter's conviction that he did not have to take abuse from the grievor and that he wanted the employee out of the plant. Mr. Jay testified that in matters of discipline a supervisor could suspend an employee for the balance of a shift. In that context, Mr. McGough's statement can only be interpreted as meaning that he had wanted the grievor suspended for the balance of the shift.

The grievor's testimony corroborated that of Mr. Jay as to what transpired although he attributed to Mr. McGough more profane language than "man" and "abuse" in Mr. McGough's initial reply to Mr. Jay.

On August 24 the grievor was handed, at his workplace and in the presence of Mr. Jay, a letter from the Postmaster, A. Jones, (Exhibit 8) reading as follows:

> The purpose of this letter is to advise you that you are being suspended from duty for a period of 6 months, from 6:35 AM August 28, 1978 to February 22, 1979, 3:05 PM.
>
> The reason for this suspension is your act of major misconduct on Friday, August 18, 1978, in that you did physically assault P.O. SUP 1, J. McGough in the Letter Carrier Section.
>
> The intention of this suspension is to impress upon you the seriousness of your present conduct. A further occurrence or breach of conduct can result in further disciplinary action, up to and including Discharge [sic].

On September 1, 1978, the grievor received a further letter (Exhibit 11) by registered mail, reading:

> This is to advise you that I hereby withdraw my letter to you of August 24th, 1978 and it will be removed from your personal file. I will be advising you further on this matter perhaps.

Later on the same day, he was called into the plant to receive the second letter of the same date which led to the filing of the grievance.

According to Mr. Jay, the six-month suspension was withdrawn the same afternoon as it was issued and "pending further investigation" by a review committee including Mr. Jones. That committee had interviewed the grievor and Mr. Jay, as well as others, before determining that a suspension of 20 days was the appropriate discipline. Such testimony is somewhat difficult to reconcile with the exhibits, but little turns on this feature of the evidence. It may be pointed out, moreover, that Mr. Jones has passed away since the issuance of the letter and, consequently, was not available to clarify the matter.

. . .

---

questions

1 What do you think of the phrasing of the issues to be adjudicated? Elaborate.
2 How would you assess the Sarnia Post Office's manner of handling this case? Elaborate.
3 Does the Sarnia Post Office have any "policy" in dealing with discipline cases?
4 What do you make of the incident that precipitated this grievance? Elaborate.
5 Should Smith, the grievor and president of the local union, have handled the incident in a different way? Elaborate.
6 Did Mr. Jay do an adequate job in assessing the seriousness of the incident? Elaborate.
7 If you had been the adjudicator, what would you have done when Clarke refused to leave the room?
8 If you had been the adjudicator, what award would you have handed down? Be concise and logical in your reply.

Fighting and the Use of a Knife*

In The Matter of an Arbitration

Between:
Canadian National Railway Company

And:
Division No. 4, Railway Employees' Department A.F. of L.-C.I.O.

And in the Matter of the Grievance of W. Ward
[The case was heard by a single arbitrator]

A hearing in this matter was held at Montreal on June 13, 1979.

Award

Joint Statement of Issue

On 6 October 1978 Electrician W. Ward was working the 1600 to 2400 hours shift in the passenger car paint shop at Transcona Main Shops. At approximately 2115 hours an altercation occurred involving Mr. Ward and Carman Apprentice R. Jacot.

During the altercation Mr. Ward drew a utility knife from his tool pouch and Mr. Jacot was cut on the little finger of his left hand.

An investigation was conducted and the electrician was discharged for his part in the altercation.

The International Brotherhood of Electrical Workers appealed the company's decision requesting that Mr. Ward be reinstated in his former position and that the discipline assessed be similar to that assessed the other persons involved in the incident.

The company declined the appeal.

From the statement of all the employees concerned, it is clear that there was a fight between the grievor and another employee, and that as a result the other employee was injured (his hand was cut) by the grievor's utility knife. What is not clear is the degree of responsibility of the various persons involved.

The grievor did participate in a fight and for that (except in clear cases of self-defence) some discipline would be warranted. He did, as well, draw from his pocket (and from the pouch protecting the blade) his utility knife. The use of any weapon, or the use of a tool as a weapon (even if its blade was very short) is obviously wrong, and for that too the grievor would be

---

*Permission to use this case was granted by Labour Canada. Minor deletions were made by the author for the purposes of this book and all names changed to prevent embarrassment to the individuals involved.

subject to discipline. I do not consider that the grievor was deliberately attacked by another employee or employees, so that he was in reasonable fear of serious injury. I do not consider, then, that there was that degree of justification which would excuse resort to such a weapon in the circumstances. Thus, for his participation in the fight, and especially for his use of a knife, I consider that the grievor would be liable to severe discipline.

It is necessary, however, in assessing the penalty imposed on the grievor to consider all the circumstances of the incident, as well as the grievor's disciplinary record. In this case the grievor, an electrician, had relatively short seniority, but had a clear disciplinary record and was regarded as a good employee. He was considered by his supervisor to be cooperative and of a good disposition. It appears that he immigrated to Canada from the Philippines a few years ago, and is of relatively slight build.

On the evening in question the grievor had been speaking to his wife on the telephone, mounted on a pillar just outside a foreman's office, with respect to their sick child. Several other employees, Carmen and Carman Apprentices, were nearby, and one of them was anxious to use the telephone. The group considered that the grievor had been too long on the telephone and began to make noise, sing songs and, it seems, beat on a garbage can. While the evidence is conflicting on the point, it seems most likely that one of the employees, Mr. Jacot, actually threw a garbage can against the pillar on which the telephone was mounted. The grievor thought, perhaps not entirely without reason, that it was aimed at him, although I doubt that it really was.

Finally, the grievor hung up the telephone and some conversation took place between him and Mr. Jacot. Mr. Jacot, a Carman Apprentice, is a younger man than the grievor and is taller and heavier. The accounts of the matter differ, but it appears to me that the most probable account of what occurred is that Mr. Jacot taunted the grievor and invited him to fight. I have no doubt, from the material before me that whatever the particular incidents may have been, Mr. Jacot was the overall aggressor, and that the grievor's conduct was provoked by the actions of the younger man and by the taunts of his companions. That the grievor was in fact frightened is, I think, the case, although obviously his reaction to the situation was an improper one.

As to the severity of the penalty imposed on the grievor, it is to be noted that there were six persons involved, to some extent, in the incident: the grievor on one hand and five other employees. Of those five, two would appear not to have been substantially implicated, and were not disciplined. Two others were assessed ten and twenty demerits, respectively, for unnecessary harassment of a fellow employee. These penalties would appear to reflect the involvement of the employees concerned. The fifth member of the group which was harrassing the grievor was Mr. Jacot, who was assessed thirty demerits and was suspended for ten days. That is a substantial penalty and was, it would appear, merited. None of the penalties just described were appealed and they are not before me for determination.

. . .

---

questions

1 Do you think that the "Joint Statement of Issue" is well presented? Elaborate.
2 What is your assessment of the actions of the "aggressors" and their possible impact on Mr. Ward?
3 Under what specific situations might the use of a knife be permitted? Elaborate.
4 Do you agree with the disciplinary measures given to the other employees? Explain.
5 If you were the arbitrator, would you uphold the company's decision? Elaborate and be as concise and logically consistent as possible.

The Use of Alcohol Making an Employee Unfit for Work*

In The Matter of an Arbitration

Between:
Charterways Transportation Limited, Air Terminal Transport Division
(Hereinafter referred to as the Company)

And:
Fuel, Bus, Limousine, Petroleum Drivers and Allied Employees,
Local Union No. 352 (Hereinafter referred to as the Union)

And in the Matter of the Grievance of D. Curtis
[The case was heard by an arbitration board]

Award

The matter before the board arises out of a grievance (Ex. 2) dated March 17, 1980 concerning the grievor's discharge on March 6, 1980. The parties agreed that the matter was arbitrable and that the board had jurisdiction to deal with the grievance.

The grievor was discharged following an incident which took place on the Company's premises on or about March 5, 1980. The board heard a great deal of evidence concerning the events of March 5th, but there appears to be relatively little dispute about the significant occurrences; therefore, the

---

*Permission to use this case was granted by Labour Canada. Minor deletions were made by the author for the purposes of this book and all names changed to prevent embarrassment to the individuals involved.

evidence will be summarized without specific reference to the witnesses who tendered it.

The grievor was scheduled to work on March 5, 1980 from 5:30 p.m. to 2:30 a.m., and had worked the same shift on March 4th. At all material times he was employed as a bus driver by the Company at its Toronto airport operation. On March 5th the grievor also performed some work for Mr. G. Fortier who was engaged in some work on behalf of a trustee in bankruptcy for a Quebec firm. The grievor began work for Mr. Fortier early that morning around 7:30 or so, and finished around 4:00 p.m. The work he performed involved getting a truck started and moved to the Avion Motor Hotel where Mr. Fortier was storing the vehicle. The work was not what one would regard as strenuous, but it did involve the grievor in standing outside for long periods of time while waiting for a tow truck to assist in starting the truck.

Around 4:00 p.m. the grievor met Mr. Fortier at the Avion Hotel and was paid his money for the work involved. Mr. Fortier bought the grievor one drink (a single) and the grievor left glass in hand. Mr. Fortier next saw the grievor some time later, offered him another drink, and was told by the grievor that he had already had another one.

After leaving Mr. Fortier, the grievor apparently joined several of his fellow employees, who had gone to the hotel for a drink and a game of darts after work. The grievor spent enough time with them to play a game of darts and have another drink, probably a double vodka. At around 5:30 p.m. the grievor said that he had to go to work and was told by at least two of his fellow employees at the table that he should not report for work because he was in no fit state to work. They apparently reached this conclusion because they believed the grievor to be unsteady on his feet.

The grievor ignored this warning, left the Hotel, got something to eat at a nearby restaurant and drove to the Company's yard. He punched in around 6:20 p.m. He was observed then by Mr. Ross who was, at all material times, employed as a security guard by the Company. Mr. Ross concluded that the grievor was intoxicated because he was unsteady on his feet, flushed, bleary-eyed, and his speech was slurred.

Sometime before 7:00 p.m. the grievor fell asleep in a chair in the office. Mr. Ross said that at that time, and for some time thereafter, the cleaners were in the office working, but that the grievor was not awakened by any of this noise.

Mr. Ross called the dispatcher at the airport, Mr. Maloney, to inform him that the grievor was in no fit condition to drive and to report on what had happened. Mr. Maloney reported this to Mr. Langley, a supervisor, who drove over to the Company's office and found the grievor "passed out" in a chair in the starter's office. Mr. Langley attempted to awaken the grievor but without success.

Shortly after Mr. Langley's arrival, Mr. West, who was then the operations manager, arrived. He said that the grievor did not wake up even though the phones were ringing in the office and the cleaners were cleaning. Mr. West arranged for the Union steward, Mr. Hyde, to come to the office. Following Mr. Hyde's arrival, Mr. West made some unsuccessful attempts to awaken the grievor by calling his name in a loud voice. Finally, after about the fourth attempt, the grievor woke up.

The preponderance of evidence suggests that he was disoriented and unsteady on his feet. By this time he had been asleep for about an hour or so, despite the activity in the office and the attempts to awaken him.

After the grievor awoke he denied he had anything to drink at all that evening, and also claimed that he had just returned to Toronto after having driven to Trois Rivières and back. There are various accounts about the grievor's appearance and the presence, or absence, of alcohol on his breath. There is no doubt however that the grievor was, at all times, unfit to drive that night, and that he misled the Union Steward and the Company representatives with his account of his previous activities that day.

The grievor's past record was introduced by the Company. The record shows three disciplinary actions taken by the Company in the two years immediately preceding the incident in question. In October, 1978 the grievor was suspended for two days for punching out early without informing the dispatcher; in November, 1978 he was warned about the number of "book-offs" without reason which he had taken, and in October, 1979 he was warned for negligently causing damage to the Company's gas pump.

The uncontradicted evidence of Mr. Stroud, the general manager, was that the incident of March 5th was regarded as very serious, and that the grievor's record was a very minor consideration. Mr. Stroud also said that before the grievor was discharged, representatives of the Company and the Union met in the grievor's presence, and that the grievor continued to deny that he had consumed any alcohol at all that day. Mr. Stroud said that he also expressed a concern that the grievor had an alcohol problem, but the grievor denied having such a problem.

Evidence was also led about an incident involving another driver named Kelly who had been given a thirty day suspension shortly before the incident involving the grievor. Mr. Kelly also had reported for work in an unfit condition and was not allowed to drive. Upon learning that he would not be able to drive, Mr. Kelly apparently became quite upset; however, the next day, when he met with Mr. Stroud, Mr. Kelly admitted to having had a couple of drinks, but explained that at the time he was also on medication which had affected him along with the alcohol. Mr. Kelly submitted that he had been foolish, said that it would never happen again and apologized. Mr. Kelly had no disciplinary record at all.

Mr. Stroud explained that he had originally intended to suspend Mr. Kelly for three months, but, after hearing his explanation about the medication and in view of all of the other factors involved, he agreed to reduce the suspension to thirty days. The suspension was accepted by Mr. Kelly.

There is no doubt, indeed it is admitted by the Union, that the grievor reported for work in an unfit condition, and that the Company has just cause to discipline him on that account. It is difficult to determine exactly whether the sole cause for his being so unfit was alcohol or fatigue. It is likely that both contributed to his condition, and it is abundantly clear that he exercised extremely bad judgment both in consuming alcohol when he was fatigued and in reporting for work after he had done this. The Company is in the business of transporting people on public roads, and any accident caused by one of its drivers while driving in an unfit condition could endanger lives as well as property. The Company was unquestionably right when it refused to let the grievor drive that night.

Before dealing with the ultimate disposition of this case, the matters raised in argument concerning the grievor's record and the Kelly case should be dealt with. Article 13.23(a) of the collective agreement deals with the use which can be made of the past disciplinary record.

> ...previous offences shall not be taken into consideration except insofar as they relate to the offence under review.

It seems from this that the parties may well have agreed to limit what may be referred to as the "culminating incident doctrine." Accepting that the Company is precluded from relying on the grievor's past record to justify the discharge because no past offences dealt with the use of alcohol or with reporting to work while unfit, the Union's case is not advanced significantly here. As I understood Mr. Stroud, he looked at the grievor's record to determine if there was anything there to help him (i.e., whether it was clear) rather than to determine the appropriate level of penalty. Even agreeing that the record cannot be relied on to help support the discharge, it can surely be looked at by the Company to determine whether it provides a justification for some other penalty short of discharge. The fact that the grievor's record was looked at does not, in these circumstances, provide a reason for varying the penalty.

There are definite parallels between this case and the Kelly situation. Both involve employees who had about five years' seniority at the time, and who reported for work in an unfit condition due at least in part, to the consumption of alcohol. Mr. Kelly, however, admitted everything to Mr. Stroud, explained what had occurred, and apologized for his actions. The grievor lied about his alcohol consumption, and persisted in this even after confronted with Mr. Stroud's knowledge that other employees had seen him drinking. The grievor also lied concerning his activities on the day and tried to give the impression that fatigue was the sole cause for the indcident. It stands to reason that those should be regarded as significant differences between this situation and the treatment given Mr. Kelly. On the other hand, it is significant that Mr. Kelly was not discharged nor was discharge considered in his case, even though both his case and the grievor's concern employees reporting for work in an unfit state due in part, at least, to the consumption of alcohol. Also, in neither case did the employee drive a Company vehicle while unfit to do so.

One must agree completely with the Company's submission that, given the nature of its business and the fact that public safety is at stake, this matter must be regarded extremely seriously and any penalty should reflect the seriousness of the grievor's actions. The similarities with the Kelly case are such that it is difficult to justify discharge without some past record of reporting in an unfit state or alcohol-related misconduct. It is particularly important in this regard that discharge was not considered in the Kelly case, even before the Company learned about the medication he was taking, and before Mr. Kelly's apology.

A significant difference between the two cases, in the Company's view, appeared to be that the grievor was suspected of having a problem with alcohol despite his denials to Mr. Stroud. It is impossible to doubt the sincerity of Mr. Stroud's belief that the grievor has a problem and his wish that the grievor seek some sort of medical assessment; however, on the basis of the evidence presented, it is difficult to determine the basis for Mr. Stroud's conclusion. If one could be persuaded on balance that the grievor may have such a problem, then it would be reasonable to compel him to have a competent medical assessment of his situation. On the other hand, once the allegation has been made and the belief is sincerely held by the Company's officers, the grievor must face the situation that if he is reinstated this cloud of suspicion may remain and may affect his future relationship with his employer. Accordingly, the best way of dealing with this situation may well be to construct a remedy whereby the grievor has the choice of whether to seek a medical assessment; but, that if he so chooses to put the Company's apprehension to rest, then that decision should be taken into account in the penalty.

. . .

questions

1 What was the first thing the arbitrator did to ensure his award would not be appealed to a court on procedural grounds? Elaborate.
2 What do you think of the condition of the grievor on the night in question and the roles of all of the people involved to witness his condition?
3 What was the employee's past record and what relevance does it have for this case? Elaborate.
4 Is the general manager in a position to make a judgment as to whether the grievor has an alcohol problem? Elaborate.
5 What impact, if any, would management's decision in the Kelly case have on the present one? Elaborate. Will the apparent fact that Mr. Kelly told the "truth" and Mr. Curtis "lied" make any difference in the disposition of the two cases? Elaborate.
6 What impact does article 13.23(a) have on Mr. Curtis' past record in this case?
7 Do you think that Mr. Curtis should be put in the position of having a choice as to whether or not he should seek medical assessment? Elaborate.
8 If you were the arbitrator in this case, what award would you hand down? Be concise and logically consistent in your reply.
9 Could you envisage a situation under which you would want to be seized of the matter for a specified period of time? Elaborate.

A Policy Grievance — Medical Evidence of Sickness for Periods Less Than 3 Days*

In The Matter of an Arbitration

Between:
The St. Lawrence Seaway Authority (Authority)

And:
The Canadian Brotherhood of Railway Transport and General Workers (Union)

1   This matter has come before me as a *policy grievance*. The Union has asked for a declaration as to the meaning of Article 23.3 of the Collective Agreement. Specifically, the Union has asked for a declaration as to whether Article 23.3 allows the Authority to require a doctor's certificate in addition to an employee's written declaration for claimed illnesses of less than three days.

Article 23.3 provides as follows:

a The granting of sick leave may be conditional upon the production of a written declaration from an employee for absences up to a total of nine (9) days in a year except for absences in excess of three (3) continuous days.

b Any absence in excess of three (3) continuous days, and all absences in excess of the nine (9) days granted conditionally upon the employee's written declaration, require a certificate from a qualified medical practitioner. Upon proof of the cost of obtaining such a certificate, an employee shall be reimbursed by The Authority.

c Any absence supported by a medical certificate is excluded from the total of nine (9) days that are granted conditionally upon the employee's written declaration.

Before proceeding further, I believe it useful to state briefly that the Union's concern arose out of the Authority's demand that five employees who all reported sick within a short period of time on August 28, 1980 produce a doctor's certificate in addition to their written declaration. At the hearing on this matter there was some considerable discussion as to whether the matter before me should be treated as a policy grievance or as one going to the specific rights of the five employees. It was agreed that the matter should be treated as a policy grievance involving a declaration by me as Arbitrator as to the meaning of Article 23.3.

2   The Authority takes the view that if there is a reasonable basis for doubt as to the claim of sickness, it may ask for a medical certificate. The failure to obtain such a certificate will allow the Authority to deny the claim made. In effect, the Authority would shift the burden on the employee to prove

*Permission to use this case was granted by Labour Canada. Minor deletions were made by the author for the purposes of this book and all names changed to prevent embarrassment to the individuals involved.

THE ST. LAWRENCE SEAWAY AUTHORITY

APPLICATION FOR LEAVE

	EMPLOYEE NUMBER

NAME (SURNAME)	(GIVEN NAMES)	BRANCH

STRUCTURE, SHOP OR OFFICE	LOCATION

PERIOD REQUESTED ▶ FROM	TO	NO. OF WORKING DAYS

ADDRESS WHILE ON LEAVE

_____
SIGNATURE OF EMPLOYEE   DATE

CHECK TYPE OF LEAVE APPLIED FOR

☐ VACATION   ☐ SICK   ☐ SPECIAL   ☐ WITHOUT PAY

☐ FURLOUGH   ☐ RETIRING   ☐ INJURY ON DUTY   ☐ COMPENSATORY

COMPLETE APPLICABLE SECTION BELOW

SICK LEAVE	SPECIAL LEAVE OR LEAVE WITHOUT PAY
NATURE OF ILLNESS:	REASON:

☐ MEDICAL CERTIFICATE ATTACHED

☐ I CERTIFY THAT I WAS ILL AND UNABLE TO WORK DURING THE ENTIRE PERIOD OF ABSENCE

_____
SIGNATURE OF EMPLOYEE   DATE

NOTE
FOR ILLNESS IN FAMILY — ATTACH MEDICAL CERTIFICATE

APPROVED BY   APPROVAL OF AUTHORITY WHEN REQUIRED

_____
OFFICER IN CHARGE   DATE

_____
TITLE

_____
DATE

A FALSE STATEMENT ON THIS FORM CAN RESULT IN DISCIPLINARY ACTION.

the claim of sickness for periods involving less than three consecutive days or nine days in any year.

In support of its position the Authority has cited *Re Salvation Army Grace Hospital, Windsor and Canadian Union of Operating Engineers and General Workers, Local 11*, 25 L.A.A. (2d) 241 (McLaren 1980). There the arbitrator dealt with a provision in the collective agreement which stated: "The Hospital reserves the right to demand a Doctor's certificate of proof of illness after an employee has been absent from scheduled duty with the Hospital for a period exceeding twenty-four (24) hours."

The grievance concerned an employee who twice asked for time off to hunt. The request was denied. The employee then reported sick at precisely the time he had requested to be off. The time reported as sick was less than that set out in the agreement relating to the right of the employer to ask for a medical certificate.

The employer did *not* ask for a medical certificate. But it did ask the employee to produce some evidence, other than his own statement, that he was indeed sick. This the employee refused to do.

Citing the collective agreement the union argued the employee was not required to do more than make a claim for sick leave. The arbitrator ruled otherwise. He said the agreement gave to the employer the right, without any cause having to be demonstrated, to ask for a medical certificate once the sick-leave time passed a certain point. For good cause shown, said the arbitrator, there was nothing in the agreement denying the employer the right to ask for *some proof of illness*. The arbitrator stated:

> The fact that the right to demand a medical certificate is reserved to the hospital in cases of illnesses greater than three days' duration suggests that this right is also present in absences of a shorter duration. In absences of greater than three days' duration this reserved power may be exercised even though there may be no grounds to think anything other than that the employee was legitimately ill. The inference, then, is that the hospital's power, in absences of a short duration, to demand proof of illness is restricted. What is that restriction? That the hospital may only require proof of illness when there is reasonable and probable grounds to query that an absence of less than three days' duration is due to reasons other than illness. Then, and only then, may the hospital demand some proof of the reason for the absence. If there is no reasonable and probable grounds to query the reason lying behind an absence, then there is no right to require of an employee proof that he was, in fact, ill.

I note and emphasize that this matter did not involve the submission of a medical certificate. Rather, it related to the employer's insistence, good cause having been shown, that the employee offer some proof beyond his word alone demonstrating his sickness.

3   The award discussed relates to an interpretation of the agreement in that matter. I must interpret the agreement in this matter. Even if I were to find the reasoning of the arbitrator in *Salvation Army Grace Hospital, Windsor, supra,*

persuasive, it would have limited bearing for the policy grievance which I have before me.

The *Salvation Army Grace Hospital, Windsor* matter related to an agreement which had only *one* provision similar to that between the Authority and the Union. That provision concerns the right of the employer to demand a medical certificate, without cause being shown, once a sick leave passed a certain point. The *Salvation Army Grade Hospital, Windsor* agreement, at least on the face of the award, differs in one material respect from the agreement between the Authority and the Union. Article 23.3(a) deals specifically with absences of less than three continuous days. It states:

> The granting of sick leave may be conditional upon the production of a *written declaration for an employee* for absences up to a total of nine (9) days in a year except for absences in excess of three (3) continuous days.

In my view the parties, that is, the Authority and the Union, have put their minds to the problem of handling certain kinds of sick leave claims (those involving less than three continuous days.) In their agreement the parties have allowed for such claims to be made on the basis of a written declaration.

4   The parties have acted under Article 23.3. Evidence was submitted indicating an unbroken line of practice implementing Article 23.3. That evidence came from S. Rowan, an Authority employee for twenty-seven years. Currently, he holds the position of Mechanical Superintendent. He has held that position for a number of years. Before that he had served for six years as local chairman of the Union.

It was the uncontradicted testimony of Mr. Rowan that any employee claiming sick leave for less than three days (within the nine-day annual allowance) would be granted such leave on executing the Application for Leave — Sick Leave (Union Exhibit 5, attached). This would be done even though Mr. Rowan might have some reasonable doubt as to the truth of the claim made.

(Mr. Rowan, again according to his uncontradicted testimony, held and carried forward the duty of approving sick leave claims. In the course of any year he estimated that among the forty employees he supervised, about 150 to 200 sick leave claims are passed on by him).

Not once did Mr. Rowan ever demand more than the written declaration for purposes of the sick leave claim.

In my view the sick leave declaration constitutes the accepted manner according to which the parties have carried out the terms of Article 23.3.

. . .

---

questions

1 a What is meant by a policy grievance, and how does it differ from a grievance of an individual?
  b Why do policy grievances usually arise?

2 What do you think of the decision of the arbitrator in the *Salvation Army Grace Hospital, Windsor and Canadian Brotherhood of Railway Transport and General Workers?* Elaborate.
3 If you were the arbitrator in this case, what decision would you hand down? Be concise and logically consistent.
4 Would the *Salvation Army Grace Hospital* case affect your decision? Elaborate.
5 Is there anything on the "Application for Leave" form that might affect your decision? Elaborate.

Glossary of Industrial Relations Terms*

Accreditation: The process used to certify an organization of employers as the bargaining agent for a unit of employers. *(Accréditation syndicale)* The parallel term for employee organizations is "certification". *(Certification)*

Adversary System: The industrial relations system seen as consisting of two necessarily opposing forces, labour and management. This viewpoint ignores the co-operative elements of the relationship. *(Régime d'antagonisme)*

Affiliation: The establishment of an organic bond between two or more organizations. In an affiliation, the organization maintains its essential character and continues to enjoy a relative autonomy within the limits established by the purpose of the affiliation. *(Affiliation)*

Affirmative Action Plan: A written program to actively eliminate employment standards and practices that tend to discriminate on the grounds of race, creed, sex or national origin. *(Programme d'action positive)*

Agreement: (See **Collective Agreement**)

Appeal: A procedure by which a party dissatisfied with a decision, award or ruling may refer the matter to a higher authority for review. *(Appel)*

Apprentice: A worker who enters into agreement with an employer to learn a skilled trade through a special training period combining practical training with related off-the-job technical instruction. Apprenticeship is sometimes regulated by statute (designated trades). *(Apprenti/ie)*

*Quoted from Labour Canada, *Glossary of Industrial Relations Terms* (Ottawa: Supply and Services Canada, 1984).

Arbitration: The procedure by which a board or a single arbitrator, acting under the authority of both parties to a dispute, hears both sides of the controversy and issues an award, usually accompanied by a written decision, which is ordinarily binding on both parties. Arbitrators are usually appointed by the parties concerned, but under special circumstances, they are appointed by the Minister of Labour. *(Arbitrage)* **Compulsory arbitration** is that required by law and is the usual procedure for settling contract interpretation disputes. *(L'arbitrage obligatoire)* The term **voluntary arbitration** indicates that the parties to a dispute agree to arbitration in the absence of statutory compulsion. *(L'arbitrage facultatif)*

Arbitrator: Third party chosen to hear a case or group of cases which are submitted for arbitration. *(Arbitre)*

Assembly-line Work: A manufacturing procedure in which many workers successively perform an operation or task while the item under production is moved along a conveyor system timed to move in accordance with the time allotted for each distinct function to be performed. *(Production à la chaîne)*

Automation: Automation is usually characterized by two major principles: (1) mechanization, i.e., machines are self-regulated so as to meet predetermined requirements (a simple example of self-regulation can be found in the operation of a thermostatically controlled furnace); (2) continuous process, i.e., production facilities are linked together, thereby integrating several separate elements of productive process into a unified whole. There are three basic kinds of automated process: (1) assembly-line automation, characteristic of the automobile industry; (2) extensive use of computers, as found in many modern offices and businesses; (3) utilization of complex electronic equipment as controls in the manufacturing and processing of products, such as in the refining industry. *(Automatisation)*

Award: In labour-management arbitration, the final decision of an arbitrator, binding on both parties to the dispute. *(Sentence arbitrale)*

Bargaining Agent: The organization that is the exclusive representative of a group of workers or employers in the process of collective bargaining. *(Agent négociateur)*

Bargaining Unit: A group of employees in a firm, plant, or industry that has been recognized by the employer and certified by a labour relations board as appropriate to be represented by a union for purposes of collective bargaining. In a craft union, this could be all members of a trade, such as all tool and die makers in a plant; in an industrial union, the bargaining unit may include all production workers in a plant or all plants in a company. *(Unité de négociation)*

Base Rate: The lowest rate of pay, expressed in hourly terms, for the lowest paid qualified worker classification in the bargaining unit. Not to be confused with **basic rate** which is the straight-time rate of pay per hour, job or unit, excluding premiums, incentive bonuses, etc. (*Taux de base*)

Blue-collar Workers: Term used to describe manual workers, i.e. production and maintenance workers. In recent years, the percentage of blue-collar workers in the labour frorce has declined considerably. (*Cols bleus*)

Boycott: An organized refusal on the part of employees and their union to deal with an employer, with the objective of winning concessions. Primary boycotts usually take the form of putting pressure on consumers not to buy the goods of an employer who is directly involved in a dispute. In the dress industry, for example, the International Ladies' Garment Workers' Union frequently boycotts the sale of non-union made dresses. Secondary boycotts are those in which pressure is exerted on employers who are not directly involved in a dispute, e.g., workers of Company A refuse to buy or handle goods of Company B, which is engaged in a labour dispute. (*Boycottage*)

Broader-based or Centralized Bargaining: A type of bargaining that aims to reduce the degree of fragmentation in the collective bargaining process and the potential conflict that can result, by combining employers on the one hand and/or unions on the other to form negotiating coalitions, thereby reducing the potential for sequential work stoppages in the same industry/company as various contracts terminate. (*Négociation sectorielle*)

Bumping: Exercise of seniority rights by workers to displace less senior union employees when business conditions require temporary layoffs or the discontinuance of departments. (*Supplantation, déplacement*)

Business Agent: A full-time union officer of a local union who handles grievances, helps enforce agreements, and performs other tasks in the day-to-day operation of a union. (*Agent d'affaires*)

Business Council on National Issues: A consultative body formed in 1970, consisting of the chief executive officers of 150 leading Canadian corporations, which meets with governments, labour unions and other interest groups to develop policy recommendations on economic and social issues. A major area of interest to the council is its task force on employment and labour relations.

Call-back Pay: Compensation, often at higher wage rates, for workers called back on the job after completing their regular shift. Contract provisions usually provide for a minimum number of hours of pay, regardless of the number of hours actually worked. (*Indemnité de rappel*)

Call-in Pay: Guaranteed hours of pay (ranging from two to eight hours) to a worker who reports for work and finds there is insufficient work for him or her to do. Provisions for call-in pay are usually spelled out in collective agreements. *(Indemnité de convocation au travail)*

Canada Labour Code: Legislation applicable to employers whose operations fall within federal jurisdiction and to their employees. The Canada Labour Code consists of Part III (Labour Standards); Part IV (Safety of Employees); and Part V (Industrial Relations). *(Code canadien du travail)*

Canada Labour Relations Board: A board whose powers and duties under the industrial relations provisions of the Canada Labour Code include the determination of appropriate bargaining units, the certification or decertification of trade unions, decisions as to unfair labour practices or failure to bargain in good faith, etc. The board is composed of a chairman, at least one vice-chairman and not less than four nor more than eight members. (See also Labour Relations Board) *(Conseil canadien des relations du travail)*

Canadian Chamber of Commerce: A national body representing business interests, which seeks to influence federal legislation by presentation of briefs; it disseminates commercial information and attempts to foster understanding and sympathy for the problems businessmen encounter. *(Chambre de commerce du Canada)*

Canadian Labour Congress (CLC): Canada's national labour body, formed in 1956 from the merger of the Trades and Labour Congress and the Canadian Congress of Labour, and representing more than half of organized labour in the country. *(Congrès du Travail du Canada (CTC)*

Canadian Manufacturers' Association: A large organization of manufacturers in every type of industry, founded in 1871, incorporated 1902, it serves as a spokesman for interests of the Canadian manufacturing industry. *(Association des manufacturiers canadiens)*

Centrale des syndicats démocratiques (CSD): A federation of Québec unions founded in 1972 by unions that broke away from the Confédération des syndicats nationaux (CSN). *(Centrale des syndicats démocratiques (CSD))*

Certification: Official designation by a labour relations board or similar government agency of a union as sole and exclusive bargaining agent, following proof of majority support among employees in a bargaining unit. *(Accréditation syndicale)*

Certified Union: A union designated by a labour relations board as the exclusive bargaining agent of a group of workers. *(Syndicat accrédité)*

Checkoff: A clause in a collective agreement authorizing an employer to deduct union dues and, sometimes, other assessments, and transmit these funds to the union. There are four main types; the first three apply to union members only: (1) Voluntary revocable; (2) Voluntary irrevocable; (3) Compulsory; (4) Rand Formula — dues deduced from both union and non-union employees. *(Précompte, retenue, prélèvement)*

Closed Shop: A provision in a collective agreement whereby all employees in a bargaining unit must be union members in good standing before being hired, and new employees must be hired through the union. *(Atelier fermé)*

Code of Ethical Practices: A declaration of principle adopted by the Canadian Labour Congress, requiring unions to try to ensure maximum attendance at meetings and general participation by membership. Under this code, no one engaging in corrupt practices may hold office in the union or in the CLC. *(Code d'éthique)*

Co-determination: A process whereby decisions are made jointly by management and workers (or their representatives). These joint decisions may be made at various levels within a company—at the board level, for example, through the appointment of worker directors, or at shop-floor level by establishing some form of labour-management committee or even by utilizing existing collective bargaining machinery. *(Cogestion)*

COLA Clause: Literally a "cost of living adjustment" (or allowance) clause. A clause built into a collective agreement which links wage or salary increases to changes in the cost of living during the life of the contract. Also termed an "escalator clause." *Clause d'échelle mobile de salaires)*

Collective Agreement: An agreement in writing between an employer and the union representing his/her employees which contains provisions respecting conditions of employment, rates of pay, hours of work, and the rights and obligations of the parties to the agreement. Ordinarily the agreement is for a definite period such as one, two, or three years, usually not less than twelve months. Under some conditions, amendments are made to agreements by mutual consent during the term of the agreement in order to deal with special circumstances. *(Convention collective)*

Collective Bargaining: Method of determining wages, hours and other conditions of employment through direct negotiations between the union and employer. Normally the result of collective bargaining is a written contract that covers all employees in the bargaining unit, both union members and non-members, for a specified period of time. More recently the term has been broadened to include the day-to-day activities involved in giving effect to or carrying out the terms of a collective agreement. *(Négociation collective)*

Bargaining in good faith refers to the requirement that the two parties meet and confer at reasonable times with minds open to persuasion with a view to reaching agreement on new contract terms. Good faith bargaining does not imply that either party is required to reach agreement on any proposal. *(Négociation de bonne foi)* The term collective bargaining is frequently prefaced with expressions such as company-wide, industry-wide or multi-employer, which serve to specify more precisely the form of bargaining. Thus **company-wide collective bargaining** *(Négociation à l'échelle de la firme)* refers to bargaining that takes place between a company with many plants and (typically) a single union representing employees of a particular craft or skill. The terms and conditions arrived at are generally uniform throughout the company. **Industry-wide bargaining** *(Négociation de branche)* refers to situations in which the terms and conditions of employment agreed to by labour and management cover an entire industry. **Multi-employer bargaining** *(Négociation multi-employeurs)* covers those situations in which bargaining takes place between a union and a group or association of employers (hence it is also termed "association bargaining"). Quite often, in fact, much so-called industry-wide bargaining is actually multi-employer bargaining, since there are relatively few industries in which collective bargaining is conducted in a genuinely industry-wide context.

Combines Investigation Act: A federal government act providing for the investigation and repression of trade combinations operating in restraint of trade and to the detriment of the public. *(Loi relative aux enquêtes sur les coalitions)*

Company Union: An employee organization, usually of a single company, that is dominated or strongly influenced by management. Company unions were wide-spread in the 1920s and early '30s. The Labour Relations Acts of the 1940s declared that such employer domination is an unfair labour practice, and company unions have since been on the decline. *(Syndicat de boutique)*

Compensation: Recompense to employees for lost wages due to delays, injury on the job, etc. **Workers' compensation** *(indemnisation des accidents du travail)* is paid to workers temporarily or permanently disabled by an accident in the workplace. Total compensation may refer to all forms of payment for work done, i.e., wages plus pensions and fringe benefits. *(Indemnité)*

Conciliation and Mediation: A process that attempts to resolve labour disputes by compromise or voluntary agreement. By contrast with arbitration, the mediator, conciliator, or conciliation commissioner does not bring in a binding award, and the parties are free to accept or reject the recommendation. The conciliator is often a government official whose report contains recommendations and is made public. Conciliation is a prerequisite to legal strike/lockout action. The mediator is usually a private individual appointed as a last resort after conciliation has failed to prevent or put an end to a strike. **Preventive mediation** *(médiation préventive)* is intervention by a neutral third party during the closed period of a collective agreement to assist in resolving contentious problems, before they reach the bargaining table. *(Conciliation et médiation)*

Confederation of Canadian Unions (CCU): Federation of unions dedicated to a Canadian union movement independent of the internationals. Founded in 1969 by B.C. pulp and paper and aluminum workers, it has affiliated unions in the five provinces west of Québec. *(Confédération des syndicats canadiens (CSC))*

Confederation of National Trade Unions (CNTU): A Quebec-based central labour body. *(Confédération des syndicats nationaux (CSN)*

Consumer Price Index: A Statistics Canada monthly statistical indicator which follows changes in retail prices of selected consumer items in major Canadian cities. The index and its monthly fluctuations are employed in calculating COLA payments (cost of living allowance) in collective agreements. *(Indice des prix à la consommation)*

Contract: A collective agreement. (See **Collective Agreement**.) *(Contrat)*

Contracting out: The use by employers of workers outside their own work force to perform tasks previously performed by the employers' own employees. *(Concession)*

Cooling-off Period: A required period of delay (fixed by federal or provincial law) following legal notice of a pending labour dispute, during which there can be neither strike nor lockout. It follows upon the unsatisfactory conclusion of compulsory conciliation attempts. Wages and conditions of work are usually frozen under conditions set by the previous contract. Every effort is made during this time to settle the dispute. *(Délai de réflexion)*

Cost of Living: Relationship of the retail cost of consumer goods and services to the purchasing power of wages. *(Coût de la vie)*

Craft: A manual occupation that requires extensive training and a high degree of skill, such as carpentry, plumbing, linotype operation. *(Métier)*

Craft Union: A union that limits its members to a particular craft. Most craft unions today, however, have broadened their jurisdiction to include many occupations and skills are not closely related to the originally designated craft. *(Syndicat de métier)*

Cyclical Unemployment: Unemployment caused by fluctuations in the economy, i.e., loss of jobs due to a downward trend in the business cycle.

Cyclical unemployment is of far greater magnitude than seasonal, technological or frictional unemployment. *(Chômage cyclique)*

Decertification: The procedure for removing a union's official recognition as exclusive bargaining representative. *(Révocation d'accréditation syndicale)*

Discrimination (at work): Unequal treatment of persons, whether through hiring or employment rules or through variation of the conditions of employment, because of sex, age, marital status, race, creed, union membership, or other activities. In many cases discrimination is an unfair labour practice under federal or provincial laws. *(Discrimination au travail)*

Dismissal Pay: (See **Severance Pay.**)

Dispute Resolution System: The process and procedures for applying third-party assistance to collective bargaining parties to reach an agreement on the matter(s) in dispute. The notion of dispute resolution includes both legislative and non-legislative elements. There is a range of possible stages in the dispute resolution process, and various mechanisms (both voluntary and compulsory) can be used to this end. *(Méthode de règlement de conflit)*

Earnings: Compensation for services rendered or time worked. *(Gains)*

Economic Council of Canada: An economic research and policy advisory agency created by an Act of Parliament in 1963. Its members represented business, labour agriculture, and other interests until 1976, when labour representatives withdrew to protest the government's anti-inflation program. *(Conseil économique du Canada)*

Employee: A person working in an industry or enterprise who is entitled to wages for labour or services performed. Not included are persons employed in certain professions or who exercise managerial functions. *(Employé)*

Employer: A person or firm having control over the employment of workers and the payment of their wages. *(Employeur)*

Equal Pay for Equal Work: The principle that wage rates should be based on the job, rather than upon the sex, race, etc., of the worker, or upon other factors not related to his/her ability to perform. *(À travail égal, salaire égal)*

Equal Pay for Work of Equal Value: The principle that workers who are performing work of equal value must receive the same pay for work in the same establishment. Equal value is determined by an analysis of the composite skill, effort, and responsibility required in the performance of such work and the conditions under which the work is performed. *(Égalité de rémunération pour un travail de valeur égale)*

Essential Industries: Industries which render such important and necessarily uninterrupted service to the general public as to warrant special regulation to prevent the stoppage of their operations by labour disputes. *(Service d'intérêt public)*

Exclusivity: The right acquired by an employee organization to be the sole representative of the bargaining unit. Exclusive representation is usually provided by labour relations statutes, although some statutes governing public employee labour relations provide alternatives such as proportional representation. Proportional representation accords bargaining rights to be one or more organizations in direct relation to the number of members in the bargaining unit who belong to or vote for the organization. *(Exclusivité)*

Expedited Arbitration: Used independently or in conjunction with the term "industry arbitration," it encompasses systems used in specific industries whereby a "permanent" arbitrator or panel of arbitrators is selected to hear grievances arising under one or more collective agreements over a period of time, as well as any procedures or mechanisms designed to expedite the grievance arbitration process. *(Arbitrage accéléré)*

Fact-finding: A formal/informal dispute resolution procedure for investigating and reporting on the facts of a situation, such as a work stoppage affecting the public. *(Enquête factuelle)*

Fair Employment Practices: The practice of employers or unions of offering workers equal employment opportunities regardless of race, national or ethnic origin, colour, religion, age, sex, marital status, conviction for which a pardon has been granted, or physical handicap. *(Pratique loyale en matière d'emploi)*

Featherbedding: The practice of extending work through the limitation of production, the amount of work to be performed or other make-work arrangements. Many such practices have come about as a consequence of workers being laid off through mechanization or technological change, which has led unions to seek some method of retaining workers even though there may be no work for them to perform. *(Sinécure ouvrière)*

Federal Jurisdiction: Authority of the federal government exercised over employees or employers in any enterprise of an interprovincial, national or international nature, such as air transport, broadcasting, banks, pipelines, railways, highway transport, shipping, and grain elevators. Generally speaking, all other enterprises fall within the jurisdiction of provincial or territorial governments. *(Compétence fédérale)*

Federation of Labour: An allied group of unions in one or several industries, covering a geographical area, such as a district, province or country. An example of a national federation is the Canadian Labour Congress (CLC)/*Con-*

grès du Travail du Canada (CTC). National federations may join to form confederations or international federations such as the International Confederation of Free Trade Unions (ICFTU). *(Fédération des travailleurs)*

Final Offer Selection: A form of arbitration used in the United States and more recently in Canada, usually after a predetermined period of unsuccessful negotiation. Both sides put forward final offers, one of which an arbitrator or board of arbitrators must choose. *(Arbitrage des propositions finales)*

Flexible Work-week or Flextime: A system which provides workers with some freedom in deciding when they start and finish work, subject to the requirement that they are present during certain "core" hours and fulfill a minimum attendance requirement each day. *(Horaire variable de travail)*

Foreman: A supervisory employee, usually classed as a part of management. A working foreman or leadman is one who regularly performs production work or other work unrelated to supervisory duties. *(Contremaître)*

Free Riders: Non-union employees who share in whatever benefits result from union activities without sharing union expenses, or union members who are 'delinquent' in paying their dues. *(Resquilleurs)*

Freeze: Government action restricting wage, salary and price increases in order to stabilize the economy. *(Blocage)*

Frictional Unemployment: Unemployment due to time lost in changing jobs rather than a lack of job opportunities. Frictional unemployment would not be reduced significantly even if there were an increased demand for workers, but might be reduced by improving the information available to job seekers about vacancies. *(Chômage frictionnel)*

Fringe Benefits: Non-wage benefits such as paid vacations, pensions, health and welfare provisions, life insurance, etc., the cost of which is borne in whole or in part by the employer. Such benefits have accounted for an increasing percentage of worker income and labour costs in recent years and have thus become an important aspect of collective bargaining *(Avantages sociaux)*

Garnishment: Attachment of an employee's wages in the hands of the employer to pay a creditor. *(Saisie du salaire)*

General Strike: A general strike is a cessation of work by all union members in a geographical area, usually as a political protest. *(Grève générale)*

Grievance: A statement of dissatisfaction, usually by an individual but sometimes by the union or management, concerning interpretation of a collective bargaining agreement or traditional work practices. The grievance machinery (i.e., the method of dealing with individual grievances) is nearly always spelled out in the contract. If a grievance cannot be handled at the shop level (where most of them are settled), and the grievance arises out of an interpretation of the contract, it must be resolved by arbitration. *(Grief)*

Guaranteed Wage Plan: A system under which an employer (a) contributes to a fund used to pay additional wages during slack periods or (b) contractually guarantees a specified number of days of work during a specific period. *(Régime de salaire garanti)*

Handicapped Workers: Workers whose earning capacity is impaired by age, physical or mental deficiency, or injury. To encourage their employment, they are sometimes given special treatment in labour statutes, for example, by permitting employment at subminimum rates. *(Travailleur handicapé)*

Harmony Pledge (Co-operation Clause): A clause in a union contract in which the employer and the union agree to co-operate on some specific subject. *(Clause de coopération)*

Hazardous Occupations: Jobs which are classified as dangerous by provincial or federal laws, and in which employment of minors is restricted or forbidden. Federal legislation provides workers with the right to refuse work that is considered hazardous to health or safety. *(Emploi dangereux)*

Hiring Hall: An office, usually run by the union, or jointly by employers and union, for referring workers to jobs or for the actual hiring operation. *(Bureau d'embauchage)*

Holidays: Days established by law or custom for which workers receive pay while absent from work. Statutory holidays *(congé statutaire)* are established by law. When the customary day falls on a weekend a moveable holiday *(congé mobile)* may be substituted for it on another day. *(Jours fériés)*

Hot Cargo: Merchandise shipped from a struck plant or by an employer on a union boycott list. *(Produit boycotté)*

Idle Time: Nonproductive time resulting from waiting for work, machinery or other breakdowns, and the like. *(Temps inoccupé)*

Illegal Strike: A strike called in violation of the law. Strikes are generally illegal when they occur as a result of a dispute over the interpretation of a collective agreement currently in force, when they occur before conciliation procedures have been complied with, or when certification proceedings are under way. *(Grève illégale)*

Independent Union: A labour organization which is not affiliated with and remains independent of any federation. *(Syndicat autonome)*

Individual Bargaining: The right of individual members of a unit for which an exclusive representative has been designated for collective bargaining purposes to present, as individuals, grievances that are not contrary to the existing union contract. *(Négociation individuelle)*

Industrial Conflict: A general term used to describe the broad areas of disagreement and difficulty between labour and management (though the government may also be involved). The strike is the most common and most visible manifestation of conflict. It may also take the form of peaceful bargaining and grievance handling, boycotts, political action and restriction of output, industrial sabotage, absenteeism or labour turnover. Several of these forms, such as restriction of output, absenteeism and turnover, may take place on an individual as well as on an organized basis, and as such they constitute alternatives to collective action. *(Conflit de travail)*

Industrial Democracy: The involvement of workers (or their representatives) in decision making within industry. The machinery of industrial democracy may involve such devices as joint labour-management committees, works councils or worker representatives in the boardroom. The development of collective bargaining is viewed by many as providing the machinery through which industrial democracy may be developed. (See also **Quality of Working Life** and **Worker Participation**.) *(Démocratie industrielle)*

Industrial Health: A branch of public health which concerns itself with the health and well-being of workers. A body of rules and practices has evolved, designed to eliminate hazards and industrial fatigue in the workplace. *(Hygiène industrielle)*

Industrial Relations: A broad term that may refer to relations between unions and management, unions themselves, management and government, unions and government, or between employers and unorganized employees. Within this definition, specific attention may be directed toward industrial conflict or its regulation through the formulation of work rules or agreements. *(Relations industrielles)*

Industrial Union: A union organized on the basis of product, i.e., along industrial lines; in contrast to a craft union organized along skill lines. *(Syndicat industriel)*

Industry-wide Bargaining: Collective bargaining that takes place on an industry-wide basis; terms and conditions of employment agreed upon cover all or a major portion of the organized employees in the industry. *(Négociation de branche)*

Initiation Fees: Fees that must be paid by new members of a union or by former employees who have left the union and wish to return. Initiation fees serve several purposes: (1) a source of revenue; (2) an equity payment by new members to compensate for the efforts older members have made in building the union; (3) a device to restrict membership (if initiation fees are very high) in those unions desiring to remain small in order to protect job opportunities. *(Droits d'adhésion)*

Injunction: A court order restraining an employer or union from committing or engaging in certain acts. An ex parte injunction is one in which the application for an injunction is made in the absence of the party affected. *(Injonction)*

Interest Dispute: A dispute arising from the negotiation of a new collective agreement or the revision of an existing agreement on expiry. *(Conflit d'intérêts)*

International Confederation of Free Trade Unions (ICFTU): An international trade union body, formed in 1949, composed of a large number of national central labour bodies such as the Canadian Labour Congress/Congrès du Travail du Canada. It represents 50 million members in 96 non-communist countries. *(Confédération internationale des syndicats libres (CISL)*

International Labour Office: The secretariat of the **International Labour Organization,** which administers and co-ordinates the activities of the ILO. *(Bureau international du travail)*

International Labour Organization (ILO): A tripartite world body representing labour, management and government. Since 1946 one of the specialized agencies of the United Nations. It disseminates labour information to workers of all countries and sets minimum international labour standards, called "conventions," offered to member nations for ratification. Its headquarters are in Geneva, Switzerland *(Organisation internationale du travail OIT)*

International Union: An international union is a union with members in both Canada and the United States. *(Syndicat international)*

Job Classification: A system designed to create a hierarchy of jobs based on such factors as skill, responsibility or experience, time and effort. The determination of the value of each job in relation to other jobs in the workplace, based on the material and content of the job and such factors as education, skill, experience and responsibility. Often used for the purpose of arriving at a system of wage differentials between jobs or classes or jobs. *(Classification des emplois)*

Job Description: A description of the nature of a particular job, its relation to other jobs, the working conditions, the degree of responsibility and the other qualifications called for. *(Description de tâches)*

Job Enrichment: The attempt to make jobs more rewarding and less monotonous for the individual worker. Procedures used may include job enlargement (including more responsibilities on the job), or job rotation (allowing the worker to move from one job to another at specific intervals). See also **Quality of Working Life**.) *(Valorisation du travail)*

Job Rotation: Used as a means to provide variety and experience for employees while creating back-up potential for performance of individual jobs. *(Rotation d'emplois)*

Job Security: A worker's sense of having continuity of employment resulting from the possession of special skills, seniority, or protection provided in a collective agreement against unforeseen technological change. *(Sécurité d'emploi)*

Job Training: A procedure whereby workers, while working, learn how to perform particular jobs. (See also "**Apprentice**.") *(Formation professionnelle)*

Joint Bargaining: Two or more unions joining forces to negotiate an agreement with a single employer. *(Front commun)*

Journeyman: A craft or skilled worker who has completed apprenticeship training and been admitted to full membership in his or her craft. Examples: journeyman plumber, journeyman carpenter. *(Compagnon)*

Jurisdiction (Union): The area of jobs, skills, occupations and industries within which a union organizes and engages in collective bargaining. International unions often assert exclusive claim to particular areas of employment. Jurisdiction has always been a problem in organized labour, since two or more unions often claim the same jurisdiction. The CLC has attempted to cope with the problem by having affiliated unions sign no-raiding agreements, in which member unions agree not to trespass on one another's jurisdiction. These agreements, however, have not been completely observed. In the case of local unions, jurisdiction refers to a region within which the local union exercises authority. *(Compétence syndicale)*

Jurisdictional Dispute — Inter-union Dispute: A conflict between two or more unions over the right of their membership to perform certain types of work. If the conflict develops into a work stoppage, it is called a jurisdictional strike. *(Conflit de compétence syndicale/Conflit intersyndical)*

Labour Canada: The federal government department responsible for disseminating information on labour-related issues and administering labour legislation within federal jurisdiction. The department's aims are to promote stable industrial relations and establish appropriate labour standards and occupational safety and health in the federal jurisdiction, to promote labour-management co-operation throughout Canada, and to co-ordinate the Canadian contribution to the improvement of labour conditions throughout the world. The government of each province has a department of labour to administer labour laws in its jurisdiction. *(Travail Canada)*

Labour College of Canada: Bilingual institution of higher education for trade union members, operated jointly by the Canadian Labour Congress, McGill University and the Université de Montréal for the purpose of providing a training ground for future trade union leaders. *(Collège canadien des travailleurs)*

Labour Council: An organization formed by a labour federation at the city level. It is organized and functions in the same manner as a provincial federation but within a city. Finances are often obtained through a per capita tax on affiliates. *(Conseil du travail)*

Labour Education: Education by unions of union members or officials in industrial relations subjects. *(Education syndicale)*

Labour Federation: An association of unions which, while retaining their autonomy, co-operate to achieve common goals. *(Fédération du travail)*

Labour Force: All persons 15 and over who are either employed, temporarily idle, or unemployed and seeking employment. *(Population active)*

Labour Law: That part of the law which treats of persons in their capacity as workers or employers; the governing of labour relations, labour and employer organizations, employment practices and conditions in the workplace. *(Droit du travail)*

Labour-Management Committee: Any committee having representation from both management and labour; discussion subjects may include safety and health, productivity, quality of working life, training, etc. *(Comité syndical-patronal)*

Labour Relations Board: A board, usually provided for under the provincial labour relations acts, which is responsible for certification of trade unions, the inclusion of dispute-settling provisions in collective agreements and investigation of complaints of bad faith in collective bargaining. (See also **Canada Labour Relations Board**.) *(Commission des relations du travail)*

Labour Turnover: Rate at which workers move into and out of employment, usually expressed as a percentage based on the number of employees leaving a plant or industry during a certain time over the average number of employees in the plant or industry during the same period. *(Roulement de la main-d'oeuvre)*

Layoff: Temporary, prolonged, or final separation from employment as a result of a lack of work. *(Mise à pied)*

Leave of Absence: Paid or unpaid time away from work, with employer's permission, to meet family or civic responsibilities. Common forms of leave include maternity leave *(congé de maternité)*, bereavement or funeral leave *(congé pour décès)*, and leave for jury duty *(congé de service judiciaire)*. *(Absence autorisée)*

Line Employee: An employee whose duties are directly related to the production and distribution of the company's products or services. *(Exécutant)*

Local Union: The unit of labour organization formed in a particular locality, through which members participate directly in the affairs of their organization, such as the election of local officers, the financial and other business matters of a local, relations with their employer(s), and the collection of members' dues. *(Section locale d'un syndicat)*

Lockout: The closing of a place of employment, a suspension of work, or a refusal by an employer to continue to employ a number of his employees, undertaken with a view to compelling them to agree to conditions of employment on his terms or to refrain from exercising their existing rights and privileges. *(Lock-out)*

Maintenance of Membership: A provision in a collective agreement stating that no worker need join the union as a condition of employment, but that all workers who voluntarily join must maintain their membership for the duration of the agreement as a condition of continued employment. (See **Union Security.**) *(Maintien de l'adhésion syndicale)*

Management Rights: These encompass those aspects of the employer's operations that do not require discussion with or concurrence by the union, or rights reserved to management which are not subject to collective bargaining. Such rights may include matters of hiring, production, manufacturing and sales. The resistance of many managers to innovations such as industrial democracy may frequently be traced to concern over the erosion of management prerogatives that such innovations sometimes entail. *(Prérogatives de l'employeur)*

Master Agreement: A collective bargaining agreement which serves as the pattern for major terms and conditions for an entire industry or segment thereof. Local terms may be negotiated in addition to the terms set forth in the master contract. *(Convention collective cadre)*

Mediation: (See **Conciliation and Mediation.**) *(Médiation)*

Mediation-Arbitration (Med-Arb): A dispute resolution procedure where the mediator is armed with the power to settle unresolved issues by binding arbitration in the event they are not settled through mediation. In such cases, the right to strike or lock out is waived by the parties. *(Médiation-arbitrage)*

Minimum Wage: The rate of pay established by statute or by minimum wage order as the lowest wage that may be paid, whether for a particular type of work, to a particular class of workers, or to any worker. *(Salaire minimum)*

Modified Union Shop: A place of work in which non-union workers already employed need not join the union, but all new employees must join, and those already members must remain in the union. (See **Union Security Clauses, Union Shop**.) *(Atelier syndical modifié)*

Monopoly: Control of a commodity or service in a particular market which enables the one having control to raise the price substantially above that fixed by free competition. *(Monopole)*

Moonlighting: The holding by a single individual of more than one paid job at the same time. *(Travail noir ou Double emploi)*

Multinational Bargaining: Bargaining between an international union or union federation and a company whose operations are international in scope. These companies, known as multinationals, pose many unique problems for organized labour. In particular, their international status gives them scope for transferring production from one country to another on a temporary or permanent basis in order to use non-union employees or break a strike. *(Négociation avec une entreprise multinationale)*

National Union: A union whose membership and locals are confined within one country. *Syndicat national)*

Nepotism: The practice of giving promotions, basic employment, higher earnings, and other benefits to employees who are relatives of management. *(Népotisme)*

Open Shop: A shop in which union membership is not required as a condition of securing or retaining employment. *(Atelier ouvert)*

Organized Labour: Consists of all unions and workers' organizations whose principal objects are the regulation of relations between workers and employers and the protection of the interests of workers; the union movement as a whole. *(Mouvement syndicat)*

Overtime: Hours worked in excess of the maximum regular number of hours fixed by statute, union contract, or custom. Clock overtime is a premium, paid for work during specified regular working hours, required by collective agreement. *(Temps supplémentaire)*

Paid Educational Leave: Leave for educational purposes granted to a worker and paid for by the employer or government. *(Congé-éducation payé)*

Part-time Employee: An employee who works fewer than the normally scheduled weekly or monthly hours of work established for persons doing similar work. There are different kinds of part-time work. For example, an employee may work regular hours that are less than full-time, or may be "on call" and work for a firm occasionally, as needed. (*Employé à temps partiel*)

Pattern Bargaining: A procedure in collective bargaining whereby a union seeks to obtain equal or identical terms from other employers as in an agreement already obtained from an important company. (*Négociation type*)

Pension Plan: Arrangement to provide definite sums of money for payment to employees following retirement. A final-earnings plan is a pension based upon length of service and average earnings for a stated period just before retirement. A contributory plan is financed by both the employer and the employees. (*Régime de pension*)

Per Capita Tax: Regular payments by a local to its national international union, labour council or federation, or by a union to its central labour body. It is based on the number of members. (*Capitation, taxe par tête*)

Picket Line: A group of workers (pickets) posted at plant entrances and gates, or marching near the entrances and gates, to inform employees of the existence of a labour dispute and to persuade and influence them not to enter the premises or do business with the employer.

Picketing: Patrolling near the employer's place of business by union members — pickets — to publicize the existence of a labour dispute, persuade workers to join a strike or join the union, discourage customers from buying or using the employer's goods or services, etc. (*Piquetage*)

Piece Rate: A predetermined amount paid to an employee for each unit of output. (*Salaire à la pièce*)

Premium Pay: A wage rate higher than straight time, payable for overtime work, work on holidays or scheduled days off, etc., or for work under extraordinary conditions such as dangerous, dirty or unpleasant work. (*Prime*)

Preventive Mediation: (See **Conciliation and Mediation**.)

Probationary Period: The initial period of employment during which a worker is on trial and may be discharged with or without cause. (*Stage*)

Productivity: Output per unit of input; a measure of efficiency. (*Productivité*)

Profit-sharing Plan: An arrangement under which employees receive a percentage of the employer's profits in addition to their wages. A cash payment plan is one under which the employees' share of the profits is paid immediately in cash. A deferred payment plan is one under which the employer deposits the employees' portion of the profits with a trustee to be paid to them at some time in the future, depending upon conditions specified in the trust. Under some schemes, profits are distributed in the form of shares. Also sometimes called gain sharing. *(Participation aux bénéfices)*

Quality Circle: A voluntary group of production workers in a workplace who meet, often with management authorization or assistance, to attempt to resolve problems affecting quality control, production and productivity. *(Cercle de qualité)*

Quality of Working Life: A process designed to assist employers, unions, and employees in implementing joint problem-solving approaches to improve the quality of working life within organizations in the interests of improved labour-management relations, organization effectiveness and employee work satisfaction. *(Qualité de la vie au travail)*

Raiding: An attempt by one union to induce members of another union to defect and joint its ranks. (See **Jurisdiction (Union).**) *(Maraudage)*

Rand Formula: A provision of a collective agreement stating that non-union employees in the bargaining unit must pay the union a sum equal to union fees as a condition of continuing employment. Non-union workers are not, however, required to join the union. *(Formule Rand)*

Rank and File: Individual union members who have no special status either as officers or shop stewards in the plant. *(Base syndicale, syndiqués de la base)*

Ratification: Formal approval of a newly negotiated agreement by vote of the union members affected, as well as by employers or employer associations. *(Ratification)*

Real Wages: The actual purchasing power of wages. Often computed by dividing money wages by the cost-of-living index. Example: if money wages increase from $1.00 to $1.25 an hour, but the cost-of-living also increases by 25 per cent, real wages having remained constant. It is by looking at the changes in real wages that changes in living standards can be observed. (See also **COLA Clause**.) *(Salaire réel)*

Recognition: Employer acceptance of a union as the exclusive bargaining representative for the employees in the bargaining unit. (See also **Certification**.) *(Reconnaissance)*

Redundancy Pay: (See **Severance Pay**.)

Reopener: A provision in a collective agreement which permits either side to reopen the contract at a specified time, or under special circumstances, prior to its expiration, in order to bargain on stated subjects such as wage increases, pensions, health and welfare schemes, etc. *(Clause de réouverture)*

Representation Vote: A vote ordered by a Labour Relations Board to determine whether employees in an appropriate bargaining unit wish to have a particular union represent them as their bargaining agent. *(Vote de représentation)*

Residual Rights: Those rights not spelled out in a collective agreement, generally considered to be management rights. *(Droits résiduaires)*

Rest Period: Specified short period, sometimes required by law, during which workers are allowed to cease work, usually on company time. *(Période de repos)*

Retirement: Permanent withdrawal from the labour force. **Delayed retirement** is withdrawal after the normal retirement date, usually with the consent or at the request of the employer. **Disability retirement** is withdrawal before the normal retirement age because of physical incapacity. **Early retirement** is withdrawal before the normal retirement date. *(Retraite)*

Retraining: The establishment of programs and training activities to educate employees in new skills or knowledge made necessary by changing technology, work rotation, reassignment, etc. *(Recyclage)*

Rights Dispute: A dispute arising from the interpretation or application of one or more of the provisions of an existing collective agreement. *(Conflit de droits)*

Right-to-Work: The right of an employee to refrain from joining a union and to keep his job without union membership or activity. *(Droit au travail)*

Safety ahd Health Committee: A committee composed of workers and management set up for the purpose of promoting a greater concern for improvement of safety and health in the workplace. *(Comité de sécurité et d'hygiène)*

Scab: (See **Strikebreakers**.)

Scanlon Plan: An incentive plan developed by Joseph Scanlon, one-time research director of the United Steelworkers and later on staff at the Massachusetts Institute of Technology. The plan is designed to achieve greater production through increased efficiency with the opportunity for the accrued savings achieved to be distributed among the workers. *(Système Scanlon)*

Seasonal Unemployment: Unemployment that is due to the seasonal nature of the work. Agricultural workers, lumber workers and some construction workers are unemployed for a part of each year because of weather conditions. *(Chômage saisonnier)*

Semi-skilled Labour: Workers who have acquired some proficiency at particular jobs but whose activities do not come within any of the traditional skilled crafts. *(Manoeuvre spécialisé)*

Seniority: An employee's standing in the plant, based on length of continuous employment. Employees with the greatest seniority are usually the last to be laid off (see **Layoff and Bumping**) and are often given certain advantages in the matters of promotion and selection of holiday periods based on seniority. *(Ancienneté)*

Severance Pay, Dismissal Pay, Redundancy Pay: A lump-sum payment by an employer to a worker whose employment is permanently ended, usually for reasons beyond the worker's control. Such payments are in addition to any back wages due to the worker. *(Indemnité de fin d'emploi)*

Shift: The stated daily working period for a group of employees, e.g., 8 a.m. to 4 p.m., 4 p.m. to midnight, midnight to 8 a.m. (See **Split Shift**.) *(Poste, quart, équipe)*

Shift Differential: Added pay for work performed at other than regular daytime hours. *(Prime de poste)*

Shop Committee: A committee of employees elected by fellow workers to represent them in considering grievances and related matters. *(Comité d'atelier)*

Shop Steward: (See **Union Steward**.) *(Délégué d'atelier)*

Sick Leave: Time off allowed for absence because of illness. *(Congé de maladie)*

Slowdown: A deliberate lessening of work effort without an actual strike, in order to force concessions from the employer. (See also **Work to Rule**.) *(Grève perlée)*

Speed-up: A union term describing situations in which workers are required to increase production without a compensating increase in wages. (See also **Stretch-out**.) *(Cadence accélérée)*

Split Shift: Division of an employee's daily working time into two or more working periods, to meet peak needs. *(Poste fractionné)*

Staff: (1) Employees of an organization. (2) Workers with administrative duties. *(Personnel)*

Standard of Living: Conditions under which a person or group of persons lives at a particular time in a particular locality, considered in relation to expenses and income. *(Niveau de vie)*

Straw-boss: A sub-foreman. *(Sous-contremaître)*

Stretch-out: A union term describing a situation in which workers are required to assume additional work duties, such as tending more machines, without additional compensation. (See also **Speed-up**.) *(Surcharge)*

Strike: A cessation of work or a refusal to work or to continue work by employees in combination or in accordance with a common understanding for the purpose of compelling an employer to agree to terms or conditions of employment. Strikes usually occur as a last resort which collective bargaining and all other means have failed to obtain the employees' demands. Except in special cases, strikes are legal only when a collective agreement is not in force. A **Rotating or Hit-and-Run Strike** is a strike organized in such a way that only part of the employees stop work at any given time, each group taking its turn. A **Sympathy Strike** is a strike by workers not directly involved in a labour dispute; an attempt to show labour solidarity and bring pressure on an employer in a labour dispute. A **Wildcat Strike** is a strike that violates the collective agreement and is not authorized by the union. *(Grève)*

Strike Benefits: Union payments, usually a small proportion of regular income, to workers during a strike. Many unions do not supply monetary aid but distribute groceries and other types of aid to needy families of strikers. *(Indemnité de grève)*

Strikebreakers: Persons who continue to work during a strike or who accept employment to replace workers on strike. By filling strikers' jobs, they may weaken or break the strike. Also known as scabs. *(Briseur de grève, jaune)*

Strike Fund: Funds held by international or local unions for allocation during a strike to cover costs of benefits, legal fees, publicity, and the like. Some international unions assess each member a small amount each month to build the fund. Other unions use the international's general fund. The amount of the fund often determines the staying power of the workers and, consequently, the success or failure of the strike. Strike funds are often designated in union financial statements as "emergency", "reserve" or "special" funds. *(Caisse de grève)*

Strike Notice: Formal announcement by a group of workers to their employer or to an appropriate government agency that on a certain date they will go on strike. *(Avis de grève)*

Strike Vote: A vote conducted among employees in a bargaining unit on the question of whether they should go on strike. *(Vote de grève)*

Struck-Work Clause: A clause in a collective bargaining agreement which permits employees to refuse to perform work farmed out by a strike-bound plant. *(Clause de refus de travail)*

Successor Rights: The rights, privileges, and duties of a union or employer that succeeds another by reason of a merger, sale, amalgamation, or transfer of jurisdiction. *(Obligation du successeur)*

Supervisor: An employee having certain management rights, such as the right to hire or fire or to recommend such action. *(Surveillant)*

Supplemental Unemployment Benefit (SUB) Plans: Private plans providing compensation for wage loss to laid-off workers, usually in addition to public unemployment insurance payments. *(Régimes d'indemnités complémentaires de chômage)*

Sweat Shop: A factory where wage rates and sanitation, safety and working conditions do not meet accepted standards. *(Atelier de pressurage)*

Sweetheart Contract: Term of derision for an agreement negotiated by an employer and a company-dominated union granting terms and conditions of employment more favourable to the contracting union than the employer would be willing to grant to a rival non-dominated labour organization, the usual purpose being to keep the rival out. *(Accord de compérage)*

Take-home Pay: The net paycheck after tax and other deductions have been made. *(Salaire net)*

Technological Change: Technical progress in industrial methods, for example, the introduction of labour-saving machinery or new production techniques. Such change can result in manpower reductions. (See **Automation**.) *(Changement technologique)*

Technological Unemployment: Unemployment that results from the introduction of labour-saving machinery. *(Chômage technique)*

Time-and-a-half: Wage payment at one and one-half times the employee's regular rate of pay or of the statutory minimum rate of pay for all hours worked in excess of a specified number per day or week. *(Taux majoré de moitié)*

Time Card: The record sheet on which, either manually or mechanically, a worker's attendance is reported. *(Fiche de présence)*

Time Clock: Clock with a mechanism to indicate on a paycard, by punch hole or other means, the time of arrival and departure of employees. *(Horlogue de pointage, horloge poinçon)*

Trade Union: (See **Union**.) *(Syndicat)*

Tripartitism (Tripartism): Consultation between representatives of labour, management and government to consider issues of mutual interest. (*Tripartisme*)

Trusteeship: (See **Union Trusteeship**.) (*Tutelle*)

Unemployed: Persons who do not have work. The official definition, for unemployment insurance purposes, described the unemployed as those persons who during the reference week: (a) were without work, had actively looked for work in the past four weeks (ending with reference week), and were available for work; (b) had not actively looked for work in the past four weeks but had been on layoff for twenty-six weeks or less and were available for work; (c) had not actively looked for work in the past four weeks but had a new job to start in four weeks or less from reference week, and were available for work. (*Chômeur*)

Unemployment Insurance: A federal program whereby eligible unemployed persons receive cash benefits for a specified period of time. These benefits are paid out of funds derived from employer, employee and government contributions. (*Assurance-chômage*)

Unfair Labour Practice: A practice on the part of either union or management that violates provisions of federal or provincial labour law. (*Pratique déloyale de travail*)

Unfair Labour Practice Proceeding: A proceeding before a labour relations board to determine whether an employer or a union has committed unfair labour practices as charged. (*Procédure en matière de pratiques déloyales de travail*)

Union: The unit of labour organization which organizes and charters locals in the industries or trades as defined in its constitution, sets general policy for its locals, assists them in the conduct of their affairs, and is the medium for co-ordinating their activities. Finances are obtained from the locals through per capita dues. Unions usually hold regular conventions of delegates from the locals at which general policy is set and at which officers are elected. A union may be affiliated with a larger labour organization (e.g., congress, federation, labour council). (*Syndicat*)

Union Dues: Periodic payments by union members for the financial support of their union. (*Cotisations syndicales*)

Union Label; Bug: A tag, imprint or design affixed to a product to show it was made by union labour. (*Étiquette syndicale*)

Union Local: (See **Local Union**.((*Syndicat local*)

Union Organizer: A person who solicits workers to join a union. (*Recruteur syndical*)

Union Scale: A rate of pay set by a union contract as the minimum rate for a job, whether or not paid to a union member. *(Tarif syndical)*

Union Security Clauses: Provisions in collective agreements designed to protect the institutional authority of the union.

Examples of union security clauses are: **closed shop**, an agreement between union and employer that the employer may hire only union members and retain only union members in the shop; **preferential hiring**, an agreement that an employer, in hiring new workers, will give preference to union members; **union shop**, an agreement that the employer may hire anyone he wants, but all workers must join the union within a specified time after being hired and retain membership as a conditions of continuing employment; **maintenance of membership**, a provision that no worker must join as a condition of employment, but all workers who voluntary join must maintain their membership for the duration of the contract in order to keep their jobs. (See also **Checkoff, Closed shop, Maintenance of Membership, Rand Formula, Union Shop, Modified Union Shop**.) *(Clause de sécurité syndicale)*

Union Shop: A place of work where every worker covered by the collective agreement must become and remain a member of the union. New workers need not be union members to be hired, but must join after a certain number of days. (See **Union Security Clauses, Modified Union Shop**.) *(Atelier syndical)*

Union Steward: Union member ordinarily elected to represent workers in a particular shop or department. His or her functions may include collecting dues, soliciting for new members, announcing meetings, receiving, investigating, and attempting the adjustment of grievances, and education. *(Délégué syndical)*

Union Trusteeship: Describes a situation in which a national or international union suspends the normal operations of a union local and takes over control of the local's assets and the administration of its internal affairs. The constitutions of many international unions authorize international officers to establish trusteeships over local unions in order to prevent corruption, mismanagement and other abuses. *(Tutelle syndicale)*

Unjust Dismissal: Dismissal of an employee in an arbitrary or unjust fashion, contrary to statute or in contravention of a collective agreement. *(Congédiement injuste)*

Unorganized Workers: Workers who do not belong to any union. *(Travailleurs non syndiqués)*

Vacation: Paid leave for a relatively extended period. Employers are required by law to give employees paid annual vacations, the length of time being dependent on length of services and provisions of the collective agreement. (*Vacances*)

Voluntary Recognition: A voluntary agreement (not involving the formal certification process) between an employer and a trade union to recognize the trade union as the exclusive bargaining agent of the employees in a defined bargaining unit. (*Reconnaissance volontaire*)

Wage and Price Controls: Government effort to restrain wage and price increases, usually through the establishment of some form of review or control agency (e.g., Anti-Inflation Board). (*Contrôle des salaires et des prix*)

Wage Determination: The practices and procedures used to fix wage rates in collective bargaining. (*Fixation des salaires*)

Wage Differentials: Variations among wage rates due to a variety of factors — job content, location, skill, industry, company, sex, etc. Unions are frequently concerned with eliminating wage differentials not based on the degree of effort or skill required in a job but considered discriminatory. (*Différence de salaire*)

Wage Parity: Equality of wages between workers in the same occupation but in different geographical areas; for workers in the same sector, e.g., the public sector, but in different occupations, e.g., policemen and firemen; or for workers in the same occupation but in different companies or countries. (*Parité*)

Walkout: A Spontaneous, co-ordinated work stoppage. (*Débrayage*)

White-collar Workers: Term used to describe non-manual workers, e.g., office, clerical, sales, supervisory, professional and technical workers. To be contrasted with blue-collar workers, e.g., maintenance and production workers. (*Cols blancs*)

Wider-based Bargaining: (See **Broader-based Bargaining**.)

Wildcat Strike: A spontaneous and short-lived work stoppage, not authorized by the union. It is usually a reaction to a specific problem in the workplace, rather than a planned strike action. (*Grève sauvage*)

Work Restriction: Limitation ordinarily placed by unions on the types or amounts of work that union members can do. (*Freinage de la production*)

Work Rules: Rules regulating on-the-job conditions of work, usually incorporated in the collective agreement. Example (1) limiting production work of supervisory personnel; (2) limiting the assignment of work outside an employee's classification; (3) requiring a minimum number of workers on a job; (4) limiting the use of labour-saving methods and equipment. *(Règles du travail)*

Work Sharing: Plan by which available work is distributed as evenly as possible among all workers when production slackens, or by which working time is generally reduced to prevent layoffs. Under the Canada Employment and Immigration Commission's Work Sharing Program, in effect since 1982, unemployment insurance benefits help compensate workers for the reduction in wages caused by such an arrangement. Under the same program, workers affected by work sharing may take part in appropriate vocational training. *(Partage du travail)*

Work Stoppage: A cessation of work resulting from a strike or lockout. *(Arrêt de travail)*

Work To Rule: A practice where workers obey to the letter all laws and rules pertaining to their work, thereby effecting a slowdown. The practice also frequently involves a refusal to perform duties which, though related, are not explicitly included in the job description. (See also **Slowdown.**) *(Grève du zèle)*

Worker Directions: Representation of employee interests by persons, usually union officials, on the board of directors of a corporation. Practised in a number of European countries, notably West Germany. *(Administrateur (travailleurs)*

Worker Participation: The opportunity for workers to share, either directly or indirectly through elected representatives, in the decision-making process. Various degrees of participation may be identified according to the amount of influence that workers are allowed to exert. Thus, **communication** refers to the simple conveyance of information to workers either before or after decisions have been made. **Consultation** involves sounding out workers' opinions, usually before decisions are made. **Co-determination** refers to a system under which workers are able to participate in a joint decision-making process. Participation is often used as a synonym for industrial democracy. *(Participation ouvrière)*

Workers' Compensation: Compensation payable by employers collectively for injuries sustained by employees in the course of their employment. Each province has a worker's compensation act. *(Indemnisation des accidents du travail)*

Working Conditions: Conditions pertaining to the worker's job environment, such as hours of work, safety, paid holidays and vacations, rest periods, free clothing or uniforms, possibilities of advancement, etc. Many of these are included in the collective agreement and subject to collective bargaining. *(Conditions de travail)*

Works Council: A form of industrial democracy found primarily in European countries, consisting of plant level committees of workers or both workers and management. Committees are involved with issues ranging from the basic rights of employees, to plans relevant to employee welfare, to full co-determination in areas such as personnel. *(Conseil d'entreprise)*

A Selected Bibliography

Aaron, B., J. R. Grodin, and J. L. Stern, eds. *Public-Sector Bargaining.* Industrial Relations Research Series. Washington: Bureau of National Affairs, Inc., 1979.

Abella, M. A. *Nationalism, Communism and Canadian Labour.* Toronto: University of Toronto Press, 1979.

Anderson, J., and M. Gunderson. *Union-Management Relations in Canada.* Don Mills: Addison-Wesley Publishers, 1982.

Arthurs, H. W., D. D. Carter, and H. J. Glasbeek. *Labour Law and Industrial Relations in Canada.* London: Kluwer, 1981. Toronto: Butterworths, 1981.

Auld, D. A. L., L. N. Christofides, R. Swidinsky, and D. A. Wilton. *The Determinants of Negotiated Wage Settlements in Canada (1966-1975): A Microeconomic Analysis.* Ottawa: Anti-Inflation Board, Supply and Services Canada, 1979.

Bacharach, S. B., and E. J. Lawler. *Bargaining: Power, Tactics and Outcomes.* San Francisco: Jossey-Bass Publishers, 1981.

Barbash, J. "Collective Bargaining and the Theory of Conflict." Vol. XVIII, No. 1, *British Journal of Industrial Relations.* March 1980, pp. 82-90.

Barrett, B., E. Rhodes, and J. Beishon, eds. *Industrial Relations and the Wider Society.* London: Collier Macmillan/The Open University Press, 1975.

Boivin, J., and G. Guilbault. *Les relations paternelles-syndicales au Québec.* Chicoutimi: Gaëtan Morin, 1982.

Brown, D. J. M., and D. M. Beatty. *Canadian Labour Arbitration,* 2nd. ed. Aurora: Canada Law Book Limited, 1984.

Canadian Industrial Relations. Report of the Task Force on Labour Relations, Chairman H. D. Woods. Ottawa: Privy Council Office, December 1968.

Chamberlain, N. W., and J. W. Kuhn. *Collective Bargaining,* 2nd. ed. New York: McGraw-Hill Book Company, 1965.

Cousineau, J. M., and R. Lacroix. *Wage Determination in Major Collective Agreements in the Private and Public Sectors.* Ottawa: Economic Council of Canada, 1977.

Crispo, John. *International Unionism: A Study in Canadian-American Relations.* Toronto: McGraw-Hill Ryerson Limited, 1967,

————— *Industrial Democracy in Western Europe: A North American Perspective.* Toronto: McGraw-Hill Ryerson Limited, 1978.

Downie, B. M. *The Behavioural, Economic and Institutional Effect of Compulsory Interest Arbitration.* Economic Council of Canada Discussion Paper 147. Ottawa: December 1979.

Finkelman, J., and S. B. Goldenberg. *Collective Bargaining in the Public Sector: The Federal Experience in Canada.* Montreal: Institute for Research on Public Policy, 1983. 2 vols.

Forsey, E. *Trade Unions in Canada: 1812-1902.* Toronto: University of Toronto Press, 1982.

Freeman, R. B., and J. L. Medoss. *What Do Unions Do?* New York: Basic Books, Inc., Publishers, 1984.

Gunderson, M., ed. *Collective Bargaining in the Essential and Public Service Sectors.* Toronto: University of Toronto Press, 1975.

Healy, J. J., ed. *Creative Collective Bargaining.* Englewood Cliffs: Prentice-Hall Inc., 1965.

Industrial Relations. Vol. 19, No. 3. California: Fall 1980.

Jamieson, S. M. *Industrial Relations in Canada,* 2nd ed. Toronto: Macmillan of Canada, 1973.

——————— *Industrial Conflict in Canada.* Economic Council of Canada Discussion Paper 142. Ottawa: December 1979. Juris, A., M. Thompson, and W. Daniels, eds. *Industrial Relations in a Decade of Change.* Industrial Relations Research Association Series. Madison: 1985.

Kochan, T. A. *Collective Bargaining and Industrial Relations.* Homewood: Richard D. Irwin, 1980.

Kumar, P. *Canadian Industrial Relations Information — Sources, Technical Notes and Glossary.* Kingston: Queen's University Industrial Relations Centre, 1979.

Logan, H. A. *Trade Unions in Canada.* Toronto: Macmillan of Canada, 1948.

Miller, R. U., and F. Isbester, eds. *Canadian Labour in Transition.* Scarborough: Prentice-Hall Canada Inc., 1971.

Ostry, S., and M. A. Saidi. *Labour Economics In Canada,* 3rd ed. Toronto: Macmillan of Canada, 1979.

Palmer, E. E. *Collective Agreement Arbitration in Canada,* 2nd ed. Toronto: Butterworths, 1983.

Peach, D. A., and B. Kuechle. *The Practice of Industrial Relations,* 2nd ed. Toronto: McGraw-Hill Ryerson Limited, 1985.

Phillips, G. E. *Labour Relations and the Collective Bargaining Cycle,* 2nd ed. Toronto: Butterworths, 1981.

Porter, J. *The Vertical Mosaic: An Analysis of Social Class and Power in Canada.* Toronto: University of Toronto Press, 1965.

Relations industrielles/Industrial Relations. Laval: quarterly.

Reynolds, L. G., S. H. Masters, and C. H. Moser, eds. *Readings in Labor Economics and Labor Relations,* 2nd ed. Englewood Cliffs: Prentice-Hall Inc., 1978.

Rose, J. B. *Public Policy, Bargaining Structure and the Construction Industry.* Toronto: Butterworths, 1980.

Rowan, R. R. ed. *Readings in Labor Economics and Labor Relations,* 4th ed. Homewood: Richard D. Irwin, Inc., 1980.

Stevens, C. M. *Strategy and Collective Bargaining Negotiation.* New York: McGraw-Hill Book Company, 1965.

Swan, K. P., and K. E. Swinton, eds. *Studies in Labour Law.* Toronto: Butterworths, 1983.

Thompson, M., and G. Swimmer, eds. *Conflict or Compromise: The Future of Public Sector Industrial Relations.* Montreal: The Institute for Research on Public Policy, 1984.

Tremblay, L. M. *Le syndicalisme québecois: Idéologies de la CSN et de la FTQ.* Montréal: Les presses de l'Université de Montréal, 1972.

Walton, R. E., and R.B. McKersie. *A Behavioral Theory of Labor Negotiations.* New York: McGraw-Hill Book Company, 1965.

Weiler, P. *Reconcilable Differences.* Toronto: The Carswell Co. Ltd., 1980.

Willes, J. A. *Contemporary Canadian Labour Relations.* Toronto: McGraw-Hill Ryerson Limited, 1984.

Wood, W. D., and P. Kumar. *The Current Industrial Relations Scene in Canada.* Kingston: Queen's University Industrial Relations Centre, annually.

Woods, H. D. *Labour Policy in Canada,* 2nd ed. Toronto: Macmillan of Canada, 1973.

Index